P9-BZS-369

# College Preparatory Mathematics 3
## (Algebra 2)

**Second Edition**
**version 5.2**

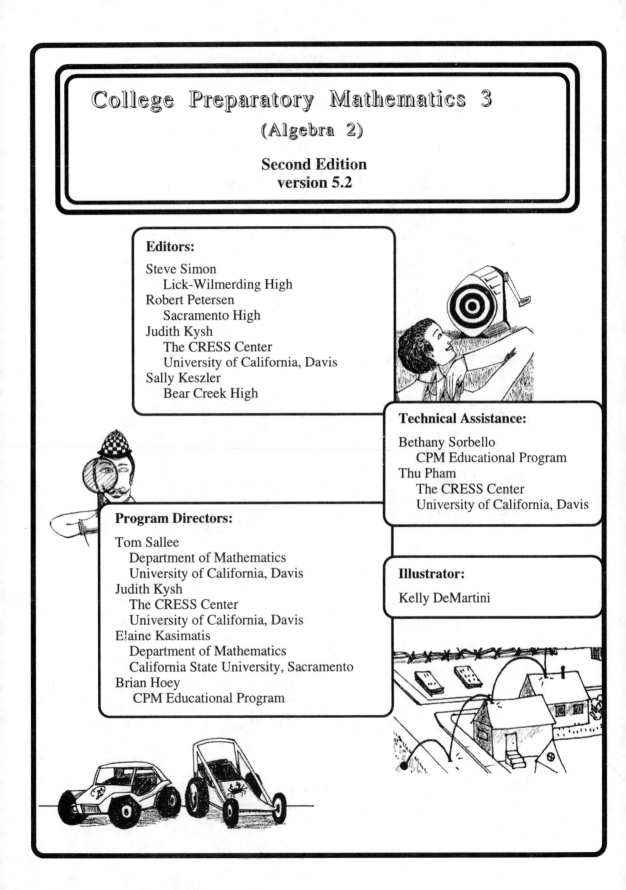

**Editors:**

Steve Simon
  Lick-Wilmerding High
Robert Petersen
  Sacramento High
Judith Kysh
  The CRESS Center
  University of California, Davis
Sally Keszler
  Bear Creek High

**Technical Assistance:**

Bethany Sorbello
  CPM Educational Program
Thu Pham
  The CRESS Center
  University of California, Davis

**Program Directors:**

Tom Sallee
  Department of Mathematics
  University of California, Davis
Judith Kysh
  The CRESS Center
  University of California, Davis
Elaine Kasimatis
  Department of Mathematics
  California State University, Sacramento
Brian Hoey
  CPM Educational Program

**Illustrator:**

Kelly DeMartini

# College Preparatory Mathematics
## Algebra 2

### Second Edition Editors: 1998-99

| | |
|---|---|
| Bob Petersen | Sacramento High |
| Steve Simon | Lick-Wilmerding High |
| Sally Keszler | Bear Creek High |

### Original Writers and Editors: First Edition 1992-95

| | |
|---|---|
| Nancy Aaberg | Yuba City High |
| Kathy Borst | Anderson Valley High |
| Tracy Brown | Luther Burbank High |
| Carlos Cabana | San Lorenzo High |
| Jonathan Compton | Belen High |
| John Cooper | Del Oro High |
| Kelly (Martin) DiLeo | Alhambra Senior High |
| Carmel Draper | Wood (Will C.) High |
| James Friedrich | Valley High |
| David Goodwin | Florin High |
| Carol Grossnicklaus | Oxnard High |
| Patty Hart | Elk Grove High |
| Gail Holt | El Camino Fundamental High |
| Karen Junker | Florin High |
| Mark Kellman | Luther Burbank High |
| Richard Melamed | El Camino Fundamental High |
| Bob Petersen | Sacramento High |
| Steve Piekarski | C.K. McClatchy High |
| Rolf Schumann | Christian Brothers High |
| Jeanne Shimizu-Yost | San Juan High |
| Clark Swanson | Sacramento High |
| Joel Teller | College Preparatory School |
| Kathy Van Liefde | Christian Brothers High |
| Joe Veiga | Elk Grove High |
| Karen Wootton | Will C. Wood High |

### and by

Judith Kysh & Tom Sallee, Project Co-Directors

### Technical Assistance
Crystal Mills, Kirk Mills, Thu Pham, and Bethany Sorbello

*Copyright © 1995, 2000, 2002 by CPM Educational Program. All rights reserved. No part of this publication may be reproduced or transmitted in any form or by any means, electronic or mechanical, including photocopy, recording, or any information storage and retrieval system, without permission in writing from the publisher. Requests for permission should be made in writing to: CPM Educational Program, 1233 Noonan Drive, Sacramento, CA 95822. E-mail: cpm@cpm.org.*

3 4 5 6 7 8 9    04 03 02

Printed in the United States of America          ISBN 1-885145-90-X

# A Note to Parent(s) and Students

The authors of the College Preparatory Mathematics Series (CPM) are all high school and middle school teachers currently in the classroom. Working along with University mathematicians, they developed and tested these materials with the dual goals of teaching the core facts and procedures of Algebra 2 AND having the mathematics contained in the course make sense. These teachers are dedicated to helping more students successfully learn and understand college preparatory mathematics.

The text provides basic skills checkpoints. These problems are marked with the Milepost icon. If a student has difficulty with a Milepost problem, he or she should refer to the Milepost practice section in the back of the book.

To provide additional support for students, the authors have written a unit by unit, *Parent's Guide with Review for Math 3 (Algebra 2)*. This document contains annotated solutions for key problems and makes suggestions about how to be successful in this course. Each unit's discussion is followed by additional practice problems. As an additional study guide, there is also a section in each unit with practice problems similar to those found on the SAT examination. Some schools make these documents available through the classroom teacher or school library. CPM sells the *Parent Guide with Review* for $20.00, including tax, shipping and handling. You may order this resource through the CPM web site at *http://www.cpm.org* or mail your request for the *Parent Guide with Review for Math 3*, **second edition**, with a check payable to "CPM Educational Program," 1233 Noonan Drive, Sacramento, CA 95822-2569. Allow ten days for delivery. This document can also be downloaded from the CPM web site at *http://www.cpm.org*.

Sometimes students find that their Algebra 1 skills need more review than an Algebra 2 course provides. Another source is the CPM *Parent Guide with Review for Math 1 (Algebra 1)*. This resource has numerous worked out examples, as well as hundreds additional practice problems arranged by topic. You may order it for $20 from the above address.

# TABLE OF CONTENTS

# CONTENTS LIST BY LESSON

# College Preparatory Mathematics
## (Algebra 2)

## Goals

Goals for Algebra 2 include all the goals stated for Algebra 1 and Geometry with emphasis on learning to:

- use problem solving strategies in conjunction with a knowledge of the inter-connections among algebra, geometry, and functions to analyze problems and formulate appropriate solutions and to extend current knowledge by making new connections;

- visualize, express, interpret, and graph functions (and their inverses, when they exist) and some relations in various positions in two dimensions. Given the graph, be able to represent it with an equation including the following:

| | | | |
|---|---|---|---|
| linear | exponential | logarithmic | circles |
| quadratic | absolute value | simple rational | ellipses |
| other polynomial | sine, cosine, tangent | square root | hyperbolas |

   as well as other functions and real world problems associated with graphs;

- use variables to represent relations from tables, graphs, verbally stated problems, and geometric diagrams and understand that algebraic relations can be tested by substitutions of numbers;

- solve any real linear or quadratic equation in one variable, mixed systems in two variables, and linear systems of equations in three or more variables;

- use ratio, proportion, and direct variation from numerical, geometric, and algebraic perspectives (percent, similarity, right triangles, slope, and probability);

- use the properties of algebra to reorganize algebraic expressions in order to put them into more useful forms;

- extend the use of trigonometry to the laws of sines and cosines and connect right triangle definitions with the trigonometric functions;

- construct convincing arguments and proofs to support or prove assertions and communicate mathematical ideas clearly using appropriate vocabulary;

- apply mathematics to problems in economics, biology, chemistry, and physics; and,

- use elementary probability and statistics to solve problems.

# WHAT DO THE BARS REPRESENT?

The bars on the opening page for each unit represent the six main threads of the course, six major areas in which you should be making progress all year long. At the beginning of each new unit take a look at the each of the bars and ask yourself, "How am I doing? What are some of the things I now know for sure in this area? What do I need to do some more work on?"

**Problem Solving:** Continues to be a major focus for learning mathematics in Math 3. You should be developing your ability to integrate your use of basic strategies such as identifying subproblems, using guess-and-check, and making organized lists with the use of algebraic procedures and your knowledge of graphing.

**Representation/Modeling:** Learning to represent situations with diagrams, graphs, equations or other models has become a much more important aspect of mathematics since the development of technologies which can carry out algorithmic procedures once a situation is represented. Being able to represent situations in several ways and to move back and forth between representations such as graphs, tables, and equations is emphasized throughout the year.

**Functions/Graphing:** Math 3 is mostly about functions: linear, exponential, quadratic, other polynomial, logarithmic, trigonometric, rational, radical, and absolute value plus others that arise out of specific situations. You'll also need to know about some non-functions such as circles, ellipses, hyperbolas, and "sleeping" parabolas and about inequalities and their graphs.

**Intersections/Systems:** Intersections (and non-intersections) of graphs of functions (and non-functions) lead to systems of equations (and inequalities) which sometimes can be solved by algebraic means and sometimes cannot. You will build on what you know about solving linear and quadratic equations to solve 3x3 systems of linear equations, 2x2 pairings of lines, circles, parabolas and other polynomials that can be solved algebraically, and some pairings of these with exponential, logarithmic, and trigonometric equations for which you will have to use estimation and graphing or some combination of methods.

**Algorithms:** As you gain familiarity through practice with some types of problems that appear routinely as subproblems in other problems, you will need to develop facility with routine procedures, including the tried and true tools of algebraic reorganization as well as others of your own devising or choice. Procedures that should become routine are identified throughout the year, often with a note to include them along with examples in the your Tool Kit.

**Reasoning/Communication:** Includes developing the ability to give clear explanations, to make conjectures, and to develop logical mathematical arguments, proofs as well as derivations. Throughout the course you will practice articulating and justifying ideas orally, in writing in both mathematical and standard language, in diagrams, and sometimes in models.

# UNIT 1

## Sharpening Pencils
### EXPLORING FUNCTIONS

# Unit 1 Objectives
## *Sharpening Pencils*: EXPLORING FUNCTIONS

We assume that students who are taking Algebra 2 are doing so to prepare for college. The reason that colleges want students to complete Algebra 2 is because the skills you learn in this course will be useful to you in many college courses—not just mathematics, but in courses as different as chemistry, economics, psychology, and zoology. What this means is that

### YOUR GOAL FOR THIS COURSE SHOULD BE <u>UNDERSTANDING</u>.

Only you will know if you understand something. We all know how easy it is to memorize something and even do well on a test without having any real idea about what is going on. If you settle for just performing well, you are cheating yourself and, when you go on to college, you will probably have to put off taking the courses you went there to take while you repeat Algebra 2. (At the University of California, which is supposed to take only the best students, approximately 30% of incoming first year students have to repeat algebra for no credit before they can take calculus, which is required for most majors.)

We have done our best to design a course to make it easy for you to try to learn <u>and</u> to understand what you have learned. But no matter what—learning is **hard work.** As the commercial says, NO (BRAIN) PAIN, NO GAIN. So if you want to do well in this course and get a good start in college there are three things which you will have to do:

1. Make <u>understanding</u> the mathematics your highest goal.
2. Discuss the questions with your team.
3. Do the homework.

If you want to understand mathematics, you will need to be willing to spend time thinking and trying out alternative approaches for solving problems. Often you won't be able to come up with the right answer on the first try, so you need to be willing to stick with it. At this level there are generally several ways to think about a topic, and you should try to see more than one of them. That is one reason why we want you to work in teams.

A second reason for working in teams is that most job situations today demand that you work in teams, discussing ideas, listening, testing, taking the good parts of one person's idea and putting them with the good parts of someone else's idea to get a solution. Many of the problems in this book will ask you to discuss your ideas with your team and to listen to other people's ideas. This is an important practice to learn so do not skip over that part of the assignment.

A third reason, which is probably the most important, is that we want the mathematics to make sense to **you**. The mathematical techniques should not seem random. The problems in this book are structured so that you and your team, with some support from your teacher, can understand much more mathematics than you could from being given a rule and then assigned a set of exercises that all look the same.

Finally, you need to do your homework. No one expects basketball players to become good (or even decent), if they just watch others play. The person has to get in there and practice. But they also need to know what to practice. In mathematics, you will often get stuck and not know what to do when you have no friend there and have no one to call to ask for help. In that situation write down what you do know about the problem, write down what you tried, and figure out what your question is. Then write down your question about the problem. This should be enough to convince your teacher that you have really tried to do the problem.

Doing this kind of work is what we mean by doing homework. In fact, the homework questions to which you should give the most attention are the ones you are not sure how to do. The questions which you can easily answer do not help you learn anything new; they are just practice. Getting stuck on a problem is your big opportunity to learn something. Analyze the problem to find out just what the hard part is. And then when you do find out how to do the problem, ask yourself, "What was it about that problem that made it hard?" Answering that question will get you ready to handle the next difficult problem so that maybe you won't get stuck, and you will have learned something.

A very useful way to help yourself learn is to use such problem solving strategies as find a subproblem, guess and check, look for a pattern, organize a table, work backwards, use manipulatives, draw a graph, write an equation, or find an easier related problem. These strategies are not only useful for solving problems, but for **learning** as well. Much of what you learn in this course will not be brand new, but will build on mathematics which you already know, even if it has a new name. You can use one of the problem solving strategies which we review in this first unit to try to go from what you know to what you need to know.

Three of your major goals for this course should be: to become a better problem solver, to become better at asking questions, and to become better at explaining your thinking and justifying your reasoning.

In Unit 1 you will have the opportunity to:

- review problem solving strategies and begin to see them as learning strategies.

- recall and use skills that you have learned in previous classes in the context of modeling and solving larger problems.

- establish good team work routines.

- start to learn what it means to investigate a function.

- become familiar with function notation and begin to see many familiar equations and graphs as functions.

Read the following problem, then go on to problem EF-1. We will do this experiment later in the unit.

---

EF-0.      Suppose you sharpened a dozen pencils so that they were all different lengths, measured them, and recorded their lengths in a data table. Then you weighed each pencil and recorded its weight in the same table. Could you write an equation that would predict the weight of any pencil if you knew its length?

---

PROBLEM SOLVING

REPRESENTATION/MODELING

FUNCTIONS/GRAPHING

INTERSECTIONS/SYSTEMS

ALGORITHMS

REASONING/COMMUNICATION

# Unit 1

*Sharpening Pencils*: **EXPLORING FUNCTIONS**

## GETTING STARTED

EF-1.    Reflect back over the preceding section, focusing on the goals of this course. Write a paragraph that outlines your goals for after high school. Include information about how this course will assist you in fulfilling your goals. Be prepared to share this with your team.

EF-2.    **YARNS**

In your team, make each of the following shapes with the yarn provided by your teacher. Show the shapes to your teacher as you complete them:

a)    square
b)    5-pointed star
c)    square based pyramid

d)    tetrahedron
e)    octahedron
f)    cube

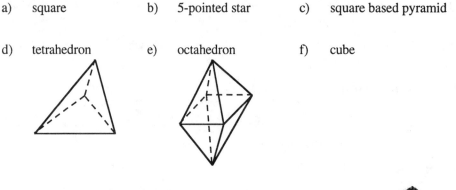

EF-3.    Write down everything you know about the equation **y = mx + b**. You should include what the equation represents and what the different letters represent. Be as thorough as you can possibly be. Tomorrow this will become the first entry in your **Tool Kit**.

> To **graph an equation** or **draw a graph** means we expect you to use graph paper, scale your axes appropriately, label key points, and plot points accurately.

EF-4.    Graph each of the following equations on separate sets of axes. Note: if you do not remember any "short cuts" for graphing, you can always make a table, choose numbers for x, figure out y, and plot the points.

a)    $y = -2x + 7$

b)    $y = \frac{3}{5}x + 1$

c)    $3x + 2y = 6$

d)    $y = x^2$

EF-5.    How is the graph in part (d) above different from the other three graphs? Explain.

   a)   What in the equation of part (d) makes its graph different?

   b)   Do you remember what the graph of part (d) is called? Share this information with your team if you do know, or ask your team members to tell you if you don't know.


EF-6.    Nafeesa graphed a line with slope 5 and y-intercept of -2.

   a)   What is the equation of her line?    b)   Find the value of  x  when  y = 0.


EF-7.    Find the error in the problem at right. Explain what the error is and show how to do the problem correctly.

$$3(x - 2) - 2(x + 7) = 2x + 17$$
$$3x - 6 - 2x + 14 = 2x + 17$$
$$x + 8 = 2x + 17$$
$$-9 = x$$


EF-8.    Solve each of the following equations.

   a)   $\frac{3}{x} + 6 = -45$      b)   $\frac{x - 2}{5} = \frac{10 - x}{8}$      c)   $(x + 1)(x - 3) = 0$


EF-9.    Write an equation to help you solve the following problem. A cable 84 meters long is cut into two pieces so that one piece is 18 meters longer that the other. Find the length of each piece of cable.


EF-10.   Uyregor has a collection of normal, fair dice. He takes one out to roll it.

   a)   What are all the possible outcomes that can come up?

   b)   What is the probability that a 4 comes up?

   c)   What is the probability that the number that comes up is less than 5?

EF-11.    **KEEPING A NOTEBOOK**

You will need to keep an organized notebook for this course. Here is one method of keeping a notebook. Ask your teacher whether you should follow these guidelines or whether there is some other system you should follow.

• The notebook should be a sturdy three-ring lose-leaf binder with a hard cover.

• The binder should have dividers to separate it into six sections:

| | |
|---|---|
| TEXT | HOMEWORK/CLASS WORK |
| NOTES | TESTS AND QUIZZES |
| TOOL KITS | GRAPH PAPER |

Because you don't want to lose your notebook, you should put your name inside the front cover. If you lose it, you will want it returned to you. Put your phone number and address (or the school's, if you don't want yours revealed) on the inside front cover. It will help to put your name in large clear letters on the outside so if someone sees it they can say, "Hey, Fred, I saw your notebook in the cafeteria under the back table."

Your notebook will be your biggest asset for this course and will be the chief way to study for tests, so take good care of it!

## INTRODUCTION TO INVESTIGATING A FUNCTION

EF-12.

As you begin investigating functions, it is important that you understand what we expect when we ask you to sketch a graph. To **sketch a graph** means you show the approximate shape of the graph in the correct location with respect to your axes and that you clearly label all key points.

Consider the following equation:
$y = \sqrt{(4 - x)} - 1$ Use a graphing calculator to help you to answer each of the following questions completely.

a)    Sketch the graph from your graphing calculator. Identify the x and y intercepts.

b)    What are all the possible values of x? Are there any values that will not work for x? What is the largest value you can use for x? Explain.

c)    Does the graph ever cross the horizontal line y = 50? How about y = 500? How do you know?

>>**Problem continues on the next page.**>>

d) What is the smallest possible value of y? What are all of the possible values of y?

e) Have you found <u>everything</u> about this equation that is important? Explain.

f) Does the line y = x intersect the graph? How could you find the point of intersection?

EF-13.  Refer back to problem EF-3 regarding a linear equation. On the Tool Kit sheet provided by your teacher, you will see several topics. Some of these topics should be familiar to you. Fill in the information that will be useful to you in understanding and remembering the topic of linear equations. We will fill in the other topics later in this unit and during Unit 2.

EF-14. Write down everything you can remember about the term **intercepts**. Discuss what you remember with your team and decide what is important. Be sure you include examples. Summarize in your Tool Kit what intercepts are and how they are found.

EF-15. Lugene's desk, the teacher's desk, and the trash can form a triangle. Lugene's desk is 10 feet from the teacher's desk. The angle he sights between the teacher's desk and the trash can is 100°. The angle the teacher sights between Lugene's desk and the trash can is 42°. If Lugene is just about to break a classroom rule and throw his gum into the trash can, about how far will he have to throw it? Do you remember the Law of Sines?

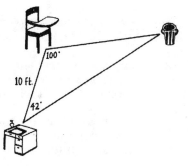

EF-16.    In ∆ABC shown below, $\overline{PQ}$ is drawn  x  units down on side $\overline{AB}$, and is parallel to $\overline{BC}$.

$\overline{AB}$ has a length of 10, $\overline{BC}$ has a length of 8.

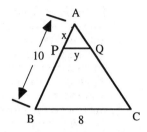

a)    If  x = 1, what is the length of  y?

b)    Suppose  x = 2.  Now what is the length of  y?

c)    Suppose  x = 3.  Now what is the length of  y?

d)    Write an equation relating  x  and  y.  Write it in the form "y =  ."

e)    Use your equation to find  y  when  x = 7.  Explain in words what this means.

f)    If you graphed your equation, what do you think the graph would look like? Explain how you know.

g)    The relationship described in this problem is often called direct variation.  Why does this description make sense?


EF-17.    In each of the equations below, what is  y  when  x = 2?  When  x = 0?  Where would the graph of each cross the y-axis?

a)    y = 3x + 15                    b)    y = 3 - 3x


EF-18.    Suppose we want to find where the lines  y = 3x + 15  and  y = 3 - 3x  cross and we want to be more accurate than the graphing calculator or graph paper will let us be.  We can use algebra to find this point of intersection.

a)    If you remember how to do this, find the point of intersection using algebra and explain your method to your team tomorrow in class.  If you don't remember, then do parts (b) - (e) below.

b)    Since  y = 3x + 15  and  y = 3 - 3x, what must be true about  3x + 15  and 3 - 3x?

c)    Write an equation which contains no y's and solve it for  x.

d)    Use the x-value you found in part (c) to find the corresponding y-value.

e)    Where do the two lines cross?


EF-19.    Find the error in the problem. Explain what the error is and re-do the problem showing a correct solution.

$$\frac{5}{x} = x - 4$$
$$x \cdot \frac{5}{x} = x - 4$$
$$5 = x - 4$$
$$9 = x$$

# SHARPENING PENCILS LAB

**EF-20.** **Introduction**

In this investigation you will be comparing weights of pencils sharpened to different lengths. While this activity, on the face of it, may not seem very inspiring or potentially enlightening, we have chosen it because it will lead to the development of mathematical models and concepts that are central to what you will be learning in Algebra 2. (A "mathematical model" might be new to you. One possible model is an algebraic equation(s) used to represent a real world situation. Knowing an equation that represents a situation allows us to make predictions based on the model.) Although this activity does not quite represent a real-world situation, it is an investigation that a large group of people can do fairly quickly in a classroom, a fact that will allow you to focus on the mathematical model this experiment will generate.

Be sure that each person in your team does a neat and accurate graph, answers all questions, and shows all work. Each of you will be keeping a portfolio in this course which will show examples of your work and problem solving skills. Your lab write-ups to these investigations will be the first pieces you will put in your portfolio.

## Directions

In this investigation you are going to sharpen pencils. You will also do some math, but throughout this investigation, remember not to use the eraser for erasing. Here's what to do:

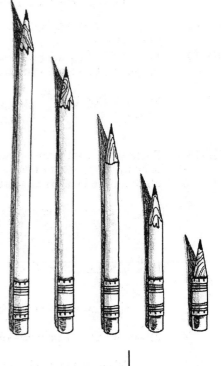

a) Start with a fresh pencil. Sharpen it just enough to be usable. Measure the length of the <u>painted</u> part (excluding the metal and eraser part) in centimeters and then weigh the pencil. Record both quantities in a table with two headings "Length of painted part (cm)" and "Mass (g)."

b) Now sharpen the pencil a bit. Measure the <u>painted</u> part and weigh it. Record your data in your table.

c) Before you gather further data, do you think the relationship will be linear or non-linear? Why?

d) Plot the data on a graph where the x-axis represents the length in centimeters and the y-axis represents the mass in grams. Use a full sheet of graph paper.

e) What should happen to the mass of the pencil as you sharpen it? How does this relate to the graph? Be clear. Collect at least ten data points. The last few should be with the pencil getting down to a little nub. Don't forget to measure, weigh, and record after each sharpening!

f) Graph your data on your graph paper. Write a sentence comparing the graph to your predictions.

EF-21.    Use a ruler to draw a straight line to fit your data and find the equation of the line that "best fits" the graph of your data.

EF-22.    Suppose you sharpened the pencil all the way down, so that no paint remained. How much would this little pencil weigh? Do you need to sharpen the pencil all the way down and weigh it to answer this question, or can you predict from your graph? Explain.

EF-23.    Suppose we took a 1 cm piece out of the middle of the pencil. What would be its mass? Use your line-of-best-fit to approximate the change in mass per 1 cm change in length? What would this value represent in your linear equation?

EF-24.    What do the y-intercept and slope of the line correspond to on the pencil? Explain your answers.

EF-25.    The x-axis on your graph represents possible lengths for the painted part of the pencil. What are acceptable values for x in this problem? Explain.

EF-26.    What do the y-values represent? What are possible values?

> Save your data and the answers to the previous questions for this investigation! You will be using them in a few days so keep this handy. The purpose of this investigation is to show how you can create an algebraic representation for the patterns you find in the data you collect.

EF-27.  James correctly completed the tables and drew the graphs below but his teacher marked each one wrong. For each problem:

a)  Identify as many mistakes as you can. Be specific.

b)  Redraw the graphs so that James knows what to do and can get full credit next time.

i)  $y = 2x + 1$

| x | y |
|---|---|
| 1 | 3 |
| 2 | 5 |
| 3 | 7 |

ii)  $y = x^2$

| x | y |
|---|---|
| 0 | 0 |
| 1 | 1 |
| 2 | 4 |
| 3 | 9 |

iii)  $y = 3x + 50$

| x | y |
|---|----|
| 0 | 50 |
| 1 | 53 |
| 2 | 56 |

iv)  $y = x^2 - 4$

| x | y |
|----|----|
| 0 | -4 |
| -1 | -3 |
| 1 | -3 |
| 2 | 0 |
| 3 | 5 |

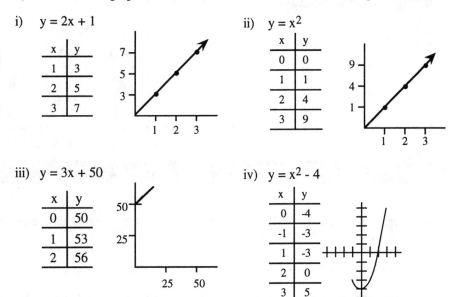

EF-28.  Rearrange these equations by solving each of them for x. Write each equation as x = ____ (y will be in your answer).

a)  $y = \frac{3}{5}x + 1$

b)  $3x + 2y = 6$

c)  $y = x^2$

EF-29.  What value of x allows you to find the y-intercept? Where does the graph of each of these equations cross the y-axis? Refer to your Tool Kit entry on intercepts if you need help. Give each answer in the form (0, _).

a)  $y = 3x + 6$

b)  $x = 5y - 10$

c)  $y = x^2$

d)  $y = 2x^2 - 4$

e)  $y = (x - 5)^2$

EF-30.  What value of y allows you to find the x-intercept? For each of the equations in parts (a) through (e) above, find where its graph intersects the x-axis. Give answers in the form (_, 0).

EF-31.    Stacie says to Cory, "Reach into this
          standard deck of playing cards, and pull out
          any card at random.  If it is the queen of
          hearts, I'll pay you $5.00."  What is the
          probability that Cory gets Stacie's $5.00?
          What is the probability that Stacie keeps her
          $5.00?  Justify your answers.

# USING THE GRAPHING CALCULATOR

EF-32.    Take out your solutions to both problems EF-29 and EF-30.  Check that your intercepts
          are correct by using the graphing calculator to display the graphs.  Considering the
          following questions may help for parts (b), (d), and (e).

          a)   What did you have to do with the equation in part (b) in order to graph it?

          b)   For part (d) use the trace button to check the x-intercepts.  How close did you get to
               $y = 0$?  Try the zoom button.  How close did you get to the actual x-intercepts?

          c)   What window adjustment did you have to make in order to see the y-intercept in
               part (e)?

EF-33.    Where do the graphs of $y = 2x - 6$ and $y = -4x + 6$ cross?  Use your graphing
          calculator to find the point.  Use your zoom key to get closer.

EF-34.    Sketch the graphs of $y = 3x - 5$ and $y = 2x + 12$.  Adjust the window and use your
          zoom-in feature to find out where they cross.  Verify your answer by solving
          algebraically.

EF-35.    What does the graph of $y = x^2 - 3x - 3$ look like?  What do we call it?  Make a sketch
          on paper.  Use the trace and/or zoom buttons to approximate the x-intercepts and
          vertex.

EF-36.    How would you set the window on the graphing calculator to graph $y = (x + 1)(x - 9)$
          so that you can see the **complete** graph?  By **complete**, we mean that we see
          everything that is important about the graph and that everything off the screen is
          predictable based on what we do see.  Explain and check.

EF-37.    Does the temperature outside depend on the time
          of day, or does the time of day depend on the
          temperature outside?  This may seem like a silly
          question, but to sketch a graph that represents
          this relationship, we need to determine which
          axis will represent what quantity.

          a)    When you graph an equation such as
                $y = 3x - 5$, as you did earlier, which
                variable, the x or the y, **depends** on
                the other?  Which is not dependent?
                (That is, which is **in**dependent?)  Explain.

          b)    Which is <u>dependent</u>:  temperature or time
                of day?  Which is <u>independent</u>?

          c)    Sketch a graph, with appropriately named
                axes, showing the relationship between temperature outside and time of day.


EF-38.    Examine each graph below.  Based on the shape of the graph and the labels of the axes,
          write a sentence to describe the relationship that each graph represents.  Then state which
          is the independent and which is the dependent variable.

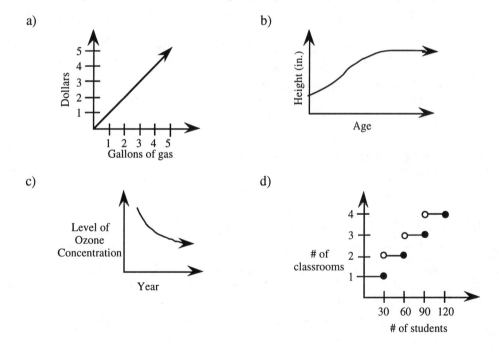

a)

b)

c)

d)


EF-39.    Find where the following pairs of lines intersect.

          a)    $y = 5x - 2$                      b)    $y = x - 4$
                $y = 3x + 18$                            $2x + 3y = -17$

EF-40. Find the error in the problem at right. Identify the error and show how to do the problem correctly.

$$4.1x = 9.5x + 23.7$$
$$-4.1x \quad -4.1x$$
$$5.4x = 23.7$$
$$\frac{5.4x}{5.4} = \frac{23.7}{5.4}$$
$$x = 4.39$$

EF-41 An average school bus holds 45 people. Sketch a graph showing the relationship between the number of students present and the number of buses required. Be sure to label the axes.

EF-42. Write down all you remember about sine, cosine, and tangent. Give examples if you can. Discuss this with your team tomorrow and enter any necessary information on your Tool Kit with appropriate drawings.

## DOMAIN AND RANGE

EF-43. Look back to your first function investigation, problem EF-12. Describe all the x-values that could be used in the equation. Were there any restrictions? Explain.

EF-44. Find your data from the sharpening pencils lab. What were the possible values for the lengths of the pencils? Could there be any other values that you did not include? Explain.

EF-45. When you sharpened and weighed pencils what was the independent variable: the length or the mass?

EF-46. Include the following definition in your Tool Kit:

> The set of possible values that the **independent variable** can take on has a special name. It is called the **DOMAIN** of the function. It consists of every number that **x** can represent for your function.

EF-47. Again look back to your first function lab, problem EF-12. What were the possible y-values you found for the equation? What did y depend on? Explain.

EF-48. What were the values for the masses of the pencils? Did the mass of the pencil depend on anything? Explain.

EF-49.    For the pencil investigation, what is the dependent variable: the length or the mass?

EF-50.    Include the following definition in your Tool Kit:

> The **RANGE** of a function is the set of possible values of the **dependent variable**. It consists of every number that **y** can represent for your function.

EF-51.    Use a set of axes to represent the domain and another to represent the range for each of the following functions.

a)                          b)                          c)                          d)

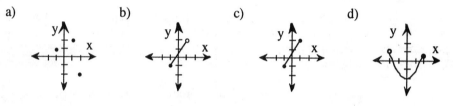

EF-52.    Graph these two lines on the same set of axes:  $y = 2x$  and  $y = -\frac{1}{2}x + 6$.

   a)    Find the x- and y-intercepts for each equation.

   b)    Shade in the region bounded by the two lines and the x-axis.

   c)    What are the domain and range of the region? State the subproblems you used to find these values.

   d)    Find the area of this region, accurate to the nearest tenth.

EF-53.    In the last problem, you needed to find the point where the two lines intersected.

   a)    Explain how to find the point of intersection for the two lines in the previous problem.

   b)    Is using the graph an accurate way to find the point of intersection? Explain.

   c)    What method do you think is the most accurate? Explain.

EF-54. Nissos and Chelita were arguing over a math problem. Nissos was trying to explain to Chelita that she had made a mistake in finding the x-intercepts of the function $y = x^2 - 10x + 21$. "No way!" Chelita yelled. "I know how to find x-intercepts! You make the y equal to zero and solve for x. I know I did this right!" Here is her work.

$$x^2 - 10x + 21 = 0, \text{ so } (x + 7)(x + 3) = 0$$

Therefore,     $x + 7 = 0$ or $x + 3 = 0$
                   $x = -7$        $x = -3$

Nissos tried to explain to her that she still had done something wrong. Who is correct? Justify and explain your answer completely.

EF-55. In Salem, 42% of the registered voters are Republicans and 44% are Democrats. The other 217 are Independents. How many registered voters are there in Salem? Write an equation that represents this problem.

EF-56. A circle has an area of $45\pi$ cm$^2$. Find its circumference (perimeter).

a) List all the "tasks" you will need to complete to solve this problem. These "tasks" are known as **subproblems**. Keep this term in mind.

b) Solve the original problem. Give your answer exactly (here it will involve $\pi$ and a square root) then use your calculator to approximate it to two decimal places.

EF-57. Find the domain and the range for each of the following functions.

a)                    b)                    c)                    d)

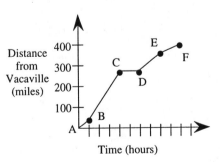

EF-58. Recently, Kalani and Lynette took a trip from Vacaville to Los Angeles. The graph at right represents their trip.

a) Explain what each stage of the graph represents.

b) About how many miles is it from Vacaville to Los Angeles? How do you know?

c) Using the graph above, sketch a graph that would represent their <u>speed</u> while traveling. Be sure to label the axes.

EF-59.  Most problems that you will meet in this course, in other mathematics courses, and in life, are made up of smaller problems whose solutions you need to put together in order to solve the original problem. These smaller problems are called **SUBPROBLEMS**. For example, you cannot solve the following problem directly. First you must solve several subproblems which are not stated explicitly but which are necessary to solve in order to solve the larger problem.

Logan's dog, Digger, was constantly digging his way under the fence, escaping from the back yard, and following Logan to school. Digger was also in big trouble with Logan's mom who enjoyed her leisure time away from her law firm by taking care of her flower garden. They decided they would have to keep Digger tied up while they were away during the day. After a long discussion about how much of the back yard Digger should be allowed to destroy, they agreed that at least **two-thirds** of the yard should be safe for planting flowers and other plants. Logan tied Digger to the corner of the shed, at point A, with a **25 foot** rope. Will this satisfy his mom?

a) Draw the region in which Digger is free to roam.

b) Before actually working out any answers, write down all of the subproblems you need to solve the problem.

c) Now solve each subproblem and answer the question.

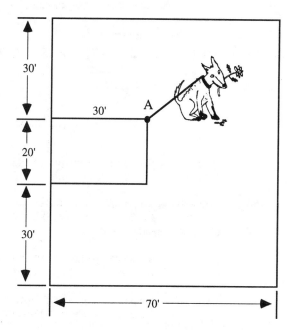

EF-60. How will your solution to the previous problem change if we lengthen Digger's rope? Explain.

EF-61. Terri's project for the Math Fair was a magnificent black box which she called a FUNCTION MACHINE. If we put a 3 into her machine, the output is an 8. If we put in a 10, it gives us a 29, and if we put in 20 it gives us a 59.

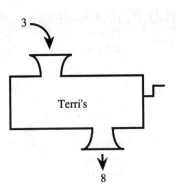

a) What would her machine do to 5? to -1? to x? A table may help.

b) Write a rule for her machine.

EF-62. Gerri made a different machine. Here are four pictures of the same machine. Find its rule.

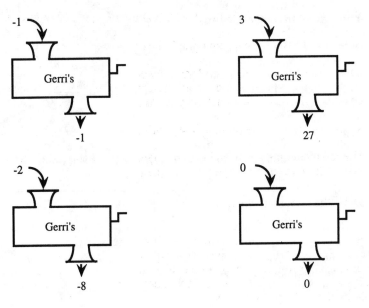

EF-63. Carmichael also made a function machine. The inner "workings" of the machine are visible. What will be the output if:

a) 3 is dropped in?

b) -4 is dropped in?

c) -22.872 is dropped in?

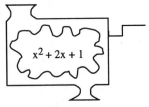

EF-64. If the number 1 is the output for Carmichael's machine, how can you find out what number was dropped in? Find the number or numbers that could have been dropped in.

EF-65. Find the error in the problem at right. Describe the error, and show how to solve the problem correctly.

$$3x + 2 = 10 - 5(x - 1)$$
$$3x + 2 = 10 - 5x - 5$$
$$3x + 2 = 5 - 5x$$
$$8x + 2 = 5$$
$$8x = 3$$
$$x = \frac{3}{8}$$

EF-66. Write an equation or two equations to help you solve the following problem. A rectangle's length is four times its width. The sum of two consecutive sides is 22. How long is each side?

EF-67. Consider the equation $4x - 6y = 12$.

a) What do you suppose the graph of this equation looks like? Justify your answer.

b) Solve the equation for $y$ and graph the equation.

c) Explain how to find the x- and y-intercepts. Be complete so that you can give your explanation to someone who is still having trouble with intercepts and he or she will be able to follow and understand your explanation.

d) Which form of the equation is best for finding intercepts quickly? Why?

e) Use the intercepts you found in part (c) to graph the line. Did you get the same line you got in part (b)? Should you? Explain.

EF-68. Have you ever wondered why so many equations are written with the variables x and y? Even if you haven't, suppose you were going to reach into a bag that contained the letters of the English alphabet, and pull out one letter at random to use as a variable in equations. What is the probability that you would pull out an x? If you got the x, now what is the probability that you pull out the y?

EF-69.    A three-foot indoor kiddy slide must meet the
          ground very gradually, making an angle of 155°
          as shown. Find the height of the slide (y) and
          the length of the floor it will cover (x).

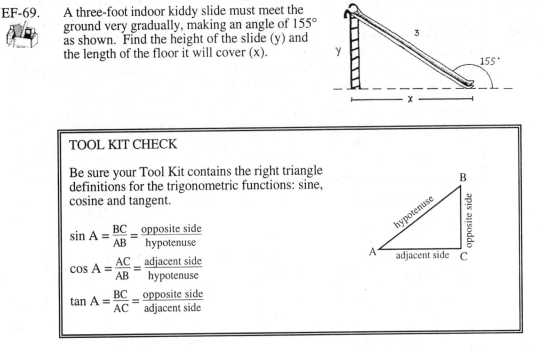

TOOL KIT CHECK

Be sure your Tool Kit contains the right triangle
definitions for the trigonometric functions: sine,
cosine and tangent.

$$\sin A = \frac{BC}{AB} = \frac{\text{opposite side}}{\text{hypotenuse}}$$

$$\cos A = \frac{AC}{AB} = \frac{\text{adjacent side}}{\text{hypotenuse}}$$

$$\tan A = \frac{BC}{AC} = \frac{\text{opposite side}}{\text{adjacent side}}$$

# INVESTIGATING FUNCTIONS

EF-70.    Working together, find out <u>everything</u> you can about the
          following equation: $y = \sqrt{(x + 16)}$. Be ready to report your
          team's findings in about 15 minutes. (Part of the problem is
          for your team to decide what we mean by "everything there is
          to know." How do you know you have found <u>everything</u>?
          Keep asking, "What else could we check?") Be sure to save
          your work as you will need it again.

EF-71.    When you use a graphing calculator for this problem, you          $y = \frac{1}{x - 3}$
          need to be careful when typing in the equation of the function.
          The calculator follows the same order of operations you have
          learned in earlier math courses, so for the graph of the equation
          at right, do you want to take the reciprocal of just the x or of
          the x - 3? What can you do to make the calculator do what
          you want? Sketch a graph of the equation at right.

EF-72.    You can use the graphing calculator to make the kind of calculations you did in problem
          EF-63 part (c) easier. As we saw, that function machine squared the number that was
          dropped in, added it to twice the number dropped in, and finally added one to all that.
          If -3 is dropped in, what comes out? Now take advantage of the graphing calculator
          and calculate the result when 23 is dropped in.

EF-73.

A convenient way to show what a function machine does is to use **FUNCTION NOTATION**. For Carmichael's machine in problem EF-63, we would write $f(x) = x^2 + 2x + 1$. The f is just the **name** of the function machine; it is not a variable. It could just as well be $Pierce(x) = x^2 + 2x + 1$ if the machine happened to be named Pierce! Warning: $f(x)$ does **not** mean f times x; we read it as "f of x." It means the output of the function f resulting from the input x. In part (c) of problem EF-63, you actually found $f(-22.872)$. Here is another example that shows how to use function notation. Add this information to your Tool Kit.

If $g(x) = 2x^2 - 5x$ then $g(-2) = 2(-2)^2 - 5(-2) = 8 + 10 = 18$.

Now use function notation to describe what each of the following machines does to x.

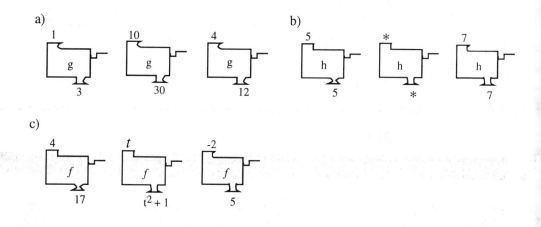

a)

b)

c)

EF-74.

How can we use the graphing calculator to make substituting values easier? Just type in exactly what you want to find. For instance, to find $f(-22.872)$ type in:

$$(-22.872)^2 + 2(-22.872) + 1$$

Do this and check your answer with problem EF-63.

EF-75.

Using the same function, find $f(-142.2)$. You can make your work even easier by substituting values on your graphing calculator and just changing the input value from -22.872 to -142.2. Be careful! Different calculators work different ways. Try this and check your result with your team.

EF-76.    Compare each of the following tables.

$f(x) = x^2 + 2x + 1$

| x | f(x) |
|---|------|
| -22.872 | 478.384384 |
| -142.2 | 19937.44 |

$y = x^2 + 2x + 1$

| x | y |
|---|---|
| -22.872 | 478.384384 |
| -142.2 | 19937.44 |

For each table, what are the independent and dependent variables? What is the difference between the two tables? What is the difference between the two rules? Explain.


EF-77.    If $g(x) = 0.01x^2 - 6.03x + 17.1$, find:

a)    g(-5.1)                               b)    g(6.23)


EF-78.    Graph the following functions and find the x- and y-intercepts.

a)    y = 2x + 3                          b)    f(x) = 2x + 3


EF-79.    Is it true that $\frac{x+2}{x+3} = \frac{2}{3}$? Explain your reasoning.


EF-80.    Write an equation for the line passing through the points (2, 0) and (0, -3). Remember that drawing a diagram, in this case the graph, can be very helpful.


EF-81.    Give a convincing argument why $\triangle ABC \sim \triangle ADE$. Then use what you know about similar triangles to complete each of the following ratios.

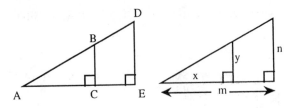

a)    $\frac{y}{x} =$ _____

b)    $\frac{n}{y} =$ _____


EF-82.    Solve for x:  $7x^2 - 3x - 4 = 0$. If you don't remember how to do this problem, ask a member of your team tomorrow if he or she remembers the Quadratic Formula.

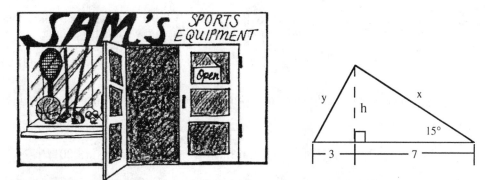

EF-83.    During a recent planning session at Sam's Outdoor Equipment headquarters, the board of directors debated whether or not they should change the design of their new *Super Push* starting block. The big debate came when they were trying to figure out how much it would cost to outline the block in leather. Help them out by finding x, y, and the perimeter. What subproblem do you need to do first?

EF-84.    Below left are the side views of three swimming pools. Below right are three graphs that show the relationship between the depth of the water (in the deep end) over time as the pool is filled at a constant rate. Match each of the following swimming pool profiles, A, B, and C, to the graph that could represent this relationship.

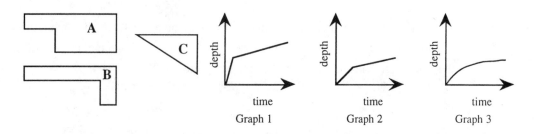

Graph 1        Graph 2        Graph 3

## INVESTIGATING FUNCTIONS WITH ASYMPTOTES

EF-85.    In problem EF-71, you sketched the graph of $y = \dfrac{1}{x - 3}$ using your graphing calculator. Here we will consider the function $h(x) = \dfrac{1}{x - 3}$ in more detail. Use a full sheet of graph paper, and set up a pair of axes with the origin near the middle of the page, vertically, and about 2 inches in from the left side. On both axes make each square on the graph paper represent 0.25 units. Now make an accurate graph of $h(x) = \dfrac{1}{x - 3}$ . Use a calculator to make the substituting and calculating easier, but make an extensive table, do not just copy the picture of the graph.

EF-86. What seems to be happening to the graph near x = 3? Did you use values like 3.5, 3.25, 2.5, and 2.75? If you didn't, do it now, and explain what is happening.

EF-87. Find each of the following values and be sure to plot them on your graph (if possible).

a)  h(2.9)          b)  h(2.99)          c)  h(2.999)

d)  h(3.1)          e)  h(3.01)          f)  h(3.001)

g)  What happens when you try x-values closer and closer to 3? Give a good explanation for this phenomenon.

EF-88. Use your results from the preceding problems to answer these questions.

a)  What are the domain and range for the function h? Explain.

b)  Where does the graph of h cross the x-axis? Compare this to your picture and justify your answer.

EF-89. As a team, come up with another equation that will have a different graph, but the same phenomenon as $h(x) = \dfrac{1}{x-3}$ . Test it out. Give it to another team to graph and find the appropriate viewing screen to be able to see the complete graph.

EF-90. I noticed my outdoor faucet dripping even after I tried to turn it off. I decided to see how much water was being wasted. I put a glass under it at 7:33 p.m. and removed it at 9:19 p.m. When I poured the water out of the glass into a measuring cup, it measured almost exactly $1\frac{1}{3}$ cups of water. About how much water leaks from that faucet each day?

EF-91. Write an equation that could represent the relationship between the number of days the faucet has been dripping and how much water has been wasted.

a)  What are the independent and dependent variables?

b)  What are the domain and range?

c)  What should the graph look like? Justify your answer.

**EF-92.** Burt takes a shower in a 40-gallon tub. His tub can drain up to 10 gallons of water per minute when the drain is clear. Unfortunately, Burt's rapid hair loss slows the drainage considerably! For each minute that Burt showers, he loses a set amount of hair and the drain becomes more and more clogged. Suppose that the water is flowing into the tub at a rate of 5 gallons per minute, that the water in the tub starts to back up after 10 minutes, and that Burt likes to take **long** showers. Make a reasonable graph of this situation showing how the gallons of water in the tub and the showering time (in minutes) are related. Label the axes, important points, and any other critical items.

**EF-93.** Make a sketch of a graph showing the relationship between the number of people on your school's campus and the time of day.

**EF-94.** The graph below shows the probabilities of a spinner coming up a red, blue or green.

a) What is the probability the spinner comes up blue?

b) What is the probability the spinner comes up green?

c) Which axis represents the <u>independent</u> axis? The <u>dependent</u> axis?

d) What is the domain? The range?

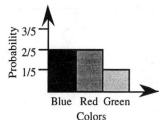

**EF-95.** Find where each of the pairs of graphs intersect.

a)   $x + y = 5$
     $y = \frac{1}{3}x + 1$

b)   $2x + y = 3$
     $y = -2x - 2$

c)   Is it necessary to actually draw the graphs to determine points of intersection in parts (a) and (b)? Explain.

**EF-96.** If $t(n) = 5 - 2(\frac{3}{4}n - 1)$, find:

a)   $t(4)$          b)   $t(-20)$          c)   $t(\frac{2}{3})$

EF-97.    You make $5.50 per hour at your job.  Approximately 30% of your wages goes for taxes, union dues, and other deductions.  How many hours do you need to work to take home $150 per week?  Use equations or explain your reasoning.

## MORE INVESTIGATIONS

EF-98.    Look back at your work on investigating functions.  Make an organized list of all the elements to consider when investigating a function.

EF-99.    Remember Logan's dog Digger?  Suppose Digger is in the middle of an enormous yard, with acres and acres of land.  Digger is roped to a stake at the center of the yard.  Consider a function where the input is the length of Digger's rope and the output is the amount of area that Digger roams.  Investigate this relationship.

EF-100.   Investigate the function $y = \dfrac{5}{(x^2 + 1)} - 1$.

EF-101.   Imagine that we add water to the beakers, A, B, and C, shown below.  Sketch a graph to show the relationship between the volume of water added and the height of the water in each beaker.  Put all three graphs on one set of axes (you may want to use colored pencils to distinguish the graphs).  What are the independent and dependent variables?

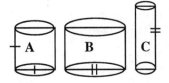

height of
liquid

volume of
water added

**EF-102.** For each of the functions below, what are the domain and range?

a)                                    b)                                    c)

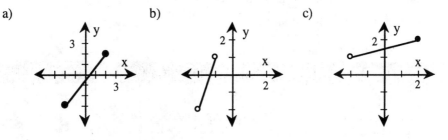

**EF-103.** Given: $f(x) = 2x - 7$

    a)   Compute $f(0)$                     b)   Solve $f(x) = 0$

    c)   What do the answers to parts (a) and (b) tell about the graph of $f(x)$?

**EF-104.** Solve each of the following equations for the indicated variable.

    a)   $y = mx + b$  (for $x$)             b)   $A = \pi r^2$  (for $r$)

    c)   $V = LWH$  (for $W$)             d)   $2x + \dfrac{1}{y} = 3$  (for $y$)

**EF-105.** If $h(x) = x^2 - 5$, where does the graph of $h(x)$ cross the x-axis? Make a sketch of the graph.

**EF-106.** Solve each of the following for $z$.

a)                                                        b)

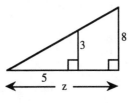 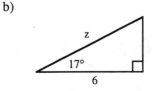

**EF-107.** If $f(x) = -x^3 + 2x^2$, find:

    a)   $f(-1)$             b)   $f(-2)$             c)   $f(2)$

    d)   $f(1)$               e)   $f(0)$              f)   $f(3)$

    g)   Draw a graph of this function.        h)   What value(s) of $x$ make $f(x) = 0$?

EF-108.* While preparing for a Sunday afternoon weather program, Mel the Meteorologist contacted his team of assistants in Chicago, Fairbanks, Melbourne (Australia), New Orleans, Salt Lake City, and San Francisco. Their task was to find the mean (average) high and low temperatures in their location for each month of the previous year. In the process of organizing this data onto graphs, Mel forgot to include the name of each location with its graph.

a) Discuss with your team what you know about each city's geographical location, and match each graph with one of the cities listed above.

b) Which location's graph is closest to linear?

c) Which location has the widest range of low temperatures for the year?

d) Estimate the range of high temperatures for Salt Lake City.

e) The range of low temperatures for New Orleans can be written as an inequality in y: $45° < y < 70°$. Write the range of high temperatures in Chicago for the year as an inequality.

f) Write the range of low temperatures in Melbourne for the year as an inequality.

g) What is the domain for these relationships?

**>>The graphs for this problem are on the next page.>>**

---

\* This problem came from a presentation by Australian Mathematics Educators at the 1991 NCTM Conference held in Salt Lake City, Utah.

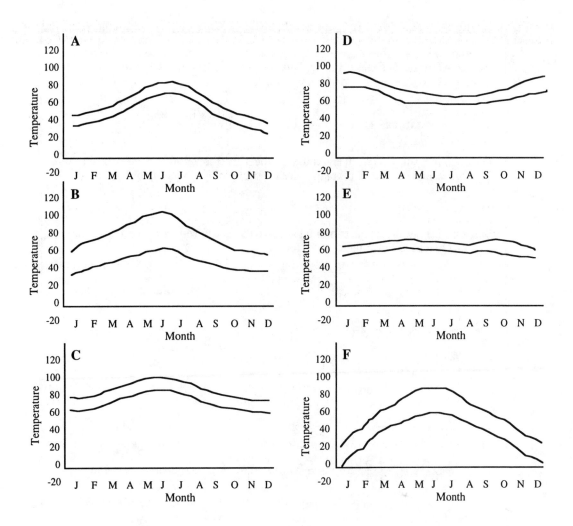

An important tool from Algebra 1 that you might have already used this year is the **QUADRATIC FORMULA**. This formula is particularly helpful for finding the x-intercepts of parabolas. The formula states

$$\text{if } ax^2 + bx + c = 0, \text{ then } x = \frac{-b \pm \sqrt{b^2 - 4ac}}{2a}.$$

For example, suppose we wanted to find the x-intercepts of $y = 2x^2 - 3x - 3$. First we would let $y = 0$ (explain why we use $y = 0$ in your Tool Kit).

$$0 = 2x^2 - 3x - 3$$

Since we cannot factor the trinomial and use the Zero Product Property, we must use the Quadratic Formula to solve for x.

$$x = \frac{-(-3) \pm \sqrt{(-3)^2 - 4(2)(-3)}}{2(2)} \qquad \text{substitute for a, b, and c}$$

$$= \frac{3 \pm \sqrt{9 + 24}}{4} \qquad \text{simplify}$$

$$= \frac{3 \pm \sqrt{33}}{4} \qquad \text{add}$$

$$\approx \frac{3 \pm 5.745}{4} \qquad \text{find } \sqrt{\phantom{x}} \text{ value}$$

$$\text{So, } x \approx \frac{3 + 5.745}{4} \text{ and } x \approx \frac{3 - 5.745}{4} \qquad \text{write values separately}$$

$$x \approx 2.18625 \text{ and } x \approx -0.68625. \qquad \text{simplify the fractions}$$

Be sure you include all the information you need about the **Quadratic Formula** in your Tool Kit.

EF-110. Solve these equations and give the solution in both radical and decimal form.

a) $x^2 + 3x - 3 = 0$          b) $3x^2 - 7x = 12$

EF-111. For each of the following graphs, state the domain and range.

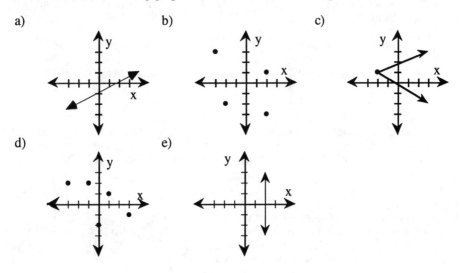

a)

b)

c)

d)

e)

EF-112. Find the slope and intercepts of $3x + 4y = 12$. Sketch a graph.

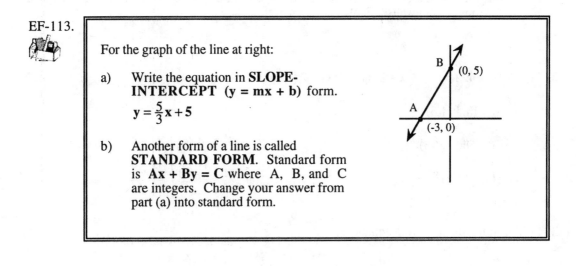

EF-113.

For the graph of the line at right:

a) Write the equation in **SLOPE-INTERCEPT** $(y = mx + b)$ form.

$$y = \frac{5}{3}x + 5$$

b) Another form of a line is called **STANDARD FORM**. Standard form is $Ax + By = C$ where A, B, and C are integers. Change your answer from part (a) into standard form.

B (0, 5)

A
(-3, 0)

EF-114. Find the length of $\overline{AB}$ in the preceding problem.

EF-115.   Suppose you have a 3 x 3 x 3 cube. It is painted on all six faces and then cut apart into 27 pieces each a 1 x 1 x 1 cube. If one of the cubes is chosen at random, what is the probability that:

a)   three sides are painted?          b)   two sides are painted?

c)   one side is painted?              d)   no sides are painted?

EF-116.   What does it mean for a shape to have a **line of symmetry**? Include several diagrams in your explanation. This might be a characteristic worth mentioning when investigating a function. Decide with your class whether or not it should be included.

EF-117.   Ayla and Sean are about to paint the side of their house facing their neighbor Brutus. Brutus tells them that since their wall is only six feet away from his, they might as well paint his wall as well. Both walls are ten feet high, and Ayla and Sean's ladder is eight feet long. If they place the ladder exactly half way between the two buildings, and let it lean against  one side and then the other (as if it were hinged on the ground), will they be able to reach the tops of both walls? Explain your answer.

EF-118.   Given:  $f(x) = -\frac{2}{3}x + 3$  and  $g(x) = 2x^2 - 5$,

a)   find:  $f(3)$                      b)   solve:  $f(x) = -5$

c)   find:  $g(-3)$                     d)   solve:  $g(x) = 9$

e)   solve:  $g(x) = 8$                 f)   solve:  $g(x) = -7$

EF-119.   Graph the following equations.

a)   $y - 2x = 3$                       b)   $y - 3 = x^2$

c)   State the x- and y-intercepts for each equation.

d)   Where do the two graphs cross? Show how to find these two points without the graphs.

EF-120.   State the domain and range of each graph.

a)                          b)                          c)

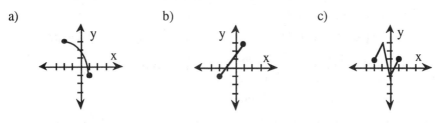

EF-121.   Look at your answers to the previous problem. If you know a specific domain and range, what do you know about the <u>shape</u> of the function?

## SUMMARY ASSIGNMENT

EF-122.   **PORTFOLIO GROWTH OVER TIME—PROBLEM #1**

On a separate sheet of paper (you will be handing this problem in separately or putting it into your portfolio) explain everything that you know about:

$$y = x^2 - 4 \text{ and } y = \sqrt{(x + 4)}.$$

EF-123.   **UNIT 1 SUMMARY ASSIGNMENT**

There are a lot of ideas covered in this unit. Some ideas should be review while others may be new to you. Answer the following questions completely and turn them in as directed by your teacher.

a)   Write down at least three major ideas of the unit and find a minimum of one problem which illustrates each idea. Be sure to include a description of the original problem and a completely worked out solution.

b)   If you had to choose a favorite problem from the unit, what would it be? Why?

c)   Find a problem that you still cannot solve or that you are worried that you might not be able to solve on a test. Write out the question and as much of the solution as you can until you get to the hard part. Then explain what it is that keeps you from solving the problem. Be clear and precise.

d)   During this unit you worked with your team daily. What role did you play in the team? (Discuss ideas similar to: were you a leader, taking charge? Did you keep your team on task? Did you ask questions? Did you just listen and copy down answers? In what ways are you a productive team member? How could you do better? Did your team work well? Why or why not?)

e)   What did you learn in this unit? Explain how your learning relates to your response in part (d).

EF-124. **SELF EVALUATION**

In this unit there were a number of problems in which you were expected to:

- solve equations.
- write the equation of a line using slope and y-intercept.
- find mathematical models to fit real life data.
- draw graphs of lines and parabolas.
- use the Pythagorean Theorem.
- set up ratios to solve problems.
- use trigonometry to find missing parts of triangles.

Write a realistic self-evaluation related to the skills in the list above. Which ones do you feel confident in performing? Which skills do you still need to work on? Decide if any of the ideas listed above need to be included on your Tool Kit.

> One of your responsibilities in this course will be to seek extra practice or assistance outside of the class to help you increase your understanding and improve your skills. You can accomplish this task by exchanging phone numbers with other students in the class or talking with your teacher about extra help resources.

EF-125. **TOOL KIT CHECK-UP**

Your Tool Kit contains reference tools for algebra. Return to your Tool Kit entries. You may need to revise or add entries.

Be sure that your Tool Kit contains entries for all of the items listed below. Add any topics that are missing to your Tool Kit NOW, as well as any other items that will help you in your study of algebra.

- Linear Equations
- Intercepts
- Quadratic Formula
- Graphing Calculator Information

- Sine, Cosine, and Tangent Ratios
- Function Notation
- Domain and Range

## EF- 126.   WHAT IS A PORTFOLIO?

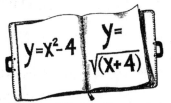

If you heard someone talking about an artist showing his portfolio of work, or an architect displaying her portfolio of designs, you would probably know what to expect to see in their portfolios.  Those portfolios represent the artist's and the architect's best work.

It is their way to demonstrate to prospective clients that they are skilled and know their trade, and that they are talented and creative in their fields.

A landscape architect might include photographs of work in progress so that he could show the stages of the job he performs.  This would give the client an idea of how hard and meticulously the landscape architect works.

Sometimes this portfolio, this record of a person's work, also shows changes in the person's work.  Maybe a product designer developed a new technique.  She might include pictures of how her products have improved and developed over time.

Keeping all these examples in mind, what would you put in your Mathematics Portfolio? You want to make sure your best work goes into it, but this does not  mean just your "neatest" or "prettiest" work.  It must show that you are knowledgeable about mathematics.  You must convince the person who reads your portfolio that you are competent, and in fact, good at mathematics!  You must not assume, however, that the reader **knows** a lot of mathematics.  We realize that most of the time the reader will be your math teacher, who does know a lot of mathematics, but you may also be showing your portfolio to your parents, other students, and other teachers, who are not familiar with this course.  You will need to show examples of the steps you went through to produce a finished piece.

Possibly, you would include examples of work that show how you have improved or have learned new mathematics.  Samples of an initial attempt followed by several revisions are important in demonstrating your ability to persevere, follow through, and grow in your understanding.

One of the reasons Algebra 2 is required by universities, in addition to providing needed preparation in mathematics, is to determine which students are willing and able to keep going when the course material is challenging.  Are you a student who is willing to persevere in working on an idea or problem that is difficult or that does not make sense at first?  Are you able to try a variety of approaches?  Are you willing to revise your work? These are all skills that can be demonstrated in a portfolio.

This year, one of your goals is to produce a Mathematics Portfolio that will be an honest reflection of the mathematics you know, have learned, and are still considering.  It should be something you would be proud to show a university admissions panel.

# UNIT 2

## The Bouncing Ball
### SEQUENCES

# Unit 2 Objectives
## The Bouncing Ball: SEQUENCES

This unit on sequences introduces some new ideas and provides some opportunities to use and review your Algebra 1 skills in a new context. As you start the unit you may use problem solving strategies such as guess and check, but you should soon move into writing the algebraic representations and combining your mathematical reasoning with your algebra skills to solve the problems. You will use and review such skills as solving for an indicated variable and solving two equations with two unknowns. In this unit we focus on the nth terms of arithmetic and geometric sequences. Later in the year, in Unit 13, we return to investigate sums of series.

This unit focuses on arithmetic and geometric sequences. Throughout this unit you will:

- continue to work in teams and use problem solving strategies as strategies for learning new mathematics.

- use patterns to make conjectures and write algebraic representations.

- become familiar with patterns and graphs of functions that are multiplicative, or geometric, as compared to additive or arithmetic.

- determine relationships between discrete functions, such as arithmetic sequences, and continuous functions, such as straight lines.

- continue to use previously learned algebraic skills in new problem contexts, particularly in solving linear and quadratic equations, solving systems of equations and using exponents.

You will calculate the rebound ratio for a super ball and then use your knowledge of geometric sequences to solve a problem similar to the following one later in this unit. In Unit 13 you will find the total vertical distance the ball would travel if it were to keep on bouncing.

Read the following problem, but do not solve it now. After you read it, go on to problem BB-1.

---

BB-0. **THE BOUNCING BALL** If you drop a super ball from a height of twenty feet and let it bounce, how high will it bounce on the tenth bounce?

---

PROBLEM SOLVING

REPRESENTATION/MODELING

FUNCTIONS/GRAPHING

INTERSECTIONS/SYSTEMS

ALGORITHMS

REASONING/COMMUNICATION

# Unit 2
## The Bouncing Ball: SEQUENCES

BB-1.    Lona received a stamp collection from her grandmother. The collection is in a leather book and currently has 120 stamps. Lona joins a stamp club which sends her 12 new stamps each month. The stamp book holds a maximum of 500 stamps.

a)    Complete the table below:

| Months (n) | Total Stamps  t(n) |
|:----------:|:------------------:|
| 0          | 120                |
| 1          | 132                |
| 2          | 144                |
| 3          |                    |
| 4          |                    |
| 5          |                    |

b)    How many stamps will she have after one year?

c)    When will the book be filled?

d)    Write an equation to represent the total number of stamps that Lona has in her collection after n months. Let the total be represented by t(n).

e)    Solve your equation for n when t(n) = 500. Will Lona be able to exactly fill her book with no stamps remaining? How do you know?

BB-2.    Samantha was looking at one of the function machines in the last unit and decided that she could create a sequence generating machine by connecting the output back into the input. She tested her generator by dropping in an initial value of 8. Each output is recorded before it is recycled.

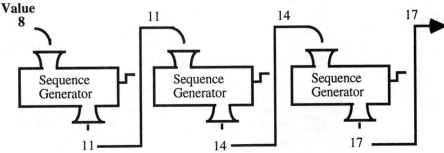

**Initial Value 8**

11    14    17

Sequence Generator    Sequence Generator    Sequence Generator

11    14    17

>>Problem continues on the next page.>>

a)  The first result is 11, then 14, then 17, etc. What operation is the sequence generator using?

b)  When Samantha uses the initial value -3 and the sequence generator "multiply by -2", what are the first five terms of the sequence?

c)  What sequence will she generate if she uses an initial value of 3 and the generator "square"?

BB-3.  Samantha has been busy creating new sequence generators and has created several sequences. Her teacher has also been busy creating sequences using his own devious methods. The following list is a mixture of Samantha's sequences and her teacher's. In your teams:

i.   Supply the next three terms for each sequence.

ii.  Describe in words how to find the next term.

iii  Decide whether the sequence could have been produced by repeatedly putting the output back into the machine as Samantha did in the previous problem.

a)  0, 2, 4, 6, 8, ...

b)  1, 2, 4, 8, ...

c)  7, 5, 3, 1, . . .

d)  0, 1, 4, 9, ...

e)  2, 3.5, 5, 6.5, ...

f)  1, 1, 2, 3, 5, ...

g)  27, 9, 3, 1, ...

h)  40, 20, 10, ...

i)  3, -1, -3, -3, -1, 3, 9, ...

j)  -4, -1, 2, 5, ...

k)  3, 6, 12, ...

l)  0, 1, 8, 27, 64, ...

BB-4.  Simplify each expression.

a)  $(x^3)(x^2)$

b)  $\dfrac{y^5}{y^2}$

c)  $\dfrac{x^3}{x^7}$

d)  $(x^2)^3$

BB-5.  Benjamin is taking Algebra 1 and cannot finish this problem. Help him by showing and explaining the remaining steps. Here is his work:

Simplify $(3a^2b)^3$.     He knows that $(3a^2b)^3 = (3a^2b)(3a^2b)(3a^2b)$.     Now what?

BB-6.    Consider the following sequence of rectangles:

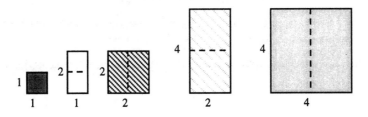

a)    On a sheet of graph paper draw a picture of the next two rectangles in the sequence of rectangles above.

b)    Describe how each figure is formed from its preceding rectangle.

c)    Write the areas of these rectangles as a sequence.


BB-7.    Write each expression below in a simpler form.

a)    $\dfrac{5^{723}}{5^{721}}$

b)    $\dfrac{3^{300}}{3^{249}}$

c)    $\dfrac{3 \cdot 4^{1001}}{7 \cdot 4^{997}}$

d)    $\dfrac{\left(6^{54}\right)^{11}}{\left(6^{49}\right)^{10}}$


BB-8.    Write the equation of a line with:

a)    a slope of -2 and a y-intercept of 7.

b)    a slope of $-\dfrac{3}{2}$ and an x-intercept of (4, 0).


BB-9.    Consider the tables below.  See if you can find some patterns within each table.

| Table 1 | | Table 2 | | Table 3 | |
|---|---|---|---|---|---|
| n | t(n) | n | s(n) | n | p(n) |
| 0 | 0 | 0 | 0 | 0 | -2 |
| 1 | 1 | 1 | 3 | 1 | 2 |
| 2 | 2 | 2 | 6 | 2 | 6 |
| 3 | 3 | 3 | 9 | 3 | 10 |

a)    How is each sequence above being generated?

b)    Find t(25), s(25) and p(25).

c)    Write a rule that will find the nth term without going through all of the previous terms (for example table 2 would have the equation  t(n) = 3n.)

BB-10.    A dart board is in the shape of an equilateral triangle with a
          smaller equilateral triangle in the center made by joining the
          midpoints of the three edges. A dart hits the board at random.
          What is the probability that:

          a)    the dart hits the center triangle? b)    the dart misses the center triangle?


BB-11.    Carmel wants to become a "Fraction Master." He has come to
          you for instruction. Help him by demonstrating and explaining          $\frac{2}{9} - \frac{1}{4}$
          every step necessary to simplify the problem at right.


          "Oh no!" exclaimed Carmel. "This is too hard for the Fraction
          Master!" Is it? Show him every step he needs to simplify the          $\frac{3}{2x} + \frac{4}{xy}$
          problem at right.


# GRAPHING SEQUENCES


BB-12.    **INTRODUCTION**

          You may want to divide this task among the members of your team. Be sure, however,
          that each team member has his or her own set of graphs drawn. For each designated
          sequence in problem BB-3, draw a separate graph on the resource sheet provided.

          ---

          **DIRECTIONS**

          You will use the sequences and their rules from
          problem BB-3 to complete parts (a), (b), and (c)
          below. Your first task will be to create a table like the
          one at right for selected parts of problem BB-3. Part
          (e) is shown as an example at right. The first term in
          the sequence is called the **INITIAL VALUE**. It is
          written as t(0). The first term after the initial value is
          t(1), t(2) is the second term, and so on. Use **n**, which
          states the position of the term after the initial value, as
          the independent variable, and the term itself, **t(n)**, as
          the dependent variable. The **GENERATOR** of the
          sequence tells what you do to each term to get the next
          term. Notice that the domain for each sequence is the
          set of whole numbers.

          | n | t(n) |
          |---|------|
          | 0 | 2    |
          | 1 | 3.5  |
          | 2 | 5    |
          | 3 | 6.5  |
          | 4 | 8    |

          **Initial value: 2,**
          **Generator:   add 1.5**


          NOTE: In this course we
          designate the first term as
          t(0). Some textbooks start
          sequences at t(1).

          ---

          a)    Create tables like the one above for the sequences from problem BB-3, parts (a),
                (b), (c), (e), (h) and (k).

          b)    Plot the points in each table on a separate set of axes on your resource page.
                **Carefully consider whether or not to connect the points on your**
                **graphs. Discuss this with the members of your team.**

          c)    Write the initial value and generator on each graph.

BB-13.   Discuss the similarities among the graphs in problem BB-12 with your team. Write down your observations in relation to the questions below.

a)   Which graphs look similar?

b)   Which graphs had similar generators?

c)   What is the significance of the initial value in each graph?

BB-14.   The graphs you drew for problem BB-12 from sequences of points might be difficult to compare and contrast. One way to learn more about the patterns is to draw "staircases" between points and label the amounts of vertical change per one unit of horizontal change. Draw a "stair-case" for each graph and briefly describe the pattern in the stair-case numbers beneath each graph in problem BB-12.

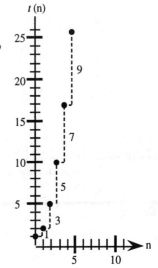

For example, the sequence 1, 2, 5, 10, 17, . . . gives this table:

| n | 0 | 1 | 2 | 3 | 4 |
|------|---|---|---|----|----|
| t(n) | 1 | 2 | 5 | 10 | 17 |

which in turn gives the graph at right. The staircases increase by 2 each time.

BB-15.   In problem BB-13, did you say that graph (c) was similar to graphs (a) and (e)? Did you say they had similar generators? How are their staircases similar? We will be particularly interested in sequences with addition generators. Explain why sequence (c) belongs in this category.

BB-16.   In problem BB-13, did you say that graph (h) was similar to graphs (b) and (k)? Did you say they had similar generators? How are their staircases similar? We will be particularly interested in sequences of this type as well. Rewrite the generator for sequence (h) so that it is the same type as graphs (b) and (k). Can you find another sequence in problem BB-3 that would belong with this group?

BB-17.    **SYSTEMS OF EQUATIONS** (A reminder from Algebra 1)

Solve each system of equations. If you remember how to do these from another course, go ahead and solve them. If you are not sure how to start, read the examples in the following boxes first. This may be something to enter into your Tool Kit.

a)  $y = 3x + 1$
    $x + 2y = -5$

b)  $4x + 2y = 14$
    $x - 2y = 1$

---

**The first subproblem in solving a system of equations is to <u>eliminate</u> one variable. One way to do this is by SUBSTITUTION:**

Consider this system:                    $10y - 3x = 14$
                                         $2x + 4y = -4.$

Look for the equation that is easiest to solve for $x$ or $y$. In this case we chose to solve the second equation for $x$. Be sure you can justify each step in the solution.

$$2x + 4y = -4$$
$$2x = -4 - 4y$$
$$x = -2 - 2y.$$

Now replace the $x$ in the <u>other</u> equation with $(-2 - 2y)$:

$$10y - 3(-2 - 2y) = 14$$
$$10y + 6 + 6y = 14$$
$$16y + 6 = 14$$
$$16y = 8$$
$$y = 0.5.$$

Find $x$ by substituting 0.5 for $y$ in either original equation:

$$x = -2 - 2(0.5)$$
$$x = -3.$$

The solution is $(-3, 0.5)$.

---

> **Some people prefer to <u>eliminate</u> a variable by ADDING the two equations.**
>
> First, rewrite the equations so that the x's and y's are lined up vertically. Next, decide what to multiply by to make the coefficients of either the x's or the y's the <u>same</u> numbers with <u>opposite</u> signs. Be sure you can justify each step in the solution.
>
> $$10y - 3x = 14$$
> $$4y + 2x = -4$$
>
> In this case we chose to make the x coefficients opposites: multiply the top equation by two and the bottom equation by three to get:
>
> $$10y - 3x = 14 \quad \text{by 2} \rightarrow \quad 20y - 6x = 28$$
> $$4y + 2x = -4 \quad \text{by 3} \rightarrow \quad \underline{12y + 6x = -12}$$
>
> $$\text{Adding eliminates x:} \quad 32y = 16$$
> $$y = 0.5.$$
>
> Finally, go back and substitute 0.5 for y in either original equation:
>
> $$10(0.5) - 3x = 14$$
> $$5 - 3x = 14$$
> $$-3x = 9$$
> $$x = -3.$$
>
> Again we get the solution: (-3, 0.5). Be sure to make note of BOTH methods in your Tool Kit.

BB-18.    Tanika made this sequence of triangles:

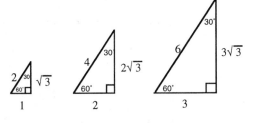

a)    What are the next two triangles in the sequence?

b)    Write a sentence to explain how to find the long leg and hypotenuse if the short leg (i.e. the base) is n units long.

BB-19.    Determine whether the points A(3, 5), B(-2, 6), and C(-5, 7) are on the same line. Justify your conclusion algebraically.

BB-20.    Find m∠a.

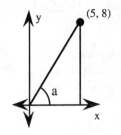

BB-21.    If these two cans hold the same
          amount of tuna, find h.

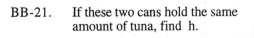

BB-22.    **Without a calculator**, perform each operation.

a)    $\dfrac{2}{3} + \dfrac{1}{4}$              b)    $\dfrac{2}{3} + \dfrac{x}{4}$

c)    $\dfrac{2}{3} + \dfrac{1}{x}$              d)    $\dfrac{2}{y} + \dfrac{3}{x}$

BB-23.    Refer back to problem BB-3 and graph sequences (d), (f), and (i). Label the staircases. Describe the pattern in each staircase. Do any of these belong in the same category as the sequences you graphed in class? Are any of them similar to each other?

BB-24.    Some sequences are named because of their common characteristics.

a)    Sequences such as parts (a), (c), (e) and (j) of problem BB-3 are called **arithmetic sequences.** Describe what these sequences have in common, and give two more examples.

b)    What do the "staircases" of the arithmetic sequences have in common?

c)    Sequences such as parts (b), (g), (h) and (k) of problem BB-3 are called **geometric sequences.** Describe what these sequences have in common and give two more examples.

d)    What do the "staircases" of the geometric sequences have in common?

e)    Sequences such as parts (d) and (i ) in problem BB-3 can be called quadratic sequences. Why? How do these quadratic "staircases" compare with those of the geometric sequences?

f)    The sequence in part (f) from problem BB-3 is special and is named after the mathematician who discovered, explored, and wrote about it. His name was Fibonacci. What is different about the stair-case of this sequence?

BB-25.    **Notation for writing sequences**. When we write a sequence such as 3, 7, 11, 15, ... , we need to have a way of describing the individual terms. The most common way to do so is to think of the sequence as a function whose domain is the non-negative integers. The expression $t(n)$ is used to generate the term, t, of the sequence as a function of n, the number of times the generator has been applied. In this example, since the initial value is 3, $t(0) = 3$. We could write this sequence as:   $t(0) = 3$;  $t(1) = 7$;  $t(2) = 11$; etc.

a)    Find $t(3)$,  $t(4)$, and  $t(5)$.

b)    Find $t(100)$.

c)    Find $t(n)$.

d)    Put information regarding function notation for sequences in your Tool Kit.

BB-26.    In the sequence 1, 4, 7, 10, 13, 16,..., we know  t(2) = 7
          and  t(5) = 16.

          a)    What is  t(8)?

          b)    What is  t(14)?

          c)    The terms  t(0), t(1), t(2), and  t(3) of this sequence
                are graphed for you at right.

          d)  What is the equation of the line that passes through these
              points?  Write your equation in the form  t(n) = _____ .

          e)    What is the significance of the initial value in terms of the graph?

          f)    What does the slope of the line represent?

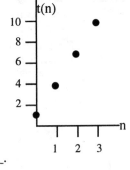


BB-27.    Solve the system at right for m and b:       $15 = 5m + b$
                                                        $7 = 3m + b$


BB-28.    Suppose we wanted to write an equation for the line containing the points (5, 15) and (3,
          7).  In previous courses you found the equation of a line by first finding the slope and
          then finding the y-intercept.  The preceding problem suggests another method.

          We know that for the correct values of  m  and  b, the points (5, 15) and (3, 7) will both
          satisfy the equation  $y = mx + b$.  The two equations in the previous problem were created
          by substituting each of the points into that equation.  For the first equation we replaced  x
          with 5 and  y  with 15.  We get the second equation by replacing  x  with 3 and  y  with 7.
          By solving the resulting linear system, you find the slope and the y-intercept of the line
          through the two points.  Use your results from that solution to write the equation of the
          line through these two points.


BB-29.    Using what you learned in the previous two problems, find the equation of the line
          through the points (2, 3) and (5, -6).  The first equation you need is  $3 = 2m + b$.


BB-30.    Sketch the graphs of  $y = x^2$,  $y = 2x^2$, and  $y = \frac{1}{2}x^2$  on the same set of axes.  Describe
          the differences between the graphs.


UNIT 2

BB-31. Given that n is the length of the bottom edge of the L-shaped figures below, what numbers are generated by the total number of dots? What is the 46th term of this sequence? The nth term?

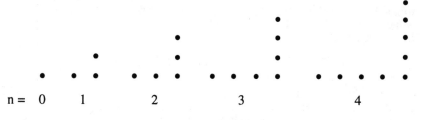

n =   0      1        2          3              4

BB-32. Classify the triangle whose vertices are A(3, 2), B(-2, 0), and C(-1, 4) by finding the length of each side. Be sure to consider all possible triangle types. Include sufficient evidence to support your conclusion.

BB-33. Find the x-intercepts for: $y - x^2 = 6x$.

BB-34. Find the missing sides of each right triangle. Write your results in simplified radical form.

a)

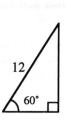

b)

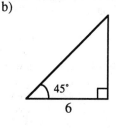

BB-35. Simplify each expression.

a)  $(2m^3)(4m^2)$

b)  $\dfrac{6y^5}{3y^2}$

c)  $\dfrac{-4y^2}{6y^7}$

d)  $(-2x^2)^3$

BB-36.   A table is very useful when analyzing a sequence to determine its pattern.  Consider the sequence  7, 10, 13, . . . in the table below:

| n | 0 | 1 | 2 | 3 | 4 | 5 | 6 |
|------|---|----|----|----|---|---|---|
| t(n) | 7 | 10 | 13 | 16 | | | |

a)   Fill in the rest of the table.

b)   What is the initial value and the generator for the sequence?

c)   The generator in an arithmetic sequence is frequently referred to as the **common difference**.  Why might this term be used?

d)   How many 3's had to be added to the initial term to get the term for  n = 4?

e)   What is an algebraic expression for the value of the nth term?

f)   Graph this function and find the slope of the line that would go through the points on the graph.

BB-37.   In the sequence of the last problem, is it possible for 30 to be a value in the  t(n)  row?  Explain your thinking.

BB-38.   What kinds of sequences have a graph whose points lie on a straight line?

BB-39.   Using what you have learned in the previous problems, find the slope of the line containing each sequence of points listed below.  Write an expression for the nth term in each case.

a)   5, 8, 11, 14, . . .          b)   3, 9, 15, . . .

c)   26, 21, 16, . . .          d)   7, 8.5, 10, . . .

BB-40.   Find the function  t(n)  where the initial value is "a" and the generator is "adding d" (the common difference).

BB-41.   Find the initial value and the common difference for the arithmetic sequence where  t(5) = -3  and  t(50) = 357.  You can use the equation you found in the previous problem and review the procedures in problem BB-28.

Enter the following definitions in your Tool Kit:

> An **ARITHMETIC SEQUENCE** is a sequence with an addition (or subtraction) generator. The number added to each term to get the next term is called the **COMMON DIFFERENCE.**
>
> A **GEOMETRIC SEQUENCE** is a sequence with a multiplication (or division) generator. The number multiplied by each term to get the next term is called the **COMMON RATIO** or the **MULTIPLIER.**

BB-43.   Write a paragraph about the relationship between an arithmetic sequence and its graph. Be sure to explain the relationships among the common difference, slope, y-intercept, and the initial value of the sequence.

BB-44.   Determine whether or not 447 is a term of each sequence below. If so, which term is it?

a)   $t(n) = 5n - 3$              b)   $t(n) = 24 - 5n$

c)   $t(n) = -6 + 3(n - 1)$         d)   $t(n) = 14 - 3n$

e)   $t(n) = -8 - 7(n - 1)$

BB-45.   Choose one of the sequences in the previous problem for which 447 was **not** a term. Write an explanation clear enough for an Algebra 1 student that describes <u>how</u> you were able to determine that 447 was not a term of the sequence.

BB-46.   Seven years ago Raj found a box of old baseball cards in the garage. Since then he has added a consistent number of cards to the collection each year. He had 52 cards in the collection after 3 years and now has 108 cards.

a)   How many cards were in the original box?

b)   Raj plans to keep the collection for a long time. How many cards will the collection contain 10 years from now?

c)   Write an expression that determines the number of cards in the collection after n years. What does each number stand for?

**BB-47.** Find the formula for t(n) for the arithmetic sequence in which t(15) = 10 and t(63) = 106.

**BB-48.** **Without a calculator**, perform each operation.

a) $\frac{3}{4} - \frac{2}{5}$

b) $\frac{3}{y} - \frac{5}{4}$

c) $\left(\frac{3m}{n}\right) \cdot \left(\frac{m}{6n}\right)$

d) $\left(\frac{5x^2}{y}\right) \cdot \left(\frac{10}{x}\right)$

**BB-49.** Find the x- and y-intercepts and the equation of the line of symmetry for:
$y = x^2 + 6x + 8$.

**BB-50.** Dr. Sanchez asked her class to simplify $x + 0.6x$.

Terry says, $x + 0.6x = 1.6x$

Jo says, $x + 0.6x = 0.7x$

Whose response is correct? Justify your conclusion.

**BB-51.** Serena wanted to examine these equations on her graphing calculator. Rewrite each of the equations so that she can enter them into the calculator in the " y = " format.

a) $5 - (y - 2) = 3x$

b) $5(x + y) = -2$

**BB-52.** Simplify each expression.

a) $\frac{6x^2y^3}{3xy}$

b) $(mn)^3$

c) $(3mn)^3$

d) $\frac{(3x^2)2}{3x}$

e) Add to your Tool Kit any Laws of Exponents you were unsure of.

| Basic Laws of Exponents | |
|---|---|
| $x^m \cdot x^n = x^{m+n}$ | $\left(x^m\right)^n = x^{mn}$ |
| $\dfrac{x^m}{x^n} = x^{m-n} \quad (x \neq 0)$ | $\left(x^m y^n\right)^k = x^{mk} y^{nk}$ |

BB-53.  Many games depend upon the players' response to the bounce of a ball. For this reason manufacturers have to make balls so that their bounce conforms with certain standards. Some standards for different balls are:

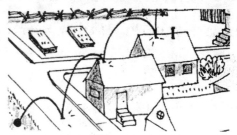

tennis ball... rebound approximately 111 cm when dropped from 200 cm
handball..... rebound approximately 63.5" when dropped from 100" at 68°F
lacrosse..... rebound approximately 47" when dropped from 72" on a wooden floor
squash ...... rebound approximately 29.5" when dropped from 100" onto a steel plate at 70° F

How can you measure "bounciness?" Which ball bounces proportionately higher than the others?

BB-54.  Designate one person in your team as recorder, one as ball dropper, and at least two as spotters. Make a table like the one below; leave the third column blank for now. Choose a starting height and record it in your table. You will need a super ball and a measuring device. Drop the ball from the chosen height and record the rebound height of the ball. **Make at least three trials from this starting height** and record **each** resulting rebound height (don't record the average rebound height). It will be easier to compare heights if you measure ALL of them to the **bottom** of the ball.

a)  What do you notice about the rebound heights?

b)  Select another 5 starting heights and repeat the procedure for each one (so you will have at least eighteen entries in your table).

**Remember to measure both heights to the bottom of the ball.**

| starting height | rebound height | |
|---|---|---|
| | | |
| | | |
| | | |
| | | |
| | | |

BB-55.  Identify the independent variable as  x  and the dependent as  y  and graph your results carefully on graph paper. What do you notice? Draw a **line of best fit**. Why should the line of best fit go through the origin? Write the equation for your line.

**BB-56.** Label the third column on your table "rebound ratio" and for each trial, calculate the ratio of the rebound height to the starting height. What do you notice?

a) How is this result related to the slope of the line of best fit?

b) Explain why it makes sense for the y-intercept to be zero.

**BB-57.** A relationship such as the one you found between the height from which the ball was dropped and the rebound height is called a **direct variation**. These are linear functions with a y-intercept of 0.

a) Choose an input (other than 0) for the equation you wrote in problem BB-55 and calculate the output. Now double the input, and examine the corresponding output. What do you notice? Try multiplying the input by some other number and see what the effect is on the output. Describe the pattern you found. This is why we say the rebound height varies directly with the starting height.

b) Does the pattern you just observed apply to linear functions in general? Choose a linear function which does not go through the origin and repeat what you did in part (a). Describe the results.

c) Think of another example of a direct variation relationship, that is, a situation where one amount is a constant multiple of some other amount. Describe it and write an equation for it.

**BB-58.** Use the information you have gathered to answer the following questions:

a) Predict how high the super ball will rebound if dropped from three meters.

b) Suppose the super ball is dropped and you notice that its rebound height is 60 cm. From what height was the ball dropped?

c) Suppose the super ball is dropped from a window 200 meters up the Empire State Building. What would you predict the rebound height to be after the first bounce?

d) How high would the ball rebound after the second bounce? the third?

**BB-59.** Recall the sequence in part (h) from problem BB-3. The sequence was 40, 20, 10, . . .

a) What kind of a sequence is 40, 20, 10, ...? Why?

b) Plot the sequence up to $n = 6$.

c) Since the sequence is decreasing, will the values ever become negative? Explain.

BB-60.    Consider the following sequences:

**Sequence 1**   **Sequence 2**   **Sequence 3**
2, 6, . . .        24, 12, . . .      1, 5, . . .

a)   Assuming that the sequences above are arithmetic, find the next four terms for each one. For each sequence, write an explanation of what you did to get the next term and write a formula for t(n).

b)   Would your terms be different if the sequences were geometric? Find the next four terms for each sequence if they are geometric. For each sequence, write an explanation of what you did to get the next term.

c)   Create a totally different type of sequence for each pair of values based on your own rule. Write your rule clearly so that someone else will be able to find the next three terms that you want.

BB-61.    Solve each of the following equations.

a)   $\dfrac{m}{6} = \dfrac{15}{18}$

b)   $\dfrac{\pi}{7} = \dfrac{a}{4}$

BB-62.    This problem is a Milepost for solving quadratic equations and for finding the x- and y-intercepts of the graph of a quadratic function.

Find the x- and y-intercepts for the graph of:   $y = x^2 + 4x - 17$.

If you needed help to solve this problem correctly then you need more practice in solving quadratic equations. Try the Milepost 1 practice problems. From this point on you will be expected to solve quadratic equations easily and accurately.

BB-63.    The equation of a line describes what the coordinates of the points on the line have in common. When what they have in common is very simple, the equation is very simple.

a)   Plot the points (3, -1), (3, 2) and (3, 4). Draw the line through them. State the coordinates of 2 more points on the line. Answer in a complete sentence: what will be true of the coordinates of any other point on this line? Now write an equation which says exactly the same thing; don't worry if it's very simple! If it accurately describes all the points on this line, it is correct.

b)   Plot the points (5, -1), (1, -1) and (-3, -1). What is the equation of the line through these points?

c)   Choose any three points on the y-axis. What must be the equation of the line that goes through those points?

## THE BOUNCING BALL (PART II)

BB-64.  Suppose we drop a super ball from a height of ten feet and let it bounce. Make a table and draw a graph of the predicted rebound height for each bounce based on the rebound ratio your team calculated in problem BB-56. The independent variable is the number of bounces. Your graph will show a record of the height for each bounce, not a picture of the ball bouncing.

    a)    Should the points on your graph be connected? Explain your thinking.

    b)    In general, how could you determine whether or not the data points on your graph should be connected? Give an example of a data set that would be connected and one that would not.

> When the points on a graph are connected, and it makes <u>sense</u> to connect them, we say the graph is **CONTINUOUS**. If it is not continuous, and is just a sequence of separate points, we say the graph is **DISCRETE**.

    c)    Look back at the graph you drew in problem BB-55. Should the graph in problem BB-55 be continuous? Explain your thinking on this.

    d)    Add the definitions of discrete and continuous to your Tool Kit.

BB-65. The heights of the ball on successive bounces form a sequence. Which sequences from problem BB-3 does it most resemble? Why?

The saga of the Bouncing Ball will continue so be sure your data is accurate, neatly organized, and readily available. You will be using your data later to answer each of the following questions: What equation could represent your graph in problem BB-64? How long will it take for the ball to stop bouncing?

BB-66. Graph linear equations.

Solve the system at right by graphing each line and finding their intersection, then solve the system algebraically to check.

$$x + y = 5$$
$$y = \frac{1}{3}x + 1$$

If you needed help to graph and find the intersection of this pair of linear equations then you need more practice. See the Milepost 2 practice problems. Be sure you know how to write the equations in y-form and use the slope and y-intercept to draw graphs efficiently.

BB-67. Perform each operation.

    a)    $\frac{m}{4} + \frac{m}{3}$                   b)    $\frac{x}{2} - \frac{x-1}{2}$

    c)    $\left(\frac{8m^2}{x}\right) \cdot \left(\frac{y}{m^3}\right)$        d)    $\left(\frac{2}{3}\right) \div \left(\frac{5}{3}\right)$

BB-68.    In 1999, Charlie received the family
          heirloom marble collection, consisting of
          1239 marbles.  The original marble
          collection was started by Charlie's great
          grandfather back in 1905.  Each year
          Charlie's great grandfather had added the
          same number of marbles to his collection.
          When he passed them on to his son he
          insisted that each future generation add
          the same number of marbles per year to
          the collection.  When Charlie's father
          received the collection in 1966 there were
          810 marbles.

a)    How many years has the collection been maintained?

b)    How many marbles are added to the collection each year?

c)    Use the information you found in part (b) to figure out how many marbles were in
      the original collection when Charlie's great grandfather started it.

d)    Write a generalized expression describing the growth of the marble collection since
      it was started by Charlie's great grandfather.

e)    When will Charlie (or his children) have more than 2000 marbles?

BB-69.    Write the range and domain for each of the following graphs.

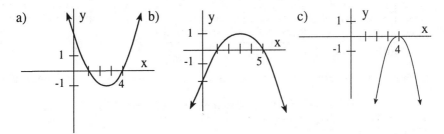

BB-70.    Simplify:

a)    $y + 0.03y$          b)    $z - 0.2z$          c)    $x + 0.002x$

BB-71. Examine each of the following sequences. State whether it is arithmetic, geometric, or neither. For those which are arithmetic, find the formula for t(n). For those that are geometric, find the multiplier (or common ratio) used to get from one term to the next.

a) 1, 4, 7, 10, 13, ...

b) 0, 5, 12, 21, 32, ...

c) 2, 4, 8, 16, 32, ...

d) 5, 12, 19, 26, ...

e) x, x + 1, x + 2, x + 3, ...

f) 3, 12, 48, 192, ...

BB-72. A dart hits each of these dart boards at random. What is the probability that the dart will land in the shaded area?

a)

b)

# GEOMETRIC SEQUENCES: COMMON RATIOS TO THE NTH TERM

BB-73. Consider the sequence 3, 6, 12, 24, . . .

a) What kind of sequence is it? How is it generated?

b) Pairing the values in the sequence with their position in the sequence creates the table below:

| n | 0 | 1 | 2 | 3 | 4 | |
|------|---|---|----|----|---|---|
| t(n) | 3 | 6 | 12 | 24 | | |

Create your own table and continue it to include the next five terms of the sequence.

c) How many times do we multiply the initial value of 3 by 2 in order to obtain the value of 24 in the sequence?

d) Is there a short cut for doing repeated multiplication? What is it?

e) The value found when $n = 6$ can be obtained by multiplying $3 \cdot 2 \cdot 2 \cdot 2 \cdot 2 \cdot 2$. Rewrite this expression using exponents

f) What will the representation be for the hundredth term of the sequence?

g) How could you represent t(n)?

BB-74. A tank contains 8,000 liters of water. Each day, one-half of the water in the tank is removed. How much water will be in the tank after:

a) the 6th day?       b) the 12th day?       c) the nth day?

BB-75. **FLU EPIDEMIC HITS TEXAS TOWN! 30% increase in cases reported this week.** Today there were 100 cases reported to begin the annual flu season. If this rate continued how many cases would be reported 4 weeks from now?

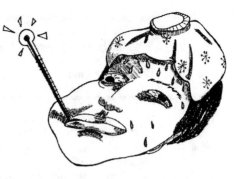

a) How many cases would be reported after 7 weeks?

b) Write a general expression that enables you to determine the number of cases reported after n weeks, assuming this rate of increase continues.

BB-76. Let's return to the Bouncing Ball problem. Refer to the data table you created when conducting the Bouncing Ball Investigation, Part II (problem BB-64). Use that data and the graph generated from the data to answer the following questions.

a) How high will the ball be after the 12th bounce?

b) How long will it take for the ball to stop bouncing?

c) Determine an equation that could represent your graph.

BB-77. Look back at the data given in problem BB-53 regarding the rebound ratio for an approved tennis ball. If you dropped your tennis ball from a height of 10 feet:

a) how high would it bounce on the first bounce?

b) how high would it bounce on the tenth bounce?

c) how high would it bounce on the nth bounce?

BB-78. Sketch $y = x^2$, $y = -3x^2$, and $y = -0.25x^2$ on the same set of axes. What does a negative coefficient do to the graph?

BB-79. What a deal! We've-Got-Shirts is having a sale: 20 percent off. Beth rushes to the store and buys 14 shirts. When the clerk rings up her purchases, Beth sees that the clerk has added the 5 percent sales tax first, before taking the discount. She wonders whether she got a good deal at the store's expense or whether she should complain to the manager about being ripped off. Your mission is to find out which is better: discount first, then tax, or tax first, then discount. Before you begin calculating, make a guess.

BB-80. In the preceding problem, suppose that Beth's shirts cost x dollars.

a)    What is the tax (in terms of x)?

b)    What is the total cost in terms of x?

---

c)    If you haven't already done so, simplify your answer to part (b), as you did in problem BB-70. This version of the answer tells you that you can increase a number by 5% simply by multiplying it by 1.05, rather than using the more obvious two-step process (multiplying the original number by 0.05, and adding that result to the original number). The number by which you multiply in order to increase something by a given percentage in one step is called the **MULTIPLIER** for that percentage increase. What would be the multiplier for a tax rate of 7%?

---

d)    Convert each of these increases to a multiplier:

3 percent                    8.25 percent                    2.08 percent

e)    Record the term **multiplier** in your Tool Kit along with an understandable definition or explanation.


BB-81. Find the values of each sequence for $n = 0$ to $n = 4$.

a)    $t(n) = 8 + 7(n - 1)$                    b)    $t(n) = -5$

c)    $t(n) = 2^{(n - 4)}$                    d)    $t(n) = (-2)^n$

e)    What is the domain for the sequences?

f)    What are the ranges for the sequences?


BB-82. A sequence is defined as $t(n) = 4n - 3$.

a)    List the first four terms.

b)    What type of sequence is this? Explain. Could you have answered this question without finding the first four terms? Explain.

c)    321 is in this sequence. What term number is it? Explain how you found this answer.

BB-83.    **RECTANGULAR NUMBERS**

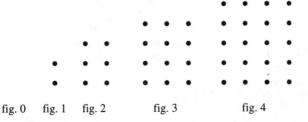

fig. 0    fig. 1    fig. 2    fig. 3    fig. 4

The sequence above has the terms 0, 2, 6, 12, 20 . . . where the value of the sequence is the number of dots in the figure. The terms in this sequence are known as the **rectangular numbers**.

a)    What is the 10th rectangular number?

b)    What is the 100th rectangular number?

c)    What is the nth rectangular number?


# MORE MULTIPLIERS AND APPLICATIONS

BB-84.    **INTRODUCTION**
Karen works for a department store and receives a 20% discount on any purchases that she makes. Today the department store is having the end of the year clearance sale where any clearance item will be marked 30% off. When Karen includes her employee discount with the sale discount, what is the total discount she will receive? Does it matter what discount she takes first? Answer the following questions to find out.

Using graph paper, separate two 10 by 10 grids as shown below.

**CASE 1** - 20% discount first          **CASE 2** - 30% discount first

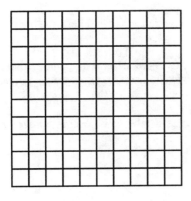          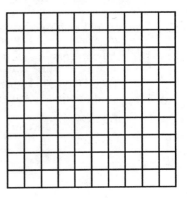

>>**Problem continues on the next page.**>>

a) Each grid has 100 squares—take the first discount in each case by shading the appropriate number of squares.

   i) How many squares remain after the first discount in case 1?

   ii) How many squares remain after the first discount in case 2?

b) Using the remaining squares in each case take the second discount. Note: you no longer have 100 squares to start.

   i) How many squares remain after taking the second discount in case 1?

   ii) How many squares remain after taking the second discount in case 2?

c) When you take a 20% discount, what percent is left?

d) When you take a 30% discount, what percent is left?

e) Multiply these two percents together. What percent do you now have? How does this relate to Karen's problem above?

BB-85. Starting with x in each case, find a simplified form for each increase or decrease. For example, a 30% increase is represented as $x + 0.3x = 1.3x$.

a) a 5% increase

b) a 12% discount

c) an 8.25% tax

d) a reduction of 22.5%

BB-86. Remember the flu epidemic in problem BB-75? It has become a statewide crisis, but you have also developed a deeper understanding of how a multiplier can help you solve a problem such as this.

a) If Dallas had 1250 cases at the start of the epidemic, with an increase of 27% per week, how many cases would be reported in Dallas after 4 weeks of the epidemic?

b) Write the general expression from which you can determine the number of cases in any week of the Dallas flu season.

c) If Health Services provided 8,000 doses of an experimental medication to fight the virus, when will the medication be used up (assume one dose per person affected)?

BB-87.    A local real estate developer decides to hire
          two high school students to rake the leaves
          along a greenbelt.  They will work a couple
          hours each afternoon until the job is
          completed.  The job is expected to take about
          three weeks.  They can choose one of two
          payment plans.  Plan A pays $11.50 per
          afternoon, while Plan B pays 2 cents for one
          day of work, 4 cents for two days of work,
          8 cents for three days of work, a total of 16
          cents for four days, and so on.  Each student
          chooses a different plan.  On which day
          would their total pay be approximately the
          same?  Support your thinking with data
          charts and/or graphs.

BB-88.    Your favorite radio station, WCPM is having a contest.  The D.J. poses a question to the
          listeners.  If the caller answers correctly, he/she wins the prize money.  If the caller answers
          incorrectly, $20 is added to the prize money and the next caller is eligible to win.  The
          question is difficult and no one has won for two days.

   a)     You were the 15th caller today and you won $735!!  How much was the prize
          worth at the beginning of today?  Be careful; think about how many times the prize
          was increased today.

   b)     Suppose the contest starts with $100.  How many people would have to guess
          incorrectly for the winner to get $1360?

BB-89.    John finished his homework last night, but his brother colored all over the paper.  All that
          remained was:

                    5, 12, 19,                                    390, 397

          He knew that 5 was the initial term and 397 the last term, but he did not remember
          anything else about the sequence.

   a)      What is the 40th term?

   b)     How many terms after the initial value is the last value in John's sequence?

BB-90.    The multiplier principle can be used if there is a percent decrease.  Suppose there is a 20
          percent discount.  Again let  x  be the original cost.

   a)     What is the discount (in terms of  x)?

   b)     What is the new price in  terms of  x?  Simplify your answer.

   c)     Just as in problem BB-79, the coefficient in (b) is the **multiplier** for a decrease of
          20%.  It is less than 1 because the discounted cost is less than the original cost.
          What would be the multiplier for a sale rate of 15% off?

BB-91.    Find the multiplier for:

a)    a 3 percent decrease.    b)    a 25 percent decrease.  c)    a 7.5 percent decrease.

BB-92.    Use the idea of a multiplier to look back at the We've-Got-Shirts problem (BB-79) and explain why both answers were the same.

BB-93.    Find the length of $\overline{AC}$.

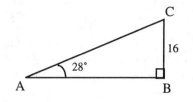

BB-94.    Place the triangle from the previous problem in the coordinate plane so that B is located at the origin.  Find the coordinates for A and C.  Find the area and perimeter of triangle ABC.

BB-95.    A grocery store is offering a sale on bread and soup.  Brian buys four cans of soup and three loaves of bread for $4.36.  Ronda buys eight cans of soup and one loaf of bread for $3.32.

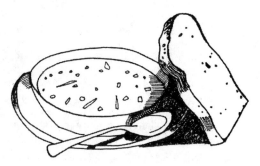

a)    Write equations for both Brian's purchase and Ronda's purchase.

b)    Solve the system to find the price for one can of soup and the price for one loaf of bread.

BB-96.    Simplify each expression.

a)    $(3x)^2$

b)    $2(3x)^2$

c)    $\dfrac{2(3x)^2}{3x^3}$

d)    $\dfrac{2(3x)^2}{(3x)^3}$

BB-97. The spiral below right is made using a sequence of right triangles, each with a leg that measures one unit, and the second leg the hypotenuse of the triangle before it. Although only four right triangles are shown, we could continue this spiral forever. As you work on this problem, **think back to previous function investigations that you have conducted. Be thorough and provide relevant data, graphs, and conclusions.** You will be investigating two functions. Each is described below:

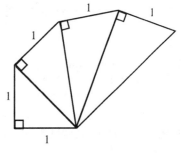

a) Investigate the function where the input is the number of right triangles in the figure, and the output is the length of the hypotenuse of the last triangle formed.

b) Investigate the function where the input is the number of right triangles in the figure, and the output is the area of the last triangle formed.

BB-98. Mai's birthday is in 18 weeks. She has no money now, but plans to start saving money **immediately** from her part time job because the car she wants to buy costs $2086. Each week she will set aside the **same amount** of money. Fortunately, her dad agreed to help her with **part** of the down payment. The car dealer has guaranteed her a 30 week payment plan which allows her to drive the car away on her birthday if she has paid $1582 by the time of her birthday. She will continue to pay the same set amount weekly for the remaining 12 weeks, at which time, the car will be paid off. How much does Mai need from her father? How much must she start saving each week?

BB-99. Fill in the missing terms of each sequence.

a) The sequence is arithmetic:

| n | 0 | 1 | 2 | 3 | 4 |
|------|---|---|----|---|----|
| t(n) | 3 | | 12 | | 21 |

b) The sequence is geometric:

| n | 0 | 1 | 2 | 3 | 4 |
|------|---|---|----|---|----|
| t(n) | 3 | | 12 | | 48 |

BB-100. The following data points show the actual score and the adjusted score for a recent Algebra 2 quiz. Graph these data points and write the equation used by the teacher to adjust the scores.

| score | 27 | 15 | 20 | 18 |
|---|---|---|---|---|
| adjusted | 91 | 55 | 70 | ? |

a) What score would have been adjusted to 82?

b) What is the adjusted score for 18?

c) What does the slope of this line represent?

BB-101. In a geometric sequence, t(0) is 5 and t(2) is 10. Find t(1) and t(3) and explain how you found the multiplier.

BB-102. Find the value of y in the sequence 2, 8, 3y + 5, . . .

a) if the sequence is arithmetic.    b) if the sequence is geometric.

BB-103. Consider the following tables:

| n | t(n) |
|---|---|
| 0 | 100 |
| 1 | 50 |
| 2 | |
| 3 | |

| x | f(x) |
|---|---|
| 0 | 50 |
| 1 | |
| 2 | 100 |
| 3 | |

a) Copy and complete each table to make the sequences arithmetic.

b) Copy and complete each table to make the sequences geometric.

c) Write the rule for each sequence in parts (a) and (b) above.

BB-104. Graph $y = x^2 + 3$ and $y = (x + 3)^2$. What are the similarities and differences between the graphs? How would these graphs compare to $y = x^2$?

BB-105. Find the domain and range for each of the following functions.

a)             b)             c)             d)

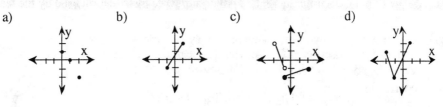

BB-106. Perform each operation.

a)    $\frac{x}{3} - \frac{x+1}{5}$

b)    $\frac{5}{x} + \frac{3}{x^2}$

c)    $\left(\frac{7x^2}{m}\right) \cdot \left(\frac{m}{x^2}\right)$

d)    $\frac{1}{3} \div m^2$

BB-107. This is a Milepost problem for using the basic rules for positive exponents.

Simplify each expression.

a)    $(2x^2y)^4$

b)    $\frac{-3x^2y^3}{(-6x)^2}$

c)    $\frac{(2x^2y)^4}{3xy^5}$

d)    $5(5xy)^2(x^3y)$

BB-108. Toss three coins in the air. Make a list of all the possible outcomes, and find the probability that:

a)    all of them land heads up.

b)    two of them land with tails up.

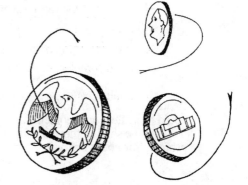

BB-109. Earlier in this unit you compared the graphs of various parabolas with different coefficients. Use what you learned to investigate $y = ax^2$. Your goal here is to examine how the value of the coefficient 'a' changes the graph of $y = x^2$. Begin by reviewing your work in problems BB-30 and BB-78.

BB-110. **SUMMARY ASSIGNMENT (BB-110 TO BB-112)**

You have looked at a variety of sequences throughout this unit. You have graphed them and analyzed their "staircases" and other characteristics such as slope and y-intercept. You have also encountered several situations in which these various sequences arise.

Write an example of each of the following:

a) An increasing arithmetic sequence.

b) A decreasing arithmetic sequence.

c) An increasing geometric sequence.

d) A decreasing geometric sequence.

Each example should include

1) The sequence.

2) A graph of the sequence.

3) An equation for the sequence.

4) A description of what the various parts of the equation represent.

5) A description of how the parts of the graph relate to its sequence.

BB-111. Write a problem that could be solved by creating and analyzing a sequence. The sequence could be arithmetic, geometric, or a combination of both. Be sure to solve your problem. You will be sharing these with members of your team who will help you to revise your problem for your portfolio.

BB-112. So far this year you have had the opportunity to work in teams with various class members. Working together gives you the opportunity to share and learn new ideas. Explaining your thinking gives you a chance to clarify your ideas and better understand the concepts. Listening to ideas gives you the chance to learn new insights into a situation. Write a few sentences that explain your own talents and qualities you feel most confident sharing with your team. Also explain how you have been assisted by other team members.

BB-113.  A rookie basketball player was recently drafted by a professional basketball team. His salary will be $673,500 for the first year, with an increase of 20% each year of his five year contract. How much will he make in the fifth year of his contract?

a)  A teammate is currently in the fourth year of a five-year contract. His current salary is $875,900, and this represents an annual raise of 15% for the life of his contract. What was his starting salary?

b)  Write the expression that describes the terms of the contract for each player. When you think you have the equations, be sure to check your answers to see if they work.

c)  What was the total amount of each five year contract for each of these players?

BB-114.  A grocery store was selling soda for $2.19 for a six pack or $3.99 for a twelve pack.

a)  Write an equation that will give the price for any number of cans based of the six-pack price. Draw its graph.

b)  Write an equation for a line through (6, 2.19) and (12, 3.99) and draw its graph on the same axes.

c)  What would be the cost of a case (24 cans) of soda based on the equation in part (b)? Would this be a good price for a store to charge? Explain your reasoning.

d)  Compare the per can cost for a six-pack, twelve-pack, and a case using the equation in part (b).

e)  What do the numbers in your equation represent? Do they always make sense? Do you think a line is a good model for this data? Discuss why or why not with your team.

BB-115.  Does the number -350 belong to the sequence 10, -50, . . .

a)  if it is arithmetic? Justify your response.

b)  if it is geometric? Justify your response.

BB-116.  Perform each operation.

a)  $\left(\dfrac{9x^2}{5}\right) \cdot \left(\dfrac{10}{3x}\right)$

b)  $\dfrac{m^2}{t} + 3m$

c)  $\dfrac{3}{y} - \dfrac{x}{y^2}$

d)  $\dfrac{3x+2}{y} - \dfrac{x+3}{2x}$

**BB-117.** **TRIANGULAR NUMBERS**

The sequence above has the
terms 0, 1, 3, 6, 10. . . where
the value of the sequence is the
number of dots in the figure.
What problem from a few days
ago would be related to this
sequence? Find it. It will be

fig. 0    fig. 1    fig. 2        fig. 3              fig. 4

very useful in figuring out the answers. The terms in the sequence above are also called
**Triangular Numbers**.

a)    What is the 15th triangular number?  b)    What is the 200th triangular number?

c)    What is the nth triangular number?

**BB-118.** **PORTFOLIO: GROWTH OVER TIME—PROBLEM #2**

On a separate piece of paper (so you can hand it in separately or
add it to your portfolio) explain **everything** that you now know
about:

$$f(x) = 2^x - 3.$$

**BB-119.** **SELF EVALUATION**

You did a self evaluation of your skills at the end of Unit 1. Here are a few more skills
for you to check. Are you confident that you can:

• solve a system of equations?

• solve any quadratic equation which has real solutions?

If you are not confident in these skills, ask for help from your team or your teacher. You
may need to seek some review help and do some extra practice outside of class time.
Find a sample problem that is worked out  completely and correctly. Enter this sample in
your Tool Kit.

**BB-120.** **TOOL KIT CHECK-UP**

Your Tool Kit contains reference tools for
algebra. Return to your Tool Kit entries.
You may need to revise or add entries.

Be sure that your Tool Kit contains entries
for all of the items listed below. Add any
topics that are missing to your Tool Kit
NOW, as well as any other items that will
help you in your study of algebra.

• Systems of Equations               • Arithmetic and Geometric Sequences

• Discrete and Continuous Graphs      • Multiplier

# UNIT 3

## Fast Cars and Depreciation
### EXPONENTIAL FUNCTIONS

# Unit 3 Objectives

## Fast Cars and Depreciation: EXPONENTIAL FUNCTIONS

In this unit, we will use what we know about geometric sequences to examine exponential functions. Exponential functions can be used to represent situations that involve growth or decay, appreciation or depreciation, so they are often very useful as mathematical models in science, business, banking, and economics.

In this unit you will have the opportunity to:

- see a relationship between geometric sequences and exponential functions that is similar to the relationship between arithmetic sequences and linear functions.

- use exponential functions to represent situations modeling growth and decay.

- develop your ability to write equations and interpret the meaning of fractional and negative exponents.

- continue to become familiar with the graphing calculator.

- continue to practice the use of basic algebraic skills in solving some not so basic problems.

The following problem is the theme problem for this unit. While it might be possible to solve it today, it will be easier to solve it later in the unit when it re-appears. For now, read it, then go on to problem FX-1.

---

FX-0. **FAST CARS:** As soon as you drive a new car off the dealer's lot, the car is worth less than what you paid for it. This is called **depreciation.** Chances are that you will sell it for less than the price that you paid for it. Some cars depreciate more than others (that is, at different rates), but most cars depreciate. On the other hand, some older cars actually increase in value. This is called **appreciation.** Let's suppose you have a choice between buying a 1999 Mazda Miata for $19,800 which depreciates at 22% a year, or a 1996 Honda Civic EX for $16,500 which only depreciates at 18% a year. In how many years will their values be the same? Should you instead buy a 1967 Ford Mustang for $4,000 that is appreciating at 10% per year? Which car will have the greatest value in 4 years? In 5 years?

---

PROBLEM SOLVING

REPRESENTATION/MODELING

FUNCTIONS/GRAPHING

INTERSECTIONS/SYSTEMS

ALGORITHMS

REASONING/COMMUNICATION

# Unit 3

*Fast Cars and Depreciation*: **EXPONENTIAL FUNCTIONS**

## MULTIPLIERS AND COMPOUND INTEREST

FX-1.    Suppose two credit unions offer to pay 8 percent annual interest. One advertises that it pays simple interest, and the other pays compound interest. We'll investigate whether it makes any difference where you invest your money.

We will consider simple interest first. Suppose you deposit $100 in the first credit union and the interest on the $100 is paid at the end of each year. The "zero" year is your initial deposit.

### SIMPLE INTEREST

| year | amount of money, in dollars |
|------|------------------------------|
| 0 | 100.00 (initial value) |
| 1 | 108.00 |
| 2 | 116.00 |
| 3 | 124.00 |
| 4 | 132.00 |

a)    By what percent had your account increased at the end of the fourth year?

b)    Continue this table for the next eight years.

c)    Draw a graph to show the relationship between years (independent variable) and amount of money in the account. Label each axis **and** state whether the graph represents an arithmetic sequence, a geometric sequence, or neither.

FX-2.    The second credit union, like most financial institutions, pays compound interest. That means that interest is paid not only on the amount you invested (called the **principal** or **initial value**) but **also** on the accumulated interest below. In other words, you get interest on your interest. To see this clearly, look at the table for compound interest. The interest rate is still eight percent per year and the principal is still $100.00.

### COMPOUND INTEREST

| year | amount of money, in dollars |
|------|------------------------------|
| 0    | 100.00 (initial value)       |
| 1    | 108.00                       |
| 2    | 116.64                       |
| 3    | 125.97                       |
| 4    |                              |

a)    Explain to other members of your team why the amount in your account at the end of the second year would be $116.64.

b)    Copy the table and enter the appropriate values for the 4th year. Be sure to round off appropriately (you can't have fractions of a cent).

c)    The simple interest that the bank paid in four years increased your account 32%. According to the table where the interest was compounded, by what percent would your account increase for this same period?

FX-3.    Extend the table of compound interest for another eight years.

a)    Draw a graph for the table of compound interest. Label each axis **and** state whether the graph represents an arithmetic (linear) sequence, a geometric sequence, or neither.

b)    Should the graphs for the last two problems be **discrete** (points only) or **continuous** (connected)? Explain.

c)    Which credit union would you use for your investment?

FX-4.    Look back at the table you just made for compound interest.

a)    Explain how to get the amount at the end of any year from the year above it.

b)    Represent the amount of money in your account after two, three, and four years using powers of 1.08.

c)    Suppose you invested $1000 in this credit union for twenty years. How much money would be in your account at the end of 20 years?

**FX-5.** Suppose you have a younger sister and yesterday was her sixth birthday. She received $100 from your grandfather and you want to convince her to put it all in a savings account at the credit union. In order to convince your sister, you need to explain to her how much money she will have by her eighteenth birthday if the credit union is paying 8% annual interest compounded <u>quarterly</u> (four times per year).

    a) If 8% is the annual interest, what is the quarterly interest? What is the quarterly multiplier?

    b) Write an expression that represents the amount of money in the account after 10 quarters.

    c) Write an expression that represents the amount of money in the account after x quarters.

    d) Write an expression that represents the amount of money in the account on your sister's 18th birthday **and** find the value of that expression.

**FX-6.** What if you could earn 12% per year compounded quarterly (3% per quarter) and you started with $356. Use the expression you wrote in the last problem as a model and write an equation for this new function where x still represents the number of quarters and y represents the amount of money you have at any time.

**FX-7.** A concert has been sold out for weeks, and as the date for the concert draws closer, the price of the tickets increases. The cost of a pair of concert tickets was $150 yesterday and today it is $162. Assuming that the cost continues to increase at this rate:

    a) what is the daily rate of increase? What is the multiplier?

    b) what will be the cost one week from now, the day before the concert?

    c) what was the cost 2 weeks ago?

**FX-8.** Solve each of the following for x.

    a) $2^3 = 2^x$                  b) $x^3 = 5^3$

    c) $3^4 = 3^{2x}$               d) $2^7 = 2^{(2x+1)}$

FX-9.     Solve $2x^2 - 3x - 7 = 0$.  Give your solutions both in radical form and as decimal approximations.


FX-10.    Write each of the following in its smallest base.
          Examples: 16 can be written as $2^4$ , and $27^2 = (3^3)^2 = 3^6$.

          a)    64                    b)    $8^3$                    c)    $25^x$

          d)    $16^{(x+1)}$          e)    $\frac{16}{81}$         f)    $81^2$


FX-11.    Solve the following systems of equations.

          Which system is most efficiently solved by substitution?  Explain.

          Which system is most efficiently solved by elimination?  Explain.

          a)    $3x - 2y = 14$              b)    $y = 5x + 3$
                $-2x + 2y = -10$                  $-2x - 4y = 10$


FX-12.    Give the coordinates of the x- and y-intercepts for each of the following functions.

          a)    $f(x) = x^2 + 6x - 72$     b)    $g(x) = -5x + 4$


FX-13.    Multiply each expression.

          a)    $2x(x + 3)$               b)    $(x + 3)(x - 5)$

          c)    $(2x + 1)(x - 3)$         d)    $(x + 3)(x + 3)$


FX-14.    Factor each expression completely.

          a)    $x^2 - 49$                b)    $4x^2 - 1$

          c)    $x^2y^2 - 81z^2$          d)    $2x^3 - 8x$


FX-15.    Explain how to find the area of the triangle shown here and find it.

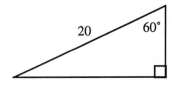

FX-16. If you flip a fair coin:

   a)    what is the probability of getting a "heads"?

   b)    what is the probability of getting a "tails"?

# APPLICATIONS: HALF LIFE

FX-17.   **THE PENNY LAB**

**The Experiment**: With your team, conduct the following experiment.

Trial #0:   Start with 100 pennies. This is your initial value.

Trial #1:   Dump the pennies in a pile on your desk. Remove any pennies that have "tails" side up. Record the number of pennies <u>left</u>.

Trial #2:   Gather the remaining pennies, shake them up, and dump them on your desk. Remove any pennies that have the "tails" side up and record the number of pennies left.

Trial #3 → Trial #?      Continue this process until the last penny is removed.

Answer the following questions.

   a)    Would the results of this experiment have been significantly different if you had removed the "heads" pennies each time?

   b)    Would the results have been significantly different if you had alternated heads/tails after each trial?

   c)    If you had started with 200 pennies, how would this have effected the results?

   d)    How does problem FX-16, about probability, relate to this investigation?

   e)    Decide what your dependent and independent variables are, clearly label them, and draw a graph of your data.

   f)    Is it possible that some team conducting this experiment might never remove their last penny? Explain.

FX-18.    When a radioactive isotope undergoes decay, it does so at a fixed rate.  The time it takes
         for half of it to decay is called the "half-life."  For example, if a substance has a half-life
         of ten years, and you start with 100 grams of it, after ten years you will have only 50
         grams.  In another ten years, half of that 50 grams will decay, and so on.

| years | amount left |
|-------|-------------|
| 0     | 100         |
| 10    | 50          |
| 20    |             |
| 30    |             |
|       |             |

a)    Make a table of values like the one shown.

b)    Extend the table for values up to 60 years.

c)    Sketch a graph to represent this situation.

d)    How much will be left after 25 years?

e)    When will this isotope disappear completely?

f)    Explain why you think most states will not allow radioactive materials to be
      dumped inside their borders.

FX-19.    Suppose a video-tape loses 60% of its value every **year** it is in a video store.  The **initial
         value** of the video-tape was $80.

a)    What is the **multiplier**?

b)    What is the value of the video after one year?

c)    What will the value be after four years?

d)    Write a function  $V(t) = ?$  to represent the value in t  years.

e)    When does the video have no value?

f)    Sketch a graph of this function.  Be sure to scale and label your axes.

**FX-20.** Two very unlucky gamblers sat down in a casino with $10,000 each. Both lost every bet they made. The first gambler bet half of his current total at each stage, while the second bet one-fourth of his current total at each stage. They had to quit betting after each of them was down under $1. How many bets did each person get to place?

**FX-21.** Find the **annual multiplier** for each of the following.

a) A yearly increase of 5% due to inflation.

b) An annual decrease of 4% on the value of a television.

c) A monthly increase of 3% in the cost of groceries.

d) A monthly decrease of 2% on the value of a bicycle.

**FX-22.** Convert each side of the equation $4^4 = 16^2$ to powers of two in order to show that $4^4$ equals $16^2$.

**FX-23.** Solve each of the following for x. For (c) and (d) use the idea from the previous problem so that you don't have to guess and check.

a) $2^{(x+3)} = 2^{2x}$

b) $3^{(2x+1)} = 3^3$

c) $9^{40} = 3^x$

d) $8^{70} = 2^x$

**FX-24.** Assume $y - 4 = 4(x - 3)$.

a) What is the slope of this line?  b) What is the y-intercept?

c) What is the x-intercept?  d) Make a quick sketch of this function.

**FX-25.** Factor each expression.

a) $2x + 8$

b) $x^2 + 4x$

c) $x^2 + 5x + 6$

d) $y^2 - 3y - 10$

FX-26.    Find the value of  x  that will make  $f(x) = 5$  where  $f(x) = \dfrac{6}{x - 1}$ .

FX-27.    Given:  $AC = BC$,  $AC = CD$, and  $m\angle ABC = 40°$.

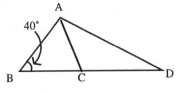

Explain how to find $m\angle ADC$.

## ZERO EXPONENTS

FX-28.    Start with a rectangular sheet of scratch paper.

a)    Now fold the paper in half.  How many times has the paper been folded?  How many rectangular regions are there?

b)    Fold it in half again.  With two folds, how many regions are there?

c)    Three folds.  How many regions?

d)    Four folds?  Five folds?  What is the pattern or rule?

e)    Write an equation to represent the rule.  Let  y  represent the number of regions and x  the number of folds.

f)    How many regions were there before you folded the paper in half the first time, in other words, when there were zero folds?  How does your equation describe this situation?

FX-29.    Consider the following pattern:

| x | 4 | 3 | 2 | 1 | 0 |
|-----|-----|-----|-----|-----|-----|
| $2^x$ | 16 | 8 | 4 | 2 | |

a)    Describe the pattern in the table, reading from left to right.

b)    Copy the table and fill in the missing value.  What should $2^0 = ?$

c)    Explain the relationship between this problem and the previous problem.

**FX-30.** **Zero Power.** In the previous problems you found the value of $2^0$ by looking at patterns. What does your calculator give for the value of $2^0$? What value(s) do you get for $3^0$, $4^0$, $10^0$, $101^0$? Experiment with lots of different values raised to the zero power (try $(-2)^0$, $(\frac{3}{5})^0$, and at least three others). Write down your results. Try more negative numbers raised to the zero power. Try fractions and decimals. Write a general rule about numbers raised to the zero power. Should this be in your Tool Kit?

**FX-31.** What are the coordinates of the y-intercepts for each of the graphs below?

a)   $y = 2^x$

b)   $y = 3^x$

c)   $y = 101^x$

d)   $y = \left(\frac{3}{5}\right)^x$

e)   What conclusion can you make about the y-intercept for the graph of $y = a^x$ for $a > 0$ ?

**FX-32.** Judy does not believe that $x^0$ could possibly have any meaning, and if it does, she can't remember it anyway. Kelly says she is sure that $x^0 = 1$ and bets her other team members that she can convince Judy. She starts with the following problems.

$$\frac{x^{10}}{x^3} = x^7 \qquad\qquad \frac{x^5}{x^3} = x^2 \qquad\qquad \frac{x^4}{x^3} = x^1$$

a)   What is the pattern for the exponents in all these problems?

b)   Use the pattern from part (a) to find t:   $\dfrac{x^3}{x^3} = x^t$ ?

c)   From arithmetic we know that $\dfrac{\text{a number}}{\text{the same number}} = ?$

d)   Use your results for parts (b) and (c) to explain why $x^0 = 1$.

**FX-33.** What is $0^0$?

a)   What does the calculator give for its value?

b)   What does $a^0$ usually equal? What does $0^a$ usually equal?

c)   Why do you think $0^0$ is undefined?

FX-34. Caren wrote the following solution, and her teacher marked it wrong but didn't tell her how to answer the problem correctly. Write an explanation of what is wrong and show Caren how to solve the problem.

$$(x + y)^2 = x^2 + y^2$$

FX-35. For each of the following situations, identify the **multiplier**, the **initial value**, and the **time**. Remember that the time must be in the same units as the multiplier.
(Example: 3% raise per quarter for two years → multiplier = 1.03, time = 8 quarters)

a) A house purchased for $126,000 has lost 4% of its value each year for the past 5 years.

b) A 1970 comic book has appreciated at 10% per year, and originally sold for 35¢. Sean wants to know its value in the year 2000.

c) A Honda Prelude depreciates at 15% per year. Six years ago it was purchased for $11,000.

d) Inflation is at the rate of 7% per year. Today Janelle's favorite bread costs $1.79. What would it have cost ten years ago?

FX-36.  Solve this system of linear equations in two variables. See the Milepost 4 problems if you need more practice.

$$5x - 4y = 7$$
$$2y + 6x = 22$$

FX-37. Find the coordinates of the x- and y-intercepts and the equation for the line of symmetry for the function at right.

$$y = x^2 + 14x + 13$$

FX-38.    Jackie and Alexandra, two sisters who love to argue, are both taking algebra. Jackie is in Algebra 1 and Al (as Alexandra prefers to be called) is in Algebra 2. They were working on homework at the kitchen table when Jackie said, "My teacher said to be careful when doing this problem because it is hard. It's not hard, in fact, it was reeeeallly easy."

"Let me see," said Al. "Silly sister, you went too fast and you were not very careful." Help Jackie find her mistakes and show how to solve the equation correctly.

This is what Jackie did:

$$(x + 4)^2 - 2x - 5 = (x - 1)^2$$

$$x^2 + 16 - 2x - 5 = x^2 + 1$$

$$16 - 2x - 5 = 1$$

$$11 - 2x = 1$$

$$-2x = -10$$

$$x = 5$$

FX-39.    Solve for x.

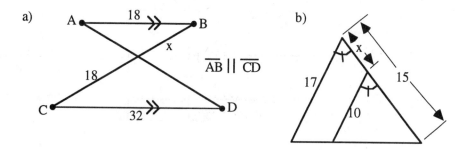

a)    $\overline{AB} \parallel \overline{CD}$    b)

FX-40.    Sketch a graph of the following situation: the distance one bicycle pedal is from the ground while you are pedaling versus time.

FX-41.    For each triangle, draw a diagram and find the required information.

a)    Find the smallest angle in a right triangle with sides 8, 15, and 17.

b)    Find the height of an equilateral triangle with sides 6.

c)    Find the measures of the angles of an isosceles triangle whose sides are 6, 6, and 8.

FX-42.    Today the class will take a "function walk" and each
student will have the opportunity to become a point on a
human graph. Your teacher will give you an integer and
an index card. Write down the integer on one side of
the index card. You will need this card, your calculator,
and a pencil for this problem.

Your teacher will give you the rest of the directions.

FX-43.    Make a table like the one below for each of the four functions from the function walk and
fill in as much as you can. Give y-values in <u>fraction</u> form and look for a pattern.

| x | $2^x$ | y |
|---|---|---|
| -4 | | |
| -3 | | |
| -2 | | |
| -1 | | |
| 0 | $2^0$ | |
| 1 | $2^1$ | 2 |
| 2 | $2^2$ | 4 |
| 3 | $2^3$ | 8 |
| 4 | | |

FX-44.    Use the table that you created for $y = 2^x$ to write explanations for the following
questions.

a)    Why should $2^0 = 1$?

b)    Why should $2^{-3} = \frac{1}{8}$? What would $3^{-3}$ equal? $3^{-4}$?

c)    Write an explanation in your Tool Kit of what a negative exponent does.

d)    Should your graphs be **discrete** (points) or **continuous** (connected)?

FX-45.    Draw a graph for each of the four functions from the function walk and give the domain
and range of each one.

FX-46. Jim does not understand negative exponents. He thinks that $4^{-2}$ is a negative number. Thu volunteers to help him out. She begins with $\frac{x^3}{x^5}$. "Simplify this two ways," she says. "First, use the subtraction rule for a division problem with exponents. Second, write out the meaning of $\frac{x^3}{x^5}$ and simplify." Write out what Thu said to do and then substitute 4 in place of x to convince Jim that $4^{-2} = \frac{1}{16}$.

FX-47. Manhattan Island (New York City) was purchased in 1626 for trinkets worth $24. The value of Manhattan in 2000 was about $34,000,000,000. Suppose the $24 had been invested instead at a rate of 6% compounded each year.

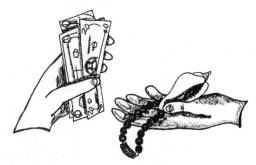

a) What is the **multiplier**?

b) What is the **initial value**?

c) What is the **time** (number of years) to find the value of the money in 2000?

d) Write a function, $V(t) = ?$, to find the **value** V of the investment at any time t.

e) What would the investment be worth in 2000?

f) How does this value compare to the 2000 value of Manhattan?

FX-48. Write each expression below as a power of the smallest integer base you can.
Example: $\frac{1}{16} = 2^{-4}$

a) $\frac{1}{125}$

b) $(\frac{1}{9})^x$

c) $(\frac{1}{32})^{(1-x)}$

FX-49. Solve each equation for x.

a) $5^x = 5^{-3}$

b) $6^x = 216$

c) $7^x = \frac{1}{49}$

d) $10^x = 0.001$

FX-50. Solve the following system of equations.
$$y = -x - 2$$
$$5x - 3y = 22$$

FX-51. Multiply each expression.

a) $(x + 2)(x - 7)$

b) $(3m + 7)(2m - 1)$

c) $(x - 3)^2$

d) $(2y + 3)(2y - 3)$

FX-52. Consider the following sequence with initial value 7:   $7, \ 6\frac{1}{3}, \ 5\frac{2}{3}, \ 5, \ ...$

a) What kind of sequence is it?

b) Write an equation that describes the sequence  $t(n) =$

c) What is the fifteenth term after the initial term,  $t(15)$?

d) Is -21 a term of the sequence?  If so, which one?

FX-53. State the coordinates of the  x- and y-intercepts      $y = -x^2 + 3x - 5$
for the graph whose equation is given at right.

FX-54. An integer between 10 and 20 is selected at random.  What is the probability that three is a
factor of that integer?

FX-55. Solve for  x.

a) $x^3 = 27$

b) $x^4 = 16$

c) $x^3 = -125$

# NON-INTEGER EXPONENTS

**FX-56.**  Is your graph for $y = 2^x$ in yesterday's assignment just a set of points or did you draw a smooth continuous curve through all the points?

a) Make a large copy of this graph and draw a smooth curve connecting the points if you have not already done so.

> This function is the simplest example of an **EXPONENTIAL FUNCTION**. An exponential equation has the general form $y = k(m^x)$, where k is the initial value and m is the multiplier. The graph of an exponential function is **continuous** because x can assume all values. Be careful. The independent variable x has to be in the exponent. For example, $y = x^2$ is **NOT** an exponential equation, even though it has an exponent.

b) Add this graph to your Tool Kit, label it EXPONENTIAL FUNCTION, and, on the graph, write the general form for an exponential function.

c) Have you seen equations of this type before? Where?

**FX-57.** Use your graph of $y = 2^x$ and your calculator to answer the following questions.

a) If $x = \frac{1}{2}$, what value do you get on your calculator (for $y = 2^x$)?

b) Does this value appear to agree with the corresponding y-value on your graph?

c) What result do you get for $x = \frac{5}{4}$ on your graph? On your calculator?

**FX-58.** Use the graph of $y = 2^x$ to approximate the value of each expression to the nearest tenth.

a) $2^{0.7}$

b) $2^{-0.3}$

c) $2^{-1}$

d) $2^{1.5}$

**FX-59.** With your team, investigate the function $y = (\frac{2}{3})^x$.

**FX-60.** Which of the following equations do you think are exponential functions? Explain.

a) $f(x) = 3x^2$

b) $h(x) = (-2)^x$

c) $y = 5(4)^x$

d) $g(x) = (2.46)^x$

e) $y = (2^x)(3^x)$

f) $y = 2^x + 3^x$

**FX-61.** Three Algebra 2 students are doing a problem in which they have to find an equation from a pattern. They get three answers: $y = 2^{-x}$, $y = \dfrac{1}{2^x}$, and $y = (0.5)^x$. Explain to these three students what has occurred.

**FX-62.** Find the **multiplier** and **time** for each of the following.

a) A yearly increase of 1.23% in population.

b) A monthly decrease of 3% on the value of a video.

c) The annual multiplier if there is a monthly decrease of 3% on the value of a video.

**FX-63.** Solve each of the following equations for x.

a) $2^{(x+3)} = 64$

b) $8^x = 4^6$

c) $9^x = \dfrac{1}{27}$

**FX-64.** When asked to solve $(x - 3)(x - 2) = 0$, Freddie gives the answer "x = 2." Samara corrects him, saying that the answer should also be x = 3. But Freddie says that when you solve an equation, you only have to find <u>one</u> value of x that works, and since 2 works, he's done. Do you agree with Freddie? Justify your answer.

**FX-65.** The area of a square is 225 sq. cm.

a) Make a diagram and list any subproblems that you would need to do to find the length of the diagonal.

b) What is the length of its diagonal?

**FX-66.** Factor completely: $5x^3y + 35x^2y + 50xy$. Show every step and explain what you did.

**FX-67.** Write the description for a situation that could fit this function: $f(t) = 2000(0.91)^t$.

FX-68. In a regular hexagon, join alternate vertices to form an equilateral triangle. Shade part of the hexagon as shown. Which is larger, the shaded area of the hexagon or the unshaded area? Explain.

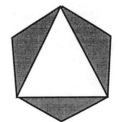

FX-69. ΔABC ~ ΔAED in the diagram shown.

a) Solve for x.

b) Find the perimeter of ΔADE

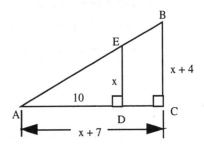

FX-70. Consider the examples below and check them in your head or on your calculator:

$9^2 = 81$ and $\sqrt[2]{81} = 9$      $8^3 = 512$ and $\sqrt[3]{512} = 8$      $7^5 = 16807$ and $\sqrt[5]{16807} = 7$

Use these ideas to compute the following without a calculator.

a) $\sqrt[2]{49} =$

b) $\sqrt[4]{81} =$

c) $\sqrt[4]{10000} =$

d) $\sqrt[5]{-32} =$

# ROOTS AND FRACTIONAL EXPONENTS

FX-71. Discuss the following question with your team. What does $\sqrt[3]{64}$ mean?

FX-72. Make a table like the one below, fill in any missing information, and complete the table.

| POWERS | in other words... | ROOTS | in other words... |
|---|---|---|---|
| $11^2 = 121$ | | | The square root of 121 is 11 |
| $5^3 = 125$ | 5 cubed is 125 | $\sqrt[3]{125} = 5$ | The cube root of 125 is 5 |
| $7^4 = 2401$ | 7 to the 4th is ____ | | The fourth root of 2401 is 7 |
| | | | The fifth root of 243 is 3 |
| | | $\sqrt[6]{64} =$ | |
| $a^n = b$ | | | |

FX-73.    In an earlier course, you learned that $x^n$ meant "n factors of x multiplied together." In this definition, the number n was a counting number. We know that $x^{-2}$ doesn't mean "-2 factors of x multiplied together" because that does not make sense. Today we want to see if we can make sense out of something like $x^{1/3}$.

   a)    You probably do not know the value of $\sqrt[3]{50}$ without using a calculator. However, it is easy to find the value of $(\sqrt[3]{50})^3$ without a calculator. What is it? Why? Explain fully.

   b)    Suppose for a moment that $50^{1/3}$ does mean "1/3 factors of 50 multiplied together," whatever that means. In that case, based on the laws of exponents for integers, what should $(50^{1/3})(50^{1/3})(50^{1/3})$ equal? What should $(50^{1/3})^3$ equal?

   c)    Look at the last result of part (b). What did you do to $50^{1/3}$? What was the result? Now compare this to your answer in part (a). What do you think $50^{1/3}$ equals?


FX-74.    Use your calculator to determine the decimal value of each of the following expressions to the nearest 0.001 (thousandth).

| COLUMN A | COLUMN B |
|---|---|
| $\sqrt[2]{9}$ | $9^{1/4}$ |
| $\sqrt[2]{12}$ | $120^{1/3}$ |
| $\sqrt[3]{125}$ | $9^{1/2}$ |
| $\sqrt[3]{120}$ | $12^{1/2}$ |
| $\sqrt[4]{9}$ | $125^{1/3}$ |

   a)    Compare the values in column A to the values in column B. What conclusions can you draw?

   b)    Using your conclusions, how else could you write $\sqrt[x]{b}$ ?

   c)    Rewrite this relationship as a rule and add it to your Tool Kit.


FX-75.    Complete the values of the following expressions, (a) through (c):

   a)    $(64^2)^{(1/3)} = ?$          b)    $(64^{1/3})^{(2)} = ?$          c)    $64^{2/3} = ?$

   d)    What can you conclude?

   e)    Write $625^{3/4}$ in two alternate forms and show how they give the same result.

FX-76. Rewrite each of the following in the form $a^b$.

a) $\sqrt[3]{5^2}$

b) $\sqrt[4]{2^5}$

c) $\sqrt[2]{7^3}$

FX-77. On your calculator evaluate $16^{3/2}$. What two calculations would you have to do to get this result without a calculator?

FX-78. Solve each equation.

a) $\left(\sqrt[3]{125}\right)^2 = x$

b) $125^{2/3} = x$

c) $\left(\sqrt{x}\right)^3 = 125$

d) $x^{3/2} = 125$

e) What do you notice about the answers to the above problems? How are the equations related to each other?

FX-79. Use the ideas from the previous problem to solve the following equations.

a) $x^{1/4} = 2$

b) $m^{1/3} = 7$

c) $r^{3/2} = 8$

FX-80. Show two steps to simplify each of the following, then calculate the value.

a) $64^{2/3}$

b) $25^{5/2}$

c) $81^{7/4}$

FX-81. Solve each of the following for x.

a) $2^{1.4} = 2^{2x}$

b) $8^x = 4$

c) $3^{5x} = 9^2$

FX-82. Consider the following pattern: $\frac{1}{2^3} = \frac{1}{8}$, $\frac{1}{2^2} = \frac{1}{4}$, $\frac{1}{2^1} = \frac{1}{2}$, $\frac{1}{2^0} = 1$.

a) Continue the pattern to find: $\frac{1}{2^{-1}}$, $\frac{1}{2^{-2}}$, $\frac{1}{2^{-3}}$, and $\frac{1}{2^{-4}}$

b) What is the value of $\frac{1}{2^{-n}}$?

c) Write this as a rule and add it to your Tool Kit (Exponent Laws).

FX-83. Factor each expression.

a)   $3y^2 + 6y$

b)   $w^2 - 5w + 6$

c)   $x^2 - 4$

d)   $9x^2 - 4$

FX-84. On the spinner at right, each "slice" is the same size. What is the probability that when you spin you will get:

a)   a one?

b)   a two?

c)   a three?

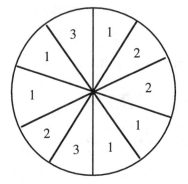

FX-85. Solve each of the following for x.

a)   $(3.25 \cdot 10^{27})^x = 1$

b)   $\left( \sqrt[7]{239^3} \right)^x = 1$

c)   $\left( \frac{287625}{1191628} \right)^x = 1$

d)   $\left[ \sqrt[3]{\pi} \left( \frac{4}{5} \right)^{-6} \right]^0 = x$

FX-86. Multiply each expression.

a)   $(2y - 7)(3y + 1)$

b)   $(x - 3)^2$

c)   $(x + 2)(x - 3)$

d)   $x(x + 2)(x - 3)$

FX-87.  Below are several situations that can be described by using exponential functions. They represent a small sampling of the situations where quantities grow or decay by a constant percentage over equal periods of time.  For each situation (a) through (f):

> i)  Find an appropriate **time** unit (days, weeks, years, etc.).
>
> ii)  State the **multiplier** that would be used for that situation.
>
> iii)  Identify the **initial value**.
>
> iv)  Write an **equation**, in exponential form:  $V(t) = k(m^t)$ **, that represents the growth or decay and  V(t)  represents the value at any given time  t.
>
> ** ($m$ = multiplier, $t$ = time, $k$ = initial value)

a)  A house purchased for $120,000 has an annual appreciation of 6% per year.

b)  The number of bacteria present in a colony is 180 at 12 noon, and the bacteria grows at a rate of 22% per hour.

c)  A 100 gram sample of a radioactive isotope decays at a rate of 6% every week.

d)  The value of a car with an initial purchase price of $12,250 which depreciates by 11% per year.

e)  For an investment of $1000 the 6% annual interest is compounded monthly.

f)  For an investment of $2500 the 5.5% annual interest is compounded daily.

FX-88.  Choose one of the exponential equations that you created in the previous problem and create a possible test question that could be solved using the equation.

FX-89.  Suppose the annual fees for attending a public university were $1200 in 1986 and the cost was increasing by 10% each year.  (Round answers to the nearest dollar.)

a)  Calculate the predicted cost for the year 1997.

b)  What was the cost in 1980? What did you have to assume?

c)  Write an equation to describe this situation.

d)  Sketch a graph of this function.

e)  By 1993 the annual cost was actually $3276.  Find this point on your graph.  How accurate was the model?  What actually happened?

FX-90. According to the U.S. Census Bureau the population of the United States has been growing at an average rate of approximately 2% per year. The census is taken every 10 years and the population in 1980 was estimated at 226 million people

    a) How many people should the Census Bureau have expected to count in the 1990 census?

    b) How many people should the Census Bureau expect to count in the census in the year 2000?

    c) If the rate of population growth in the U.S. were to continue at about 2%, in about what year would the population in the United States reach and surpass one billion?

FX-91. Solve each of the following equations for x. Notice the variety in the equations today! Each one requires some different thinking.

    a) $2^{(x-1)} = 64$             b) $4.7 = x^{1/3}$

    c) $8^{(x+3)} = 16^x$          d) $9^3 = 27^{(2x-1)}$

    e) $x^6 = 29$               f) $25^x = 125$

FX-92. Rewrite $16^{3/4}$ in as many different forms as you can.

FX-93. Write and describe a situation that would fit the following function.

$$g(t) = 0.05(1.16)^t$$

FX-94.    For each of the problems below, find the initial value.

a)    Five years from now, a bond that appreciates at 4% per year will be worth $146.

b)    Seventeen years from now, Ms. Speedi's car, which is depreciating at 20% per year, will be worth $500.


FX-95.    Factor each expression.

a)    $x^2 + 8x$                         b)    $6x^2 + 48x$

c)    $2x^2 + 14x - 16$              d)    $2x^3 - 128x$


FX-96.    Find the lengths of each of the sides labeled x in the triangles below.

a)                                               b)


FX-97.    Consider this sequence:

|    | 0  | 1 | 2 | 3 | 4 |
|----|----|---|---|---|---|
|    | 10 | 5 | 2 | 1 | 2 |

a)    Predict the next three terms.

b)    Graph this sequence. Is it arithmetic, geometric, or something else?

c)    Is your graph discrete or continuous?


FX-98.    Multiply and simplify.

a)    $(x - 3)^2$                         b)    $(2m + 1)^2$

c)    $x(x - 3)(x + 1)$              d)    $(2y - 1)(y^2 + 7)$

FX-99.    Elwina and Marc were doing their homework when they came across the following
         equation. The directions said, "Solve for z."

$$\frac{1}{x} + \frac{1}{y} = \frac{1}{z}$$

Elwina said, "Well that's easy. You just turn them all over, and it's just $z = x + y$."
"Hmmm," said Marc. "I don't think so. Because if $z = x + y$, then you'd be saying that
$\frac{1}{x} + \frac{1}{y}$ was the same as $\frac{1}{x + y}$, and . . ."

"Oops!" said Elwina, "We know that's not what you get when you add the two
fractions. You have to use the common denominator, xy."

a)    Add the two fractions $\frac{1}{x} + \frac{1}{y}$ correctly.

b)    Now your answer to part (a) is the reciprocal of z. What does z equal?


FX-100.   When we say "x = 3" are we talking about a point or a line? Explain.


FX-101.   Graph each of the following.

a)    $y < 2x + 3$                     b)    $y \geq -3x - 1$


## MORE APPLICATIONS OF EXPONENTIAL FUNCTIONS

FX-102.   Suppose your state legislature passes a law that allows
         the fees for the State University system to increase by
         5% per year without approval by the public or the
         legislature (larger increases have to be approved).
         Suppose the annual fees for the university are
         currently $1000. The Smiths just had a baby girl and
         wanted to plan for her college education. They
         figured that, in 18 years, their daughter would be
         attending one of the state universities. Since 5% of
         $1000 is $50, they figured the increase in fees in 18
         years will be 18 times $50, or $900; therefore, when
         she starts college the annual fees will be $1900.
         Explain to the Smiths why they may need to save
         more than they are anticipating.

FX-103. If you can purchase an item that costs $10.00 now and inflation continues at 4% per year (compounded yearly), when will the cost double? Show how you would compute this cost.

FX-104. Bill just graduated from college and started work with a base pay of $32,000. Each year Bill receives a 5% raise.

a) Write an expression using an exponent for Bill's income in three years.

b) What is Bill's annual income in five years?

c) When will Bill's income exceed $70,000?

d) What was the **multiplier**? What was the **initial value** (principal)? Write a function, **I(t)**, to express Bill's income **I** at any time **t**.

e) After 30 years of service, Bill retires. He receives an annual pension equal to his last year's salary. What is Bill's annual pension? (Note: Bill received a total of 29 raises.)

FX-105. In the previous problem, assume that the cost of living due to inflation goes up 4% each year.

a) Write the equation that shows what Bill's $22,000 starting salary inflation must increase to as the years go by just to keep up with inflation.

b) What salary after 30 years would be equivalent in buying power to Bill's starting salary?

c) In how many years after retirement will Bill's fixed yearly income be equivalent, after accounting for inflation, to his starting salary?

FX-106. Find the annual rate of growth on an account that was worth $1000 in 1996 and was worth $1400 in 1999.

FX-107. Find the monthly rate of decay on a radioactive sample that weighed 100 grams in May and weighs 50 grams in November.

FX-108. Graph the system of equations below. In the first graph be sure to include a value between 0 and 1 and a value between -1 and 0.

$$y = x^3 \quad \text{and} \quad y = x$$

a)    How many times do these functions cross?

b)    What are the coordinates of their intersections?

c)    Solve the equation $x^3 = x$ for $x$ by making the equation equal to zero and then factoring.

d)    How are the solutions to the equation in part (c) related to the points of intersection in part (b)?


FX-109. Kristin's grandparents started a savings account for her when she was born. They invested $100 in an account that pays 8% interest compounded annually.

a)    Write an equation to express the amount of money in the account on Kristin's $x$th birthday.

b)    How much is in the account on her 16th birthday?

c)    What are the domain and range for the equation that you wrote in part (a)?


FX-110. Solve each of the following for $x$. Again, each problem requires different thinking.

a)    $81 = 3^{2x}$         b)    $x^5 = 243$         c)    $(2x)^3 = -216$


FX-111. Rewrite each of the following in y-form so that they are in the correct format for use on a graphing calculator.

a)    $2x - 3y = 7$                    b)    $2(x + y) = x - 4$


FX-112. This is a Milepost for multiplying polynomials.

Multiply and simplify.

a)    $(x + 1)(2x^2 - 3)$                b)    $(x + 1)(x^2 - 2x + 3)$

c)    $2(x + 3)^2$                        d)    $(x + 1)(2x - 3)^2$

FX-113.    The area of square A is 121 square
           units, the perimeter of square B is
           80 units.  Find the area of square C.

FX-114.    Solve the following systems of equations.

a)    $2x + y = -7y$          b)    $3s = -5t$
      $y = x + 10$                  $6s - 7t = 17$

FX-115.    Factor each expression.

a)    $m^2 + 8m + 16$         b)    $2m^2 + 16m + 32$

c)    $x^3 + 8x^2 + 16x$      d)    $2y^2 + 11y + 5$

FX-116.    The probability of landing on blue on a three-color spinner is $\frac{2}{5}$.  What is the probability
           that you will land on blue on both of the next two spins?

## FAST CARS PORTFOLIO

Fast Cars and Depreciation: Exponential Functions

FX-117. As soon as you drive a new car off the dealer's lot the car is worth less than what you paid for it.  This is called **depreciation;** so, you will sell it for less than the price that you paid for it.  Some cars depreciate more than others (that is, at different rates), but most cars depreciate.  On the other hand, some older cars actually increase in value.  This is called **appreciation.**  Let's suppose you have a choice between buying a 1999 Mazda Miata for $19,800 which depreciates at 22% a year, or a 1996 Honda Civic EX for $16,500 which only depreciates at 18% a year.  In how many years will their values be the same?  Should you instead buy a 1967 Ford Mustang for $4,000 that is appreciating at 10% per year?  Which car will have the greatest value in 4 years?  In 5 years?

[ "Lap" means "part" (because it's about cars).]

**Lap 1:**   What is the multiplier for the Miata?  For the Honda?  For the Mustang?

**Lap 2:**   Make a table like the one below and calculate the values for each car for each year.

| year | Mazda Miata | Honda Civic EX | Mustang |
|------|-------------|----------------|---------|
| 0 | $19,800 | $16,500 | |
| 1 | $15,444 | $13,530 | |
| 2 | | | |
| 3 | | | |
| 4 | | | |
| 5 | | | |
| • | | | |
| • | | | |
| • | | | |
| 10 | | | |
| • | | | |
| • | | | |
| • | | | |
| n | | | |

**Lap 3:**   Write two functions to represent the depreciation of the Miata and the Civic and draw the graphs on the same set of axes.  Are the graphs linear?  How are they similar?  How are they different?

**Lap 4:**   When will the values of the two cars be the same?

**Lap 5:**   Write an equation and graph the results for the Mustang on the same axes with the Miata and the Civic.

**For the Checkered Flag:**  Using the graph, which of the 3 cars—the Mazda, the Mustang, or the Civic—is worth the most after 4 years?  After 5 years?  After 10 years?

**Victory Lap:**  (Evaluation)  After doing this problem what you have learned?  Has this problem changed your view of buying cars?  Pick one of the three cars and explain why you would buy it.

**Extra Lap:**  Check a newspaper for the price of cars that have been made for 10 model years.  Examples:  Ford Mustangs, Toyota Corollas, Ford Thunderbirds, Chevy Camaros.  Does a 1967 Ford Mustang cost more than a 1980 Ford Mustang?  Bring in a car ad to prove your point.

FX-118. "Half-life" applies to other situations besides radioactivity. It can apply to practically anything that is depreciating or decaying.

a) From the table of values in the previous problem, estimate the half-life of the value of the Mazda and the Honda.

b) According to the mathematical model (not necessarily corresponding to reality), when will each car have <u>no</u> value?

FX-119. Examine the figure at right.

a) Find the measures of arcs AB, BC, and AC.

b) Find the diameter, circumference, and the area of the circle.

c) Find the lengths of each arc AB, BC, and AC.

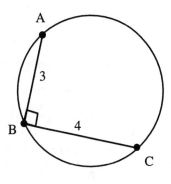

FX-120. Add this information to your tool kit if you have not done so already. Check your examples with the ones included here.

---

**SUMMARY OF EXPONENTS**

$x^0 = 1.$   Examples:  $2^0 = 1,$     $(-3)^0 = 1,$     $(\frac{1}{4})^0 = 1.$

$x^{-n} = \frac{1}{x^n}.$   Examples:  $x^{-3} = \frac{1}{x^3},$     $y^{-4} = \frac{1}{y^4},$     $4^{-2} = \frac{1}{4^2} = \frac{1}{16}.$

$\frac{1}{x^{-n}} = x^n.$   Examples:  $\frac{1}{x^{-5}} = x^5,$     $\frac{1}{x^{-2}} = x^2,$     $\frac{1}{3^{-2}} = 3^2 = 9$

$x^{\frac{a}{b}} = (x^a)^{\frac{1}{b}} = \sqrt[b]{x^a}$          Examples:     $5^{\frac{1}{2}} = \sqrt{5},$

**or**

$x^{\frac{a}{b}} = (x^{\frac{1}{b}})^a = (\sqrt[b]{x})^a$

$16^{\frac{3}{4}} = (\sqrt[4]{16})^3 = 2^3 = 8$

$4^{\frac{2}{3}} = \sqrt[3]{4^2} = \sqrt[3]{16}$

---

FX-121.  Solve each of the following for x.

a)  $25^{(x+1)} = 125^x$  b)  $\sqrt{27^x} = 81$  c)  $8^x = 2^5 \cdot 4^4$

FX-122.  Factor each expression.

a)  $x^2 - x - 72$  b)  $9x^2 - 100$

c)  $2x^2 - 8$  d)  $3x^2 - 11x - 4$

FX-123.  To what power do you have to raise:

a)  3, to get 27?  b)  2, to get 32?  c)  5, to get 625?

d)  64, to get 8?  e)  81, to get 3?  f)  64, to get 2?

g)  $(x^2)$, to get $x^1$?  h)  $(x^3)$, to get $x^{12}$?  i)  x, to get $x^a$?

FX-124.  If  $f(x) = 3(2)^x$, find

a)  f(-1)  b)  f(0)  c)  f(1)

d)  What value of  x  gives  f(x) = 12?

e)  Where does the graph of this equation cross the x-axis?  The y-axis?

FX-125.  Solve the following system of equations for D, E, and F.

$$F = -5ED^2$$
$$D = 3$$
$$6E = 2F - 32$$

FX-126.  Sketch a graph of the temperature of a hot cup of coffee left sitting in a room for a long period of time.

FX-127.  Sketch the graphs of three different parabolas with x-intercepts at (4, 0) and (8, 0). What generalization can you make about the vertex of your parabolas?

FX-128. For each step, (a) through (g), explain what mathematical operation or relationship to use to get the next result. Show both the solution steps and your explanations on your paper.

a) Problem: $\dfrac{2+x}{3} - \dfrac{x-5}{2} = \dfrac{x}{4}$

b) $12\left(\dfrac{2+x}{3} - \dfrac{x-5}{2}\right) = 12\left(\dfrac{x}{4}\right)$

c) $12\left(\dfrac{2+x}{3}\right) - 12\left(\dfrac{x-5}{2}\right) = 12\left(\dfrac{x}{4}\right)$

d) $4(2+x) - 6(x-5) = 3x$

e) $8 + 4x - 6x + 30 = 3x$

f) $-2x + 38 = 3x$

g) $38 = 5x$

Answer: $\dfrac{38}{5} = x$

# ASYMPTOTE EXPLORATION

FX-129. Your teacher will give you an integer and a sticky dot or an index card. Remember your integer. You will need this integer, your calculator, an a pencil for this problem.

With the whole class you will be graphing functions such as $y = 2^x$, $y = \dfrac{1}{x}$, $y = \dfrac{1}{x^2}$, and $y = \dfrac{x+1}{x-1}$.

FX-130. With your team:

a) Discuss what it means for a function to have a horizontal asymptote.

b) Discuss what it means for a function to have a vertical asymptote.

c) What is happening to the functions as the curve approaches these asymptotes?

d) Make copies of the functions that were graphed. Label each graph with the equation, domain and range, intercepts (if any), and clearly indicate the locations of all asymptotes.

e) Record your preliminary description of an asymptote in your Tool Kit. Include an example that shows clearly how a graph can get closer and closer to a line called an **asymptote**.

FX-131.   Investigate the family of functions  $y = a^x$  for different values of  a.  Be sure that you try enough values of  a.

FX-132.   Two weeks ago a sample of bacteria weighed 4.2 grams. Last week it weighed 4.326 grams.

   a)   What is the weekly rate of growth? b)   What is the weight **now**?

FX-133.   Last year the principal's car was worth $28,000.  Next year it will be worth $25,270.

   a)   What is the annual rate of depreciation?

   b)   What is the car worth now?

FX-134.   If  $a = k(m)^{-1}$ and $b = k(m)^1$,

   a)   what is **ab**?                b)   what is **k**?

FX-135.   Jonnique is writing a puzzle problem.  She wants the values for  x  and  y  in the second equation to be the same as in the first.  She originally wanted the values to be whole numbers so they could be guessed and checked, but the whole numbers she has tried do not work.  Show a method, other than guess-and-check, for figuring out what numbers will work.

   Jonnique's equations:      $(2^x)(2^y) = 64$         and      $2^{3x} = 16^y$

FX-136.   A sequence is given by  $t(n) = 2(3)^n$.

   a)   What are t(0), t(1), t(2), t(3)?

   b)   Graph this sequence.  What are the domain and range?

   c)   On the same set of axes, graph the function  $f(x) = 2(3)^x$.

   d)   How are these graphs similar?  How are they different?

FX-137.   Solve the following for  x.

   a)   $1^x = 5$                b)   $2^x = 9$

FX-138.  Write the description of a situation that could fit the function below.

$$g(x) = 2.79 \cdot 10^6 (0.92)^x$$

FX-139.  This is a Milepost problem for factoring quadratic expressions.

Factor each expression.

a)    $4x^2 - 1$                          b)    $4x^2 + 4x + 1$

c)    $2y^2 + 5y + 2$                     d)    $3m^2 - 5m - 2$

FX-140.  Solve each of the following for $x$ and $y$ where $x$ and $y$ are whole numbers.

a)    $2^x 3^y = 72$                      b)    $2^{(x+y)} 3^{(x-y)} = 24$

FX-141.  Write each of the expressions below in an equivalent form without negative or fractional exponents and then give the value.  You should be able to do all of these problems without your calculator!

a)    $5^{-2}$                            b)    $4^{-3}$

c)    $9^{1/2}$                           d)    $64^{2/3}$

FX-142.  You have $5000 in an account that pays 12% annual interest.  Compute the amount in the account at the end of one year if:

a)    the interest is compounded annually (once)

b)    the interest is compounded quarterly

c)    the interest is compounded monthly

FX-143.  Find an equation of decay for a radioactive sample in the form $f(t) = km^t$, where $f(t)$ is the amount of the sample at time $t$, if $f(0) = 100$ and $f(5) = 50$.

FX-144.  Rewrite each equation in y-form and then find the point(s) of intersection.

$$2x - 5y = 10 \text{ and } 4(x - y) + 12 = 2x - 4$$

FX-145. **TOOL KIT CLEAN-UP**

Tool Kits often need to be reorganized to continue to be useful. Your Tool Kit contains entries from units 1, 2, and 3.

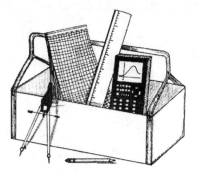

Examine the list of Tool Kit entries from this unit. Add any that you are missing.

Identify which concepts that you understand.

Choose entries to create a Unit 1 - 3 Tool Kit that is shorter, clear, and useful.

- Exponential Function
- Horizontal Asymptote
- Vertical Asymptote

- Meaning of Zero, Negative, and Fractional Exponents

FX-146. Many Algebra 1 students think that $2^{-2} = -4$. However you know that $2^{-2} = \frac{1}{2^2} = \frac{1}{4}$ .

Explain, so that an Algebra 1 student can understand, why $2^{-2} = \frac{1}{4}$ .
Do not just state a rule.

FX-147. **UNIT 3 SUMMARY ASSIGNMENT**

In this unit you have worked with exponential functions in many contexts.

a) Make up a real situation that can be represented by an exponential function.

b) Give the equation that describes the situation and tell how you arrived at the equation.

c) Draw the graph of the equation. Be sure to include all important information about the graph. How did you decide if the points on the graph should be connected or not?

d) Make up a question that can be solved by using your equation or your graph. Clearly show how to answer the question.

# UNIT 4

## The Gateway Arch
### PARABOLAS AND OTHER PARENT GRAPHS

# Unit 4 Objectives
## The Gateway Arch: PARABOLAS AND OTHER PARENT GRAPHS

The first part of this unit is all about parabolas. You will learn how to change the size, orientation, and location of parabolas on the coordinate axes and see how parabolas are mathematical models of physical situations. In addition we will investigate some other non-linear functions. You will use your graphing calculator daily as a tool to help you experiment, organize data, and recognize patterns. Just as in science, you will write up your observations and conclusions in lab reports.

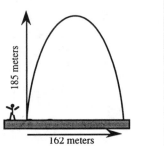

In Unit 4, you will have the opportunity to:

- become familiar with an extended set of parent equations and their graphs. These will include the parabola, absolute value, circle, cubic, and hyperbolic functions.

- relate the numbers in an equation to the location and stretch of each parent graph.

- develop your ability to visualize graphs when you know their equations and to write equations when you know their graphs.

- develop your ability to make generalizations about functions as you move from specific examples to more abstract general equations.

- develop your ability to ask questions to generate more information and to justify and explain your reasoning.

The Gateway Arch in St. Louis, Missouri is actually in the shape of a catenary curve, but we can approximate the shape with another more familiar function.

---

PG-0. **THE GATEWAY ARCH** Some bungee jumpers dream of jumping off the Gateway Arch in St. Louis, Missouri. No one has ever done this, and we are not recommending it, but it makes a challenging problem for us to consider. The most daring jumper might jump off the very top of the Arch, but this is 185 meters high. Jumpers who are more sensible might prefer to start at a lower point on the Arch. Find a rule that will tell us about how high the Arch is at <u>any</u> point so that a jumper would know how long a bungee cord to use.

185 meters

162 meters

---

| PROBLEM SOLVING |
| REPRESENTATION/MODELING |
| FUNCTIONS/GRAPHING |
| INTERSECTIONS/SYSTEMS |
| ALGORITHMS |
| REASONING/COMMUNICATION |

# Unit 4

## *The Gateway Arch*: PARABOLAS AND OTHER PARENT GRAPHS

## THE SHRINKING TARGETS LAB

PG-1.    Refer to the diagram of the Gateway Arch in problem PG-0.

    a)    What kind of curve could be used to approximate the Arch, that is, what kind of equation has a graph with a shape like this?

    b)    Actually, the Arch is the shape of a catenary or hyperbolic cosine, but we can approximate it with the more familiar curve you named in part (a). What is the simplest equation for that curve that you know of?

    c)    The graph of the equation you gave in part (b) is different from the diagram in problem PG-0, even though they have the same shape. In this unit you will learn how changes in the equation translate into changes in the graph. How must the graph of $y = x^2$ be changed in order to make it a better match for the graph of the Arch? Discuss your ideas with your team and be ready to share them with the class in a few minutes. We will return to this problem at the end of the unit.

PG-2.    **Shrinking Targets Lab**
(problems PG-2 to PG-4)

On a sheet of cardboard or an old file folder, find and mark the <u>exact</u> center. With a compass, draw the largest circle you can on the cardboard, and cut it out. Draw about nine more concentric circles on this circular disc (<u>not</u> equally spaced), but <u>do not</u> cut them out yet!

    a)    Set up a table with headings, "Length of radius (cm)" and "Mass of disc (g)." Record the length of the radius of each circle in the first column. Then cut out each circle, STARTING FROM THE OUTSIDE, and weigh the disc of cardboard each time, recording the information in the table. When your table is complete, you will graph the results.

    b)    Before you graph the results, what do you think the graph will look like?

    c)    Carefully graph your results and sketch in the smooth curve that seems to fit the points best (a "best-fit" curve).

    d)    What kind of curve does your graph seem to be? What kind of equation will it have? Save this graph. We will return to it later to determine its equation more accurately.

    e)    Predict the mass of a circle with a radius twice as large as your largest circle. Explain how you figured this out.

PG-3. For the data shown in your table in part (a) above, what is the domain? (That is, what are acceptable lengths for the radius?) What is the range?

PG-4. Does your graph in part (c) above have x- or y-intercepts? If so, what are they and what do they represent? If not, explain completely why not.

PG-5. Your results from this problem will be useful in the Parabola Investigation which you will do tomorrow.

    a) Draw the graph of $y = (x - 2)^2$. If you are doing the graph by hand be sure to use the domain: $-1 \le x \le 5$.

    b) How is this graph different from the graph of $y = x^2$? What difference in the equation accounts for the difference in the graphs?

    c) Based on your observations in part (b), write an equation with a graph that "sits on" the x-axis at the point $(5, 0)$.

PG-6. Consider the sequence with the initial value 256, followed by 64, 16, . . .

    a) Write the next three terms of this sequence. Then find a rule.

    b) If you were to keep writing out more and more of the sequence, what would happen to the terms?

    c) Sketch a graph of the sequence. What happens to the points as you go farther to the right?

PG-7. Write the equation for each graph:

a)

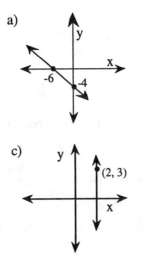

b)

c)

d)

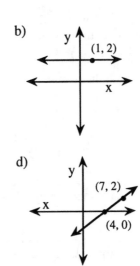

PG-8.    Imagine spinning the rectangle in the diagram about
         the y-axis.  Think of a rectangular flap hinged to the
         y-axis so it will revolve around it.

         a)    Draw the shape you would get.

         b)    Find the volume of this shape.

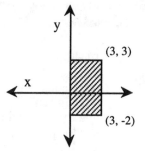

PG-9.    What is a *line of symmetry*?

         a)    Draw a figure that has a line of symmetry.

         b)    Draw a figure that has <u>two</u> lines of symmetry.

         c)    Can you find a basic geometric shape that has an
               infinite number of lines of symmetry?

PG-10.   Find the point where  $y = 3x - 1$  intersects  $2y + 5x = 53$.

PG-11.   Suppose your parents spend an average of $150 each month for your food.

         a)    In five years, when you're living on your own, how much will you be spending on
               food each month if you're eating about the same amount and inflation averages
               about 4% per year?

         b)    Write an equation that represents your monthly food bill  x  years from now if both
               the rate of inflation and your eating habits stay the same.

# PARABOLA INVESTIGATION

PG-12.  **Parabola Investigation:** For this investigation we have not provided a worksheet because we want you to gain some practice in efficiently keeping and effectively organizing your notes in order to recognize patterns and describe them. As you use the graphing calculator to investigate each question be sure to keep track of all the equations you try along with their resulting graphs. What doesn't work in one case may be the key to another question that will come later.

a) Graph the parabola $y = x^2$. Make an accurate sketch of the graph. Be sure to label any important points on your graph. In addition to x- and y-intercepts be sure to label the lowest point which is called the vertex.

b) Find a way to change the equation to make the same parabola _open downward_. The new parabola should be congruent (the same shape and size) to $y = x^2$, with the same vertex, except it should open downward so its vertex will be its highest point.

Record the equations you tried, along with their results. Write down the results even when they are wrong—they may come in handy below.

c) Find a way to change the equation to make the $y = x^2$ parabola _stretch vertically_ (it will appear steeper). The new parabola should have the same vertex and orientation (i.e., open up) as $y = x^2$.

Record the equations you tried, along with their results and your observations.

d) Find a way to change the equation to make the $y = x^2$ parabola _compress vertically_ (it will appear as if the points in $y = x^2$ move toward the x-axis).

Record the equations you try, their results, and your observations.

e) Find a way to change the equation to make the $y = x^2$ parabola _move 5 units down_. That is, your new parabola should look exactly like $y = x^2$, but the vertex should be at (0, -5).

Record the equations you try, along with their results. Include a comment about moving the graph up as well as down.

f) Find a way to change the equation to make the $y = x^2$ parabola _move 3 units to the right_. That is, your new parabola should look exactly like $y = x^2$, except that the vertex should be at the point (3, 0). Review problem PG-5 for help getting started. Record the equations you try, along with their results. Tell how to move the parabola to the left as well as how to move it to the right.

g) Find a way to change the equation to make the $y = x^2$ parabola _move 3 units to the left_ and _stretch vertically_, as in part (c). Your new parabola might look like $y = 4x^2$, except that the vertex should be at the point (-3, 0).

Record the equations you try, along with their results. Comment about how to move the parabola to the left as well as how to move it to the right.

>>Problem continues on the next page.>>

h)     Finally, find a way to change the equation to make the $y = x^2$ parabola _vertically compressed_, _open down_, _move 6 units up_, and _move two units to the left_. Where is the vertex of your new parabola?

Record the equations you try, their results, and your comments on how each part of the equation affects its graph.

PG-13.    For each equation below, predict the <u>vertex</u>, the <u>orientation</u> (open up or down?), and tell whether it is the same as a <u>vertical</u> <u>stretch</u> or <u>compression</u> of $y = x^2$. Before using the graphing calculator, sketch a quick graph based on your predictions.

a)   $y = (x + 9)^2$

b)   $y = x^2 + 7$

c)   $y = 3x^2$

d)   $y = \frac{1}{3}(x - 1)^2$

e)   $y = -(x - 7)^2 + 6$

f)   $y = \frac{5}{2}(x - 2)^2 + 1$

g)   $y = 2(x + 3)^2 - 8$

h)   $4y = -4x^2$

i)   $y = 4x - 4$

j)     Check your predictions for the equations in parts (a) through (i) on your graphing calculator. If you made any mistakes, correct them and briefly describe why you made the mistake (what incorrect idea you had). Then make a neat and accurate graph for each function.

PG-14.    Take out your Tool Kit. Write some notes for yourself on how to move, flip, and stretch/compress a parabola. Include a **general** **equation** for all parabolas.

PG-15.   Your friend is taking an algebra class at a different school where she is not allowed to use a graphing calculator. Explain to her how she can get a good sketch of the graph of the following function without a calculator <u>and</u> without having to substitute a lot of different numbers for x and do numerous calculations.

$$y = 2(x + 3)^2 - 8$$

a)     Be sure to explain how to locate the vertex, whether the parabola should open up or down, and how its shape is related to the shape of $y = x^2$.

b)     Your friend also needs to know the x- and y-intercepts. Show her how to get those without having to draw an accurate graph or use a graphing calculator.

PG-16. Solve for z:

a) $4^z = 8$

b) $4^{2z/3} = 8^{(z+2)}$

c) $5^{(z+1)/3} = 25^{1/z}$

PG-17. Lettie just got her driver's license. Her friends soon nicknamed her "Leadfoot" because she's always going 80 mph on the freeway.

a) At this speed, how long will it take her to travel 50 miles?

b) How long would it take her if she drove the 50 miles at 65 mph?

c) Speeding tickets carry fines of about $200 and usually increase the cost of insurance. If Lettie gets a ticket on this trip, what would be her cost per minute of time saved?

PG-18. Daniela, Kieu, and Duyen decide to go the movies one hot summer afternoon. The theater is having a summer special: Three Go Free (if they each buy a large popcorn and a large soft drink). They take the deal and end up spending $19.50. The next week, they go back again, only this time, they each pay $2.50 to get in, they each get a large soft drink, but they share one large bucket of popcorn. This return trip also costs them a total of $19.50.

a) Find the price of a large soft drink and the price of a large bucket of popcorn.

b) Did you write two equations or did you use another method? If you used another method, write two equations now, and solve them. If you already used a system of equations, skip this part.

PG-19.    Solve for the indicated value.

a)    x = _____

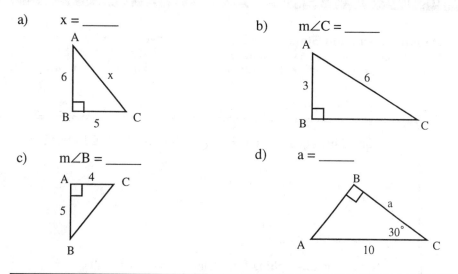

b)    m∠C = _____

c)    m∠B = _____

d)    a = _____

---

### INVERSE TRIGONOMETRIC FUNCTIONS

Remember that the trigonometric functions sine, cosine, and tangent match an angle measure with a decimal that represents the ratio of two sides in a right triangle.

**Question**: If you know the decimal value for the sine, cosine, and tangent, how do you use the calculator to find out what the angle is?

**Answer**:  Remember, what sin does, $\sin^{-1}$ undoes.  Use the "arc" or "inverse" trigonometric buttons on your calculator.

---

PG-20.    Simplify each expression.

a)    $\sqrt{8} = \sqrt{4}\sqrt{2} =$

b)    $\sqrt{50}$

c)    $\sqrt{72}$

d)    $\sqrt{45}$

PG-21    Use what you learned in the Parabola Investigation to write an equation for each of the parabolas described below.

a)    A parabola just like  $y = x^2$  but shifted 8 units right and 5 units down.

b)    A parabola with a stretch factor of 10, sitting with its vertex on the  x-axis at (-6, 0).

c)    A downward opening parabola with vertex (-7, -2) with a vertical compression of 0.6.

**PG-22.** **Graphing Form and Standard Form** As you have worked with quadratic functions, equations, and expressions you have regularly seen two forms. One is known as **graphing (or vertex) form**, the other is known as **standard form**.

---

A quadratic equation in **GRAPHING** or **VERTEX FORM** looks like:

$$y = a(x - h)^2 + k.$$

For example, the equation

$$y = 3(x - 1)^2 - 5$$

is in graphing form where $a = 3$, $h = 1$, and $k = -5$.

---

NOTE: The equations you found in the parabola investigation (problem PG-12) should be in graphing (or vertex) form.

The following quadratic equation represents the same parabola as $y = 3(x - 1)^2 - 5$, but it is written in what is generally called **standard form.**

---

A quadratic equation in **STANDARD FORM** is written as $y = ax^2 + bx + c$.

For $y = 3x^2 - 6x - 2$, $a = 3$, $b = -6$, and $c = -2$.

---

a) Use your graphing calculator to verify that the two equations $y = 3(x - 1)^2 - 5$ and $y = 3x^2 - 6x - 2$ are equivalent.

b) Show algebraically that these two equations are equivalent by starting with the graphing form and showing step by step how to get the standard form.

c) Notice that the value for a is 3 in both forms of the equation, but that the numbers for b and c are different from the numbers for h and k. Why do you think the value for a would be the same number in both forms of the equation?

PG-23.    Ms. Speedi, who teaches Algebra
2 as well as Algebra 1, knew she
would not be at school on Friday
because she would be attending a
mathematics conference. Before
leaving school Thursday, she
wrote on the board a list of ten
parabola equations in graphing
form, with instructions for her
fourth period Algebra 2 class.
The instructions said:

TEAM QUIZ
Use what you learned yesterday
about the graphing form of
quadratic equations to sketch the
graphs of these parabolas *without
using your graphing calculators.*

On Friday morning the substitute arrived late, and the custodian let the first period
Algebra 1 class into the room. Several eager students saw the assignment on the board
and thought it was for them. They immediately went to the board and started doing the
one thing they had learned so far, multiplying out the squared expression and
simplifying. They had just finished replacing the last equation with its simplified form
when the substitute arrived with a completely different assignment for them.

When the students in the fourth period Algebra 2 class arrived, they read the instructions
and saw the list of equations, all in standard form. The first one was: $y = x^2 - 8x + 7$

Making xy-tables and plotting point-by-point would take forever. They had to find
another way. Enrico said, "We need that other form of the equation that tells us the
vertex. How do we get that?"

a)    Jessica suggested, "We know how to get the coordinates of the x-intercepts." What are
the coordinates of the x-intercepts for this equation?

b)    Kevin said, "And parabolas are symmetric, so the vertex is mid-way between them."
How could you find the x-value of the vertex? Find it.

c)    Kenya volunteered, "And if we know the x-value, we can find the y-value that goes
with it." Find the y-value.

d)    "We've got the vertex. Now we can make a sketch!" they all said together. Make
a sketch of this function, label the intercepts and the vertex, and draw in a line of
symmetry.

e)    "How can we be sure we're right?" asked Jessica. "Couldn't we write the graphing
form equation then work it out to see if we get the original one in standard form?"
Enrico suggested. Use the vertex to write the equation in graphing form. Show
your work to verify that it is the same as the original by squaring and simplifying.

The Gateway Arch: Parabolas and Other Parent Graphs

PG-24. The following four functions were also part of Ms. Speedi's Quiz. For each function do parts (a) through (e) as in the previous problem in order to write and verify the graphing form:

a) $p(x) = x^2 - 10x + 16$

b) $f(x) = x^2 + 3x - 10$

c) $g(x) = x^2 - 4x - 2$

d) $h(x) = -4x^2 + 4x + 8$

PG-25. On Friday afternoon the custodian erased all the boards, so when Ms. Speedi returned on Monday, she assumed that her Algebra 2 students had just started with the graphing forms. She never realized that her class had figured out their own method for changing the equation from standard form to graphing form.

Based on your work with the two preceding problems, describe the students' method for finding the vertex without drawing the graph and for figuring out the graphing form of the equation of a parabola from the standard form. With your team, make up another example, and show how to use the method you described.

PG-26. Explain what the differences are between:

(1) an accurate sketch  and  (2) a careful graph.

PG-27. Solve each of the following equations *without using the quadratic formula.*

a) $y^2 - 6y = 0$

b) $n^2 + 5n + 7 = 7$

c) $2t^2 - 14t + 3 = 3$

d) $\frac{1}{3}x^2 + 3x - 4 = -4$

e) Zero is one of the solutions of each of the above equations. What do all of the above equations have in common that causes them to have zero as a solution?

PG-28. Find the vertex of each of the following parabolas by averaging the x-intercepts. Then write each equation in graphing form.

a) $y = (x - 3)(x - 11)$

b) $y = (x + 2)(x - 6)$

c) $y = x^2 - 10x + 16$

d) $y = (x - 2)^2 - 1$

PG-29.  Did you need to average the x-intercepts to find the vertex in part (d) of the preceding problem?

    a)      What are the coordinates of the vertex for part (d)?

    b)      How do these coordinates relate to the equation?

> The **vertex** of a parabola locates its position on the axes. The **vertex** serves as a **LOCATOR POINT** for a parabola. The other shapes we will be investigating in this course also have locator points. These points have different names but the same purpose for each different type of graph.

    c)      Add **Locator Point** to your Tool Kit. Use a parabola and its vertex as one example. You may wish to leave room for another example if you find one later.

PG-30.  More practice in solving for one variable in an equation or formula involving two or more variables is available in the Milepost 7 problems. Rewrite the following equations so that you could enter them into the graphing calculator. In other words, solve for y.

    a)   $x - 3(y + 2) = 6$               b)   $\dfrac{6x - 1}{y} - 3 = 2$

    c)   $\sqrt{y - 4} = x + 1$           d)   $\sqrt{y + 4} = x + 2$

    e)      Find the x- and y-intercepts for each of the graphs created by the calculator forms of the equations in parts (a) through (d).

PG-31. Scientists can estimate the increase in carbon dioxide in the atmosphere by measuring increases in carbon emissions. In 1998 the annual carbon emission was about eight gigatons (a gigaton is a billion metric tons). Over the last several years annual carbon emission has been increasing by one percent.

    a)      At this rate how much carbon will be emitted in 2005?

    b)      Write a function $C(x)$ to represent the amount of carbon emitted in the year 2-thousand-X.

# SOME MATHEMATICAL MODELING: PARABOLAS

PG-32.    Parabolas are good models for all sorts of things in the world.  Indeed, many animals and insects jump in parabolic paths.

This diagram shows a jackrabbit jumping over a three foot high fence. In order to just clear the fence, the rabbit must start its jump at a point 4 feet from the fence.

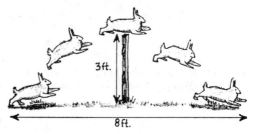

a)    Decide, as a team, where to put the x- and y-axes on this diagram.

b)   Find the equation of a parabola that models the jackrabbit's jump.

c)    Did you solve part (b) by guess-and-check or some other method?  This is an example of a problem where guessing and checking can actually make your work harder.  As a hint to avoid further guessing and checking, how could you check your answer without the graphing calculator?

d)    What do the dependent and independent variables represent in this situation?

e)    What are the domain and range of your equation?  What parts of the domain and range are appropriate for the actual situation?

PG-33.    A fireboat in the harbor is assisting in putting out a fire in a warehouse along the pier.  Use the same process as in the previous problem to find the equation of the parabola that models the path of the water from the fireboat to the fire, if the distance from the barrel of the water cannon to the roof of the warehouse is 120 feet and the water shoots up 50 feet above the barrel of the water cannon.

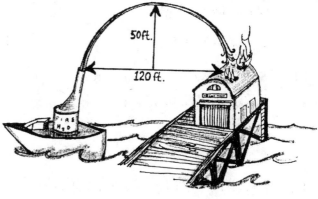

PG-34.    Make predictions about how many places the graph of each equation below will touch the x-axis.  You may want to first rewrite some of the equations in a more useful form.

a)    $y = (x - 2)(x - 3)$      b)    $y = (x + 1)^2$        c)    $y = x^2 + 6x + 9$

d)    $y = x^2 + 7x + 10$      e)    $y = x^2 + 6x + 8$      f)    $y = -x^2 - 4x - 4$

g)    Check your predictions with your calculator.

h)    Write a clear explanation describing how you can tell whether the equation of a parabola will touch the x-axis at only one point.

PG-35.    Draw accurate graphs of $y = 2x + 5$, $y = 2x^2 + 5$, and $y = \frac{1}{2}x^2 + 5$ on the same set of axes.  Label the intercepts.

     a)    In the equation $y = 2x + 5$, what does the 2 tell you about the graph?

     b)    Is the 2 in $y = 2x^2 + 5$ also the slope? Explain.

PG-36.    Do the sides of a parabola ever curve back in like Figure A at right?  Give a reason for your answer.

PG-37.    Do the sides of the parabola approach straight vertical lines as shown in Figure B at right  (in other words, do parabolas have asymptotes)? Give a reason for your answer.

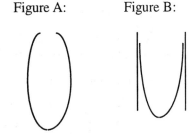

Figure A:       Figure B:

PG-38.    Find the x- and y-intercepts of:

     a)    $y = 2x^2 + 3x - 5$             b)    $y = \sqrt{2x - 4}$

PG-39.    Sketch graphs for each of the following equations.  Remember that a sketch includes the labeled locator point.

     a)    $y = 3x^2 + 5$               b)    $f(x) = -(x - 3)^2 - 7$

PG-40.    If $g(x) = x^2 - 5$, find:

     a)    $g(0.5)$                      b)    $g(h + 1)$

PG-41.    If $g(x) = x^2 - 5$, find the value(s) of x so that:

     a)    $g(x) = 20$                b)    $g(x) = 6$

PG-42.    While watering his outdoor plants, Maurice noticed that the water coming out of his garden hose followed a parabolic path.  Write the equation of a parabola that describes the path of the water from the hose to the plant.

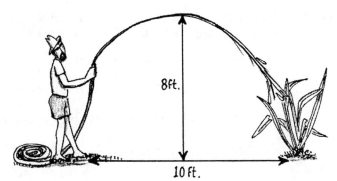

8ft.

10 ft.

PG-43.    Use the method from problem PG-23 to find the vertex of $y = x^2 + 7x - 8$ and write the equation in graphing form.

PG-44.    Write an equation of a parabola that fits the description of a parabola below.

domain: $-\infty < x < \infty$,  and range: $y \geq 2$.

PG-45.    Plot each pair of points and find the distance between them. You may use graph paper or draw generic triangles. Give answers in both square root form and as decimal approximations.

a)     (3, -6) and (-2, 5)                    b)     (5, -8) and (-3, 1)

c)     (0, 5) and (5, 0)                       d)     Write the distance you found in part (c) in simplified square root form.

# COMPLETING THE SQUARE

PG-46.    **INTRODUCTION**  In problems PG-23 and PG-24, you found that one way to change a quadratic function from the standard form $y = ax^2 + bx + c$ to the graphing form $y = a(x - h)^2 + k$ is to figure out the vertex by using the average of the x-intercepts and then to substitute the coordinates of the vertex for **h** and **k**. Ms. Speedi, who did not know her students had already figured out the method of averaging the intercepts, had a different method she planned to teach them, called **completing the square.**

Jessica was at home struggling with her Algebra 2 homework and grumbling about how she just didn't get this new method they were supposed to be learning. She didn't see how she could get from $y = x^2 + 8x + 10$ to the graphing form without figuring out the vertex first, and Ms. Speedi kept talking about something called "Completing the Square." Then her precocious younger sister, who was playing with algebra tiles, said, "Hey, I bet I know what they mean." Anita's Algebra I class had been using tiles to multiply and factor binomials. Anita explained:

$x^2$ represents the area of a square tile with dimensions  x by x,
x   represents the area of a rectangle with dimensions  x by 1, and
1   represents the area of a  square with dimensions  1 by 1.

"Yes," said Jessica, "I took Algebra I too, remember?"

Then Anita went on to say, "Good, so $x^2 + 8x + 10$ would look like this:

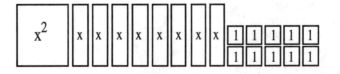

and <u>you</u> need to make it into a square!"

>>Problem continues on the next page.>>

"OK," said Jessica. "I'll have to do this:"

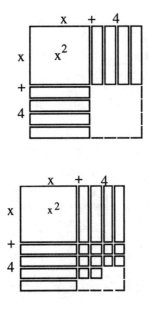

"Oh, whoa," said Jessica. "So with the 8 x's, then I just need 16 small squares to fill in the corner."

"But you only have 10," Anita reminded her.

"Okay, okay, so I only have ten," Jessica muttered. She put in the 10 small squares then completed the outline of the whole composite square and said,

"The complete square...... Oh, I get it! The **complete square** is $(x + 4)^2$, but what I started with is six less than that, so it's $(x + 4)^2$, minus 6."

"Oh, I see," said Anita. "You started with $x^2 + 8x + 10$, but $(x + 4)^2$ has six extras so $x^2 + 8x + 10 = (x + 4)^2 - 6$."

a)     Where is the vertex of the parabola $y = (x + 4)^2 - 6$?

b)     Sketch the graph.

PG-47.   The next problem looked almost the same as the previous case. It was $y = x^2 + 4x + 9$. Anita quickly grabbed the blocks and laid out one large square, four rectangles, and 9 small squares. She arranged a large composite square with the big square in the upper left corner and split the 4 rectangles so she could put two on the right of the big square and two on the bottom. Then she filled in the lower right-hand corner with the small squares and looked up with a puzzled expression. "Oh, oh," she said, "we can't complete the square this time. We have too many small squares."

But Jessica just smiled and said, "This is easier than the first one. I'll just write an expression describing what I see, a complete square and some extras."

a)     What equation did Jessica write? (You may want to draw the picture.)

b)     Name the vertex, and sketch the graph.

PG-48. How could you **complete the square** of the quadratic expression and find the vertex for:

$$f(x) = x^2 + 5x + 2?$$

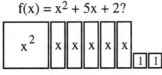

What about the five x-bars? Use force! Split one bar in half. See Figure A.

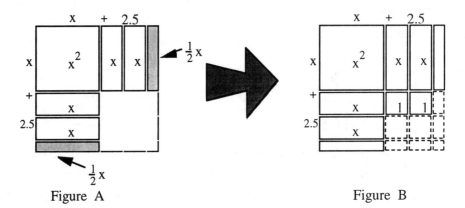

Figure A                    Figure B

a) How many 1 by 1 squares, including parts of squares are we missing? Figure B should help.

b) What expression represents the complete square?

c) Write the graphing form of the equation.

d) Name the vertex and sketch the graph.

e) Use your observations in the last three problems to summarize the method known as **COMPLETING THE SQUARE** and add it to your Tool Kit.

PG-49. For each quadratic function use the idea of completing the square to write it in the graphing form. Then state the vertex of each parabola.

a) $f(x) = x^2 + 6x + 7$

b) $y = x^2 + 4x + 11$

c) $f(x) = x^2 + 10x$

d) $y = x^2 + 7x + 2$

PG-50. Represent the number of small squares you would have to add to an expression of the form $x^2 + bx$ to make a complete square. Use drawings and examples if they help to clarify. Add this information to your Tool Kit entry.

**PG-51.** Challenge: write the graphing form for $y = x^2 + bx + c$:

a) when c is more than the number of small squares needed for a complete square.

b) when c is less than the number of small squares needed for a complete square.

c) How does your answer for part (b) differ from your answer to part (a)? Are the two results algebraically different?

**PG-52.** Simplify each expression.

a) $\sqrt{24}$

b) $\sqrt{18}$

c) $\sqrt{3} + \sqrt{3}$

d) $\sqrt{27} + \sqrt{12}$

**PG-53.** Use a generic triangle to find the slope of the line through the two given points and then find the distance between the two points.

An explanation and more practice in using the formula for the distance between two points is available in the Milepost 8 problems.

a) (0, 0) and (4, 4)

b) (-2, 4) and (4, 7)

c) (12, 18) and (-16, -19)

d) (0, 0) and (25, 25)

**PG-54.** Harvey's Expresso Express, a drive through coffee stop, is famous for its great house coffee, a blend of Colombian and Mocha Java. Their arch rival, Jojo's Java, sent a spy to steal their ratio for blending beans. The spy returned with a torn part of an old receipt that showed only the total number of pounds and the total cost, 18 pounds for $92.07. At first Jojo was angry, but then he realized that he knew the price per pound of each kind of coffee ($4.89 for Colombian and $5.43 for Mocha Java). Show how he could use equations to figure out how many pounds of each type of beans Harvey's used.

**PG-55.** Lilia wants to have a circular pool put in her back yard. She wants the rest of the yard to be cement.

a) If her yard is a 50 ft. by 30 ft. rectangle, what is the largest radius pool that can fit in her yard?

b) If the cement is to be 8 inches thick, and costs $1.00 per cubic foot, what is the cost of putting in the cement? (Reminder: Volume = (Base Area) • Depth)

# MOVING OTHER FUNCTIONS

PG-56. Each person will need two full sheets of graph paper (you will use the front side only). Divide each sheet into six equal sections as shown in the figure at right.

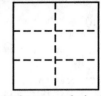

Working as a team, sketch a graph of each of these equations and identify each graph with its equation.
Label the coordinates of intercepts or any other important points that are relatively easy to find. You may split up the work in any way you think is fair, but each person should have a task to perform.

a) $y = x^3$

b) $y = 2^x$

c) $y = \frac{1}{x}$

d) $y = \frac{1}{x} - 4$

e) $y = (x - 1)^3$

f) $y = 2^x - 4$

g) $y = 2^{(x-4)} - 3$

*h) $y = \frac{1}{x + 3} + 1$

*i) $y = \frac{2}{x - 3}$

j) $y = (x - 2)^3 + 1$

k) $y = 2^{(x+3)}$

l) $y = \frac{1}{2}(x + 2)^3$

\* Be sure to use parentheses when entering these kinds of equations in a calculator.

PG-57. Separate (cut) your graphs along the fold lines and then discuss possible methods of sorting the graphs; which graphs seem to belong together? Once your team has decided on a sorting method, sort the graphs into appropriate stacks.

a) How did you decide which graph went in which stack? What are the similarities and differences among the graphs in each stack?

b) What are the similarities and differences among the <u>equations</u> of the graphs in each stack?

c) Which graph, in each pile, has the simplest equation?

d) Each person in your team should carefully graph the simplest equation from each stack to keep for themselves (keep these graphs with your answers to this problem). You will each need these graphs later in this unit.

PG-58. Look at your graph of $y = x^3$. This curve, called a "**cubic**," has an important point at the origin. As you will find out in Calculus, points like these are called "inflection points." If you are curious, ask your teacher for a definition of an inflection point. Find all the other graphs that have inflection points. Write down their equations and the coordinates of their inflection points.

PG-59. Find all of the graphs that have asymptotes. Write down their equations, along with the equations of the asymptotes. If a graph has two asymptotes that intersect each other, write down the point where they intersect.

PG-60.   A few days ago you explored how to change the equation of $y = x^2$ to shift the graph up and down, left and right. Explain the relationship between that lab and today's graphs.

PG-61.   Sketch a graph of each of these equations (include the y-intercept and "locator point" for each; approximate the x-intercepts where appropriate).

a)   $y = x^3 + 5$

b)   $f(x) = (x - 10)^3$

c)   $g(x) = \dfrac{1}{x} + 7$

d)   $y = \dfrac{1}{x + 8}$

e)   $y = 2^x + 7$

f)   $h(x) = (x - 2)^3 - 6$

PG-62.   Jessica's new dilemma is the following problem:

> Use the idea of completing the square to write the following quadratic function in graphing form:
> $$y = x^2 - 6x - 2.$$

As usual Anita was looking over Jessica's shoulder as she read the problem. "You can't do that one with the tiles," she announced.

"Why not?," asked Jessica.

"Because it has negatives in it, and our teacher said the tiles are only a good model for positive numbers, but not negatives," Anita assured her.

"Who needs the tiles?" said Jessica. "I can use the **idea** of completing the square algebraically. See, the complete square for $x^2 - 6x$ is $(x - 3)^2 = x^2 - 6x + 9$ So, I just have to subtract 11 to get that expression to equal $x^2 - 6x - 2$."

a)   Based on Jessica's method above, what is the graphing form of this equation? State the vertex and sketch the graph.

b)   Use the idea of completing the square to write the function $f(x) = x^2 - 4x - 5$ in graphing form. Give the vertex and sketch the graph.

PG-63.   Use the method of averaging the intercepts to find the vertex and write the graphing form for each of the functions in parts (a) and (b) of the preceding problem.

PG-64.   Now that you have seen and used two different approaches for converting a quadratic expression from standard form to graphing form—the students' method of averaging x-intercepts and Ms. Speedi's way of algebraically completing the square—which do you prefer? What do you see as the advantage of one over the other?

PG-65.    The graph of $y = x^2$ is shown in dashed lines.
Estimate the equations of the two other parabolas.

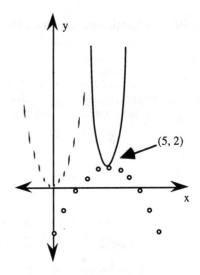

(5, 2)

PG-66.    Use the method you prefer to write the equation in
graphing form and find the x- and y-intercepts and
the vertex (locator point) of $y = x^2 + 2x - 80$.
Then sketch the graph.

PG-67.    You are standing outside the school, waiting to cross the street, when you hear a
booming car stereo approaching.

a)    Sketch a graph that shows the relationship between how far away from you the car
is and the loudness of the music.

b)    Which is the dependent variable and which is the independent variable?

PG-68.    Simplify each expression.

a)    $\sqrt{75} + \sqrt{27}$

b)    $\sqrt{x} + 2\sqrt{x}$

c)    $(\sqrt{12})^2$

d)    $(3\sqrt{12})^2$

PG-69.    Use the locator points to write a possible equation for each graph:

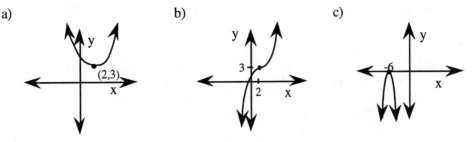

a)

(2,3)

b)

3

2

c)

-6

PG-70.    Find the domain and range for each of the graphs in the previous problem.


PG-71.    Complete the square to get an equivalent expression for each of the following
          expressions:

          a)   $x^2 + 2x$                           c)   $x^2 - 10x + 21$

          b)   $x^2 - 4x - 2$                        d)   $x^2 - 7x + 12.5$


PG-72.    Ryan thinks that completing the square is only good for changing quadratic <u>functions</u> into
          graphing form, but cannot be used for solving quadratic <u>equations</u>.

          Show him how to complete the square to rewrite $x^2 + 6x - 10 = 0$. Then use the new
          form to solve for x.


PG-73.    If the slope of line AB is $\frac{5}{9}$ and the coordinates of point B are (18, 6), what is the
          y-intercept of line AB ?

**PG-74.** What is the simplest equation of a parabola you can think of?

Most people would probably say that $y = x^2$ is the simplest parabola. The simplest version of a whole family of equations is called its **PARENT GRAPH**. So $y = x^2$ is the parent for all parabolas. We can get the equation of any other parabola just by moving, flipping, or stretching $y = x^2$.

a) What do you think is the parent for all lines? All exponentials?

---

Some families of functions are so important that they will come up over and over again throughout this course. So it will come in handy to have a **PARENT GRAPH** Tool Kit, a special Tool Kit where we will keep a catalog of parents of important equations and shapes. The parents we have seen so far are as follows:

| Parent Equation | Family |
|---|---|
| $y = x$ | **Lines** |
| $y = x^2$ | **Parabolas** |
| $y = x^3$ | **Cubics** (This is just one type of cubic. There are other cubic equations that don't have $y = x^3$ as a parent, which you will see later.) |
| $y = 2^x$ | **Exponential Form** |
| $y = \dfrac{1}{x}$ | **Hyperbolas** (There are also other parent hyperbolas.) |

---

b) Get two Parent Graph Tool Kit pages from your teacher and put in the information about each of these functions. For each one, include its name, a careful graph that is clearly labeled, a domain and range, and all the other things involved in investigating a function. Describe the locator point, but do not try to enter a general equation; that will come later.

**PG-75.** Picky Patrick doesn't think that $y = 2^x$ should be the parent of all exponentials. "The parent is supposed to be the *simplest* equation you can get," Patrick says. " I think either $y = 1^x$ or $y = 0^x$ is simpler than $y = 2^x$, so one of those two should be the parent of all exponentials. What do you think?

PG-76.    For each function below:

i)   state the equation of the parent.

ii)  create a reasonable sketch of the graph, including intercepts (you should try this without a graphing calculator, but feel free to use one to check your ideas).

iii) give the domain and range.

iv)  find the coordinates of the vertex or other locator point, if any.

v)   indicate the location of any asymptotes (and where they intersect each other).

Note: these may be easier to figure out if you put them all in y-form.

a)   $y + 1 = x^2$           b)   $y + 4 = x^3$           c)   $y + 6 = (x + 2)^3$

d)   $y + 2 = 2^x$           e)   $y = \dfrac{1}{x - 3}$           f)   $y = \dfrac{1}{x} + 2$

g)   $y - 3 = (x - 4)^3$     h)   $y + 2 = (x - 3)^2 + 1$   i)   $y - 5 = 2^{(x+4)}$

PG-77.    Two of the families of functions in the preceding problem had graphs with **asymptotes**.

a)    Check your tool kit to be sure you have examples and a description of asymptotes.

So far we have graphed functions from two families that have vertical or horizontal **ASYMPTOTES**.  The following examples are from the $y = 2^x$ and the $y = \dfrac{1}{x}$ families.

$y = 2^x - 5$ has a horizontal asymptote, the line $y = 5$.

$y = \dfrac{1}{x+3} - 2$ has a horizontal asymptote $y = -2$ and vertical asymptote $x = -3$.

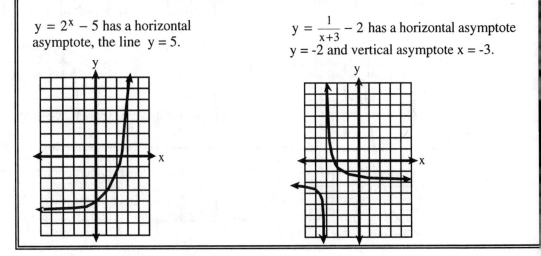

b)    For each graph explain why you think the equation will continue to generate values closer and to the asymptote(s).  Tables of values may help.

PG-78.    Multiply the expressions in parts (a) through (c) to remove the parentheses.

a)    $(x - 1)(x + 1)$           b)    $2x(x + 1)(x + 1)$           c)    $(x - 1)(x + 1)(x - 2)$

d)    Find the x- and y-intercepts of $y = x^3 - 2x^2 - x + 2$.  The factors in part (c) should be useful.

The Gateway Arch: Parabolas and Other Parent Graphs                                                    131

PG-79. Write a possible equation of each of these graphs. Assume that one mark on each axis is one unit. When you are in class, check your equations on a graphing calculator and compare your results with your teammates.

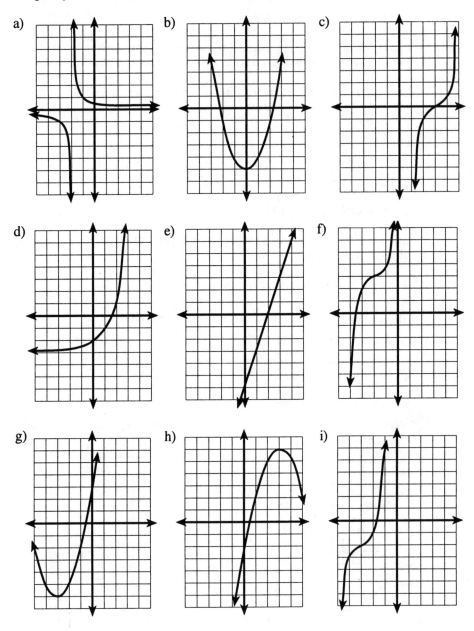

PG-80.    Consider a line with a slope of 3 and a y-intercept at (0, 2).

   a)    Sketch the graph of this line.

   b)    Write the equation of the line.

   c)    Find the initial term and the next three terms of the sequence $t(n) = 3n - 1$. Plot the terms on a new set of axes next to your graph from part (a) above.

   d)    Explain the similarities and differences between the graphs and equations in parts (a) - (c). Are both continuous?


PG-81.    The gross national product (GNP) was $1.665 \times 10^{12}$ dollars in 1960. If the GNP increased at the rate of 3.17% per year until 1989:

   a)    what was the GNP in 1989?

   b)    write an equation to represent the GNP t years after 1960, assuming that the rate of growth remained constant.

   c)    do you think the rate of growth remains constant? Explain.


PG-82.    Simplify each expression.

   a)    $\sqrt{x} + \sqrt{y} + 5\sqrt{x} + 2\sqrt{y}$              b)    $(2\sqrt{8})^2$

   c)    $\dfrac{\sqrt{50}}{\sqrt{2}}$                                    d)    $\sqrt{\dfrac{3}{4}}$

PG-83.   Write the equations of three different parabolas with a common vertex at (4, 0).

PG-84.   Now that you have had some experience with graphs that are generated from $y = x^2$, we will look at graphs that come from $y = x^3$.

   a)   Draw an accurate graph of $y = x^3$. (x-values from -2 to 2 will be sufficient!)

   b)   Now imagine <u>stretching</u> this graph just like you stretched a parabola. Sketch in what you think the stretched graph would look like.

   c)   Imagine <u>compressing</u> $y = x^3$. Sketch in what you think the compressed graph would look like.

   d)   How can you change the equation $y = x^3$ so that the graph is stretched or compressed? Experiment with a graphing calculator until you're confident that you can write a complete answer to this question.

PG-85.   Now consider $y = -x^3$.

   a)   Predict what the graph of $y = -x^3$ will look like. Add a sketch of this function to your $y = x^3$ graph. Explain how you decided what this function looks like.

   b)   Graph $y = -x^3$ on your calculator. How does this graph compare with your sketch?

PG-86.    One way of writing a **general equation** for a **parabola** is $y = a(x - h)^2 + k$. This equation tells us how to start with the parent $y = x^2$ and shift or stretch it to get any other parabola.

   a)   Explain what each letter (a, h, & k) represents in relation to the graph of $y = x^2$. Add this information to your Tool Kit.

   b)   Write a general equation for a <u>cubic</u> with parent graph $y = x^3$, and explain how each letter in your general equation affects the stretch or location. Make sure everyone in your team agrees, and be ready to present your ideas to the class.

PG-87.   Sketch a graph of these cubics without a graphing calculator. Then use your calculator to check your thinking.

   a)   $f(x) = 3(x - 2)^3 + 2$          b)   $y + 3 = \frac{1}{3}(x + 1)^3$

PG-88. Take out your Parent Graph Tool Kit. As a team, write **general equations** for each parent. Be ready to explain how your general equations work; that is, tell what effect each part has on the graph: openness and direction, horizontal location (left/right shift), vertical location (up/down shift). Include an example with a sketch.

PG-89. Explain the difference between the graphs of $y = \frac{1}{x}$ and $y = 4\left(\frac{1}{x + 5}\right) + 7$.

PG-90. How is $y = 2^x$ different from $y = -(2^x)$? Sketch the graph of $y = -(2^x)$.

PG-91. Sketch the graph of $y = 2(x - 1)^2 + 4$.

a) Now rewrite the equation $y = 2(x - 1)^2 + 4$ without parentheses. That is, perform whatever algebra is necessary to get rid of the parentheses. Remember order of operations!

b) What would be the difference between the graphs of the two equations above? This is sort of a trick question, but do explain your reasoning.

c) What is the parent of $y = 2(x - 1)^2 + 4$?

d) What is the parent of $y = 2x^2 - 4x + 6$?

PG-92. Use the technique of completing the square to express $y = x^2 - 5x + 7$ in graphing form and state the vertex.

PG-93. Find the coordinates of the intercepts for each of the following functions:

a) $g(x) = (x + 3)^3$          b) $y - 1 = 3^x$

PG-94. If $h(x) = (x + 2)^{-1}$, find:

a) $h(3)$      b) $h(-3)$      c) $h(a - 2)$

PG-95. The point $(3, -7)$ is on a line with slope $\frac{2}{3}$. Find another point on the line.

PG-96.   **Target Lab Revisited**  Look back at your Target
Lab graph.  When you decided what kind of equation
could represent the data did you say $y = ax^2$?  You
might have said $y = x^2$, which would have been
sufficient at that time, but now we can be more
accurate and get a better version of the equation to
represent the curve you drew.

    a)   Find a convenient point on the curve you drew
and substitute the x- and y-coordinates for x
and y in the equation $y = ax^2$.  Solve for a.
Then use that result to write a more accurate equation for your graph.

    b)   Graph your equation from part (a) on your graphing calculator.  Compare this
graph with your graph of the actual data.  Explain the similarities and differences in
terms of the difference in the domain for the real situation and the domain for the
purely mathematical representation of the equation.

PG-97.   **The Fireboat Again**  The equation
below is one possibility for the parabola
formed by the water canon on the
fireboat in problem PG-33:

    $f(x) = a(x - 60)^2 + 50$

    a)   Will the value of a be positive
or negative?

    b)   Check to see whether you got
exactly $-\frac{1}{72}$ for a. If you did not, then calculate the value for a by substituting
the coordinates of some known point other than the vertex and then write the
complete equation.

    c)   Why wouldn't it work to substitute the coordinates of the vertex in part (b)?  If
you're not sure, try it.

PG-98.    Imagine a sphere being inflated so that it gets larger and larger, but remains a perfect sphere. Consider the function defined this way: the inputs are the various radii of the sphere, and the outputs are the corresponding volumes. You may remember from your previous math course that the formula for the volume of a sphere is $V(r) = \frac{4}{3}\pi(r)^3$.

   a)   What is the parent of this function?       b)   What is the stretch factor?
        Explain how you decided.

   c)   If the radius is measured in centimeters,   d)   Make a sketch of this function.
        what are the units for the volume?

   e)   What are the domain and range?


PG-99.    The cables that hold up a suspension bridge (like San Francisco's Golden Gate Bridge) also have the shape that can be approximated by a parabola. Find an equation to model the section of cables between the towers of the bridge in the diagram. Be sure to tell where you put the origin.

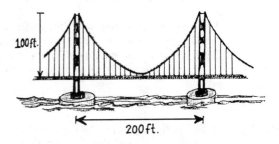


PG-100.   Tasha is experimenting with her graphing calculator. She claims that $y = \frac{1}{x}$ is the parent of $y = \frac{4}{x}$. Do you agree? If not, tell why not. If you do agree, what change (shift, stretch, or compress) could you make to $y = \frac{1}{x}$ to get $y = \frac{4}{x}$?


PG-101.   The amount of profit (in millions) made by Scandal Math, a company that writes math problems based on tabloid articles, can be found by the equation $P(n) = -n^2 + 10n$, where n is the number of textbooks sold (also in millions). Find the maximum profit and the number of textbooks that Scandal Math must sell in order to attain this maximum profit.


PG-102.   Carefully graph $y = x^3 - 4x^2 - 3x + 18$ for $-4 < x < 4$.

   a)   How many x-intercepts does it have and what are their coordinates?

   b)   What <u>small</u> change could you make in the equation so that the graph would have:

        (i)   one x-intercept.    (ii)   three x-intercepts.    (iii)   four x-intercepts.

PG-103. Draw the graph of $y = 2x^2 + 3x + 1$.

    a)    Find the x- and y-intercepts.

    b)    Where is the line of symmetry of this parabola? Write its equation.

    c)    Find the coordinates of the vertex.


PG-104. Change the equation in the previous problem so that the parabola has only one x-intercept.


PG-105. Shortcut Shuneel claims he has an easier way of changing the equation so that the parabola has only one x-intercept.

He just changed $y = 2x^2 + 3x + 1$ to $y = 0x^2 + 3x + 1$. What do you think of his method?


PG-106. Consider equations in the form $y = ax^2 + bx + c$, where a, b, and c are constants (numbers).

    a)    Make up three examples of functions that are in this form. What is the parent of each one?

    b)    Is $y = ax^2 + bx + c$ always a parabola no matter what a, b, and c are? Explain fully with examples to support your ideas.


PG-107. Writers of standardized college entrance tests sometimes write problems with weird symbols in them to test your symbolic reasoning skills.

Suppose that $A \clubsuit B$ means $\dfrac{A^2 - B^2}{A - B}$.

    a)    Find:

        i)  $5 \clubsuit 3$     ii)  $10 \clubsuit 9$     iii)  $28 \clubsuit 2$     iv)  $17 \clubsuit 17$     v)  $x \clubsuit y$

    b)    Write a conjecture about $A \clubsuit B$. Then test your conjecture with $5 \clubsuit 5$. Does it work? Revise your conjecture if necessary.

    c)    How could you show algebraically that your conjecture works for almost any value of A and B?

PG-108. Remember function machines? Each of the following pictures shows how the same machine changes the given x-value into a corresponding f(x)-value. Find the rule for this machine:

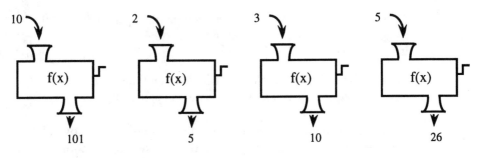

PG-109. If $x^2 + kx + 18$ is factorable, what are the possible values for k?

PG-110. Andrew likes to make up weird sequences and name them after himself. He made up these two:     $A(n) = 2(n - 1) + 3$   and   $a(n) = 2(n - 1)^2 + 3$.

a)     Are his sequences arithmetic, geometric, or something else?

b)     What would their graphs look like?

## ABSOLUTE VALUE

PG-111. Jamal's little brother Rashaad was watching Jamal make function machines. He decided to invent one of his own. Here are four examples of what Rashaad's machine does:

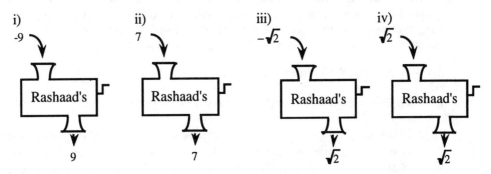

What is Rashaad's rule?  (It is okay just to describe the rule in words.)

PG-112. The mathematical name for Rashaad's machine is ABSOLUTE VALUE, and we write the rule for his function using a special symbol: $f(x) = |x|$.  With this in mind, find:

a)     $f(-6)$

b)     $f(13)$

c)     $f(-\frac{3}{5})$

d)     $f(-\pi)$

e)     $f(0)$

f)     $f(n)$

PG-113. The following problem is a chance for you to demonstrate what you've learned so far in this unit. Try to be accurate and thorough.

a) Investigate $y = |x|$. Use a full sheet of graph paper, and be sure to include all the elements of a function investigation.

b) Take out your Parent Graph Tool Kit. Do you think that any of the equations you already have is the parent of $y = |x|$? Why or why not?

c) How can we change the equation $y = |x|$ to move it up, down, left, or right? How can we stretch it or compress it, or to make it open down? Include several examples, and write a general equation for $y = |x|$.

PG-114. Add $y = |x|$ to your Parent Graph Tool Kit. Include everything you found in your investigations.

PG-115. For what values of $x$ does:

a)  $|x| = 8$ ?          b)  $|x| = 4$ ?

c)  $|x| = 0$ ?          d)  $|x| = -4$ ?

PG-116. Olivia's team was working on the problem $|x + 1| = 6$. The other three people in her team all got $x = 5$ as their answer, but Olivia got a different answer. Her teammates all tried to convince Olivia that her answer was wrong, but Olivia knew that it was correct because she checked it. She said that <u>both</u> answers were right.

a) What was Olivia's answer?

b) Explain why both answers are correct and show how you could get both solutions.

c) Make a sketch of $f(x) = |x + 1|$ and use the graph to show why there are two answers. Identify on your graph what two x-values give a corresponding y-value of 6.

PG-117. Graph $f(x) = |x - 3|$ and $x = 3$ on the same set of coordinate axes. Write a description of the relationship between the two graphs.

PG-118.  Compare these two expressions: $|\,11 - 5\,|$ and $|\,5 - 11\,|$.

    a)    How would you simplify each of them?

    b)    Explain why you get the same answer.


PG-119.  For what values of x does:

    a)    $|\,x - 7\,| = 50$ ?             b)    $|\,x + 7\,| = 50$ ?

    c)    $|\,10 - x\,| = 12$ ?           d)    $|\,2x + 1\,| = \text{-}3$ ?

    e)    What numbers are a distance of 50   f)    What numbers are a distance of 12
          units from 7 on the number line?              units from 10 on the number line?

    g)    Your answers to parts (a) and (c) should be the same as those for parts (e) and (f). Let's investigate why. What numerical expression gives the distance on the number line between 47 and 19? What expression gives the distance between 47 and 632? In general, how do you find the distance between two points on the number line? Be very specific.

    h)    Suppose you wanted to write an expression for the distance between 47 and x, without knowing whether x is greater or less than 47. You would have to write something that says "subtract x and 47, so that the result is positive," and that expression is $|\,x - 47\,|$ or $|\,47 - x\,|$. So part (a) above could be stated as "the distance between x and 7 is 50." Write and solve an equation that says "the distance between x and -9 is 15."


PG-120.  Explain the difference between $f(x) = |\,x\,|$ and $y = |\,x\,|$.


PG-121.  Sketch a graph and draw the line of symmetry for the equation $y + 3 = 2|\,x - 4\,|$. What is the equation of the line of symmetry?.


PG-122.  Find the intercepts, the locator point, and give the domain and the range for each of the following functions:

    a)    $y = |\,x - 4\,| - 2$           b)    $y = \text{-}|\,x + 1\,| + 3$


PG-123.  By mistake Jim graphed $y = x^3 - 4x$ instead of $y = x^3 - 4x + 6$. What should he do to his graph to get the correct one?

PG-124. Simplify each expression.

a) $(3\sqrt{2})^2$

b) $\sqrt{\dfrac{9}{4}}$

c) $\sqrt{\dfrac{1}{3}}$

d) $(3 + \sqrt{2})^2$

## NON-FUNCTIONS: THE SLEEPING PARABOLA

PG-125. Think about the equation $x = y^2$. How is the equation $x = y^2$ different from other equations we've investigated?

a) Investigate $x = y^2$.

b) We want to learn how to change the equation $x = y^2$ in order to shift and stretch or compress its graph. You may think you already know how to do this, but the patterns you've learned were always used with equations in "y =" form. Prepare to be surprised!

(i) Convert the equation $x = y^2$ to "y =" form. Now change the equation to move its graph up 2 units. Finally, convert this equation back to "x=" form.

(ii) Repeat part (i), but this time move its graph 6 units to the right.

(iii) With your team compare your answers in (i) and (ii) to the original equation $x = y^2$, and discuss how shifting a graph in "x=" form differs from shifting a graph in "y =" form. Write a clear paragraph describing what you observed.

(iv) Figure out how to change the equation $x = y^2$ so that the parabola opens to the left. Check your answer by converting to y-form and graphing on your calculator.

PG-126. Use your ideas from the previous problem to write a general equation for all parabolas that open sideways (think of them as "sleeping parabolas"). Add the sleeping parabola to your Parent Graph Tool Kit.

PG-127.

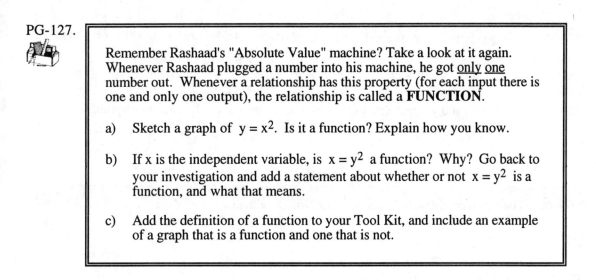

Remember Rashaad's "Absolute Value" machine? Take a look at it again. Whenever Rashaad plugged a number into his machine, he got only one number out. Whenever a relationship has this property (for each input there is one and only one output), the relationship is called a **FUNCTION**.

a)  Sketch a graph of $y = x^2$. Is it a function? Explain how you know.

b)  If x is the independent variable, is $x = y^2$ a function? Why? Go back to your investigation and add a statement about whether or not $x = y^2$ is a function, and what that means.

c)  Add the definition of a function to your Tool Kit, and include an example of a graph that is a function and one that is not.

PG-128.  Curtis, who lives on a farm and likes cows, has invented a weird type of machine, which he calls *"Curtis' Cow Machine."* Each picture represents the same machine.

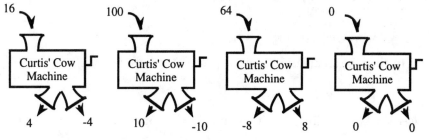

a)  Is this machine a <u>function</u> machine? Explain.

b)  Draw a graph that represents his machine. Remember that the numbers on top are the inputs and the numbers that come out of the cow machine are the outputs.

c)  Write a rule for Curtis's Cow Machine.

PG-129.  Anne says that $y = x^2$ is not a function, because when she plugs in 3 for x, she gets 9, and when she plugs in -3 she gets 9 too. Two different inputs give her the same output. Brooke says that Anne has the function idea all mixed up. Help! Explain who's right. Is $y = x^2$ a function or not? Why?

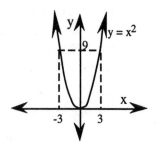

PG-130.  Return to your Parent Graph Tool Kit and for each parent graph state whether or not it is a function.

The Gateway Arch: Parabolas and Other Parent Graphs

PG-131. The Quadratic Formula can be used in solving $4x^3 + 23x^2 - 2x = 0$. Show or explain how.

PG-132. Find the x- and y-intercepts and the locator points, then write each in graphing form.

    a)   $y - 7 = 2x^2 + 4x - 5$              b)   $x^2 = 2x + x(2x - 4) + y$

PG-133. The two rectangles shown at right are similar. Find the width of each.

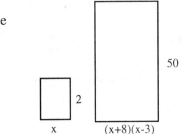

PG-134. Consider this system of equations:    $3y - 4x = -1$
                                                 $9y + 2x = 4$

    a)    What is the parent of each equation?

    b)    Solve this system.

    c)    Find where the two lines intersect.

    d)    Explain the relationship between parts (b) and (c) above.

PG-135. Solve each equation for $x$ (that is, put in "x =" form).

    a)   $y = 2(x - 17)^2$             b)   $y + 7 = \sqrt[3]{x + 5}$

PG-136. Multiply each of the following expressions:

    a)   $2x^3(3x + 4x^2y)$           b)   $(x^3y^2)^4(x^2y)$

    c)    There are several subproblems to do before "multiplying." Factor, factor, factor.

$$\frac{x^2 - 9}{2x} \cdot \frac{x^2 + x}{x^2 - 2x - 3}$$

PG-137. A line passes through the points $(0, 2)$ and $(1, 0)$. Find:

    a)    The slope of the line.          b)    The slope of a line parallel to the given line.

    c)    The slope of a line perpendicular to   d)    What is the product of the slopes of the given line.                              two perpendicular lines?

# ANOTHER NON-FUNCTION: THE CIRCLE

PG-138. Use what you learned in the sleeping parabola investigation ($x = y^2$) to graph the equation $x^2 + y^2 = 9$ on your graphing calculator. What equation(s) did you use?

PG-139. Is the point $(0, -3)$ on your graph of $x^2 + y^2 = 9$? Explain why it should be. If it isn't, then your graph is incomplete. If that is the case, go back to the previous problem, figure out how the complete graph should look, and how to make it look that way on the calculator.

PG-140. Investigate $x^2 + y^2 = 9$. Along with all the usual elements of an investigation, discuss also whether this equation is or is not a function.

PG-141. What would be the equation of a circle with radius 10? With radius 12? With radius $r$?

PG-142. You know how to shift the graphs of equations which are in "x=" form or in "y=" form. Now it's time to shift the graph $x^2 + y^2 = 9$, which is in neither form.

a) Without actually graphing, describe the graph of $y = \pm\sqrt{9 - (x - 4)^2} - 2$. What is the center of the circle, and what is the radius? Now check your answer on the graphing calculator.

b) Transform the equations in part (a) into one equation in the form

$$(\text{something})^2 + (\text{something})^2 = 9.$$

This is an example of the **graphing form of the equation of a circle**.

c) How would you change the equation $x^2 + y^2 = 9$ so that the center is at $(-3, 0)$? $(0, 5)$? $(h, k)$? Give your answers in graphing form. How would you change these equations to make the radius $= 5$?

PG-143.

> Rewrite the last equation from problem PG-142, part (c), so that the radius could be any length. You now have a **general equation** for a **circle** in **graphing form,** from which you can read its radius and locator point (i.e. its center). Add a circle and all of the associated information to your Parent Graph Tool Kit.

PG-144. Factor each of the following. Look for the difference of squares and common factors.

a) $4x^2 - 9y^2$

b) $8x^3 - 2x^7$

c) $x^4 - 81y^4$

d) $8x^3 + 2x^7$

PG-145. For each of the following equations, explain what $d$ does to the shape, size, and/or location of the equations' graphs:

a) $y = d \mid x \mid$

b) $y = 3x^2 - d$

c) $y = (x - d)^2 + 7$

d) $y = \frac{1}{x} + d$

PG-146. A parabola has vertex $(2,3)$ and contains $(0,0)$.

a) If this parabola is a function find its equation.

b) Suppose this parabola is not a function. It is a "sleeping" parabola. Find its equation.

PG-147. Solve for x: $ax + by^3 = c + 7$

PG-148. Jasper and Jennifer were doing their homework when they came across a problem they had never seen before. It asked them to sketch the graph of:

$$x^2 + y^2 - 4x + 6y - 3 = 0$$

"How are we supposed to graph this?" asked Jennifer. "It's a mess. It's got both $x^2$ and $y^2$ and x's and y's and everything!"

"Well, we know it's not a line," said Jasper.

"Thanks a lot," replied Jennifer. "It can't be a parabola either, because there's more than one thing squared."

At that moment they both looked up and said, "Hey! It's got to be a circle."

Then Jasper said, "Look, there's both an $x^2$ and a $y^2$ and ..."

"But, what about the other stuff?" Jennifer interrupted.

"What if we write it like this?" asked Jasper.

$$x^2 - 4x + \underline{\phantom{xx}} + y^2 + 6y + \underline{\phantom{xx}} = 3$$

**>>Problem continues on the next page.>>**

"The $x^2 - 4x$ part looks like what we had when we completed the square," said Jennifer.

"Exactly!" said Jasper.

"So, can we complete the square twice in one problem?" asked Jennifer.

"Why not?" Jasper replied.

a) Help them to rewrite the equation. Complete the square twice, once for $x^2 - 4x$ and once for $y^2 + 6y$.

b) The radius should turn out to be 4. If your radius turned out to be something different, multiply out your complete square versions of $x^2 - 4x$ and $y^2 + 6y$ to make sure that they are correct.

c) Sketch a graph of your result.

PG-149. This is a Milepost for use of function notation and describing domains and ranges.

Given $g(x) = 2(x + 3)^2$. State the domain and range.

a) Find g(-5).

b) Find g(a + 1).

c) If $g(x) = 32$, figure out what number x can be.

d) If $g(x) = 0$, figure out what number x can be.

PG-150. The slope of line AB is 5, with points A(-3, -1) and B(2, n). Find the value of n and the distance between points A and B.

**PG-151.** **THE GATEWAY ARCH** Remember why we wanted to move parabolas around in the first place? We wanted the specific equation of a parabola that would model the Gateway Arch. This is your opportunity to show off all you have learned so far. The complete problem is printed below. Write out your work in good detail, explaining your ideas where necessary.

Would you ever go bungee jumping? Beginners jump off bridges over water, or off cranes over a big air cushion. But true daredevils (some call them crazy) dream of jumping off the Gateway Arch in St. Louis, Missouri, which has no soft landing area in case the bungee cord breaks. No one has ever done this, and we are not recommending it, but it makes a challenging problem for us to consider. The most daring jumper might jump off the very top of the Arch, but this is 185 meters high. Jumpers who are more sensible might prefer to start at a lower point on the Arch. Find a rule that will tell us about how high the Arch is at any point, so they'll know how long a bungee cord to use.

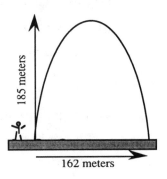

PG-152. Write an explanation relating a graph to its parent graph so that someone new to this class would understand how to tell whether the stretch factor of its equation was:

a)   positive or negative.

b)   less than 1 or greater than 1.

PG-153. Each of the general equations in your Parent Graph Tool Kit has a **locator point**. For each parent:

a)   describe the locator point.

b)   Write an equation for each parent with locator point (3, -4) and sketch each graph.

PG-154. Look back over your work on the labs and investigations that you did in this unit. Write several paragraphs summarizing what you've learned. What new mathematics did you learn? What were the key ideas? What conclusions, conjectures and generalizations can you make? What unanswered questions do you still have?

PG-155. **TOOL KIT CHECK-UP**

Your Tool Kit contains reference tools for algebra. Return to your Tool Kit entries. You may need to revise or add entries.

Be sure that your Tool Kit contains entries for all of the items listed below. Add any topics that are missing to your Tool Kit NOW, as well as any other items that will help you in your study of algebra.

REGULAR TOOL KIT

- Graphing Form and Standard Form
- Function
- Locator Point

Your PARENT GRAPH TOOL KIT should include complete entries for:

- Parabola
- Exponential
- Absolute Value
- Circle
- Cubic
- Hyperbola
- Sleeping Parabola

In addition, add the following information to your Tool Kit:

**>>Problem continues on the next page.>>**

## GENERAL EQUATIONS

If $y = f(x)$ is any parent equation, then the general equation for that function is given by

$$y = af(x - h) + k$$

where $(h, k)$ is the point corresponding to $(0, 0)$ in the parent graph and, relative to the parent graph, the function has been:

- vertically stretched if the absolute value of $a$ is greater than 1.
- vertically compressed if the absolute value of $a$ is less than 1.
- reflected across the x-axis if $a$ is less than 0.

For the equation of a circle of radius $r$ with parent equation $x^2 + y^2 = r^2$, the general equation is given by

$$(x - h)^2 + (y - k)^2 = r^2$$

where $(h, k)$ is the center of the circle. In general, the center of the graph is shifted to the point $(h, k)$ by replacing x by $(x - h)$ and y by $(y - k)$.

PG-156. People who live in isolated or rural areas often have their own tanks for gas to run appliances like stoves, washers, and water heaters. Some of these tanks are made in the shape of a cylinder with two hemispheres on the ends. (A hemisphere is half a sphere, or half a ball, and the volume of a sphere is found by using $V = \frac{4}{3}\pi r^3$.)

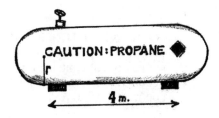

The Inland Propane Gas Tank Company wants to make tanks with this shape, but make different models of different sizes. The cylinder part on all tanks will be 4 meters long. However, the radius $r$ will vary among different models.

a) One of their tanks has a radius of 1m. What is its volume?

b) When the radius doubles (to 2m), will the volume double? Explain. Then figure out the volume of the larger tank with $r = 2m$.

c) Write an equation that will let Inland Propane Gas Tank Company determine the volume of a tank with any size radius.

PG-157. For each of the following, write an equation and sketch a graph for the circle with:

a) locator point $(0, 0)$, radius 5.      b) locator point $(2, 3)$, radius 5.

c) locator point $(-1, -4)$, radius 5.

PG-158. Sketch a graph of $g(x) = x^2 - 6x$.

    a)    Is it a function? How do you know?

    b)    What are the coordinates of its vertex?

    c)    What are its domain and range?

    d)    What else do you know about this equation and its graph?

PG-159. Given: $f(x) = x^3 + 1$ and $g(x) = (x + 1)^2$,

    a)    sketch the graphs of the two functions.

    b)    find $f(3)$.             c)    solve $f(x) = 9$.

    d)    find $g(0)$.            e)    solve $g(x) = 0$.

    f)    solve $f(x) = -12$.      g)    solve $g(x) = -12$.

PG-160. Find the intercepts (both x- and y-) and inflection points or vertex of each function in the previous problem. Then find the equations of any lines of symmetry.

PG-161. Write an equation for this graph, assuming that it has y-intercept $(0, 1)$.

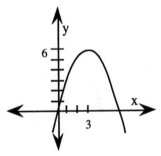

PG-162. Sketch a graph of:

    a)    $g(x) = (x + 3)^3$

    b)    $y - 1 = 3^x$

    c)    $(x + 2)^2 + (y - 1)^2 = 25$

PG-163. If $p(x) = x^2 + 5x - 6$, find:

    a)    where $p(x)$ intersects the y-axis      b)    where $p(x)$ intersects the x-axis

    c)    Now suppose $q(x) = x^2 + 5x$. Find the intercepts of $q(x)$ and compare the graphs of $p(x)$ and $q(x)$.

PG-164.  **Portfolio Growth Over Time—Problem #1**

On a separate sheet of paper (you will be handing this problem in separately or putting it into your portfolio) explain everything that you know about:

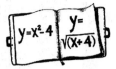

$$y = x^2 - 4 \ \text{and} \ y = \sqrt{(x + 4)}.$$

This is the second time you have done this problem. Be sure to include everything you included the first time plus what you have learned since then.

# UNIT 5

## The Toy Factory
### LINEAR SYSTEMS AND MATRICES

# Unit 5 Objectives
## The Toy Factory: LINEAR SYSTEMS AND MATRICES

The key to this unit is your understanding that the graph of a
function represents all those points whose coordinates satisfy
its equation. You will graph inequalities and solve larger
systems of equations, first using methods you already know
and then using a new method, matrices.

In this unit you will have the opportunity to:

- extend your knowledge of solving systems of
  equations to problems involving three variables
  and three equations.

- see how graphs of systems of inequalities form
  the basis for a method to solve more complicated
  application problems.

- learn about matrices and how they can be used to solve systems of equations.

- develop renewed appreciation for the value of teamwork in solving problems.

This unit includes several problems that will require pulling together your knowledge about solving
and graphing in order to address the kind of questions posed by business professionals and
biologists. The actual questions are designed to be solvable without the use of elaborate technology
so they are necessarily over-simplified both in the size of the numbers and in complication, but the
tools and the thinking you use to solve them will be representative of the tools and thinking needed in
a real situation.

Read the following problem, but do not try to solve it now.

---

LS-0.   **THE TOY FACTORY**

Otto Toyom builds toy cars and toy trucks. Each car needs 4 wheels, 2 seats, and
1 gas tank. Each truck needs 6 wheels, 1 seat, and 3 gas tanks. His storeroom
has 36 wheels, 14 seats, and 15 gas tanks. He needs to decide how many cars and
trucks to build so he can maximize the amount of money he makes when he sells
them. He makes $1.00 on each car and $1.00 on each truck he sells. (This is a
very, very small business, but the ideas are similar for much larger enterprises.)

---

PROBLEM SOLVING
REPRESENTATION/MODELING
FUNCTIONS/GRAPHING
INTERSECTIONS/SYSTEMS
ALGORITHMS
REASONING/COMMUNICATION

# Unit 5
## *The Toy Factory*: LINEAR SYSTEMS AND MATRICES

## COMPARING LINEAR PAYMENT PLANS

LS-1.  Since she had been doing so well in her Algebra 2 class, Lorrel's parents agreed to let her have her own phone line on the condition that she pays for the service. Lorrel's boyfriend just moved to Chicago, and she needs to choose a long distance plan. The phone company offers two plans: Normal Rate, which will cost $6 for each hour of use, or High Use Rate which has a monthly fee of $6 plus $5 for each hour of use.

   a)  Write two equations, one for each plan, that will represent Lorrel's long distance cost based on the number of hours she calls her boyfriend.

   b)  Graph each of the equations you wrote in part (a) on the same set of axes. Under what conditions is it better for Lorrel to use the Normal Rate? When is it better to use the High Use Rate?

   c)  When could either of the company's plans be used for the same price? What is the significance of this value? How does it relate to the graph?

LS-2.  Sue and John are going to the junior prom. They agree that Sue will pay $75 for the bid and dinner. John will pay for the limousine rental. ComfortCar rents limos for $50 plus $3 per hour. SmoothRide rents them for $25 plus $10 per hour. Write an equation to represent each company's cost using hours as the independent variable. Graph both equations on the same set of axes. Be sure to label the axes.

   a)  For what number of hours can John rent from either company for about the same cost? (Find your answer to the nearest $\frac{1}{2}$ hour.) How much is the cost?

   b)  If John rents a car for 7 hours, which company should he use? How much is the cost?

   c)  John wants to spend the same amount as Sue. Which company should he use to get the most time? How long will they have the car?

**LS-3.** Why is 238 + -487 a negative number? Many people say it's because -487 is bigger than 238; that's not right, but we understand what they mean! They mean that it would be bigger if you ignored the negative. It moves you farther in the negative direction than 238 moves you in the positive direction. We say -487 has greater magnitude than 238; another term for magnitude is absolute value. One thing the absolute value of a number tells us is how far the number is from zero, without regard to direction. Using this idea, describe all the x's which solve the following inequalities. You may use words or inequalities.

a) $|x| \leq 7$                  b) $|x| > 4$

**LS-4.** Does -8 solve the inequality in part (b) above? Is it included in your answer? If not, go back and try again. Think about all the numbers with magnitude greater than 4. Once you've solved the problems above, others like them are easy. Assume that k is some positive number, and using inequalities this time, describe the x's that satisfy:

a) $|x| \leq k$                  b) $|x| > k$

**LS-5.** Once you understand the preceding two problems, you can also solve more complicated problems such as $|2x - 17| > 9$. When you said that, for positive k, $|x| > k$ is the same as $x > k$ or $x < -k,$* the letter x was irrelevant. (*You did say that, didn't you? If you left out the word "or," go back and add it. This is not a system; we want numbers that satisfy *either* inequality.) What you are really saying is that if the absolute value of anything is more than k, then that thing must be above k or below -k. In this new problem, "anything" is the quantity 2x - 17.

a) If the absolute value of 2x - 17 is greater than 9, what numbers could 2x - 17 be equal to? Use inequalities to express your answer.

b) Solve those two inequalities. The result is the solution to the inequality $|2x - 17| > 9$.

**LS-6.** Describe the graphs of:

a) $y = 3$      b) $x = -2$      c) Where do they cross?

**LS-7.** Find the equation of the line through (0, 2) and (5, 2).

a) What would be the equation of the x-axis?

b) What would be the equation of the y-axis?

**LS-8.** Solve this system of equations:      $2x + 6y = 10$
                                        $x = 8 - 3y$

a) Describe what happened.      b) Draw the graph of the system.

c) How does the graph of the system explain what happened with the equations? Be clear.

LS-9. Choose the appropriate symbol (>, <, or =) to complete the comparison to make a true statement.

  i)  -2 _?_ 3          ii)  6 _?_ 4               iii)  -5 _?_ -1

  a)  Multiply both sides of each inequality by 5. Write the result. Are the inequalities still true?

  b)  Multiply both sides of the original inequalities by -1. Are the inequalities still true?

  c)  If we multiply both sides of each inequality from part (a) by -5, are the inequalities true now?

  d)  Write a conjecture about what you observed.


LS-10. In the previous problem you determined that multiplying both sides of an inequality by a negative number makes the inequality false. What can you do to the inequality sign to make the inequality true again?


LS-11. The conjectures you made in the previous problems will help you transform inequalities to y-form accurately.

  a)  Choose a value of $y$ that makes the inequality $-2y < 6$ obviously true.

  b)  Write the inequality in y-form (that is, solve for $y$). Test the value you chose in part (a) on your transformed inequality. Is it still true? What must you do to make it true again?

  c)  Repeat this test on the following inequalities. Choose a value that makes the inequality true, write the inequality in y-form, then test the value again to be sure that you have adjusted the inequality correctly to keep it true.

  i)  $-3y + 1 > 4$          ii)  $2y + 7 > 5$               iii)  $6 - 4y < 0$

  d)  Write a rule about multiplying and dividing inequalities by negative numbers.


LS-12. The same idea used in problem LS-5 applies to $|5x + 8| < 20$. The only difference is that the original inequality of the form $|\text{quantity}| < k$ translates to the continued inequality, or betweenness statement: $-k < \text{quantity} < k$. If you think it is okay to isolate x by performing the same operation on all three elements of the inequality, you're right. Convert $|5x + 8| < 20$ to a betweenness statement, and solve for x.

LS-13.    Solve the following inequalities:

a)    $|x + 4| < 9$

b)    $|\frac{1}{2}x - 45| \geq 80$

c)    $|2x - 5| \leq 2$

d)    Enter the following information in your Tool Kit:

---

### INEQUALITIES WITH ABSOLUTE VALUE

If  k  is any positive number, an inequality of the form:

- $|f(x)| > k$  is equivalent to the statement  $f(x) > k$  or  $f(x) < -k$
- $|f(x)| < k$  is equivalent to the statement  $-k < f(x) < k$

---

## LINEAR INEQUALITIES

LS-14.    When solving an inequality, what causes the inequality symbol to reverse its order?

LS-15.    Add the following information to your Tool Kit.

---

### SOLVING LINEAR INEQUALITIES

Inequalities can be solved or rearranged using the same rules you have used for equations with one exception.  Multiplying or dividing both sides of an inequality by a negative number reverses the relationship.  For example:

Given:  $-8x < 44$

You would want to multiply by  $-\frac{1}{8}$  (or divide by -8).

$\left(-\frac{1}{8}\right)(-8x) > 44\left(-\frac{1}{8}\right)$  Note that  <  becomes  >.

$x > -5.5$

---

**LS-16.** Remember that, when drawing the graph of $y > 3x - 1$, we begin by graphing the line $y = 3x - 1$ with a dashed line. People decided to use a dashed line instead of a solid line for problems like this one. Do you think that was a good idea? Why would it be important to use something different from a regular line?

| Point | Location (above, below, or on) | $y > 3x - 1$ (true or false) |
|---|---|---|
| A(0, 0) | | |
| B(3, 4) | | |
| C(-1, -4) | | |
| D(-2, 3) | | |
| $E(-\frac{2}{3}, -4)$ | | |

a) Graph the line (dashed) and plot the points from the table above on the same set of axes. Label each point.

b) Complete the table. Which of these points makes $y > 3x - 1$ true?

c) Which region of your graph should be shaded to represent all the points for which $y > 3x - 1$ is true? Describe the region and shade it.

**LS-17.** Simone has been absent and does not know the difference between the graph of $y \leq 2x - 2$ and the graph of $y < 2x - 2$. Explain thoroughly so that she completely understands what points are excluded from the second graph.

**LS-18.** Graph the solution to each of the following inequalities on a different set of axes (but you should be able to fit all four on one side of the graph paper). Label each graph with the inequality as given and with its y-form. Choose a test point and show that it gives the same result in both forms of your inequality.

a) $3x - 3 < y$

b) $3 > y$

c) $3x - 2y \leq 6$

d) $x^2 - y \leq 9$

**LS-19.** Ted needs to find the point of intersection for the lines $y = 18x - 30$ and $y = -22x + 50$. He takes out a piece of graph paper and then realizes that he can solve this problem without graphing. Explain how Ted is going to accomplish this and find the intersection point.

LS-20.    Your family plans to buy a new air
          conditioner.  They can buy the
          Super Cool X1400 for $800 or they
          can buy the Efficient Energy X2000
          for $1200.  Both models will cool
          your home equally well, but the
          Efficient Energy model is less
          expensive to operate.  The Super
          Cool X1400 will cost $60 a month
          to operate while the Efficient Energy
          X2000 costs only $40 a month to
          operate.

a)    Write an equation that will represent the cost of buying and operating the
      Super Cool X1400.

b)    Write an equation that will represent the cost of buying and operating the
      Efficient Energy X2000.

c)    How many months would your family have to use the Efficient Energy model to
      compensate for the additional cost of the original purchase?

d)    Figuring your family will only use it 4 months each year, how many years
      will you have to wait to start saving money overall?


LS-21.    Find the x- and y-intercepts.

a)    $2x - 3y = 9$                         b)    $3y = 2x + 12$


LS-22.    Graph each of the following equations.  (Keep them handy; you will need them later.)

a)    $y = |x|$                            b)    $|y| = x$

c)    How are the two graphs similar or different?

d)    What is the domain and range of each?


LS-23     Graph the inequalities below on the same set of axes.  Shade the solution of each one.

          $y \geq -4x - 2$            $3x + 2y < 6$

a)    Test the following points in both inequalities and label them on your graph.  Indicate
      which ones are solutions to both inequalities.

          $A(0, 4)$        $B(0, 0)$        $C(-1, -1)$        $D(4, 3)$

b)    What does the area where the graphs overlap represent?

LS-24.    Rewrite as an equivalent expression using fractional exponents.

a)    $\sqrt[2]{5} =$            b)    $\sqrt[3]{9} =$            c)    $\sqrt[8]{17^x} =$

## SYSTEMS OF LINEAR INEQUALITIES

LS-25.    Take out your solution to problem LS-23 from yesterday's homework. Discuss your
solutions with your team. Answer the following questions.

a)    When do we use a dashed line instead of a solid line?

b)    What determines where the final region is shaded?

LS-26.    Graph the four inequalities below on the same set of axes. Before you begin it would be
a good idea for the team to discuss the most efficient way to graph a line. Be very careful
to compare your answers as you work through the parts.

i)    $2y \geq x - 3$                    ii)    $x - 2y \geq -7$

iii)    $y \leq -2x + 6$               iv)    $-9 \leq 2x + y$

a)    What type of polygon is formed by the solution of this set of inequalities? Write a
convincing argument to justify your answer.

b)    Find the vertices of the polygon. If your graph is very accurately drawn you will be
able to determine the points from the graph. If it is not, you will need to solve the
systems (pairs) of equations that represent the corners of your graphs.

LS-27.    Find the area of the polygon that you graphed in the last problem.

LS-28.    Consider the graph of the equation $y = \sqrt{x}$.

a)    Change the equation so its graph is vertically stretched and moved 6 units to the
right.

b)    Change the original equation so its graph is vertically compressed and moved 9
units down.

c)    Write a general equation for the family of functions that have $y = \sqrt{x}$ as a
parent.

d)    For the general equation that you found in part (c), choose numbers to make a
representative example and draw its accurate graph. Include all of the important
information.

e)    Add "Square Root" equations to your Parent Graph Tool Kit.

The Toy Factory: Linear Systems and Matrices                                                     161

LS-29. Write the three inequalities that will form the triangle shown at right.

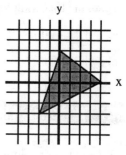

LS-30. Use these three equations to solve for x, y, and z.

$$3x + 8 = 2$$
$$7x + 3y = 1$$
$$\frac{1}{2}x + y - 8z = 8$$

LS-31. Macario's salary is increasing by 5% each year. His rent is increasing by 8% each year. Currently, 20% of Macario's salary goes to pay his rent. Assuming that Macario does not move or change jobs, what percent of his income will go to pay rent in 10 years? Think about this problem and if you see a way to solve it, do it. If not, complete the four parts below.

a)  If x represents Macario's current salary write an expression to represent his salary ten years from now.

b)  Use x in an expression to represent Macario's rent now.

c)  Use what you wrote in part (b) to write an expression for the rent ten years from now.

d)  Now use the expressions that you wrote in parts (a) and (c) to write a ratio that will help you answer the question.

LS-32. Each cube is 1 cm on a side.

a)  Based on the pattern, find the volume of figure (III).

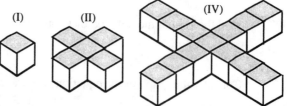

b)  The pattern continues. Write an expression to represent the volume of figure N. What kind of sequence is this?

LS-33. Rewrite each expression as an equivalent expression without negative exponents.

a)  $5^{-2}$

b)  $xy^{-2}$

c)  $(xy)^{-2}$

d)  $a^3b^4a^{-4}b^6$

**LS-34.** Solve the following inequalities and draw a number line graph to represent each solution.

a) $|2x + 3| < 5$

b) $|2x + 3| \geq 5$

c) $|2x - 3| < 5$

d) $|2x - 3| \geq 5$

e) $|3 - 2x| < 5$

f) $|3 - 2x| \geq 5$

g) Describe any relationships you see among these six problems.

**LS-35.** Refer back to the graphs you did for problem LS-22. Use those graphs to help you to graph each of the following inequalities.

a) $y \leq |x|$

b) $|y| \geq x$

LS-36. **The Toy Factory**

Otto Toyom builds toy cars and toy trucks. Each car needs 4 wheels, 2 seats, and 1 gas tank. Each truck needs 6 wheels, 1 seat, and 3 gas tanks. His storeroom has 36 wheels, 14 seats, and 15 gas tanks. He needs to decide how many cars and trucks to build so he can maximize the amount of money he makes when he sells them. He makes $1.00 on each car and $1.00 on each truck he sells. (This is a very, very small business, but the ideas are similar for much larger enterprises.) We will divide this problem into subproblems.

a) Otto's first task is to figure out what his options are. For example, he could decide to make no cars and no trucks and just keep his supplies. On the other hand, because he likes to make trucks better, he may be thinking about making five trucks and one car. Would this be possible? Why or why not? What are all the possible numbers of cars and trucks he <u>can</u> build, given his limited supplies? This will be quite a long list. An easy way to keep your list organized and find some patterns is to plot the points that represent the pairs of numbers in your list directly on graph paper. Use the x-axis for cars and the y-axis for trucks. Make a fairly large, neat first quadrant graph. (Why the first quadrant?) We will need to use this graph later in this problem and in the next one.

b) In part (a) you figured out all the possible combinations of numbers of cars and trucks Otto could make. Which of these give him the greatest profit? Explain how you know your answer is right. You have to convince Otto, who likes trucks better.

c) New scenario: Truck drivers have just become popular because of a new TV series called "Big Red Ed." Toy trucks are a hot item. Otto can now make $2.00 per truck though he still gets $1.00 per car. He has hired you as a consultant to advise him, and your salary is a percentage of the total profits. What is his best choice for the number of cars and the number of trucks to make now? How can you be sure? Explain.

LS-37.    In the last problem you probably had to carry out a lot of calculations in order to convince Otto that your recommendation was correct. In this problem we will take another look at Otto's business using some algebra and graphing tools we already know.

a)    The first task is to write three inequalities to represent the relationship between the number of cars, x, the number of trucks, y and the number of:

   i)    wheels.                ii)    seats.                iii)    gas tanks.

b)    Carefully graph this system of inequalities (assume $x \geq 0$ and $y \geq 0$. Why?) on the same set of axes you used for the last problem. Shade the region of intersection lightly.

c)    What are the vertices of the pentagon that outlines your region? Explain and show exactly how and why you could use the five equations below to find those five points. In many problems these points are difficult to determine from the graph alone.

$$x = 0 \qquad\qquad 2x + y = 14$$
$$y = 0 \qquad\qquad x + 3y = 15$$
$$4x + 6y = 36$$

d)    Part (c) shows how we could get an outline of the region of points that represents possible numbers of cars and trucks. Are there some points in the region that seem more likely to give the maximum profit? Where are they? Why do you think they are the best coordinates? How can you represent the total profit if Otto makes $1.00 on each car and $2.00 on each truck?

e)    What if Otto ended up with a profit of $8? Write an equation for the profit when it is $8.00. Use the graph of just one of your teammates and draw the graph of this equation on it. Do you think from looking at this graph that $8 is the maximum Otto could make? Why or why not? Try some other possibilities ($9, $10, $11, $12). Write an equation and draw a graph for each (continue to use just one person's paper.) Find the maximum and justify your answer for Otto.

f)    What did all the lines you drew in parts (d) and (e) have in common? What was different? What were you trying to do? Ask your teacher for a transparency, place it on top of some graph paper and draw just a y-axis and one line with the same slope as your profit lines. Now put the transparency on top of one of your team's graphs and align the y-axis. How could you physically slide the transparency over the graph to find the maximum profit? Try it on another teammate's graph and explain why this method should work.

LS-38.    Use the method you developed in the last problem to find Otto's maximum possible profit if he gets $3.00 per car and $2.00 per truck.

LS-39.    At Wet World there is an 18-ft long water slide. The angle of elevation of the slide is 50°. At the end of the slide is a 6-ft drop into a pool. After you climb the ladder to the top of the slide, how many feet above the water level are you? Make a diagram.

LS-40. Graph the inequalities and calculate the area bounded by them.

$$y \le 2x + 6 \qquad y \le -x + 3 \qquad y \ge -2$$

LS-41. Visualize the figure for $n = 4$.

a) How many cubes are in the figure for $n = 4$?

b) How many cubes are in the figure for $n = 1$?

c) Find the general equation for the number of cubes for any given n. Verify your formula with the cases of $n = 1$ and $n = 5$.

d) Is the sequence arithmetic or geometric? Explain why or why not.

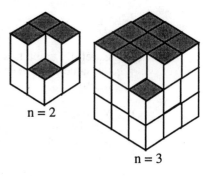

n = 2

n = 3

LS-42. Solve the system of equations at right:

$$2^{(x+y)} = 16$$
$$2^{(2x+y)} = \frac{1}{8}$$

LS-43. Lexington High School has an annual growth rate of 4.7%. Three years ago there were 1500 students at the school.

a) How many students are there now?

b) How many students were there 5 years ago?

c) How many in students will be there in n years?

LS-44. Paul states that $(a + b)^2$ is equivalent to $a^2 + b^2$. Joyce thinks that something is missing. Help Joyce show Paul that the two expressions are not equivalent. Explain using at least two different approaches: diagrams, algebra, numbers, or words.

LS-45. Factor each of the following expressions:

a) $bx + ax$ 

b) $x + ax$

Factor and reduce each of these expressions:

c) $\dfrac{ax + a}{x^2 + 2x + 1}$ 

d) $\dfrac{x^2 - b^2}{ax + ab}$

LS-46. **Sandy Dandy Dune Buggies**
The Sandy Dandy Dune Buggy Company makes two models of off-road vehicles: the *Sand Crab* and the *Surf Mobile*. They can get the basic parts to produce as many as 15 Sand Crabs and 12 Surf Mobiles per week, but two

parts have to be special ordered: a unique exhaust manifold clamp and a specially designed suspension joint. Each Sand Crab requires 5 manifold clamps and 2 suspension joints. Each Surf Mobile requires 3 manifold clamps and 6 suspension joints. The maximum number of clamps available is 81 per week and the maximum number of joints is 78 per week.

It takes 20 hours to assemble one Sand Crab and 30 hours to assemble one Surf Mobile. The company has 12 employees who each work a maximum of 37.5 hours per week.

Sandy Dandy, Inc. has hired your team as consultants to advise them on how many Sand Crabs and how many Surf Mobiles they should make each week in order to maximize their profit. They know their profit margin on each Sand Crab is $500 and on each Surf Mobile $1000. Prepare a complete report including your graphs and an explanation to justify your conclusions.

Our goal in this problem is not simply to solve the problem, but to see how it might be solved by using a particular method, **Linear Programming**, that relies on you using your algebraic and graphing skills.

You may choose to work on this problem without further suggestions or you can use the set of questions below as a guide.

a) First you need to use the information in the problem to decide how many combinations of numbers of vehicles can be built. You could do this point by point but it probably is more efficient to write five inequalities and graph them. Work in teams of four, but each pair of students should make a large, neat graph with equations written along the lines they represent.

Let x represent the number of Sand Crabs built in one week.
Let y represent the number of Surf Mobiles built in one week.

b) You can assume $x \geq 0$ and $y \geq 0$. Why? What kind of polygon did you get? What would be useful to know about this polygon? Find them.

c) What expression can you write to represent the profit? How can you use this expression and your graph to find the maximum possible profit and the number of Sand Crabs and Surf Mobiles that will produce it? Do it, and complete your report.

LS-47. Solve the following system of equations. What subproblems did you need to solve?

$$x + 2y = 4$$
$$2x - y = -7$$
$$x + y + z = -4$$

LS-48.    Consider the arithmetic sequence 2, a - b, a + b, 35, . . . Find the value of a and b.

LS-49.    Marvelous Mark's Function Machines. Mark has set up a series of three function
          machines that he claims will surprise you:

          a)    Try a few numbers. Were you surprised?

          b)    Carrie claims she was not surprised and
                she can show why the sequence of
                machines does what it does by simply
                dropping in a variable and writing out
                step-by-step what happens inside each
                machine. Try it (use something like c or
                m). Be sure to show all the steps.

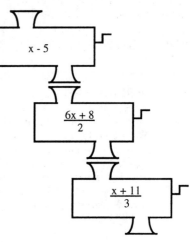

LS-50.    Give the equation of each circle in graphing form:

          a)    center (0, 0) and radius 6          b)    center (2, -3) and radius 6

          c)    $x^2 + y^2 - 8x + 10y + 5 = 0$

LS-51.    A square target 20 cm on a side contains 50 non-overlapping circles each 1 cm in
          diameter. Find the probability that a dart which hits the board at random hits one of the
          circles.

LS-52.    Think about the axis system in the two-dimensional coordinate plane. What is the
          equation of the x-axis? What is the equation of the y-axis?

LS-53.    Write the linear equation for each line defined below.

          a)    The line through points (-1, 4) and (2, 1).

          b)    The line through points (6, 3) and (5, 5).

Matrices are simply tables of numbers, but the rise of modern computing has made them increasingly important in science, economics, computer science, and mathematics. Matrices have their own notation and form, **and their own unique arithmetic** which you'll need to become familiar with before proceeding further. Once you understand the mechanics, the computations are straightforward, and your calculator can even do them for you! Matrices have many applications, and we'll see how they tie together with systems of equations later in the unit.

LS-54. Otto Toyom's toy factory has become extremely successful. His cars and trucks are selling like crazy. He now has three major stores selling his toys: Bull's Eye Discount Outlet, JC Nickles, and Marcey's Department Store. He needs an efficient way to keep track of his profits, the number of cars ordered, and number of parts needed to complete his orders. He begins by writing down a simple matrix to represent the number of wheels, seats, and gas tanks needed to build his cars and trucks.

$$\text{vehicles} \begin{array}{c} \text{parts} \\ \begin{bmatrix} 4 & 2 & 1 \\ 6 & 1 & 3 \end{bmatrix} \end{array}$$

a) Otto is definitely going to need the help of a skilled algebra student. He has asked for your help. Copy the matrix and the words "parts" and "vehicles;" title it the "vehicle x parts matrix." Use the words **cars** and **trucks** to label the matrix rows (rows run across) and use the words **wheels, seats,** and **gas tanks** to label the supply columns (columns run up and down).

b) **This matrix is called a "2 x 3" matrix because it has 2 rows and 3 columns.** If this matrix represents the special parts needed to build one car and one truck, what do you think $\begin{bmatrix} 4 & 2 & 1 \\ 6 & 1 & 3 \end{bmatrix} + \begin{bmatrix} 4 & 2 & 1 \\ 6 & 1 & 3 \end{bmatrix}$ would represent, and what matrix would it equal?

c) Just as we use letters to represent numbers, we can use letters to represent matrices (capital letters). We'll use A to represent our vehicles x parts matrix. How would you represent the matrix of parts needed to build 5 cars and 5 trucks?

d) Write the matrix that would represent this information.

LS-55.    Otto has a question for you. "I don't always want to build equal numbers of cars and trucks. Bull's Eye just gave me this week's order. They want 20 cars and 25 trucks. How many special parts will I need to complete that order?"

a)    Make a 1 x 2 , store x vehicles, matrix to represent the number of cars and trucks Otto wants to build. Label this matrix B. Make sure you label the row "BE" for Bull's Eye and again use cars and trucks to label the columns.

b)    Write matrix A to the right of matrix B. Now use the information in the two matrices to calculate the total number of wheels Otto needs to build the cars and trucks requested by Bull's Eye.

c)    Now use the information in the two matrices to calculate the total number of seats and the total number of gas tanks Otto needs to complete the order.

d)    Record the numbers of wheels, seats, and gas tanks Otto needs to complete the order in a 1 x 3 matrix, a store x parts matrix. Call this matrix C and label the row and columns appropriately.

e)    Add a summary of the procedure outlined below to your Tool Kit.

---

### MATRIX MULTIPLICATION, PART 1

Congratulations!! You have just performed a new operation, Matrix Multiplication. To find the total supplies needed, you multiplied matrices B and A together to get matrix C. Algebraically it is written $BA = C$.

In order to find the total number of wheels needed, you had to use the row of matrix B that contained the number of cars and trucks requested by Bull's Eye, and the column of matrix A that contained the number of wheels needed per car and per truck. For this to work, the row of matrix B had to match (i.e. have the same number of entries as) the column of matrix A.

$$\text{BE} \begin{array}{c} c \quad t \\ [20 \quad 25] \end{array} \qquad \begin{array}{c} \quad\quad w \ \ s \ \ g \\ c \\ t \end{array} \begin{bmatrix} 4 & \_ & \_ \\ 6 & \_ & \_ \end{bmatrix}$$

$$\downarrow \ \ \downarrow \ \ \downarrow$$

$$= \qquad \begin{array}{c} w \ \ \ s \ \ \ g \\ \text{BE} \ [230 \ \_ \ \_] \end{array}$$

The product matrix gives you the number of wheels needed to complete the Bull's Eye order.

---

f)    Describe **CAREFULLY** what you had to do to find each of the entries in matrix C. Pay close attention to the labels on the numbers you multiply, "Number of cars times number of wheels on a car," etc.

LS-56.    Suppose a store requests x cars and y trucks. Then the matrix multiplication looks like the equation below. Fill in the entries of the product matrix C in terms of x and y.

$$[x \ \ y] \begin{bmatrix} 4 & 2 & 1 \\ 6 & 1 & 3 \end{bmatrix}$$

$$[\_ \ \_ \ \_]$$

This process of multiplying-then-adding that you used to get each entry in the product matrix is the fundamental operation of matrix multiplication. We'll refer to it as **multiplying a row into a column**.

LS-57.    You have just astounded Otto with your use of matrices. He is at your doorstep again
          with more questions. JC Nickels Department store has called to place an order this week.
          They would like 15 cars and 30 trucks by the end of the week. Otto would like you to
          show him how to represent this information with matrices.

          a)    Add a row to matrix B to include the quantities requested by JC Nickles. Be sure to
                label rows and columns appropriately.

          b)    Calculate the number of each special part (wheels, seats, gas tanks) that Otto needs
                to build the toys for JC Nickels and expand matrix C to include this information.
                Rewrite the new C matrix with all the appropriate labels.

          c)    With the expanded versions of B and C, we can still say that $BA = C$. Rewrite this
                equation using the complete matrices. This example, in which each matrix has more
                than one row, shows the more general case of matrix multiplication. Describe how
                each entry in matrix C is calculated from B and A; you may refer to the operation
                "multiplying a row into a column" in your explanation.


LS-58.    Using your new matrix, C, what does the entry in the 2nd row-3rd column mean?
          Note: a shorthand notation for this is $c_{2,3}$.


LS-59.    Now that you have used matrices a bit, let's consider some notation and terminology.
          At the end of this problem, record the new definitions in your Tool Kit along with
          some examples.

---

### MATRICES

A **MATRIX** is a rectangular array of numbers or algebraic expressions enclosed in
square brackets. (Some math texts use parentheses instead.) Usually, a matrix is
denoted by a capital letter. The plural of matrix is **matrices**. Each matrix has **ROWS**
and **COLUMNS**. In mathematics we are very precise: **rows are horizontal, and
columns are vertical**. If matrix M has 2 rows and 3 columns, we say the
**dimensions** of M are $2 \times 3$, or M is a 2 by 3 matrix. $m_{2,1}$ is the **ENTRY** in the
second row and first column of matrix M; in general, $m_{r,c}$ is the entry in the $r$th row
and $c$th column.

---

          a)    Shown at right are some examples of
                matrices. Specify the dimensions of
                each matrix.

$$M = \begin{bmatrix} -6 & 12 & 0.4 \\ 3.9 & 0 & -2x \end{bmatrix} \quad N = \begin{bmatrix} 8 & x & 3y \end{bmatrix}$$

$$P = \begin{bmatrix} 5 & -9 \\ \frac{3}{7} & 12 \end{bmatrix} \quad Q = \begin{bmatrix} 1 \\ 0 \end{bmatrix} \quad R = \begin{bmatrix} 2 \end{bmatrix}$$

$$S = \begin{bmatrix} 5 & 9 \\ 1 \end{bmatrix} \quad T = \begin{bmatrix} 6 & 1 \\ & 3 & -2 \end{bmatrix}$$

          b)    The objects shown at right are <u>not</u>
                matrices. Explain why not for each
                one.

$$U = \begin{matrix} y \\ 1 \\ 0 \end{matrix} \quad V = \begin{bmatrix} \text{Fred} & \text{Barney} \\ \text{Wilma} & \text{Betty} \end{bmatrix}$$

LS-60.    Let F be the matrix shown at right.

a)    What is $f_{1,3}$ ?

$$\begin{bmatrix} 16 & 3 & -4 & 21 \\ 19 & 31 & 12 & 17 \\ 25 & -6 & 8 & 11 \end{bmatrix}$$

b)    Two matrices can be added only if they have the same dimensions.  Matrix G can be added to matrix F. What must be the dimensions of **G**?

c)    All the entries of the zero matrix are 0.  Write the zero matrix with the same dimensions as F.

d)    Write the matrix you would add to matrix F to get the zero matrix.  What would be the logical name for your new matrix?

LS-61.    Shola's Bakery uses sugar, eggs, and butter in all of its cakes, as well as in the frosting. Matrix C shows how many eggs, cups of sugar, and ounces of butter are used in each Angel Food cake and in each Devil's Food cake.  Matrix F shows how many eggs, cups of sugar, and ounces of butter are used in the frosting for each cake.

$$C= \begin{matrix} & \begin{matrix} e & s & b \end{matrix} \\ \begin{matrix} af \\ df \end{matrix} & \begin{bmatrix} 6 & 1 & 5 \\ 3 & 1.5 & 4 \end{bmatrix} \end{matrix} \quad F= \begin{matrix} & \begin{matrix} e & s & b \end{matrix} \\ \begin{matrix} af \\ df \end{matrix} & \begin{bmatrix} 2 & 1 & 2 \\ 1 & 2 & 4 \end{bmatrix} \end{matrix}$$

a)    Write the matrix C + F, being sure to label the rows and columns, and explain what it represents.

b)    Write the matrix 3C, with labels, and explain what it represents.

c)    Leora orders three Angel Food and two Devil's Food cakes, without frosting, from Shola's Bakery, as represented in matrix $L = \begin{matrix} \begin{matrix} af & df \end{matrix} \\ \begin{bmatrix} 3 & 2 \end{bmatrix} \end{matrix}$. Use matrix multiplication to write a matrix that shows how much sugar, eggs, and butter Shola will need to fill Leora's order.

LS-62.    Solve the system at right algebraically and explain what the solution tells you about the graphs of the two equations.

$$4x - 6y = 12$$
$$-2x + 3y = 7$$

LS-63.    Draw the graph of the system of inequalities at right.

$$y \geq | x | - 3$$
$$y \leq - | x | + 5$$

a)    What polygon does the intersection form?  Justify your answers.

b)    What are its vertices?          c)    Find the area of the intersection.

LS-64.    Solve each equation for  y  so that it could be entered in a graphing calculator.

a)    $5 - (y - 3) = 3x$                     b)    $4(x + y) = -2$


LS-65.    Janelle inadvertently conducted an experiment by leaving her bologna sandwich at school
over the winter break.  Much to her surprise, her sandwich (or what used to be a
sandwich) was much larger than it was when she left it.

After inspecting it, her science teacher said the sandwich had produced great quantities of
a seldom seen bacteria, bolognicus sandwichae.  Based on a sample taken from the
sandwich, they determined that there were approximately 72 million bacteria present.
Janelle was greatly surprised by this number. Her science teacher informed her that this is
not too surprising since the number of bacteria triples every 24 hours.  Janelle thought
that the sandwich must have been loaded with bacteria initially since it had been made
only 15 days ago.

Janelle is making plans to sue the meat company because she learned that the food
industry standard for the most bacteria a sandwich could have at the time it was made was
100.  Find out how many of the bacteria were present when the sandwich was made to
determine if Janelle has a case.


# MULTIPLYING MATRICES

LS-66.    Your work yesterday in helping Otto with his toy orders has motivated him to offer you a
full time position with his company.  He would like you to expand yesterday's
store x vehicle matrix, B,  to include his third retailer, Marcey's Department Store. For
this week, they have requested 12 cars and 24 trucks.   Make sure you label every row
and column appropriately, and pay close attention to the row and column labels as you
multiply.

a)    Use the new matrix B and matrix A and find their product C, to represent the
number of wheels, seats, and gas tanks per store.

b)    What does the entry in the 2nd row-2nd column represent?

c)    In matrix B, the rows represent stores and the columns represent vehicles. As a
result, we can refer to matrix B as a stores x vehicles matrix.  Matrix A can be
referred to as a  vehicles x parts matrix.  What row x column words describe matrix
C?  Describe the relationships of the labeling of the rows and columns in B and A to
the labeling in the result C.

LS-67.    Because each store sells its toys for a different amount, Otto has instructed you to keep all the ordering information sorted by stores. He would like you to figure out his cost to fill each store's order. Each car costs Otto $2.75 to make, and a truck costs him $3.10. Make 2 new matrices to represent these costs, one a 1 x 2 matrix and the other a 2 x 1 matrix.

a)    Using the descriptive word labels for row x column, what does the 1 x 2 matrix represent?

b)    What does the 2 x 1 matrix represent?

c)    You need to multiply one of these matrices, call it matrix D, with matrix B to find Otto's cost to supply each store. It is not always possible to multiply two matrices together. Which matrix would you use and in what order would you have to write the multiplication problem to make matrix multiplication possible? Use the relationship you found in LS-66 part (c).

d)    Find this product and label the matrix appropriately. Call this matrix E.

e)    What does the entry in the 3rd row-1st column of matrix E represent?

LS-68.    Otto wants to figure out his profit on this week's order. Because he has expanded his business he now charges an 86% markup beyond his costs on the vehicles he sells to Bull's Eye, 74% on the vehicles he sells to JC Nickles, and a whopping 93% on the items he sells to Marcey's.

a)    Make a matrix to represent Otto's profit percentages by store. Label it appropriately.

b)    Multiply this profit x stores matrix with matrix E. What does this matrix represent?

The kind of computations you did in the last few problems occur so often that it is useful to formally describe the process. In fact, we can multiply matrices of any size as long as they "fit" right. You get the entries of the product matrix by finding "sums of products" of rows of the first matrix with columns of the second. Here is a more formal description:

>>Problem  continues  on  the  next  page.>>

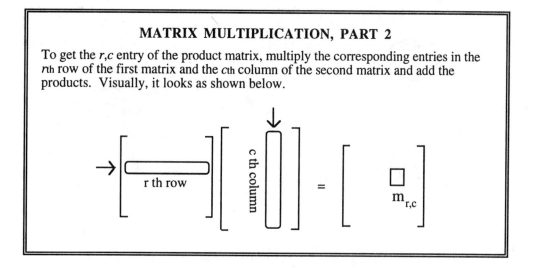

## MATRIX MULTIPLICATION, PART 2

To get the *r,c* entry of the product matrix, multiply the corresponding entries in the *r*th row of the first matrix and the *c*th column of the second matrix and add the products. Visually, it looks as shown below.

**LS-69.** Let $A = \begin{bmatrix} 1 & 2 \\ 3 & 4 \end{bmatrix}$ and $B = \begin{bmatrix} 5 & 6 \\ 7 & 8 \end{bmatrix}$.

a) Let C be the product of matrix A with matrix B (in symbols, C = AB). Find C. (Even though no units are specified for the matrix entries, a product of matrices always refers to the matrix multiplication method described in the previous problem.)

b) Now find BA. Be careful. This time use the rows of B with the columns of A.

c) Since ab = ba for any numbers a and b, we say multiplication of numbers is *commutative*. (This word is related to "commuting," as in going back and forth to work.) Is multiplication of matrices commutative? How do you know?

**LS-70.** Copy and complete: In order for matrix multiplication to work, the number of entries in each row of the first matrix must be the same as the number of entries in ___ _____ of the _____ matrix.

**LS-71.** Abe, Barbara and Cassie work at "Budding Success" Flower Shop. Each day, they plan to make bouquets in three styles in the quantities indicated in matrix W, a "workers"x"bouquets" matrix, shown at right.

$$\text{Workers} \begin{array}{c} A \\ B \\ C \end{array} \begin{bmatrix} 6 & 4 & 7 \\ 4 & 8 & 5 \\ 5 & 6 & 6 \end{bmatrix}$$

Bouquet Styles
#1 #2 #3

a) How many #2 bouquets will Cassie make each day?

b) Who makes the most bouquets?

c) If all the workers make their quota each day for a full work week (Monday through Friday), write a matrix which shows how many bouquet styles each worker made.

d) Represent your answer to part (c) in terms of W.

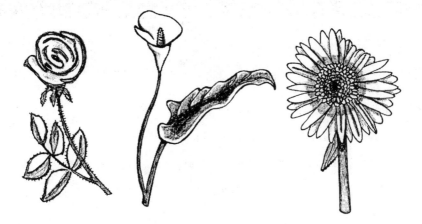

LS-72. Each #1 bouquet has 5 lilies, 4 roses and 3 daisies. Each #2 bouquet has 4 lilies, 3 roses and 3 daisies. Each #3 bouquet has 4 lilies, 6 roses and 6 daisies.

a) Arrange this information in a new matrix whose rows are bouquet styles. What will be the columns of this new matrix? Label the rows and columns of the matrix and call this matrix B.

b) Using the row x column labels, what will matrix B represent?

LS-73. Which matrix product makes sense, BW, or WB? Find this matrix. What does it represent?

LS-74. Compare and contrast the graphs of $y > x^2$ and $y > (x - 4)^2 + 2$ and shade their overlapping region.

LS-75. Given these two points (-2, 0) and (0, 1):

a) Find the slope of the line.

b) Find the slope of the line perpendicular to the given line.

c) Describe the relationship between the slopes of perpendicular lines.

LS-76. Find the equation for each line in the form of $y = mx + b$.

a) A certain line with slope $\frac{1}{2}$ goes through the point (6, 1).

b) The line $y = 2x + b$ goes through the point (1, 4).

**LS-77.**  You can enter and manipulate matrices with your graphing calculator, but you may have to be careful because the notation is different. Some calculators allow you to use A to represent a matrix, but some require that you use brackets around A, [A], and some put the brackets in automatically.

Look back at problems LS-71 and LS-72.

a) Enter W and B into your graphing calculator.

b) Use your calculator to find W*B. Compare this with your answer for LS-73.

c) Find B*W. Write down what happened and explain?

**LS-78.**  Let A = matrix [1  1  1]. Enter A in your graphing calculator .

a) Find A*W.

b) What does this product represent?

**LS-79.**  Suppose A is an m x n matrix and B is a p x q matrix.

a) If AB is a valid matrix product, what must be true?

b) What will be the dimensions of AB?

c) Add this information to your Tool Kit.

**LS-80.** When discussing matrices, a number or expression is called a **SCALAR** to distinguish it from a matrix.

a) Add **scalar** to your Tool Kit.

b) Identify the scalars in the following list: $[7]$    7    $[5 \quad x]$    x

**LS-81.**  Suppose you needed to multiply $\begin{bmatrix} 2 & 3 \\ 4 & 5 \end{bmatrix}\begin{bmatrix} 1 & 2 \\ 3 & 4 \end{bmatrix}$. Which is faster, with or without a calculator? Have members in your team try it each way and see.

**LS-82.** To your Tool Kit add directions for how to:

1. multiply matrices by a scalar.
2. add two matrices.
3. multiply two matrices together.

Check your definitions with the other members in your team.

LS-83.    At Budding Success
          Flower Shop, three
          different bouquet styles,
          each consisting of lilies,
          roses, and daisies are
          assembled as shown in
          matrix B to the right.

Flowers
L R D

$$\begin{array}{r} \#1 \\ \text{Bouquet Styles } \#2 \\ \#3 \end{array} \begin{bmatrix} 5 & 4 & 3 \\ 4 & 3 & 3 \\ 4 & 6 & 6 \end{bmatrix}$$

a)    Suppose lilies cost $0.30 each, roses cost $0.45 and daisies cost $0.60. Write this
      information as a matrix in such a way that it can meaningfully multiply matrix B on
      the right. (B * (your matrix) must make sense.) Title and label it as usual.

b)    Do the matrix multiplication and interpret the result.

LS-84.    Perform the following matrix multiplication without a calculator:

$$\begin{bmatrix} 2 & 3 & 7 \\ 5 & 1 & 0 \end{bmatrix} \begin{bmatrix} 4 \\ 6 \\ 1 \end{bmatrix}$$

LS-85.    In the previous problem, the first matrix had dimension $2 \times 3$ and the second matrix had
          dimension $3 \times 1$. What is the dimension of the product matrix?

LS-86.    Perform each of the following matrix operations without a calculator, or say impossible
          and explain why.

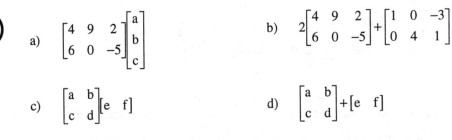

a)    $\begin{bmatrix} 4 & 9 & 2 \\ 6 & 0 & -5 \end{bmatrix} \begin{bmatrix} a \\ b \\ c \end{bmatrix}$

b)    $2\begin{bmatrix} 4 & 9 & 2 \\ 6 & 0 & -5 \end{bmatrix} + \begin{bmatrix} 1 & 0 & -3 \\ 0 & 4 & 1 \end{bmatrix}$

c)    $\begin{bmatrix} a & b \\ c & d \end{bmatrix} \begin{bmatrix} e & f \end{bmatrix}$

d)    $\begin{bmatrix} a & b \\ c & d \end{bmatrix} + \begin{bmatrix} e & f \end{bmatrix}$

LS-87.    Suppose you have to multiply a $5 \times 11$ matrix times a $c \times d$ matrix.

a)    For what value of c will the multiplication be defined?

b)    Given this value of c, what will be the dimensions of the product matrix?

LS-88.    Solve the system at right.                 $x + 3y = 16$
                                                      $x - 2y = 31$

Now, rewrite the system and replace $x$ with $x^2$. What effect will this have on the solution to the system? Solve the new system.

LS-89.    A line intersects the graph of $y = x^2$ twice, at points whose x-coordinates are -4 and 2.

a)    Draw a sketch of both graphs, and find the equation of the line.

b)    Find the measure of the angle that the line makes with the x-axis.

LS-90.    Three red rods are 2 cm longer than two blue rods. Three blue rods are 2 cm longer than four red rods. How long is each rod?

LS-91.    Sketch the graph of the following equations and inequality on separate pairs of axes.

a)    $y + 5 = (x - 2)^2$      b)    $y \le (x + 3)^3$      c)    $y = 4 + \dfrac{1}{x - 3}$

LS-92.    Susan and JT are water polo coaches for Sunford University. They are excellent coaches, but terrible bookkeepers. After a recent four-day tournament, they were asked to record three items: the cost of a room per player per night, the amount spent on a player for food daily, and the spending money per player allotted per day.

"I know that for the four days, Elissa spent the total of $136, which included room, food, and daily expenses," said Susan. "Ellen spent only three nights with the team, received two days of meals, but four days of spending money for a total of $95."

"Well I remember that Heather spent only one night with the team because she slept at home, but did receive two days of meals and three days of spending money for a total of $56," stated JT. "How can we figure this out?"

a)    Write a system of equations in three variables (one equation for each player) to represent this problem. Let $x$ = the cost of a room per night, $y$ = the cost spent on food per day, and $z$ = the amount of the daily allowance given to each player.

b)    You already know everything you need to know to solve this system. This problem simply has a few more subproblems. Simplify each equation as much as possible and, as with two equations, you need to decide on one variable to ELIMINATE.

c)    Next, select any pair of equations from the above set of three. Use your knowledge of solving systems of equations with two variables to eliminate your chosen variable.

d)    Then select a different pair of equations (the one you have not used yet and one you already used) and eliminate the same variable again.

e)    You have modified the original system so that now you have a familiar situation; two equations with two variables. Rewrite and solve this system.

f)    You now know two of the three variables, but you are not finished. What is missing? Complete the solution.

g)    Check your solution in each of the original equations.

**LS-93.** Solve this system of equations and then check your solution in each equation. Be sure to keep your subproblems well organized.

$$x - 2y + 3z = 8$$
$$2x + y + z = 6$$
$$x + y + 2z = 12$$

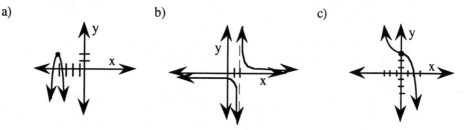

**LS-94.** Write a system of inequalities for the graph at right.

**LS-95.** Find reasonable equations which will generate each graph. You may want to look at your Parent Graph Tool Kit.

a)

b)

c)

**LS-96.** Is $y = \dfrac{1}{x}$ the parent of $y = \dfrac{1}{x^2 + 7}$? Explain your reasoning.

**LS-97.** Solve each of the following equations for $x$:

a) $2x + x = b$   b) $2ax + 3ax = b$   c) $x + ax = b$

LS-98. Mark has been busy. Now he claims to have created another sequence of three function machines that always gives him the same number he started with.

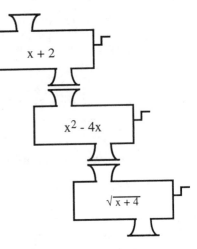

a) Test out his machines. Do you think he is right?

b) Be sure to test negative numbers. What happens for negative numbers?

c) Mark wants to get his machine patented but he has to prove that it will always do what he says it will, at least for positive numbers. Show Mark how to prove his machines work by dropping in a variable, for example n, and writing out each step the machines must take.

d) Why do the negative numbers come out positive?

LS-99. The cost of food has been increasing about 4% per year for many years. To find the cost of an item 15 years ago, Heather said "Take the current price and divide by $(1.04)^{15}$." Her friend Elissa said "That might work, but it's easier to take the current price and multiply by $(.96)^{15}$!" Explain who is correct and why.

LS-100. Solve for w.

a) $w^2 + 4w = 0$
b) $5w^2 - 2w = 0$
c) $w^2 = 6w$

# APPLICATIONS OF SYSTEMS OF EQUATIONS

LS-101. We already know how to find the equation of a line given two points. First we find the slope of the line and then we find the y-intercept. There is another way to think about this problem. If we consider the equation of any line as $y = ax + b$, we can solve this problem using a system of equations.

a) The fact that a line goes through two points (-3, 4) and (-2, -1) means those values for (x, y) make the equation $y = ax + b$ true. Use this information to write two equations in which a and b are the variables.

b) Use your equations from part (a) to find the equation of the line through the points (-3, 4) and (-2, -1). (That is, solve for a and b, not x and y.)

LS-102.   A parabola with a vertical line of symmetry can be represented by $y = ax^2 + bx + c$. It takes just two points to determine a line. How many points do you think it would take to determine such a parabola? Discuss the question with your team before reading part (a).

a)   Use the idea you used in the previous problem about the line to find an equation for a parabola that passes through the points $(2, 3)$, $(-1, 6)$, and $(0, 3)$. You can start by writing three equations in which a, b, and c are the variables.

b)   Solve the system of three equations and use the results to write the equation of a parabola.

LS-103.   Find the equation of the parabola through the points given:

a)   $(3, 10)$, $(5, 36)$, and $(-2, 15)$.          b)   $(2, 2)$, $(-4, 5)$, and $(6, 0)$.

LS-104.   What happened in part (b) in the last problem? Why did this occur? (If you are not sure, plot the points.)

LS-105.   Write the system of inequalities which will give you the graph at right.

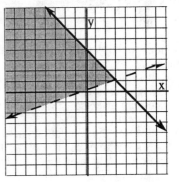

LS-106.   Arthur was supposed to solve the following system of equations.

$$5x + y + 2z = 6$$
$$3x - 6y - 9z = -48$$
$$x - 2y + z = 12$$

Arthur decided to solve this system by eliminating x. He started with the second and third equations and realized that he could divide both sides of the second by -3 to get $x + 2y + 3z = 16$.   He then combined this result with the third equation to get

$$\begin{array}{l} -x + 2y + 3z = 16 \\ \underline{x - 2y + z = 12} \\ \phantom{xxxxx} 4z = 28 \\ \phantom{xxxxxx} z = 7 \end{array}$$

"Wow! Two with one shot!" said Arthur. But then he didn't know what to do next. What should he do to find x and y? Do it.

LS-107.   Solve for x:       $1 - \dfrac{b}{x} = a$

LS-108.   Compare and contrast the graphs of $y = (x - 3)^2$ and $y = x^2 - 3$.

LS-109.    A stick two feet long is accidentally broken.  Assume the stick is equally likely to break anywhere.

   a)    What is the probability that each of the pieces is at least 9 inches long?

   b)    Write an expression to represent the probability that each of the pieces is at least x inches long.

LS-110.    This is a Milepost problem for slopes of parallel and perpendicular lines.

   Find an equation for each of the lines described below.

   a)    The line with slope $\frac{1}{3}$ through the point $(0, 5)$.

   b)    The line parallel to $y = 2x - 5$ through the point $(1, 7)$.

   c)    The line perpendicular to $y = 2x - 5$ through the point $(1, 7)$.

   d)    The line through the point $(0,0)$ so that the tangent of the angle it makes with the x-axis is 2.

## USING MATRICES TO REPRESENT SYSTEMS OF EQUATIONS

The solutions to the systems of equations that you have done the past two days required many calculations. Many applications in advanced mathematics and technology such as computer drawing programs or switching and circuitry problems in telephone communications can lead to a hundred equations in one hundred unknowns and involve solving systems of equations.  Next you'll learn how matrices can make solving these systems much easier.

LS-111.    Solving three equations in three unknowns is sometimes as difficult as it is useful. Fortunately, matrices can help, but first we must express the original system as a matrix equation.

$$9x - 3y + z = -7$$
$$x + y + z = -3$$
$$16x + 4y + z = 21$$

The original system is shown above. Copy it and the matrix equation below it onto your paper.  Fill in the missing entries to express the system as a matrix equation.  Then check by multiplying out the matrices.

$$\begin{bmatrix} 9 & -3 & 1 \\ 1 & 1 & 1 \\ 16 & 4 & 1 \end{bmatrix} \begin{bmatrix} \ \\ \ \\ \ \end{bmatrix} = \begin{bmatrix} \ \\ \ \\ \ \end{bmatrix}$$

We can abbreviate this matrix equation as $AX = B$, where A is the $3 \times 3$ matrix of coefficients, X is the single column matrix of variables, and B is the single column matrix of the constants.

LS-112.    Write this system as a matrix equation and identify the matrices A, X and B.

$$2x + 7y + 5z = 15$$
$$3x + y + 4z = 41$$
$$6x + 9z = 34$$

LS-113.   Imagine that the subtract key on your calculator is broken.

   a)   What would you do to both sides of the equation to solve $x+149 = 237$?  Why?

> Adding -149 to both sides of the equation above works because opposites add up to zero, and $x + 0 = x$.  Because zero is the number that does nothing when you add it, it is called the **identity element for addition** or the **additive identity** (Identity means self, and any number plus zero equals itself).  Since things that undo each other are called inverses, another term for opposites is **additive inverses**.

   b)   What is the **identity element for multiplication**? What is the multiplicative inverse of 4? of 0.1?  What is the familiar name for "**multiplicative inverse**"?

LS-114.   What matrix is the additive identity for $2 \times 2$ matrices?

LS-115.   Show that $\begin{bmatrix} 1 & 1 \\ 1 & 1 \end{bmatrix}$ is <u>not</u> the multiplicative identity for $2 \times 2$ matrices.  That is, show that

   when you multiply $\begin{bmatrix} 1 & 1 \\ 1 & 1 \end{bmatrix}$ by $\begin{bmatrix} 3 & 5 \\ 1 & 2 \end{bmatrix}$ it does not equal $\begin{bmatrix} 3 & 5 \\ 1 & 2 \end{bmatrix}$.

LS-116.   Even though order matters when you multiply matrices, there is still a multiplicative identity matrix called I, for $2 \times 2$ matrices, that works whether you multiply by it on the left or on the right.  With your team and with your knowledge of how matrix multiplication works, guess what this identity matrix, I, might be.  Check with your calculator.  Use variable entries a, b, c and d  as entries of the matrix M to show that $MI = IM = M$ for any $2 \times 2$ matrix M.

LS-117.   In the last problem, you found the (right <u>and</u> left) multiplicative identity for $2 \times 2$ matrices.

   a)   Guess the multiplicative identity for $3 \times 3$ matrices.

   b)   Replace the blank matrix with your guess.  Then check whether the matrix equations are true.

$$\begin{bmatrix} 2 & 7 & 5 \\ 3 & 1 & 4 \\ 6 & 0 & 9 \end{bmatrix} \bullet \begin{bmatrix}  &  &  \\  &  &  \\  &  &  \end{bmatrix} \overset{?}{=} \begin{bmatrix} 2 & 7 & 5 \\ 3 & 1 & 4 \\ 6 & 0 & 9 \end{bmatrix} \qquad \begin{bmatrix}  &  &  \\  &  &  \\  &  &  \end{bmatrix} \bullet \begin{bmatrix} 2 & 7 & 5 \\ 3 & 1 & 4 \\ 6 & 0 & 9 \end{bmatrix} \overset{?}{=} \begin{bmatrix} 2 & 7 & 5 \\ 3 & 1 & 4 \\ 6 & 0 & 9 \end{bmatrix}$$

LS-118. Let $A = \begin{bmatrix} 4 & -1 \\ 7 & 2 \end{bmatrix}$ and $B = \begin{bmatrix} -5 & 0 \\ 3 & -8 \end{bmatrix}$. Find:

a)  A - B  b)  5A  c)  AB  d)  BA

LS-119. Write each system as a matrix equation and find the matrices A, X and B in each case.

a)  $p + 2q = 7$
$3p + 4q = 11$

b)  $4m - 5n = -2$
$-3m + 4n = 9$

c)  $4x - y + z = -5$
$2x + 2y + 3z = 10$
$5x - 2y + 6z = 1$

d)  $7w - 3x + 2z = 41$
$-2w + x - z = -13$
$4w + y - 2z = 12$
$w - 3z = 1$

LS-120. Juan, Huang, and Danusha have pencils and pens in their backpacks. Juan has 3 pencils and 2 pens, Huang has 4 pencils and 5 pens, and Danusha has 6 pencils and 4 pens.

a)  Represent this information in a $3 \times 2$ matrix. Label rows and columns.

b)  Each pencil is worth 10 cents and each pen is worth 25 cents. Represent this information in a matrix in such a way that you can multiply the first matrix by this one. Label rows and columns.

c)  Find the product matrix and interpret the 2,1 entry.

LS-121. Suppose the entries in the first 3 x 2 matrix are a, b, c, d, e, f (reading across the rows), and the entries in the second 2 x 1 matrix are g, h. Write the product matrix in terms of these letters.

LS-122. If x is a number, represent its reciprocal using exponents and not fractions.

LS-123. Cheri has forgotten how to change a quadratic equation from standard form to graphing form. She remembers something about averaging intercepts and completing squares, but she is really confused. Clearly show Cheri **both** methods by changing $y = x^2 + 4x - 7$ into graphing form.

LS-124. Factor completely:

a)  $25x^2 - 1$

b)  $5x^3 - 125x$

c)  $x^2 + x - 72$

d)  $x^3 - 3x^2 - 18x$

LS-125. As you learned in problem LS-111, a system of equations can be represented by a single *matrix* equation of the form AX = B. If you can find the matrix X which makes this equation true, you will have the values of x, y, and z which solve the original system of equations. Solving matrix equations is very similar to solving "normal" equations; we try to get X by itself. One complication is that there is no way to divide matrices, so you will need to learn about the **multiplicative inverse of a matrix.**

a) Think about what you've learned about additive and multiplicative inverses for numbers. What should you get when you multiply a matrix by its multiplicative inverse?

b) Why would the multiplicative inverse of a matrix be useful in solving the matrix equation AX = B?

---

**INVERSE OF A MATRIX**

If $A = \begin{bmatrix} 2 & 7 & 5 \\ 3 & 1 & 4 \\ 6 & 0 & 9 \end{bmatrix}$ is a matrix, then the symbol for its

**MULTIPLICATIVE INVERSE** is $A^{-1} = \begin{bmatrix} 2 & 7 & 5 \\ 3 & 1 & 4 \\ 6 & 0 & 9 \end{bmatrix}^{-1}$ . Note that $A^{-1}$ does

<u>not</u> mean $\frac{1}{A}$, because a number (1) cannot be divided by a matrix (A). Instead, $A^{-1}$ is the matrix with the property that
$$AA^{-1} = A^{-1}A = I,$$
where I is the identity matrix. The identity matrix for $3 \times 3$ matrices is shown at right. Only square matrices can have inverses, and $A^{-1}$ must have the same dimension as A. $\begin{bmatrix} 1 & 0 & 0 \\ 0 & 1 & 0 \\ 0 & 0 & 1 \end{bmatrix}$

---

c) Show without a calculator that $\begin{bmatrix} 3 & 5 \\ 1 & 2 \end{bmatrix}$ and $\begin{bmatrix} 2 & -5 \\ -1 & 3 \end{bmatrix}$ are inverses (for matrices, inverse means multiplicative inverse). Careful: this requires two matrix calculations.

LS-126. The process of finding $A^{-1}$ is complicated and takes more time than we can spend in this course. Fortunately, your graphing calculator can do it with ease! Your Matrix Function Resource Page will show you how. Use it to find the inverse of matrix A in the previous problem. To fit it easily on one screen, display the matrix entries as fractions.

LS-127. To check, compute $[A][A]^{-1}$ and $[A]^{-1}[A]$. Why are there entries like 1 E -13 and -1 E -14? What should these entries be?


LS-128. Now you are ready to solve the system of equations in problem LS-111 by solving the equivalent matrix equation AX = B.

a) Enter the matrices A and B from LS-111 in your calculator. Then use what you learned in problem LS-125 to get X by itself, and find the values of x, y, and z which solve the system. Check your answer in two ways: use your calculator to verify that AX = B, and show that the values of x, y, and z solve the original system. If you think your method makes sense, but you can't get answers because your calculation says "ERROR" (and something like "DIMENSION MISMATCH"), don't panic; go on to part (b).

b) It makes sense that in order to get X by itself, you would multiply both sides of the equation by $A^{-1}$. The problem is that when dealing with matrices, the word "multiply" isn't specific enough! It takes some getting used to, but in general AB gives a different matrix product from BA (assuming both products are possible), so if someone tells you to multiply matrices A and B together, there may be two different answers possible.

> As a result of this, when we're dealing with matrices, we don't use the word "multiply" by itself; we use the terms **right-multiply**, and **left-multiply**. So if the product we want is BA, we say either "right-multiply B by A", or "left-multiply A by B."

What must you do to both sides of the equation AX = B in order to put it in the form "X = "?

c) In general, if AX = B is a matrix equation, then what does X equal? Enter this in your Tool Kit.


LS-129. Write the linear system to the right as a matrix equation of the form AX = B. Then enter matrices A and B in your graphing calculator and use the method of the previous problem to solve the system.

$$4x + 4y - 5z = -2$$
$$2x - 4y + 10z = 6$$
$$x + 2y + 5z = 0$$

LS-130. Professor Zipthrough wants to prove that the method of problem LS-128 always works to solve equations of the form AX = B. He has written the steps on the board, but he wants you to explain the justification for each step. Fill in the reasons that each equation can be turned into the one below it.

$AX = B$

1. ________________

$A^{-1}(AX) = A^{-1}B$

2. ________________

$(A^{-1}A)X = A^{-1}B$

3. ________________

$IX = A^{-1}B$

4. ________________

5. $X = A^{-1}B$

LS-131 Use the matrix method to solve the equations shown at right.

$$\begin{aligned} -4x + 7y - 12z &= -3.8 \\ 5x - 8y \phantom{{}+9z} &= -14.8 \\ x - 4y + 9z &= 7.6 \end{aligned}$$

LS-132. Show that each of the following pairs of matrices are inverses.

a) $\begin{bmatrix} 1 & 2 \\ 3 & 4 \end{bmatrix}$ and $\begin{bmatrix} -2 & 1 \\ 1.5 & -0.5 \end{bmatrix}$

b) $\begin{bmatrix} 4 & -5 \\ -3 & 4 \end{bmatrix}$ and $\begin{bmatrix} 4 & 5 \\ 3 & 4 \end{bmatrix}$

LS-133. Use matrices to solve these systems. Check your answers by substituting them in the original equations. You will not need a calculator if you use the results of the previous problem.

a) $$\begin{aligned} p + 2q &= 7 \\ 3p + 4q &= 11 \end{aligned}$$

b) $$\begin{aligned} 4m - 5n &= -2 \\ -3m + 4n &= 9 \end{aligned}$$

LS-134. Let $P = \begin{bmatrix} 2 & -1 & 5 \\ -4 & 0 & 7 \end{bmatrix}\begin{bmatrix} -3 & 2 \\ 1 & -6 \\ 0 & 1 \end{bmatrix}$. Do each calculation or explain why it cannot be done.

a) P

b) $p_{1,2}$

c) $p_{2,3}$

LS-135. If M is as shown below, find a matrix I such that MI = IM = M, or say impossible and explain.

a) $M = \begin{bmatrix} 2 & -1 & 5 \\ -4 & 0 & 7 \end{bmatrix}$  b) $M = \begin{bmatrix} 2 & -1 \\ -4 & 0 \end{bmatrix}$  c) $M = \begin{bmatrix} 2 & -1 & 5 \\ -4 & 0 & 7 \\ 6 & -2 & 8 \end{bmatrix}$

LS-136. The cubic function $g(x) = px^3 + qx^2 + rx + s$ passes through the points (-2, -22), (1, 2), (2, -2) and (5, 118).

a) Set up four equations using unknowns p, q, r, and s as variables.

$$-8p + 4q - 2r + s = -22$$
$$p + q + r + s = 2$$
$$8p + 4q + 2r + s = -2$$
$$125p + 25q + 5r + s = 118$$

b) Write these four equations as a single matrix equation.

c) When you have access to a graphing calculator, finish the problem by finding g(x).

LS-137. Add or subtract and simplify.

a) $\dfrac{3}{(x - 4)(x + 1)} + \dfrac{6}{x + 1}$

b) $\dfrac{3x}{x^2 + 2x + 1} + \dfrac{3}{x^2 + 2x + 1}$

c) $\dfrac{x + 2}{x^2 - 9} - \dfrac{1}{x + 3}$

d) $\dfrac{3}{x - 1} - \dfrac{2}{x - 2}$

e) Write a justification for each step you used in simplifying the expression in part (d).

LS-138. Find the equation of a parabola with x-intercepts (3,0) and (15,0) that passes through (6,-162).

LS-139. A spaceship is approaching a star and is caught in its gravitational pull. When the ship's engines are fired the ship will slow down, momentarily stop, and then, hopefully, pick up speed, move away from the star, and not be pulled in by the gravitational field. The engines were engaged when the ship was 750 thousand miles away from the star. After one minute the ship was 635 thousand miles away from the star. After two minutes the ship was 530 thousand miles away from the star.

a) Find three points from the information above where x = the time since the engines were engaged and y = the distance (in thousands of miles) from the star.

b) Plot the points in part (a). We want the distance to reach a minimum and then increase again, over time. What kind of model follows this pattern?

c) Find the equation of the parabola that fits the three points you found in part (a).

d) If the ship comes within 50 thousand miles of the star, the shields will fail and the ship will burn up. Use your equation to determine whether the space ship has failed to escape the gravity of the star.

LS-140. Sid Sickly has contracted an infection and has gone to the doctor for help. The doctor takes a blood sample and finds 900 bacteria per cc. ("cc" stands for cubic centimeter which is equal to 1 milliliter.) Sid gets a shot of a strong antibiotic from the doctor. The bacteria will continue to grow for a period of time, reach a peak, and then decrease as the medication succeeds in overcoming the infection. After 10 days, the infection has grown to 1600 bacteria per cc. After 15 days it has grown to 1875.

a) What are the three data points?

b) Make a rough sketch that will show the number of bacteria per cc over time.

c) Find the equation of the parabola that contains the three data points.

d) Based on the equation, when will Sid be cured?

e) Based on the equation, how long had Sid been infected before he went to the doctor?

LS-141.  Solve for integers x, y, and z: $\left(2^x\right)\left(3^y\right)\left(5^z\right) = \left(2^3\right)\left(3^{x-2}\right)\left(5^{2x-3y}\right)$.

LS-142.  Given $f(x) = 2x^2 - 4$ and $g(x) = 5x + 3$, find:

   a)   $g(-2)$.

   b)   $f(-7)$.

   c)   Find $f\big(g(-2)\big)$.

   d)   Find $f\big(g(1)\big)$.

LS-143.  Find the measure of $\angle CPM$.

   List any subproblems that were
   necessary to solve this problem.

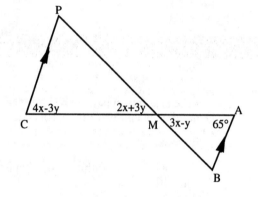

LS-144.  Solve each equation for y so that it could be entered in the graphing calculator.

   a)   $x^2 = x(2x - 4) + y$

   b)   $x = 3 + (y - 5)^2$

LS-145.  Describe how the graph of $y + 3 = -2(x + 1)^2$ is different from $y = x^2$.

LS-146.  Sketch each graph:

   a)   $(x - 2)^2 + (y + 3)^2 = 9$

   b)   $(x - 2)^2 + (y + 3)^2 \geq 9$

LS-147.   You are standing 60 feet away from a five story building in Los Angeles, looking up at its roof top. In the distance you can see the billboard on top of your hotel but the building is completely obscured by the one in front of you. If your hotel is 32 stories tall and the average story is 10 feet high, how far away from your hotel are you?

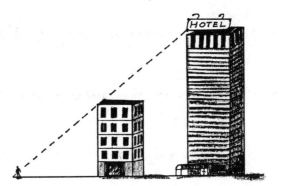

## REVIEW AND SUMMARY

LS-148.   Sensible Sally has a job that is 35 miles from her home. She needs to be at work by 8:15 a.m. Sally wants to maximize her sleep time by leaving as late as possible but still get to work on time. From experimentation, Sally discovered that if she left at 7:10, it would take her 40 minutes to get to work. If she leaves at 7:30, it will take her 60 minutes to get to work. If she leaves at 7:40, it will take her 50 minutes to get to work. Since her commute time increases and then decreases, Sally decides to use a parabola to model her commute. Assume the time it takes to get to work varies quadratically with the number of minutes after 7:00 that Sally leaves.

a)   Let x = the number of minutes after 7:00 that Sally leaves.
Let y = the number of minutes it takes Sally to get to work.

b)   One ordered pair is (10, 40). What are the other two ordered pairs given in the problem?

c)   Write three equations in three variables based on the general formula of the quadratic equation $ax^2 + bx + c = y$.

d)   Solve the system to find a, b, and c. Write the particular quadratic equation for this function. Round your answer to 3 decimal places.

e)   Use your equation to find how long it would take to get to work if Sally left at 7:20.

f)   According to your equation, how long would it take to get to work if she left at 7:58? Does this make sense? Why?

g)   Find reasonable limitations for the domain of the function assuming a maximum average speed of 60 mph.

h)   What time(s) does Sally need to leave to spend at most 45 minutes in her car?

i)   What is the latest time, keeping in mind the restrictions on the domain, that Sally can leave in order to get to work by 8:15?

**LS-149.** Milepost 12 problems provide more practice graphing linear inequalities.

For this system of inequalities:

$$y \le -2x + 3 \qquad y \ge x \qquad x \ge -1$$

a) Draw the graph.

b) Find the area of the shaded region.

**LS-150.** Graph each system and shade the solution:

a) $y \ge x^2 - 4$
   $y < \frac{1}{3}x + 1$

b) $y < 2x + 5$
   $y \ge |x + 1|$

**LS-151.** Write each number as a power of 2.

a) 16

b) $\frac{1}{8}$

c) $\sqrt{2}$

d) $\sqrt[3]{4}$

**LS-152.** Perform the following operations if possible:

a) $3\begin{bmatrix} 3 & 2 \\ 6 & 4 \end{bmatrix} + \begin{bmatrix} 2 & 5 \\ 3 & 1 \end{bmatrix} =$

b) $\begin{bmatrix} 2 \\ 4 \\ 3 \end{bmatrix}\begin{bmatrix} 1 & 2 & 3 \\ 2 & 4 & 3 \end{bmatrix} =$

c) $\begin{bmatrix} 2 & 3 \end{bmatrix}\begin{bmatrix} 1 & 3 \\ 4 & 2 \end{bmatrix} =$

d) $3\begin{bmatrix} 3 & 6 \end{bmatrix} + \begin{bmatrix} 2 & 5 \end{bmatrix} =$

**LS-153.** Given $f(x) = 2x^2 - 4$ and $g(x) = 5x + 3$ find:

a) $f(a)$

b) $f(3a)$

c) $f(a + b)$

d) $f(x + 7)$

e) $f(5x + 3)$

f) $g(f(x))$

**LS-154.** Solve the system of equations at right:

$$5x - 4y - 6z = -19$$
$$-2x + 2y + z = 5$$
$$3x - 6y - 5z = -16$$

LS-155.  If a movie ticket now averages $6.75 and has been increasing an average of 15% per year, compute the cost:

a)    in 8 years                    b)    8 years ago


LS-156.  Graph the solution of:            $y > (x - 2)^2$
                                           $y \le (x - 2)^3 + 2$


LS-157.  Consider the parabola that passes through the points (2, 6), (-1, 12), and (0, 6).

a)    Find the equation of the parabola.    b)    Find the vertex of the parabola.


LS-158.  You have a bag with 60 black jelly beans and 240 red ones.

a)    If you draw one jelly bean out of the bag, find the probability that it is black.

b)    If you add 60 black jelly beans to the original bag and draw out a bean, what is the probability that it is black?

c)    How many black beans do you need to add to the original bag to double the original probability of drawing a black bean?

d)    Write an equation that represents the problem in part (c).


LS-159.  **PORTFOLIO: GROWTH OVER TIME—PROBLEM #2**

On a separate piece of paper (so you can hand it in separately or add it to your portfolio) explain **everything** that you now know about:

$$f(x) = 2^X - 3.$$

This is the second opportunity to solve this problem. Be sure to include everything you included the first time plus all that you have learned since then.


LS-160.  Write an explanation for someone just coming into the class about how to use subproblems to solve a system of four linear equations with four unknowns. Give such a clear and convincing explanation that your teacher will never ask you to actually solve one.

## LS-161.  SUMMARY ASSIGNMENT

a)  Create or select two systems of linear equations. Make one of them a system that you would want to use matrices to solve and the other a system you would prefer to use other algebraic methods to solve.  Show how to solve both systems.

b)  On graph paper draw a polygon.  Label its vertices then write the set of inequalities for which the intersection will be the area inside the polygon you drew.  You can do an easy one, a triangle, or you can consider this a challenge and see how interesting a figure you can represent.

c)  What were the most difficult parts of this unit?  List sample problems and discuss the hard parts.

d)  What problem did you like best and what did you like about it?


## LS-162.  PORTFOLIO ASSIGNMENT

a)  Find what you believe to be your two best pieces of work for this unit.  Explain why you are particularly proud of these assignments.  Be sure to include a restatement of the original problem or a copy of it.

b)  Select two problems from the year that you are still having difficulty with.  Copy each problem and solve as much of it as you can.  Explain what part of the problem you do not understand.


## LS-163.  TOOL KIT CHECK-UP

Your Tool Kit contains reference tools for algebra. Return to your Tool Kit entries. You may need to revise or add entries.

Be sure that your Tool Kit contains entries for all of the items listed below.  Add any topics that are missing to your Tool Kit NOW, as well as any other items that will help you in your study of algebra.

- Inequalities with Absolute Value
- Matrices
- Solving Matrix Equations

- Solving Linear Inequalities
- Matrix Multiplication

# UNIT 6

## The Case of the Cooling Corpse
### LOGARITHMS AND OTHER

# Unit 6 Objectives
## The Case of the Cooling Corpse:
## LOGARITHMS AND OTHER INVERSES

In this unit you will undo everything you have done so far, that is, you will learn to find functions that reverse the order of operations of given functions.

In this unit you will have the opportunity to:

- learn to how write algebraic expressions and draw graphs for inverse functions.

- learn about a new function, the undoing or inverse function for an exponential function.

- develop properties of logarithms based on your knowledge of exponents.

- use logarithms for solving equations and other problems.

Once again a graphing calculator will be a valuable tool and you will continue to need at least a scientific calculator for homework.

---

CC-0.     **THE CASE OF THE COOLING CORPSE**
Think about how you would solve this equation: $1.04^x = 2$.

As it turns out solving an equation like this will provide a key piece of information that will enable you to solve the Case of the Cooling Corpse. Try solving this equation now. Is it easy? Did you use guess and check? One of the goals of this unit is to provide you with more of the algebraic tools you will need to solve problems where the exponent is the variable.

---

PROBLEM SOLVING
REPRESENTATION/MODELING
FUNCTIONS/GRAPHING
INTERSECTIONS/SYSTEMS
ALGORITHMS
REASONING/COMMUNICATION

# Unit 6

**The Case of the Cooling Corpse: LOGARITHMS AND OTHER INVERSES**

## UNDOING MACHINES

CC-1. At right is a picture of Anita's function machine. When she put a 3 into the machine, the machine put out a 7. When she put in a 4, the machine gave her a 9, and when she put in a -3, out came -5.

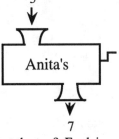

a) Explain in words what this machine does to a number.

b) What if it were possible to turn the crank the opposite direction, causing the machine to pull 7 back up into it? What do you think would come out the top? Explain.

c) Suppose Anita wants to build another machine that will **undo** the effects of her first function machine. That is, she wants a machine that will take seven and turn it back into three, take nine and turn it back into four, and so on. Write a rule that she should program into this new machine to make it do this.

CC-2. The function machine to the right, f, follows the rule:

$$f(x) = 5x + 2.$$

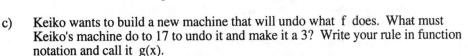

a) What is f(4)?

b) If the crank is turned backwards, what number should be pulled up into the machine in order to have a 4 come out the top?

c) Keiko wants to build a new machine that will undo what f does. What must Keiko's machine do to 17 to undo it and make it a 3? Write your rule in function notation and call it g(x).

CC-3. Find the undo rules for each of the functions below. Write your answers in function notation, but be sure to use a name that is different from the function name. For example, if the function is named f(x), you can't use f(x) for the undoing machine too. You'll need to use some other letter, like g(x).

a) $f(x) = 3x - 2$

b) $h(x) = \dfrac{x + 1}{5}$

c) $p(x) = 2(x + 3)$

d) $q(x) = \dfrac{x}{2} - 3$

CC-4.    Diane claims that $f(x) = \dfrac{3}{x}$ is its own undo rule.  Is her conjecture correct?  Show how you know.

CC-5.    Your teacher will give you a handout describing your long-range project entitled **REPORT ON GROWTH**.  Be sure to keep this handout in a safe place, as you will need to refer to it periodically.  You might want to put this information in your Tool Kit so that you can find it later.

CC-6.    Nossis has been working on his geometry homework and he is almost finished.  His last task is to solve $\sin x = 0.75$.  Nossis cannot figure out what $x$ is!  Explain to him how he can figure out what $x$ is and show him that it does work.

CC-7.    Antonio's function machine is shown at right:

   a)    What is $A(2)$?

   b)    If 81 came out, what was dropped in?

   c)    If 8 came out, what was dropped in?  Be accurate to two decimal places.

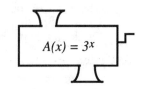

CC-8.    If $10^x = 10^y$, what is true about $x$ and $y$?  Justify your answer.

CC-9.    Gary has a function $g(x) = 10^x$ and Amy has her function $a(m) = 10^m$.  Each person is going to choose a whole number at random from the numbers 1, 2, 3, . . ., 10, and substitute it into his or her respective function.  After they do this, what is the probability that $g(x) = a(m)$?

CC-10.   Solve each of the following equations.

   a)    $\dfrac{x}{3} = \dfrac{4}{5}$

   b)    $\dfrac{x}{x + 1} = \dfrac{5}{7}$

   c)    $\dfrac{6}{15} = 2 - \dfrac{x}{5}$

   d)    $\dfrac{2}{3} + \dfrac{x}{5} = 6$

CC-11.   Sketch the solution of this system of inequalities.

$$y > x^2 - 5$$

$$y < -(x - 1)^2 + 7$$

CC-12. Graph $y = \frac{1}{2}x - 3$ and its undoing function on the same set of axes.

a) What is the equation of the undoing function?

b) Does this graph, including both lines, have a line of symmetry? If so, what is the equation of the line of symmetry?

CC-13. Given the following matrices: $C = \begin{bmatrix} -2 & 3 \\ -1 & 5 \end{bmatrix}$; $P = \begin{bmatrix} 1 & 4 & 0 \\ 2 & -3 & 1 \end{bmatrix}$; $M = \begin{bmatrix} -2 \\ -5 \end{bmatrix}$, compute:

a) CP

b) CM

c) C + M

CC-14. Solve for x: $x^2 = 91$.

CC-15. The angle of elevation of the sun at 10:00 a.m. is 29°. At that point, a tree's shadow is 32 feet long. How tall is the tree?

# GRAPHS OF INVERSES

CC-16.

The formal mathematical name for an undoing function is **INVERSE**. Record this in your Tool Kit.

Find the inverse for each of the functions below. Then graph each function and its inverse on the same set of coordinate axes. In other words, use one set of axes for part (a), a new set for part (b), etc. This is NOT a good time to divide up the graphing among your teammates. Make sure each of you does the work for each part. Check with each other as you go.

a) $f(x) = 2x + 4$

b) $f(x) = -\frac{2}{3}x$

c) $y = \frac{1}{3}x + 2$

d) $y = x^3 + 1$

CC-17. When you have completed all the pairs of graphs, look for patterns in the graphs. What relationships do you see between the graph of a function and the graph of its inverse? Do the pairs of graphs have a line of symmetry? Justify your answer.

CC-18.    Use a full sheet of graph paper.  Put the axes in the center of the page, and label each
          mark on each axis as one unit.  Use pencil (the softer the lead the better.)

   a)    Graph $y = (\frac{x}{2})^2$ over the domain $0 \le x \le 8$.  Label the graph with its equation.
         Trace over the graph with the pencil until the graph is heavy and dark.  Crayon
         works even better than pencil.

   b)    On the same graph paper, graph $y = x$ using ball-point pen (use a straightedge, and
         press down hard).

   c)    What is the equation of the inverse of this parabola?

   d)    Using a ruler as an edge, fold the paper along the line $y = x$, with the graphs on the
         **inside** of the fold.  Put the folded paper on your desk top.  You will be able to see
         the darkened graph of the half-parabola through the paper.  Now press the paper
         with a hard object, such as the back of your fingernail or the top of a pen, so that
         you are rubbing the graph from the back of the paper.  The purpose is to make a
         "carbon copy" of the graph of the parabola, reflected across the line.  Then open the
         paper and fill in the picture if it is not completely copied.  Write your observations
         on the graph.

   e)    Find three points (x, y) that satisfy the equation you wrote in part (c).  Find each point
         on the "carbon copy" graph.  Each <u>should</u> be a point on this graph.  Explain why.


CC-19.    Wanda and Samantha have found a useful pattern between functions and their inverses.
          They didn't remember any shortcuts for graphing lines, so they made a table to graph
          $f(x) = 2x + 4$ and its inverse.  That's when they made their discovery.

   a)    Make and complete the two tables and see if you can find their pattern.

| x  | f(x) |
|----|------|
| 0  | 4    |
| 1  |      |
| 2  |      |
| -1 |      |
| -2 |      |

| x | g(x) |
|---|------|
| 4 | 0    |
| 6 |      |
| 8 |      |
| 2 |      |
| 0 |      |

   b)    If (10, 27) is a point on the graph of the function, what point do you automatically
         know is on the inverse graph?  Answer the same questions for
         (3.5, 14), (a, b), and (x, y).


CC-20.    Solve the following system using elimination or matrices.

$$x + y + z = 2$$
$$2x - y + z = -1$$
$$3x - 2y + 5z = 16$$


CC-21.    Solve the equation $3 = 8^x$ for x, accurate to two decimal places.

CC-22.    Solve the system below using matrices or elimination.

$$\begin{aligned} a - b + 2c &= 2 \\ a + 2b - c &= 1 \\ 2a + b + c &= 4 \end{aligned}$$

a)    What happened?  What does this mean?

b)    What does the solution tell you about the graphs?


CC-23.    Dana's mother gave her $175 on her sixteenth birthday.  "But you must put it in the bank and leave it there until your eighteenth birthday," she told Dana.  Dana already had $237.54 in her account, which pays 3.25% annual interest, compounded quarterly.  What is the minimum amount of money she will have on her eighteenth birthday if she makes no withdrawals before then?  Justify your answer.


CC-24.    If $2^{(x+4)} = 2^{(3x-1)}$, what is x?


CC-25.    Write the equation of a circle with a center at (-3, 5) that is tangent to the y-axis. Sketching a picture will help.


CC-26.    Perform each operation.  Factoring will help you to simplify.

a)    $\dfrac{(x+2)(x-3)}{(x+1)(x-4)} \cdot \dfrac{(x+1)}{x(x+2)}$

b)    $\dfrac{x^2 + 5x + 6}{x^2 - 4} \cdot \dfrac{4}{x+3}$

c)    $\dfrac{2x}{x+4} + \dfrac{8}{x+4}$

d)    $\dfrac{x}{x+1} - \dfrac{1}{x+1}$


CC-27.    Samy has a 10-foot wooden ladder which he needs to climb to reach the roof of his house.  The roof is 12 feet above the ground.  The base of the ladder must be at least 1.5 feet from the base of the house.  How far is it from the top step of the ladder to the edge of the roof?  Draw a sketch.


CC-28.    Later, the ladder fell and broke into two pieces.  Samy needed a piece at least 4 feet long to wash a window.  At the same time, his neighbor, Elisa, needed to borrow a ladder, and she **also** needed one that was at least four feet long.  What is the probability that the ladder broke in a spot so that both he and Elisa would be able to use a ladder at least four feet long?

# INVERSE AND INTERCHANGE

CC-29. Kalani began to think that this method of **graphing** the inverse of a function might help him find the **equation** of the inverse. "If you can just interchange x and y to find points on the graph of the inverse, why not just switch x and y in the equation itself to find the equation of the inverse?" he said to his friend Macario.

"Well, I think I see what you are saying. A function and its inverse are reflected across the line y = x, and in the table of values, the values for the independent and dependent variables are just switched. But what makes you think we can do the same thing with the equation?" Macario asked.

"Think about it: an equation represents **all** the points on the line, so if you can interchange all of the x and y values, why not interchange the x and y variables?"

a) Try interchanging the x and y variables on y = 3x - 1, then solve the new equation for y.

b) Did this method work? Show how you know.

c) The inverse of a function could be called the **x-y interchange** of the function. Give a good reason why someone might want to call it that.

CC-30. Find the inverse of each of the functions below. Write your answers in function notation. Remember to use a new name for the new function.

a) $f(x) = 8x + 6$

b) $f(x) = 3x^5$

CC-31. Uyregor's math teacher is really demanding.

He gave Uyregor the function $f(x) = \frac{3}{5}x + 9$ and told him that he is supposed to find the inverse of this function and call it g(x). That's the easy part. Once he has done that, he is supposed to find f(1), f(2), f(3), . . . , f(50)! But wait! That's not all! Then he is supposed to substitute those results into g(x)! Since you have such a **nice** teacher, you can help Uyregor out. Explain to him why he should already know all of the final results.

CC-32. The graphs of some functions are sketched below. For each function, sketch the graph of the inverse. Then state the domain and range for each function and for its inverse. The dotted line is y = x.

a)    b)    c)

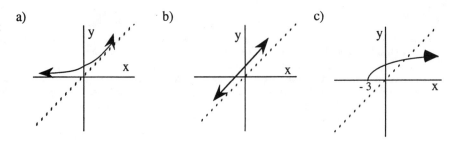

CC-33.    Trejo says that if you know the x-intercepts, y-intercepts, domain, and range of an equation, then you automatically know the x-intercepts, y-intercepts, domain, and range for the inverse. Hilary disagrees. She says you know the intercepts, but that is all you know for sure. Who is correct? Justify your answer.

CC-34.    Lacey and Richens each have their own personal function machines. Lacey's, L(x), squares the input and then subtracts one. Richens' function, R(x), adds 2 to the input, and then multiplies the result by three.

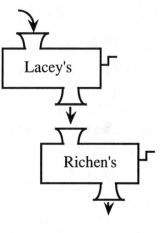

a)    Write the equations that represent L(x) and R(x).

b)    Lacey and Richens decide to connect their two machines, so that Lacey's output becomes Richens' input. Eventually, what is the output if 3 is the initial input?

c)    What if the order of the machines was changed. Would it change the output? Justify your answer.

CC-35.    Two function machines, f(x) = 5x - 3 and g(x) = (x - 1)$^2$, are shown at right.

Suppose f(3), (not x = 3!), is dropped into the g(x) machine. This is written as g(f(3)).

What is this output?

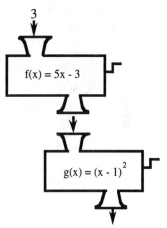

CC-36.    Using the same function machines as in the previous problem, what is f(g(3))? Be careful! The result is different from the last one because the <u>order</u> in which you use the machines has been switched! With f(g(3)), first you will find g(3), then you substitute that answer into the machine named "f".

CC-37.

When we push two (or more) function machines together, we say we have a new function which is the **COMPOSITION** of the two functions. The composition can be written different ways, as $f(g(x))$ or sometimes as $f \circ g(x)$. Does it seem to matter in what order you use the functions? Does $f(g(x))$ necessarily equal $g(f(x))$? Explain.

If $f(x) = 2x + 1$ and $g(x) = \frac{1}{2}x^2$, find $f \circ g$ and $g \circ f$ and simplify.

a) $f \circ g(x) = f(g(x)) =$

b) $g \circ f(x) = g(f(x)) =$

CC-38. Solve each of the following equations.

a) $\dfrac{3x}{5} = \dfrac{x - 2}{4}$

b) $\dfrac{4x - 1}{x} = 3x$

c) $\dfrac{2x}{5} - \dfrac{1}{3} = \dfrac{137}{3}$

d) $\dfrac{4x - 1}{x + 1} = x - 1$

CC-39. Rebecca thinks that she has found a quick way to graph an inverse of a function. She figures that if you can interchange $x$ and $y$ to find the inverse, she will interchange the x- and y-axes by flipping the paper over so that when she looks through the back the x-axis is vertical and the y-axis is horizontal as shown below. Copy the graph on the right on a separate sheet and try her technique. What do you think?

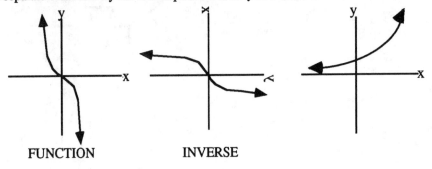

FUNCTION                    INVERSE

**CC-40.**

FRACTION BUSTERS REVISITED! Another way to use fraction busters is to simplify complicated expressions like the one below. Instead of multiplying both sides by the common denominator, we can multiply the numerator and denominator of the large fraction by the common denominator of the smaller fractions. In the example below, we can multiply the top and bottom by **ab** to clear the fractions in the numerator and the denominator (provided neither a nor b is equal to 0).

$$\frac{\frac{a}{b}}{1 - \frac{1}{a}} \quad \text{multiply top and bottom by \textbf{ab} (common denominator of all the fractions).}$$

$$\frac{\left(\frac{a}{b}\right)}{\left(1 - \frac{1}{a}\right)} \cdot \frac{\frac{ab}{1}}{\frac{ab}{1}} = \frac{\frac{a^2 b}{b}}{ab - \frac{ab}{a}} \quad \text{Now simplify.} \qquad \frac{\frac{a^2 \cancel{b}}{\cancel{b}}}{ab - \frac{a\cancel{b}}{\cancel{a}}} = \frac{a^2}{ab - b} \text{ or } \frac{a^2}{b(a-1)}$$

Use the Fraction Buster technique to simplify each problem below:

a) $\dfrac{x}{1 - \frac{1}{x}}$

b) $\dfrac{\frac{1}{a} + \frac{1}{b}}{\frac{1}{b} - a}$

**CC-41.** Complete the square to write the equation in graphing form and sketch the graph of

$$x^2 + y^2 - 4x - 16 = 0.$$

**CC-42.** Parts (a) and (c) are the Milepost problems for multiplication and division of rational expressions.

Think about factoring first, then perform each operation. Simplify when it is helpful.

a) $\dfrac{x^2 + 5x + 6}{x^2 - 4x} \cdot \dfrac{4x}{x + 2}$

b) $\dfrac{y^2}{y + 4} - \dfrac{16}{y + 4}$

c) $\dfrac{x^2 - 2x}{x^2 - 4x + 4} \div \dfrac{4x^2}{x - 2}$

d) $\dfrac{x^2 - 6x}{x^2 - 4x + 4} + \dfrac{4x}{x^2 - 4x + 4}$

e) For each step you took in part (c), list the property or properties of numbers that justify that step.

# MORE ON INVERSE RELATIONS

CC-43.     Danny was having trouble finding the undo function
           (the inverse) for $g(x) = x^2$. So he graphed the
           function $y = x^2$ and used the carbon copy method to
           get the interchanged graph at right.

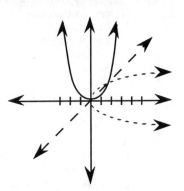

  a)     "Aha!" he said, "Now I know the interchange
         function." What equation was he thinking of?

  b)     "But wait!" said Regis. "$x = y^2$ is not a
         function." "Picky, picky, picky," Danny replied,
         "It works doesn't it?" What do you think? Why
         can't $y = x^2$ have an inverse <u>function</u>?

  c)     Think of another function that does not have an inverse function. Discuss this with
         your team.


CC-44.     As you saw in the previous problem some functions do not have inverse <u>functions</u>.
           There may be an inverse equation that works, but it is not a function. In these cases, in
           order to get an inverse <u>function</u> we use only a <u>part</u> of the original function. Let's examine
           the previous problem again.

           Graph the original function and its inverse function and find the equation of the undoing
           function for parts (a) and (b) below.

  a)   $f(x) = x^2$ with domain $x \geq 0$        b)   $g(x) = (x - 2)^2$ with domain $x \geq 2$


CC-45.     Graph each of the following functions on a separate pair of axes. Clearly label the
           equation of the graph.

           i)      $y = -\frac{2}{3}x + 6$

           ii)     $y = \frac{1}{2}(x + 4)^2 + 1$ with domain $x \geq -4$

           iii)    $y = \frac{1}{x}$

  a)     For each of the functions above, state the x-intercepts, y-intercepts, domain, and
         range.

  b)     Graph the inverse of each function by using the "carbon copy" method or by
         interchanging points. Clearly label the inverse.

  c)     State the x-intercepts, y-intercepts, domain, and range for each of the inverse
         graphs.

  d)     Find the "undoing" equation for each equation above and write it next to the graph
         of the inverse function.

CC-46. Amanda's favorite function is $f(x) = 1 + \sqrt{x + 5}$. She has built a function machine that performs these operations on the input values. Her brother Eric is always trying to mess up Amanda's stuff, so he created the inverse of $f(x)$, called it $e(x)$, and programmed it into a machine.

a) What is the equation of $e(x)$, Eric's function, which is the inverse of Amanda's? (Remember, it must <u>undo</u> Amanda's machine.)

b) What happens if the two machines are pushed together? What is $e(f(-4))$? Explain why this happens.

c) If $f(x)$ and $e(x)$ are graphed on the same set of axes, what would be true about the two graphs?

d) Draw the two graphs on the same set of axes. Be sure to notice the restricted domain and range of Amanda's function.

CC-47. If $g(x) = 4x + 7$, find the equation of a machine $f(x)$ so that $f(x)$ is the inverse of $g(x)$. Explain completely how you got your function and show that it works for at least three different numbers.

CC-48. The figure at right shows a tree casting a shadow of length s feet when the angle of elevation is a°. In a 24 hour period, what are the possible values for:

a) s?

b) a?

CC-49. Solve each of the following equations.

a) $\frac{x}{3} = x + 4$

b) $\frac{x + 6}{3} = x$

c) $\frac{x + 6}{x} = x$

d) $\frac{2x + 3}{6} + \frac{1}{2} = \frac{x}{2}$

CC-50. Sketch the solution to this system of inequalities.
$$y \geq (x + 5)^2 - 6$$
$$y \leq -(x + 4)^2 - 1$$

**CC-51.** Make a sketch of a graph showing the change in temperature of a cup of coffee as it sits on the kitchen table to cool.

    a) What are the independent and dependent variables?

    b) What is the domain and range?     c) Is there an asymptote? Explain.

**CC-52.** Solve each of the following equations for x.

    a) $x^2 = 27$                      b) $2^x = 27$

**CC-53.** Adam keeps getting negative exponents and fractional exponents confused. Help him by explaining the difference between $2^{1/2}$ and $2^{-1}$.

**CC-54.** Solve and graph or graph and solve each inequality on a number line.

    a) $|x| < 3$          b) $|2x+1| < 3$          c) $|2x+1| \geq 3$

# INTERCHANGING AN EXPONENTIAL FUNCTION

**CC-55.** **SILENT BOARD GAME**

Do this individually and silently (don't discuss it with your team). Figure out the rule for this function. The table is written on the board. As you figure out a number that fits, go up and fill in the number (silently). If it is not the correct number, your teacher will erase it. Only one number from each person, please. Copy the table at the side of a full sheet of graph paper.

| x | 8 | $\frac{1}{2}$ | 32 | 1 | 16 | 4 | 3 | 64 | 2 | 0 | 0.25 | -1 | $\sqrt{2}$ | 0.2 | $\frac{1}{8}$ |
|------|---|---------------|----|---|----|---|---|----|---|---|------|----|-----------|-----|---------------|
| g(x) | 3 | -1 | | 0 | | | | 6 | | | | | | | |

**CC-56.** When the Silent Board Game table is filled in, discuss in your teams how you found the entries and write a brief description of the method.

    a) Write your rule for the function in symbols.

    b) $x = 1024$ is not in the table. What is $g(1024)$?

CC-57.    Using a full sheet of graph paper, put the axes in the center of the page and label each
          mark on each axis as one unit.

    a)    Draw the graph of the function from the Silent Board Game by plotting the table of
          values.  On the same axes, in a contrasting color, graph $y = 2^x$ and label it with its
          equation.

    b)    What would happen if you reflected the graph $y = 2^x$ across the line $y = x$?
          Reflect it by the "carbon copy" method if you would like to check it.  On the graph,
          answer this question and write any other observations you can make about the two
          graphs.

CC-58.    We will call the function $x = 2^y$ the **inverse exponential
          function, base 2**.  Label the graph with this name.  Then
          describe this function as completely as possible; more
          precisely, investigate it.  Write all the important information on
          the graph paper.

CC-59.    Suppose we label the inverse exponential function, base 2, $g(x)$.  Refer back to the Silent
          Board Game table and your graph to evaluate $g(x) = y$ below.  What is $y$ and/or $x$ in
          each of the following cases?

    a)  $g(32) = y$            b)  $g\left(\frac{1}{2}\right) = y$            c)  $g(4) = y$

    d)  $g(0) = y$             e)  $g(x) = 3$            f)  $g(x) = \frac{1}{2}$

    g)  $g\left(\frac{1}{16}\right) = y$            h)  $g(x) = 0$            i)  $g(8) = y$

CC-60.    Sketch the graph of $y + 3 = 2^x$.

    a)    What is the domain and range of this function?

    b)    Does this function have a line of symmetry?  If so, what?

    c)    What are the x and y intercepts?

    d)    Change the equation so that the graph of the new equation has no x-intercepts.

CC-61.    What is the equation of the inverse of $f(x) = \sqrt{5x + 10}$?  Make a graph of both the
          function and its inverse on the same set of axes.

CC-62.    Write the equation of an increasing exponential function, which has a horizontal
          asymptote at $y = 15$.

CC-63. On Howie's math homework last night, he had to solve for x in several equations. He did fine on all of the problems involving numbers, but he just didn't believe that the methods he used for problems such as $5 \cdot 4 + 2(x)^3 = 8 + 7$ would work on problem such as $ay + bx^3 = c + 7$. Show Howie how he can use the same basic steps he used for the first problem to solve the second.

CC-64. What is the difference between the graphs of:

$$y + 3 = (x - 1)^2 \quad \text{and} \quad x + 3 = (y - 1)^2?$$

Explain completely enough so that someone who does not know how to graph either equation could graph them after reading your description. Are the two graphs inverses of each other? Are they both functions? Justify your answer.

CC-65. Which is larger, $n - 1$ or $n - 2$? Is your answer the same regardless of the value you chose for n? Explain.

CC-66. Solve each of the following equations for x.

a) $x^3 = 243$ 

b) $3^x = 243$

CC-67. Write the equation for each circle graphed below:

a)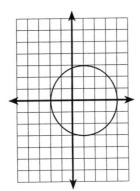

b)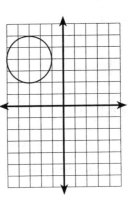

CC-68. Add or subtract and simplify.

a) $\dfrac{x^2}{x - 5} - \dfrac{25}{x - 5}$

b) $\dfrac{a^2}{a + 5} + \dfrac{10a + 25}{a + 5}$

c) $\dfrac{x^2}{x - y} - \dfrac{2xy - y^2}{x - y}$

d) $\dfrac{x}{x + 1} + \dfrac{1}{x - 1}$

e) For each step you wrote in part (a), list the properties that justify that step.

CC-69.    If $x = 2^y$, how can you solve for $y$ and make it say "$y =$"? Discuss this with your team and be prepared to report to the class what you think.

CC-70.

> When mathematicians cannot solve a problem or do not have the tools to do a particular problem, do you know what they usually do? They invent a tool to do what they need! Of course this invention has to be consistent with all the existing mathematical rules. In this case they invented a new operation, the **inverse exponential function, base 2**. Henceforth they said (at one point in history) the inverse exponential function base 2 will be known as **LOGARITHM, BASE 2**. Why did they select "logarithm" when thousands of other names were possible? That is a question to investigate on the internet. You graphed this function in problem CC-58 (we called the graph the inverse exponential function, base 2). Find your graph and label it "logarithm, base 2." Add the graph and its equation $y = \log_2 x$ to your Parent Graph Tool Kit.
>
> Logarithm base 2 is usually abbreviated as log, base 2 and is usually written $\log_2$. When we see this symbol, we read it aloud as "log, base 2." The comma means we pause a bit when we say it. Since it is a function, we can use function notation, such as $g(x) = \log_2 (x)$. Notice that the base number, 2 in this case, is always written a little lower, which is called a **SUBSCRIPT**.

Use your graph of $g(x)$ to find each of the missing values:

a)   $\log_2(32) = ?$

b)   $\log_2\left(\frac{1}{2}\right) = ?$

c)   $\log_2(4) = ?$

d)   $\log_2(0) = ?$

e)   $\log_2( \ ? \ ) = 3$

f)   $\log_2( \ ? \ ) = \frac{1}{2}$

g)   $\log_2\left(\frac{1}{16}\right) = ?$

h)   $\log_2( \ ? \ ) = 0$

i)   $\log_2(8) = ?$

CC-71.    How do your answers in the previous problem relate to those in problem CC-59?

CC-72.    Let $y = \log_2 (x)$. Rewrite this so that it is solved for $x$. Think about how we defined $y = \log_2 (x)$ for a hint. Put a large box around both equations. Do the two equations look the same? Do the two equations mean the same thing? Are they equivalent? How do you know? This is very important. Don't rush; think about it.

CC-73.    If $x = 3^y$, what do you think you would write to solve for $y$? Explain.

CC-74.    Solve for x in the following problems.

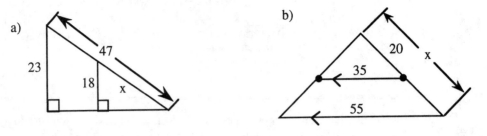

a)

b)

CC-75.    Ramin is trying to evaluate an expression and he cannot get the negative sign to work on his calculator. Explain to Ramin how he can simplify $\dfrac{7 \cdot 4^{-2001}}{2 \cdot 4^{-1997}}$ without using a calculator.

CC-76.    Solve each of the following rational equations.

a)    $\dfrac{x}{3} = \dfrac{4}{x}$

b)    $\dfrac{x}{x-1} = \dfrac{4}{x}$

c)    $\dfrac{1}{x} + \dfrac{1}{3x} = 6$

d)    $\dfrac{1}{x} + \dfrac{1}{x+1} = 3$

CC-77.    An investment counselor advises a client that a safe plan is to invest 30% in bonds and 70% in a low risk stock. The bonds currently have an interest rate of 7% and the stock has a dividend rate of 9%. The client plans to invest a total of x dollars.

a)    Write an expression for the annual income that will come from the bond investment.

b)    Write an expression for the annual income that will come from the stock investment.

c)    Write an equation and solve it to find out how much the client needs to invest to have an annual income of $5,000.

CC-78.    Solve for x:   $2^x = 3$. Be accurate to three decimal places.

CC-79. Although the Quadratic Formula always works when solving quadratic equations, for many problems it is not the most efficient method. Sometimes it is faster to factor or complete the square or even just "out-think" the problem. For each equation below, choose the best method to solve the equation and explain your reason. You do **not** actually have to solve the equation.

a) $x^2 + 7x - 8 = 0$

b) $(x + 2)^2 = 49$

c) $5x^2 - x - 7 = 0$

d) $x^2 + 4x = -1$

CC-80. If a point inside the figure is chosen at random, what is the probability that it is in the shaded region?

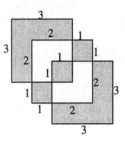

CC-81. Solve for n: $n^3 = 49$.

CC-82. A circle has the equation $x^2 + (y + 2)^2 = r^2$. If the circle is shifted 2 units to the left, 5 units up and the radius is doubled, what will be the new equation?

# LOGARITHMS

CC-83. Make a table like the one below and fill in the missing numbers.

a)

| x | f(x) |
|---|---|
| 81 | 4 |
| $\frac{1}{3}$ | |
| 3 | |
| 27 | |
| 1 | 0 |
| -1 | |
| 0 | |
| 9 | 2 |
| $\frac{1}{9}$ | |
| $\sqrt{3}$ | |

b) Consider the equation for the function in part (a). There are two ways to write this equation; one uses exponents, and one uses the word "log." Write the equation in both ways.

CC-84. Suppose $h(x) = 3^x$ and $k(x) = \log_3(x)$. What is $k(h(x))$? What about $h(k(x))$? Start with a few numbers to convince yourself. Explain completely why this is true.

CC-85. Since a logarithm is the interchange (or inverse) of an exponential function, each logarithmic function has a particular base. Note that we write the base <u>below</u> the line (like a subscript). For example, we write $\log_2(x)$. This looks a bit confusing, since the "x" is above the 2. It almost looks like $2^x$, but it isn't. When you write it, make it very clear. Most log equations can be written as an exponential equation and vice versa, as you saw in the previous problem. Copy each equation shown below. Then rewrite each equation in the other form.

a) $y = 5^x$

b) $y = \log_7(x)$

c) $8^x = y$

d) $A^K = C$

e) $K = \log_A(C)$

f) $\log_{1/2}(K) = N$

CC-86. On Wednesdays at Tara's Taqueria four tacos are the same price as three burritos. Last Wednesday the Lunch Bunch ordered five tacos and six burritos, and their total bill was $8.58 (with no tax or drinks included). Nobody in the Lunch Bunch can remember the cost of one of Tara's tacos. Help them figure it out.

CC-87. Barnaby's grandfather is always complaining that back when he was a kid, he used to be able to buy his girlfriend dinner for only $1.50. If that same dinner that Barnaby's grandfather purchased for $1.50 sixty years ago now costs $25.25, and the increasing amounts form a geometric sequence, write an equation which will give you the costs at different times.

CC-88. Make a sketch of a graph that is a decreasing exponential function with the x-axis as the horizontal asymptote.

Now make a similar sketch, but this time the horizontal asymptote is the line $y = 5$.

CC-89.   If $f(x) = x^4$ and $g(x) = 3(x + 2)$, what is:

a)   f(2)?

b)   g(2)?

c)   f(g(2))?

d)   g(f(2))?

e)   If f(x) = 81, what is x?


CC-90.   At the Write-a-Text Factory, workers spend grueling hours at computer terminals trying to be creative writing textbooks. One day, during a brief bout of boredom, Karna and Carlos decided to play a trick on Darell as he worked on his document. They implanted a strange code in his computer so that as soon as he had entered 60,000 characters, 10% of his document, starting at the beginning, would be deleted every hour. Just as the clock struck 5:00 and he was anxiously waiting for the whistle to blow telling him he could go home, Darell typed in his 60,000th character. He left and did not return until 8:00 a.m. the next day.

a)   How many characters were left when he returned the next morning?

b)   If Darell starts typing 3600 characters per hour when he arrives, will he increase the size of his document faster than the mutant code can decrease it, or vice-versa?


CC-91.   A triangle is formed by a line which has a slope of 2 and the x- and y-axes. The area of the triangle is 30 square units. Find the equation of the line. A diagram would be helpful.


CC-92.   Ever eat a maggot? Guess again! The FDA publishes a list, the Food Defect Action Levels list, which indicates limits for "natural or unavoidable" substances in processed food (*Time*, October 1990). So in 100 g of mushrooms, for instance, the government allows 20 maggots! The average rich and chunky spaghetti sauce has 350 grams of mushrooms. How many maggots is that?


CC-93.   Some of the following algebraic fractions have common denominators and some do not. Add or subtract the expressions and simplify, if possible.

a)   $\dfrac{3}{(x - 4)(x + 1)} + \dfrac{6}{x + 1}$

b)   $\dfrac{5}{2(x - 5)} - \dfrac{3x}{x - 5}$

c)   $\dfrac{x}{x^2 - x - 2} - \dfrac{2}{x^2 - x - 2}$

d)   $\dfrac{x + 2}{x^2 - 9} - \dfrac{1}{x + 3}$

e)   For each step you took in part (a), list the property or properties that justify that step.

## LOGARITHM AND EXPONENTIAL NOTATION

Logarithmic expressions are just a new way of writing exponential expressions. In the same way that $x = \sqrt[3]{5}$ is equivalent to $x^3 = 5$, $\log_2(8) = m$ is equivalent to $2^m = 8$. It is the same relationship written a different way. The same pairs of numbers make the two equations true. In general,

$$\log_b(n) = m \quad \text{means} \quad b^m = n \quad (\text{if } b > 0).$$

The $\log_b(n)$ is the exponent which must be used on the base $b$ to equal $n$.

Examples: $\log_4(64) = 3$ because $4^3 = 64$

$\log_4(\frac{1}{64}) = -3$ because $4^{-3} = \frac{1}{64}$

$\log_9(3) = \frac{1}{2}$ because $9^{\frac{1}{2}} = 3$

Complete these logarithm equations, which are true for any base $b > 0$.

a)  $\log_b(b) =$                    b)  $\log_b(1) =$

# LOGARITHM INVESTIGATION

CC-95.   There is a "log" key on your calculator. On a normal scientific calculator, you enter the number first, then press the log key. On the graphing calculator, however, it is entered just as you would write it or say it (press "log" first, then the number). But you will notice that the base is omitted. Unfortunately, you do not get the option of putting in any base you want. Instead, the calculator's log has a fixed base. Your task is to figure out this base. As a hint, try entering log (2), log (3), etc. Keep track of your results. Use complete sentences to write an explanation of the problem and your solution.

CC-96.   Investigate the family of functions $y = \log_b(x)$. Be complete and be sure to include several appropriate graphs.

CC-97.

---

**LOGARITHM NOTATION**

When we compute with logarithms using the calculator, what base must we use?

Since the calculator's base for logs is always 10, and since the calculator is so useful in computations, we save time by making this agreement: When we write **log (x)**, *without writing a base*, we mean $\log_{10}(x)$.

Log is a function and, like any function, its inputs should be in parentheses like f(x). But since logs are so useful and written so frequently, some people omit the parentheses, and just write log x (or $\log_N$ x if the base is not 10).

---

CC-98.   Copy these log equations and solve for x. Obtain a numerical answer without a calculator if possible.

a)   $\log_5 (25) = x$

b)   $\log_4 \left(\frac{1}{4}\right) = x$

c)   $3 = \log_x (343)$

d)   $\log_6 (0) = x$

e)   $3 = \log_5 (x)$

f)   $\log_9 (x) = \frac{1}{2}$

g)   $x = \log_{64} (8)$

h)   $\log_{11} (x) = 0$

i)   $x = \log_{10} (0.01)$

CC-99.   Your friend is not quite sure how to rewrite exponential equations as log equations, and vice-versa. Write out an explanation for your friend. It might be easier to use equations, symbols, and letters of the alphabet in addition to sentences. What you are really doing here is developing a definition of logarithm. If you need help, rewrite the equations from the previous problem without the "log" to see a pattern.

CC-100.    Late last night, as Agent 008
negotiated his way back to
headquarters after a long day, he saw
the strangest glowing light. It came
closer and closer until finally he could
see what was creating the light. It was
some kind of spaceship! He was
frozen in his tracks. It landed only 15
feet from him, and a hatch slowly
opened. Four little creatures came out
carrying all sorts of equipment,
including calculators and what
appeared to be laser beams. They did
not seem to notice that Agent 008 was
there; that is, until he sneezed!
Suddenly, the creatures turned around,
looking very startled. They dashed
into the spaceship, closed the hatch, and rocketed into the night. Could he believe what
he had seen? Was it just a dream? After a few minutes of standing there dazed and
confused, he started walking on, his eyes glazed over. He was just coming to his
senses when he stepped on something strange. He picked it up and to his surprise it
was one of the creature's calculators! What a prize! He started playing with it as he
walked on. Boy! Headquarters is going to love this! It appeared to have a log button
and as he played with it he noticed something interesting: log 10 did not equal 1 as it did
on his calculator. With this calculator, log 10 ≈ 0.926628408! He tried some more:
log 100 ≈ 1.853256816, and log 1000 ≈ 2.779885224. This was most peculiar.
Obviously, the creatures did not work in base 10!

a)    What base do the space creatures work in? Explain how you got your answer. You
may want to rewrite the problem as $\log_b 10 = 0.926628408$ and try to figure out
the value of b.

b)    How many fingers do you think these space creatures have?


CC-101.    Solve for x. Your answer must be accurate to three decimal places.

$$2 = 1.04^x$$


CC-102.    Delores has two big bags of hard candies that she is planning to put into small packages
for the Ides of March picnic. One bag contains 450 assorted fruit flavored candies; the
other contains 500 coffee-toffees. She figures that the children will like the fruit candies
better, and the adults will prefer the coffee-toffees. She plans to make little bags of 2
coffee-toffees and 6 fruit candies for the children and of 5 coffee-toffees and 3 fruits for
the adults. She is trying to figure out what numbers of child and adult candy packets she
can make. Help her out by writing two inequalities and drawing their graphs. Let x be
the number of bags for children and y the number for adults. If sixty children and 70
adults go to the picnic will there be enough bags of candy?


CC-103.    If $10^{3x} = 10^{(x-8)}$, solve for x. Show that your solution works by checking your
answer.

CC-104.    For $f(x) = 3 + \sqrt{2x - 1}$, do each of the following:

    a)    What are the domain and range for $f(x)$?

    b)    What is $f(x)$'s inverse (or interchange)? Call it $g(x)$.

    c)    What are the domain and range of $g(x)$?

    d)    Calculate $f(g(6))$.

    e)    Calculate $g(f(6))$. What do you notice? Why does this happen?


CC-105.    Which of the following statements are true? If untrue, show why each statement is false.

    a)    $\dfrac{x + 3}{5} = \dfrac{x}{5} + \dfrac{3}{5}$  b)                      $\dfrac{5}{x + 3} = \dfrac{5}{x} + \dfrac{5}{3}$


CC-106.    Two congruent overlapping squares are shown. If a point inside the figure is chosen at random, what is the probability that it will <u>not</u> be in the shaded region?

CC-107.    While working on his Algebra 2 homework, Pietro came across this problem:

"For $F(x) = 3^{(-x)} - 1$, find $F(2)$, $F(3)$, $F(4)$ and $F(5)$. Then explain what happens as larger and larger numbers are substituted for $x$."

He had no idea how to do the problem.

    a)    Help him out by calculating $F(2)$, $F(3)$, $F(4)$, and $F(5)$.

    b)    Plot the points and draw the graph of $F(x)$. Be sure to continue the graph for $F(-1)$, $F(-2)$, etc. Use an appropriate scale.

    c)    Use your graph to explain to Pietro what happens to $F(x)$ as $x$ gets larger and larger.


CC-108.    Solve for $m$: $m^5 = 50$.

# TRANSLATING THE GRAPHS OF LOGARITHMIC FUNCTIONS

CC-109. Using a full sheet of graph paper, make a fairly accurate graph of $f(x) = \log(x)$. Clearly write the equation on the graph.

CC-110.  On the same set of axes, but in another color, graph $g(x) = 5 + \log(x)$. How is this graph different from the first? Explain. Use what you know about parent graphs (perhaps referring to your Tool Kit notes from Unit 4) and you can do these graphs more efficiently than with a graphing calculator.

CC-111.  On the same set of axes, but in a third color, graph $h(x) = 5 \log(x)$. How is it different? Explain.

CC-112.  Next graph $j(x) = \log(x + 5)$ in a fourth color. How is it different? Explain.

CC-113. Finally, graph $k(x) = \log(x - 5)$ in a fifth color. How is it different? Explain.

CC-114. In your Parent Graph Tool Kit write a general equation for the logarithm graph. Prove to your teacher that you are the expert log grapher! Explain completely, so that even an Algebra 1 student can follow your work, how to graph $y = 2 + 7 \log(x + 4)$.

CC-115. Graph $y = |\log(x)|$.

CC-116. Copy these equations and solve for x. You should be able to do all these problems without a calculator.

a) $\log_x (25) = 1$  b) $x = \log_3 (9)$  c) $3 = \log_7 (x)$

d) $\log_3 (x) = \frac{1}{2}$  e) $3 = \log_x (27)$  f) $\log_{10} (10000) = x$

CC-117. Complete the following calculator investigation.

a) Compute the decimal values for the following pairs of logarithmic expressions:

$4 \log (2)$ and $\log (2^4)$     $2 \log (3)$ and $\log (9)$     $3 \log (5)$ and $\log (5)^3$

b) What do you notice in all three examples? Explain completely. Rewriting the number within the parentheses as a power might help.

c) Try $\log 1000^5$ and $5 \log 1000$ and $\log (10^3)^5$.

d) Make up three examples of your own; use unusual numbers in one of them.

CC-118. Solve for x. Your solution must be correct to **four** decimal places.

$$2 = 1.04^x$$

CC-119. Randomly choose a point on $\overline{AB}$ and label it X. Draw $\overline{XC}$ and $\overline{XD}$ to form $\triangle XCD$. If a dart is thrown and lands inside the square, what is the probability that it landed inside $\triangle XCD$? Does it matter where you place x on $\overline{AB}$ ?

CC-120. Is it true that $\log_3 (2) = \log_2 (3)$? Justify your answer.

CC-121. Consider the general form of an exponential function: $y = km^x$.

a) Solve for k.      b) Solve for m.

CC-122.  Graph the two functions at right on the same set of axes.      $y = 3(2^x)$
$y = 3(2^x) + 10$

a)  How do the two graphs compare?

b)  Suppose the first equation is $y = k \cdot m^x$ and the graph is shifted up  b  units.  What is the new equation?

CC-123.  Solve each equation or inequality.

a)  $|x - 1| = 9$

b)  $2|x + 1| + 3 = 9$

c)  $|x - 1| < 3$

d)  $|x + 5| \geq 8$

CC-124.  Milepost 15 is addition and subtraction of rational expressions.

a)  $\dfrac{2 - x}{x + 4} + \dfrac{3x + 6}{x + 4}$

b)  $\dfrac{3}{(x + 2)(x + 3)} + \dfrac{x}{(x + 2)(x + 3)}$

c)  $\dfrac{3}{x - 1} - \dfrac{2}{x - 2}$

d)  $\dfrac{8}{x} - \dfrac{4}{x + 2}$

e)  For each step you take in part (d), list the property or properties that justify it.

CC-125.  Discuss with your team how you solved  $2 = 1.04^x$  accurate to four decimal places.  Lay out the subproblems or key ideas.

CC-126.  It would certainly be useful to have an easier method than guess and check to do problems like the one above.  Actually, you already know most of the steps to do so. You just need to put some ideas together.  Note that one possible approach to solving $2 = 1.04^x$  would be to convert this equation from exponential form to log form: $x = \log_{1.04}(2)$.  However, our calculators are still useless here, so this approach leads to a dead end.

a)  Consider the equation  $4^x = 8^{(x+2)}$.  Recall that the strategy here is to rewrite the equation using the same base on both sides.  What base should you use in this case?

b)  Rewrite the equation in part (a) so that both sides are powers of the same base and solve it.

CC-127. The equation in the preceding problem was chosen so that it would be easy to make the bases the same; 4 and 8 are both powers of 2. Now you know enough to solve any equation of this form. The base you'll use is 10 (can you guess why?). Follow the steps below to solve $2 = 1.04^x$.

    a)    Without guess and check and without your calculator, solve the equation $2 = 10^m$ for m, then use your calculator to get a decimal answer.

    b)    Next solve $1.04 = 10^n$ for n and get a decimal answer.

    c)    The results of parts (a) and (b) tell you how to express the numbers 2 and 1.04 as powers of 10. Use those results, and substitution, to rewrite the original problem $2 = 1.04^x$ so that both the 2 and the 1.04 are powers of 10. What can you conclude from this version of the equation?

    d)    Finish solving the problem and check your answer.

    e)    You probably rounded off your answers to parts (a) and (b), but to get the most accurate answer to $2 = 1.04^x$ you need to use the unrounded versions. Show how you could tell your calculator what operations to do without getting long decimal answers along the way. Write down your directions to your calculator.

    f)    Explain why this process will work for any equation of the form $a^x = b$, as long as a and b are positive numbers.

CC-128. Use the ideas from problem CC-127 to solve this equation. Be accurate to three decimal places.
$$5 = 1.04^x$$

CC-129. Solve each of the following (nearest 0.001):

    a)    $25^x = 145$         b)    $(1.28)^x = 4.552$         c)    $240(0.95)^x = 100$

CC-130. If gasoline now costs \$1.25 per gallon and is increasing at 5% per year, how long will it be before it costs \$2.00 per gallon? Write an equation and solve.

CC-131. Use the idea from problem CC-117 to write three different but equivalent expressions for each of the following logs. For example: $\log 7^{3/2}$ can be written as $\frac{3}{2}\log 7$, $\frac{1}{2}\log 7^3$, $3 \log \sqrt{7}$, etc.

    a)    $\log 8^{2/3}$         b)    $-2 \log 5$         c)    $\log (na)^{ba}$

CC-132.  Margee thinks she can use logs to solve $56 = x^8$ since logs seem to make exponents disappear. Unfortunately, Margee is wrong. Explain the difference between equations like $2 = 1.04^x$, in which you can use logs, and $56 = x^8$, in which you don't need logs.

CC-133.  Complete this investigation.

a)  What can we multiply 8 by to get 1?

b)  What can we multiply x by to get 1?

c)  By using the rules of exponents, find a way to solve $m^8 = 40$. Remember logarithms will not be useful here, but the exponent key on your calculator will. (Obtain the answer as a decimal approximation using your calculator. Check your result by raising it to the $8^{th}$ power.)

d)  Now solve $n^6 = 300$.

CC-134.  What is the equation of the line of symmetry of the graph of $y = (x - 17)^2$? Justify your answer.

CC-135.  Solve each system below. (Don't forget that you can use matrices if you have a graphing calculator.)

a)  $-4x = z - 2y + 12$
$y + z = 12 - x$
$8x - 3y + 4z = 1$

b)  $3x + y - 2z = 6$
$x + 2y + z = 7$
$6x + 2y - 4z = 12$

c)  What does the solution in part (b) tell you about the graphs?

CC-136.  Integral and rational exponents

Use integer or rational exponents to write each of the following as a power of x.

a)  $\sqrt[5]{x}$

b)  $\dfrac{1}{x^3}$

c)  $\sqrt[3]{x^2}$

d)  $\dfrac{1}{\sqrt{x}}$

## WRITING EQUATIONS OF EXPONENTIAL FUNCTIONS

CC-137.  As you learned in Unit 3, an exponential function has the general form $y = km^x$.

   a)  Does this type of equation have an asymptote? If so, what?

   b)  A particular exponential function goes through the points (2, 36) and (1, 12) and has the x-axis as a horizontal asymptote. Substitute these values into $y = km^x$, for x and y to create two equations with two unknowns, the unknowns being k and m.

   c)  Solve one of your equations for k or m. Substitute that result into the remaining equation. You should now be able to figure out one of the variables. Once you know one of the variables, you should be able to find the other.

   d)  What is the exponential function that passes through (2, 36) and (1, 12)?

CC-138.  I'd like to have $40,000 in 8 years, and I only have $1000 now.

   a)  What interest rate would I need that, when compounded yearly, will reach my goal?

       To help me solve this, set up an exponential equation: let y = amount of money, let x = number of years, and let m be the multiplier. Since interest rate problems are best modeled by exponential functions, the equation is to be in the form $y = km^x$. Find the rate.

   b)  Suppose I start with $7800 and I want to have $18,400 twenty years from now. What interest rate do I need (compounded yearly)?

   c)  Which of these two scenarios described in parts (a) and (b) do you think is more likely to happen? Justify your response.

CC-139.  An exponential function contains these two points: (3, 12.5) and (4, 11.25).

   a)  Is the exponential function increasing or decreasing? Justify your answer.

   b)  This exponential function does not have the x-axis as a horizontal asymptote. The horizontal asymptote for this function is the line $y = 10$. Make a sketch of this graph showing the horizontal asymptote.

   c)  If this function has the equation $y = km^x + b$, what would be the value of b? Explain.

   d)  Substitute the known points into the equation $y = km^x + 10$ and solve the system for k and m.

   e)  What is the equation of the function?

CC-140. Solve each of the following equations (to the nearest 0.001).

a) $(5.825)^{(x-3)} = 120$

b) $18(1.2)^{(2x-1)} = 900$

CC-141. The economy has worsened to the point that the merchants in downtown Hollywood cannot afford to replace the light bulbs when they burn out. On average about thirteen percent of the light bulbs burn out every month. Assuming there are now about one million outside store lights in Hollywood, how long will it take until there are only 100,000 bulbs lit? Until there is only one bulb lit?

CC-142. A dart hits each of these dart boards at random. What is the probability that the dart will not land in the shaded area?

a)

b)

CC-143. Given the function $y = 3(x + 2)^2 - 7$, how could you restrict the domain to give "half" of the graph?

a) Find the equation for the inverse function for your "half - a - function."

b) What are the domain and range for the inverse function?

CC-144. Eniki has a sequence of numbers given by the formula $t(n) = 4(5^n)$.

a) What are the first three terms of Eniki's sequence?

b) Chelita thinks the number 312,500 is a term in Eniki's sequence. Is she right? Justify your answer by either giving the term number or explaining why it isn't in the sequence.

c) Elisa thinks the number 94,500 is a term in Eniki's sequence. Is she right? Explain.

CC-145.   Below right is a graph of $y = \log_b x$.  Find a reasonable value for b.

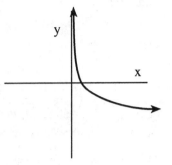

CC-146.   Simplify the following fractions:

a)   $\dfrac{\dfrac{1}{a} - \dfrac{1}{b}}{\dfrac{1}{a} + \dfrac{1}{b}}$

b)   $\dfrac{x + y}{\dfrac{1}{x} + \dfrac{1}{y}}$

CC-147.   Describe the transformation and sketch the graph of $y = \log_3 (x + 4)$.

# SOLVING A MURDER MYSTERY: AN APPLICATION OF LOGARITHMS

CC-148.   **THE CASE OF THE COOLING CORPSE**

The coroner's office is kept at a cool 17°C.  Agent 008 kept pacing back and forth trying to keep warm as he waited for any new information about his latest case.  For over three hours now, Dr. Dedman had been performing an autopsy on the Sideroad Slasher's latest victim, and Agent 008 could see that the temperature of the room and the deafening silence were beginning to irritate even Dr. Dedman.  The slasher had been creating more work than Dr. Dedman cared to investigate.

"Dr. Dedman, don't you need to take a break?  You've been examining this dead body for hours!  Even if there were any clues, you probably wouldn't see them at this point," Agent 008 queried.

"I don't know."  Dr. Dedman replied.  "I just have this feeling something is not quite right.  Somehow the slasher slipped up with this one and left a clue.  We just have to find it."

**>>Problem continues on the next page.>>**

"Well, I have to check in with HQ," 008 stated. "Do you mind if I step out for a couple of hours?"

"No, that's fine." Dr. Dedman responded. "Maybe I'll have something by the time you return."

"Sure," 008 thought to himself. Someone always wants to be the hero and solve everything himself. The doctor just doesn't realize how big this case really is. The Slasher has left a trail of dead bodies through five states! 008 left, closing the door quietly. As he walked down the hall, he could hear the doctor's voice fade away, as he described the victim's gruesome appearance into the tape recorder.

The hallway from the coroner's office to the elevator was long and dark. This was the only way to Dr. Dedman's office. Didn't this frighten most people? Well, it didn't seem to bother old Ajax Boraxo who was busy mopping the floor, thought 008 . . . most of the others wouldn't notice, he reminded himself.

He stopped briefly to use the restroom and bumped into one of the deputy coroners. "Dedman still at it?" "Sure is, Dr. Quincy. He's totally obsessed. He's certain there is a clue." As usual, when leaving the court house, 008 had to sign out.

"How's it going down there, Agent 008?" Sergeant Foust asked. Foust spent most of his shifts monitoring the front door, forcing all visitors to sign in, while he recorded the time next to the signature. Agent 008 wondered if Foust longed for a more exciting aspect of law enforcement. He thought if he were doing Foust's job he would get a little stir-crazy sitting behind a desk most of the day. Why would someone become a cop to do this?

"Dr. Dedman is convinced he will find something soon. We'll see!" Agent 008 responded. He noticed the time: Ten minutes to 2:00. Would he make it to HQ before the chief left?

"Well, good luck!" Foust shouted as 008 headed out the door.

Agent 008 sighed deeply when he returned to the court house. Foust gave his usual greeting: "Would the secret guest please sign in?" he would say, handing a pen to 008 as he walked through the door. Sign in again, he thought to himself. Annoying! 5:05 p.m. Agent 008 had not planned to be gone so long, but he had been caught up in what the staff at HQ had discovered about that calculator he had found. For a moment he saw a positive point to having anyone who came in or out of the court house sign in: he knew by quickly scanning the list that Dr. Dedman had not left. In fact, the old guy must still be working on the case.

As he approached the coroner's office, he had a strange feeling that something was wrong. He couldn't hear or see Dr. Dedman. When he slowly opened the door, the sight he saw inside stopped him in his tracks. Evidently, Dr. Dedman was now the newest victim of the slasher. But wait? The other body, the one the doctor had been working on, was gone! Immediately, the security desk, with its annoying sign-in sheet came to mind. Yes there were lots of names on that list, but if he could determine the time of Dr. Dedman's death, he might be able to just scan the roster to find the murderer! Quickly, he grabbed the thermometer to measure the Doctor's body temperature. He turned around and hit the security buzzer. The bells were deafening. He knew the building would be sealed off instantly and security would be there within seconds.

"My God!" Foust cried as he rushed in. "How did this happen? Who could have done this? I spoke to the Doctor less than an hour ago. What a travesty!"

>>Problem continues on the next page.>>

As the security officers crowded into the room, Agent 008 explained what he knew, which was almost nothing. He stopped long enough to check the doctor's body temperature: 27°C. That's 10°C below normal. He figured that the doctor had been dead at least an hour. Then he remembered: the tape recorder! Dr. Dedman had been taping his observations; that was standard procedure. They began looking everywhere for that blasted thing. The slasher must have realized that the doctor had been taping and taken that as well. Exactly an hour had passed during the search and Agent 008 noticed that the thermometer still remained in Dr. Dedman's side. The thermometer clearly read 24°C. Agent 008 knew he could now determine the time of death precisely.

| Coroner's Office - Please Sign In | | |
|---|---|---|
| Name | Time In | Time Out |
| Lt. Borman | 12:08 | 2:47 |
| Alice Bingham | 12:22 | 1:38 |
| Chuck Miranda | 12:30 | 2:45 |
| Harold Ford | 12:51 | 1:25 |
| Ajax Boraxo | 1:00 | 2:30 |
| D. C. Quincy | 1:10 | 2:45 |
| Agent 008 | 1:30 | 1:50 |
| Ronda Ripley | 1:43 | 2:10 |
| Jeff Dangerfield | 2:08 | 2:48 |
| Stacy Simmons | 2:14 | 2:51 |
| Brock Ortiz | 2:20 | 2:43 |
| Pierce Bronson | 3:48 | 4:18 |
| Max Sharp | 3:52 | 5:00 |
| Maren Ezaki | 3:57 | 4:45 |
| Caroline Cress | 4:08 | 4:23 |
| Milly Osborne | 4:17 | 4:39 |
| D.C. Quincy | 4:26 | 4:50 |
| Vinney Gumbatz | 4:35 | |
| Cory Delphene | 4:48 | 4:57 |
| Max Crutchfield | 5:04 | |
| Agent 008 | 5:05 | |
| Security | 5:12 | |

a) Make a sketch showing the relationship between body temperature and time. What type of function is it? Justify your answer.

b) What is the asymptote for this relationship? Explain.

c) Use your data and the equation $y = km^x + b$ to find the equation that represents the temperature of the body at a certain time.

d) When did Dr. Dedman die?

e) Who is the murderer?

CC- 149.   Using your calculator, compare each expression in Column A with its paired expression in Column B.

|  | Column A | >  <  =  ? | Column B |
|---|---|---|---|
|  | log (30) |  | log (5) + log (6) |
|  | log (27) |  | log (9) + log (3) |
|  | log (24) |  | log (2) + log (12) |
|  | log (132) |  | log (12) + log (11) |

a)   Write a conjecture (a statement you think is true) based on the pattern you noticed.

b)   What is another way of expressing log (65)?

c)   Make up three more examples of your own, and check them.

CC-150.   Using your calculator, compare the expressions in these two columns.

|  | Column C |  | Column D |
|---|---|---|---|
|  | log (30) |  | log (300) - log (10) |
|  | log (27) |  | log (81) - log (3) |
|  | log (8) |  | log (24) - log (3) |
|  | log (12) |  | log (60) - log (5) |

a)   Write a conjecture based on the pattern you noticed.

b)   What is another way of expressing log (13)?

c)   Make up three more examples of your own, and check them.

CC-151.   Using your calculator, compare the expressions in these two columns.

|  | Column E |  | Column F |
|---|---|---|---|
|  | log $(3 \cdot 4)$ |  | log (3) + log (4) |
|  | log $(\frac{72}{8})$ |  | log (72 - log (8) |

a)   What is another way of expressing  log $(a \cdot b)$?

b)   What is another way of expressing  log $(\frac{a}{b})$ ?

CC-152. Use the rules of exponents to argue that what you wrote for parts (a) and (b) in the preceding problem is true for all $a > 0$ and $b > 0$. That is, prove parts (a) and (b).

CC-153. Refer back to problem CC-117 and write a rule for $\log (a)^m$. Then use the idea of powers of ten from problem CC-127 to argue that your rule works for any $m$ and all values of $a > 0$.

CC-154. Give a numerical example for each of the listed properties. Add this information to your Tool Kit.

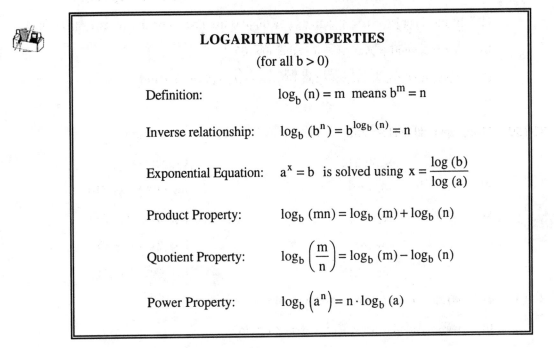

**LOGARITHM PROPERTIES**

(for all $b > 0$)

Definition: $\log_b (n) = m$ means $b^m = n$

Inverse relationship: $\log_b (b^n) = b^{\log_b (n)} = n$

Exponential Equation: $a^x = b$ is solved using $x = \dfrac{\log (b)}{\log (a)}$

Product Property: $\log_b (mn) = \log_b (m) + \log_b (n)$

Quotient Property: $\log_b \left(\dfrac{m}{n}\right) = \log_b (m) - \log_b (n)$

Power Property: $\log_b \left(a^n\right) = n \cdot \log_b (a)$

CC-155. A rule-of-thumb used by car dealers is that the trade-in value of a car decreases by 20% each year.

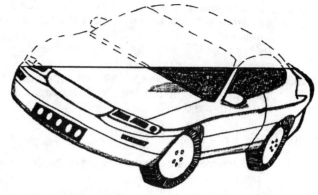

a) Explain how the phrase "decreases by 20% each year" tells you that the trade-in value varies **exponentially** with time (i.e., can be represented by an exponential function).

b) Suppose the initial value of the car is $23,500. Write an equation expressing the trade-in value of your car as a function of the number of years from the present.

c) How much is the car worth in four years?

d) In how many years will the trade-in value be $6000?

e) If the car is really 2.7 years old now, what was its trade-in value when it was new?

CC-156. Solve for x. (Do it without a calculator.)

a) $x = \log_{25}(5)$

b) $\log_x(1) = 0$

c) $23 = \log_{10}(x)$

CC-157. Solve to the nearest 0.001 on your calculator:

a) $x^6 = 125$

b) $x^{3.8} = 240$

c) $x^{-4} = 100$

d) $(x + 2)^3 = 65$

e) $4(x - 2)^{12.5} = 2486$

CC-158. Find the inverse of each of the functions below. Write your answers in function notation.

a) $p(x) = 3(x^3 + 6)$

b) $k(x) = 3x^3 + 6$

c) $h(x) = \dfrac{x + 1}{x - 1}$

d) $y = \dfrac{2}{3 - x}$

CC-159. Kirsta was working with her function machine, but when she turned her back her little brother Caleb dropped a number in. She didn't see what was dropped in, but she did see what fell out: 9. What operations must she perform on 9 to undo what her machine did? Use this to find out what Caleb dropped in.

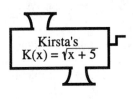

Kirsta's
$K(x) = \sqrt{x + 5}$

CC-160. Write a rule for a machine that will undo Kirsta's machine. Call it c(x).

CC-161. Is the graph at right a function? Explain.

a) Make a sketch of the inverse of this graph. Is the inverse a function? Justify your answers.

b) Must the inverse of a function be a function? Explain.

c) Describe what is characteristic about functions that do have inverse functions.

(You might want to add this to your Tool Kit.)

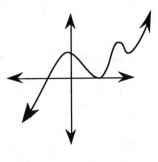

CC-162. The half-life of uranium is 1000 years. If 50 grams of uranium is sealed in a box,

a) how much is left after 10,000 years?

b) how long will it take to reduce to 1% of the original amount?

c) how long will it take until all of the original mass of uranium is gone? Support your answer.

CC-163. A two-bedroom house in Nashville is worth $110,000. If it appreciates at a rate of 2.5% each year,

a) what will it be worth in 10 years?

b) when will it be worth $200,000?

c) In Homewood, houses are depreciating at a rate of 5% each year. If a house is worth $182,500 now, how much would it be worth two years from now?

CC-164. Give an example of an equation that would require the use of logarithms to solve it.

CC-165. Consider the equation: $y = (x + 6)^2 - 7$.

    a)      Explain completely how to get a good sketch of the graph of $y = (x + 6)^2 - 7$.

    b)      Explain how to change the graph to represent the graph of $y < (x + 6)^2 - 7$.

    c)      Given the original graph, how can you get the graph of $y = |(x + 6)^2 - 7|$?

    d)      Restrict the domain of the original parabola to $x \geq -6$ and graph the inverse function.

    e)      What would be the inverse function if we restricted the domain to $x \leq -6$?

CC-166.   **TOOL KIT CLEAN-UP**

Tool Kits often need to be reorganized to continue to be useful. Your Tool Kit contains entries from units 1 through 6.

Examine the list of Tool Kit entries from this unit. Add any that you are missing.

Identify concepts that you understand and the skills you are ready to use at any time.

Choose entries to create a Unit 1 - 6 Tool Kit that is shorter, clear, and useful.

- Inverses
- Logarithm Base 2, Base 10
- Composition of Functions

- Fraction Busters for Complex Fractions
- Logarithm Notation
- Logarithm Properties

CC-167.   **UNIT 6 SUMMARY ASSIGNMENT**

    a)      Explain inverse functions. Tell everything you know about them. Use examples. Make sure you include information about graphs, tables of values, (x, y) pairs, domain and range.

    b)      Explain what a logarithm is. Be very clear and thorough, and include examples and graphs of logarithm functions.

    c)      Explain the relationship between the two main topics of this unit: inverse functions, and logarithms. (You may skip this if you already answered it in part (b).)

    d)      Show and explain, step by step, how to use logarithms to solve equations like $7 = 4^x$.

# UNIT 7

## At the County Fair
### POLYNOMIALS AND GENERAL SYSTEMS

# Unit 7 Objectives
## At the County Fair: POLYNOMIALS AND GENERAL SYSTEMS

In this unit you will investigate polynomial functions beyond linear and quadratic functions. You will go back to looking at where a curve intersects the line $y = 0$. Then you will investigate what happens when there are no real numbers to make a polynomial equal zero. This work leads to the introduction of imaginary numbers.

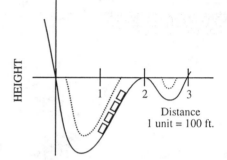

In this unit you will have the opportunity to:

- explore polynomial equations and their graphs.

- find intersections of non-linear functions and other equations both graphically and algebraically.

- discover that some systems of equations cannot be solved algebraically. Their solutions can only be approximated by graphing and estimating.

- learn that other equations which, at first glance, could not be solved can be solved when we expand the set of numbers we can use.

- expand your thinking in order to work with numbers composed of real and imaginary parts.

- summarize the important ideas from the course.

Keep a graphing calculator handy—you will be surprised at how useful, even necessary, it will be in solving many of these problems, especially equations that cannot be solved using algebraic methods.

---

CF-0. **THE GAME TANK** The Mathamericaland Carnival Company wants to make a special game to premiere at this year's county fair. The game will consist of a tank filled with ping pong balls. Most are ordinary white ones, but there are a limited number of orange, red, blue, and green prize ping pong balls. The blue ones have a prize value of $2; the reds, $5; the orange ones, $20; and the green ping pong ball (there's only one!) is worth $1000. There are 1000 blue ping pong balls, 500 red ones, and 100 orange ones. Fairgoers will pay $1 for the opportunity to crawl around in the tank while blindfolded for a set amount of time, trying to find one of the colored ping pong balls.

The owner of the company thinks that she will make the most profit if the tank has maximum volume. In order to cut down on the costs of building this new game, she hires you to find out what shape to make the tank.

---

PROBLEM SOLVING
REPRESENTATION/MODELING
FUNCTIONS/GRAPHING
INTERSECTIONS/SYSTEMS
ALGORITHMS
REASONING/COMMUNICATION

# Unit 7

*At the County Fair*: **POLYNOMIALS AND GENERAL SYSTEMS**

## INTRODUCTORY TOPICS

CF-1.　Solve each of the following for x:

a)　$(x - 1) = 0$　　　b)　$(x - 1)(x + 1) = 0$　　c)　$(x - 1)^2 = 0$

CF-2.　Sketch a graph of each of the following functions and indicate where each intersects the x-axis:

a)　$y = (x - 1)$　　　b)　$y = (x - 1)(x + 1)$　　c)　$y = (x - 1)^2$

CF-3.

> By this time in the course, we hope you have realized that the two previous problems are basically asking for the same thing. In the Parabola Lab, you discovered how to make a parabola "sit" on the x-axis, and you also looked at ways of making parabolas intersect the x-axis in two specific places. These x-intercepts for the graph of the function are often called the **ROOTS of the function** and sometimes can be found by factoring. Another name for roots of the function is **ZEROS of the function** because at the root or x-intercept, the value of the function is zero. Add **roots** and **zeros** to your Tool Kit.

CF-4.　Find the **roots** of each of the following functions:

a)　$y = x^2 - 6x + 8$　　b)　$f(x) = x^2 - 6x + 9$　　c)　$y = x^3 - 4x$

CF-5.　For the equations in this problem, make tables from -2 to 2 and draw the graph.

a)　$y = (x - 1)^2(x + 1)$　　　　　b)　$y = (x - 1)^2(x + 1)^2$

c)　$y = x^3 - 4x$　　　　　　　　d)　Do we have the parent graphs for these equations in the Parent Graph Tool Kit?

The algebraic expressions in the previous problem are called **POLYNOMIALS.** Polynomials are expressions that can be written as a sum of terms of the form: (any number)$\cdot x^{(\text{whole number})}$. The highest power of x in any of these terms is called the **DEGREE** of the polynomial, and the terms are usually arranged with the powers of x in order, starting with the highest, left to right. The numbers which multiply the powers of x are called the **COEFFICIENTS** of the polynomial.

| These are polynomial functions | These are not polynomial functions |
|---|---|
| a) $f(x) = 8x^5 + x^2 + 6.5x^4 + 6$ | d) $y = 2^x + 8$ |
| b) $y = \frac{3}{5}x^6 + 19x^2$ | e) $f(x) = 9 + \sqrt{x} - 3$ |
| c) $P(x) = 7(x - 3)(x + 5)^2$ | f) $y = x^2 + \dfrac{1}{x^2 + 5}$ |

The general equation of a second degree (quadratic) polynomial is often written: $ax^2 + bx + c$. The general equation of a third degree (cubic) polynomial is often written: $ax^3 + bx^2 + cx + d$.

If the polynomial has degree n, we do not know how many letters we will need for the coefficients, so we use subscripts: $(a_n)x^n + (a_{n-1})x^{(n-1)} + \ldots + (a_1)x^1 + a_0$

This general polynomial has degree n and coefficients $a_n, a_{n-1}, \ldots, a_1, a_0$. For example:

in $7x^4 - 5x^3 + 3x^2 + 7x + 8$, n = 4, therefore . . .

$a_n = a_4 = 7$,     $a_{n-1} = a_3 = -5$,     $a_{n-2} = a_2 = 3$,     $a_1 = 7$   &   $a_0 = 8$

a) What is the degree of example (a) in the box above? example (b)? example (c)?

b) Why are (d), (e) and (f) <u>not</u> polynomial functions?

c) Find the degree and identify the coefficients $a_0$ through $a_n$ for the polynomial in part (a) of the preceding problem. You need to do a subproblem to be able to answer this question.

CF-7. Describe the possible numbers of intersections for each of the following pairs of graphs. Sketch a graph for each possibility. For example, in part (b), a parabola could intersect a line twice, once, or not at all. Your solution to each part should include all of the possibilities and a sketched example of each one.

a) Two different lines.

b) A line and a parabola.

c) Two different parabolas.

d) A parabola and a circle.

CF-8.    Solve the following system:          $y = x^2 - 5$
                                              $y = x + 1$


CF-9.    How did you solve the previous problem?  If you did not use algebra, try to solve the
         system algebraically.  Show your work or explain why it cannot be solved that way.


CF-10.   Describe the difference between the graphs of $y = x^3 - x$  and  $y = x^3 - x + 5$.


CF-11.   Artemus was putting up the sign at the
         County Fair Theater for the movie "ELVIS
         RETURNS FROM MARS."  He got all of
         the letters he would need and put them in a
         box.  He reached into the box and pulled
         out a letter at random.

         a)    What is the probability that he got the first letter he needed when he reached
               into the box?

         b)    Once he put the first letter up, what is the probability that he got the second
               letter he needed when he reached into the box?


CF-12.   Which of the following equations are polynomial functions?  For each one that is not,
         give a brief justification as to why it is not.

         a)    $y = 3x^3 + 2x^2 + x$                    b)    $y = (x - 1)^2(x - 2)^2$

         c)    $y = x^2 + 2^x$                          d)    $y = 3x - 1$

         e)    $y = (x - 2)^2 - 1$                      f)    $y^2 = (x - 2)^2 - 1$

         g)    $y = \dfrac{1}{x^2} + \dfrac{1}{x} + \dfrac{1}{2}$         h)    $y = \dfrac{1}{2}x + \dfrac{1}{3}$


CF-13.   Sam thinks that the equation  $(x - 4)^2 + (y - 3)^2 = 25$  is equivalent to the equation
         $(x - 4) + (y - 3) = 5$, because you can just take the square root of both sides of the first
         equation. Are the two equations equivalent?  Explain why or why not.


CF-14.   Solve the equations below (remember "fraction busters").

         a)    $\dfrac{3x}{x + 2} + \dfrac{7}{x - 2} = 3$                    b)    $\dfrac{x - 7}{x - 5} - \dfrac{6}{x} = 1$

CF-15.    An arithmetic sequence starts out   -23, -19, -15, . . .

a)    What is the rule?

b)    How many times must the generator be applied so that the result is greater than 10,000?


## POLYNOMIAL FUNCTIONS LAB

CF-16.    **Polynomial Functions Lab (CF-16 & CF-17)**  We are going to be doing an investigation of polynomial functions, but first we will do one example as a class. The example function we will work with is  $P_1(x) = (x - 2)(x + 5)^2$.

a)    Graph the function on a graphing calculator using the standard viewing window.

b)    As you can see, we do not get the best view of the function in the standard window. We will use the zoom features of the graphing calculator to obtain a better view of the graph. What should we be looking for when we zoom?  Start by zooming out. You may have to do this more than once to get the complete graph. Next use the box feature to select the portion of the graph which you would like to view. Sketch this graph on the second set of axes. It helps to label the important points of the graph such as the intercepts.

c)    Find the roots.

d)    On the number line mark the roots with open circles and then shade the regions where the function outputs are positive (the graph is above the x-axis).

e)    Describe the graph and its relation to the equation. Make sure that you include the degree and the intercepts as part of your description. Pay close attention to the way the function curves.


CF-17.    Use the approach you used for  $P_1(x)$  to investigate the following five polynomials.

a)    $P_2(x) = 2(x - 2)(x + 2)(x - 3)$        b)    $P_3(x) = 0.2x(x + 1)(x - 3)(x + 4)$

c)    $P_4(x) = (x + 3)^2(x + 1)(x - 5)$        d)    $P_5(x) = -0.1x(x + 4)^3$

e)    $P_6(x) = x^4 - x^2$


CF-18.    Sketch a graph of  $y = x^2 - 7$.

a)    How many roots does this graph have?

b)    What are the roots of the function?

CF-19.    Solve: $x^2 + 2x - 5 = 0$.

a)    How many x-intercepts does $y = x^2 + 2x - 5$ have?

b)    What are they?

c)    Approximately where does the graph of $y = x^2 + 2x - 5$ cross the x-axis?


CF-20.    Are parabolas polynomial functions? Are lines polynomial functions? Are cubics? Exponentials? Circles? In all cases, explain why or why not.


CF-21.    **The County Fair Ferris Wheel**

Consider this picture of a Ferris Wheel. The Wheel has a 60' diameter and is drawn on a set of axes with the Ferris Wheel's hub at the origin. Use a table like the one below and draw a graph that relates the angle (in standard position) of the spoke leading to your seat to the approximate height of the top of your seat above or below the height of the central hub. The table below starts at -90°, your starting position before you ride around the wheel.

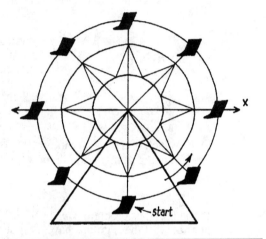

| x, the angle measure | -90° | -45° | 0° | 45° | 90° | 135° | 180° | .... | 270° |
|---|---|---|---|---|---|---|---|---|---|
| y, the height | -30' | -21.2' | 0' | | | | | | |

a)    The wheel goes around (counter-clockwise) several times during a ride. How could you reflect this fact in your graph? Update your graph.

b)    What is the maximum distance above or below the center that the top of your seat attains during the ride?


CF-22.    Graph the inequality $x^2 + y^2 \le 25$, then describe its graph in words.


CF-23.    Find x if $2^{p(x)} = 4$ where $p(x) = x^2 - 4x - 3$.


CF-24.    Start with the graph of $y = 3^x$, then write new equations that will shift the graph:

a)    down 4 units.                b)    to the right 7 units.

CF-25. Look back at the work you did on the **Polynomial Functions Lab.** Then answer the following questions.

    a) What is the maximum number of roots a polynomial of degree 3 can have? Sketch an example.

    b) What do you think is the maximum number of roots a polynomial of degree n can have?

    c) Can a polynomial of degree n have fewer than n roots? Under what conditions?

    d) For each function below, state the minimum degree its polynomial equation could have.

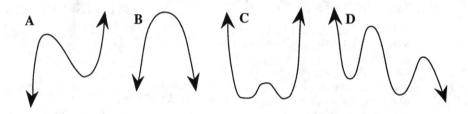

    e) Which of the graphs above have a negative orientation? (They are opposite of their parent graphs.) Explain how you determine the orientation of a graph.

CF-26. In the previous problem, we specified how to find the minimum degree. It may be possible that these graphs have a higher degree.

Look at the graphs of $y = x^2$ and $y = x^4$.

    a) How are these graphs similar? How are they different?

    b) Could graph **B** (previous problem) have degree 4?

    c) Could it have degree 5? Explain.

CF-27. In the first example from the **Polynomial Functions Lab** $(x + 5)^2$ is a factor. This produces what is called a **double root.**

    a) What effect does this have on the graph?

    b) In $P_5(x)$ (problem CF-17, part (d)) there is a **triple root.** What does the equation have that lets us know it has a "triple root?"

    c) What does this do to the graph?

CF-28. The following number lines show where the output values of each polynomial function (a), (b), (c), and (d) are positive, that is, where the graph is above the x-axis. Sketch a possible graph to fit each description. Note: each number line represents a different polynomial.

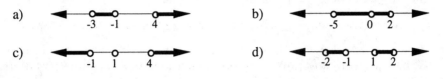

a)  -3  -1  4

b)  -5  0  2

c)  -1  1  4

d)  -2  -1  1  2

CF-29. Without using a graphing calculator, sketch rough graphs of the following functions. Refer to your Polynomial Functions Lab.

a)  $P(x) = -x(x + 1)(x - 3)$

b)  $P(x) = (x - 1)^2(x + 2)(x - 4)$

c)  $P(x) = (x + 2)^3(x - 4)$

CF-30. Where does the graph $y = (x + 3)^2 - 5$ cross the x-axis?

CF-31. If you were to graph the function $f(x) = (x - 74)^2(x + 29)$, where would the graph of $f(x)$ intersect the x-axis?

CF-32. What is the degree of each of these polynomial functions?

a)  $P(x) = 0.08x^2 + 28x$

b)  $y = 8x^2 - \frac{1}{7}x^5 + 9$

c)  $f(x) = 5(x + 3)(x - 2)(x + 7)$

d)  $y = (x - 3)^2(x + 1)(x^3 + 1)$

CF-33. A sequence of pentagonal numbers is started at right.

a)  Find the next 3 pentagonal numbers.

b)  What kind of a sequence is formed by the pentagonal numbers?

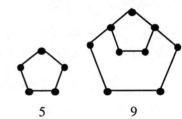

1        5        9

c)  What is the equation for the nth pentagonal number?

CF-34.    A circle with its center on the line $y = 3x$ (1st quadrant) is tangent to the y-axis.

a)    If the radius is 2, what is the equation of the circle?

b)    If the radius is 3, what is the equation of the circle?

CF-35.    A contractor working for the county failed to complete the new County Fair Pavilion within a specified time. According to his contract, he is compelled to forfeit $10,000 a day for the first ten days of extra time required, and for each additional day, beginning with the eleventh, the forfeit is increased by $1000 a day. If he lost a total of $255,000, how many days did he overrun the stipulated completion date? What kind of sequence do his fines form starting after the tenth day?

CF-36.    Sketch the graph of each function below on the same set of axes.

a)    $y = 2^x$              b)    $y = 2^x + 5$              c)    $y = 2^x - 5$

# NON-LINEAR SYSTEMS

CF-37.    Consider the equation $2^x = x + 3$.

a)    Discuss in your team methods you could try to solve this equation. How many different ways can you think of?

b)    Solve the equation.

c)    Be sure you found two solutions. How can you be certain there are no more than two?

CF-38.    When solving systems of equations, it is important to recall the significance of the solution. What does the solution represent in terms of:

a)    The equations?                    b)    The graphs of the equations?

CF-39.    Consider the following system:                    $y = 2^x + 1$
                                                                              $y = x + 6$

a)    What kind of equation is $y = 2^x + 1$?

b)    What kind of equation is $y = x + 6$?

c)    In how many points might a linear graph and an exponential graph intersect? Must they intersect? (This will tell us how many solutions we can expect.)

d)    Solve the system by any method that your team discussed for the previous problem.

CF-40.    Cindy needs to graph $y = \log_2 x$ and wants to use her graphing calculator. She figures that she can change the equation into exponential form by converting both sides to base 10, and then re-solving for y. Here is what she did:

$$y = \log_2 x$$

$$2^y = x$$

$$(10^{\log 2})^y = 10^{\log x} \qquad \text{(Remember that this is now log base 10.)}$$

$$y \cdot \log (2) = \log (x)$$

$$y = \frac{\log (x)}{\log (2)}$$

a)    Will this work for any base? Show the method for $y = \log_7 x$.

b)    How would you change $y = \log_3 (x + 5)$ to be able to graph it on a graphing calculator?

c)    How would you change $y = \log_2 x - 3$ to be able to graph it on a graphing calculator?


CF-41.    Find where the graphs of $y = \log_2 (x - 1)$ and $y = x^3 - 4x$ intersect.


CF-42.    Solve $\log_2 (x - 1) = x^3 - 4x$.


CF-43.    The systems that you have been solving today are non-linear systems.

a)    What does "non-linear" mean?

Some non-linear systems may be **impossible** to solve algebraically; others may just be extremely difficult.

b)    What other methods do we have to solve these systems?


CF-44.    Sketch a graph of the equation $y = x^2 + 4$.

a)    Where does the graph cross the x-axis?

b)    Solve the equation $x^2 + 4 = 0$ and explain how this relates to the answer you found in part (a).

c)    What occurred when you tried to solve the equation in part (b) that let you know that it has no real solution?

**CF-45.**

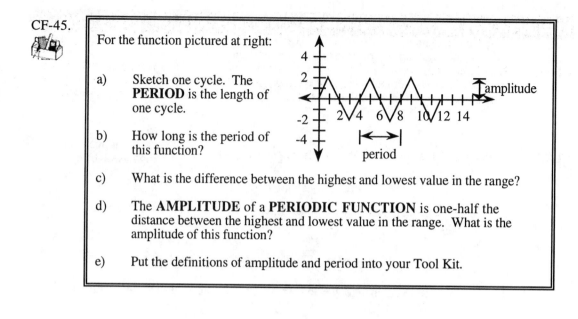

For the function pictured at right:

a) Sketch one cycle. The **PERIOD** is the length of one cycle.

b) How long is the period of this function?

c) What is the difference between the highest and lowest value in the range?

d) The **AMPLITUDE** of a **PERIODIC FUNCTION** is one-half the distance between the highest and lowest value in the range. What is the amplitude of this function?

e) Put the definitions of amplitude and period into your Tool Kit.

**CF-46.** Sketch the graphs and find the area of the intersection of:

$$y > |x + 3|$$
$$y \leq 5$$

**CF-47.** Determine if $x = -2$ is a solution to the equation $x^4 - 4x = 8x^2 - 40$. Show why or why not.

**CF-48.**

A circle with a radius equal to 1 is called a **UNIT CIRCLE**.

a) Draw a sketch of a unit circle centered at the origin. What is the equation of the circle?

b) What is the area of the circle?

c) What is the circumference of the circle?

**CF-49.** Solve the following equation for $x$:

a) $\dfrac{x + 3}{x - 1} - \dfrac{x}{x + 1} = \dfrac{8}{x^2 - 1}$

b) In part (a) the result of solving the equation is $x = 1$, but what happens when you substitute 1 for $x$? What does this mean in relation to solutions for this equation?

CF-50. Sketch the circle $(x + 2)^2 + (y + 1)^2 = 9$ and the line $y = x + 4$ on the same set of axes. Find and clearly label the point(s) of intersection of the line and the circle. You may use your graph to estimate the solutions but show how to find the solutions algebraically.

CF-51. Sketch the circle $x^2 + y^2 = 25$, and the parabola $y = x^2 - 13$.

a) How many points of intersection are there for this parabola and the circle?

b) Find the coordinates of these points algebraically. Remember that the key to solving systems is to eliminate a variable.

c) Explain how the graph helps you with the algebraic solution.

CF-52. Solve this system of equations, and explain your method: $(x - 1)^2 + y^2 = 16$
$$y = 2^x$$

CF-53. Solve this system of equations. Be sure to sketch the graphs on your paper.
$$(x - 2)^2 + y^2 = 25$$
$$y = x^3 - 9x$$

a) How many solutions does this system have? Are you sure?

b) Zoom in or set up a new range with x-values close to -3, and y-values a little greater than zero. Now what do you think?

CF-54. Verify that the graphs of the equations $x^2 + y^3 = 17$ and $x^4 - 4y^2 - 8xy = 17$ intersect at (3, 2). Then:

a) give an equation of the vertical line through this point.

b) give an equation of the horizontal line through this point.

CF-55.    The equation for the circle at right is $x^2 + y^2 = 1$.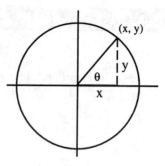

a)    What is the radius of the circle?

In terms of the labels on the graph, what is:

b)    sin (θ)?

c)    cos (θ)?

d)    [sin (θ)]² + [cos (θ)]² = ?

CF-56.    Each year the Strongberg Construction company builds twenty more houses than in the previous year. Last year they built 180 homes. Acme Homes business is increasing by 15% each year and they built 80 homes last year.

a)    Assuming that you don't have a graphing calculator with you now, what can you do to solve this problem with just a scientific calculator?

b)    Write equations for each construction company and find the year in which both construction companies will build the same number of homes.

CF-57.    Each of the dart boards below is a target at the County Fair dart throwing game. What is the probability of hitting the **shaded** region of each target? Assume you always hit the board but the location on the board is random.

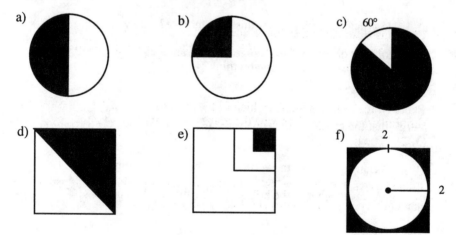

CF-58.    Use the graph at right to answer the questions below.

a)    What is the **amplitude** of this function?

b)    What is the **period** of this cyclic function?

c)    How many **cycles** are represented on this graph?

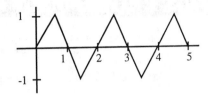

CF-59.    A general equation is an equation that can be used to describe a group of equations or functions with similar characteristics (sometimes called a **family of equations** or **family of functions**). For example, circles with centers at (-3, 5) can be written as $(x + 3)^2 + (y - 5)^2 = k^2$. Here k can be any positive number. Find the general equation for each of the following and sketch a couple of examples of each type.

a)    Lines parallel to  y = 6x - 7.

b)    All parabolas with a vertex at (4, 3).

c)    All parabolas with roots of 2 and -5.

CF-60.    Choosing your own values for k, sketch on the same set of axes five different examples of graphs which fit the equation: $(x - 3)^2 + (y - 5)^2 = k$. Then describe the graphs in words.

CF-61.    Choosing different values for  k  and  j, sketch three different examples of graphs which fit the equation  $(x - k)^2 + (y - j)^2 = 9$. Then describe the graphs in words.

CF-62.    Sketch three different graphs which fit the equation: $(x - d)^2 + (y - 5)^2 = 16$  by choosing different values of  d.  Describe the graphs in words.

CF-63.    Julianna says that $\dfrac{a}{x + b} = \dfrac{a}{x} + \dfrac{a}{b}$. Fred is not sure; he thinks that the two expressions are not equivalent. Who is correct?  Justify your answer.

CF-64.    The area of $\triangle ABC$ is 24 square inches. If $\overline{AB} \perp \overline{BC}$  and BC = 8 in., find  AC.

# INTRODUCTION TO COMPLEX NUMBERS
# (WHEN GRAPHS DO NOT INTERSECT)

CF-65.    Consider the graphs whose equations are $y = x^2$ and $y = 2x - 5$.

   a)    Use algebra to find the intersection of the graphs.

   b)    Sketch the graphs and label the intersection.


CF-66.    Discuss the previous problem with your team. What happened when you tried to solve the system algebraically?


CF-67.    Solve: $x^2 = 3$.

---

### COUNTY FAIR INFORMATION BOOTH: HISTORICAL NOTE

In Ancient Greece, people believed that all numbers could be written as fractions of whole numbers (what we call rational numbers). Many individuals realized later that some numbers could not be written as fractions (such as the result you just calculated) and challenged the accepted beliefs. Some of these people were exiled or outright killed over these challenges. As you can see, the Greeks took their mathematics very seriously. It was known that for a one unit square, the length of the diagonal, squared, yielded 2; when it was shown that no rational number could do that, they accepted the existence of what we call irrational numbers, and invented symbols like $\sqrt{2}$ to represent them. The problem above also has no rational solutions; fractions can never work exactly. The rational (i.e., decimal) solutions that calculators and computers provide are only approximations; the exact answer can only be represented in radical form.

---

   a)    How do you "undo" squaring a number?

   b)    When you solved $x^2 = 2$, how many solutions did you get?

   c)    How many x-intercepts will $y = x^2 - 2$ have?

   d)    Write your solutions both as radicals and as decimal approximations.

CF-68.   Mathematicians throughout history have resisted the
notion that some equations were not solvable.  Still,
it made sense that $x^2 + 1 = 0$ was not solvable,
because the graph of $y = x^2 + 1$ has no
x-intercepts.

a)   What happens if we try to solve $x^2 + 1 = 0$?

In some ways, each person's math education parallels the history of mathematical
discovery.  When you were much younger, if you were asked, "How many times does 3
go into 8?" or "What is 8 divided by 3?" you might have said, "3 doesn't go into 8."
Then you learned about numbers other than whole numbers, and the question had an
answer.  Of course, in some situations you are only interested in whole numbers, and
then the first answer is still the right one.  Later, if you were asked "what number squared
makes 5" you might have said "no number squared makes 5".  Then you learned about
numbers other than rational numbers, and you could answer that question.

Similarly, until about 500 years ago, the answer to the question "what number squared
makes -1" was "no number squared makes -1."  Then something remarkable happened.
An Italian mathematician named Bombelli used a formula for finding the roots of third
degree polynomials.  Within the formula was a square root, and when he applied the
formula to a particular equation the number under the square root came out negative.
Instead of giving up, he got a brilliant idea.  He knew the equation had a solution, so he
decided to see what would happen if he pretended that there *was* a number you could
square to make a negative.  Remarkably, he was able to continue the calculation, and
eventually the "imaginary" number disappeared from the solution.  More importantly the
resulting answer worked; it solved the equation he had begun with.  This led to the
acceptance of these so-called imaginary numbers, though the name stuck, and
mathematicians came to believe that equations like the one above do have solutions.  Of
course, in some situations we are only interested in real numbers (that is to say not having
an "imaginary" part) and then the original answer, that there is no solution, is still the
right one.

---

**COUNTY FAIR INFORMATION BOOTH: DEFINITIONS**

The set of numbers that solve equations of the form $x^2 =$ (a negative number) are
called **IMAGINARY NUMBERS**.  They are not positive, negative, or zero.
The collection (set) of positive and negative numbers (integers, rational numbers
(fractions), and irrational numbers), along with 0, are referred to as the **REAL
NUMBERS**.  In particular, the imaginary number that solves the equation
$x^2 = -1$ is named **i**, so $i^2 = -1$.  In general, **i** follows the rules of real number
arithmetic (e.g. $i + i = 2i$).  The sum of two imaginary numbers is imaginary
(unless it $= 0$); the same is true of the product of a real number and an imaginary
number.  In fact, multiplying the imaginary number **i** by every possible real
number yields all the imaginary numbers.  Record this information in your Tool
Kit.

---

b)   If we let $i = \sqrt{-1}$, and we define $i^2 = -1$, then what would be the value of
$\sqrt{-16} = \sqrt{16i^2} = ?$

CF-69.    Use the definition of **i** to show that:

a)    $\sqrt{-4} = 2i$

b)    $(2i)(3i) = -6$

c)    $(2i)^2(-5i) = 20i$

d)    $\sqrt{-25} = 5i$


CF-70.    Consider the function $y = x^2 - 4x + 5$. Its graph does not cross the x-axis, so the equation $x^2 - 4x + 5 = 0$ has no real solutions. Show that applying the quadratic formula to this equation yields the solutions $x = 2 + i$ and $x = 2 - i$. Check one of these solutions by substituting it for x and simplifying the result.

> The sum of a real number and an imaginary number, such as $2 + i$, is neither real nor imaginary. Numbers such as these, which can be written in the form $a + bi$, where $a$ and $b$ are real numbers, are called **COMPLEX NUMBERS**. These numbers constitute all of the "non-real" numbers. Each complex number has a real component, $a$, and an imaginary component, $bi$. Note that according to this definition, the real numbers are also complex numbers; they are the ones with a 0 imaginary part. Record this definition in your Tool Kit.

CF-71.

> If all the numbers on the number line are real numbers, where are the complex numbers located? The real and imaginary parts are independent, so the complex numbers are a two-dimensional number system. To represent them, we need a plane. Real numbers are on the horizontal axis and imaginary numbers are on the vertical axis. Complex numbers are graphed using the same method that coordinate points are: the number $2 + 3i$ is located at $(2, 3)$, the number i or $0 + 1i$ is located at $(0, 1)$.
> The number -2 or $-2 + 0i$ is located at $(-2, 0)$. This representation is called the **COMPLEX PLANE.** Enter this into your tool kit and include an example of how to graph complex numbers.

CF-72.    In solving the system at right, we need to solve the equation $x^2 = 2x - 5$. Use the Quadratic Formula to find a solution which includes **i**.

$y = x^2$
$y = 2x - 5$


CF-73.    Simplify the following (write in $a + bi$ form):

a)    $-18 - \sqrt{-25}$

b)    $\dfrac{2 \pm \sqrt{-16}}{2}$

c)    $5 + \sqrt{-6}$

CF-74. Explain why $i^3 = -i$. What does $i^4 = ?$

CF-75. Solve for x: $16^{(x+2)} = 8^x$.

CF-76. Is $(x - 5)^2$ equivalent to $(5 - x)^2$? Explain briefly.

CF-77. Evaluate each of the following:

i) $(\sqrt{7})^2$        ii) $(\sqrt{18.3})^2$        iii) $(\sqrt{d})^2$

a) Using what you observed above, evaluate: $(\sqrt{-1})^2$

b) What does $i^2 = ?$

c) Is this consistent with part (a)?

CF-78. Calculate each of the following:

a) $\sqrt{-49}$        b) $\sqrt{-2}$

c) $(4i)^2$        d) $(3i)^3$

CF-79. A function $g(x)$ that "undoes" what another function $f(x)$ does is called its inverse. In the last unit, for example, we saw that $\log_2 x$ is the inverse of $2^x$. We often use a special notation for this relationship and, instead of giving the inverse function a different name, such as $g(x)$, write $f^{-1}(x)$ (read " f inverse of x"). In other words, whatever f does to x, $f^{-1}$ undoes.

a) If $f(x) = 2x - 3$, then $f^{-1}(x) = ?$        b) If $h(x) = (x - 3)^2 + 2$, then $h^{-1}(x) = ?$

CF-80. Consider a circle located at the origin with a radius of 5.

a) If you make a quick sketch of this graph, how many points on the graph do you know are accurate? Explain.

b) Find other points which will satisfy the equation $x^2 + y^2 = 25$. To get you started, consider (-4, 3). Look for a total of 12 points with integer coordinates.

CF-81.     When a graph crosses the x-axis, these x-values are sometimes referred to as the **roots** of the equation ( in other words, when $y = 0$). We have seen that solutions to equations can be real or complex, so it must be possible for **roots** be either real or complex.

a)    Sketch the graph of $y = (x + 3)^2 - 4$. What are the roots?

b)    Sketch the graph of $y = (x + 3)^2$. What are the roots?

c)    Sketch the graph of $y = (x + 3)^2 + 4$. Find the roots by solving $(x + 3)^2 + 4 = 0$. Where does the graph cross the x-axis?

CF-82.     Show by purely algebraic methods that the graphs of $y = \frac{1}{x}$ and $y = -x + 1$ do not intersect. What are the complex solutions? Check the graphs on a graphing calculator.

CF-83.     Find the roots of each of the following quadratic functions by solving for x when $y = 0$. Do any of the graphs of these functions intersect the x-axis?

a)    $y = (x + 5)^2 + 9$.

b)    $y = (x - 7)^2 + 4$.

c)    $y = (x - 2)^2 + 5$.

CF-84.     What do you notice about the complex solutions of the equations in the previous problem? Describe any patterns you see. Discuss these with your team and write down everything you can think of.

CF-85.     Look for patterns as you find the products for parts (a) through (d). Then use your pattern to answer parts (e) and (f).

a)    $(2 - \mathbf{i})(2 + \mathbf{i})$

b)    $(3 - 5\mathbf{i})(3 + 5\mathbf{i})$

c)    $(4 - \mathbf{i})(4 + \mathbf{i})$

d)    $(7 - 2\mathbf{i})(7 + 2\mathbf{i})$

e)    Find a complex number by which you can multiply $(3 + 2\mathbf{i})$ to get a real number.

f)    Find a complex number by which you can multiply $(a + b\mathbf{i})$ to get a real number.

CF-86.

The complex numbers 2 - **3i** and 2 + **3i** are called **COMPLEX CONJUGATES**. What is the complex conjugate of:

a)    4 + i?

b)    2 + 7i?

c)    3 - 5i?

Put examples of complex conjugates in your Tool Kit. Explain what happens when you multiply them and when you add them.

CF-87. If $f(x) = x^2 + 7x - 9$, calculate:

a)    f(-3)

b)    f(**i**)

c)    f(-3 + **i**)

CF-88. Verify that 5 + 2**i** is a solution to $x^2 - 10x = -29$.

CF-89. Another useful tool in finding some inverse functions is a table. When the formula has only one x in it we can describe it with a sequence of operations, each applied to the previous result. Consider the following table for $f(x) = 2\sqrt{x - 1} + 3$:

|  | 1st | 2nd | 3rd | 4th |
|---|---|---|---|---|
| what f does to x: | subtr. 1 | $\sqrt{\ }$ | mult. by 2 | adds 3 |

Since the inverse must undo these operations, in the opposite order, the table for $f^{-1}(x)$ would look like:

|  | 1st | 2nd | 3rd | 4th |
|---|---|---|---|---|
| what $f^{-1}$ does to x: | subtr. 3 | div. by 2 | $(\ )^2$ | adds 1 |

a)    Copy and complete the following table for $g^{-1}(x)$ if $g(x) = \frac{1}{3}(x + 1)^2 - 2$:

|  | 1st | 2nd | 3rd | 4th |
|---|---|---|---|---|
| what g does to x: | adds 1 | $(\ )^2$ | div. by 3 | subtr. 2 |
| what $g^{-1}$ does to x: |  |  |  |  |

b)    Write the equations for $f^{-1}(x)$ and $g^{-1}(x)$.

CF-90.   Consider the following graph:

a)   What is the parent for this function?

b)   What are the coordinates of the locator point?

c)   Write an equation for this graph.

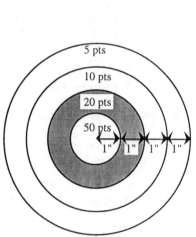

CF-91.   In one of the games at the County Fair, people pay to shoot a paint pistol at the target shown at right. The center has a radius of one inch. Each concentric circle has a radius one inch larger than the preceding circle. Assuming the paint pellet hits the target randomly, what is the probability it hits:

a)   the 50 point ring?

b)   the 20 point ring?

CF-92.   Kahlid is going to make a table to graph $y = \sqrt{x^2}$ but Aaron says that it would be a waste of time to make a table because the graph is the same as y = x.

a)   Use Kahlid's equation to make the table and draw the graph.

b)   As you can see, Aaron was wrong, but you did get a graph that you have seen before. What other equation has the same graph? Explain why this is reasonable.

# FINDING THE EQUATIONS OF POLYNOMIAL FUNCTIONS

CF-93.   Find reasonable equations for each of the following polynomial functions:

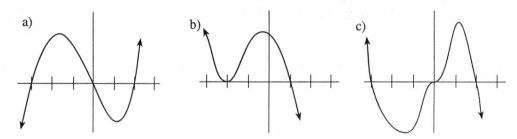

a)     b)     c)

**CF-94.** What is the difference between the graphs of the functions $y = x^2(x - 3)(x + 1)$ and $y = 3x^2(x - 3)(x + 1)$?

**CF-95.** Find a possible equation for the graph at right:

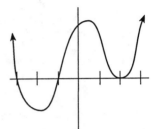

a) If the equation were multiplied by 5, how would that alter the graph?

b) The polynomial for this graph can be written as $P(x) = a(x + 3)(x + 1)(x - 2)^2$. Find the value of $a$ if you know that the graph goes through the point $(1, 16)$.

**CF-96.** **The County Fair Coaster Ride**

The Mathamericaland Carnival Company has decided to build a new roller coaster to use at this year's county fair. The new coaster will have the special feature that part of the ride will be underground. The designers will use polynomial functions to describe various sections of the track. Part of the design is shown below:

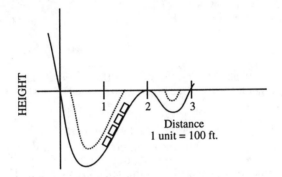

The numbers along the x-axis are in hundreds of feet. At 250 feet, the track will be 20 feet below the surface. This will give the point (2.5, -0.2).

a) What degree polynomial is demonstrated by the graph?

b) What are the roots?

c) Find an exact equation of the polynomial that will generate this curve.

d) Find the deepest point of the tunnel.

CF-97.    Write an exact equation for each of the following graphs.

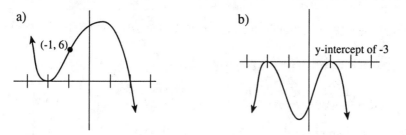

a)

(-1, 6)

b)

y-intercept of -3

CF-98.    $y = \frac{1}{2}$ and $y = \frac{16}{x^2 - 4}$. Find the coordinates where the graphs of the functions intersect.

CF-99.    A circle is tangent to the lines $y = 6$, $y = -2$ and to the y-axis. What is the equation of the circle? Draw a picture!

CF-100.   Use algebra to solve the system of equations:          $y = x^2 + 5$
          Confirm your solutions by sketching the graphs.         $y = 2x$

CF-101.   You are given the equation $5x^2 + bx + 20 = 0$. For what values of b does this equation have real solutions?

CF-102.   The function $h(x)$ is defined by the operations in the following table:

| | 1st | 2nd | 3rd |
|---|---|---|---|
| what h does to x: | adds 2 | $(\ )^3$ | subtract 7 |
| what $h^{-1}$ does to x: | | | |

a)    Copy and complete the table for $h^{-1}(x)$.

b)    Write equations for $h(x)$ and $h^{-1}(x)$.

CF-103.   Find the center and radius of the following circles:

a)    $(y - 7)^2 = 25 - (x - 3)^2$          b)    $x^2 + y^2 + 10y = -9$

c)    $x^2 + y^2 + 18x - 8y + 47 = 0$          d)    $y^2 + (x - 3)^2 = 1$

CF-104.    Based of the following graphs, how many **real** roots does each polynomial function have?

Something is added to each function and each graph is translated upward resulting in the graphs below.  How many **real** roots does each of these polynomial functions have?

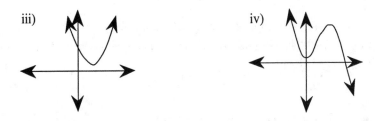

The polynomials in (iii) and (iv) do not have fewer roots.  Polynomial (iii) still has **two** roots, but now the roots are complex.  Polynomial (iv) has **three** roots: **two** are complex and only **one** is real.

CF-105.    Recall that a polynomial function with degree  n  crosses the x-axis at most  n  times. For instance,  $y = (x + 1)^2$  intersects the x-axis once, while  $y = x^2 + 1$  does not intersect it at all.  The function  $y = x^2 - 1$  intersects it twice.

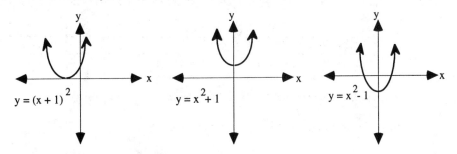

$y = (x + 1)^2$    $y = x^2 + 1$    $y = x^2 - 1$

a)    A third-degree equation might intersect the x-axis 1, 2, or 3 times.  Make sketches of all these possibilities.

b)    Why can't a third-degree equation have 0 real roots?

CF-106.    Now consider $x^3 - 3x^2 + 3x - 2 = 0$.  Since the number of different real solutions is the same as the number of points of intersection of $y = x^3 - 3x^2 + 3x - 2$ with the x-axis, how many real solutions could this have?

   a)    Check to verify that $x^3 - 3x^2 + 3x - 2 = ( x - 2 )( x^2 - x + 1 )$.  How many real solutions does $x^3 - 3x^2 + 3x - 2 = 0$ have?  How many non-real (complex)? What are all the solutions?

   b)    How many roots does $y = x^3 - 3x^2 + 3x - 2$ have?  How many real and how many non-real (complex)?  How many times does the graph intersect the x-axis?  Check it out.

CF-107.    In our example with the parabolas (problem CF-105), $(x + 1)^2 = 0$ has one real solution, and $x^2 - 1 = 0$ has two real solutions.

   a)    How many solutions of what type(s) does $x^2 + 1 = 0$ have?  Solve for x.  How does this relate to the graph of $y = x^2 + 1$?  Explain.

   b)    Consider the factors of the three polynomials:  $(x + 1)^2$, $x^2 - 1$, and $x^2 + 1$.  What is the relationship between the factorization and the number and kind of roots?

CF-108.    For each polynomial function $f(x)$, the graph of $f(x)$ is shown.  Based on this information, tell how many linear and quadratic factors the factored form of its equation should have and how many real and complex (non-real) solutions $f(x) = 0$ might have. (Assume a polynomial function of the lowest possible degree for each one.)

EXAMPLE:

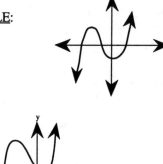

f(x) will have three real linear factors, therefore three real roots and no complex roots.

a)

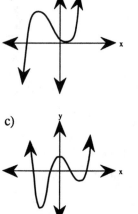

b)

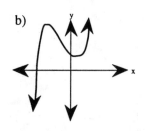

c)

d)

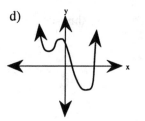

CF-109. Make a sketch of a graph $f(x)$ so that $f(x) = 0$ could have the indicated number and type of solutions.

a)   5 real solutions.

b)   3 real and 2 complex.

c)   4 complex.

d)   4 complex and 2 real.

e)   For parts (a) through (d), what is the smallest degree each function could be?

CF-110. Add some examples to your Tool Kit that illustrate the fact that the degree depends on the number of linear and quadratic factors and that the number of roots will be less than or equal to the degree of the polynomial since some factors may be repeated.

CF-111. Consider the function $y = x^3 - 9x$.

a)   What are the roots of the function? (Factoring will help!)

b)   Sketch a graph of the function.

CF-112. Which of the following equations have real roots and which have complex roots?

a)   $y = x^2 - 6$

b)   $y = x^2 + 6$

c)   $y = x^2 - 2x + 10$

d)   $y = x^2 - 2x - 10$

e)   $y = (x - 3)^2 - 4$

f)   $y = (x - 3)^2 + 4$

CF-113. Graph the following system:      $y = x^2 + 5$
$y = 2x$

a)   Refer back to your algebraic solution in problem CF-100.

b)   How does your graphical solution relate to your algebraic solution?

CF-114. Raul claims he has a shortcut for deciding what kind of roots a functions has. Jolene disagrees. She says you just have to solve the quadratic equation to find out. They are working on $y = x^2 - 5x - 14$.

Jolene says, "See, I just start out by trying to factor. This one can be factored $(x - 7)(x + 2) = 0$ so the equation will have two real solutions and the function will have two real roots."

"But what if it can't be factored?" Raul asked. "What about $x^2 + 2x + 2 = 0$?"

"That's easy, I just use the Quadratic Formula," said Jolene. "And I get,...let's see, negative two plus or minus the square root of...two squared, that's 4, minus...eight..."

"Wait!" Raul interrupted. "Right there, see, you don't have to finish. $2^2$ minus $4 \cdot 2$, that gives you -4. That's all you need to know. You'll be taking the square root of a negative number so you will get a complex result."

"Oh, I see," said Jolene. "I only have to do <u>part</u> of the solution, the part you have to take the square root of."

Use Raul's method to tell whether the each following functions has real or complex roots.

a)  $y = 2x^2 + 5x + 4$        b)  $y = 2x^2 + 5x - 3$

CF-115. Consider this geometric sequence: $i^0, i^1, i^2, i^3, i^4, i^5, ..., i^{15}$.

a)  You know that $i^0 = 1$, and $i^1 = i$, and $i^2 = -1$. Calculate the result for each term up to $i^{15}$, and organize your answers so a pattern is obvious.

b)  Use the pattern you found in part (a) to calculate $i^{396}, i^{397}, i^{398}$, and $i^{399}$.

CF-116. Use the pattern from the previous problem to help you to evaluate the following:

a)  $i^{592} =$        b)  $i^{797} =$        c)  $i^{10,648,202} =$

CF-117. Describe how you would evaluate $i^n$ where **n** could be any integer.

CF-118. The management of the Carnival Cinema was worried about breaking even on their movie ELVIS RETURNS FROM MARS. To break even they had to take in $5000 on the matinee. They were selling adult tickets for $8.50 and children's tickets for $5.00. They knew they had sold a total of 685 tickets. How many of those would have to have been adult tickets for them to meet their goal?

CF-119. Sketch graphs of each of the following polynomial functions. Be sure to label the x- and y-intercepts:

a) $y = x(2x + 5)(2x - 7)$

b) $y = (15 - 2x)^2(x + 3)$

CF-120. Multiply each of the following:

a) $(x - 3)^2$

b) $2(x + 3)^2$

c) $(a - b)(a^2 + ab + b^2)$

CF-121. Show that each of the following is true:

a) $(i - 3)^2 = 8 - 6i$

b) $(2i - 1)(3i + 1) = -7 - i$

c) $(3 - 2i)(2i + 3) = 13$

# THE GAME TANK LAB

CF-122. The Mathamericaland Carnival Company wants to make a special game to premiere at this year's county fair. The game will consist of a tank filled with ping pong balls. Most are ordinary white ones, but there are a limited number of orange, red, blue, and green prize ping pong balls. The blue ones have a prize value of $2, the red ones $5, the orange ones $20, and the green ping pong ball (there's only one) is worth $1000. There are 1000 blue ping pong balls, 500 red balls, and 100 orange balls. Fairgoers will pay $1 for the opportunity to crawl around in the tank for a set amount of time while blindfolded, trying to find one of the colored ping pong balls.

The owner of the company thinks that she will make the most profit if the tank has maximum volume. In order to cut down on the labor and materials costs of building this new game, she hires you to find out what shape to make the tank.

The tank will be rectangular, open at the top, and will be made by cutting squares out of each corner of an 8.5 meter by 11 meter sheet of specially processed, heavy-duty transparent material.

We can model this problem by using a sheet of paper. You will need to write a report with your findings to the Carnival Company. The report needs to include the following:

a)  The data and conjectures found in the experiment making the paper tanks.

b)  A well drawn diagram of the tank with the dimensions clearly labeled with appropriate variables.

c)  A graph of the volume function that you found with notes on a reasonable domain and range.

d)  An equation that matches your graph.

e)  An estimate of the number of ping pong balls that will be needed and your adjusted recommendation based on this information.

f)  Your final conclusions and observations.

The following problems (CF-123 through CF-128) will help guide you through the various aspects of the project.

CF-123. Use a full sheet of 8-1/2" x 11" paper, which is the same shape as the material for the tank (at a slightly smaller scale!). Each member of your team should cut a different size square out of each corner. Measure the side of the square you cut out and write along the edge of the large piece of paper. Use either inches or centimeters. Your paper should look like the figure at right:

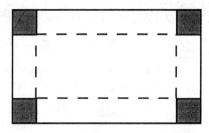

Fold the paper up into an open box (fold on the dotted lines). Then tape the cut parts together so that the box holds its shape. Measure the dimensions of the tank. Record the dimensions directly on the model tank.

CF-124. Make a table like the one below, then calculate the volume of your tank, write it on the tank, and record all of the data in your table. Next, add the data from each of the other members of your team to your table. Finally, get the data from four more students, possibly by having pairs of teams exchange data. Make sure that you consider "extreme" tanks, the ones with the largest possible cutout and the smallest possible cutout (do not actually try to build them; that would be physically impossible. You cannot cut a square that is 1/100th of an inch on a side, but you can **imagine** cutting a square out of each corner zero inches on a side.)

| Tank height | Tank width | Tank length | Tank volume |
|---|---|---|---|
|  |  |  |  |

a) Discuss with the other members of your team (experimenting if you wish) what happens if the cutouts are not square.

b) Examine the data in the table from the different sizes of cutout squares and discuss it with your team. Make some conjectures about how to find the maximum volume.

c) Label the height as x. Using x for the height, find expressions for the length and the width.

d) Find an equation for the volume of the tank.

e) Sketch the graph of your function by using the roots and determining the orientation.

CF-125. Graph the function on your calculator. Make sure you find appropriate values for the range on the graphing calculator.

a) Make a large accurate graph on graph paper with appropriate labels. Locate and label the points from your data table on the graph. (What did 'x' represent?)

b) Find the maximum for the volume and the dimensions of the tank that will generate this volume.

CF-126. Use your graph and your tank model to carefully answer the following questions.

    a)    Which points on the graph represent tanks which can actually be made? Explain.

    b)    How are the dimensions of the tank related? In other words, what happens to the length and width as the height increases?

    c)    Make a drawing of your tank. (You may want to use isometric dot paper.) Label your drawing with its dimensions and its volume.

CF-127. The carnival company decides to follow your recommendation on the dimensions of the tank and to fill the tank to a depth of 1.2 meters in order to avoid losing the ping pong balls that might bounce out. At the retail price of six for $2 the ping pong balls would cost a fortune, but the carnival owners have found a bargain on army surplus ping pong balls at $20 per case of 1000. A standard ping pong ball has a diameter of 3.7 cm (1.45 inches). Estimate the number of ping pong balls they will need and the cost.

CF-128. The company realizes that it was overly ambitious (or greedy) in planning a tank with maximum dimensions. They have only budgeted $8000 for ping pong balls. They decide to reduce the size of the tank, but keep the tank proportions the same.

    a)    Find the dimensions of the reduced tank, if the new height is 1.2 meters.

    b)    The company decides that it will only fill the new tank to a level 0.4 meters below the top, to keep the balls from bouncing out. Can they fill the new tank with ping pong balls to a level of 0.8 meters for under $8000?

    c)    Based on your scaled down tank, what is the probability of winning a prize?

CF-129. A polynomial function has the equation: $P(x) = x(x - 3)^2(2x + 1)$. What are the x-intercepts?

CF-130. Sketch a graph of a fourth-degree polynomial that has no real roots.

CF-131. In this unit you have learned that the roots of a polynomial correspond to its linear factors; for each root $x = a$ there is a factor $(x - a)$ and vice versa. This makes sense to Elijah, but one day he found himself puzzled.

"Can you factor $x^2 + 4x + 1$?" he asked his friend Kelly.

"Let me see. . .two numbers that multiply to make 1 and add up to 4? Don't think so!" he said.

"But look what happens when I graph it. It crosses the x-axis in two places, so it must have two linear factors, right?"

"It should. Let's see what the roots are."

a) Find the roots of Elijah's equation as accurately as you can.

b) Using what you have learned in this unit, what should be the factors of $x^2 + 4x + 1$?

"Wow," said Kelly, "It works! There *are* two numbers that multiply to make 1 and add up to 4."

c) What are the numbers to which Kelly is referring?

In the past, when you were asked to factor, it was understood that you were only to use integers as the coefficients in your factors. This restriction meant that many expressions were unfactorable. If we allow other numbers (such as fractions and irrationals) as coefficients, many more expressions can be factored. In fact, if we allow complex numbers as coefficients, every quadratic polynomial can be factored!

Use Kelly and Elijah's method to factor the following polynomials:

d) $x^2 - 10$

e) $x^2 - 3x - 7$

f) $x^2 + 4$

g) $x^2 - 2x + 2$


CF-132. Draw a unit circle (that's a circle with radius 1) centered at the origin.

a) Find the circumference of the circle. Keep your answer in terms of $\pi$.

b) What is the length of the arc that lies in the first quadrant? Answer in terms of $\pi$.

c) What is the measure of the angle formed by the positive x- and y-axes?

d) What is the length of the arc that lies in the first and second quadrants?

e) What is the measure of the angle that forms the arc?

f) Suppose the arc has length $2\pi$. What is the measure of the angle that forms the arc?


CF-133. Sketch a graph of the following system:  $x^2 + y^2 \leq 25$
$x - 2y > 5$

CF-134. **PORTFOLIO: GROWTH OVER TIME—PROBLEM #1**

On a separate piece of paper (so you can hand it in separately or add it to your portfolio) explain **everything** that you now know about the function below. Be sure to add everything that you have learned since the last time you did this problem, and don't leave out any important information that you included in your earlier attempts.

$$f(x) = x^2 - 4 \quad \text{and} \quad g(x) = \sqrt{x + 4}.$$

CF-135. Growth Over Time Reflection. Look at your three responses to the growth-over-time problem above. Write an evaluation of your growth based your responses. Consider the following when writing your answer:

a) What new concepts did you include the second time you did the problem? In what ways was your response better than your first attempt?

b) How was your final version different from the first two? What new ideas did you include?

c) Did you omit anything in the final version that you used in one of the earlier problems? Why did you omit that item?

d) Rate your three attempts by making three bars like those below and shading each bar to represent how much you knew on each attempt.

| First Attempt: | |
| Second Attempt: | |
| Final Attempt: | |

e) Is there anything you would add to your most recent version? What would it be? Discuss this with your team.

CF-136. Consider the equation $x^2 = 2^x$. Use inspection and a graphing calculator to answer:

a) How many solutions does the equation have?

b) What are the solutions?

CF-137. A polynomial function has the equation $y = ax(x - 3)(x + 1)^2$ and goes through the point (2, 12). Use the coordinates of the point to figure out what 'a' must equal and write the specific equation.

CF-138.    **Unit 7 Summary Assignment**

Identify with your team five main topics from this unit. For each topic, rewrite or create a problem that represents the main ideas in that topic. Carefully solve and explain the solution to each of those five problems so that someone else, someone who didn't know what to do, could use these problems and solutions as example problems to help them through the unit. This should be done on a separate sheet of paper to be included with your portfolio.

CF-139.    Find the width of the river in the figure at right if AB is 33 meters.

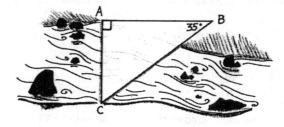

CF-140.    Verify that $x = -2 + 5i$ is a root of the quadratic function $y = x^2 + 4x + 29$.

CF-141.    Carmel picks an integer from 1 to 12 as a value for $c$ in the equation $y = x^2 + 4x + c$. What is the probability that his equation will have complex roots?

CF-142.    A parabola has intercepts at $x = 2$, $x = -4$, and $y = 4$. What is the equation of the parabola? There are at least three ways to solve this problem. Show as many ways as you can.

CF-143.    Solve each of the following quadratic equations.

a)    $x^2 - 4x + 3 = 0$

b)    $x^2 - 8x + 25 = 0$

c)    $x^2 - 4x + 20 = 0$

d)    $x^2 + 100 = 0$

CF-144.    Write an explanation, including an example, of how to find out what $f^{-1}$ does to $x$ if you know what $f$ does to $x$.

CF-145. Find the point where the graph of $y = 2^x + 5$ will intersect the line $y = 50$. Find your answer to three decimal places.

CF-146. Write equations for these circles:

a)  center (9, -3), radius 4

b)  center (-5, 0), radius $\sqrt{23}$

## COURSE SUMMARY

CF-147.  **Course Summary Assignment**

Identify with your team at least six, but no more than ten big ideas from units 1-7. After describing each big idea, rewrite or create one or two problems that illustrate the main point(s). Just as you did in the Unit Summaries, solve and explain the solution to each of these problems. This should also to be done separately from your homework and should be included with your portfolio.

CF-148. You are given the equation $ax^2 + bx + c = 0$.

a)  What are the roots of this equation?

b)  What part of the equation determines whether they are real or complex roots?

c)  When will the roots be real?

d)  When will the roots be complex numbers?

For any quadratic equation $ax^2 + bx + c = 0$, you can determine whether the roots are real or complex by examining the value of $b^2 - 4ac$, known as the **DISCRIMINANT**. The roots are real when $b^2 - 4ac \geq 0$ and complex when $b^2 - 4ac < 0$.

CF-149. Solve for $x$ and $y$ in each of the following systems:

a)  $2x + y = 12$
$xy = 16$

b)  $y = -2x + 12$
$xy = 20$

c)  What is the difference between the graphs of the two systems? (If you are not sure, you may want to graph them.)

CF-150. Farmer Ted grows alfalfa and he has been losing more of his crop each month because of the growth of the rabbit population. Ted has been advised to have the rabbits destroyed, but he feels he can simply increase his production to compensate for the alfalfa destroyed by the rabbits. Currently Ted produces 600 tons of alfalfa each month and he plans to increase his production by 5 tons each month. Last month the rabbits destroyed 3 tons of the crop. The rabbit population around Ted's farm is increasing by 15% each month. If Ted allows the rabbits to continue to destroy part of his crop, at what point will they eat everything he produces? Write a system of equations to represent his dilemma and estimate how long it will take.

CF-151. A fifth-degree polynomial has exactly two x-intercepts. What does this tell you about the roots of the function? Try sketching several different examples.

CF-152. By looking at the graph of the function at right:

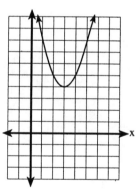

a) What can you tell about the roots?

b) What is the equation of the function if the y-intercept is 13?

c) Find the roots of the function you found in part (b).

d) Find the average of the roots. How does it relate to the equation?

e) Using the domain $1 \leq x \leq 4$, what are the maximum and minimum values of the function?

CF-153. Explain what the relationship is between the solutions of $3x = x^2 + 5x$ and the x-values where the graphs of $y = 3x$ and $y = x^2 + 5x$ intersect.

CF-154. If a system of equations has only complex number solutions, what do we know about the graphs of the equations?

CF-155. Judy claims that since $(xy)^4$ is $x^4y^4$, it must be true that $(x + y)^4$ is $x^4 + y^4$. What do you think? Explain your reasoning.

CF-156. Write the equation for the circle with center (-4, 7) that is tangent to the y-axis. Sketching a graph will help.

CF-157. If $f(x) = \frac{1}{2}\sqrt{3(x-1)} + 5$, then $f^{-1}(x) = ?$

CF-158. **TOOL KIT CHECK-UP**

Your Tool Kit contains reference tools for algebra. Return to your Tool Kit entries. You may need to revise or add entries.

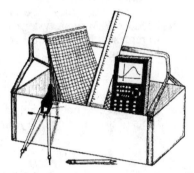

Be sure that your Tool Kit contains entries for all of the items listed below. Add any topics that are missing to your Tool Kit NOW, as well as any other items that will help you in your study of algebra.

- Roots/Zeros of a Function
- Polynomial and Degree
- Amplitude and Period
- Unit Circle

- Complex Numbers
- Complex Plane
- Complex Conjugates
- Discriminant

# UNIT 8

## The Circle of Terror
### CIRCULAR FUNCTIONS

# Unit 8 Objectives
### The Circle of Terror: CIRCULAR FUNCTIONS

What do all of the following situations have
in common?

- pedaling a bicycle
- the motion of the tides
- riding a Ferris Wheel
- your heartbeat
- the orbit of the Space Shuttle
- the length of each day (sunrise to sunset) as
  we move through the year from January to
  December
- the motion of a bouncing spring

The word "cycle" is a clue to answering the
previous question, but probably you <u>didn't</u> say that they are all periodic. That's what mathematicians
call situations which go through the same cycle over and over again. None of the parent graphs
you've encountered so far are appropriate for mathematically representing or modeling periodic
behavior.

In this unit, before pedaling your bicycle off into the sunset, you will have the opportunity to:

- use a circle to create some very important cyclic curves.

- become familiar with the Parent Graphs of circular functions.

- use what you know about Parent Graphs and translating, compressing, or expanding
  their graphs to model a variety of situations.

- learn how "DEG" and "RAD" on your calculator are related to each other and explain that
  relationship.

The theme problem for this unit includes gathering data on an imaginary amusement park ride. You
will ride with Sally and Steve for several days in order to develop some very important and useful
ideas about circular functions. Read the problem below, then go on to problem CT-1.

---

CT-0. **THE CIRCLE OF TERROR** Great Hemisphere Amusement Park has a new
ride for the new century. The Circle of Terror is a circular track, half above
ground and half below. The track rises to a height of 1 kilometer and descends to
a depth 1 km below the ground. Sally dares Steve to try it. Steve boards the ride
at ground level, buckles in, and glances up to see a display that says, "ALTITUDE
0 km." As the ride begins, he clutches the rail in front of him and focuses on the
track ahead. Is there a relationship between the height of his seat and the distance
he has traveled on the circular track?

---

PROBLEM SOLVING

REPRESENTATION/MODELING

FUNCTIONS/GRAPHING

INTERSECTIONS/SYSTEMS

ALGORITHMS

REASONING/COMMUNICATION

# Unit 8

## *The Circle of Terror*: CIRCULAR FUNCTIONS

## THE CIRCLE OF TERROR (PART 1)

CT-1.    It's January 1, 2100, and Great Hemisphere Amusement Park has a
new ride for the new century: The Circle of Terror. It is on a circular
track, half above ground and half below, and it rises to a height of 1
kilometer and descends to a depth 1 km below the ground. Sally dares
Steve to try it. Steve boards the ride at ground level and glances up to
see a display that says, "ALTITUDE 0 km." As the ride begins, Steve
clutches the rail in front of him and focuses on the track ahead. He notices that the
distance along the track is marked every kilometer, and to distract himself from his rising
anxiety he begins to pay attention to the relationship between the distance he's traveled
along the track and the altitude above or below ground level displayed on the panel
overhead. At home later he found himself wondering about the relationship he observed
while on the ride.

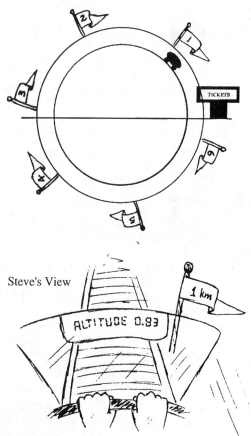

Steve's View

a)    Is the relationship between the
distance traveled and the altitude
a function? Does it matter
which quantity is the
independent variable and which
is the dependent?

b)    There are four points at which
you know Steve's exact altitude.
What are they, and how far had
he traveled when he was at each
of those altitudes? Use your
knowledge of circles to express
these distances in exact form.

c)    Make a table of values for the
function Steve observed. Use
the diagram on the resource page
provided to estimate Steve's
altitude at the distances indicated
and include the four points you
found in part (b). Use negative
numbers to represent altitude
below ground level.

d)    We'll call Steve's function $S(x)$.
Continue investigating this
function. Be sure to include **all**
of the usual information involved
with investigating functions.

**CT-2.** Steve brought his investigation to school the next day. He wanted to convince his teacher that riding the "Circle" had been a mathematical experience. Sally looked at Steve's table of values for his function and decided to challenge him (she knew he didn't have a formula for his function).

    a) "So, what's $S(5.5)$?" she asked. Use the graph you made in problem CT-1 to estimate this value. Then describe what this tells about the Circle of Terror ride.

    b) Undaunted, Sally tried again. "Solve the equation $S(x) = \frac{1}{2}$," she said. Use your graph to solve Sally's equation.

    c) Explain what the solution(s) to this equation tell about the Circle of Terror.


**CT-3.** While Steve was presenting his investigation to the class, Sally interrupted, saying, "But we've already seen that kind of function. It's a third degree polynomial!"

    a) Explain why Sally might think $S(x)$ is a third-degree polynomial. Find a possible equation of the third-degree polynomial that looks like $S(x)$ on the domain of Steve's graph. Do you think that is the equation of $S(x)$? Why or why not?

    b) Cynthia thought $S(x)$ was made by gluing together two semi-circles. Do you agree? Why or why not?


**CT-4.** What is a Unit Circle? What is its equation? Check your Tool Kit if you don't remember.


**CT-5.** 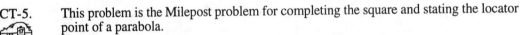 This problem is the Milepost problem for completing the square and stating the locator point of a parabola.

Write the equation in graphing form and sketch a graph of $y = 2x^2 - 4x + 5$. Then label the coordinates of all intercepts and write the equation of its line of symmetry.


**CT-6.** Find the equation of the parabola that passes through the points $(0, 0)$, $(3, 9)$, and $(6, 0)$.


**CT-7.** Find the inverse functions for:

    a) $y = \sqrt[3]{4x - 1}$                     b) $y = \log_7 x$


**CT-8.** Find the x- and y-intercepts of $y - 7 = 3^{(x+4)}$.

CT-9.    Copy the triangles at right.

a)    Finish labeling the lengths of the sides.
      Use radical form to give exact values.

b)    The 30-60-90 triangle is also called a
      half-equilateral. Draw a picture to
      illustrate this, and explain how it can be
      used to help label the missing sides in part (a).

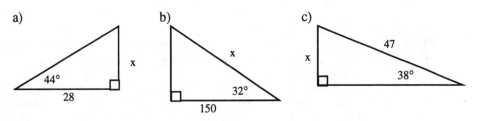

CT-10.   In each of the following triangles, find the length of the side labeled x:

a)                          b)                          c)

CT-11.   Calculate $(2 + i)(3 - 5i) - (1 - 4i)^2$.

# THE CIRCLE OF TERROR (PART II)

CT-12.   Steve was now more
         curious than ever about his
         Circle of Terror
         investigation. He decided
         that his data was incomplete.
         Ignoring the queasiness he
         still felt from yesterday's
         adventure, Steve decided to
         head for the park and ride
         the "Circle" again to gather
         more information. He paid
         the ride operator double to
         allow him to make **two**
         complete circles instead of
         the usual one.

Reluctantly, Steve boarded the ride for the second time. To his relief, he noticed that the
data he collected for the first rotation of the ride had not changed. However, now, after
one complete rotation, he had to be careful. Help Steve out. He's terrified, his head is
spinning, and he must concentrate to collect the correct data.

a)    After one complete rotation, how far has he traveled along the track? (Give both the
      approximate and the <u>exact</u> distance.)

>>**Problem continues on the next page.**>>

b) After one complete rotation, what is his altitude?

c) When he passes the **1 km** marker for the second time, how far has he really traveled along the track? What is his altitude?

d) Continue the table of values of $S(x)$ to include the following values of x:
$2\pi + 1$, $2\pi + 2$, $2\pi + 3$, $2\pi + 4$, $2\pi + 5$, $2\pi + 6$, $2.5\pi$, $3\pi$, $3.5\pi$, $4\pi$.

e) On the resource page make a new graph of $S(x)$ that shows the data for distance traveled and altitude for Steve's second ride.

f) How does the new graph compare to the original one?

CT-13. Steve was excited with his findings and shared his new data with his classmate Sally. Intrigued by the investigation, Sally volunteered to gather more data. "Instead of going for a third rotation, I want to try something different," she said, " I wonder if the Circle of Terror goes in reverse?" "Oh no," said Steve. "That will make everything confusing. How will we be able to tell which points were collected when the ride was going forward, and which were taken when the ride is traveling in reverse?" "Simple," stated Sally. "We'll use negative numbers to represent distance traveled in the opposite direction." After talking with the ride operator, Sally climbed into a seat and made one complete revolution going in reverse.

Sally found that the ride was built to go in both directions, so there were also distance markers facing her as she went around in reverse. On the diagram on your resource page, add dots to show the distances around the circle as she traveled in reverse. Make a table of values that shows Sally's distances and altitudes using the opposites of all the $x$ values you used in problem CT-1. Extend your graph from the previous problem to include these points.

CT-14. What is the domain of the entire graph of $S(x)$?

CT-15. Suppose we extend $S(x)$ to include all possible distances traveled along the track, in either direction, and the resulting altitudes.

a) Describe what this graph would look like.

b) The question Sally raised in problem CT-3 is an important one: could $S(x)$ be an example of any of the functions we know already? Explain why $S(x)$ cannot be a polynomial function.

**CT-16.**

> A function like $S(x)$, which repeats the same pattern endlessly in both directions, is called a **PERIODIC FUNCTION**. The function pictured in problem CF-45 is also a periodic function, assuming that the pattern continues forever to the left and right. Add **periodic function** to your Tool Kit, and make sure you also have the definitions of **period** and **amplitude** from problem CF-45.

a) What is the period of $S(x)$?

b) What is the amplitude?

**CT-17.** Copy the triangles and label the missing side lengths.

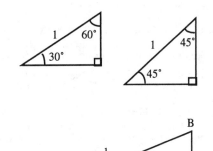

**CT-18.** Find the measure of angle A.

**CT-19.** State the degree of $f(x) = (x + 4)(x + 1)^2(x - 2)$, then sketch its graph.

**CT-20.** Find the equation of a polynomial that has the roots 3, 2, and -1 and goes through the point (1, 1).

**CT-21.** On her way back from the amusement park Sally was going 80 miles per hour when she passed a parked highway patrol car. By the time she was half a mile past the patrol car, the officer was chasing her at 100 miles per hour. If these rates remain constant, how long did it take the officer to overtake Sally? Write an equation to represent this situation.

# EVALUATING THE S(X) FUNCTION

CT-22. **INTRODUCTION**

*S(x)* will turn out to be a very important function, so you need to learn more about how the input and output values are related. You may already be irritated by the fact that you had to estimate from a diagram in order to make tables of values. In the next few problems you will learn how you can use your calculator to be more precise. You'll also discover a very close relationship between *S(x)* and trigonometry.

To begin, evaluate $S(\frac{\pi}{3})$. (This may seem like a difficult number to use for x, but it turns out to be easier than numbers like 1 or 2.) The first thing you'll need to do is figure out where you are when you have traveled $\frac{\pi}{3}$ km around the circle. You already know that $\pi$ km takes you around the upper semi-circle. Now see if you can find $S(\frac{\pi}{3})$. If you are not sure how to start, complete the steps below.

a) On the diagram of the Circle of Terror on the resource page, find the point $\frac{\pi}{3}$ km around the circle. (Recall that $\frac{\pi}{3}$ is the same as $\frac{1}{3}$ of $\pi$.) Label this point A. If we think of the Circle of Terror diagram as a graph on a set of xy-axes with its center at the origin, what is $S(\frac{\pi}{3})$ in relation to the point A?

b) Draw the line segment connecting point A to the center of the circle. What is the measure of the angle formed by that line segment and the x-axis? (Remember that you have traveled one-third of the way around the upper semi-circle. How many degrees are in the semi-circle?) Now can you find $S(\frac{\pi}{3})$?

c) Next draw the line segment from point A straight down to the x-axis. The length of that segment is the value of $S(\frac{\pi}{3})$. Use your knowledge of trigonometric ratios to find that length. Use the diagram on your resource page to make sure your answer is reasonable.

CT-23. Use the process from the previous problem to calculate $S(\frac{3\pi}{4})$. Again, $\frac{3\pi}{4}$ may seem like a strange number to use for x, but it turns out that numbers like this, expressed as multiples of $\pi$, are the distances around the circle that lead to central angles with convenient numbers for their measures. Remember that $\frac{3\pi}{4}$ is the same as $\frac{3}{4}\pi$ and that x = $\pi$ corresponds to traveling half way around the circle. Use the unit circle (on the resource page) which is divided into eighths.

CT-24.    Now find the precise value of $S(1)$. If you are not sure how to begin, complete the following steps.

a)    Write a fraction that represents the portion of the upper half of the Circle of Terror that Steve had covered when he passed the 1 km point.

b)    Draw the line segment from the center to the point at the 1 km mark. Use your fraction from part (a) to find the angle between the x-axis and this segment. Don't forget there are 180° in the semi-circle.

c)    What trigonometric ratio relates this angle to the y-coordinate (i.e. height) of the point at the 1 km mark? Explain how to use your calculator to find $S(1)$.


CT-25.    You may have realized that you could find the value of $S(\frac{\pi}{3})$ without using trigonometry, once you found the measure of the central angle, because the triangle formed is one of the "special" right triangles. Show how to use a special triangle with hypotenuse equal to 1 (see problem CT-17) to find $S(\frac{\pi}{3})$.


CT-26.    Calculate:

a)    $S(\frac{\pi}{4})$                                 b)    $S(\frac{2\pi}{3})$


CT-27.    Calculate:

a)    $S(4)$                                          b)    $S(\frac{4\pi}{3})$


CT-28.    In problem CT-2 you used the graph of $S(x)$ to approximate the solutions to $S(x) = 0.5$. Use the sine ratio or special right triangles to find the exact values of those solutions.


The Circle of Terror: Circular Functions                                           283

CT-29.    Complete the table of values for $f(x) = \dfrac{x^2 + 4x - 5}{x - 1}$.

| x | -2 | -1 | 0 | 1 | 2 | 3 |
|---|----|----|---|---|---|---|
| y |    |    |   |   |   |   |

a)    Graph the points. What kind of function does it appear to be? Why is it not correct to connect all the dots?

b)    Look for a simple pattern for the values in the table. What appears to be the relationship between x and y? Calculate f(0.9) and f(1.1), and add the points to your graph. Is there an asymptote at x = 1? If you're not sure, calculate f(0.99) and f(1.01), also.

c)    Simplify the formula for f(x). What do you think the complete graph looks like?

CT-30.    The measure of ∠ROS in Δ ROS is 60°.

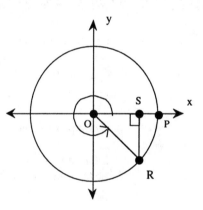

a)    The curved arrow represents the rotation of $\overline{OR}$, beginning at the positive x-axis. Through how many degrees has $\overline{OR}$ rotated?

Use the special right triangle relationships to give exact answers for the following in radical form.

b)    If OR = 1, what is OS? SR?

c)    What are the coordinates of point R?

d)    Find the distance around the circle, traveling counterclockwise, from P to R. Now find S(x) for that value.

CT-31.    In 1998, Terre Haute, Indiana had a population of 72,000 people. In 2000, the population had dropped to 70,379. The city officials expect the population to eventually level off at 60,000.

a)    What kind of function would best model the population over time?

b)    Write an equation that would model the population.

CT-32.    A semi-circular tunnel is 26 feet high. A road 48 feet wide is centered under the tunnel. Bruce needs to move a house on a trailer through the tunnel. The load is 22 feet wide and 24 feet high. Will he make it? Draw a diagram and explain why or why not. Show all your work.

CT-33. Mr. Ron Keis, math teacher extraordinaire, loves challenging his talented Algebra 2 students. He writes the following problem on the board and tells his class, "No calculators please. Simplify. You have thirty seconds!"

$$\left(\frac{13^{12}}{14^{23}}\right)\left(\frac{27^3}{13^{11}}\right)\left(\frac{2^{10}}{27^4}\right)\left(\frac{14^{22}}{13}\right)\left(\frac{27}{2^9}\right)$$

Time yourself and simplify the expression. What is the answer? Did you meet the challenge?

CT-34. Verify that $3 + i\sqrt{2}$ is a solution of $x^2 - 6x + 11 = 0$.

# SINE: A NEW PARENT GRAPH

CT-35. In previous problems you uncovered a relationship between the function $S(x)$ and the sine ratio you use to solve triangles. Each value of x leads to a point on the unit circle (radius = 1) and that point determines a central angle of the circle. The Greek letter $\theta$ (pronounced "theta") is commonly used to represent the measure of this angle.

a) Explain how to find $\theta$ when you know x.

b) Explain how to find $S(x)$ when you know $\theta$. You will need to adjust your rule for each quadrant of the graph.

CT-36.

> The fact that values of $S(x)$ can be found from the sines of angles reveals the connection between the function $S(x)$ and the sine ratio. Because of this, the official name of the function $S(x)$ is the **SINE FUNCTION**, abbreviated **SIN X**, and in fact the sin key on a calculator can be used to find values of $S(x)$ directly for any value of x. However, the sin key operates in two different modes. You are familiar with the **degree mode**, and this mode is used to find missing sides and angles of triangles (though you will find later that it also can be used on the unit circle.)
>
> The mode that tells your calculator to interpret x as a distance traveled around the unit circle is called **RADIAN MODE**. Enter this in your Tool Kit, and make sure you know how to set the mode of your calculator. When your calculator is in radian mode, the sin key represents exactly the function we have been calling $S(x)$. Put your calculator in radian mode, and use it to check some of the entries in the table of values you made in problem CT-1.

CT-37. Take out your Parent Graph Tool Kit. Add **y = sin x.** Remember to include statements about domain and range, intercepts, asymptotes, symmetry, period, amplitude, etc. Sin x is the parent graph for most periodic (i.e. cyclic or infinitely repetitive) behavior. Not only does sin x go back and forth, changing directions at regular intervals, but it does so in a way that mirrors cyclic behavior in the physical world.

a) Imagine a pendulum swinging back and forth, or a train that shuttles between two stations, changing direction without turning around, or an athlete doing wind sprints in a gym, running back and forth as fast as he can and stopping at each end to touch the line on the floor. Where in its cycle will each of these back-and-forth travelers be going the fastest? Why? What must each of them do as they approach a turn-around point? What will they do just after they change directions?

b) Now look at your graph of sin x, and think about riding the Circle of Terror. When is the height, relative to the distance traveled, changing the fastest? How can you see this on the graph? When is the height changing slowly? How can you see that on the graph?

c)

> The periodic functions you are learning about in this unit are called **CIRCULAR FUNCTIONS**. Why do you think sine is called a circular function?

CT-38. Imagine the graph y = sin x shifted up one unit.

a) Sketch what it would look like.

b) What do you have to change in the equation y = sin x to move the graph up one unit? Write the new equation.

c) What are the intercepts of your new equation? Label them with their coordinates on the graph. It may help to look at the graph from problem CT-12 and imagine shifting it up one unit.

d) When you listed intercepts in part (c), did you list more than one x-intercept? Should you have?

CT-39. The graph at right was made by shifting one cycle of $y = \sin x$ over to the left.

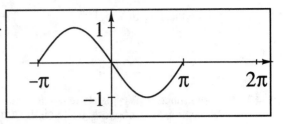

a) How many units to the left was it shifted?

b) Figure out how to change the equation of $y = \sin x$ so that the graph of the new equation will look like the one in part (a). Keep in mind that you may need to change the viewing window. If you don't have a graphing calculator at home, sketch the graph and check your answer when you get to class.

CT-40.  You have seen that you can calculate values of the sine function (formerly known as $S(x)$) using right triangles formed by the radius of the unit circle. Values of x that result in 30°- 60°- 90° or 45°- 45°- 90° triangles are used very frequently on exercises and tests because their sines can be found exactly without a calculator. You should learn to recognize these values of x and find their corresponding central angles quickly and easily. The same is true for values of x that correspond to the x- and y-intercepts of the unit circle.

The central angles that correspond to these "special" values of x are: 30°, 45°, 60°, 90°, 120°, 135°, 150°, 180°, 210°, 225°, 240°, 270°, 300°, 315°, and 330°. What these angles have in common is that they are all multiples of 30° or 45°, and some of them are also multiples of 60° or 90°.

a) You already know that $x = \pi$ corresponds to $\theta = 180°$. So $\frac{\pi}{2}$, which is half of $\pi$, corresponds to 90°, and $\frac{\pi}{4}$, which is half of $\frac{\pi}{2}$, corresponds to 45°. Similarly, $\frac{\pi}{3}$, which is one-third of $\pi$, corresponds to 60°, and $\frac{\pi}{6}$, which is half of $\frac{\pi}{3}$, corresponds to 30°. Since all the special angles are multiples of 30°, 45°, 60°, or 90°, all the special values of x are multiples of $\frac{\pi}{6}, \frac{\pi}{4}, \frac{\pi}{3},$ or $\frac{\pi}{2}$. Thus, you can recognize a special value of x because it will have a multiple of $\pi$ in the numerator, and 2, 3, 4, or 6 as its denominator. To find the corresponding angle for one of these values of x, think of the fraction as a whole number times $\frac{\pi}{6}, \frac{\pi}{4}, \frac{\pi}{3},$ or $\frac{\pi}{2}$, and then replace the fraction with its corresponding angle measure. For example: $\frac{5\pi}{6} = 5(\frac{\pi}{6}) => 5\ (30°) = 150°$.

b) Copy and complete the table below. Try to do the calculations in your head.

| x | $\frac{5\pi}{6}$ | $\frac{2\pi}{3}$ | $\frac{3\pi}{4}$ | $\frac{4\pi}{3}$ | $\frac{7\pi}{6}$ | $\frac{11\pi}{6}$ |
|---|---|---|---|---|---|---|
| $\theta$ | 150° | | | | | |

CT-41. Graph the system at right: $1 + x - y \geq 3x - 2y - 4$

$$y < 2x^2 + 1$$

CT-42. Some function W(x) is sketched at right. Make your own copy, then sketch the graph of the inverse of W(x).

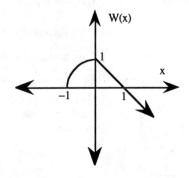

a) Is the inverse a function?

b) Explain.

CT-43. Solve for x: $\dfrac{1}{ax} + \dfrac{1}{b} = \dfrac{1}{x}$

CT-44. While trying to measure the height of a tree, Julie noticed that a 3.5 foot post had a 4.25 foot shadow. If the tree's shadow is 100 feet long, how tall is the tree?

CT-45. Show and explain why the equation $2^x = 5 - x$ has only one real solution.

CT-46. Sketch a graph of at least one cycle of y = sin x. Label the intercepts. With your team:

a) Write an equation whose parent graph is y = sin x, but is:

   i)   shifted 3 units up.            ii)  reflected across the x-axis.

   iii) shifted 2 units to the right.   iv)  vertically stretched.

---

b) Check your answers to part (a) with your graphing calculator. Then sketch each graph and label it with its equation. **For each sketch**, include the points that represent:

   i)   the locator point (the start of the first cycle);

   ii)  the end of the first cycle;

   iii) the middle point of the first cycle;

   iv)  the point one quarter of the way through the first cycle (halfway between the first point and the middle point); and

   v)   the point three quarters of the way through the first cycle (halfway between the middle point and the last point). This is important. Don't rush through it.

Note: We call the steps above the **FIVE-POINT METHOD** for graphing periodic functions. Here is how it looks when applied to y = sin x:

locator point for y = sin x · 1/4 cycle · full cycle · half cycle · 3/4 cycle

c) Write a general equation for y = sin x. Explain what each letter that you use represents or how it affects the graph.

---

d) Add these examples to your Tool Kit. Be sure to list the five key points for each.

$$y = \sin\left(x + \frac{\pi}{3}\right) \quad \text{and} \quad y = \sin(x - 1)$$

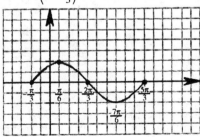
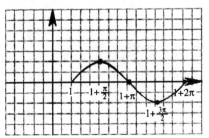

CT-47. Use the five point method to sketch each of the following graphs without using your graphing calculator. Label the coordinates of all five points.

a) $y = \sin\left(x + \frac{\pi}{4}\right)$

b) $y = -2 \sin (x - 1) + 0.5$

c) $y = 3 \sin (x + \frac{\pi}{3}) - 2$

d) $y = a \sin (x - h) + k$ (Put the locator at a random point and label the other four points in terms of $h$ and $k$.)

CT-48. Find an equation for each graph:

a)

b)

c)

d)

CT-49. Great Hemisphere Amusement Park has a crisis. Government inspectors have shut down the Circle of Terror out of fear that it could collapse during an earthquake. The park has decided to rebuild the ride so that most of it is underground. The center of the circle will be one-half km underground and passengers will ride an elevator 1.5 km underground in order to board at the lowest point. As before, there will be markers visible to show how far you have traveled from your starting point and a digital read-out to tell your altitude relative to ground level. Once again, altitude is a function of distance traveled from the starting point. Make a sketch of this function and then write a formula for it.

CT-50. What central angle corresponds to a distance around the unit circle of $x = \frac{7\pi}{3}$? What other value of $x$ takes you to the same point on the circle? Make a sketch of the unit circle showing the resulting right triangle and use what you know about special right triangle to find $\sin(\frac{7\pi}{3})$ exactly.

CT-51. Suppose you were to bend two whole sheets of $8\frac{1}{2}$ x 11 paper to form two cylinders (a tall, skinny one and a short, wide one).

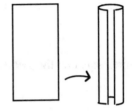

a) Do the two cylinders have the same volume? Prove your answer.

b) Is the result different if you start with $8\frac{1}{2}$ x $8\frac{1}{2}$ paper?

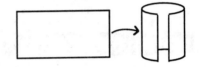

CT-52. Here is a sequence of doodles, with some numbers to go with them:

180    120    90    72

a) Draw the next two, and write the numbers to go with them.

b) What number would go with the 99th doodle? With the nth doodle?

CT-53. Find the roots of each of the following quadratic functions and state the x- and y-intercepts.

a) $y = 3x^2 + 6x + 1$    b) $y = -2x^2 + 5x - 7$

CT-54. Write each of the quadratic functions in the preceding problem in graphing form. If you need help getting started, read parts (a) and (b) for some assistance.

a) In part (a) above the roots give the x-intercepts of the graph, so you can use the method of averaging the intercepts to figure out the vertex.

b) In part (b) above the roots are complex so they do not tell you where the graph crosses the x-axis; however, you can use the average of the roots to figure out the vertex. Try it, but be sure to check your answers.

CT-55. Solve for x: $3^x + 5 = x^2 - 5$. If you do not have a graphing calculator, show your work to approximate a solution and check it in class.

CT-56. Solve $\left(\frac{1}{8}\right)^{(2x-3)} = \left(\frac{1}{2}\right)^{(x+2)}$ .

CT-57. Dolores says that the solutions for $x^2 - x + 1 = 0$ are $\frac{1}{2} \pm \frac{i\sqrt{3}}{2}$. Is she correct? Explain your answer.

## CHANGING THE LENGTH OF THE PERIOD OF THE SINE FUNCTION

CT-58. Put your graphing calculator in radian mode. Set the domain and range of the viewing window so that you would see just one complete cycle of $y = \sin x$. What is that domain? Range?

a) Graph **y = sin x**, **y = sin (0.5x)**, and **y = sin (2x)** simultaneously, but make sure you know which is which. Answer these questions for each equation:

i) How many cycles of each graph appear on the screen?

ii) What is the amplitude of each graph?

iii) What is the period of each graph?

iv) Is each equation a function?

b) Make a conjecture about the graph of $y = \sin (bx)$ with respect to each of the questions (i), (ii), (iii), and (iv) above. If you can't make a conjecture yet, try more examples.

c) Create at least <u>three</u> of your own examples to check your conjectures. Be sure to include sketches of your graphs.

CT-59.  **Without** using a graphing calculator, describe each of the following functions by stating the amplitude, period, and locator point and then sketch the graph. **After** you have completed each graph, check your sketch with the graphing calculator and correct and explain any errors.

a)  $y = \sin 2(x - \frac{\pi}{6})$

b)  $y = 3 + \sin(\frac{1}{3}x)$

c)  $y = 3 \sin(4x)$

d)  $y = \sin \frac{1}{2}(x + 1)$

e)  $y = -\sin 3(x - \frac{\pi}{3})$

f)  $y = -1 + \sin(2x - \frac{\pi}{2})$

CT-60. Philip was surprised! He predicted that the equation in part (e) of the previous problem would have its locator point at $(\frac{\pi}{2}, -1)$, but that was not what he saw when he graphed it. Instead, the x-coordinate of his locator was $(\frac{\pi}{4}, -1)$. Philip began to wonder if this was an exception to the pattern he had been using successfully in the other problems. Explain to him why it is not an exception, and rewrite the equation from part (e) so that it does fit the pattern of the other problems.

CT-61. Write the equation of a sine graph with period $6\pi$, amplitude 2, and locator point $(\pi, 1)$. Use the five-point method to sketch the graph.

Take out your Parent Graph Tool Kit and revise the general equation for $y = \sin x$ to reflect what you found in the previous problems.

CT-62. Based on your explorations in class, complete the following tasks.

a)  Describe what the graph of $y = 3 \sin(\frac{1}{2}x)$ will look like compared to the graph of $y = \sin x$.

b)  Use the five point method to sketch both graphs on the same set of axes based on your hypothesis.

c)  Explain the differences between the two graphs. How are they the same?

CT-63. What is the period of $y = \sin(2\pi x)$? Use the five point method to sketch each of the following:

a)  $y = \sin(2\pi x)$

b)  $y = 3 \sin(\pi x)$

c)  $y = 3 \sin(2\pi x) + 1$

CT-64.    Match each equation with the appropriate graph.  Do this without a graphing calculator.

a)    $y = \sin\left(x + \frac{\pi}{2}\right)$

b)    $y = \sin(2x)$

c)    $y = 2\sin\left(\frac{x}{2}\right)$

d)    $y = \sin(x) - 3$

e)    $y = -\sin 2\left(x - \frac{\pi}{8}\right)$

CT-65. Ceirin's teacher had promised a quiz for the next day, so he phoned Adel to review what they had done in class.

"Suppose I have y = sin 2x," said Ceirin, "What will it look like?"

"It will be horizontally compressed by a factor of 2," replied Adel, "so the period is π."

"Okay, now suppose I want to shift it one unit to the right. Do I just subtract 1 from x, like always?"

"I think so, " said Adel, "but let's check on the graphing calculator."

They proceeded to check on their calculators, and after a few moments they both spoke at once.

"Rats," said Ceirin, "it isn't right."

"Cool," said Adel, "it works."

When they arrived at school the next morning, they compared the equations they had put in their graphing calculators while they talked on the phone. One had

$$y = \sin 2x - 1$$

while the other had

$$y = \sin 2(x - 1).$$

Which equation was right? Did they both subtract 1 from x? Explain. Describe the rule for shifting a graph one unit to the right in a way that avoids this confusion.

CT-66. Solve each equation.

a) $\dfrac{3}{x+1} = \dfrac{4}{x}$

b) $\dfrac{3}{x+1} + \dfrac{4}{x} = 2$

c) $\dfrac{3}{x+2} + 5 = \dfrac{3}{x+2}$

d) Explain why part (c) has no solution.

CT-67. **A Satellite's Path**

The CPM satellite (set up by students to beam solutions to problems around the world) follows an orbit in which it is over the northern hemisphere half of the time and the southern hemisphere the other half. You have been asked to help the observers on the ground locate the satellite by giving them a formula for the location at any time after the launch.

You know the following information:

- The satellite's greatest distance north of the equator is 4500 kilometers, which it reaches two hours after the launch.

- Six hours later, a bit more than half-way through its orbit, the satellite reaches its greatest distance south of the equator, which is also 4500 kilometers.

- The satellite takes twelve hours to complete an orbit.

a) Sketch a graph showing the satellite's distance from the equator over time, labeling the information you know.

b) Find an equation to model the satellite's distance from the equator over time. Be sure to tell what your variables represent so that even a NASA engineer would approve.

c) Use your model to predict the satellite's distance from the equator at:

   i) 1 hour              ii) 6 hours              iii) 11 hours

d) What does your answer to (iii) imply about the location of the satellite at that time?

CT-68. Write an equation for each of the following graphs. If you have a graphing calculator use it to check your equation (be sure to set your window to match the picture). Otherwise, check when you get to class.

a)

b)

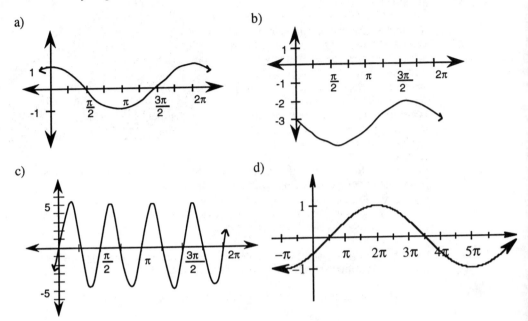

c)

d)

CT-69. Sketch a graph of:

a) $y = -2(x - 2)^2 + 3$

b) $y = (x - 1)^3 + 3$

CT-70. Write the equation of a line parallel to $3x - y = 2$. Then write the equation of a parabola that intersects your line but not the graph of $3x - y = 0$.

CT-71. Solve each of the following equations for x:

a) $171 = 3(5^x)$

b) $171y = 3(x^5)$

CT-72. A 5' x 4' x 3' box is made for the purpose of storage. What is the longest pole that can fit in the box?

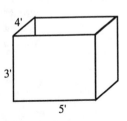

CT-73.    Which of these situations (if any) is best modeled by a circular function? Explain your reasoning.

a)    The number of students in each year's graduating class.

b)    The temperature outside your classroom window over the course of several years.

c)    The high tide level at a point along the sea coast.


CT-74.    What interest rate is needed to double your investment in 15 years?


CT-75.    Phana's garden is 2 m wide and 5 m long. She puts a walkway of uniform width around her garden. If the area of the walkway is 30 m², what are the outer dimensions of the walkway? Drawing a diagram will be very helpful.


CT-76.    Parts (c) and (d) are the Milepost problems for solving equations and inequalities involving absolute value.

a)    $2(x - 1)^2 = 18$                                    b)    $2^x + 3 = 10$

c)    $2|2x + 3| = 10$                                       d)    $-|x + 3| < 10$


## SINE OF AN ANGLE

CT-77.    The sine function is based on the unit circle. In radian mode, the input tells it how far around the circle to go, and the output gives the height of the corresponding point on the circle.

When you've used the sine key on your calculator in degree mode, sine meant something different: the sine *ratio*. The input represented the measure of an acute angle of a right triangle, and the output gave the ratio of the opposite leg to the hypotenuse of the triangle. Today you'll see how the sine *function* can also work in degree mode, because angle measure can also be used to specify a point on the circle.

a)    Make a graph of a unit circle, using 10 units on your graph paper to represent one unit, or use the resource page. Using a protractor, draw a radius in the second quadrant which makes a 150° angle with the positive x-axis. Set your calculator to degree mode and use it to find sin (150°). What do you get? Explain the meaning of this result in terms of the sine *function*.

b)    Now use your calculator to find sin (200°). Explain the meaning of this result in terms of the sine function.

c)    Finally, use your calculator to find sin (-160°). What do you notice? Explain what this means in terms of the sine function.

CT-78.

In the previous problem, sin (200°) gave the y-coordinate of a point on the unit circle in the third quadrant. In geometry you focused on angles less than 180°, but we can imagine a radius beginning at (1,0) and rotating counter-clockwise about the origin to a point in the third quadrant. If it then makes a 20° angle with the negative side of the x-axis, it makes sense to say that it rotated 200°, where each degree represents $\frac{1}{360}$ of a complete rotation. Rotations measured in this way, with the understanding that we begin at (1,0), and that counter-clockwise is the direction of positive rotation, are referred to as **ANGLES OF ROTATION IN STANDARD POSITION.** When we draw an angle in standard position, the positive x-axis is called the **INITIAL RAY**, and the radius that determines the angle is called the **TERMINAL RAY.** Add these terms to your Tool Kit.

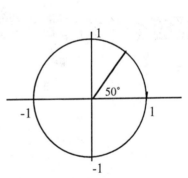

With this understanding, the sine function has the same definition in degree mode as it does in radian mode. The input tells how far around the circle to go and the output tells the height (y-coordinate) of the corresponding point on the circle.

Use this definition to find the following **without a calculator:**

a)   sin (0°)      b)   sin (90°)      c)   sin (270°)      d)   sin (450°)

CT-79.    Hank wasn't happy about this latest development. "If I'm asked for the sine of an angle, how do I know if they want $\frac{opposite}{hypotenuse}$ or height on the unit circle?"

"Good question," said Paula. "At least if the angle is negative, or more than 90°, we know it means height on the unit circle. When the angle is between 0 and 90°, I'm not sure."

Paula chose to investigate the situation using a 50° angle. She drew it in standard position, as shown at right. Then she used her calculator to find sin (50°).

"Hmmm, sin (50°) is about 0.77. That looks about right to be the height of the point on the circle," she said.

"But look," replied Hank, "It's $\frac{opposite}{hypotenuse}$ , too!"

Copy the circle and draw the right triangle Hank sees, and then explain why $\frac{opposite}{hypotenuse}$ is the same as the y-coordinate of the point on the circle, whenever θ is between 0° and 90°.

CT-80. Now that we have two different modes for the sine function, representing two different ways of measuring travel around the unit circle, it is helpful to be able to switch from one to the other.

a) If you start at (1, 0) on the unit circle, and rotate 4/10 of the way around the circle, what will be the degree measure in standard position of the resulting angle?

b) Steve and Sally's rides on the Circle of Terror can be described in terms of angles in standard position. When they travel 144° around the circle, what fraction of the way around the track have they gone? Explain how to calculate how many km they've traveled along the track if you know what fraction of the circle they've covered.

c) Add this information to your Tool Kit.

---

**MEASURING IN RADIANS**

From parts (a) and (b) you can conclude that $\sin(144°) = \sin\left(\frac{4}{5}\pi\right)$. Why? (Note: When there's no degree symbol (°), we assume radian mode.) For any angle $\theta°$ in standard position there is a value of $x$ for which traveling $x$ units around the unit circle takes you to the same place as rotating $\theta°$. Because of this, we can use distance around the unit circle as a way to measure angles of rotation. The distance around the unit circle that corresponds to any angle of rotation is called the **RADIAN MEASURE** of the angle. Enter this in your Tool Kit. What is the radian measure of 180°?

---

d) You may have answered something like 3.14159 radians for the previous question, but it is traditional and convenient to leave that in symbolic (and exact) form as $\pi$ radians. What would be the exact radian measure of each of the following angle measures? (It is very helpful to remember that $180° = \pi$ radians.)

i)    60°

ii)    90°

iii)    120°

iv)    270°

CT-81. A 70° angle is drawn for you in the unit circle at right.

a) Label the coordinates of point R.

b) How could you represent the <u>exact</u> coordinates of point R?

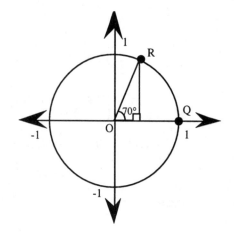

CT-82.    Evaluate without a calculator:

a)    sin (180°)                              b)    sin (360°)

c)    sin (-90°)                              d)    sin (510°)  (Use a special triangle.)


CT-83.    Colleen and Jolleen are twin sisters. They
have the same clothes, same hairstyles,
same math class, and same calculators.
When Luis asked them to find sin 30°,
Colleen (who has been absent the last few
days) got sin 30° = -0.9880316241 on her
calculator, but Jolleen got sin 30° = 0.5 on
hers. They tried it several times and got
the same results. They quickly forgot
about Luis and started trying to figure out what was wrong.  Is one of their calculators
broken, or is something else going on?  Why did they get different answers?

CT-84.    Convert each of the following, expressing radians in terms of $\pi$.

a)    $\pi$ radians to degrees    b)    $3\pi$ radians to degrees    c)    30 degrees to radians

d)    $\frac{\pi}{4}$ radians to degrees    e)    225 degrees to radians    f)    $\frac{3\pi}{2}$ radians to degrees


CT-85.    Simplify each of the following (write the expression without parentheses) and express the
result with positive exponents:

a)    $(x^3 y^{-2})^{-4}$                          b)    $-3x^2(6xy - 2x^3 y^2 z)$


CT-86.    Sketch a graph of $y = \frac{1}{2}(x + 1)^3$.  Then sketch its inverse and write the equation of the
inverse.


CT-87.    Write the quadratic function $f(x) = 2x^2 - 16x + 34$ in graphing form.


CT-88.    Six-Hundred Flags Amusement Park has decided to do the Circle of Terror one better.
Their ride will consist of a circular track with a radius of one km, but the center of the
circle will be 0.5 km underground, and passengers will board at the highest point, so they
begin with a blood-curdling drop.  As in the Circle of Terror, there will be markers
visible to show how far riders have traveled from their starting point and a digital read-out
to show their altitude relative to ground level.  Write a formula for the function that relates
these variables.

# THE COSINE FUNCTION

**CT-89.** You may be wondering if the cosine can also be interpreted as a circular function. The answer, of course, is "Yes."

a) Use your calculator to find cos (150°), cos (200°), and cos (-160°). Now look at the unit circle you made for problem CT-77, which has these angles drawn on it. What does the cosine represent on the unit circle?

b) Evaluate each of the following cosines without a calculator:

   i) cos (90°)    ii) cos (540°)    iii) cos $(-\frac{5\pi}{2})$    iv) cos ( 8π )

c) As in the case of sine, the cosine of an angle between 0° and 90° can be interpreted as previously studied as a ratio of triangle sides, or in the way you discovered in part (a). Refer to problem CT-79 and explain why both interpretations lead to the same value.

d) Sketch a graph of the cosine function in radian mode.

e) Describe how the cosine graph differs from the sine.

**CT-90.** Make a conjecture about what will happen to the graph of y = cos (bx) when you vary the value of b. Then test your conjecture for at least three values of b (include values both greater and less than one) and sketch your results. Does your conjecture hold? If not, revise it and test again.

**CT-91.** It's time to investigate the cosine function. First, be careful when you think about the variable x. Since the cosine represents the x-coordinate of the point on the unit circle, it can be very confusing to also use x to represent the distance around the circle, which is what we are doing if we write y = cos (x). Instead, we will

choose a different variable for the function. We will use θ, with the understanding that θ can be degrees or radians, depending on whether or not it has a ° on it. In general, θ is used to represent angles rather than distances, but it may be used for both purposes because the radian measure of the angle in standard position is the same as the distance around the unit circle. Investigate the function y = cos (θ). Be sure to include all the information you gave when you investigated the sine function. Add this information to your Parent Graph Tool Kit.

CT-92. The division of the circle into 360° is ancient and somewhat arbitrary. One theory says that 360 was chosen because many numbers divide into it evenly. Mathematicians have found that radian measure is more useful.

Earlier in this unit, the Circle of Terror diagram showed an angle of one radian.

a) Imagine a circle with a radius of 1 cm, with an angle of 1 radian drawn in standard position. As you learned in geometry, a piece of a circle is called an arc. What is the length of the arc cut off by this angle?

b) Now imagine the circle is enlarged so that its radius is 1 inch. What is the length of the arc?

c) Enlarge again to make the radius 1 foot. What is the length of the arc?

d) Now suppose you have a circle whose radius is 3 feet. You are asked to draw an angle of exactly 1 radian, and you only have a tape measure. How can you do it? Explain clearly.

e) Describe a general method for creating an angle of 1 radian.

CT-93. There are several angles with sine and cosine values that you can figure out exactly based on your knowledge of 30°–60°–90° and 45°–45°–90° triangles.

We recommend using a whole sheet of graph or lined paper, a protractor, a ruler, and a compass for this problem so you can keep it in your Tool Kit for easy future reference.

a) Neatly draw a set of x-y axes and a large unit-circle in the center of the paper.

b) Use your protractor to measure a 30° angle and label it in both degrees and radians. Use your knowledge of the special right triangles to label the coordinates on the circle that are $\cos\frac{\pi}{6}$ and $\sin\frac{\pi}{6}$ as $\left(\frac{\sqrt{3}}{2}, \frac{1}{2}\right)$. Then draw and label three other angles whose cosines and sines have the same absolute values. For example, one of the other angles would be $\frac{7\pi}{6}$ (or 210°) and the coordinates for $\left(\cos\frac{7\pi}{6}, \sin\frac{7\pi}{6}\right)$ are $\left(\frac{-\sqrt{3}}{2}, -\frac{1}{2}\right)$.

c) Follow directions similar to those in part (b) for $\frac{\pi}{4}$.

d) Follow directions similar to those in part (b) for $\frac{\pi}{3}$.

e) Fill in the coordinates for the cosine and sine values for multiples of $\frac{\pi}{2}$.

f) The angle $\frac{\pi}{6}$ is called the **reference angle** for all other angles whose cosine and sine have the same absolute values. In part (a) you saw that $\frac{\pi}{6}$ was the reference angle for $\frac{5\pi}{6}$, $\frac{7\pi}{6}$, and $\frac{11\pi}{6}$. Name two additional angles for which $\frac{\pi}{6}$ would be the reference angle.

CT-94.

**REFERENCE ANGLE**

For every angle of rotation there is an angle in the first quadrant $0 \le \theta \le \frac{\pi}{2}$ whose cosine and sine have the same absolute values as the cosine and sine of the original. This first quadrant angle is called a **reference angle**.

What reference angle would you use to find each of the following?

a) $\sin\frac{11\pi}{6}$

b) $\cos 120°$

c) $\cos\frac{8\pi}{9}$

d) $\cos 203°$

e) $\sin 310°$

f) $\sin 113°$

CT-95. Draw a picture of an angle that measures 6 radians.

a) Approximately how many degrees is this?

b) Estimate, from your picture, the sine of 6 radians.

CT-96. Explain your method for converting degree measure to radian measure and vice-versa. Refer to problem CT-80 if you are having trouble getting started.

CT-97. The temperature of a pizza, after it has been delivered, depends on how long it has been sitting on the family room table.

a) Sketch a reasonable graph of this situation. Be sure to label your axes.

b) Should your graph have an asymptote? Why?

CT-98. Graph the following inequality: $y < \frac{1}{x + 5}$

CT-99. Using separate axes, sketch $y = \sin \theta$ and $y = \cos \theta$. Draw at least one full cycle of each. Then label the coordinates of the x-intercepts in <u>both</u> degrees <u>and</u> radians.

CT-100. In the function $y = 4 \sin (6\theta)$, how many cycles of sine are there from 0 to $2\pi$? How long is each cycle? (i.e., what is the period)?

Find the period and locator point and then use the five point method to sketch each of the following graphs.

a) $y = \sin\left(\frac{1}{3}\theta\right)$

b) $y = \cos 3(\theta - \frac{\pi}{2})$

c) $y = 1 + \cos 4\theta$

CT-101. Compute each complex product.

a) $(1 + i)^2$

b) $(1 + i)^3$

# MATHEMATICAL MODELING USING CIRCULAR FUNCTIONS: DAY CYCLES

CT-102. The chart below lists the number of hours of daylight in Denver, Colorado at various dates during the year. The data was collected every 15 days.

| DATE | HOURS OF DAYLIGHT | DATE | HOURS OF DAYLIGHT |
|------|-------------------|------|-------------------|
| Jan. 01 | 9.37 | Jul. 01 | 14.98 |
| Jan. 16 | 9.63 | Jul. 16 | 14.78 |
| Jan. 31 | 10.08 | Jul. 31 | 14.32 |
| Feb. 15 | 10.68 | Aug. 15 | 13.73 |
| Mar 02 | 11.23 | Aug. 30 | 13.18 |
| Mar 17 | 11.93 | Sept. 14 | 12.47 |
| Apr. 01 | 12.57 | Sept. 29 | 11.28 |
| Apr. 16 | 13.23 | Oct. 14 | 11.17 |
| May 01 | 13.83 | Oct. 29 | 10.65 |
| May 16 | 14.37 | Nov. 13 | 9.97 |
| May 31 | 14.77 | Nov. 28 | 9.57 |
| June 15 | 15.02 | Dec. 13 | 9.35 |
| | | Dec. 28 | 9.38 |

a) Draw a graph showing days (independent) compared to hours of daylight (dependent). Use a full sheet of graph paper and make a neat graph.

b) What type of function could be used to model this data? Justify your choice.

c) Would it be easier to model the data starting with a sine function or a cosine function? Explain.


CT-103. The Day Cycles graph you just made would be a useful tool if you had an equation that approximated it. Then you could estimate, fairly accurately, the number of hours of daylight on any given day of the year.

a) Find an equation whose graph roughly fits the data. (Pretend the minimum daylight occurs on day 0, and there are 360 days in the year.)

b) Use your equation to approximate the number of hours of daylight on the 120th day of the year.

c) How could you make your equation more accurate?

CT-104. Can we use a circle with the radius not equal to 1 to evaluate the sine and cosine functions? Yes, and here's how: The graph at right shows the point P at (-3, 4) on the circle of radius 5. Point P determines an angle in standard position. Call this angle θ.

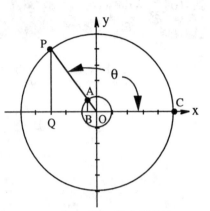

a) Triangles PQO and ABO are similar. On the resource page, find the lengths of the sides of △PQO and write the length on each side. What is the ratio of the sides of △ABO to the sides of △PQO? If you know the length of a side of △PQO, what would you do to that number to find the length of the corresponding side of △ABO? Find the lengths of the sides of △ABO and label them on your resource page.

b) What are the coordinates of point A? What are the values of sin (θ) and cos (θ)?

c) Select any other point on the larger circle and label it (a, b). Draw a segment from that point to the origin. What are the coordinates of the point where that segment intersects the unit circle?

d) Any point in the plane (other than the origin) determines an angle in standard position by connecting it to the origin. If a point at (x, y) is r units from the origin, what is the sine of the angle it determines? What is the cosine?

CT-105. How would the graph of the number of hours of darkness (Night Cycles) compare to the graph of the number of hours of daylight? (Refer to problems CT-102 and CT-103.)

CT-106. Carefully sketch one cycle each of sine and cosine on the same set of axes.

a) Where do the two graphs intersect? Write your answers in both degrees and radians.

b) Draw a unit circle or use one from a resource page. In your circle, sketch the angles you found in part (a). The rays you just drew should be collinear. What is the equation of the line formed by the two rays?

c) Explain why the values of θ for which sin θ and cos θ intersect should be on the line you found in part (b).

CT-107. Give the locator point for each of the following equations then use the five-point method to sketch each graph.

a) y = 3 sin (x + 90°)          b) y = -2 sin (4x)

CT-108.    Write a possible equation for the graph at right.

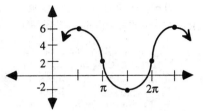

CT-109.    Convert each of the following angle measures:

a)    $\frac{7\pi}{6}$ radians to degrees    b)    $\frac{5\pi}{3}$ radians to degrees    c)    45 degrees to radians

d)    100° to radians    e)    810° to radians    f)    $\frac{7\pi}{2}$ radians to degrees

CT-110.    Copy the following definition into your Tool Kit, then answer the questions that follow:

---

### SINE AND COSINE FUNCTIONS

For any real number θ, the **sine of** θ, denoted sin θ, is the y-coordinate of the point on the unit circle reached by a rotation of θ radians in standard position. The **cosine of** θ, denoted cos θ, is the x-coordinate of the point on the unit circle reached by a rotation of θ radians in standard position.

---

Without your calculator, use the definition above to state whether each of the following values is positive, negative, or zero:

a)  sin 6    b)  cos 4    c)  $\sin \frac{3\pi}{2}$    d)  $\cos \frac{3\pi}{2}$

e)  Explain how to determine whether a given value of sine or cosine will be positive or negative.

CT-111.  This problem is a milepost for writing and solving exponential equations.

When rabbits were first brought to Australia, they had no natural enemies. There were about 80,000 rabbits in 1866. Two years later, in 1868, the population had grown to over 2,400,000!

a) Why would an exponential equation be a better model for this situation than a linear one? Would a sine function be better or worse? Why?

b) Write an exponential equation for the number of rabbits  t  years after 1866.

c) How many rabbits do you predict would have been present in 1871?

d) According to your model, in what year was the first pair of rabbits introduced into Australia? Is this reasonable?

e) Is your exponential model useful for predicting how many rabbits are there now? Explain.

CT-112. Susan knew how to shift  $y = \sin x$ to get the graph at right, but she wondered if it would be possible to get the same graph by shifting  $y = \cos x$.

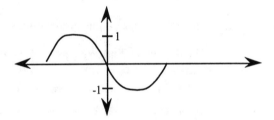

a) What do you think?

b) If you think it's possible, find the equation that does it. If you think it's impossible, explain why.

c) Adlai said, "I can get that graph **without** shifting to the right or left." What equation did he write?

CT-113. David Longshot loves playing golf after a long day of teaching mathematics. He is known for his long drives, and today he drove the ball 250 yards. He estimated that the ball reached a maximum height of 15 yards. Find a quadratic equation that would model the parabolic path of the golf ball.

CT-114. Linda and Francis need to find an equation to fit this graph. Linda wants to use $y = \sin x$, but Francis thinks that starting with $y = \cos x$ will be easier.

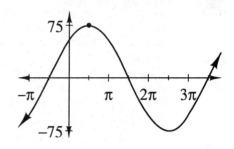

a) Which do you think is easier? Why?

b) Find equations both ways. That is, starting first with $y = \sin x$ and then with $y = \cos x$, find two different equations to fit the graph.

c) Test your ideas on your graphing calculator. Revise your equations if necessary, and make a note about what caused any error.

CT-115. Average daytime temperatures in Sidney, Australia are given below for four days during the year.

| Date | January 1st | April 1st | July 1st | October 1st |
|---|---|---|---|---|
| Temperature | 92° | 70° | 50° | 72° |

a) Sketch a graph of the temperature vs. time of year for Sidney.

b) Find an equation to approximate your graph.

CT-116. The pedal shaft on a standard bicycle is about 7 inches long and the center of the bottom bracket to which the pedal shaft is attached is about 11 inches above the ground. Sketch a graph that shows the relationship of the angle of the shaft (for one pedal) in standard position (as if the point of attachment were the origin of a set of x-y axes shifted up 11 units) to the height of one pedal above the ground as the pedal is turned.

Write an equation for a function that represents your graph.

CT-117. Solve for x: $x^2 - 5 = 2^{-x}$

CT-118. Find the x- and y-intercepts for each of the following equations.

a) $y = 2x^3 - 10x^2 - x$

b) $y + 2 = \log_3 (x - 1)$

CT-119. Too Tall Thomas has put Rodney's book bag on the pump house roof. Rodney goes to borrow a ladder from the school custodian. The tallest ladder available is 10 feet long and the roof is 9 feet from the ground. He places the ladder's tip at the edge of the roof. The ladder is unsafe if the angle it makes with the ground is more than 60°. Is this a safe situation? Explain.

CT-120. Deniz and Christina are at it again! This time Christina has broken into Deniz's computer and infected it with a virus. At first the virus will slowly erase information from Deniz's hard drive. As time goes on, the amount of information erased will increase. In t minutes after the virus starts erasing information, $5,000,000(\frac{1}{2})^t$ bytes of information remain on the hard drive.

a) Before the virus starts erasing, how many bytes of information are on Deniz's hard drive?

b) After how many minutes will there be 1,000 bytes of information left on the drive?

c) When will the hard drive be completely erased?

CT-121. Claudia graphed $y = \cos x$ and $y = \cos (x + 360°)$ on the same set of axes. She didn't see any difference in their graphs at all. Why not?

CT-122. Should $y = \sin x$ and $y = \cos x$ both be parent graphs, or is one the parent of the other? Give reasons for your decision.

CT-123. Simplify each value without using a calculator:

a) $25^{-1/2}$

b) $\left(\frac{1}{27}\right)^{-1/3}$

c) $9^{3/2}$

d) $16^{-3/4}$

**CT-124.** **Tangent Investigation**

The third trigonometric ratio you have used to solve triangles is the tangent. As you may have guessed, the tangent can also be interpreted as a circular function. The first thing you need to do is find out how it is related to the unit circle.

a) To investigate, take out a unit circle graph and draw an angle in standard position of 114° and another of 143°. The terminal rays can be extended to form lines. Use what you've learned in this unit to find the coordinates of a point where each line intersects the unit circle, and then use the coordinates of that point to write the equation of the line.

b) Next use your calculator to find tan 114° and tan 143°. What do you notice? We know that sin θ gives the y-coordinate on the unit circle at an angle of θ in standard position and cos θ gives the x-coordinate. What rule could you use to calculate tan θ ?

c) As in the case of sine and cosine, the tangent of an angle between 0° and 90° can be interpreted as a ratio of triangle sides. It can also be seen as the slope of a line through the origin. Make a unit circle sketch and explain why both interpretations lead to the same value.

**CT-125.** The graph of tan θ is very different from those of sine and cosine. To begin investigating, copy and complete the following table of values, using your calculator. Be sure to use the π key with your calculator in radian mode.

| x | $-\dfrac{\pi}{2}$ | $-\dfrac{5\pi}{12}$ | $-\dfrac{\pi}{3}$ | $-\dfrac{\pi}{4}$ | $-\dfrac{\pi}{6}$ | $-\dfrac{\pi}{12}$ | 0 | $\dfrac{\pi}{12}$ | $\dfrac{\pi}{6}$ | $\dfrac{\pi}{4}$ | $\dfrac{5\pi}{12}$ | $\dfrac{\pi}{2}$ | $\dfrac{7\pi}{12}$ | $\dfrac{2\pi}{3}$ |
|---|---|---|---|---|---|---|---|---|---|---|---|---|---|---|
| tan x | | | | | | | | | | | | | | |

a) Why is the tangent undefined at certain values? What does this indicate about the terminal ray for those angles? Find two other values of θ (in radians) for which tan θ will be undefined.

b) Find some values of tan θ when θ is very close to $\frac{\pi}{2}$. What happens to the values of tan θ as θ gets close to $\frac{\pi}{2}$ and $-\frac{\pi}{2}$. Why? (Think about the coordinates of the point on the unit circle.)

c) Plot the points from your table of values to sketch a graph of tan θ for θ from $-\frac{\pi}{2}$ to $\frac{\pi}{2}$. (Note that the θ-values in the table are evenly spaced.) Leave room to extend the graph up to θ = $\frac{3\pi}{2}$.

**>>Problem continues on the next page.>>**

d) Why are the values of tan for $\theta = \frac{7\pi}{12}$ and $\frac{2\pi}{3}$ the same as for $\theta = -\frac{5\pi}{12}$ and $-\frac{\pi}{3}$?

e) What values of x in the table are the same as those for $\theta$ between $\pi$ and $\frac{3\pi}{2}$? Use these values to extend your graph up to $\theta = \frac{3\pi}{2}$.

f) Is $y = \tan \theta$ periodic? Why or why not? If so, what is its period?

CT-126. Set the domain of your graphing calculator's viewing window to show $-\frac{\pi}{2} \leq x \leq \frac{\pi}{2}$ and the range to show $-10 \leq y \leq 10$. Then graph $y = \tan x$. Use radians.

a) What other function does the graph resemble?

b) Each of the sections of $y = \tan x$, separated by asymptotes, is called a branch of the function. Some people think that the branches of tan x are copies of $y = x^3$. Graph $y = x^3$ in the same window with $y = \tan x$. See if you can alter $y = x^3$ to match $y = \tan x$. What happens?

c) With the same window, graph the function $y = \frac{\sin x}{\cos x}$. What do you notice? Explain why this is so.

CT-127. Finish investigating $y = \tan x$. Be sure to include a general equation with a description of how the constants in it affect the graph. Add tan x to your Parent Graph Tool Kit.

CT-128. Make up a situation that could be accurately modeled using a circular function. Justify why you think a circular function would make a good model.

CT-129. Copy the following information into your Tool Kit, and answer the questions that follow.

> ### CONVERTING BETWEEN RADIANS AND DEGREES
>
> If an angle of rotation has radian measure R then the degree measure, D, is given
>
> by the equation: $D = \dfrac{R}{\pi}(180°)$ Likewise, R is given by the formula: $R = \dfrac{D}{180°}(\pi)$

a) Write a careful paragraph, using complete sentences, to explain why the formulas above make sense.

b) As you have seen, angles which are multiples of 30° and 45° are used very frequently in working with circular functions because their sines and cosines can be found exactly using special right triangles. For these angles there are shortcuts for applying the formulas above.

You should know that $30° = \dfrac{\pi}{6}$ radians, $45° = \dfrac{\pi}{4}$ radians, $60° = \dfrac{\pi}{3}$ radians, and 90°

$= \dfrac{\pi}{2}$ radians. If you don't know them, memorize them now.

A shortcut for converting radian measures which are multiples of these values to degrees is described in problem CT-40. Look back at that problem and refresh your memory.

For angles given in degrees, divide by the largest of the numbers 30, 45, 60, or 90 that goes into it evenly. Then multiply that number by the radian equivalent of the degree value you divided by. For example, consider the first one below. Since 210° is 7 x 30°, and $30° = \dfrac{\pi}{6}$ radians, the radian measure of 210° is7 x $\dfrac{\pi}{6}$. Do the rest of the conversions without a calculator, writing the steps as shown in the examples below.

$210° = 7\,(\,30°\,) = 7\left(\dfrac{\pi}{6}\right) = \dfrac{7\pi}{6}$          $\dfrac{3\pi}{4} = 3\dfrac{\pi}{4} = 3(45°) = 135°$

$270° =$          $\dfrac{5\pi}{3} =$

$450° =$          $\dfrac{11\pi}{3} =$

$150° =$          $\dfrac{7\pi}{2} =$

$240° =$          $\dfrac{7\pi}{4} =$

$330° =$          $\dfrac{7\pi}{3} =$

CT-130.   Rip-Off Rentals charges $25 per day plus 50¢ per mile to rent a mid-sized car. Your teacher will rent you his/her family sedan and charge you only 3¢ if you drive one mile, 6¢ if you drive two miles, 12¢ if you drive three, 24¢ for four, and so on.

a)   Write a rule that will give you the cost to rent each car.

b)   If you plan to rent the car for a two-day road-trip, which is the better deal if you drive: 10 miles? 20 miles? 100 miles?

CT-131.   Solve for x:  $|x + 5| = |x| - 5$. To find all solutions you will probably need to graph two functions.

CT-132.   Eddie was solving the equation

$$\cos(4x) = (\cos x) + 1.$$

His solution is shown at right.

a)   Check his answer in both degrees and radians. Is he right?

b)   If he is wrong, find his mistake and explain how <u>you</u> would solve his equation. You do not actually have to solve it—just explain how you would do it.

$$\cos(4x) = (\cos x) + 1$$

$$\frac{\cos(4x)}{\cos} = \frac{\cos x}{\cos} + 1$$

$$4x = x + 1$$

$$3x = 1$$

$$x = \frac{1}{3}$$

CT-133.   Solve for x:  $\log_2 x = 2^x$.

CT-134.   Sketch a graph of  $x^2 + y^2 = 100$.

a)   Is it a function?

b)   What are its range and domain?

c)   In your circle, make a central angle that measures $\frac{2\pi}{3}$ radians. If you remove this wedge of the circle, what is the left-over area?

CT-135.    Daniel sketched these graphs for $y = \sin x$ and $y = \cos x$.

Unfortunately, he forgot to label which is which, and now he can't remember. Help him out. Explain how he can tell (and remember!) which graph is sine and which is cosine.

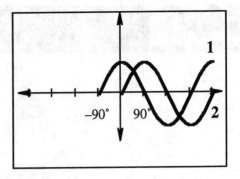

CT-136.    Make sure that your parent graph Tool Kit accurately contains the following information. Then answer the questions below.

The **GENERAL EQUATION FOR THE SINE FUNCTION** is

$$y = a \sin b(x - h) + k$$

This function has amplitude = a, period = $\frac{2\pi}{b}$, and locator point (h, k).

The **GENERAL EQUATION FOR THE COSINE FUNCTION** is

$$y = a \cos b(x - h) + k$$

This function has amplitude = a, period = $\frac{2\pi}{b}$, and locator point (h, k + 1).

A circular function has a "peak" at (2, 3). (The technical name for such a point where a function changes direction is a **relative maximum**.) From that point it decreases to a low point, or **relative minimum**, at (5, -11).

a)    Find the amplitude of the function.

b)    Find the period of the function.

c)    Write the formula for this graph using a cosine function .

# MODELING AND TRANSFORMATIONS WITH THE TANGENT FUNCTION

| time | meters |
|------|--------|
| 0 | 0 |
| 0.3 | 200 |
| 0.7 | 400 |
| 1.3 | 600 |
| 2.5 | 800 |
| 5.3 | 1000 |
| 16.8 | 1200 |
| 24.7 | 1250 |
| 34.1 | 1300 |
| 46.0 | 1400 |
| 52.9 | 1600 |
| 54.9 | 1800 |
| 55.9 | 2000 |
| 56.5 | 2200 |
| 56.8 | 2400 |
| 57.1 | 2600 |
| 57.3 | 2800 |

CT-137. Eoin (pronounced like Owen) lives near the seashore, and ever since he was little, he has been mesmerized by watching the beam of light from the lighthouse move along the shore as the light rotates. There is a straight sidewalk at the base of the seawall that runs along the beach. When Eoin was younger he would run along the sidewalk and try to race the beam as it moved across the wall along side him. He found that he could win the race for a while, but then the beam would move faster and faster and leave him behind. He realized that when the light first appeared on the wall far down the shore it moved very fast, then it slowed down as it came toward him and sped up again as it moved off into the distance.

As he grew older, he found ways to collect data so he could understand how the beam behaved. There were openings in the wall where the streets intersected the sidewalk. He determined that they were 200 meters apart. He realized that he could use the wall as a number line. He chose one of the openings in the wall near where the beam first became visible each time around and wrote 0 in chalk on the wall there. Then he rode his bike along the sidewalk from that point, writing chalk numbers at each opening in the wall to make his number line. Finally he was ready. He borrowed a stopwatch, started it when the light hit the 0 mark, and recorded how long the beam took to reach points along the wall. Some of the data he collected is listed in the table above right.

a) Enter the data that Eoin collected into your graphing calculator and using time as the independent variable, graph it. Estimate the locator point. What do you think could be the parent graph? Why does it make sense to use a periodic function?

b) Eoin realized he had more information. He noticed that the light made one full revolution in exactly 2 minutes (120 seconds) and that it only pointed toward the shore for half that time. How does this apply to the function that will best fit Eoin's data?

c) Help Eoin out. Find a function to fit his data. Check it on your graphing calculator.

CT-138.   Graph the function g(x) = cos 4x - sin 2x.

a)   Why does it make sense that this function is periodic?  What is its period? How many cycles does cos 4x complete in that interval?  How many cycles does sin 2x complete?

b)   Combinations of trigonometric functions are used to represent more complicated cycles.  Consider the following graph of an average person's blood pressure over time:

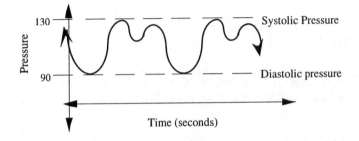

This represents blood pressure of 130 over 90 (130 systolic, 90 diastolic).  Think of g(x) as the parent graph for the graph above and adjust the function g(x) above to make it fit the graph shown.

CT-139.   Compare the graphs of  y = - sin x  and  y = sin (-x).  What do you notice?  Use the Circle of Terror to explain why.

CT-140.   Give the locator point for each of the following functions then use the five-point method to sketch each graph.

a)   y = sin (0.5(x - π ))          b)   y = 10 sin(3x) - 2

c)   y = 5 cos (x + $\frac{\pi}{4}$)          d)   y = cos (2(x - $\frac{\pi}{4}$))

CT-141.   Sketch a unit circle.  In your circle, sketch in an angle that has:

a)   a positive cosine and a negative sine.

b)   a sine of -1.

c)   a negative cosine and a negative sine.

d)   a cosine of about -0.9 and a sine of about 0.3.

e)   Could an angle have a sine equal to 0.9 and cosine equal to 0.8?  Give an angle or explain why not.

CT-142. For the system of equations at right,
$$x^2 + y^2 = 25$$
$$y = x^2 + 36$$

find the intersection of the graphs. To find the algebraic solution of the system you need to solve for x and y. In this case which variable is easier to solve for first: x or y? Do it. Now try to solve for the other variable first. What caused you to get stuck?

CT-143. Sketch a graph of $y = -x^2(x-2)^2(x+2)^2$.

CT-144. Inverse functions

Find the equation for the inverse of the following function: $y = 2\sqrt{3(x-1)} + 5$. Sketch the graph of both the original and the inverse.

## REVIEW AND SUMMARY

CT-145. Last week Tim was sitting in his math class playing with an ant (what else?) instead of working on circular functions with his team. He was trying to force the helpless ant to scurry in a perfect square. Luckily for the ant, Tim's teammates stopped him. Tim apologized, and to show him there were no hard feelings, the team let him help with one of their math problems. "OK, Tim," they said. "Look at the diagram. Here's a sketch of that poor ant you were pestering. It's walking along that square, on which we have conveniently put a set of axes. The ant starts at (1, 0) and walks counterclockwise."

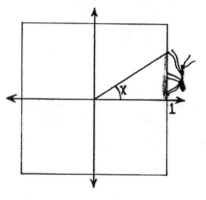

Consider a function (or non-function) where the input is the angle the ant makes with the positive x-axis and the output is the ant's <u>distance from the y-axis</u>. With your team, **investigate this function or non-function**. Be sure to include the usual information: intercepts, domain, asymptotes, etc.

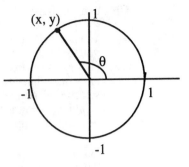

CT-146. In problem CT-141, part (e) you found that it is not possible for an angle to have a sine equal to 0.9 and cosine equal to 0.8. In fact, the sine and cosine are so closely linked that once you know the sine of an angle you can calculate the absolute value of the cosine, and vice versa. Look at the unit circle graph at right.

    a)    What equation must x and y satisfy if they are coordinates of a point on the unit circle?

    b)    What do you know about the relationship between x and θ? Between y and θ?

    c)    You now have three equations in three variables, one from part (a) and two from part (b). Use substitution to eliminate x and y and create an equation in terms of only θ .

    d)    This important equation is called the **Pythagorean Identity**. Use it to answer the following question: If the cosine of an angle is 0.8, what are the possible values of the sine of that angle?

CT-147. Given the points O(0, 0) and R(-5, -12), we will find the measure of the angle formed by $\overline{OR}$ in standard position.

    a)    What is the sine of the angle formed by $\overline{OR}$ in standard position?

    b)    Use your calculator (in degree mode) to find the measure of an angle whose sine is the number you found in part (a). Is this the angle formed by $\overline{OR}$ in standard position?

    c)    How many angles in standard position are there which have a sine equal to the number you found in part (a)?

    d)    Can the calculator know which is the one you're looking for? Which one do you think it gives you? How can you use that answer to find the angle formed by $\overline{OR}$?

CT-148. In problem CT-139 you found that sin (-x) = -sin x by comparing the graphs of y = sin (-x) and y = -sin x. Is a similar relation true for cos (-x)? What does cos (-x) equal? Why?

CT-149. Trigonometry means measurement of triangles and refers to the use of sine, cosine, and tangent to find unknown sides or angles of triangles. The study of circular functions is also referred to as trigonometry. What is the relationship between coordinates on the unit circle and the familiar opposite-adjacent-hypotenuse ratios of right triangle trigonometry?

CT-150. **UNIT 8 SUMMARY ASSIGNMENT**

a)  What are circular functions? Give a definition as you understand it. Then summarize the important new ideas of this unit, including an example for each one, along with a complete solution. In selecting examples, you should create at least three original problems that represent important concepts developed in the unit and show their solutions.

b)  What topics of trigonometry/circular functions do you have questions about and what do you think you understand well?

c)  Since the start of this course you have been learning about mathematics as a tool for modeling. Tell what you know about mathematical modeling so far. What is it? Why would someone want to do this? What functions might someone use for modeling? Describe types of situations that fit each of the functions we have studied so far.

CT-151.  Add the following information to your Tool Kit and answer the question below:

---

**THE TANGENT FUNCTION**

For any real number $\theta$, the **TANGENT of** $\theta$, denoted tan $\theta$, is the slope of the ray which represents a rotation of $\theta$ radians in standard position. It is also equal to the ratio $\frac{y}{x}$, where (x, y) is the point reached by a rotation of $\theta$ radians on the unit circle. In addition, $\tan x = \frac{\sin x}{\cos x}$. The general equation for the tangent function is

$$y = a \tan b(x - h) + k$$

This function has period $= \frac{\pi}{b}$, vertical asymptotes at $\frac{\pi}{2b} + h \pm \frac{n\pi}{b}$ for n = 1, 2, . . ., and locator point (h, k).

---

Without a calculator, sketch the graph of $y = \tan \frac{1}{3}(x - \pi) - 2$. Show at least 2 cycles and be sure to show the asymptotes.

CT-152.  Add the following information to your Tool Kit, and answer the question below.

---

**THE PYTHAGOREAN IDENTITY**

For any value of x,   $\sin^2 x + \cos^2 x = 1$

(Note that $\sin^2 x$ is an abbreviated way to write $(\sin x)^2$.)

---

If $\sin x = \frac{1}{3}$, find the values for cos x.

CT-153. Consider the system of equations at right. Can the system be solved by substitution? By the addition/subtraction method? By graphing?

$$y = \cos x$$
$$y = -1$$

a) If x is measured in degrees, list at least five solutions

b) Write several solutions if x is measured in radians.

c) Consider the lists of solutions you wrote in parts (a) and (b) as sequences and write a rule for each sequence of solutions as a way to represent ALL possible solutions.

CT-154. Write the equation of a circular function that has an amplitude of 7 and a period of $8\pi$. Sketch its graph.

CT-155. Sketch a graph of $y = x^3(x - 2)(x + 2)^2$.

CT-156. Find the solutions, real or complex, of the system at right:

$$y = x^2 + 2x + 5$$
$$y = 2x^2 + 4x + 7$$

CT-157. **TOOL KIT CHECK-UP**

Your Tool Kit contains reference tools for algebra. Return to your Tool Kit entries. You may need to revise or add entries.

Be sure that your Tool Kit contains entries for all of the items listed below. Add any topics that are missing to your Tool Kit NOW, as well as any other items that will help you in your study of algebra.

REGULAR TOOL KIT

- Five-Point Method for Graphing Periodic Functions

- Angles of Rotation

- The Sine and Cosine Functions

- The Tangent Function

- Radian Mode

- Radian Measure

- Converting between Radians and Degrees

- The Pythagorean Identity

PARENT GRAPH TOOL KIT should include complete entries for:

- Sin x

- Cos x

- Tan x

CT-158. **PORTFOLIO: GROWTH OVER TIME - PROBLEM #2**

On a separate piece of paper (so you can hand it in separately or add it to your portfolio) explain **everything** that you now know about the function below. Be sure to add everything that you have learned since the last time you did this problem and do not leave out anything that you included in your earlier attempts.

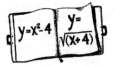

$$f(x) = 2^x - 3.$$

CT-159. **Growth Over Time Reflection** Look at your three responses to the growth-over-time problem above. Write an evaluation of your growth based your responses. Consider each of the following while writing your answer.

a) What new concepts did you include the second time you did the problem? In what ways was your response better than your first attempt?

b) How was your final version different from the first two? What new ideas did you include?

c) Did you omit anything in the final version that you used in one of the earlier problems? Why did you omit it?

d) Rate your three attempts by making three bars like those below and shading each bar to represent how much you knew on each attempt.

| | |
|---|---|
| First Attempt: | |
| Second Attempt: | |
| Final Attempt: | |

e) Is there anything you would add to your most recent version? If so, what is it?

# UNIT 9

# The Search for Sunken Treasure
## MORE TRIANGLES AND TRIGONOMETRY

# Unit 9 Objectives
## The Search for Sunken Treasure: MORE TRIANGLES AND TRIGONOMETRY

This unit uses what you have learned about trigonometry and circular functions to develop further the trigonometry of triangles. You will also learn more about trigonometric functions and their inverses.

In this unit you will have the opportunity to:

- develop the Law of Sines, which will allow you to determine missing parts of some triangles.

- develop the Law of Cosines, which, with the Law of Sines, will allow you to determine missing parts of any triangle.

- investigate inverse functions for trigonometric functions.

The following problem is the theme problem for this unit, but there is not enough information given for you to solve it now. To solve it you will need to use the Laws of Sines and Cosines.

---

ST-0.     **THE SEARCH FOR SUNKEN TREASURE**   Sandy Salvage has heard that a ship loaded with gold just sank off the coast of Florida in international waters. This means whoever gets there first can claim the gold. Getting there first is not a problem since Sandy has two of the best and fastest ships in the world, the Goldrush and the Goldfish.

Sandy's problem is that Blackbeard also wants the treasure. Blackbeard's ship, the Surging Skurge, is an old wreck. The only way Blackbeard will get his hands on the treasure is to let Sandy get the treasure aboard and then attack Sandy's ship. Sandy has decided that if he sends a decoy ship he will have a 50% chance of getting away with the treasure.

Your team has been captured by Blackbeard. You must determine which of Sandy's ships is the treasure ship. If your team finds the treasure ship Blackbeard will spare your lives. If you pick the wrong ship, you walk the plank!

The only information that Blackbeard gives you is a note from one of his spies with an angle of descent of 2.18° from the seaport to the location of the treasure.

---

PROBLEM SOLVING

REPRESENTATION/MODELING

FUNCTIONS/GRAPHING

INTERSECTIONS/SYSTEMS

ALGORITHMS

REASONING/COMMUNICATION

# Unit 9

## *The Search for Sunken Treasure*: MORE TRIANGLES AND TRIGONOMETRY

## THE LAW OF SINES

ST-1.    Think back to your knowledge of right triangle trigonometry. For the triangle at right, answer the following questions.

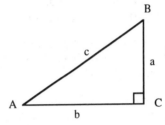

a)    What is the ratio for sin A?

b)    What is the ratio for cos A?

c)    What is the ratio for tan A?

ST-2.    For the triangle at right with side lengths a, b, and c:

 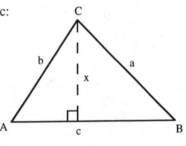

a)    Solve for x in terms of a and ∠B.

b)    Solve for x in terms of b and ∠A.

c)    What can we conclude?

d)    Show how your answer to part (c) leads to the formula: $\dfrac{\sin A}{a} = \dfrac{\sin B}{b}$ .

e)    What do you think is probably true of $\dfrac{\sin C}{c}$ ? Explain how you could show it.

f)    Add the information the box below to your Tool Kit.

>>**Problem continues on the next page.**>>

In parts (a) through (e) above, you derived the **LAW OF SINES**.

For <u>any</u> ΔABC, it is always true that:

$$\frac{\sin A}{a} = \frac{\sin B}{b} = \frac{\sin C}{c}$$

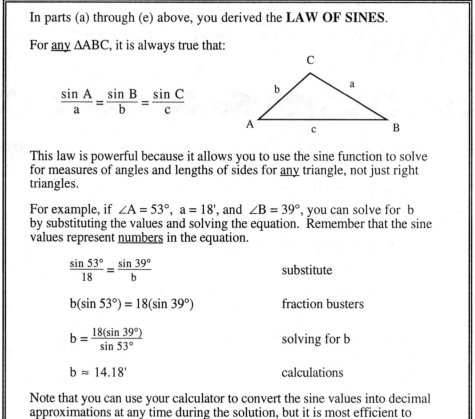

This law is powerful because it allows you to use the sine function to solve for measures of angles and lengths of sides for <u>any</u> triangle, not just right triangles.

For example, if ∠A = 53°, a = 18', and ∠B = 39°, you can solve for b by substituting the values and solving the equation. Remember that the sine values represent <u>numbers</u> in the equation.

$$\frac{\sin 53°}{18} = \frac{\sin 39°}{b}$$          substitute

$$b(\sin 53°) = 18(\sin 39°)$$          fraction busters

$$b = \frac{18(\sin 39°)}{\sin 53°}$$          solving for b

$$b \approx 14.18'$$          calculations

Note that you can use your calculator to convert the sine values into decimal approximations at any time during the solution, but it is most efficient to wait until the end of the problem.

ST-3.    Michelle pointed out to Jodi that the ratios $\frac{\sin A}{a} = \frac{\sin B}{b} = \frac{\sin C}{c}$ could also be written $\frac{a}{\sin A} = \frac{b}{\sin B} = \frac{c}{\sin C}$. Is Michelle correct? Why or why not?

ST-4.    Nathan lives 200 ft. down the river from Tong. Both live across the river from Amy. Nathan views the other two houses at a 100° angle while Tong sees them at 38°.

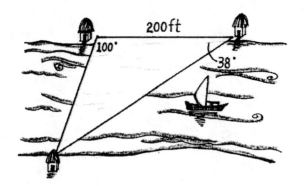

a)    Find the distance between Nathan's and Amy's house.

b)    Find the distance between Tong's and Amy's house.

ST-5.    Use the Law of Sines to find x and y. Be sure to
show how you set up the equation.

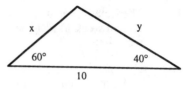

ST-6.    ΔPQR is an isosceles triangle with base angles of 46° and equal sides of length 26 cm.
Draw a diagram and use the Law of Sines to complete parts (a) through (c).

a)    Find the length of its base.          b)    Find the length of its perimeter.

c)    Find its area.

ST-7.    Sketch the graphs of each of the following on separate axes.

   i)    $y = (x + 3)^2 - 6$      ii)    $y = |(x + 3)^2 - 6|$      iii)    $y < (x + 3)^2 - 6$

a)    What are the domain and range for the graph in part (*i*)?

b)    What are the domain and range for the graph in part (*ii*)?

c)    How is the graph in part (*iii*) different from the other two parts?

ST-8.     Without graphing on a graphing calculator, find where the graph $y = 5 \cdot 2^x$ crosses
the line $y = 6$? Show your method.

ST-9.    Calculate the product $(3 + i)(1 + 2i)$. Illustrate with a sketch of the complex plane
showing both factors and the product.

ST-10.    The points (0, 6), (0, 0) and (4, 6) are connected with straight lines to enclose a region.
Imagine spinning this region about the y-axis.

a)    Describe the shape of the solid you get.  Make a sketch.

b)    Compute the volume of the figure.

ST-11.    The Lincoln's new business is doing very well. The first week they took in $1000, the second week $1100, the third week $1200, and each week thereafter $100 more than the week before.

a)    Decide what they started with and find an equation that describes the amount of money taken in for any week.

b)    How much did they take in during the 20th week?

ST-12.    Use elimination or matrix multiplication to solve
this system of equations:

$$x + \ y - z = 12$$
$$3x + 2y + z = 6$$
$$2x + 5y \ - z = 10$$

ST-13.    Jeanne Marie bought a sweater originally priced at $50 for 35% off. How much did she pay for the sweater?


## AREA FROM THE LAW OF SINES

ST-14.    How do you find the area of a triangle? List as many ways as you can with examples.

a)    Suppose in the triangle at right you knew the length of the base but not the length of the altitude. What could you do to find the area?

b)    Could you find the area if you knew neither the base nor the altitude?

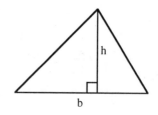

ST-15.    Explain completely how the Law of Sines could help you find the area of the triangle at right.

ST-16.    Given any ΔABC with altitude  x
(an example is shown below right):

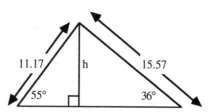

a)    draw a diagram and label it in the same way as the one at right, then represent the area of the triangle.

b)    what is the ratio for  sin A? Solve this expression for  x.

c)    substitute this expression for  x  into your area equation in part (a).

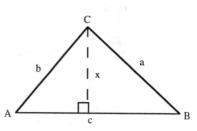

ST-17.  Using the triangle from the previous problem:

a)  Represent the area of the triangle algebraically.

b)  What is the ratio for sin B? Solve this expression for x.

c)  Substitute this expression for x into your area equation (in part (a)) to get another formula for the area of ΔABC.


ST-18.  Based on the same triangle you used in the last two problems, discuss with your team how to write an area formula that uses sin C. Based on your discussion, write a step-by-step explanation of how to find the area of a triangle when given the lengths of two sides and the measure of the angle between them. You may want to put this new way to find the area of a triangle in your Tool Kit.


ST-19.  An isosceles triangle has a perimeter of 42 inches. A base angle measures 62°. What is the area of the triangle?


ST-20.  Compute the area of these triangles using the information given:

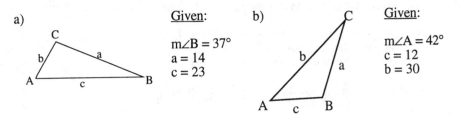

a)

Given:

m∠B = 37°
a = 14
c = 23

b)

Given:

m∠A = 42°
c = 12
b = 30


ST-21.  Have you ever wondered why the TV weather-person reports the temperature and the humidity at the same time? When it is hot and very humid, you feel hotter. When it is not very humid, you feel cooler. Suppose the temperature reaches its daily maximum at 3 p.m., and the humidity level reaches its daily maximum at 9 p.m.

a)  Sketch a graph of the temperature over a three-day period. You can assume daily cycles of highs and lows and use the five-point method to outline your graph.

b)  Sketch a graph of the humidity level over a three-day period.

c)  Imagine combining these two graphs into one which would represent "the discomfort level." When do you think is the most uncomfortable time of the day for most people?

ST-22.    Solve the system at right for  x  and  h:          $x^2 + h^2 = 25$

$(7 - x)^2 + h^2 = 36$

ST-23.    A seven foot board is cut into two pieces.  If one piece is  x  feet long, how long is the other piece?

ST-24.    Graph $y = x^{3/2}$.  You can find enough points using a regular scientific calculator.

a)    Graph the inverse.

b)    State the domain and range for each function.

c)    How many point(s) of intersection are there for the two equations?  What are they?

ST-25.    A function, f(x), is shown at right.

a)    If this is a complete graph, what are the domain and range of f(x)?

b)    Make a sketch of what f(x + 3)  would look like.

c)    Make a sketch of what  3·f(x)  would look like.

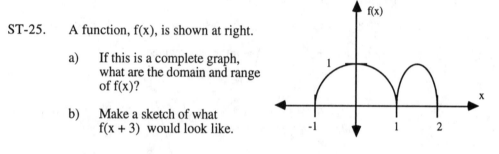

ST-26.    Solve for  x.

a)    $2x^3 = 75$                     b)    $2(3)^x = 75$

# APPLICATIONS OF AREA AND LAW OF SINES

ST-27.    The towns of Lake Forest and Greenville are 12 miles apart.  The angles of elevation to a balloon directly between the towns are 12° and 33° respectively.

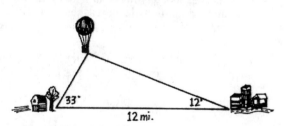

a)    Find the altitude of the balloon.

b)    How far would you have to drive from Greenville to the balloon if there were no wind and the balloon came straight down?

**ST-28.** Kaun Kreit, the cement contractor, has a job to pour cement for a patio that already has a sidewalk down the middle. The measurements that Kaun got from the owner were from a picture like the one at right. In the picture all of the lengths are in inches.

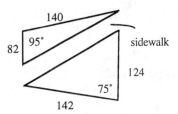

a)  Find the area of the top surface of each piece of patio in square feet.

b)  If the concrete is to be 4 inches thick, find the volume of concrete needed for the job.

c)  If concrete costs $60 per cubic yard, how much will Kaun have to pay for the load of concrete?

**ST-29.** Mathematicians invent symbols and abbreviations, called notation, to represent mathematical concepts. Sometimes the notation is more difficult to understand than the concepts! Consider the functions $y = \sin^{-1} x$ and $y = \dfrac{1}{\sin x}$.

a)  Use your graphing calculator to graph the equation $y = \sin^{-1} x$ (use the $\sin^{-1}$ button) and sketch the graph.

b)  Use your graphing calculator to graph the equation $y = \dfrac{1}{\sin x}$ and sketch the graph.

c)  Are these graphs the same? Now graph the equation $y = (\sin x)^{-1}$. Which two graphs are the same? Why does this make sense?

**ST-30.** Consider this sequence of triangles.

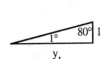

Triangle 1          Triangle 2          Triangle 3

a)  What would the $n^{\text{th}}$ triangle look like?

b)  Write a general equation for the length of $y_n$.

c)  Suppose a function is defined as follows: using the pattern generated above, the input is the triangle number and the output is $y$ for that triangle. Write a formula for this function. What are the domain and range for this function?

d)  If you have a graphing calculator, use it and make a sketch of the graph.

ST-31.    Find the area of the shaded figure if $\angle BAC = 30°$
          and $r = 5$.

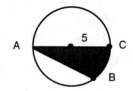

ST-32.    A fire is spotted by two lookout stations
          that are 10 miles apart. The Smoky
          Ridge station measures an angle of 78°
          between the fire and the Firesight station.
          Firesight measures an angle of 43°
          between the fire and Smoky Ridge.

          a)    How far is the fire from Firesight
                Station?

          b)    How far is the fire from Smoky Ridge?

ST-33.    On January 1st, the student population at Awl R. Smart High School, a year-round
          school, was 1368 students. Three months later, on April 1st, the population seems to
          have declined exponentially, and is 1124 students.

          a)    Assuming that the population is declining exponentially, write an equation which
                will give the student population at time $x$ in months.

          b)    Will the population ever reach zero?

          c)    The school board will shut the school down if the student population drops below 100
                students. When will this happen?

ST-34.    Write $(a^{-1} + b^{-1})^{-1}$ as a single fraction with positive exponents.

ST-35.    Solve each quadratic equation and then graph the solutions in the complex plane.

          a)    $x^2 + 4x + 5 = 0$                    b)    $x^2 - 6x + 13 = 0$

ST-36.    Here is another funny rule: If $A ¤ B ¤ C$ means $\dfrac{A^{(B-C)}}{A^{(C-B)}}$. What is:

          a)    $2 ¤ 3 ¤ 4$?          b)    $4 ¤ 3 ¤ 2$?          c)    $A ¤ A ¤ A$?

ST-37. If a 4-cm cube is first painted red and then cut into sixty-four 1-cm cubes, what is the probability that a cube chosen at random will be painted on:

a) 0 sides?  b) 1 side?  c) 2 sides?

d) 3 sides?  e) 4 sides?  f) all 6 sides?

ST-38. Solve each of the following for x and/or y.

a) $5 \cdot 4^x = 12$

b) $x^2 + y^2 = 16$
$y = x^2 - 4$

ST-39. Draw examples of:

a) a regular polygon.  b) a regular pyramid.

c) a right cylinder.  d) a cone.

# SOLVING TRIANGLES GIVEN THREE SIDES

ST-40. The lengths of the sides of a triangle are 3, 4, and 5.

a) Is this triangle a right triangle? Justify your answer.

b) Sketch a picture of this triangle.

c) Find the measures of the other parts (i.e. the three angles) to the nearest hundredth of a degree.

ST-41. Suppose that you want to find the measures of the angles in a triangle with sides measuring 5, 6, and 7.

a) Is this a right triangle? Justify your answer.

b) Explain what happens if you try to find the measures of the other parts, the three angles, by using the Law of Sines.

**ST-42.** Since the Law of Sines doesn't seem to help us in cases like the one in the preceding problem, we need to develop another method to find the measures of the angles.

a) In the picture at right, if the length of $\overline{AP}$ is x, what expression represents the length of $\overline{PB}$?

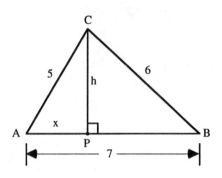

b) Use the Pythagorean Theorem to write a system of two equations: one using 5, x and h and the other using the length of $\overline{PB}$, h, and 6.

c) Solve your system of two equations for x and h.

**ST-43.** Now that you have found the lengths of the sides of the smaller **right** triangles, you can find the measures of the angles. What are the measures of the angles to the nearest tenth?

**ST-44.** Find the measures of each of the angles in a triangle with sides of length:

a) 5, 7, and 9.

b) 6, 8, and 10.

**ST-45.** In this problem use the same steps (using the Pythagorean Theorem) as you used to solve the previous problems. This time you will use only variables.

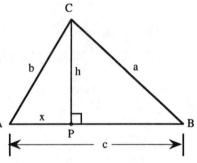

a) Write two appropriate equations using the smaller right triangles.

b) Solve the system for x. Your solution should contain a, b, and c.

c) Use your result in part (b) as a substitute for x and solve for h. The result should contain a, b, and c and will look very messy.

**ST-46.** Solve the following equations for x. Round answers to the nearest 0.1°

a) $8 = 5 + 2 \tan x$

b) $4^2 = 5^2 - 2(4) \tan x$

c) $6 - 2 \tan x = 4 + 5 \tan x$

ST-47.    Macario just completed part (a) of the previous problem. After writing the original
         statement, his first step was to write $8 = 7 \tan x$ and then he divided by 7 to get
         $1.143 = \tan x$. Is there anything wrong with the method that he is using? Explain.


ST-48.    Shawn was working on simplifying an answer that he got to a physics problem. His
         original solution was:

$$a = \sqrt{70^2 + 25^2 - 2(70)(25)(\cos 50°)}$$

$$a = \sqrt{4900 + 625 - 3500(\cos 50°)}$$

$$a = \sqrt{2025(\cos 50°)}$$

$$a = \sqrt{2025(0.642788)}$$

$$a = \sqrt{1301.6}$$

$$a \approx 36.1$$

What is wrong with this solution? What is the correct value of a?


ST-49.    Consider the sequence where 87 is the initial value:

$$87 \qquad 71 \quad 55 \quad 39 \quad \ldots$$

a)    What are the next three terms?

b)    Write a formula for the $n$th term after the initial value.


ST-50.    A population of bacteria cells grows at the rate shown in the table below.

a)    How many cells are there after six hours?

| Hours | Cells (in thousands) |
|-------|----------------------|
| 0     | 5                    |
| 1     | 15                   |
| 2     | 45                   |

b)    Write a formula which will give the number
      of cells at hour n.


ST-51.    Where do these three planes intersect?

$$3x + 4y = 19$$
$$2y + 3z = 8$$
$$4x - 5z = 7$$

**ST-52.** As grain is being unloaded from a freight car, the rising pile forms the shape of a cone. The pile grows as more and more grain is unloaded, but the cones at different stages are always similar. After ten minutes the height of the cone is five feet and the radius of the base is nine feet. After thirty minutes, the height is twelve feet. How much area, on the ground, does the pile cover at this point?

**ST-53.** Compute each complex product.

a) $\left(1+i\sqrt{3}\right)^2$

b) $\left(1+i\sqrt{3}\right)^3$

## THE LAW OF COSINES

**ST-54.** Recall from yesterday the problem where we wanted to find the angles in a triangle with side lengths 5, 6, and 7. In order to solve that problem it was necessary to solve a system of quadratic equations. Although you were able to solve this problem, it involved many subproblems. We would like to turn this long series of subproblems into a shorter method by developing a general rule or formula.

Consider the figure at right:

a) Find e in terms of c and d.

b) Split the figure into **two right triangles** and make clearly labeled sketches of the new triangles.

c) Use the Pythagorean Theorem with each **right triangle** to find two equations (one for $b^2$ and one for $a^2$), but don't use e. Use what you found in part (a) as a substitution for e.

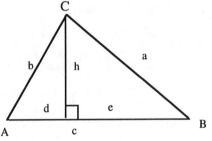

**ST-55.** Using the **smaller right triangle** above, what is the ratio for cos A?

ST-56. Our goal is to create an equation, similar to the Pythagorean Theorem, which tells how the lengths of the sides of the original triangle are related even when the triangle is not a right triangle. The lengths we are interested in are a, b, and c.

a) Look at the equations you found in problem ST-54 part (c). To find the formula we seek, which variables need to be eliminated?

b) Using the techniques you have learned for solving systems of equations, eliminate h from this system (i.e., combine the two equations to make one equation in which the $h^2$ term no longer appears).

c) Solve the resulting equation for $a^2$. Simplify the result by expressing it without parentheses and combining similar terms.

d) What does this expression remind you of?

e) What do you think is the significance of the term -2cd?

f) Solve the equation in problem ST-55 for d, then substitute for d in your answer to part (c) above.

g) Explain why it makes sense that, in order to find $a^2$, you need to know angle A, as well as lengths b and c.

---

In the previous problem you derived one version of **LAW OF COSINES**.

For <u>any</u> $\triangle ABC$, it is always true that: $a^2 = b^2 + c^2 - 2bc \cos A$.

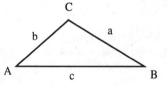

This law is very useful because it allows you to use the cosine function to solve for measures of angles and lengths of sides for <u>any</u> triangle, not just right triangles.

---

ST-57. The Law of Cosines can be thought of as the Pythagorean Theorem with a correction term for non-right triangles. To investigate, suppose b = 3 and c = 4.

a) What is the value of a when m∠A = 90°?

b) Find 'a' when m∠A = 40°. How does this value compare to the 'a' in part (a)?

c) Find 'a' when m∠A = 110°. How does this value compare to the 'a' in part (a)?

d) What relationship do you notice between the size of ∠A and the "correction term"?

ST-58. Rewrite the Law of Cosines in the form "cos A = "; that is, solve for cos A.

ST-59. You are a surveyor who needs to lay out a triangular lot at the corner of an intersection. The two streets bounding the lot make an angle of 70°. The lengths of the two sides of the lot on these streets are 140 feet and 112 feet.

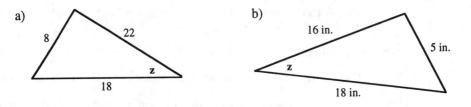

a) Decide whether or not there is exactly one lot which can have the required properties and explain why you made this decision.

b) Find the length of the third side of the lot.

c) Find the other two angles of the lot.

ST-60. Suppose that the city of Eau Claire passes an ordinance that corner lots cannot be larger than 7200 square feet in area. Would the lot in the preceding problem be approved in Eau Claire? Justify your answer.

ST-61. Substitute the known sides and angle into the Law of Cosines to find the missing side x to the nearest hundredth.

a)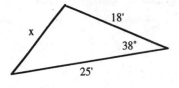
18'
x
38°
25'

b)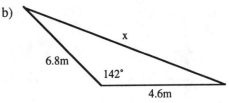
x
6.8m
142°
4.6m

ST-62. The Law of Cosines can be used to solve for missing angles as well. Refer to your result in problem ST-58, then solve each of the following problems for z:

a)
8
22
z
18

b)
16 in.
5 in.
z
18 in.

ST-63. Let $f(x) = (x + 3)^3(x^2 - 4x)$. Find the roots of $f(x)$ and make a rough sketch of the graph.

ST-64.   Refer to the Quadratic Formula for solving $ax^2 + bx + c = 0$.  Under what conditions will the equation have:

a)   one real solution?     b)   two real solutions?     c)   no real solutions?

ST-65.   Write each of the following as a single fraction:

a)   $\dfrac{2}{x} + \dfrac{4}{y}$                    b)   $\dfrac{1}{x - 2} - \dfrac{1}{x + 2}$

c)   Justify each of the steps you took in part (b).

ST-66.   McGumper is locked in a shrinking room.  The initial dimensions are 10 feet by 10 feet by 10 feet.  After one minute the room is 9.5 feet long, 9.5 feet wide and 9 feet high.

a)   What is the initial volume of the room?

b)   What is the volume after one minute?

c)   If the dimensions of the room continue to change at this constant rate, what is the volume of the room after  n  minutes?

d)   Sketch a graph to show how the volume changes as time passes.

e)   McGumper needs a minimum of 100 cubic feet of space and 6 minutes to escape.  Will McGumper make it out safely?

ST-67.   To find the height h of a small mountain in the California Coast Range, two angle measurements were taken 1200 feet apart along a direct line toward the mountain. With this information, find the height of the mountain.

ST-68.   Triangle ABC has m∠A = 65°, m∠C = 45° and BC = 10 cm.  Find the length(s) of $\overline{AC}$.  Hint: draw a diagram!

ST-69.   In a major league baseball diamond, which is in fact a square, the bases are 90 feet apart, and the pitcher's mound is exactly 60 feet 6 inches from home plate.

a)   Draw a diagram of the baseball diamond.

b)   Find the distance between the pitcher's mound and third base.

ST-70.   An isosceles triangle has an area of 60 square centimeters and a base of 10 centimeters. Draw a sketch of such a triangle.

a)   Draw the line segment from the midpoint of the base to the opposite vertex to get two smaller triangles.  List everything you know about these smaller triangles.

b)   Find the lengths of the two congruent sides of the isosceles triangle.

c)   List the subproblems that you had to solve to answer part (b).

ST-71.   Tuan Nguyen noticed that during the winter, even with his heater running, the temperature in his house would rise and fall throughout a 24 hour period.  Here are some temperatures he recorded at different times.

| time | Midnight | 4:00 a.m. | 8:00 a.m. | Noon | 4:00 p.m. | 8:00 p.m. |
|---|---|---|---|---|---|---|
| temperature | 63° | 59° | 63° | 71° | 75° | 71° |

Using Tuan's recorded amounts:

a)   graph the data.

b)   write an equation which could model this data.

ST-72.    In geometry, we had several methods for showing that two triangles are congruent. (For example, we could use the **SSS** congruence property.)

a)    List as many methods as you can remember.

b)    Suppose you know three sides of a triangle (**SSS**). Would you want to use the Law of Sines, the Law of Cosines, or some other techniques from trigonometry to compute the three angles of the triangle? Creating an example might help you to think about this.

c)    Use whatever technique you decided on in part (b) to compute the angles of a triangle with sides 3, 6 and 7.


ST-73.    Al needs to drill a water well for his new home in the hills. Becky, who lives in the valley below said that she had to drill 84 feet before she struck water. The distance straight up the hill to Al's cabin is 3150 feet. If the angle of inclination for the hill averages 15°, how far down will Al have to drill assuming the water is at the same level as it was for Becky? Do you think this situation is, in reality, likely to occur?


ST-74.    Hue was making $6.50 an hour working at Burger Delite and looking to move up.

a)    When she was made night manager, her salary went up 40%. How much was she making then?

b)    Hue figured she was on easy street and began arriving late for work, so she was demoted and had her salary reduced by 40%. What does she make now?

c)    Forty per cent was added then taken off. Why is Hue's new salary lower than her original salary?


ST-75.    Solve for  x  if  $x^3 + 4x = 0$.


ST-76.    Let $z = \dfrac{(a^3 b^{-2})^{-3}}{ab^3}$ .

a)    Write  z  as a fraction using only positive exponents.

b)    Write  z  as a fraction using only negative exponents.


ST-77.    The junior class at Pohatsa High School decided it would be more cost effective to buy CD's and tapes for their school dances than to hire a DJ. Danielle found that six CD's cost the same as ten cassette tapes while Kris found that 12 CD's and 15 tapes cost $272.73. Find the cost per CD and the cost per tape.

ST-78.    Plot the following eight values of the polynomial function f(x) given below on one set of axes. This function has at least how many roots?

$$f(-5) = -1 \qquad f(-3) = 3 \qquad f(-1) = 6 \qquad f(5) = 0$$

$$f(0) = 5 \qquad f(1) = -1 \qquad f(3) = -4 \qquad f(9) = 8$$

ST-79.    Simplify each of the following expressions:

a)   $2^x \cdot 2^x$

b)   $\dfrac{2^x}{2}$

ST-80.    Factor:  $2^x + 2$.

ST-81.    John thinks that  $\log (A^n) = \log (A) + n$  and here is his proof. Examine each step and if it correct, tell why. If it incorrect, change it so that it is correct.

Let    x = log A.

That means that    $A = 10^x$.

Then it is true that  $(A)^n = (10^x)^n = 10^{x+n}$

If  $(A)^n = 10^{x+n}$, then  $\log (A)^n = \log 10^{x+n} = x + n$

So finally        $\log (A)^n = x + n = \log (A) + n$

ST-82.     Consider △ABC at right:

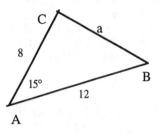

a)   Why is this a well-defined triangle?  What theorem ensures that all triangles with this given information will be congruent?

b)   Find the length of the missing side  a.

c)   Use the Law of Sines to find m∠C.  Then use subtraction to find m∠B. Record your answers.

d)   Now use the Law of Sines to find ∠B first and then use subtraction to find  ∠C. Record your answers.

e)   Which triangle is correct?  Explain how you can tell.

ST-83.     What happened in the previous problem?  Does the order in which we find the angles really matter?  On a Unit Circle resource page, draw ∠C (the correct  ∠C!) from problem ST-82 in standard position.  What type of angle is this?

a)   Find the sine of ∠C.  Record that value on your paper and show it on the unit circle.

b)   You know how to use the sin⁻¹ key to find the measure of an angle when you know its sine.  What would you expect to get if you find sin⁻¹ of your answer to part (a)?  Do it.  What do you actually get?  Does it look familiar?  Record this angle on your paper and draw it on the same unit circle.

c)   What relationship do these two angles have? Why do they have the same sine?

d)   Make a conjecture about your findings.

ST-84.     ## USE SIN⁻¹ WITH CAUTION!

a)   What kind of angle is 110°?  Find the sine of 110° and record this value. Using the sin⁻¹ key, find sin⁻¹ of the value you just recorded.  What angle did you get?  What is the relationship between these two angles?

b)   When you find sin⁻¹(0.9397) on your calculator, you are essentially asking "What is **the** angle whose sine is 0.9397?"  But there isn't just one such angle, and the calculator can only give you one answer.  In general, which answer does it give you?

c)   Every time you use the Law of Sines to find the measure of an angle, you must consider the possibility that the angle you are looking for is not the one the calculator gives you!  What must you do to make sure that your answer is correct?

d)   Record your answer to part (c) in your Tool Kit.

ST-85. Sometimes you can't tell whether the missing angle is acute or obtuse. This happens when the triangle is not uniquely defined by the information given. Consider a triangle, ABC, with $\angle A = 30°$ and side $c = 10$. Using the Law of Sines, and each value of 'a' given below, determine the measure of $\angle C$.

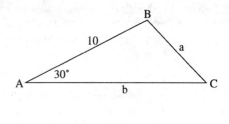

a)    $a = 5$              b)    $a = 3$              c)    $a = 7$

d)    Sketch a picture to illustrate your answer to part (a). Use it to explain your answer to part (b).

e)    Did you get two answers in part (c)? Perhaps you assumed that b is the longest side, so $\angle C$ must be acute, but the drawing is deceptive; we don't know the length of side b. Draw another version of the triangle, with m$\angle A$ still 30°, $c = 10$ and $a = 7$, but with $\angle C$ the largest angle. It helps to imagine side 'a' hinged at vertex B, since $\angle B$, $\angle C$, and side b are all unknown. Label this drawing with the correct measures of its angles.

ST-86. We could describe problem ST-85 as an example of SSA: finding the missing parts of the triangle when given two sides and an angle other than the one between the known sides.

a)    For each of the following SSA cases, draw as many different triangles fitting the data as you can. The sides and angles are listed in order as you go around the triangle:

i)    40°, 5, 7              ii)    40°, 7, 5              iii)    30°, 10, 5

b)    SSA should not be one of the congruence theorems you listed in problem ST-72. Explain why SSA is not a congruence theorem.

ST-87. Write out several sentences explaining how to use the Law of Sines to find all possible solutions to a triangle for which you know two sides and an angle that is not included between them (SSA). Make sure your answer applies to all three examples in problem ST-86 (a).

ST-88. Investigate the SSA case of 30°, 11, 5. Make a sketch, and use the Law of Sines to find one of the missing angles. Explain the result.

ST-89. Are there any other combinations of three angles and/or sides that could be given to mislead you into thinking there was a triangle when there wasn't? If so, what are they?

ST-90.    For each of the congruence methods you listed in part (a) of problem ST-72, decide whether you can find the other three parts of the triangle using only the Law of Sines, only the Law of Cosines, or if you will need to use both?

ST-91.    A trapezoid has an altitude of 6 cm and bases of length 20 cm and 8 cm.

   a)    Find its area.

   b)    The original trapezoid is cut by a line parallel to and halfway between its parallel edges to make two new trapezoids. Find the area of each.

ST-92.    A circle of radius 10 cm cut out of cardboard weighs 120 gm.

   a)    How much would a 60° sector weigh?

   b)    How much would a circle of radius 15 cm cut out of the same cardboard weigh? *Think carefully! This is not as simple as it may appear!*

ST-93.    Write each of the following expressions as a single fraction:

   a)    $\dfrac{2}{5} + \dfrac{4}{x}$

   b)    $\dfrac{x^2}{x + 1} - \dfrac{2}{x}$

ST-94.    In the figure at right, solve for x.

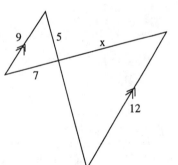

ST-95.    Consider the triangle below right.

   a)    Using the given information, could you draw a non-congruent triangle? What congruence property justifies your answer?

   b)    Find the lengths of the unknown sides and the measure of the missing angle.

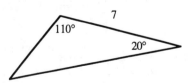

ST-96.     It was another lazy day in southern
Florida.  Sandy Salvage, the
famous underwater explorer (he's
the only diver ever to have gone to
a depth of 1 kilometer in just scuba
gear) and treasure hunter of The
Golden Mind Company, has heard
that a ship loaded with gold just
sank off the coast of Florida in
international waters.  All Sandy has
to do is be the first company to get
to the wreck site and he can claim
the underwater treasure.  Getting
there first is, of course, not a

problem since Sandy has two of the best and fastest ships in the world, the Goldrush
and the Goldfish.

Sandy's problem is that Blackbeard, the famous pirate of the high seas, also wants the
treasure.  Blackbeard's ship, the Surging Skurge, is an old wreck herself, and the only
way Blackbeard will get his grimy hands on the treasure is to wait until Sandy gets the
treasure aboard, then attack Sandy's ship.  Sandy has decided that if he sends a decoy
ship, he will have a 50% chance of not having to fight off the villain.

Your team, which has been captured by Blackbeard (because of your mathematical
power), must determine which of Sandy's ships has been chosen to be the treasure ship.
You must help Blackbeard get the treasure.  If your team finds the correct ship Blackbeard
has promised to spare your lives.  If you pick the wrong ship, you walk the plank!

The only information that Blackbeard could give you was a note from one of his spies
with the angle of descent  of 2.18° from the seaport to the actual location of the treasure.

Be sure to read each part of the following three problems carefully and refer back to this
introduction if necessary.

ST-97.     The Goldrush left port on a due east heading for 15
km then turned toward the north 55° from east for 27
km.  The Goldrush dropped anchor there, but sent a
mini submarine in the same direction as a line going
directly from the port <u>through</u> the Goldrush.  The sub
descended at a 48° angle for 2 kilometers.

a)    How far from port was the Goldrush when it
dropped anchor?

b)    How far was it from the shore to the final
location of the sub?

c)    What was the angle of descent from the shore to the final location of the sub?

ST-98. The Goldfish left the port at the same time and headed 15° south of due east for 20 kilometers. From that heading the crew turned toward the north 80° for 38 kilometers. At that point the Goldfish dropped anchor and the diver-down flag went up. The treasure appeared to be directly beneath the ship.

a) What is the distance between port and the Goldfish when it dropped anchor?

b) What is the depth of the water if this is where the treasure is located?

c) How far is it from the shore to the possible location of the treasure?

ST-99. Well, you scurvy barnacles, make your decision! Are you spared, or do you walk the plank? Which ship do you send Blackbeard after, the Goldrush or the Goldfish? Explain your reasoning.

ST-100. A quadrilateral has its vertices at A(0, 0), B(8, 1), C(6, 7), and D(-1, 9).

a) Sketch the figure on graph paper. b) Find the length of the longer diagonal.

c) Explain in a sentence or two how you could find the measure of angle A. (Don't do it—just tell <u>how</u> you would do it.)

ST-101. Find the acute angle formed by the intersection of the lines $y = -\frac{1}{5}x + 4$ and

$y = -\frac{4}{5}x + 1$. Starting with a precise graph might be helpful.

ST-102. In a Modoc High School production, the stage crew must build a model of the Leaning Tower of Pisa. The model will be 15 feet long, but when they stand it up it will not reach that altitude since it will be leaning 10° from the vertical. A wire which will hold the tower in place is attached to the floor 20 feet from the bottom of the Leaning Tower model. How long must the wire be to reach the top of the Leaning Tower of Pisa?

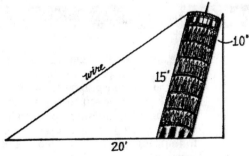

ST-103. Plot the points (0, 2), (3, 4) and (6, 9).

a) Find the equation of the line that best fits these points.

b) Find the equation of the parabola which best fits these points.

c) Find the equation of the exponential function which best fits these points.

ST-104.    Find the angles in the triangle formed by the points  A(-2, 6),  B(4, 3), and  C(4, -3).

ST-105.    Make a sketch of the graph of each of the equations below.  On the same set of axes, sketch the inverse.  Then algebraically find the equation of the inverse.

a)    $y = x^3 + 5$

b)    $y = 4 \cdot 2^x$

ST-106.    Of the inverses you found in the previous problem, which are functions?  Justify your answer.

ST-107.    Solve each of the following for  x:

a)    $\log_2 \left( \frac{3x}{x + 1} \right) = -1$

b)    $\log_3 \left( \frac{2x + 28}{x} \right) = 2$

ST-108.    Solve the following system for  x  and  y:    $\begin{array}{l} 2x - y = 7 \\ x + 2y = 9 \end{array}$

ST-109.    Find the value of  $(3y - 5)^2$  if  $2y + 2 = 16$.

# INVERSE TRIGONOMETRIC FUNCTIONS

ST-110.    Take out two full, clean sheets of graph paper.  On each page, set up x- and y-axes, centered on the page.  Let the units on your x-axis be in radians.  On one graph, make a neat and accurate graph of  $y = \sin x$  and on the other a graph of  $y = \cos x$.  Do them in thick, heavy pencil and include two full cycles, one on each side of the origin.  Use the technique of folding the page along the line  $y = x$  to make a graph of the <u>inverse</u> of each of these functions.  What is the formula for each of these graph?  Label each graph with its formula.

ST-111.    Investigate the two inverses.

ST-112.    Using your graphing calculator, try to find an equation which, when graphed, will give the inverses you have on the graph paper.  Why do you get only a portion of the graph of the inverse?  Explain completely.

ST-113. You have been using the function $y = \text{Sin}^{-1} x$ on your calculator for some time, but as you saw in the previous problem this function is not precisely the inverse of $y = \sin x$, since that inverse is not function. Instead, $y = \text{Sin}^{-1} x$ is the inverse of a part of the sine function; to see which part, graph the inverse of $y = \text{Sin}^{-1} x$. In this piece of the sine function (or restricted sine function, because $x$ has been restricted to certain values), each value in the range appears exactly once, so that when you take the inverse of *this* function it will be a function; for each $x$ between -1 and 1 inclusive, there will be exactly one angle $y$ whose sine is $x$. That angle is referred to as the **principal angle whose sine is x**, and this function in addition to being called the **Inverse Sine of x**, denoted $y = \text{Sin}^{-1} x$, is also called the **Arcsine of x**, denoted **y = Arcsin x**. (Warning: what in this case looks like an exponent of -1 **does not** mean $\frac{1}{\sin x}$. See problem ST-29.) Refer to the graphs of $x = \sin y$ and $y = \text{Sin}^{-1} x$ from problems ST-110 and ST-112. You may also use the Circle of Terror diagram.

a) Find four solutions to the equation $\sin y = 0.5$. Which of these is $\text{Sin}^{-1} 0.5$?

b) Find four solutions to the equation $\sin y = -0.5$. Which of these is $\text{Sin}^{-1} -0.5$?

c) Of all the values of $y$ for which $\sin y = x$ for a given $x$, which is the *principal value* of $y$ whose sine is $x$? (i.e., which one is $\text{Sin}^{-1} x$?) How is this related to the restricted sine function?

d) What is the domain of $y = \text{Sin}^{-1} x$? Why?

ST-114. The situation for the inverse of the cosine is similar, but not identical, to that for sine. The **Inverse Cosine of x**, denoted $y = \text{Cos}^{-1} x$, is also called the **Arccosine of x**, or **y = Arccos x**, and the output it gives is the **principal angle whose cosine is x.**

a) $Y = \text{Cos}^{-1} x$ is the inverse of part of $y = \cos x$, but which part? Make a graph of the inverse of $y = \text{Cos}^{-1} x$ (this is the restricted cosine function). What is the domain of this graph? Is it the same as the domain of the inverse of $y = \text{Sin}^{-1} x$? Explain.

b) Find four solutions to the equation $\cos y = 0.5$. Which of these is $\text{Cos}^{-1} 0.5$?

c) Find four solutions to the equation $\cos y = -0.5$. Which of these is $\text{Cos}^{-1} -0.5$?

d) Of all the values of $y$ for which $\cos y = x$ for a given $x$, which is the *principal value* of $y$ whose cosine is $x$? (i.e., which one is $\text{Cos}^{-1} x$?)

ST-115. In each of the following equations, x is in **radians**. Solve for x. Each equation has infinitely many possible solutions; your teacher will tell you which of them to list.

a) $3 + 2 \sin x = 2$

b) $(\cos x + 1)(3 \cos x - 1) = 0$

c) $(\sin x - 2)(5 \sin x - 3) = 0$

The Search for Sunken Treasure: More Triangles and Trigonometry

ST-116.   Graph $y = \tan x$ and $y = \text{Tan}^{-1} x$ (also known as **Arctan x**) on your graphing calculator. Make a sketch of what you see.

a)   $Y = \text{Tan}^{-1} x$ is the inverse of which part of $y = \tan x$? This is the restricted tangent function; what is its domain?

b)   Of all the values of $y$ which solve $\tan y = x$ for a given value of $x$, which one is the principal angle whose tangent is $x$?

ST-117.   For what value(s) of $k$ does the quadratic equation $x^2 - 4x + k = 0$ have:

a)   one solution?                b)   two real solutions?

c)   no real solutions?

ST-118.   For what value(s) of $m$ does $x^2 + 2mx + 9 = 0$ have:

a)   one real solution?                b)   two real solutions? This may require some careful thinking.

ST-119.   Sketch the graph of each of the following equations without using a graphing calculator:

a)   $y = -2 + \sin (x - \frac{\pi}{4})$                b)   $y = 3 - 4 \cos (x + \frac{\pi}{3})$

ST-120.   All three sides are given in the triangle at right. Calculate the measures of all the angles.

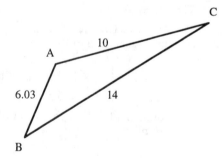

ST-121.   A newly planted tree is supported by guy-wires attached to its trunk at a point 14 feet above the ground. There are three wires, each making a 60° angle with the ground. The stakes that attach them to the ground are at the vertices of an equilateral triangle. Find the sides of this triangle and the length of each guy-wire. (Draw a picture.)

ST-122.   Convert each of the following angles from radians to degrees.

a)   $\frac{\pi}{5}$                b)   $\frac{-2\pi}{3}$                c)   $\frac{13\pi}{12}$

ST-123.  Why is the domain of Arcsin the same as the domain of Arccos? Why is the domain of Arctan different ?

ST-124.  Add the following information to your Tool Kit:

---

### INVERSE CIRCULAR FUNCTIONS

**Y = ARCSIN X** is the name for the Inverse Sine Function. It means the same as $Sin^{-1} x$ or "find the principal angle whose sine is x." In other words, it gives the angle of rotation between $-\frac{\pi}{2}$ and $\frac{\pi}{2}$ radians or between -90° and 90° that has x as its sine.

**Y = ARCCOS X** is the name for the Inverse Cosine Function. It means the same as $Cos^{-1} x$ or "find the principal angle whose cosine is x." In other words, it gives the angle of rotation between 0 and $\pi$ radians or between 0° and 180° that has x as its cosine.

**Y = ARCTAN X** is the name for the Inverse Tangent Function. It means the same as $Tan^{-1}$ or "find the principal angle whose tangent is x." In other words, it gives the angle of rotation between $-\frac{\pi}{2}$ and $\frac{\pi}{2}$ radians or between -90° and 90° that has x as its tangent.

---

ST-125.  Graph the functions $y = \tan^2 x + 1$ and $y = \frac{1}{\cos^2 x}$ on your calculator. What do you notice? Explain. You'll need another way to express tan x and the Pythagorean Identity. Use your Tool Kit!

ST-126.  Find three values of x ( in radians) such that $x = \tan x$.

ST-127.  **UNIT 9 SUMMARY ASSIGNMENT**

Now that you have learned a little bit more trigonometry, we want you to answer a question again: what is trigonometry? Give a definition as you understand it now. Then summarize the important new ideas of this unit, including an example for each, along with a complete solution. In your examples, you should give at least two original problems of your own creation that represent important concepts developed in this unit and show their solutions. Finally, on what topics do you still have questions? What do you think you understand well?

ST-128.    Find all the missing parts for each of the following triangles:

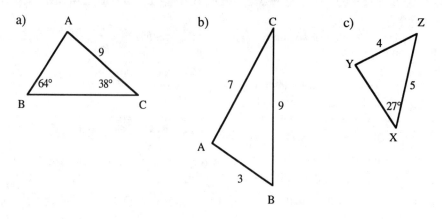

a)

b)

c)

ST-129.    Solve the following system for  x,  y, and  z.

$$x + 2y + 3z = 1$$
$$2x - y - 3z = 11$$
$$y + z = -1$$

ST-130.    A rectangle has an area of 240 cm$^2$ and its length is 3 times its width.  Compute the length of its diagonal.

ST-131.    Solve for  y  if  $3^{(y^2 - 4y)} = 1$.

ST-132.    Use the Pythagorean Identity to simplify  $\dfrac{\sin x}{\cos x} + \dfrac{\cos x}{\sin x}$ .

ST-133.    Solve each equation.

a)    $\dfrac{1}{x} + \dfrac{1}{3x} = 6$

b)    $\dfrac{1}{x} + \dfrac{1}{x+1} = 3$

ST-134.    Solve exactly for  x  if  $\left(x + 2\right)\left(x - \dfrac{3}{x}\right) = \left(x - 2\right)\left(x + \dfrac{3}{x}\right)$.

ST-135.    Simplify the following:  $\log_2\left(4^{10} \div 8^3\right)$.

ST-136.    Sketch the graph of each of the following.

   a)    $y = \log_2 (x + 2)$        b)    $y = 2 + \log_2 x$        c)    $y = |\log_2 x|$


ST-137.    Solve the following problems for  x.

   a)                                b)                                c)

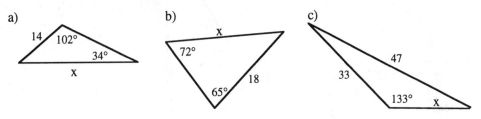


ST-138.    Solve each equation.  Give answers in **degrees**.

   a)    $\tan^2 x - 3 = 0$    b)    $2 \cos x \cdot \sin x + \cos x = 0$   c)    $3 \sin^2 x + 4 \sin x + 1 = 0$


ST-139.    **TOOL KIT CLEAN-UP**

Tool Kits often need to be reorganized to
continue to be useful.  Your Tool Kit
contains entries from units 1 through 9.

Examine the list of Tool Kit entries from
this unit.  Add any that you are missing.

Identify the concepts that you understand.

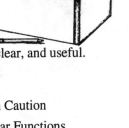

Choose entries to create a Unit 1 - 9 Tool Kit that is shorter, clear, and useful.


   •   Area of SAS Triangles              •   Use $\text{Sin}^{-1}$ with Caution

   •   Law of Cosines                     •   Inverse Circular Functions


ST-140.    **COURSE SUMMARY ASSIGNMENT**
Since the start of this course you have been learning about
mathematics as a tool for solving many problems.  Tell what you
think are the five or six most important concepts in mathematics
you have learned this year.  How have you used these concepts
this year?  Give specific problems with solutions to illustrate your choices.

# UNIT 10

## Policy Making
### PROBABILITY

# Unit 10 Objectives
## Policy Making: PROBABILITY

In this unit you will learn about probability through two visual representations: tree diagrams and area models. These representations make conditional probability understandable and lead to the consideration of decision making in relation to some important policy issues such as mandatory testing for drugs and diseases.

In this unit, you will have the opportunity to:

- use tree and area diagrams to represent multiplication, particularly the multiplication of probabilities expressed as fractions, decimals, and percents.

- use tree and area diagrams to model problems of conditional probability.

- compute expected values and determine whether games are fair.

- apply matrices to probabilities.

- learn about some ways in which a knowledge of probability can provide valuable information in relation to important policy decisions.

An understanding of probability is valuable in relation to important policy issues that are often decided for political reasons. As the issues get more complicated, a knowledge of probability and statistics could make a big difference in the decisions each of us will help to make. The following hypothetical problem is one example. Read through the problem now. We will complete it later in the unit.

---

PM-0. **AIDS TESTING AND MULTIPLICATION:** With the growth of the number of AIDS cases, some people have called for mandatory testing for the HIV virus with public disclosure of the results. Others argue that mandatory testing would jeopardize the lives and livelihood of many people who do not have the disease and is therefore an unwarranted and unjust invasion of their privacy. Furthermore, they argue that if testing is not mandatory, more people who are at risk will volunteer for testing, increasing the likelihood of identifying and helping people who have the disease.

If the test for HIV is 99% accurate on the population to be tested (suppose that in this case doctors, dentists and other health practitioners would be tested) and 100 out of 100,000 people in that group actually are HIV positive, what percentage of those who are tested will be false-positive? In other words, what is the probability that a health practitioner would be identified as having the AIDS virus who actually did not?

---

PROBLEM SOLVING
REPRESENTATION/MODELING
FUNCTIONS/GRAPHING
INTERSECTIONS/SYSTEMS
ALGORITHMS
REASONING/COMMUNICATION

# Unit 10
## Policy Making: PROBABILITY

PM-1.    When you first learned to add you probably did addition by counting.  You could combine a set of four buttons with a set of three buttons and count seven buttons.  A **discrete** model looked something like:

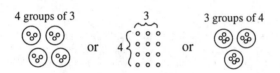

Later on you learned to measure and learned number names for parts of a whole number, so you could use a **continuous** model:

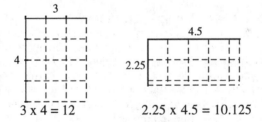

Then you mastered multiplication.  For example, to compute 4 x 3, you at first used discrete arrangements of four groups of three:

4 groups of 3            3            3 groups of 4

or    4 {           or

Later you may have used a continuous model related to area.

3

4

3 x 4 = 12

4.5

2.25

2.25 x 4.5 = 10.125

Area is a useful way to think about multiplying fractions.

One day when Alfred and Fritz were mowing neighboring lawns to earn money, Al yelled over to Fritz, "Let's take a break.  How much have you done?"  Fritz yelled back, "Oh, about three-quarters of a half."  "Huh?" said Alfred.

Use an area model to explain to Alfred what Fritz meant when he said he had finished mowing $\frac{3}{4}$ of $\frac{1}{2}$ of his rectangular lawn.  Then explain how this model relates to the product $\frac{3}{4} \cdot \frac{1}{2}$.

PM-2. There is another way to visualize four groups of three. Think of branches of a tree: start with four branches, then add three branches on each of those four. (Read the model at right from bottom to top.)

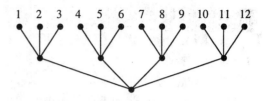

An advantage of this model is that it is easy to extend to multiply three or more numbers. For example, 4 x 2 x 3 starts with four branches, then expands with two branches on each of those four, then extends three branches on each of the eight from the 4 x 2 part. (We can draw our trees sideways or upside down.) There should be 24 endpoints in the figure at right.

Think about the following situation:

Maryanne said she was late to class on Monday because she couldn't decide what outfit to wear. On Sunday, her birthday, she received two new pairs of jeans: one white, the other faded blue; three tops: one plain, one striped, and one print; and two jackets: one lightweight and one heavier. On Monday morning she realized everything color-coordinated with everything else.

a) Draw a multiplication tree to represent all the possible outfits she could wear: jeans, tops, and jackets.

b) How many different completely new outfits did she have to choose from?

c) If she chose randomly, what is the probability she chose the print top and the white jeans?

d) What is the probability that the striped top was part of her outfit.

e) In what other ways could you have organized the information in this problem?

Both the AREA and TREE models for multiplication should be useful as you work on the problems in this unit.

PM-3.    You will need to work in a team of four. Have one person act as recorder while the other three act as players.

a)   List the names of the people in your team alphabetically.  The first person on the list is player A, the next is player B, the third is C, and the fourth is the recorder.  Write down who has each role.

b)   Play "Rock - Paper - Scissors" at least 20 times. Each time all three players match, player A gets one point. Each time two of the three players match, player B gets a point. If none of the players match, then player C gets a point.  Record the players' points.

c)   If you could choose to be any player, A, B, or C, which would you choose?  As a team, prepare a justification for your choice.  A tree model might help, or you may just want to make a well-organized list.

d)   What is the probability that A will win?  B?  C?

e)   What can you do to make the game fair, that is, so that each person has an equally likely chance of winning?  Write up your plan and justify it.

PM-4.    Use the averaging method to find the vertex of each parabola.

a)    $y = x^2 + 8x + 12$                    b)    $y = x^2 - 2x + 3$

PM-5.    Use what you know about locator points to find the vertex of each parabola:

a)    $y = (x + 4)^2 - 4$                     b)    $y = (x - 1)^2 + 2$

c)   Compare your answers in this problem with the previous one.  They should be the same even though the problems look different.  Show why both parts (b) should give the same answer, even though the zeros for problem PM-4 (b) are complex.

PM-6.    Complete the square to convert to graphing form.  Give the vertex and sketch the graph.

a)    $f(x) = x^2 + 6x + 7$                   b)    $f(x) = x^2 - 10x$

PM-7.    Complete the square twice to convert the equation $x^2 + 8x + y^2 - 12y = 12$ to graphing form, then describe the graph.

Policy Making: Probability

PM-8.    Spud has a problem. He knows the solutions for a quadratic equation are
x = 3 + 4i and x = 3 - 4i but in order to get credit for the problem he was supposed to
have written down the equation. Unfortunately he lost the paper with the original
equation on it. His friends are full of advice.

a)    Alexia says, "Look, just remember when we did polynomials. If you wanted 7 and
4 to be the answers, you just used (x - 7)(x - 4). So you just do x minus the first
one times x minus the other."

b)    Hugo says, "No, no, no. You can do it that way, but that's too complicated. I think
you just start with x = 3 + 4i and work backwards. So x - 3 = 4i, then, hmmm.
Yeah, that'll work."

Help Spud figure out the original equation. You may want to use the advice of either or
both friends.

PM-9.     **Without a calculator**, solve each equation below for $0 \le x \le 2\pi$.
(Some parts have two answers!)

a)    $\sin x = -1$

b)    $2 \cos x - 1 = 0$

c)    $\tan x = 1$

d)    $2 \sin x = 4 \sin x + 1$

PM-10.    Solve each of the following equations:

a)    $\dfrac{x}{x + 1} = \dfrac{5}{7}$

b)    $\dfrac{2}{y} = \dfrac{3}{y + 5}$

c)    $\dfrac{x}{x + 1} + \dfrac{2}{x - 1} = \dfrac{8}{x^2 - 1}$

d)    $\dfrac{2}{y + 5} - \dfrac{3}{y} = \dfrac{3}{y + 5}$

PM-11. **PENCILS AND ERASERS**

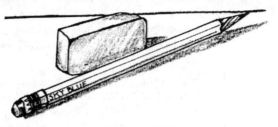

Penny Ante's teacher has a box
with pencils and erasers in it.
There are currently three yellow,
one blue, and two red pencils in it
along with one yellow and two
red erasers. She has just bet her
friend a dime to his dollar that she could walk by the teacher's desk and, without looking,
grab a blue pencil and a red eraser from the box. Should her friend accept this challenge?

Your task is to determine the probability that Penny will walk away with a blue pencil and
a red eraser. There are several ways to organize this problem.

Gerri suggests making a list of all the possible
color combinations, pencil first then eraser.

|     |     |     |
|-----|-----|-----|
| RY  | BY  | YY  |
| RR  | BR  | YR  |

"So," says Gerri, "the answer is $\frac{1}{6}$."

"That doesn't seem quite right," Says Marty. "There are more yellow pencils in there
than blue ones. I don't think the chance of getting a yellow pencil and a red eraser should
be the same as getting a blue pencil and a red eraser. Maybe we need to account for all
three yellow pencils with $Y_1, Y_2, Y_3$."

a) Make a tree diagram or a well-organized complete list of all the possibilities, using
subscripts to account for the colors for which there is more than one pencil or eraser.

b) Use the tree or list to find the probability of Penny snatching the blue-red
combination.

c) Should Penny's friend take the bet? Why or why not?

PM-12. From your tree diagram or list in the preceding problem it should now be easy to find the
probability for each of the six color combinations of a pencil and eraser that Marty named.
Make a list of the correct probabilities for Gerri. For example, $P(BR) = \frac{1}{9}$.

PM-13. What are the outcomes of rolling two dice, one red and one white? So far we have used tree diagrams to organize our thinking about sample spaces or possible outcomes.

a) Think about what would be involved in drawing a tree to show the outcomes, then go on to part (b).

b) In part (a) we said "think about" for a good reason. Most of the people who try to draw a tree diagram for this problem end up with a mess on their paper because they didn't anticipate the amount of space it would take. Sometimes an area diagram is easier to draw and at least as useful. In the area diagram at right the X indicates that the red die shows a 2 and the white die a 5. What does square A represent?

c) In the diagram, what does B represent?

d) What does C represent?

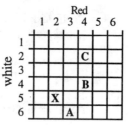

PM-14. Use graph paper and make diagrams similar to the one above. For each of the following situations shade the appropriate squares and give the probability of the specified outcome of rolling a red die and a white die.

a) Shade in the squares that show the red die is a 3. Find the probability that the red die comes up three.

b) Shade in the squares that show either the red or white die is a 3. Find the probability that at least one of the dice comes up three.

c) Shade in the squares that show the red and white dice came up the same number. Find the probability of getting the same number on both dice.

d) Shade in the squares that show the sum of the numbers on the red and white dice is 8. Find the probability of the sum being 8.

PM-15. Look at the diagram for problem PM-13.

a) What do the 36 different squares in the diagram represent? Explain why there must be 36.

b) If you rolled two identical dice, would you still get 36 possible outcomes?

362                                                                                UNIT 10

PM-16.    Suppose you roll two dice.

   a)   What is the probability that exactly one of them shows a 2?

   b)   What is the probability that both of them show a 2?

   c)   What is the probability of at least one 2?

   d)   What is the probability of no 2's?


PM-17.    Suppose you roll two dice but one of them has two 6's and no 1's.

   a)   Draw an area diagram of the possible outcomes.

   b)   Find the probability that the sum of the numbers on the two dice is 8.


PM-18.    Suppose you have the two ordinary dice. For each integer $n = 2, 3, 4, ..., 12$, calculate $p(n)$, the probability that the sum on the two dice is $n$ points. For example, since there are two ways to make 3 points, $p(3) = \frac{2}{36}$. Did you use a tree or an area diagram?


PM-19.    Solve the following equations.

   a)   $\frac{3}{x} + \frac{5}{x - 7} = -2$          b)   $\frac{2x + 3}{4} - \frac{x - 7}{6} = \frac{2x - 3}{12}$


PM-20.    Solve these systems of equations.

   a)   $x - 2y = 7$          b)   $\frac{x + 4y}{3} - \frac{6y - x}{4} = -3$
        $2x + y = 3$                $\frac{x}{10} + 5y = 2$


PM-21.    Solve for $x$ and $y$ if:

   a)   $2x + y = 12$          b)   $2x + y = 12$
        $xy = 16$                    $xy = 20$

   c)   Explain how the graphs of (a) and (b) relate to the solutions of each system of equations.


PM-22.    At McDugal's Golden Parabola, Ramona bought four hamburgers and two milkshakes for $4.10. Inez bought three hamburgers and one milkshake and spent $2.80. What is the cost of a hamburger? A milkshake?

**PM-23.** The line $y = 3x - 4$ is perpendicular to another line which goes through the origin. What is the relationship between the slopes of perpendicular lines? If you do not remember, sketch a careful graph of a line with slope 3, and a line perpendicular to it to see what the slope must be. Find the equation of the perpendicular line through the origin.

**PM-24.** Calculate the total surface area and volume of the prism at right.

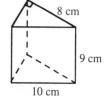

8 cm

9 cm

10 cm

**PM-25.** Solve the equations below for $x$. Show and justify all steps leading to your solution. Answers will contain $a$, $b$, and/or $c$.

a)  $cx - a = b$

b)  $\frac{x}{a} - b = c$

c)  $(x - a)(x - b) = 0$

d)  $ax^2 - acx = 0$

e)  $\frac{x}{a + b} = \frac{1}{c}$

f)  $\frac{1}{x} + a = b$

# MORE TREES AND AREA MODELS

**PM-26.  PENCILS AND ERASERS AGAIN**

There are still two red, one blue, and three yellow pencils and one yellow and two red erasers in the box. Show and explain how you could use this area diagram to figure out the probabilities for all the pencil-eraser color pairs. What is the probability of getting the yellow pencil and red eraser combination?

erasers

| | R₁ | R₂ | Y₁ |
|---|---|---|---|
| Y₁ | $\frac{1}{18}$ | | |
| Y₂ | | | |
| Y₃ | | | |
| R₁ | | | |
| R₂ | | | |
| B | | | |

pencils

**PM-27.** The area diagram at right could be used to represent the probabilities in the pencil/eraser problem. Explain how it is related to the one in the preceding problem.

$p(Y) = \frac{1}{2}$

$p(R) = \frac{1}{3}$

$p(B) = \frac{1}{6}$

$p(R) = \frac{2}{3}$    $p(Y) = \frac{1}{3}$

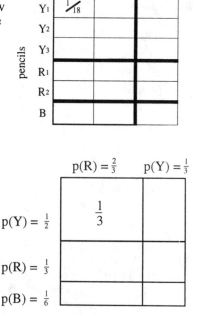

$\frac{1}{3}$

PM-28.    Another way to organize the pencil and eraser problem is to draw a simpler tree diagram
          based on the probabilities:

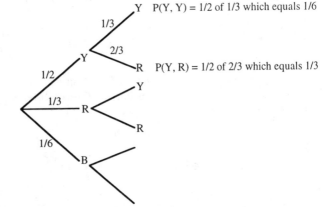

          a)   Copy and complete
               the probability tree
               shown at right.

          b)   Describe what you
               did to find the
               probabilities for the
               color combinations.

          c)   Explain how the
               second tree is a
               shortcut for the tree
               or list you made in
               problem PM-11.

---

### INDEPENDENT EVENTS

In the pencils and erasers problem, you saw that the probability of drawing a blue
pencil and a red eraser equaled the product of the pencil probability and the eraser
probability   P(blue pencil and red eraser) = P(blue pencil) x P(red eraser)

$$\frac{1}{9} = \frac{1}{6} \times \frac{2}{3}$$

When the probability of two events happening equals the product of their probabilities
the events are said to be **independent**.

---

PM-29.    How are the tree diagram in problem PM-28 and the area diagram in problem PM-27
          related?  Which method of diagramming did you like best for solving the pencil-erasers
          problem?  Explain your reasons.

PM-30.    A Nevada roulette wheel has 38 slots numbered 00, 0, 1, 2, 3, ..., 36.  Eighteen of the
          numbers 1, 2, ..., 36 are red and 18 are black; 0 and 00 are green.

          a)   What is the probability of landing on red?

          b)   What is the probability of not landing on red?

          c)   The bettor put his money on red twice in a row.  Use an area or a tree diagram to
               show how to find the probability that he won both bets.

PM-31.    Harold had several jars of specially sorted jelly beans.
          They were specially sorted because he likes the purple
          ones best and the black ones next best so these were
          both in one jar.  His next favorites were yellow,
          orange, and white, in that order, and these were in
          another jar.  The rest were in the garbage.  Harold
          allowed himself only one jelly bean from each jar per
          day.  He also wore a blindfold when he selected his
          jelly beans so as not to eat all of the best ones first.

          What is the probability that Harold gets his favorite jelly bean from each jar if jar #1 has
          60% purple and 40% black, and jar #2 is 30% yellow, 50% orange, and 20% white?  Be
          sure to show and explain your solution.

PM-32. Use the method of completing the square to reorganize these equations for easy graphing. State the locator point and sketch the graph.

a)  $f(x) = x^2 + 4x + 6$          b)  $x^2 + 6x + y^2 - 8y = 0$

PM-33. Betty's Quick Stop makes 15% profit on its lunches and 22% profit on its dinners. If Betty took in $2,700 on Tuesday and made $513.01 profit, how much was spent at lunch? Write one or two equations, then solve.

PM-34. Solve each of the following ratio problems for x.

a)  Forty-two percent of  x  is 112.      b)  Forty-two is  x  percent of 112.

c)  Twenty-seven is  x  percent of 100.   d)  Twenty-seven percent of 500 is  x.

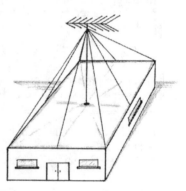

PM-35. The Flat family's roof is 32 feet wide and 60 feet long. Their TV antenna rises 25 feet above the center of the roof and the wires are attached to the top of the antenna. Guy wires are attached at each corner of the roof and at the midpoint of each edge. What is the total length of wire needed (without counting any extra needed for attaching it)?

PM-36. In the previous problem, suppose that the height of the antenna is  x  feet. Represent the total length of the guy wires in terms of  x.

PM-37. In the original antenna problem, find the angle that the guy wires to the corners make with the roof.

PM-38. Solve $\sqrt{x^2 + 6} = x + 2$.

PM-39. Find the inverse of  $g(x) = (x + 1)^2 - 3$  with the domain  $x \geq -1$. Sketch both graphs and tell the domain and range of the inverse function.

PM-40. Suppose you roll two dice, one red and one blue, and get a sum of 10.

a) List the different ways this can occur.

b) Sketch an area diagram and shade these possibilities.

c) What is the probability of getting a sum of 10?

d) Suppose you know the sum is 10 but not what is on each die. Explain why the probability that you rolled two 5's would be $\frac{1}{3}$.

PM-41. Suppose you roll two dice and the sum is more than 8.

a) Shade the squares on an area diagram where this outcome could occur.

b) What is the probability that both dice show the same number?

c) What is the probability that exactly one 6 is showing?

d) What is the probability that at least one 5 is showing?

e) In part (d) you calculated the conditional probability that a five will show given that the sum on the dice is greater than eight. Here is another way to think of the problem.

> Event A is sums that contain at least one 5
> Event B is sums greater than 8
> Event AB is the intersection of events A and B, that is sums that contain at least one five and are greater than 8.

Then we can compute P(A/B), the **conditional probability** that at least one five was showing given that the sum was greater than 8, by using the probabilities P(AB) and P(B)

$$P(A/B) = \frac{P(AB)}{P(B)}$$

Complete this calculation and compare this method and result with part (d).

PM-42. A spinner comes up blue, red, and green with a probability of $\frac{1}{3}$ for each color.

a) Sketch an area diagram for spinning twice.

b) Shade the region on your area diagram that corresponds to getting the same color twice.

c) What is the probability that both spins give the same color?

d) If you know that you got the same color twice, what is the probability the color was blue?

PM-43.　A spinner comes up red 25% of the time and green 25% of the time. The rest of the time it lands on blue.

　　a)　Draw an area diagram for spinning twice, and shade the region on your area diagram corresponding to getting the same color twice. A neat and accurate diagram on this problem will help in understanding the next several problems. What are the dimensions of the whole diagram?

　　b)　What is the probability that both spins give the same color?

　　c)　If you know that you got the same color twice, what is the probability the color was blue?

PM-44.　Guess what? Another spinner. This time the spinner lands on red half of the time and on green one-third of the time. The rest of the time it lands on blue.

　　a)　Draw an area diagram for spinning twice, and shade the region that corresponds to getting the same color on both spins.

　　b)　Suppose you know that the spinner landed on the same color twice. What is the probability that color was green?

---

If you have difficulty with problems PM-45 or 46, the first thing to do is go back and think about what you did in problems PM-42, 43, and 44.

---

PM-45.　A spinner has just two colors, red and blue. The probability the spinner will land on blue is  x.

　　a)　What is the probability it will land on red?

　　b)　Sketch an area diagram  for spinning twice.

　　c)　When it is spun twice, what is the probability it will land on the same color both times?

　　d)　Given that it lands on the same color twice, what is the probability that it landed on blue both times?

PM-46.　On a spinner with blue, red, and green sectors, blue occurs a fraction  x  of the time and red occurs the same fraction.

　　a)　Write an expression to represent the fraction of time green occurs.

　　b)　Sketch an area diagram of spinning twice.

　　c)　Shade the region on your area diagram corresponding to getting the same color twice.

　　d)　What is the probability that both spins give the same color?

　　e)　If you know that you got the same color twice, what is the probability the color was blue?

PM-47.    Solve each of the following for  x. What are the three methods used for finding unknown
          parts of triangles?  Refer to your Tool Kit if necessary

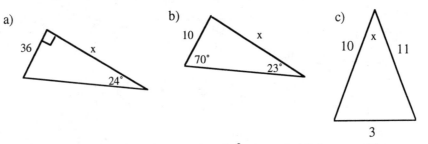

a)

36

x

24°

b)

10

x

70°

23°

c)

10

x

11

3

PM-48.    For what values of n  does the equation  $2x^2 + nx + 9 = 0$  have exactly one root?

PM-49.    Sketch the graph of  $y = (x + 2)^3 + 4$.

  a)   Rewrite the equation  $y = (x + 2)^3 + 4$  without parentheses.  Remember order of
       operations.

  b)   How would the graph in part (a) differ from the graph of the original equation?

  c)   What is the parent of  $y = (x + 2)^3 + 4$?  Of  $y = x^3 + 6x^2 + 12x + 12$?

PM-50.    Julio runs  $\frac{3}{10}$  mile in  $1\frac{1}{2}$  minutes.  If he keeps running at that rate, how long will it take
          him to run 2 miles?  **m**  miles?

PM-51.    Where do these graphs intersect?  You should be able to do these without a graphing
          calculator.

  a)    $2x + y = 10$
         $x + y = 25$

  b)    $2x + y = 10$
         $x^2 + y^2 = 25$

PM-52.    We can add, subtract and multiply complex numbers by essentially treating  **i**  as a
          variable and using standard rules of algebra, but dividing is trickier.  Suppose we want to
          divide  5 + 6i  by  3 + 4i  or, in other words, simplify this fraction: $\frac{5 + 6i}{3 + 4i}$.  What we
          mean here is: what number times 3 + 4i equals 5 + 6i?  The direct way to solve this is to
          write the equation (3 + 4i)(a + bi) = 5 + 6i.

  a)   Multiply out the left side of this equation.  This will result in both real and imaginary
       terms.  The real terms must equal 5, and the imaginary must equal 6i.  This results in
       two equations that can be solved for  a  and  b.  Do this, and state the answer to the
       division problem.

  b)   The process in part (a) is important in understanding complex division, but there is
       an easier way.  See what happens when you multiply the numerator and denominator
       of the fraction by the conjugate of  3 + 4i.

  c)   How does the result for part (b) compare to your answer to part (a)?  What do you
       need to do to show they are the same?

PM-53.    Divide the following complex numbers by multiplying the numerator and denominator by the conjugate of the denominator.  Write the answer in the form  a + bi.

a)  $\dfrac{5}{3-4i}$

b)  $\dfrac{4+2i}{1-i}$

c)  $\dfrac{2-3i}{1+2i}$

PM-54.    If $A = \begin{bmatrix} 3 & 2 \\ -1 & 0 \\ 1 & -3 \end{bmatrix}$ and $B = \begin{bmatrix} 2 & -1 \\ 3 & 0 \end{bmatrix}$ compute the following if possible.

a)  AB

b)  BA

c)  $B^2$

PM-55.    Using a graph of  $y = \sin x$  for reference, graph  $y = |\sin x|$.

## MORE CONDITIONAL PROBABILITY

PM-56.    On the midway at the County Fair there are many popular games to play.  One of them is Flip-to-Spin-or-Roll.  You start by flipping a coin.  If heads comes up, you get to spin the big wheel, which has ten equal sectors: three red, three blue, and four yellow.  If the coin shows tails, you get to roll a cube with three red sides, two yellow sides, and one blue side.  If your spin lands on blue or the blue side of the cube comes up, you win a stuffed animal.

a)    Draw **both** an area diagram and a tree diagram to represent Flip-to-Spin-or-Roll.

b)    Which diagram was easiest to make?  From which diagram is it easiest to tell what result is most likely?

c)    What is the probability of winning a stuffed animal?

d)    Tyler won a stuffed animal.  What is the probability that he started off with heads?  From which diagram was it easiest to find this?

e)    About how many times would you expect to have to play this game in order to win a stuffed animal?

f)    If it cost a dollar to play the game, and the stuffed animal could be purchased at the Bob's Bargain Basement for $3.50, was it worth it?  Explain.

PM-57. In the children's game, Build-a-Farm, each player first spins a spinner. Half of the time the spinner comes up red. Half of the time the spinner comes up blue. If the spinner is red, you reach into the red box. If the spinner is blue, you reach into the blue box. The red box has 10 chicken counters, 10 pig counters, and 10 cow counters, while the blue box has 5 chicken counters, 4 pig counters and 1 cow counter.

a) Sketch an area diagram for the situation where a child spins and then draws. Note that the parts corresponding to the two boxes of animal markers will be quite different.

b) Shade the parts of the diagram corresponding to getting a pig counter. What is P(pig)?

c) Find the probability of getting a cow counter.

d) Find the probability that if you got a cow counter you also spun red.

e) Find the probability that if you got a cow counter you also spun blue.

f) Would this have been easier with a tree model? Try it and decide.

g) **CONDITIONAL PROBABILITY**

The probabilities you computed in parts (c) and (d) are **conditional probabilities**. In part (c) you calculated the probability that you spun red given that you got a cow counter. P(R/C) is short for P(Red/Cow), "probability of red given cow."

One way to compute the probability is to write P(Red/Cow) = P(Red cow)/P(cow)

$$P(R/C) = \frac{P(RC)}{P(C)} = \frac{\frac{1}{6}}{\frac{13}{60}} = \frac{1}{6} \times \frac{60}{13} = \frac{10}{13}$$

Use the above method to calculate P(B/C) and compare your result with your answer to part (e).

PM-58. If Letitia studies for her math test tonight, she has an 80% chance of getting an "**A**." If she does not study, she has a 10% chance. Whether she can study or not depends on whether or not she has to work at her parents' store. Earlier in the day Frank, who usually works weekdays, said he was feeling sick and there is only a 50% chance he will be there tonight.

a) Draw a tree diagram of the situation.

b) Draw an area diagram of the situation.

c) Shade the parts of the area diagram corresponding to Letitia getting an "**A**."

d) Find the probability Letitia gets an "**A**."

e) If Letitia got an "**A**," what are the chances she studied?

PM-59. La Troy has been studying very hard for his English test. He thinks that given any question he has a 99% chance of getting it right.

    a)   What is the probability that he gets the first three questions right?

    b)   If the test has fifty questions, what is the probability he gets them all correct?

    c)   Suppose La Troy wanted a 90% chance he would get every question on the test. What would his chances have to be of getting each question correct?

    d)   If you didn't already, write an equation to represent part (c) and solve it.

PM-60. Two similar triangles are cut out of the same piece of sheet metal. The smaller weighs 250 g and the larger weighs 400 g. If the shortest side of the smaller triangle is 26 mm, how long is the shortest side of the larger triangle?

PM-61. Find the volume of the trapezoidal prism at right. Show all subproblems.

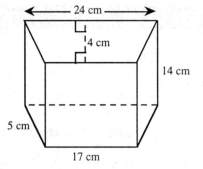

PM-62. Find the equation of the line that is perpendicular to $y = \frac{1}{2}x - 3$ and passes through (10, 14).

PM-63. For $y = 5x^2 + 4x + 20$:

    a)   find the roots.

    b)   find the vertex and rewrite the equation in graphing form.

PM-64. A sequence starts 24, 12, . . .

If it is arithmetic:

    a)   Find t(3) = ?    t(n) = ?

    b)   What shape is the graph?

    c)   What term is -624?

If it is geometric:

    d)   Find t(3) = ?    t(n) = ?

    e)   What shape is the graph?

    f)   What term is $\frac{3}{128}$?

PM-65. Solve each of the following equations for x.

    a)   $1234x + 23456 = 987654$

    b)   $\frac{10}{x} + \frac{20}{x} = 5$

    c)   $5x^2 - 6x + 1 = 0$

    d)   $x^3 - 3x^2 + 2x = 0$

PM-66. Solve each equation for $0° \le \theta \le 360°$. You may need your calculator but remember that your calculator only gives ONE answer. Most (all?) of these have more than one answer. Think about the quadrants.

a) $\sin \theta = 0.5$

b) $\cos \theta = -0.5$

c) $4 \tan \theta - 4 = 0$

d) $3 \sin^2 \theta = 1$

PM-67. Factor each expression and simplify it.

a) $\dfrac{x^2 - 4}{x^2 + 4x + 4}$

b) $\dfrac{2x^2 - 5x - 3}{4x^2 + 4x + 1}$

c) Justify each step in simplifying the expression in part (a).

# EXPECTED VALUE

PM-68. Add a brief explanation of **expected value** to your Tool Kit, then complete parts (a) through (d) below.

> To calculate the **EXPECTED VALUE** of an event, multiply the probability of each possible outcome by the value of that outcome, and add the results together.
>
> For example, suppose a game show contestant rolls one die to determine her grand prize. If she rolls a 6, she wins $10,000 and if she rolls anything else she wins $1000. Her expected value is :
>
> (the probability of a six)($10,000) + (the probability of not rolling a six)($1000)
>
> $= \dfrac{1}{6}(\$10,000) + \dfrac{5}{6}(\$1000) = \$2,500.$
>
> In a **FAIR GAME** with several people, the expected values are equal. If you pay to play a game, then it is fair if the cost to play equals the expected value.

Double Spin is a new twist on the Wheel of Few Bucks. You get to spin the spinner twice, and you have to match the amounts to win. The $100 sector is $\dfrac{1}{8}$ of the circle.

a) What is the probability of winning $100?

b) What is the probability of winning anything at all?

c) What is the expected value for a winner of this game? You'll need to solve four subproblems to answer this.

d) If it costs $3.00 to play this game, is it worth playing?

## PM-69.  BASKETBALL: SHOOTING ONE-AND-ONE FREE THROWS

Rimshot McGee has a 70% free throw
average.  Rimshot is at the foul line in a
one-and-one situation with seconds left in
the game.  The opposing team is ahead by
one point.

a)  What do you think is the most likely
outcome for Rimshot: zero points,
one point, or two points?  Discuss
this with your team and see what
people think before you proceed.

b)  The majority of people, when asked
the question in part (a), say one point,
but if you set up a model you may
change their minds.  Use an area
model or a tree diagram to argue
which outcome is most likely.

c)  What is Rimshot's expected value in
terms of points?  Could this answer
be the cause of confusion or the
reason most people would think
one point was most likely?  Explain your answer.

d)  What is the difference between "most likely" and "expected value?"


PM-70.  Dunkin' Delilah Jones has a 60% free throw average.

a)  What would be the most likely result when she shoots one-and-one?

b)  Try at least three other possible free throw percentages, and make a note of the most
likely outcome.

c)  Is there some free throw percentage that would make two-points and zero-points
equally likely outcomes?  Find it.

d)  If you did not already do so, draw an area or tree diagram for part (c) using  x  as the
percentage and write an equation to represent the problem.  Write the solution of the
equation in simplest radical form.

e)  The result in part (d) is a well known number.  Ask your teacher to explain other
circumstances in which it appears.


PM-71.  Find all values of  'a'  for which the equation  $ax^2 + 5x + 6 = 0$  has a solution that is a
real number.  Express  'a'  in terms of one or more inequalities.

PM-72.    On a spinner, blue occurs a fraction  x  of the time while red and green are equal.  There
          are no other colors.

   a)   Represent the probability that the spinner will land on green.

   b)   Sketch an area diagram for spinning twice.

   c)   Shade the region on your area diagram corresponding to getting the same color twice.

   d)   What is the probability that both spins give the same color?

   e)   If you know that you got the same color twice, what is the probability the color was
        blue?


PM-73.    Where do  $x^2 - y = 4$  and  $y = 2x - 1$  intersect?


PM-74.    If  $\log_b 5 = 3$, compute  $\log_b 2$.


PM-75.    Using a graph of  $y = \cos x$  for reference, graph  $y = |\cos x|$.


PM-76.    Find the measures of the angles that the graph of  $y = \frac{3}{5}x + 11$  makes with the x-axis
          (to the nearest 0.01).


PM-77.    Multiply and simplify:

   a)   $( 3 + 2i )( 4 + i )$                  b)   $( 2 + 3i )( 2 - 3i )$

   c)   $( 5 - 2i )( 5 + 2i )$                 d)   $( a + bi )( a - bi )$


PM-78.    Change each of the following complex fractions into a single fraction.

   a)   $\dfrac{1 + \frac{1}{x}}{x}$                b)   $\dfrac{\frac{1}{2}}{1 - \frac{1}{x}}$

   c)   Justify each step you used in part (b).

PM-79. When he was in first grade, Harvey used to love games with spinners. One game he especially liked had two spinners and several markers that you moved around a board. You were only allowed to move if your color came up on BOTH spinners. Harvey always chose purple because that was his favorite color and, after all, he was only six years old.

a) What was the probability that Harvey could move his marker?

b) What was the probability for the better choice of color?

c) How often did no one get to move?

d) There are at least two ways to figure out part (c). Discuss your method of solution with your team and show a second way to solve part (c).

PM-80. Sometimes it is easier to figure out the probability that something will **not** happen than the probability that it **will**. Show two ways to do this problem and decide which is easier.

Crystal is spinning this spinner and claims she has a good chance of having the spinner land on red at least once in three tries. What is the probability that the spinner will land on red at least once in three tries.

PM-81.

> The set of all possible outcomes of an event is called the **SAMPLE SPACE**.

a) If you flipped three coins, would a tree diagram or an area model be better for determining the sample space?

b) How many outcomes are there?

c) What is the probability of flipping:

(i) three heads?

(ii) at least two heads?

(iii) one head and two tails?

(iv) at least one tail?

(v) exactly two tails?

(vi) at least one head and one tail?

(vii) Which is more likely, flipping at least two heads or at least two tails? Explain.

PM-82. Eddie told Alfred, "I'll bet if I flip three coins I can get exactly two heads." Alfred replied, "I'll bet I can get exactly two heads if I flip four coins!" Eddie scoffed, "Well, so what? That's easier." Alfred argued, "No, it's not. It's harder." Who is right? Show all your work and be prepared to defend your conclusion.

PM-83. One way to win in a game with two dice is to throw a sum of six before getting a sum of seven. (Anything else that happens—sums of 2, 3, 4, 5, 8, 9, 10, 11, or 12—is ignored.)

a) How many ways are there to get a sum of six?

b) How many ways are there to get seven?

c) How many possible outcomes are important in this problem?

d) What is the probability of getting a six before a seven?

PM-84. Use the five-point method to graph at least one full cycle of each graph.

a) $y = 2 \sin x$

b) $y = \cos (2x)$

c) $y = -1 + 2 \cos x$

d) $y = -1 + 2 \sin (x + \frac{\pi}{2})$

PM-85. Show how to solve these exponential problems <u>without</u> using your calculator. You will have radicals or logarithms in your answers.

a) $3^x = 17$

b) $x^3 = 17$

PM-86. Write a brief explanation of how you would divide one complex number by another and give at least two examples. You may want to refer to problem PM-52.

PM-87. Consider the function $y = x^2 + 5x + 7$.

a) Complete the square to find the vertex.

b) Find the y-intercept.

c) Use the vertex, the y-intercept, and the symmetry of parabolas to find a third point and sketch the graph.

PM-88. If Emily bought three pounds of oranges and four pounds of bananas for $2.67 and Beth bought four pounds of oranges and two pounds of bananas for $2.46, how much should Jenel expect to pay for nine pounds of oranges and seven pounds of bananas?

PM-89.    Sam says, "log (AB) = log A + log B. Joe says, "log (AB) = (log A)(log B) and I can
Ⓔ        prove it." Examine Joe's proof and determine if he is correct or if there is something
         wrong. Explain completely. Is either person correct?

First:    If x = log A, then $10^x$ = A and if y = log B, then $10^y$ = B.

Second:   AB = $10^x 10^y$ = $10^{xy}$  so log (AB) = xy.

Finally:  log (AB) = xy = (log A)(log B).


PM-90.    Suppose three people were solving a geometry problem involving similar right triangles.
          One got an answer of $\sqrt{48}$, another got $4\sqrt{3}$, and the third got $\dfrac{12}{\sqrt{3}}$. Would they realize
          that all three answers are equal? To make it easier to compare answers, it is useful to
          write square roots in "simplest form." "Simplest" means:

              (1) getting the square root part as small as possible by taking out square factors and

              (2) only dividing by integers.

          For example:

$$\sqrt{48} = \sqrt{16} \cdot \sqrt{3} = 4\sqrt{3} \qquad\qquad \frac{12}{\sqrt{3}} = \frac{12}{\sqrt{3}} \cdot \frac{\sqrt{3}}{\sqrt{3}} = \frac{12\sqrt{3}}{3} = 4\sqrt{3}$$

          Simplify what you can, then perform the indicated operations:

          a)   $\sqrt{3}(\sqrt{18} + \sqrt{32})$                b)   $\sqrt{98} + \sqrt{27} + \sqrt{147} + \sqrt{18}$

          c)   $\dfrac{\sqrt{5}}{\sqrt{10}}$


PM-91.    The congruent sides of an isosceles triangle are labeled  2x + 5  and  3x - 8  units,
          respectively. Find the length of each of the congruent sides.

Both of the following problems would be good to put into your portfolio.

PM-92. An understanding of probability is valuable in relation to important policy issues that are often decided for political reasons. As the issues get more complicated, a knowledge of probability and statistics could make a big difference in the decisions each of us will help to make. For example, with the growing number of AIDS cases, some people have called for mandatory testing for the HIV virus with public disclosure of the results. Others argue that mandatory testing jeopardizes the lives and livelihood of many people who do not have the disease and is therefore an unwarranted and unjust invasion of their privacy. Furthermore, they argue if testing is not mandatory, more people who are at risk will volunteer for testing, increasing the likelihood of identifying and helping people who do have the disease.

In order to explore these issues further we will consider a hypothetical situation. Suppose that the currently used test for HIV is 99% accurate (current tests are not this accurate), and suppose that in the population to be tested (in this case it is doctors, dentists, and other health practitioners) 100 out of 100,000 people actually are HIV positive. The question is: what is the probability that a health practitioner would be identified as having the AIDS virus who actually did not?

a) Make a diagram for this situation.

b) How does the number of people who are HIV positive compare with the number of people who will be told they are HIV positive but really are not?

c) If a randomly tested health practitioner's test comes back positive, what is the probability that he is **not** actually HIV positive? In other words, if you are told that you are sick, what is the probability that you are not sick?

d) Write up your conclusions. In other words, what would you do if you were in a position to decide about mandatory testing of health practitioners and why? What about mandatory testing for other groups?

PM-93.   **LUNCH WITH A CALCULATING SWINGER**

George is in a zebrawood tree deep in an
Amazon rain forest. He spies a bunch of
bananas in a tree below. At the same time he
notices movement on the jungle floor. He is
12 meters above the ground, holding onto a
vine. If he jumps, his distance from the
ground will get smaller, then larger. He
figures that a quadratic function is a
reasonable mathematical model. But the
movement he saw was Praether the local
panther who, if he times it well, could leap
to a height of three meters to snag George at
the bottom of his swing. One second after
he jumps, he will be 8.5 meters above the
ground, and 3 seconds after he jumps he
will be 4.5 meters above the ground.
Should George go for the bananas?

a)   Define independent and dependent
     variables and name three points that would be on the graph.

b)   Find an equation for this function.

c)   What is the minimum height of his swing? Knowing the vertex will give the
     answer to this question. To be able to see the vertex in the equation, first multiply
     $y = 0.5x^2 - 4x + 12$ by 2 to get $2y = x^2 - 8x + 24$. Then complete the square.
     When you are done, multiply both sides by $\frac{1}{2}$.

d)   Sketch the graph of this function, and advise George regarding lunch.

PM-94.   If $f(x) = x^2 + 7x$, calculate:

a)   $f(2)$          b)   $f(-3)$          c)   $f(\mathbf{i})$          d)   $f(-3.5 + 1.5\mathbf{i})$

e)   solve $f(x) = 0$

PM-95.   Make a sketch of a graph $f(x)$ which has the indicated number and type of roots.

a)   5 real roots.                    b)   3 real and 2 complex.

c)   4 complex.                       d)   4 complex and 2 real.

PM-96.    Draw a circle and a line tangent to it at any point x on the circle.  Now draw a line from the center of the circle through point x.

a)    What do we know about these two lines?

b)    What do we know about their slopes?


PM-97.    Write the equation of the line tangent to the graph of $(x - 7)^2 + (y - 2)^2 = 169$ at the point (12, 14).  (A diagram will certainly help in organizing this problem.)


PM-98.    Without graphing, find where each of the following curves crosses the x-axis.  (Find the **exact** points!)

a)    $f(x) = x^2 - x - 12$

b)    $f(x) = 2x^2 - 3x - 9$

c)    $f(x) = 2x^2 + x - 7$

d)    $f(x) = 3x^2 - 2x + 7$

e)    $f(x) = 3x^3 + 2x^2 - 8x$

f)    $f(x) = 2x^3 + 2x^2 + 13x$


# APPLYING MATRICES TO PROBABILITY

PM-99.    **HOME OWNERS AND RENTERS IN MINIOPOLIS**

Every year some families who have been renting manage to purchase a home or condominium. Conversely, some families (frequently older ones) sell their homes and move into rental properties.  A recent study has found that in Miniopolis each year 40% of the renters become homeowners, while 10% of homeowners become renters.  Of course, that also means that 60% of renters continue to rent, and 90% of homeowners remain owners.

Currently there are 140,000 renters and 160,000 homeowners in the city.  City planners want to know how these numbers will change over the next 20 years and they will pay top dollar to find out.  Can you help?

a)    How many homeowners will there be in Miniopolis next year, assuming that the percentages stated above remain true?

b)    How many renters will there be next year?

c)    How many homeowners and renters will there be after one more year?

PM-100.   It's easy to see that a shortcut will be helpful if we want to find the numbers after 20 years. You may already see the pattern, but we'll use some variables to make it clear. Let $H(n)$ = the number of homeowners after n years, and let $R(n)$ = the number of renters after n years. Suppose you don't know the initial numbers of homeowners and renters. Write expressions for $H(1)$ and $R(1)$ in terms of $H(0)$ and $R(0)$.

PM-101.   Does problem PM-100 remind you of matrix multiplication? It should! Make three matrices: T, C, and N, so that C contains the current numbers of homeowners and renters, N contains next year's numbers of homeowners and renters, and $N = CT$. It may be helpful to review how you express a system of linear equations as an equivalent matrix equation. The matrix T is called the transition matrix.

PM-102.   Since each number of homeowners and renters will become the basis for calculating the next year's numbers, we will let $D_n$ represent the matrix of homeowners and renters after n years. The matrix equation becomes $D_{n+1} = D_n T$ (we call $D_n$ a distribution matrix). Find $D_5$, and explain its meaning.

PM-103.   To find $D_5$ did you also have to find $D_4$, $D_3$, $D_2$, and $D_1$? Perhaps you found the shortcut. Think back to your work on sequences in Unit 1.

   a)   What is the generator for this sequence of matrices?

   b)   Which type of sequence is this?

   c)   If you have the sequence 3, 15, 45, . . ., how can you represent and find $t(100)$ without finding all the terms up to that one?

   d)   Apply that same reasoning to find $D_5$.

   e)   Did you get the same answer? Now find $D_{10}$ and $D_{20}$. What appears to be happening? What will you tell the city planners about what to expect over the long term?

PM-104. In the Miniopolis situation there were only two categories (homeowner and renter), and the probability of proceeding from one category to another depended only on the former condition. The matrix method we used for modeling this situation is called a **MARKOV CHAIN** because it was developed by the Russian mathematician, Andrei Andrevich Markov (1856 - 1922). Here's a more complex example:

In Bigg City there are estimated to be 120,000 homeowners, 200,000 renters, and 5,000 homeless families. Studies have shown that from one year to the next, among homeowners, 10% will become renters and the rest remain owners. Among renters, 20% will become homeowners, 1% will fall on hard times and become homeless, and the rest remain renters. And among the homeless, 50% become renters and the others remain homeless.

a) Find the number of owners, renters, and homeless families after one year.

b) Create a transition matrix T so that $D_n = D_0 T^n$, where $D_n$ contains the number of residents in each category after n years.

c) Write and label the Initial Distribution matrix for this situation.

d) Investigate what will happen over the long term.


PM-105. Let $T_n$ be the sum of the first n counting numbers.

a) To the right are diagrams of $T_1 = 1$, $T_2 = 1 + 2 = 3$, $T_3 = 1 + 2 + 3 = 6$, $T_4 = 1 + 2 + 3 + 4 = 10$. The letter T is used because these are called **triangular numbers**. Why?

n=1   n=2   n=3   n=4

b) $T_n = an^2 + bn + c$ is a quadratic function of n. Use the first three triangular numbers to write three equations in a, b, and c.

c) Write a matrix equation you could use to solve for a, b, and c. Explain how to solve it.

PM-106. Sunshine Hospital has four categories for the status of its patients: well (W) (about to be discharged), good (G), critical (C), and deceased (D). Sunshine's patients move from one category to another each day according to the probabilities shown below.

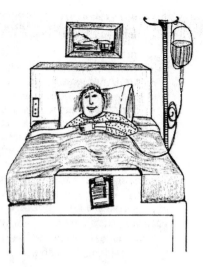

$$
\begin{array}{c c c c c}
 & W & G & C & D \\
W & \begin{bmatrix} 1 \\ 0.5 \\ 0.1 \\ 0 \end{bmatrix} & \begin{matrix} 0 \\ 0.3 \\ 0.2 \\ 0 \end{matrix} & \begin{matrix} 0 \\ 0.1 \\ 0.6 \\ 0 \end{matrix} & \begin{matrix} 0 \\ 0.1 \\ 0.1 \\ 1 \end{matrix} \end{array}
$$

a)  Explain the meaning of each of the numbers in the second row.

b)  The numbers in the distribution matrices can also be seen as probabilities. If Maura enters Sunshine Hospital in critical condition, her "initial distribution" matrix is [ 0 0 1 0 ]. Multiply this matrix by T, the transition matrix above, and explain the meaning of the answer in terms of probabilities.

c)  How can Maura find the probability that she will be well after three days? How can you find the probability that another patient will get well eventually? If you have a graphing calculator, find those probabilities.

d)  What happens to the probability of "G" or "C" in the long run?

e)  This Markov Chain has two states called **absorbing states**. What are the two absorbing states, and what does this term mean?

f)  In light of your answers to parts (c) and (d), how do you account for the fact that there are always plenty of people in critical condition in Sunshine Hospital?

PM-107. For the function $f(x) = \dfrac{\sqrt{x + 4}}{2} - 1$:

a)  sketch the graph and the inverse.

b)  find the equation of the inverse function.

c)  determine the domain and range of the inverse.

d)  compute $f^{-1}(f(2))$.

PM-108. Compute the volume of the solid at right.

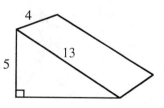

PM-109. A bowl contains three candies, two red ones and a green one. Work with a partner and decide who is player A and who is player B. Then take turns choosing a candy from the bowl without looking. Player A takes one and keeps it, then player B takes one. If the colors match, player A gets a point; if they differ, player B gets a point. Is this a fair game? First try the game experimentally, then show your analysis of the probabilities.

PM-110. Now put four candies in the bowl, three of one color and one of another. Will this game be fair? Again, check experimentally then give your analysis using probabilities.

PM-111. Are there other ways to put different numbers of two colors of candy in the bowl that would lead to a fair game while keeping the rest of the rules the same as in previous two problems? Try a number of different possibilities, analyze each one using probability, make some hypotheses, and report any conclusions or generalizations that you can justify mathematically.

**Evaluation**:

Problem PM-111 is, of course, the most important part of this investigation. Your report will be evaluated based on:

- The number and variety of cases you investigate and analyze.

- Your organization of the data, your analyses, and your general conclusions.

- The extent to which you can mathematically justify any generalizations you make.

## PM-112.  THE PROBABILITY OF WINNING A CASINO DICE GAME

To play this game you roll two dice. If your total is 7 or 11 points, you win. If your total is 2, 3, or 12 points, you lose. For any other number (4, 5, 6, 8, 9, or 10), that number becomes your point. You continue to roll until your point comes up again or a 7 comes up. If your point comes up first, you win. If 7 comes up first, you lose.

a)   As a team, play the game ten times. Record how many wins and losses your team has. Combine your information with that of the class. Are the results fairly even or were there many more wins or losses?

b)   List the number of ways to get each sum 2, 3, ..., 12.  (Do they total 36?)

**For the remaining parts of the dice game, leave answers in fraction form.**

c)   Find the probability you win on the first throw?

d)   Find the probability you lose on the first throw?

e)   Find the probability the game ends on the first throw?

PM-113.   Besides getting a 7 or 11, another way to win is to roll a 4 (your point) then another 4 before you roll a 7.

a)   Find the probability of a 4.

b)   Find the probability of a 4 before a 7.

c)   Find the probability of rolling a 4 and then rolling another 4 before a 7. Check your answer before going on.

d)   Find the probability of a 5.

e)   Find the probability of a 5 before a 7.

f)   Find the probability of a 5 and another 5 before a 7.

g)   Find the probabilities for winning with the sums 6, 8, 9, and 10. Look for symmetry.

PM-114.   List the ways to win the dice game. This is a fairly long list but it will be helpful for the next question.

a)   What is the probability of winning? Look for symmetry as you do this.

b)   If you won the game, what is the probability that you won by throwing 7 or 11 on the first throw?

c)   What is the probability of losing this game?

PM-115.    Solve each equation.

a)    $2^{(x-1)} = 64$

b)    $9^3 = 27^{(2x-1)}$

c)    $x^6 = 29$

d)    $6^x = 29$


PM-116.    In a certain county, weather service records based on the last 120 years show that if it rains or snows on a given day, there is a 70% chance that it will do so the next day as well.  If it does not rain or snow on a given day, there is a 20% chance that it will rain or snow the following day.

a)    Make a transition matrix to represent the information above.  Label the rows and columns.

b)    Suppose it rains today.  The distribution matrix that represents this beginning state is $D_0 = [\ 0\ \ 1]$ or $D_0 = [\ 1\ \ 0\ ]$, depending on how you arranged your transition matrix. Which of these fits yours?

c)    Find the product $D_1 = D_0\ T$, and explain what the entries mean.

d)    If it is clear on Monday, show how to find the probability that it will rain on Friday.  .


PM-117.    Sally's mother has two bags of candy but she says that Sally can only have one piece. Bag #1 has 70% orange candies and 30% red ones.  Bag #2 has 10% orange, 50% white, and 40% green candies.  She closes her eyes, randomly chooses one bag, and pulls out one candy.

a)    Draw a diagram.

b)    Find the probability of getting a red candy.

c)    Find the probability of getting an orange candy.

d)    If Sally got an orange candy, what is the probability that she chose bag #1?


PM-118.    Solve for x.

a)
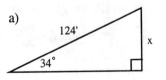

b)
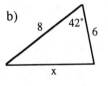

PM-119. In the summer of 1994, a couple were going through their attic and found a $1000 bond issued by the State of Nevada in 1865. It read "Pay to the Bearer" (whoever has possession.) States issue bonds when they need to borrow money. In 1865, Nevada was a new state and in great need of cash so it issued this bond at an interest rate of 24%.

a) Why do you think that the Supreme Court of the State of Nevada refused to authorize payment of the bond?

b) If $1000 were invested at 24% from 1865 until 1994, how much would it be worth? If you didn't have an answer to part (a) before, do you now?

c) What is the place value of the first digit in the answer to part (b)?

PM-120. In tennis, a player is allowed two serves. If the first one is in, the ball is played until someone wins the point. If the first serve is out, the player serves again. If the second serve is out, the player serving loses the point. If the second serve is in, the ball is played until someone wins the point. Joe Racquet gets his first serve in about 70% of the time. When this happens, he wins the point about 80% of the time. If he misses his first serve, his second serve goes in about 97% of the time. When this happens he wins the point about 40% of the time.

a) Find the probability that Joe wins a point when he is serving. Show clearly how you found it.

b) If you know Joe won a point while serving, what is the probability his first serve went in?

c) Which type of diagram did you use to answer (a) and (b)? Why?

PM-121. **TOOL KIT CHECK-UP**

Your Tool Kit contains reference tools for algebra. Return to your Tool Kit entries. You may need to revise or add entries.

Be sure that your Tool Kit contains entries for all of the items listed below. Add any topics that are missing to your Tool Kit NOW, as well as any other items that will help you in your study of algebra.

- Tree and Area Diagrams
- Expected Value
- Independent Events

- Fair Game
- Sample Space
- Conditional Probability

**UNIT 10 SUMMARY PROBLEM**

Choose two problems that represent the important concepts of this unit. Copy each problem (or a restatement of it) and show how to do each problem in more than one way. Your explanations should be clear enough so that someone who is not in this class can understand them.

# UNIT 11

## The Ice Cream Shoppe
### COUNTING AND SAMPLING

# Unit 11 Objectives
## *The Ice Cream Shoppe*: COUNTING AND SAMPLING

In this unit we will consider questions that involve many numbers. For example, phone number is made up of an area code and is followed by seven digits. Each town or area of a city usually has the same first three digits. Have you ever thought about whether there are enough phone numbers for everyone in your city or town? If a city has a population of 75,000, would there be enough phone numbers for everyone using six prefixes? The fact that the phone company has been splitting area codes in many metropolitan areas is evidence that they do run out of numbers.

Problems such as the phone number situation described above are known as counting problems, because we need to **count** how many different phone numbers are available. Counting problems arise in all sorts of situations and applications. In this unit you will have the opportunity to:

- Learn some general techniques for counting as well as develop formulas for permutations and combinations.

- Use these counting techniques to solve a variety of probability problems.

- Improve your problem solving skills to help you solve any counting problem whether or not you know a technique or a formula.

- Learn how to use what you know about counting to write the result of raising a binomial to an integral power.

Read the following problem and think about the different ways you can request three scoops of ice cream, keeping in mind that it can be on a cone or in a bowl. Then go on to problem IC-1.

IC-0. **THE ICE CREAM SHOPPE** On the eighth day of temperatures above 100°, Millie Zmelt's Easy Ice Cream Shoppe had only five flavors left. As usual, some customers ordered their ice cream in cones and some in a dish, but everyone ordered three scoops, the maximum Millie was allowing that day to ensure that her inventory would last. Millie had also considered allowing no more than one scoop of a particular flavor per customer in order to keep a balanced variety on hand. The number of choices available to customers would depend on whether they chose a cone or a dish and on the decision of the MZE Shoppe's management as to whether to allow more than one scoop of the same kind of ice cream. There are four counting problems here (at least). For each possible situation, how many choices does the customer have?

PROBLEM SOLVING
REPRESENTATION/MODELING
FUNCTIONS/GRAPHING
INTERSECTIONS/SYSTEMS
ALGORITHMS
REASONING/COMMUNICATION

# Unit 11
## *The Ice Cream Shoppe*: COUNTING AND SAMPLING

### SAMPLE SPACES AND BRANCHING DIAGRAMS

IC-1.      Suppose that you were going to flip three coins: a penny, a nickel, and a dime.

     a)      Make an organized list that shows all the possible outcomes. This list of all the possible outcomes is known as the **sample space** for this experiment.

     b)      How many outcomes are there?

     c)      What is the probability of flipping:

         i)   three heads?             ii)   at least two heads?

         iii)   one head and two tails?      iv)   at least one tail?

         v)   exactly two tails?           vi)   at least one head and one tail?

     d)      Which is more likely: flipping at least 2 heads or at least 2 tails? Explain your answer.

     e)      Remember that one way to create an organized list to represent this sample space is to make a **tree diagram**. The first coin, the penny, can either come up heads or tails. From there, we show the possible outcomes as **branches**. If you did not do so already, represent this sample space as a tree diagram.

IC-2.      You have decided to take a vacation. You want to go from Los Angeles to San Francisco and then to Hawaii, and you have all summer for your trip. To get from Los Angeles to San Francisco you can choose to drive, fly, take a bus, or take the train. From San Francisco to Hawaii you can fly, cruise, or sail.

     a)      Make a tree diagram to represent the possible choices in this problem.

     b)      How many choices do you have for the first leg of your trip? How many for the second?

     c)      In how many different ways can you travel from Los Angeles to Hawaii?

     d)      If you randomly choose your means of transportation, what is the probability of flying both times?

IC-3.    While playing Scrabble®, you need to make a word out of the letters  A  N  P  S.

   a)    How many arrangements of these letters are possible?

   b)    Of those arrangements, how many are words?  What are they?

   c)    What is the probability of a two-year-old randomly making a word using the four letters?


IC-4.    A typical counting problem might read: "How many four-digit numbers can be made using the digits  1, 2, 3, 4, 5, 6, 7  if it is okay to repeat a digit in a number?"  In order to solve this problem, you could take a variety of approaches.

   a)    Try to make a list (sample space) of the possibilities.  What is the difficulty here in trying to create a sample space?

         Try to make a tree diagram for this problem.  What is the difficulty here in trying to make a tree diagram?

   b)    A better method for organizing this problem is to condense it into a **decision chart**.  Start by asking, "How many decisions (or choices) do I need to make in this problem?"  In this case, the problem asks for <u>four-digit</u> <u>numbers</u> so there are **four** decisions.  You can set up a chart for the four decisions as follows:

         _____   _____   _____   _____
         1st digit     2nd digit     3rd digit     4th digit

   c)    How many choices do you have for the first digit?

   d)    The problem states that it is okay to repeat digits.  What does that imply?

   e)    How many choices do you have for the second digit?  the third?  the fourth?  Visualize a tree diagram.

   f)    Explain how to find the answer to the original question.  Justify your reasoning.


IC-5.    Refer back to the Scrabble® problem (IC-3).  Make a tree diagram **and** a decision chart for that problem.

   a)    Discuss with your team the similarities between the tree diagram and the decision chart.

   b)    Explain how you can determine the number of arrangements by looking at the tree diagram.

   c)    How do you get the same answer from the decision chart?

IC-6.     Make a decision chart to help you answer the following question:

          "How many four-digit numbers could you make with the digits 1, 2, 3, 4, 5, 6, 7 if you could not repeat the use of any digit?"


IC-7.     Use decision charts to answer parts (a) and (b) then explain the similarities and differences in the two situations.

          a)   A child's game contains nine discs, each with one of the numbers 1, 2, 3, ..., 9 on it. How many different 3-digit numbers could be formed by choosing any three discs?

          b)   A new lotto game called Quick Spin has three wheels, each with the numbers 1, 2, 3, ..., 9 equally spaced around the rim. Each wheel is spun once and the number the arrow points to is recorded. How many three digit numbers are possible?


IC-8.     Rondal High School had a student enrollment of 1245 in 1997, 1328 in 1998, and 1413 in 1999. School officials predicted that the 2000 enrollment would be 1505. The capacity of the school is 1800 students.

          a)   Graph this data. Determine the line of best fit and write a possible equation for that line.

          b)   What do the slope and y-intercept of the line represent?

          c)   Based on this information, when do you predict that the school will reach its capacity?

          d)   According to your graph and data, estimate the enrollment of Rondal High in 1992.

          e)   When do you think that Rondal High was built? Explain your thinking.


IC-9.     What is the probability that $x^2 + 7x + k$ will factor if $0 \le k \le 20$ and $k$ is an integer?

IC-10.    Earthquake magnitudes are measured by
          the amount of energy that is released.
          Since the amount of energy released from
          a large earthquake can be millions of times
          greater than the energy released by a small
          quake, a scale was created (the Richter
          scale) to give magnitudes in numbers that
          are easy to use.  An earthquake measuring
          3.4 on the Richter scale, for example, has
          an energy release of $10^{3.4}$ kilo joules.

   a)    How many times more energy is
         released by an earthquake that
         measures 5.5 on the Richter scale
         than one that measures 4.5?

   b)    How many times more energy is
         released by an earthquake that
         measures 4.1 than one that measures
         3.9?  Give your answer as a power
         of 10 and as a decimal.

   c)    What would the magnitude be of an earthquake that released half as much energy as
         a quake measuring 8.6 on the Richter scale?


IC-11.    Represent the integer that is:

   a)    one less than  n.                    b)    one more than  n.

   c)    one less than  n - 1.                d)    one less than  n - 4.


IC-12.    Verify algebraically that  $g(x) = \dfrac{2x - 3}{5}$  is the inverse function of  $f(x) = \dfrac{5x + 3}{2}$ .


IC-13.    Solve this system for  y  and  z:

          $$\frac{z + y}{4} + \frac{z - y}{2} = 1 \quad \text{and} \quad \frac{3z - y}{4} + \frac{4z + 2y}{11} = 3$$


IC-14.    Convert the following measurements in degrees to radians.

   a)    45°                                   b)    75°

   c)    -15°                                  d)    450°

IC-15. Arissa's sample is disappearing! Originally she had 59,049 elements in her sample, but at the end of each hour that passes only one-third of the previous amount remains.

 a) Write a formula to represent the number of elements in her sample space after t hours.

 b) After ten hours, she hopes to use her sample space in an experiment. How many elements remain after ten hours?

IC-16. Write a quadratic equation with roots $x = 3 \pm 5i$.

# FROM BRANCHES TO FACTORIALS

IC-17. Marcos is selecting classes for next year. He plans to take English, Physics, Government, Pre-calculus, Spanish and Journalism. His school has a six-period day. In how many different ways might the school arrange his day?

 a) Make a decision chart for this problem.

 b) What is the probability that Marcos will get first period Pre-calculus?

 c) What is the probability that Marcos will get both first period Pre-calculus and second period Physics?

IC-18. On your calculator, see if you can find a button like $\boxed{n!}$.

 This is the **factorial** function button.

 a) Find the values of 8 factorial (written 8!, then 7!, then 6!, . . ., 1!

 b) Which one of these is the same as the number of Marcos' possible schedules?

IC-19.  **FACTORIAL** is a shorthand for multiplication of a list of consecutive, descending whole numbers:  $n! = n(n - 1)(n - 2) \cdots (3)(2)(1)$.

For example,  4 factorial $= 4 \cdot 3 \cdot 2 \cdot 1 = 24$ and $6! = 6 \cdot 5 \cdot 4 \cdot 3 \cdot 2 \cdot 1 = 720$.

a) Explain why 6! gives the correct solution to the possible number of ways to arrange Marcos' schedule.

b) Explain why 4! gives the correct solution to the possible number of ways to arrange the letters **M   A   T   H**.

IC-20. How many distinguishable batting orders can be made from the nine starting players on a baseball team?

IC-21. How many distinct rearrangements of the letters in the word FRACTIONS are there?

IC-22. Five students are running for Junior Class President. They must give speeches before the election committee. In how many different orders could they give their speeches?

IC-23. Remembering what n! means can help you do some messy calculations quickly, as well as help you do problems that might be too large for your calculator. For instance, if we wanted to calculate

$$\frac{9!}{6!}$$

we could use the n! button on our calculator and find that $9! = 362880$, and $6! = 720$, so

$$\frac{9!}{6!} = \frac{362880}{720} = 504.$$

But, if we remember that $9! = 9 \cdot 8 \cdot 7 \cdot 6 \cdot 5 \cdot 4 \cdot 3 \cdot 2 \cdot 1$ and $6! = 6 \cdot 5 \cdot 4 \cdot 3 \cdot 2 \cdot 1$ then we can write

$$\frac{9 \cdot 8 \cdot 7 \cdot \cancel{6} \cdot \cancel{5} \cdot \cancel{4} \cdot \cancel{3} \cdot \cancel{2} \cdot \cancel{1}}{\cancel{6} \cdot \cancel{5} \cdot \cancel{4} \cdot \cancel{3} \cdot \cancel{2} \cdot \cancel{1}} = 9 \cdot 8 \cdot 7 = 504$$

Use this idea to simplify each of the following problems before computing the result.

a) $\frac{10!}{8!}$     b) $\frac{20!}{18!2!}$     c) $\frac{7!}{4!3!}$     d) $\frac{75!}{73!}$

IC-24.     If $f(n) = n!$, evaluate each of the following:

a)     $\dfrac{f(5)}{f(3)}$          b)     $\dfrac{f(6)}{f(4)}$          c)     $\dfrac{f(9)}{f(7) \cdot f(2)}$


IC-25.     What is the probability that $x^2 + kx + 12$ will factor if $0 \le k \le 8$ and $k$ is an integer?
           Make an organized list (sample space) to help you determine the probability.


IC-26.     Consider the following situation:

           You must park in a parking garage that charges \$3.00 for the first hour and \$1.00 for
           each hour (or any part of that hour) after that.

a)     How much will it cost to park your car for 90 minutes?

b)     How much will it cost to park your car for 118 minutes?   119 minutes?

c)     How much will it cost to park your car for 120 minutes?   121 minutes?

d)     Graph the cost in relation to the length of time your car is parked.

e)     Is this function continuous?


IC-27.     Victoria is playing with her balance scale and balances 3 blue blocks and 2 red blocks on
           one side with 5 blue blocks and a red block on the other.  Later, her brother balances 2
           red blocks and a blue block with 40 g.  How much does each block weigh?


IC-28.     Factor and reduce to simplify: $\dfrac{5x + 10}{x^2 + 6x + 8}$ . Justify each step.


IC-29.     Use an idea from the previous problem to simplify and add these fractions.  Justify each
           step.
$$\dfrac{x - 2}{x + 2} + \dfrac{2x - 6}{x^2 - x - 6}$$


IC-30.     Change the angles that are given in radians to degrees and the angles that are given in
           degrees to radians.

a)     $108°$          b)     $320°$          c)     $\dfrac{7\pi}{9}$

d)     $\dfrac{19\pi}{12}$          e)     $\dfrac{17\pi}{2}$          f)     $260°$

IC-31.    How many solutions are there to the system of
          equations at right. Justify your response.

$$y = x^2 - 2x + 2$$
$$y = 2x - 2$$

IC-32.    Graph each inequality and find the area of the enclosed region:

$$y \geq |x - 2| \quad \text{and} \quad y \leq 4 - |x|$$

IC-33.    A conveyor belt carries grain to the top of a barn,
          where it drops the grain allowing it to fall in a pile
          on the ground.  The pile is in the shape of a cone.
          Recall that $V = \frac{1}{3}\pi r^2 h$ is the volume for a cone.

   a)     Find the volume when the height is ten feet
          and the radius of the base is four feet.

   b)     The cone-shaped piles at each stage are all
          similar.  If the radius of the base is four feet
          when the height is ten feet, what is the radius of the base when the height is 15 feet?

   c)     Consider the angle the side of the cone-shaped pile makes with the ground.  Is this
          angle changing?  Justify your answer.  If not, what is the measure of the angle?

## FACTORIALS TO PERMUTATIONS

IC-34.    Jasper finally managed to hold on to some money long enough to open a savings account
          at the credit union.  When he went in to open the account, the accounts manager told him
          that he needed to select a 4-digit **pin** (personal **i**dentification **n**umber).  She also said that
          he could not repeat a digit but that he could use any of the digits 0, 1, 2,..., 9 for any
          place in his 4-digit code.

   a)     Make a decision chart for this problem.

   b)     How many digits does he have to choose from for the first place?

   c)     Once he chooses a digit to use for the first place, how many does he have to choose
          from for the second?  the third?  the fourth?

          Notice that the decision chart looks like the beginning of 10! but it doesn't go all of the
          way down to one.  We can use factorials to represent this problem, but we must
          compensate for the factors that we do not need.

   d)     Reduce, and leave in factored form:  $\frac{10!}{6!}$ .

   e)     How does the solution to part (d) relate to the decision chart in part (a)?

IC-35.    Twenty-five art students submitted sculptures to be judged at the county fair. Awards are going to be given for the six best sculptures. You have been asked to be the judge. You must **choose and arrange in order** the best six sculptures.

a)    Make a decision chart for this problem.

b)    How many sculptures do you have to choose from for the first place award?

c)    Once you have chosen a sculpture for first place, how many do you have to choose from for second place? the third? the fourth?

d)    Show the numerical simplification of $\frac{25!}{19!}$.

e)    Explain how the solution to part (d) relates to the original problem and the decision chart in part (a).

f)    Where did the 19 come from? How could you get 19 from the numbers in the original problem? Why did 19! in the denominator become an important step in coming up with an answer to the problem? Discuss this with your team.


IC-36.    With your team, discuss how you could use factorials to express each of the following solutions:

a)    Fifty-two contestants are vying for the Miss Teen pageant crown. In how many different ways can the judges pick the next Miss Teen and her three runners-up?

b)    The volleyball team is sponsoring a mixed-doubles sand court volleyball tournament and sixteen pairs have signed up for the chance to win one of the seven trophies and cash prizes. In how many different ways can the teams be chosen and arranged for the top seven slots?

c)    Carmen is getting a new locker at school and the first thing she must do is decide on a new combination. The three number combination can be picked from the numbers 0-35. How many different locker combinations could she make up if none of the numbers can be repeated?

Problems about batting orders and questions about how many numbers you could make without repeating any digits are called **PERMUTATIONS**. The following lists give some more examples and some non-examples.

Permutations:

- All the arrangements of the letters ABC.

- The possible 4-digit numbers you could make if you had square tiles, one with each number 2, 3, 4, 5, 6, 7, 8.

- From a group of 8 candidates, one will become president, one vice president, and one secretary of the school senate.

Not-permutations:

- All the possible license plate letter triples that could be made using A, B, C.

- The possible 4-digit numbers you could make if you could choose any digit from 2, 3, 4, 5, 6, 7, 8.

- From a group of 8 candidates, three will be selected to be on the executive committee.

a) List some possible license plate letter triples using A's or B's or C's that would not be in the list of arrangements of the cards lettered A, B, and C.

b) Compare the two lists of 8 candidates. How do they differ?

c) What are the important characteristics that a counting problem has to have in order to classify it as a permutations problem?

d) Discuss with your team a general method for solving the examples on the left above, and write a description for your general method that would work for any problem that could be identified as a permutations problem.

## PERMUTATIONS, A SPECIAL NOTATION

**Problem**: Eight people are running a race. In how many different ways can they come in first, second, and third?

This is a problem of counting **permutations**, and the result can be represented $_8P_3$, which means the number of ways to **choose <u>and</u> arrange** three things from a set of eight.

$$_8P_3 = 8 \cdot 7 \cdot 6 = 336$$

A more complicated but more compact way to write this is:

$$_8P_3 = 8 \cdot 7 \cdot 6 = \frac{8 \cdot 7 \cdot 6 \cdot 5 \cdot 4 \cdot 3 \cdot 2 \cdot 1}{5 \cdot 4 \cdot 3 \cdot 2 \cdot 1} = \frac{8!}{5!} = \frac{8!}{(8-3)!}$$

In general, $_nP_r = \frac{n!}{(n-r)!}$ for n items chosen r at a time. Record this notation and what it stands for in your Tool Kit.

IC-39.    The basketball cheerleaders printed large letters on cards that spell out your school's mascot. Each card has one letter on it and each cheerleader is supposed to hold up one card. At the end of the first quarter, they realize that someone has mixed up the cards.

a)    How many ways are there to arrange the cards?

b)    If they hadn't noticed the mix up, what would the probability be that the cards would have correctly spelled out the mascot?


IC-40.    Mr. Dobson is planning to give a quiz to his class tomorrow. Unfortunately for his students, Mr. Dobson is notorious for writing quizzes that seem to have no relevance to the subject whatsoever. With this in mind, his students know that their efforts will be purely guesswork. If the quiz contains ten questions that the students will have to match with ten given answers, what is the probability that Randy Random will get all ten questions matched correctly?


IC-41.    The first four factors of 7! are  7, 6, 5, 4  or  7, (7 - 1), (7 - 2), (7 - 3):

a)    What are the first four factors of 12! ?

b)    What are the first six factors of n! ?

c)    What are the first five factors of (n - 3)! ?

d)    What are the first five factors of (n + 2)! ?


IC-42.    A state is chosen at random from the 50 states. Find the probability that it:

a)    is on the east coast.

b)    has at least one representative in the house of representatives.

c)    has three U.S. senators.

d)    does not border an ocean or the gulf of Mexico.

IC-43.    Which is bigger:  (5 - 2)!  or  (5 - 3)! ? Justify your answer.


IC-44.    Find the value of each permutation:

a)    $_5P_3 = ?$          b)    $_7P_4 = ?$          c)    $_8P_2 = ?$

IC-45.     What do you think 0! will equal?

   a)     Try it on your calculator to see what you get.

   b)     What does $_8P_8$ mean? What *should* $_8P_8$ be equal to? Write $_8P_8$ using the factorial formula. Why is it necessary to have $0! = 1$?

   c)     Remember how we showed that $2^0 = 1$? One way was to go down the sequence of powers of 2: $\frac{2^4}{2} = 2^3$, $\frac{2^3}{2} = 2^2$, $\frac{2^2}{2} = 2^1$, $\frac{2^1}{2} = 2^0$, but $\frac{2^1}{2} = 1$, so $2^0 = 1$. We can use a similar argument for $0!$. Explain why $\frac{5!}{5} = 4!$. Use that pattern to construct an argument for why $0!$ should equal 1.


IC-46.     Compute the quotient $(4 - 7i) \div (8 - 9i)$. Refer to problem PM-52 if you need help.


IC-47.     The Postal Service requires 33 cents postage on a first class letter weighing less than but not equal to 1 ounce. An additional 22 cents is added for each ounce or part of an ounce above that. Graph the relationship between price and weight for first class mail.


IC-48.     How many of the following are in a standard deck of cards? This is information you will need to know in order to solve some future problems.

   a)     cards                          b)     diamonds

   c)     twos                           d)     face cards


IC-49.     Graph $y = \sqrt{4 - x^2}$. Imagine revolving this around the x-axis, faster and faster, so that it appears to form a three dimensional figure.

   a)     Make a sketch of the three dimensional figure. What is it called?

   b)     Use $V = \frac{4}{3}\pi r^3$ to find the volume of the three dimensional figure.

> The following problem is a good example to keep for future reference and you may want to add it to your portfolio.

IC-50.    Five members of the Spirit Club have volunteered for the club governing board. These members are: Al, Betty, Carl, Darla, and Eugene. The club members will select three of the five as board members for the next year. One way to do this would be to elect a governing committee of three in which all members would have the same title. A second way would be to select a president, vice-president, and secretary.

   a)    How many different slates of officers are possible? (This means a president, vice-president, and a secretary are chosen. Al as president, Betty as vice-president, and Carl as secretary is considered a different slate from Al as president, Betty as secretary, and Carl as vice-president. )

   b)    How many different governing committees are possible? Don't try to calculate this; just make a list of all the possibilities.

   c)    The Spirit Club expects many more members will join during the second semester and there will be more volunteers for the governing board. The club members have voted to have a governing committee (all three members have the same title), and they'd like a way to calculate how many different committees of three are possible from any number of volunteers. They know that listing all the possibilities will take a long time.

   Jaime, another member of the club, was assigned to answer the question. He decided to start with his favorite problem-solving strategy: solving a smaller problem. He began by finding how many committees of two could be formed from four volunteers and he started by making a list of all the possibilities.

   Ngan was looking over Jaime's shoulder and asked, "Why not make a decision chart? There are four choices for the first member, and three choices for the second, so there should be 12 possible committees. Fred showed her his list which only had 6 committees and asked, "Where are the others?"

   Make your own list and see if you can find more than 6 committees. If not explain why Ngan's method gave too many. It may help to make a tree diagram for her method.

   d)    Jaime and Ngan figured out what was wrong with Ngan's method, but they didn't have any other ideas for calculating an answer without a list or a tree, so they decided to see if they could find a way to adapt Ngan's method to make it work.

   Ngan said, "My method gave 12 committees, but there were only 6, so let's just do it my way, and then divide by 2."

   Jaime was more cautious. "Let's try that on another example, say, committees of three people chosen from four volunteers."

   "Okay," said Ngan, "My way gives 24."

   "I made a list, and there are only four possibilities. I'm sure I got them all," Jaime replied.

   Show how Ngan got 24, and explain why her method gives <u>six</u> times the actual number here, but only gave twice the correct number in the previous example.

**>>Problem continues on the next page.>>**

e) Finally they felt ready to tackle the big problem: suppose you had n volunteers from whom r people would be chosen for the governing committee. They started with Ngan's method, which they realized was the same as finding how many ways they could make a slate of officers (president, vice-president, secretary, etc.).

Use permutation notation to express this number, and explain what they must divide by to get the number of committees.

Create a formula using permutation notation and factorials and test it on the original question from part (b).

f) Add the following information to your Tool Kit.

---

In selecting committees, we care about who is selected but we do **not** care about the **order** of selection or any **arrangement** of the groups. Selections of committees, or of subsets of items from a larger set without regard to the order of the group selected, are called **COMBINATIONS**.

Lists in which the order of selection is important, but selections cannot be repeated are called **PERMUTATIONS**.

---

IC-51. In the California state lottery there are 51 numbers to choose from. How many ways are there to choose 6 of the 51 numbers? How many **combinations** of 6 numbers can be chosen from the list of 51?

As in the committee problem, order is not important. We can start with factorials, find the number of permutations $_{51}P_6$ and then divide by the number of arrangements of each group, 6!.

Our numerator represents the total number of ways to arrange six numbers (out of 51 numbers) where the order matters. Each group of the same six numbers is counted $6! = 720$ times. Since they are the same and grouped together, we need to divide to find out how many combinations there are without regard to order.

a) Find the number of possible combinations for the California Lottery.

b) What is the probability of selecting the six winning numbers?

IC-52. Five cards are drawn from a standard deck of 52 cards.

a) Show a decision chart for the number of choices for the first card, second card, and so forth up to the fifth card, and write the total number of arrangements of the cards that you found using permutation notation.

b) How many ways can you arrange the five cards selected? Write your answer both as a number and using a factorial.

c) Since order generally does not matter when playing cards, we need to divide out the number of repetitions of the same set of five cards. Calculate the number of five card hands that can be selected from a deck of 52 cards.

**IC-53.**

"This is strange," said Nora. "First we learned factorials, which count the number of ways to arrange a group of objects in order. Then we learned permutations, which count ways to *choose* **and** *arrange* a subgroup from a larger group. Now we're learning combinations, which count ways to just choose a subgroup from a larger group. Why didn't we learn how to choose before we learned how to choose-and-arrange?"

"I see!" said José. "The permutation formula was based on a decision chart: how many ways to pick the first object, times how many ways to pick the second, etc. So we were choosing and arranging at the same time. We didn't choose, then arrange."

"But why **can't** we choose, then arrange?" said Nora. "It should be a simple decision chart:

$$\underset{\substack{\text{Number of ways to} \\ \text{choose and arrange}}}{\underline{\qquad {}_nP_r \qquad}} = \underset{\text{number of ways to choose}}{\underline{\qquad\qquad\qquad}} \bullet \underset{\substack{\text{number of ways to arrange} \\ \text{what was chosen}}}{\underline{\qquad\qquad\qquad}}$$

Fill in the blanks in Nora's decision chart.

---

### COMBINATIONS: A SPECIAL NOTATION

Let's see how Nora's idea fits in with what you've learned so far. Consider the following problem.

**Problem**: Ten people are running for the prom committee. In how many different ways can a committee of 4 be chosen?

To begin, this is a problem of counting **combinations**. Since the order does not matter, it will help to have a notation for combinations. We use $_{10}C_4$ to represent the number of ways to **choose** four things from a set of ten. (This is often read as "10 choose 4.")

Rewrite Nora's decision chart equation for the prom committee problem, using our notations for permutations, combinations, and arrangements.

Solve the equation for $_{10}C_4$.

Explain why the equation above can also be written as $_{10}C_4 = \dfrac{10!}{(6!)(4!)}$.

Finally, write a general formula, in two different versions, for $_nC_r$, the number of ways to choose $r$ things from a total of $n$. Remember, Nora was right:

(number of ways to choose)(number of ways to arrange) =
(number of ways to choose and arrange)

**therefore:**

(number of ways to choose) = $\dfrac{\text{(number of ways to choose and arrange)}}{\text{(number of ways to arrange)}}$.

$$_nC_r = \frac{_nP_r}{r!} = \frac{n!}{(n-r)!r!}$$

---

IC-54.    There are twelve people signed up to play darts during lunch.  How many ways can a three-person dart team be chosen?


IC-55.    Find the value of each of the following:

a)    $_{10}C_8 = ?$             b)    $_{12}C_7 = ?$             c)    $_7C_1 = ?$


IC-56.    On the 6-person bowling team only four players bowl at one time.  How many different four-person teams can be made?


IC-57.    How many different bowling line ups can be made in the previous problem?


IC-58.    What is 0! ?

a)    How many ways are there to choose all five items from a group of five items?  What happens when you substitute into the factorial formula to compute $_5C_5$?  Since you know (logically) what the result has to be, use this fact to explain why mathematicians decided that 0! equals 1.

b)    On the other hand, how many ways are there to choose **nothing** from a group of five items?  And what happens when you try to use the factorial formula to compute $_5C_0$?

c)    In order to extend the use of the formula for combinations to the examples described in parts (a) and (b) mathematicians agreed that  0!  must equal  1.

| **Definition:   0! = 1** |
| --- |
| Some would argue that there is logic to this if you think of selecting zero items from a list.  There is just **one** way to do this, which is to leave them all unselected. |


IC-59.    Two cards are dealt from a randomly shuffled deck (a regular deck of 52 cards).  To establish the sample space for this problem you need to think of choosing two from a set of 52.

a)    How many ways are there to do this?

b)    How many diamonds are there?  How many ways to choose two diamonds out of all the diamonds in the deck?  What is the probability of dealing two diamonds from the whole deck of 52 cards?

c)    If you did not already do so, express your solution to part (b) in the form $\frac{_aC_b}{_dC_e}$ .

d)    What is the probability of dealing two face cards?

e)    If you did not already do so, express your solution to part (d) in the form $\frac{_aC_b}{_dC_e}$ .


408                                                                                          UNIT 11

IC-60.    Given seven points in a plane, no three of which are collinear:

    a)    how many different lines are determined by these points?

    b)    how many distinct triangles can be formed?

    c)    how many distinct quadrilaterals can be formed?


IC-61.    Explain why the answers to parts (b) and (c) of the preceding problem are the same.


IC-62.    Graph:  $y = 1 + \tan (x - \frac{\pi}{4})$


IC-63.    If $n > 3$, how could you write $n \cdot (n - 1) \cdot (n - 2) \cdot (n - 3)!$  more efficiently?


IC-64.    Simplify:

    a)    $3^{-2} \cdot 3^4$          b)    $3^{-4} \cdot 3^4$          c)    $(3^{-1} + 3^{-3}) \cdot 3^4$


IC-65.    You can use part (c) of the previous problem to get the answer to this problem or you can use other methods, but be careful about the order in which you do the operations.

$$\frac{3^{-2} - 3^{-1}}{3^{-3} + 3^{-4}}$$


IC-66.    Consider the following two sequences.  The initial value is underlined in each sequence:

    **Sequence 1**: 52, 54, 56, 58, . . .
    **Sequence 2**: 1, 2, 4, 8, 16, . . .

    a)    Which sequence is arithmetic and which is geometric?  Justify your answer.

    b)    Write a formula for the $n^{th}$ term of each sequence.

    c)    Do these sequences have any terms in common?  If so, what are they (and prove it)? If not, why not?


IC-67.    Compute:

    a)    $\left(\frac{\sqrt{2}}{2} + \frac{i\sqrt{2}}{2}\right)^2$          b)    $\left(\frac{-\sqrt{2}}{2} - \frac{i\sqrt{2}}{2}\right)^2$

    c)    Use the results from parts (a) and (b) above to solve $x^2 = i$ for x. (the square roots of i.)

# OTHER COUNTING TECHNIQUES

> Permutations? No! Combinations? No! Then what? What other kinds of counting problems are there?

IC-68.   Andrea has just purchased a 5-digit combination lock (mathematicians might call some of these locks permutation locks), and it allows her to set up her own combination. She can use the numbers 0 - 9 for her combination and she must have five of them.

a)   How many 5-digit combinations can she make so that no digit is repeated?

b)   How many 5-digit combinations are possible if she **can** repeat the digits?

IC-69.   Joaquin is getting a new locker at school and the first thing he must do is decide on a new combination. The three number combination can be picked from the numbers 0 through 21.

a)   How many different locker combinations can Joaquin choose if none of the numbers can be repeated?

b)   If he can let the numbers repeat, how many locker combinations can he choose from?

IC-70.   Another school nightmare: Monday morning brings a surprise quiz with nine true or false questions. Fortunately the teacher writes a bonus problem on the board: How many different true-false answer patterns could there be for the nine questions on the quiz?

IC-71.   How many different ways can you have your quarter pound hamburger prepared if you can have it prepared with or without mustard, ketchup, mayonnaise, lettuce, tomatoes, pickles, cheese, and onions?

IC-72.   What has been different about the last four problems? Did you solve them with permutations? With combinations? What method did you use to solve them?

IC-73.    Yesterday in chemistry class Alberto took a four question quiz. The four questions were true/false and he had forgotten to study, so he had to guess. Using '**W**' for wrong and '**R**' for right:

a)    Create a sample space for the sequences of wrong and right solutions that are possible for this quiz.

b)    Create a tree diagram for this problem.

c)    What is the probability that Alberto will get:

    i)    4 right?           ii)    3 right?           iii)    2 right?

    iv)    1 right?          v)    0 right?

d)    What score should Alberto expect to get on his quiz?


IC-74.    The Colorado Rookies and the Tampa Bay Demons have made it into the World Championship. After four games, the Rookies are leading the series three to one. The Series is a "best of seven" situation (the first team with four wins, wins). Assume that each team is equally likely to win an individual game.

a)    What is the probability that the Rookies will win the World Championship?

b)    What is the probability that the Demons will win the World Championship?


IC-75.    A member of the U.S. Public Health Service came up with a list of words from which impressive sounding 3-word phrases can be formed if you choose one word at random from each of these three columns.

| | | |
|---|---|---|
| integrated | management | options |
| total | organizational | flexibility |
| systematized | monitored | capability |
| parallel | reciprocal | mobility |
| functional | digital | programming |
| responsive | logistical | concept |
| optional | transitional | time-phase |
| synchronized | incremental | projection |
| compatible | third-generation | hardware |
| balanced | policy | contingency |

a)    How many different three-word phrases can be constructed from the list?

b)    How many different three-word phrases can be constructed if each column had only four words in it?

c)    How many different 3-words phrases can be constructed if each column has fourteen words?

d)    Try it out. Write a sentence containing one of the three-word phrases.


The Ice Cream Shoppe: Counting and Sampling

IC-76.    Sai Chiam and one of his friends were chosen to be captains of the A and B soccer teams
during PE.  Their PE teacher asked each of them to pick a number from 1 to 10.  What is
the probability that:

a)    Sai Chiam's number is greater than his friend's number?

b)    His number is equal to his friend's number?

c)    His number is less than his friend's number?

d)    Be prepared to explain your method for figuring out these probabilities.

IC-77.    A biologist wanted to find out how many trout were
in a lake.  He caught 250 trout, tagged them and
returned them to the lake.  If he later came back and
caught 200 trout and 5 of them had tags, how many
trout can the biologist expect the lake to contain.

IC-78.    Simplify:

a)   $\dfrac{n!}{(n-1)!}$

b)   $\dfrac{(n+2)!}{n!}$

IC-79.    Use your knowledge of how to solve  $2y^2 + 5y - 3 = 0$  in order to solve for  x:

$$2 \sin^2 x + 5 \sin x - 3 = 0.$$

IC-80.    Josephina thinks that she has discovered a new pattern.

$$\frac{x-1}{x-1} = 1 \implies \frac{x^2-1}{x-1} = x+1 \implies \frac{x^3-1}{x-1} = x^2+x+1 \implies \frac{x^4-1}{x-1} = x^3 +x^2+x+1$$

a)    Check her equations above by multiplying.  Does her pattern work?

b)    Based on her pattern, what does  $\dfrac{x^5-1}{x-1}$  equal?  Is it true?  Justify your answer.

c)    Make a conjecture about how to represent the result for $\dfrac{x^n-1}{x-1}$.  You will probably
need ", . . .," in the middle of your expression.

IC-81.    Water boils at 100°C or 212°F.  Water freezes at 0°C or 32°F.  Write a linear equation to
calculate the temperature of water in Fahrenheit if you know the temperature in Celsius.

# THE ICE CREAM SHOPPE

This problem is definitely one you should keep as an example for later reference. It would also be a good problem for your portfolio.

IC-82. After seven days of temperatures above 100°, Millie Zmelt's Easy Ice Cream Shoppe had only five flavors left: chocolate fudge, French vanilla, maple-nut, lemon custard, and blueberry delight. On the eighth day of the heat wave, some customers ordered their ice cream in cones and some in a dish, but everyone ordered three scoops, the maximum Millie was allowing that day to ensure that her inventory would last. Millie had also considered allowing no more than one

scoop of a particular flavor per customer in order to keep a balanced variety on hand. The number of choices available to customers would depend on whether they chose a cone or a dish and on the decision of the MZE Shoppe's management as to whether to allow more than one scoop of the same kind of ice cream. For a cone the order in which the scoops are served makes a difference; for a dish the order does not matter. There are four counting problems here (at least). For each possible situation, how many possibilities does the customer get to choose from?

IC-83. Make a chart organizing and describing types of counting problems you solved in the previous problem along with their solutions. One of the problems is a set of permutations, another is combinations, the remaining two have no particular names, but for one of them there is an easy way to write a formula for its solution. For which ones can you give a formula for counting? It would be a good idea to make a neat, organized copy of your conclusions to keep for future reference in your Tool Kit.

IC-84. Millie Zmelt decided it was okay to serve cones with multiple scoops of the same flavor and you sent your friend Randy Random to get a cone for you.

a) What is the probability he would bring you a cone with **all** three scoops the same? (Assume he made a random selection).

b) What is the probability he would get all three different?

IC-85. With your team, find another situation where four types of counting problems could be involved. Write a short paragraph describing such a problem.

IC-86.    A pizza parlor has 12 toppings other than cheese. How many different pizzas can they create with five **or fewer** toppings?

IC-87.    John has to graph a set of parabolas of the form $y = x^2 - 4x + 2^n$ where $n$ is an integer and $0 \le n \le 6$. What is the probability that one of these parabolas, chosen at random, will have:

a)    one x-intercept?          b)    two x-intercepts?

c)    no x-intercepts?

IC-88.    Another pizza parlor is having a lunch special. They have a rack of individual pizzas each with three different toppings. The price is really low because they forgot to indicate on the boxes what toppings were on the pizza. If they only have ten ingredients, and if each pizza has a different combination of three ingredients, and all three-combinations were used: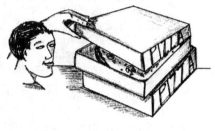

a)    how many pizzas are on the rack?

b)    how many have Canadian bacon, pineapple, and one other ingredient?

c)    what is the probability of getting a pizza that has mushrooms on it?

IC-89.    Write an explanation of the difference between a combination and a permutation so your friend, who is taking Pre-calculus and doesn't understand counting techniques, can understand.

IC-90.    Without using a graphing calculator, graph $y = \sin x$ and $y = \cos x$ on the same set of axes. Use $0 \le x \le 2\pi$. On the same axes and in a different color, graph $y = \sin x + \cos x$ by mentally adding the two approximate y-values for a sufficient number of x-values.

IC-91.    Simplify:

a)  $\dfrac{(n - 3)!}{(n - 5)!}$          b)  $\dfrac{n!}{(n - 2)!}$

IC-92.    Solve for x.

$$\frac{x}{2x+1} - \frac{1-x}{2x-1} = \frac{2x+7}{4x^2-1}$$

414                                                                                    UNIT 11

IC-93.     Solve for x in the figure at right.

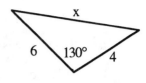

IC-94.     Joanne was making repairs to her deck and needed to buy some supplies. She purchased 2 posts, 3 boards and 4 piers for $52. Needing more materials she went back to the lumber yard and bought one post and 5 boards for $13. Realizing she did not need the piers she made a third trip where she bought 3 more boards, returned the 4 piers and ended up with a refund of $34. What was the cost of each item?

IC-95.     A tree casts a 12 m shadow when the angle of elevation of the sun is 42°. How tall is the tree?

## TWISTS ON PERMUTATIONS AND COMBINATIONS

IC-96.     For some counting problems, it is important to do some thinking before you start. For example, in the problem below, the number must be less than 500, so you need to use what you know about the hundreds digit first. Don't forget to count two digit and one digit numbers as well.

   a)     How many numbers less than 500 can you make using the digits 0, 1, 3, 5, 7, if no digit may be repeated? Identify the subproblems and solve each subproblem to find the answer.

   b)     Let's change the problem slightly.

          How many numbers less than 500 are there if the digits can be repeated? Identify the subproblems and solve each subproblem to find the answer to this question.

> The following problems will require some thought. While combinations, permutations, and factorial formulas are necessary and useful, you cannot do them without common sense and good problem solving skills. Discuss and debate choices of methods with your team.

IC-97.     How many permutations of the letters in the word SQUARE begin with SQ?

   a)     What was different about this problem that you had to consider?

   b)     What method did you use to solve this problem? Explain why you chose this method.

IC-98.    Five teenagers go to the movies.  They want to sit together in a row with a student on
          each aisle (assume the row is 5 seats wide including 2 aisle seats).

          a)    How many ways can they sit in the row?

          b)    If Kris wants to sit in an aisle seat, how many ways can they all sit in the row?

          c)    If Patrice wants to sit on an aisle seat with Beth next to her, how many ways can the
                five students sit?


IC-99.    **Anagrams**

          a)    How many distinct ways can the letters in the word MASH be arranged?

          b)    How many distinct ways can the letters in the word SASH be arranged?
                Be careful!

          c)    How many distinct ways can the letters in the word SASS be arranged?

          d)    What makes these counts different?


IC-100.   How many permutations of all the letters in the word PYRAMID do not end with D?


IC-101.   Your teacher gave you a list of ten questions to study for a test and told you that the test
          would consist of six questions chosen from the list.  When you got home, you realized
          that you wouldn't have time to study for all ten questions, so you picked the seven that
          you thought were most likely to be on the test.  When you got to school the next day, you
          found out that your teacher had randomly chosen six questions to put on the test.

          a)    The teacher could have picked 4 from the 7 that you studied and 2 from the three
                you did not.  Represent each of these in combination notation.

          b)    To find the number of tests the teacher might have constructed this way, what should
                you do with these two results:  Multiply?  Add?  Discuss this with your team.

          c)    In how many ways could your teacher have randomly selected six of the ten
                questions?  Express this in combination notation.

          What is the probability that you will have studied:

          d)    six of the selected questions?

          e)    five of the selected questions?

          f)    three of the selected questions?

          g)    Assuming you get correct all the questions that you studied for and miss all the ones
                you did not study for, what is you expected score on the test?

IC-102.    Consider this puzzle:

a)    How many ways are there to arrange the letters in each of the two scrambled clues on the left?

b)    How many ways are there to arrange the letters in each of the two scrambled clues on the right?

c)    Unscramble each of the clues to find the letters in the circles.

d)    How many ways are there to arrange the circled letters that complete the MISQUOTE?

e)    Unscramble the circled letters to find the MISQUOTE.

## SCRAMBLES

REDOR

ANMDRO

IGTDI

PMEASL

Where the probability teacher said he wants to build a home;

" on ⬚⬚⬚⬚⬚⬚⬚ "

MISQUOTE

IC-103.    A wildlife biologist is given the task of estimating the population of blacktail deer on Southfork Mountain. She uses a tranquilizer gun to capture, tag, and release unharmed 50 does and 15 bucks over a period of several months. She returns to the mountains the following year and makes the following observations:

"I saw 70 does this week and only 4 of them had tags."

"Of the 40 bucks I observed, 15 had been tagged."

a)    Estimate the number of does on Southfork Mountain.

b)    Estimate the number of bucks on Southfork Mountain.

IC-104. We know that $_nC_r = \dfrac{n!}{(n-r)!r!}$ and $_nC_r = \dfrac{_nP_r}{r!}$, but these are not really different formulas. Show that they really amount to the same thing.

IC-105. You are given a bag that you are told contains 8 marbles. You draw a marble, record its color, and put it back.

a) If you do this eight times and you don't record any red marbles, can you conclude that there aren't any red marbles in the bag? Explain.

b) If you do this 100 times and you don't record any red marbles, can you conclude that there are no red marbles in the bag? Explain.

c) How many times do you have to draw marbles (putting them back in each time) to be absolutely certain that there are no red marbles in the bag?

IC-106. Simplify the following expressions so that they do not have negative exponents:

a) $\dfrac{x^{-2} - y^{-2}}{x^{-1} + y^{-1}}$

b) $(x^{-2} - 5y^{-1})^{-1}$

IC-107. Sketch the graph of $y = 2^{(x+3)}$. Then write the equation of the graph that is four units to the right and five units down from this one.

IC-108. Solve each inequality for $x$ and represent each solution on a number line. Assume that $c > 0$ and $a > 0$.

a) $|x - b| \le c$

b) $|ax - b| \ge c$

IC-109. Consider the system at right: How many solutions does this system have? Justify your answer.

$$x = (y - 3)^2 + 2$$
$$y = (x - 5)^2 + 3$$

IC-110. Multiply each of the following. The first one is already done for you.

a) $(x + y)^1 = x + y$

b) $(x + y)^2$

c) $(x + y)^3$

IC-111. "These counting problems are driving me crazy," Alex complained as he tossed his book bag on the chair. "They don't have anything to do with real algebra." Alex had been to see his counselor and arrived after his team had started to work.

"I'm glad you said that," commented José. "Guess what we're doing today?"

"Impossible!" said Alex.

"Remember the last problem on last night's homework?" Marcia asked. "Today's first problem is to expand $(x+y)^4$ and $(x+y)^5$."

"I'm just going to use my answer from last night and multiply by another factor of $(x + y)$," Melvin suggested.

"I'm just going to add another bunch of branches to my tree diagram." José added.

"To your WHAT?" the others shouted all at once.

"To my tree diagram," said José. They all looked to see what he had.

"See, when you multiply $(x + y)(x + y)$, you multiply the $x$ in the first factor by each term in the second factor, and you multiply the $y$ in the first factor by each term in the second factor. So you get $x \cdot x$, $x \cdot y$, $y \cdot x$, and $y \cdot y$, just like in the tree above right.

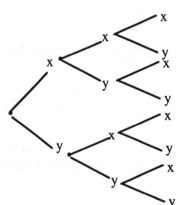

"Then for $(x + y)^3$, everything in the first answer gets multiplied by x and also by y, so you just add another set of branches and count up: there is one $x^3$, three $x^2y$, three $xy^2$, and one $y^3$."

"Oh, cool," said Melvin. "Now I see why, in $(x+y)^3$, the total of the powers of $x$ and $y$ in each term is always 3."

a)  Explain Melvin's last statement.

Then Marcia said, "And I see why there are three $x^2y$ branches! To get to the end of a branch, you start at the left, at the first junction, and choose $x$ or $y$. Then at the second junction you choose $x$ or $y$ again, and then one more time. If you choose $x$ twice and $y$ once, you wind up with $x^2y$, and there are three ways to do that."

b)  Make a copy of the $(x + y)^3$ tree, and trace the paths that end in $x^2y$. Explain why there can only be three. Explain why there can only be one branch each of

$x^3$ and $y^3$. How many branches are there of $xy^2$? Explain how you can tell without going through the tree.

**>>Problem continues on the next page.>>**

José said, "To be honest, I'm not sure how I'm going to fit another layer of branches on my tree. Besides, we'll probably have to do $(x + y)^{20}$ or something. Maybe Marcia is on to a shortcut here. Let's see if we can figure out $(x + y)^4$."

c)  In $(x + y)^3$, it took 3 x-y choices to get to the end of a branch, so all the branches ended in $x^3$, $x^2y$, $xy^2$, or $y^3$. What will the branches of $(x + y)^4$ end in?

Alex said, "It's pretty easy to see how many branches will end in $x^4$ and $y^4$. And I think I even see how many there will be that only have one power of x or one power of y, because this time it takes four choices of x or y to get through the tree."

d)  What did Alex see? How many branches will end in $x^4$, $y^4$, $x^3y$, $xy^3$? If you're not sure, make the tree.

Now it was Melvin's turn to jump back in. "The $x^2y^2$ one is the tricky one. I'm making a list of all the ways to get it. I'll just say which two of the four choices are x, and let the other two be y. It could be choices 1 and 2, 1 and 3, 1 and 4, 2 and 3, 2 and 4, or 3 and 4. I think that's all of them. So there will be 6 $x^2y^2$."

e)  Write out the expansion of $(x + y)^4$.

"Wait," said José, "Is making all these lists really going to be faster for $(x + y)^5$ than multiplying $(x + y)^4$ by $(x + y)$? And what about $(x + y)^{20}$? And why are we doing this in this unit anyw...WAIT! "

"I see it! In $(x + y)^5$, you go through five junctions to get to the end of a branch. To get, say, $x^2y^3$, you have to choose x at two of the five junctions. To find how many of those paths there are, we need to count how many different ways there are to pick two out of the five junctions to be the ones where you choose x, just like the list Melvin made: it could be junctions 1 and 2, 1 and 3, 2 and 4, etc... and we learned how to do that in this unit! And, we learned how to do it on our calculators!

f)  Use what you've learned in this unit to find the coefficients of $x^5$, $x^4y$, $x^3y^2$, $x^2y^3$, $xy^4$, and $y^5$ in the expansion of $(x + y)^5$, and write out the expansion.


IC-112.  Write the expansion for $(x + y)^8$. Use you calculators to find the coefficients


IC-113.  Describe a method for figuring out the binomial expansion for $(x + y)^n$ without having to multiply factor by factor or draw a tree diagram.


IC-114.  Five cards are dealt from a shuffled deck of 52 playing cards. A royal flush is the AKQJ10 all of the same suit. What is the probability of getting a royal flush?

IC-115.	In several states, standard license plates have one digit (1 to 9), then three letters, then three digits (0 to 9). How many license plates of this type are possible? What is the probability of getting one containing ALG 2?

IC-116.	Expand $(x + y)^7$.

IC-117.	The array of numbers at right is known as Pascal's Triangle.

$$
\begin{array}{c}
1 \\
1\ 1 \\
1\ 2\ 1 \\
1\ 3\ 3\ 1 \\
1\ 4\ 6\ 4\ 1 \\
1\ 5\ 10\ 10\ 5\ 1
\end{array}
$$

a)	There are many patterns in the triangle, which continues indefinitely. Describe as many as you can find (at least 3).

b)	Look at your work on expanding binomials (problems IC-106 and 107). What is the relationship between $(x + y)^n$ and the nth row of the triangle, if you count the 1 at the top as row 0?

c)	Each row of the triangle can be figured out from the row directly above it. Find the rule.

d)	Charlie wanted to find $_{10}C_3$ and he didn't have a calculator. But he knew $_9C_3$ and $_9C_2$. ($_9C_3 = 84$ and $_9C_2 = 36$.)

He had just finished calculating the number of two- and three-person committees that could be selected from the nine spirit club volunteers when the executive council informed him that they were only interested in three-person committees and that one more person had volunteered. He needed to calculate $_{10}C_3$ and he had left his calculator at a friend's house.

Then he had an inspiration! He thought, I already have the number of three-person committees the new volunteer will <u>not</u> be on because they would be selected from the other nine. What number is that? Give the answer in combination notation as well as a number.

AND I also know how many committees the new volunteer <u>will</u> <u>be</u> on because I can just add his name to each of my two-member committees. How many possible committees include the new volunteer?

Explain how Charlie calculated $_{10}C_3$ without a calculator (and without multiplying or dividing).

e)	The answers to parts (b), (c), and (d) are all related. Explain how.

IC-118.	How many <u>distinct</u> <u>permutations</u> are there of the word "**bookkeeper**?"

IC-119. Consider the function $C(r) = {}_8C_r$ .

    a) What is an appropriate domain for this function?

    b) What is the range?

IC-120. If you put $100 in the bank at an annual rate of 3%, compounded monthly, how long will it take to be worth $1000?

IC-121. What is the inverse of $f(x) = -x + 6$? Justify your answer.

IC-122. Find all of the roots of $f(x) = x^3 + 3x$.

# BUILDING A BETTER BIOME

> This is a large problem that will pull together systems of equations and sampling techniques. It will make a good portfolio entry, and it could serve as a summary problem because it brings together many ideas from throughout the course.

IC-123. **The Bird Biome Investigation**

A biologist is trying to determine how the number of birds of three species, A, B, and C, in a particular biome compares to the optimum combined number that the region might support. She has tagged birds in the biome to estimate the numbers of each species already there. She had collected the information given below before an unfortunate encounter with a thundering herd of turtles landed her in the hospital. You have been given the task of completing the analysis of the region based on her notes.

    **Week 1**: Three species of birds: A, B, and C. Estimate of food supply: approx. 3.5 kg of food per 10 m$^2$. Dimensions of biome are 325 m by 400 m.

                     **>>Problem continues on the next page.>>**

**Week 2:** Research has shown that each nesting pair of species A requires 30 kg of food (during the season) and defends an area of 60 m². Each nesting pair of species B requires 25 kg of food and defends an area of 100 m². Each nesting pair of species C requires 40 kg of food and defends an area of 300 m². In addition, species A and C prefer to build their nests in a particular type of pine tree, and there are only about 1100 of these trees in the biome. Neither will choose a tree that already has a nest.

**Week 3:** Caught and tagged 280 adult males of species A, 100 adult males of species B.

**Week 4:** Caught 140 adult males of species A—44 had tags. Caught 120 adult males of species B—48 had tags.

**Week 5:** Completed count of species C nests; a total of 12 active nesting pairs were found within the biome.

Questions you should consider but are not limited to (be sure to show all of your reasoning):

a) Approximately how many pairs (assume that each adult male has a mate) of each species of birds are currently living in this biome?

b) What is the optimal combination of pairs of birds that could live in this biome?

c) How does the existing population compare with the maximum combined number of nesting pairs the biome can support?

d) Summarize your results for parts (a), (b), and (c) in a letter to the biologist for whom you completed the work. In the letter you need to demonstrate mathematically your various conclusions. Then based on your results, think of at least two questions the biologist might want to explore further in relation to this biome. Be sure to include these questions in your letter. It is important to note that the mathematics does not give us answers here but can be helpful in identifying problems or new questions.

IC-124. If five cards are dealt from a shuffled deck of playing cards:

a) What is the probability of getting a five card hand that is all red?

b) Express your solution to part (a) in the form: $\frac{_aC_b}{_dC_e}$ .

c) What is the probability of getting a five card hand that is all clubs?

d) Express your solution to part (c) in the form: $\frac{_aC_b}{_dC_e}$ .

e) What is the probability of getting a flush (5 cards from any one suit)?

IC-125. A license plate is composed of three letters followed by three numbers. What is the probability of getting a license plate containing **ALG 2** on it if:

a) it is okay to repeat the digits and the letters?

b) it is not okay to repeat the digits nor the letters?

IC-126. The new track coach has a very mathematical mind!

a) How many ways can the track coach pick a four-person 100-meter relay team from a group of nine sprinters?

b) How many ways can the coach organize the team that was chosen in running order?

IC-127. Expand the binomial: $(a + b)^8$

IC-128. Sketch both graphs below on the same set of axes. What is the solution to the system?

$$f(x) = (x - 3)^2 + 2 \qquad \text{and} \qquad g(x) = 2 + \log_2 (x - 2)$$

IC-129. An isosceles triangle has sides of lengths 10, 10, and 5 cm. What are the measures of the three angles?

IC-130. Here's a strange rule:

$$A \, \Omega \, B \, \Omega \, C = \sqrt[C]{A^B}$$

a) What is: $8 \, \Omega \, 2 \, \Omega \, 3$?

b) What is: $-1 \, \Omega \, 2 \, \Omega \, 4$?

c) If $A > 1$, when does $A \, \Omega \, B \, \Omega \, C = A$?

IC-131. If $m > n$, is $x^m > x^n$ for every positive x? Justify your answer.

IC-132. Points are placed on a circle in such a way that $\overarc{AB} = 10°$, $\overarc{BC} = 20°$, $\overarc{CD} = 30°$, and so on around the circle, stopping once one complete revolution is made. Copy and complete the circle to the right. If two of the labeled points are chosen at random from the circle, what is the probability that the segment joining the points forms a diameter of the circle?

## EXPLORING WITH COMBINATIONS

IC-133. For the purposes of this problem, we will include the "trivial" subgroups: the one containing nothing, and the one containing all three things.

a) How many subgroups of any size can be made from a group of three things?

b) Generalize part (a): How many ways are there to choose n or fewer things from a group of n things? This is actually simpler than finding how many subgroups there are of a particular size. You can experiment with some other values of n (though you probably don't want to go beyond n = 5 if you're listing all the possibilities!) Or you can think of a decision chart. What decision must you make for each of the n things?

IC-134. Duong noticed that $_1C_0 + {_1C_1} = 2^1$. He tried $_2C_0 + {_2C_1} + {_2C_2} = 2^2$ and found that it worked also.

a) Does $_3C_0 + {_3C_1} + {_3C_2} + {_3C_3} = 2^3$ ?

b) Does $_4C_0 + {_4C_1} + {_4C_2} + {_4C_3} + {_4C_4} = 2^4$ ?

c) Explain why $_nC_1 + {_nC_2} + ... + {_nC_n} = 2^n$. How does this relate to the previous problem?

IC-135. Jean Luc's favorite Asian restaurant has six dishes on its lunch menu. He wants to get their three item combo for lunch and is reminded by the counter-person that he can repeat a selection. How many different ways could he order lunch?

IC-136. Make a quick sketch of each of the following functions:

a) $y = (x - 1)^2(x - 3)^3(x - 5)^2$

b) $y = -(x - 1)^2(x - 3)^3(x - 5)^2$

IC-137. You roll three different colored dice and use the numbers on the dice to determine the lengths of the sides of a triangle. <u>Example</u>: 3, 3, 5 would be an isosceles triangle with base 5.

What is the probability of building a right triangle?

IC-138. Given the function $h(x) = -2(x + 3)^2 + 2$:

a)    what are the intercepts?

b)    what are the domain and range?

IC-139. Expand the binomial:  $(y + z)^5$

IC-140.

> We have distinguished sequences from other functions by using t(n) rather than f(x). Another common way to denote a sequence is with subscripts; instead of t(n) we write $t_n$ to mean the same thing. Sometimes the rule for a sequence only tells how to get each term from the ones that came before it; this is called a **RECURSIVE DEFINITION**. When defining a sequence this way it is also necessary to specify one or more of the beginning terms of the sequence. For example, the sequence 1, 3, 5, . . . could be defined by the rule  $t_n = t_{n-1} + 2$; $t_0 = 1$. This says that the nth term is the previous, or (n - 1)st, term plus two, and the initial term is one.

For each of the following recursively defined sequences, list the first four terms, and state whether the sequence is arithmetic, geometric, or neither.

a)    $t_n = t_{n-1} - 11$; $t_0 = 98$.

b)    $a_n = 2a_{n-1} + 1$; $a_0 = 0$.

IC-141. Last Autumn, Julia noticed something interesting as she blew up spherical balloons for Harris's birthday party.

a)    If the radius of the balloon is 4 cm, what is the volume of the balloon?  In case you have forgotten, the volume of a sphere with radius r is $\frac{4}{3} \pi r^3$.

b)    If the radius of the balloon is 8 cm (**double** the size as in part (a)), what is the volume?

c)    Is the volume twice as big when the radius is doubled?

d)    Julia did figure out a pattern.  What is it?

IC-142.   Imagine a circle with radius 4 units and a center at (5, 6). This circle is rotated around the x-axis, always staying the same distance from the axis. It sweeps out a three dimensional figure. What shape is formed? Make a sketch.

IC-143.   Your teacher has decided one person in your class can take one week off from doing homework. The lucky person has been narrowed down so it is between you and Newton. The teacher says, "I'm thinking of a number between 0 and 10. Whoever can choose the number closest to it gets the holiday from homework. Quickly, Newt yells out "Three!" Assuming he did not hit the number exactly, what number would you choose? Justify and explain your answer.

IC-144.   Solve for x. Give answers in degrees or radians but think about the possible quadrants.

$$2 \sin x \cos x + \cos x = 0$$

# SUMMARY AND REVIEW

IC-145.   **Unit 11 Summary Assignment**

a)   If you were going to write the test for this unit, what kinds of problems would you include? Describe each type of problem and explain why you would choose it.

b)   Find your favorite problem from this unit. If it is one you completed as a portfolio entry, describe the problem and explain what makes it your favorite. Otherwise write out the complete question (or summarize the information), write out your complete solution process, and then explain what makes it your favorite problem.

c)   Find a problem that you still cannot solve or that you are worried that you might not be able to solve on a test. Write out the question and as much of the solution as you can until you get to the hard part. Then explain what it is that keeps you from solving the problem. Be clear and precise.

d)   What did you learn in this unit?

e)   Turn all this in to be included in your portfolio according to your teacher's instructions.

**IC-146.** **Triangles By Chance: An Investigation**

Obtain three dice from your teacher. You may also want some string, linguini, a compass or some other building material. Roll the three dice and use the numbers on the dice to represent the lengths of sides of a triangle. Build (or draw) the triangle. Record the three numbers in a table according to the type of triangle formed (scalene, isosceles, equilateral). For example, if 3, 3, and 5 came up on the dice, you would record 3, 3, 5 under the heading ISOSCELES since a triangle with sides of length 3, 3, and 5 is isosceles. Repeat this ten times, then add your information to the class list on the board.

Examine the data from the whole class and discuss it with your team. Based on the class results and on your discussion, estimate:

a)   the probability of being able to build an equilateral triangle.

b)   the probability of being able to build an isosceles triangle.

c)   the probability of being able to build a scalene triangle.

d)   the probability that no triangle is formed.

e)   Explain how you came up with each of your estimates.

f)   Calculate the **actual probabilities** for each part (a) through (d) above. Show and explain your reasoning for all of your work.

g)   Record your results to all of the above in either a report or on a poster based on your teacher's instructions. Examine the grading rubric to be sure you include everything your teacher expects.


**IC-147.** The local theater is offering a "moviefest." Patrons can watch three different movies for the price of one and they can watch them in any order. In how many different ways can you arrange the order in which you see the three movies?


**IC-148.** Next June Joanna is taking a vacation. She will make four stops while she is gone. They will be Pittsburgh, Washington, D.C., Philadelphia, and New York City. Joanna is not sure in what order to visit these places. In how many different ways can she organize her vacation?


**IC-149.** Ms. Hart has three different math books, four different chemistry books and six different history books to arrange on a shelf.

a)   How many ways can she arrange all the books in any order?

b)   How many ways can she arrange the math books?

c)   How many ways can she arrange the chemistry books?

d)   How many ways can she arrange the history books?

e)   How many ways can she arrange the books if each subject is grouped together?

IC-150.     How many <u>distinct</u> ways can you arrange the letters in the word CAR?  POP?


IC-151.     In an algebra class of 28 students, in how many different ways can a 4-student study teams be formed?


IC-152.     A license plate is composed of a number followed by three different letters followed by three different digits.  All letters and the numbers 0 through 9 can be used in any respective position.  What is the probability of getting a license plate with your initials on it?


IC-153.     What is the probability of getting a full house (three of one kind of card and two of another kind of card, assuming "kinds" are 1, 2, ..., Q, K) from five cards dealt from a shuffled deck of 52 playing cards?  Express your answer in combination form.


IC-154.     You are given a bag that you are told contains 8 marbles, 4 red and 1 each of four other colors.  Express in the form $\frac{_aC_b}{_dC_e}$ the probability that two marbles, drawn together, will:

   a)   be the same color.                         b)   be different colors.


IC-155.     A coin is flipped four times.  What is the probability of getting two tails if the first two flips were two heads?


IC-156.     Expand each binomial:

   a)    $(x - y)^3$                          b)          $(x - y)^4$


IC-157.     **TOOL KIT CHECK-UP**

   Your Tool Kit contains reference tools for algebra. Return to your Tool Kit entries. You may need to revise or add entries.

   Be sure that your Tool Kit contains entries for all of the items listed below.  Add any topics that are missing to your Tool Kit NOW, as well as any other items that will help you in your study of algebra.

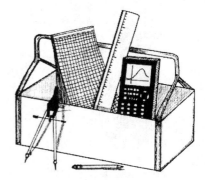

   - Decision Chart
   - Factorial
   - Recursive Definition
   - Pascal's Triangle

   - Permutations
   - Combinations
   - Binomial Expansion
   - Other Counting Techniques

# UNIT 12

## Closest to the Pin
### DESCRIPTIVE STATISTICS

# Unit 12 Objectives
## *Closest to the Pin*: DESCRIPTIVE STATISTICS

We see data represented in many forms. Whether we see it as a representation of an athlete's performance or the public's opinion on a particular issue, it is displayed as a daily part of our lives. We call these displays or numerical summaries of data "statistics." Advertisers often make references to statistics to persuade consumers to purchase their products, and political parties use statistics to persuade voters to support their candidates. In these examples the data is frequently collected or presented in a biased way in order to sway the reader. One of the goals of this unit is  to analyze conclusions drawn from data with a critical eye. When you encounter a presentation based on statistics, you should first consider the way the data was gathered.

In this unit you will have the opportunity to:

- consider and discuss issues that might cause bias in data gathering and its reporting.

- use measures of central tendency (the mean and median) and measures of dispersion (the mean and standard deviation) to compare sets of data.

- convert data into z-scores, standard scores, and percentiles in order to make comparisons across data sets easier.

- use stem-and-leaf plots and box-and-whisker plots to display and compare sets of data.

Read the following problem and discuss with your team the question: "Now that we have accepted the job, what should we do?" Write down a few ideas.

---

DS-0. **CLOSEST TO THE PIN** The Hookenslise Corporation is having its annual golf tournament. Each year it gives away numerous prizes, including a new car. The corporate theme for the year has been, "Consistency and Hard Work Pay Off." In keeping with this theme, the corporate president wants this year's "Closest to the Pin Award" to go to the player who is consistently close to the hole on five designated par three holes. (This way they hope to award the prize to the "best" player, not merely the luckiest one.) They need to know how to make this determination. Your team has been hired to find the best method to analyze the data they have gathered so far.

---

PROBLEM SOLVING
REPRESENTATION/MODELING
FUNCTIONS/GRAPHING
INTERSECTIONS/SYSTEMS
ALGORITHMS
REASONING/COMMUNICATION

# Unit 12

*Closest to the Pin*: DESCRIPTIVE STATISTICS

## DATA GATHERING

DS-1.    In your teams, discuss how the following issues can bias a survey. Be prepared to share your thoughts with the class.

a)    Where was the survey taken?        b)    Who took the survey?

c)    How were the survey questions asked?    d)    When was the survey taken?

e)    What was the question?

DS-2.    **Closest to the Pin Lab** If you have not yet read problem DS-0, read it now.

To test your ideas, we need some data. Let's simulate the golf shots by tossing coins at a target. Your teacher has set up a target. From a distance of five feet, each team member should toss the coin five times.

a)    Measure each distance from the target to the final position of the tossed coin to the nearest centimeter. Measure from the center of the target to the center of the coin. Record all of your data on a chart as shown below. **Do not discard any toss.**

b)    For each set of data, calculate both the **MEAN** (average score) and the **MEDIAN** (middle score). Record the results on your chart. **Save this data; you will use it throughout the unit.**

| Name | Toss 1 | Toss 2 | Toss 3 | Toss 4 | Toss 5 | Mean | Median |
|------|--------|--------|--------|--------|--------|------|--------|
|      |        |        |        |        |        |      |        |
|      |        |        |        |        |        |      |        |
|      |        |        |        |        |        |      |        |
|      |        |        |        |        |        |      |        |

DS-3.    Which average (the mean or the median) do you think best meets the needs of the corporation? Why?

DS-4.  Have one team member record all of your tosses on the class histogram provided by your instructor. (A **HISTOGRAM** is a bar graph showing the frequency with which data values occurred.) Sketch the shape of the histogram.

DS-5. Data points that are quite removed from the rest of the data are called **OUTLIERS**. Does the class data have any outliers? What may have caused them?

DS-6. Is this an accurate model for the "Closest to the Pin" contest? What factors may cause some of your data to be biased?

DS-7. The following are test scores from a difficult chemistry test. Calculate the mean and median from each set of data:

a)  62, 68, 75, 60, 72, 62, 67        b)  60, 62, 96, 68, 72, 62, 67

c)  The highest score in the second set is 96. What effect does this score have on the mean and median for the set?

DS-8. Create a set of data in which:

a)  the median is <u>much</u> higher than the mean.

b)  the mean is <u>much</u> higher than the median.

DS-9. The Davidsons took a trip to Minneapolis and left on Friday afternoon in the middle of the rush hour traffic. Because of all of the traffic, they averaged 40 mph on the way to the city. They returned Sunday morning when traffic was much lighter. They averaged 60 mph on the way home.

a)  What was their average speed?

b)  The Davidsons live 120 miles from Minneapolis. How long did it take for them to drive to the city?

c)  How long did it take to return?

d)  Find the average speed by calculating rate $= \frac{\text{Total Distance}}{\text{Total Time}}$. Does this answer agree with your results from part (a)? If not, which one is correct?

e)  If the total distance from the Davidsons' home to Minneapolis were 300 miles, what would be the average speed?

f)  If the total distance were n miles, what would be the average speed?

DS-10. Brandon's little brother spilled orange juice on his calculator and now he's stuck in radian mode and the $\pi$ button won't work.

He needs to evaluate $\pi + \cos \frac{\pi}{5}$. Explain how he can still use <u>his</u> calculator to evaluate the value.

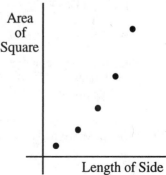

DS-11. Read the information in the box below and add it to your Tool Kit.

---

### SERIES AND SUMMATION NOTATION

A **SERIES** is the sum of the terms of a sequence. An example of a simple arithmetic series in expanded form is $2 + 4 + 6 + 8 + 10$. A convenient way to indicate a series is to use **SUMMATION NOTATION**: $\sum\limits_{n=1}^{5} 2n$. This notation is read, "The sum of numbers of the form $2n$ as $n$ goes from 1 to 5." The **INDICES**, $n = 1$ and 5, show that n is to be replaced successively by $1, 2, \ldots, 5$. The symbol $\sum$ (the Greek letter sigma) means that the terms resulting from successive replacements are to be added together, that is, summed.

Therefore, $\sum\limits_{n=1}^{5} 2n = 2(1) + 2(2) + 2(3) + 2(4) + 2(5) = 30$.

---

a) Find $\sum\limits_{n=1}^{5} 3n$.

b) Find $\sum\limits_{n=1}^{4} (2n+1)$.

DS-12. Dan Domain's teacher had him make several squares on centimeter paper. Then he had to make a graph that compared the <u>side length</u> and the <u>surface area</u> of the squares.

a) Dan's teacher asked him to find a curve to fit the data (shown at right), so Dan used a quadratic. Is a quadratic a good choice? How could you tell <u>without</u> looking at the graph?

b) After doing all that work, Dan's teammate claimed that a parabola is not a very good model, since a parabola is U-shaped and this data isn't. What do you think?

c) Describe another example where the domain of the situation is not the same as the domain of the equation that models that situation.

Area of Square

Length of Side

DS-13.   Solve for c:   $c + \sqrt{c+1} = 5$

# WHAT IS AVERAGE?

DS-14.   Using the data gathered from the "Closest to the Pin"
lab, find the mean and median for your team.

a)   Is it true that the mean for your team is the
average (mean) of the means of the
individual members?  Will this always be the
case?  Explain in a few sentences or using algebra to show why you came to this
conclusion.  What kind of reasoning did you use, inductive or deductive?

b)   Is it true that the median for your team is the average (median) of the medians of the
individual members?  Will this always be the case?  Explain in a few sentences or
using algebra to show why you came to this conclusion.

DS-15.   For this simulation, your whole class represents our "population of interest," that is, the
corporation's golfers.  Your team is a **sample** of that population.  When we take the
mean of a sample, we hope that it will approximate the mean of the population.  How
does your team's mean compare to the class mean that your teacher put on the board?

DS-16.   Do you think that every team in the class will have the same result?  Explain.

DS-17.   We are going to gather all of the mean scores and the median scores and display them on
two new histograms.  Your teacher has two master graphs.  On the graph  labeled
MEAN, record all of the mean scores from the individuals in your team.  On the graph
labeled MEDIAN, record all of the median scores from the individuals in your team.

DS-18.   Look at the mean graph created by the class.  Where is the graph centered? What is the
shape of the curve?  How does it differ from the class histogram you sketched in
problem DS-4?

DS-19.   Look at the median graph.  Where is the graph centered? What is the shape of the curve?
How does it differ from the class histogram you sketched in problem DS-4?

DS-20.   Suppose we had a class of 100 students.  What would change for these two graphs?

DS-21.    If each person did 100 tosses instead of just 5, what would change for the two graphs? Why?


DS-22.    A teacher is trying to decide which 32-point exam to use. She randomly chooses five students to take both of the exams. The scores of the exams are shown below:

**Form A:** 20, 22, 24, 26, 28      **Form B:** 10, 22, 24, 32, 32

a)    What is the mean for each form?

b)    What is the median for each form?

c)    Are the two tests equivalent? If not how are they different?

d)    Which form do you think she should use? Why?


DS-23.    The Hookenslise Corporation is in the midst of union negotiations. Labor claims that the company's average salary is $28,000 while management claims it is $32,000. If they are using the same set of data, how can their averages be different? How could such a large difference have occurred?


DS-24.    Look back at your team data from the "Closest to the Pin" problem. How many scores (from your team) are below your individual median score? What percent of the scores are below that value?


DS-25.    Find $\displaystyle\sum_{n=2}^{6}(3n-2)$.

DS-26.    Read the information below about notation and add it to your Tool Kit.

---

**STATISTICAL VARIABLES**

In statistics there are some standard variables used to represent certain values. When data refers to the entire group (which is called the **POPULATION**) the variables are written using lower-case Greek letters such as $\mu$ (pronounced "mu") and $\sigma$ (pronounced "sigma"). When the data refers to a **SAMPLE** from the population, the data is written using standard (English) letters.

Examples:

If the members of our class were our population then a subgroup consisting of every fifth member of our class would be a sample.

If the set of all words written in English were our population, the words on page 25 of your history book could be a sample (although perhaps a biased one).

The following are variables we have used so far:

  **n**   total number of data values in your sample

  **x**   an individual value from a set of data

  $\overline{\mathbf{x}}$   sample mean

  $\mu$   *(mu)* population mean

Here are two variables that we will be using in the next few days.

  **s**   sample standard deviation

  $\sigma$   *(sigma)* population standard deviation

Note: $\Sigma$ is capital sigma, $\sigma$ is lower case sigma.

---

DS-27.    Suppose the mean $(\overline{\mathbf{x}})$ SAT score for a random sample of students is 960.

a)    What does this tell you about the actual mean $(\mu)$ for all students who took the SAT?

b)    Would another sample have the same mean?

c)    For different samples, does $\mu$ change? Does $\overline{\mathbf{x}}$ change?

d)    How do $\overline{\mathbf{x}}$ and $\mu$ compare numerically?

DS-28.    Assuming $n$ is an integer greater than 1 and $A$ is a positive real number, which is larger: $\frac{A}{n}$ or $\frac{A}{n-1}$ ? Justify your answer algebraically.

DS-29.    Write the following series in expanded form and find the sum: $\displaystyle\sum_{n=1}^{6}\left(\frac{1}{2}n+10\right)$

DS-30.    Simplify if possible; justify each step.

a)    $\dfrac{2x-3x^2}{4x^3}$

b)    $\dfrac{2x^{-1}-3x^{-2}}{4x^{-3}}$

# SPREADS: RANGE, MEAN DEVIATION, STANDARD DEVIATION AND VARIANCE

DS-31.    Look back at problem DS-22.

a)    What makes the two tests different? Discuss in your team a method for describing the difference between the two sets of data.

b)    Find a way to numerically represent this difference.

DS-32.    Try your method for the following two sets of data. Does your method still help to distinguish between the two sets of data?

**Set A:** 10, 30, 39, 40, 43, 48, 70        **Set B:** 10, 20, 30, 40, 50, 60, 70

DS-33.    One way to measure the spread of data is to calculate the **RANGE** (high score - low score), but the previous problem shows that this measure may not give a good sense of the spread.

> Another method for measuring the spread is to calculate the average (mean) distance from the mean called the mean deviation. In general,
>
> $$\text{MEAN DEVIATION} = \frac{\sum |(x - \overline{x})|}{n}$$
>
> Use this formula to calculate the mean deviation for Set A in the previous problem. You may need to refer back to problems DS-11 or DS-26 to interpret the symbols used in the formula.
>
> Note: Many statistical formulas that use $\Sigma$ (summation notation) will not use indexed values. It is always assumed that all the data values (x) will be used in the formula. In this case, we know that there are "n" data values that need to be summed.
>
> Using indexed values, the formula is written $\dfrac{\sum\limits_{i=1}^{n} |x_i - \overline{x}|}{n}$ .

DS-34.    Find the mean deviation for your tosses on the "closest to the pin" problem. Compare your result with those of the other members of your team. Who appears to be the most "consistent" player in your team?

DS-35.    Notice how we used absolute value to calculate the mean deviation. What would happen if we did not use absolute value? Use your data to demonstrate.

DS-36.

Although the mean deviation gives a fairly reliable measure of the dispersion, the use of absolute value leads to problems with the development of more advanced mathematical computations. Therefore, the **STANDARD DEVIATION**, which uses squaring to retain positive differences is more generally used.

$$\sigma = \sqrt{\frac{\sum (x - \bar{x})^2}{n}}$$

In any set of data at least 75% of the points will lie within two standard deviations of the mean, and if the data are normally distributed 68% will be found within one standard deviation of the mean and 95% will be within two standard deviations. This information can be very useful in interpreting data and is another reason that people choose to use the standard deviation.

Calculate the standard deviation for your tosses on the "closest to the pin" problem. Once again, compare your result with those of the other members of your team. What does the standard deviation tell you about your data?

DS-37. Is the formula above equivalent to $\frac{\sum |x - \bar{x}|}{\sqrt{n}}$ ? Justify your answer with an explanation or a counterexample.

DS-38. How do the mean deviation and the standard deviation from your tosses compare?

DS-39. The set of data at right is organized in a frequency table. Although we do not know the source of the actual data, we can still make an estimate of the mean and other statistical quantities.

| Class | Frequency |
|---------|-----------|
| 0 - 9 | 5 |
| 10 - 19 | 16 |
| 20 - 29 | 12 |
| 30 - 39 | 8 |
| 40 - 49 | 5 |
| 50 - 59 | 3 |
| 60 - 69 | 1 |

a) 4.5 is the best single value representative for the first class of data (0-9). Explain why you think that this would be true.

b) Using this quantity, make an estimate of the sum of all the scores in the first class.

c) Find the midpoint of each of the other classes and make estimates for the sum of all the scores in each class. Then find an estimate for the total of all of the scores.

d) How many total scores were there?

e) Make an estimate for the mean.

f) In what class will the median occur?

DS-40.    Consider the following set of data: 8, 10, 15, 25, 34, 36

      a)    Find the mean.           b)    Calculate the mean deviation.

      c)    Calculate the standard deviation.    d)    How do your answers from parts (b) and (c) compare?


DS-41.    Ms. Hilling teaches two geometry classes. On the last test both classes had a mean of 78, but the standard deviation for her first class was 8 while the standard deviation for her second class was 15. What does this information tell you about the performance of the two classes on that test?

> Still another measure of spread or dispersion or variation is the **VARIANCE**, which is simply the square of the **standard deviation.**
>
> $$\sigma^2 = \frac{\sum (x-\bar{x})^2}{n}$$
>
> Sometimes it is more convenient to use the **variance** in making calculations.
>
> What is the **variance** for each of Ms. Hilling's two Geometry classes? Do you think this calculation gives you any better information?


DS-42.    Remember Brandon's problem with his calculator? The $\pi$ button still doesn't work but now it's stuck in degree mode. Explain how he can evaluate the problem $\pi + \cos\left(\frac{\pi}{5}\right)$ where $\frac{\pi}{5}$ is in radians.


DS-43.    Ms. Shimizu brought in a big bowl of hard candy for her class. She walked around the room letting each student take a handful, but she started with the students with the smallest hands and went in order of increasing hand size.

      a)    Sketch a graph of this situation, comparing the number of pieces of candy in the bowl over time.

      b)    Is this situation an example of a discrete function or a step function or neither? Justify your choice.

DS-44.    Kisha has graphed  $y = x(6 - x)$  in a standard window.

a)    What is the best name for the graph?

b)    Jamal has bet Kisha that he can make the graph look like a horizontal line without changing, adding, or deleting functions.  Kisha doesn't think he can do it, but Jamal is sure he can.  What strategy does Jamal have in mind?

DS-45.    Show that  $\cos 2x \neq 2 \cos x$.

## STATISTICS ON A CALCULATOR

DS-46.    This problem introduces the STAT features on your calculator.  Your teacher will provide a resource page.  Enter the following set of data:

22, 8, 33, 19, 27, 23, 15, 35, 38, 16, 19, 24, 17, 37

a)    Use your calculator to sort the data.  Use this sorted list to find the median.

b)    Use the 1-Var statistic feature and record all of the variables that are displayed.  What do each of the variables stand for?

c)    What is the mean of the data?

d)    What is the standard deviation?

DS-47.    Enter your team's data for "Closest to the Pin."  Use the statistics features to calculate the mean and standard deviation for your team.

DS-48.    Most graphing calculators will draw histograms  from your statistical data.  Use your calculator to draw the histogram.  Change the x-scale to view different kinds of histograms.

DS-49.    The frequency table at right represents all scores on a 10 point quiz.

a)    Find the mean score.

b)    Find the standard deviation of the scores.

c)    Draw the histogram of the scores.

| Score | Frequency |
|-------|-----------|
| 4     | 2         |
| 5     | 4         |
| 6     | 8         |
| 7     | 15        |
| 8     | 22        |
| 9     | 8         |
| 10    | 4         |

DS-50.
Data can be represented graphically in many forms. A useful organizational tool is the **STEM-LEAF PLOT**. In its simplest form for two digit data, the tens digits are listed vertically in numerical order in the first column. The ones digits are recorded to the right of the corresponding tens digit as you read through the list. Consider the data: 25, 38, 25, 30, 60, 42, 17, 22, 55, 69, 42, 100, 52, 12.

a) Complete the preliminary stem-leaf for this information. (The first five numbers have already been entered, in addition to all the tens digits.)

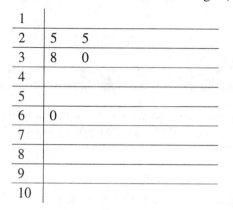

```
 1  |
 2  | 5   5
 3  | 8   0
 4  |
 5  |
 6  | 0
 7  |
 8  |
 9  |
10  |
```

b) Rewrite the stem-leaf in final form putting the ones digits on each line in increasing order.

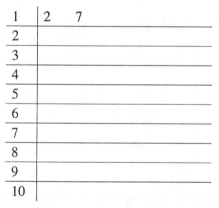

```
 1  | 2   7
 2  |
 3  |
 4  |
 5  |
 6  |
 7  |
 8  |
 9  |
10  |
```

DS-51.
While straightening up the living room, Calvert's mom came across a Spanish test on which he had earned a score of 42. Before she assumes that he failed the test, what questions does she need to ask him? List at least three.

DS-52.
Your end-of-unit project is to write a report for the corporation that hired your team at the beginning of this unit. (Remember "Closest to the Pin?") Go back and reread the initial project and write down some ideas about completing parts of this project. Consider the statistical tools we have studied so far: mean, median, spread, and standard deviation. Your task is to devise a method to determine the most consistently accurate golfer. How do each of these statistical tools help you to develop your project?

DS-53.    Tara's family took a casual drive through the country one Saturday. They drove slowly
          to enjoy the scenery, so they averaged 30 mph.  On the way home, they took the same
          route, but because everyone was tired they drove at the speed limit of 55 mph.

          a)    What was their average rate for the whole trip (50 miles each way)?

          b)    What would be their average rate if they drove at the same speeds for 100 miles
                each way?

          c)    What conclusions can you make?


DS-54.    Suppose you walk the 3000 miles from San Francisco to New York City at 3 mph.  Then
          you fly back at 500 mph.

          a)    What is your average speed for the whole trip?

          b)    Explain, in words, why your average speed is much closer to 3 mph than to 500
                mph.  Use as few numbers as possible and absolutely no algebra in your
                explanation.


DS-55.    Without a calculator, evaluate: $\left(\dfrac{4}{9}\right)^{3/2}$

(7, 5)
(3, 3)
-5
5
-5


DS-56.    Write an equation for the curve at right.
          Is it a function?  Justify your answer.


DS-57.    Solve for x, correct to three decimal places.

          a)    $27 = 6^x$                           b)    $27 = \dfrac{1}{6^x}$

          c)    $27 = \dfrac{1}{\left(\frac{1}{6}\right)^x}$              d)    Show that $\dfrac{1}{\left(\frac{1}{6}\right)^x} = 6^x$ .

**DS-58.**     Consider two sets of test data:

| | | | | |
|---|---|---|---|---|
| Test A | 57 | 76 | 76 | 95 |
| Test B | 29 | 94 | 95 | 95 |

a)     Find the mean and standard deviation ($\sigma$) of each set.

b)     Who would have more reason to rejoice: the person who earned a 95 on Test A or on Test B?  Explain using your results from part (a).

**DS-59.**

> If you earned 42 points out of 50 on a particular test, 42 is called your **RAW SCORE**.  Raw scores are often converted to **Z-SCORES**, because then you can tell how far a particular score is from the mean.  A z-score of 1 is 1 standard deviation above the mean.  A z-score of 2.5 is $2\frac{1}{2}$ standard deviations above the mean.

a)     What does a z-score of 0 indicate?     b)     What does a z-score of -1 indicate?

**DS-60.**     A set of data has a mean of 92 and a standard deviation of 8.

a)     How many standard deviations above the mean is a raw score of 104?

b)     If a student has a raw score of 110, what is his z-score?

c)     What z-score corresponds to a raw score of 88?

d)     What raw score corresponds to a z-score of -1.75?

**DS-61.**     Consider the following scores on a geometry test:  75, 86, 94, 89, 80, 72, 17,100, 56, 80, 91, 71, 79, 57, 94, 90, 58, 60, 100, 75, 83, 86, 53, 93, 92, 60, 81, 100, 94, 69, 89, 86, 42, 76, 75.  Just from looking at the numbers, how do you think the class did on the test?

**DS-62.**     Find the mean and the standard deviation of the scores in problem DS-61.

**DS-63.**     What do you think caused the standard deviation to be so high?  Test your hypothesis and share it with your team.

DS-64.    In some large classes, teachers use z-scores to assign grades.  For example 1.5 standard deviations below the mean might be the highest F and 1.5 above the mean might begin the A's.  According to this grading policy, which scores on the geometry test would fail the test?  Which would get A's?


DS-65.    Would it be to your advantage if your teacher graded your next test on this type of a curve?  Explain.


DS-66.    On a recent 250 mile trip, Felicia averaged 50 mph over the first 125 miles.  What should be her average speed for the second half of her trip if she wants to average 60 mph over the whole journey?


DS-67.    Write possible equations for each of these four graphs.  Notice that you will need to account for the scaling of the axes for graphs (c) and (d).

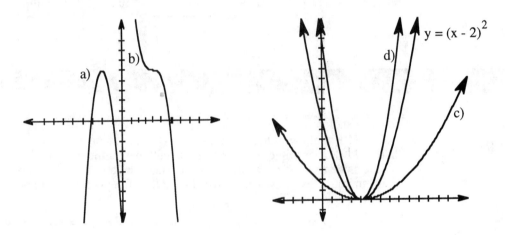


DS-68.    For the sequences listed below, state whether each is arithmetic or geometric, whether the terms are increasing or decreasing, and find a formula for the nth term after the initial term.  The initial term for each sequence is in bold print.

a)    **1**, 3, 5, 7, . . .

b)    **1**, 3, 9, 27, . . .

c)    **10**, 5, $\frac{5}{2}$, $\frac{5}{4}$, . . .

d)    **16**, 12, 9, . . .

DS-69.    Given the points O(0, 0) and R(-5, -12):

     a)    What is the equation of the circle centered at point O and passing through R?

     b)    What is the measure of the angle formed by $\overline{OR}$ and the positive x-axis?  Answer in both radians and degrees.

     c)    Graph your circle in part (a) and  $x^2 + y^2 = 25$  on the same set of axes.  Shade the region between the circles.

     d)    If we use these circles as a dart board and the dart is certain to hit randomly somewhere within the largest circle, what is the probability of hitting the shaded region?


DS-70.    The volume of an open-top box is 30 in³.  The length of the base is twice its width.

     a)    Sketch and label a diagram.

     b)    Express the total outside surface area  S in terms of the width  x.  Simplify.


# PERCENTILES

DS-71.

A **PERCENTILE** ranking indicates the percentage of students who scored *below* that score.  For example, if you are at the 90th percentile in your class, 90 percent of the students at your grade level have a GPA below yours.  If there are 320 students in your class, how many would be at the 90th percentile or above? Add this definition to your Tool Kit.


DS-72.    Ryan had a score of 76 on the geometry test in problem DS-61.  What is his percentile?

**DS-73.**

Another representation of data is the **BOX AND WHISKER** diagram. This diagram shows the high and low values, as well as the values at the 75th, 50th, and 25th percentiles. The four groups between these percentiles are called **QUARTILES**. In the box and whisker diagram, the highest and lowest quartiles are the whiskers, and the middle two quartiles are the boxes.

The diagram at right represents the data   1, 3, 5, 6, 6, 7, 8, 9

The numbers 1, 4, 6, 7.5, and 9 have special significance on this box and whisker diagram. Why? Discuss this with your team What do each of the numbers represent?

**DS-74.** On your calculator, plot the data in the previous problem using a box and whisker diagram.

**DS-75.** What percentage of the data falls in each section: A, B, C, and D?

**DS-76.** Make a stem-leaf and a box and whisker diagram for the geometry test scores in problem DS-61. Use the box and whisker diagram to describe the performance of the class on that test.

**DS-77.** Compare your results for the preceding problem with your answer to problem DS-61. Which methods do you think provide the best description of the data? Why do you think so?

**DS-78.** Recall these two ways to write a general equation for a parabola:

$$y = a(x - h)^2 + k \qquad \text{and} \qquad y = ax^2 + bx + c$$

Veronica is confused. "If there are two different general equations for a parabola, how do you know which one to use and when?" Help her out by answering the questions below.

a) Are they really two different equations? Prove that you can always change one into the other by expanding $y = a(x - h)^2 + k$ so that it is in $y = ax^2 + bx + c$ form (multiply it out and combine like terms). Represent the values of a, b, and c in terms of a, h, and k.

b) Answer Veronica's question: How do you know which of these equations to use?

c) Does the 'a' represent the same thing in both equations? Do the 'k' and 'c' both represent the y-intercept? Explain your thinking.

DS-79.  Driving from San Antonio to Dallas, Erin averaged 60 mph for the first 2 hours, 20 mph the next hour (rush hour), and 65 mph the final 3 hours of his journey.

   a)  Can you determine how fast he was going after one hour based on these data? If so, find his speed; if not, explain why not.

   b)  What was his average rate for the entire 6 hour trip?

DS-80.  Consider the function $y = 3 \sin (x + \frac{\pi}{2}) - 4$.

   a)  How is its graph different from $y = \sin x$?

   b)  Sketch the graph.

DS-81.  If $p = 3t - 5t^2$:
   a)  find $p$ when $t = 0$.         b)  find $t$ when $p = 0$.

DS-82.  Each labeled point on this graph is either a maximum or a minimum.

   a)  Find the period and amplitude of the graph.

   b)  Find an equation for the graph.

   c)  Use one of the given points to check your equation.

(15,23)

(81,–17)

DS-83.  Sketch a temperature vs. time graph of these situations (with time as the independent variable):

   a)  A cup of hot coffee is left on a table.    b)  A glass of ice tea is left in the sun.

   c)  What kind of function would you use to model these situations? Give a reason for your choices.

DS-84.  Solve $\dfrac{\sqrt{8m^2}}{\sqrt{2m}} = 6$.

DS-85.  Find the equation of the line that passes through (-2, 5) and is perpendicular to $y = -5x + 2$.

DS-86.    Solve for x: $\dfrac{1}{x+2} - \dfrac{1}{x} = 2$.


DS-87.    Solve this system:    $(x-3)^2 + (y+2)^2 = 100$   and   $y + 2 = (x-3)^2$

    a)    Sketch the graph of the two equations on the same set of axes.

    b)    Find the points of intersection algebraically and label them on your graph.


# TRANSFORMATIONS OF Z-SCORES

DS-88.    A recent 90-point algebra test resulted in the following raw scores: 85, 63, 77, 56, 57, 80, 69, 46, 57, 86, 77, 67, 67, 90, 68, 89, 87, 43, 65, 57, 68, 47, 52, 75, 73. The instructor has asked for your help in analyzing the results.

    a)    Organize the material in a stem-leaf plot.

    b)    Use the stem-leaf plot to make a box and whisker diagram of the data. Mark the mean and the median on the plot.

    c)    Write a summary of how you think the class did. Refer to the box and whisker plot.


DS-89.    Danielle's score on the above test was an 86. In what percentile did she fall? What was her z-score?


DS-90.    While z-scores are very useful because they indicate the distance from the mean, they have a psychological difficulty. Even if you know you scored 1 standard deviation above the mean, how does it feel to be told that you have a score of 1?

    We can combat that problem by making a linear transformation of the data using $y = Ax + B$. Let y represent the new score, and x represent the old z-score. The equation would read: **New Score = A (z-score) + B.** $(y = mx + b)$

    If you scored the mean, a score of 50 would feel better than a z-score of 0, so let's find a scoring system that lets 50 be the mean and 10 be the standard deviation.

    a)    Explain why a z-score of 0 will be transformed to a new score of 50.

    b)    Explain why a z-score of 1 will transformed to a new score of 60.

    c)    If x represents the z-score and y represents the new score, we have two points: $(0, 50)$ and $(1, 60)$. Find the linear function that makes this transformation.

    d)    In the equation that you found, what does the y-intercept represent? What does the slope represent?

DS-91. SAT scores use a similar transformation. They use a mean of 500 and a standard deviation of 100. What is the linear transformation $(y = Ax + B)$ that converts z-scores to SAT score.

DS-92. Aimee has been tutoring her brother, Logan, for the past two weeks. As an incentive, she promised to take him out to dinner if he earns an A on his next test. (His teacher has announced that to earn an A, one's z-score must be $\geq 1.5$.) The day came and Logan scored 42 out of 60. If the class average was 30 with a standard deviation of 8, did Logan earn his dinner? Explain.

DS-93. Take out your team data from our original "Closest to the Pin" problem.

a) Make a histogram and a box and whisker diagram of the individual scores.

b) Describe the advantages and disadvantages of each type of graph.

DS-94. Multiply:

a) $(a + b)(a^2 - ab + b^2)$

b) $(x - 2)(x^2 + 2x + 4)$

c) $(Y + 5)(Y^2 - 5Y + 25)$

d) $(x - y)(x^2 + xy + y^2)$

e) What did you notice about these products?

f) Make up another multiplication problem that will follow the same pattern.

DS-95. Parts (a) and (d) of the preceding problem represent a general pattern known as the **sum and difference of cubes**. Use this pattern to factor each of the following polynomials:

a) $x^3 + y^3$

b) $x^3 - 27$

c) $8x^3 - y^3$

d) $x^3 + 1$

e) Make up another sum or difference of cubes problem and show how to factor it.

DS-96. Use the sum or difference of cubes pattern and what you already know about factoring to factor the following as completely as possible.

a) $x^5 + 8x^2y^3$

b) $8y^6 - 125x^3$

c) Start with $x^6 - y^6$. This one is tricky. If you start it as the difference of two cubes you will not be able to factor it completely. Think of it as the difference of two squares and then factor the factors as the sum and difference of two cubes.

DS-97. Add some notes to your Tool Kit about how to factor the sum and the difference of two cubes.

DS-98. Find the equation of a cubic function that has $y = x^3$ as its parent, an inflection point at (-6, -10), and that passes through the origin.

DS-99. Write an equation for this curve. Then sketch the graph of the inverse of this graph and write its equation.

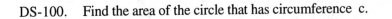

(5, 4)

(3, 3)

5

−5

5

DS-100. Find the area of the circle that has circumference c.

DS-101. Find the domain and range for each function.

a) $f(x) = \dfrac{x}{x^2 - 4x}$

b) $f(x) = \dfrac{1}{\sqrt{x} - 5}$

# SAMPLING TECHNIQUES

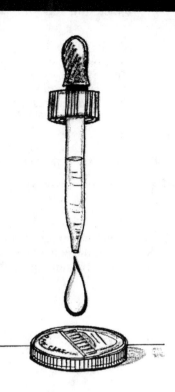

DS-102.  How many drops of water do you think a penny can hold? Using your supplies, count the number of drops of water your penny can hold before it overflows. Record your results on a class stem-leaf plot, then make a box and whisker diagram.

DS-103.  Look at the box and whisker diagram generated by this data. Why is the data so spread out? Discuss as a class **exactly** how you did the experiment. Did you all do it exactly the same way? What instructions could be given at the beginning of the experiment that would help make the results more uniform?

DS-104.  As a class, decide on uniform instructions and repeat the experiment.

DS-105.  Is the data more uniform this time around? Which experiment better answered the original question, "How many drops of water can a penny hold before it overflows?"

DS-106.  When gathering data it is important that the question be clearly worded to eliminate conditions that would bias the results. (For example, the height from which you used the dropper.) Rewrite the instructions for the penny and water experiment with this in mind.

DS-107.  In the last unit (problems IC-111 through IC-113) you developed a method based on counting combinations to write out the expansion of binomial expressions raised to powers without having to do all of the multiplication. Use your method to expand the following:

a)   $(x - y)^6$                           b)   $(a + bc)^4$

DS-108.  How can you use Pascal's Triangle to expand $(x + 2y)^3$ ?

a)   What substitution can be made? Use it to expand the binomial.

b)   Now try $(5x - 2y)^3$.

DS-109.

## THE BINOMIAL THEOREM

The method of using combinations to write the expansion of expressions of the form $(x + y)^n$ is called the **BINOMIAL THEOREM**. When it is written out in general the notation for combinations makes it look very complicated.

$$(x + y)^n =$$
$$_nC_n x^n + {}_nC_{n-1}x^{n-1}y + {}_nC_{n-2}x^{n-2}y^2 + \ldots + {}_nC_1 xy^{n-1} + {}_nC_0 y^n$$

Add some examples to show how you can use the Binomial Theorem and Pascal's Triangle to your Tool Kit.

DS-110.    Extend your copy of Pascal's triangle to the tenth row.

a)   Explain how to figure out $_{12}C_5$ without writing out two more whole rows.

b)   If you knew $_{19}C_4$ and $_{19}C_3$ how could you figure out $_{20}C_4$ ?

c)   Show by writing out the numerical calculations using the formula $_nC_r = \dfrac{_nP_r}{r!}$ that your answer to part (b) is correct.

d)   In general, why should $_{n+1}C_r = {}_nC_r + {}_nC_{r-1}$?

DS-111.    Bias can take many forms. Sometimes it is created unintentionally by conditions in an experiment. Other times it is more intentional. For each example below, comment on its possible bias.

a)    In a TV commercial an interviewer asks people on the street to name their favorite radio station. All five that he asked claimed WCPM as their favorite.

b)    A university campus wants to increase fees in order to build a new recreation hall. It surveys students to determine support. Survey booths are placed outside the university gym. The resulting survey showed overwhelming support.

c)    A study shows that many more accidents occur on I-95 during the day than at night. Is it therefore safer to drive at night?

d)    An active citizens' group claimed that a nuclear facility was operating at below average standards and therefore should be shut down.

DS-112.    A district attorney claims that local officials received $32,515 in bribes from organized crime. What problem do you see in this report? Explain.

DS-113. The streets in Squaresville are neatly laid out as shown in the diagram below. The city is sponsoring a race from 1st and A to 5th and E. They want to know how many "shortest-path" routes are possible.

a) Since there is only one shortest path to get to 1st and B, write a little 1 at that corner. There is also only one way to get to 2nd and A, so write a little 1 at that corner.

b) How many shortest paths are there to get to 2nd and B? Write the appropriate number at that corner.

c) At each intersection on the grid, write the number of shortest paths a runner can take to reach it. Look for a familiar pattern in the numbers.

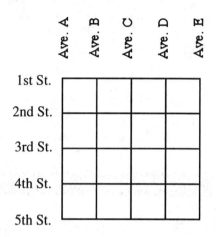

d) Continue in this manner to solve the original problem.

DS-114. What's the name of the pattern you used to solve the last problem?

DS-115. What does it mean if someone has a negative z-score?

DS-116. Solve for g: $\sqrt{2g+1} - 7 = -g$.

DS-117. Write an equation for this curve.

a) Make a statement about the end behavior of this function. What happens to y as x gets larger and larger?

b) Write the equation of the vertical asymptote. What happens as x gets closer and closer to 3?

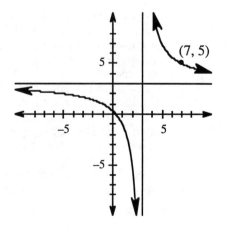

DS-118.    Do not use a calculator and do not convert to exponential form.  Instead, do the
           problems mentally.

    a)    $\log 1$                  b)    $\log 10^3$               c)    $10^{\log 4}$

    d)    $10^{3\log 4}$            e)    $\log 0$                  f)    $\log 10$

    g)    $\log \sqrt{10}$          h)    $10^{(2/3)\log 27}$       i)    $\log (-10)$


## BIAS IN SAMPLING AND REPORTING

DS-119.    On the square piece of paper provided by your teacher, write down an integer from 1 to
           4.  Tape it to the board to form a histogram.


DS-120.    What numbers were picked most frequently?  Discuss in your teams why this might have
           happened.


DS-121.    Statistical results can be affected by psychological issues.  In the previous activity, logic
           might have suggested that each number would be equally likely to be picked, but statistics
           shows us that this is not the case.  Researchers who conduct experiments need to
           eliminate sources of bias for their statistical analysis to be meaningful.  Discuss in your
           teams the potential causes of bias in the following samples.

    a)    Cola #2 did a taste test comparing itself to Cola #1.  Participants were asked to pick
          their favorite drink—one labeled  m  and the other  q.  The majority of participants
          picked the drink labeled  m, which was Cola #1.

    b)    A survey was conducted in the following manner: "The Bill of Rights guarantees
          the right to bear arms so that we can protect our families and our country.  Recently,
          attempts have been made to enact stricter gun controls.  Do you want these
          restrictions?"

    c)    Another survey was conducted in the following manner: "Last year over 15,000
          people were murdered by handguns.  That was 68% of all murders.  Recently,
          attempts have been made to enact stricter gun controls.  Do you want these
          restrictions?"

DS-122. Another interesting oddity of statistics is called the "Simpson's Paradox." Consider the following example based on a recent case: The Cooson Corporation formed two new departments which required massive hiring. Department A had 500 male and 250 female applicants. From this pool, they hired 250 men and 150 women. Department B had 100 male and 400 female applicants. They hired 25 of the men and 108 of the women. A few months later a suit was filed against them charging that their hiring practices discriminated against women. How could this be? Let's take a closer look.

a)  What percentage of the total males who applied were hired? What percentage of the total females who applied were hired? Which group appears to be favored?

b)  In Department A, what percentage of the males who applied were hired? What percentage of the females who applied were hired? Which group appears to be favored?

c)  In Department B, what percentage of the males who applied were hired? What percentage of the females who applied were hired? Which group appears to be favored?

d)  What is the paradox?

e)  Is the suit justified? Explain briefly.


DS-123. Uri's friend's father needs to have surgery. Hospital Alpha has a 100% success rate with that procedure, but has only performed it five times. Hospital Beta has a performed the operation 400 times and has an 90% success rate. Which hospital would you recommend? Explain.


DS-124. Let $f(x) = 2^x(x^2 + 4)$. Find the roots of $f(x)$.


DS-125. On a test with a mean of 66 and a standard deviation of 15, a z-score of 1 corresponds to what raw score?


DS-126. If Josh received a percentile ranking of 20% on a standardized test, what percentage of test takers scored above him?

DS-127. Decide whether each of the following is always, sometimes, or never true when the variables represent real numbers. For the ones that are sometimes true explain when.

a) $\dfrac{1}{x} + \dfrac{1}{y} = \dfrac{1}{x+y}$

b) $\sqrt{a^2 + b^2} = a+b$

c) $\sqrt{x^2} = x$

d) $\sqrt{x^2} = -x$

e) $2^x = 0$

f) $(4 - x)^2 < 0$

g) $(x + y)^2 = x^2 + y^2$

h) $\sqrt{x^2} = |x|$

i) $\dfrac{x}{2} + \dfrac{y}{3} = \dfrac{x+y}{5}$

j) $\dfrac{x}{2} + \dfrac{y}{4} = \dfrac{x+y}{6}$

k) $\dfrac{1}{x} + \dfrac{1}{y} = \dfrac{x+y}{xy}$

DS-128. Expand $(a - 2b)^4$ using Pascal's Triangle.

DS-129. During the same week of the 1996 presidential campaign, one poll claimed Clinton had a 20% lead over Dole while another claimed that Clinton had only a 6% lead. If both statistics are accurate, how is this possible?

DS-130. Simplify $(a^{-1} - b^{-1})^{-1}$.

DS-131. Solve for x if $-2\pi \le x \le 2\pi$.

a) $4 \sin^2 x = 1$

b) $3 \tan^2 x = 1$

DS-132. A bag of popping corn contains $\frac{2}{3}$ white kernels and $\frac{1}{3}$ yellow kernels. Only $\frac{1}{2}$ of the white kernels will pop, whereas $\frac{2}{3}$ of the yellow ones will pop. A kernel is selected at random from the bag, and pops when placed in the popper. What is the probability that the kernel selected was white?

DS-133. Reread the "Closest to the Pin" problem from the beginning of the unit. It's time to start writing your report. Be sure to use the statistical methods you have learned in this unit to support your decision.

DS-134. A test was given that had some extreme scores. The median was 52 and the mean was 63. Were the extreme scores very high or very low? Explain.

DS-135. In a labor dispute using the same set of data, management reported an average company salary of $68,000, while labor reported an average company salary of only $48,000. Both averages were accurate. How is this possible? Explain the discrepancy.

DS-136. Bill and Karen have a $5 bet on who will have the better grade on a physics test. Unfortunately they take the test from two different instructors and each instructor made up her own test! Bill had a score of 53 where the test had a mean score of 42 with standard deviation of 12. Karen earned a score of 118 where the mean score was 102 with a standard deviation of 19. Who should win the bet? Explain.

DS-137. A music company wants to know the music preference of people in Cleveland. Their surveyor asks people who are walking out of a business office building, "What is your favorite type of music?" What kind of problems may arise that will not produce accurate results? (List as many problems as you can.)

DS-138. A group of 30 students took a college placement test with the scores listed below. Make a box and whisker diagram for the data.

| 42 | 58 | 89 | 74 | 87 | 83 | 96 | 38 | 65 | 48 |
| 62 | 85 | 80 | 71 | 90 | 24 | 77 | 63 | 68 | 85 |
| 88 | 80 | 73 | 78 | 71 | 84 | 73 | 56 | 67 | 75 |

DS-139. If Eugene had a score of 83 on the college placement test in the previous problem, find both his percentile in the class and his standard z-score.

DS-140. The mean for the set of scores in problem DS-138 is 71 and the standard deviation is approximately 16.4. The teacher wants to assign new scores to the tests so that the mean is 100 and the standard deviation is 20.

a) The original score of 71 will now be _____.

b) An original score of 90 will now be _____.

c) If the new score is 78, what was the original score?

DS-141. Expand $(2 - 3x)^3$ and simplify your answer.

DS-142. For the final exam in this course we are considering two options. You can take a 100-point test worth 15% of your grade or a 300-point test worth 10% of your grade. Which testing option would have a greater impact on your grade? Explain.

DS-143. Solve this system of equations: $x^2 + y^2 = 16$
$$y = x^2 - 4$$

DS-144. Find the area of the triangular region formed by the intersection of the graphs of the inequalities at right:

$$y \le -\frac{1}{2}x + 5$$
$$y \ge x - 1$$
$$y \le \frac{5}{2}x + 5$$

DS-145. A cannon shoots a cannon ball into the air. The barrel of the cannon is located 6 feet above the ground. After 2 seconds the ball is 102 feet above the ground. After 4 seconds it is 70 feet above the ground. Find the equation of the parabola that models the path of the cannon ball.

DS-146. An exponential function has an asymptote at $x = -10$. If the graph goes through the points $(2, 8)$ and $(4, 30.5)$, find the equation of the function.

DS-147.  **TOOL KIT CHECK-UP**

Your Tool Kit contains reference tools for algebra. Return to your Tool Kit entries. You may need to revise or add entries.

Be sure that your Tool Kit contains entries for all of the items listed below. Add any topics that are missing to your Tool Kit NOW, as well as any other items that will help you in your study of algebra.

- Mean and Median
- Series and Summation Notation
- Mean Deviation
- Stem-Leaf Plot
- Percentile
- Binomial Theorem

- Outliers
- Statistical Variables
- Standard Deviation
- Raw Scores and Z-Scores
- Box-and-Whiskers and Quartiles
- Histogram

# UNIT 13

## Return of the Bouncing Ball and Other Topics
### REVISITING AND EXTENDING EARLIER TOPICS

# Unit 13 Objectives
### Return of the Bouncing Ball and Other Topics: REVISITING AND EXTENDING EARLIER TOPICS

The topics of this unit extend and build on topics you studied in Units 2, 4, and 7. This unit has three main parts. The first part builds on sequences from Unit 2, moving on to sums of arithmetic and geometric sequences and introducing the idea of an infinite sum. Formulas for sums lead to an introduction to proof by induction. The second part extends the work you started in Unit 4 with parabolas and circles to include ellipses and hyperbolas. The third topic draws upon your expertise in factoring polynomials and uses the factor theorem, which is central to Unit 7 to develop a method for dividing polynomials.

In this unit you will have the opportunity to:

- Learn formulas for computing sums of arithmetic sequences and both finite and infinite geometric sequences.

- Learn a new method of proof called mathematical induction.

- Learn about two more conic sections, the ellipse and the hyperbola, and the relationship of their geometric properties to their equations.

- Add division of polynomials to your Tool Kit for finding the roots of polynomial functions.

One of the problems we will solve in this unit will be to find the vertical distance traveled by a bouncing ball.

---

RE-0. **RETURN OF THE BOUNCING BALL** A ball with a rebound ratio of 0.6 (each bounce is 0.6 times as high as the previous one) is dropped from a height of 10 meters and allowed to bounce repeatedly. When the ball hits the ground for the 10th bounce, what vertical distance has it traveled? If the ball continued to bounce and bounce and bounce . . ., what vertical distance would it travel?

---

PROBLEM SOLVING
REPRESENTATION/MODELING
FUNCTIONS/GRAPHING
INTERSECTIONS/SYSTEMS
ALGORITHMS
REASONING/COMMUNICATION

# Unit 13

## *Return of the Bouncing Ball and Other Topics:*
## REVISITING AND EXTENDING EARLIER TOPICS

### SUMS OF ARITHMETIC SEQUENCES

RE-1.

Becky's grandfather said that if she does all her homework he will give her money to help her buy a used car when she gets her driver's license. Grandfather has noticed that Becky is very diligent at the beginning of each semester but becomes less consistent as the weeks go on, so he has decided to add an incentive for persistence. He will give her $5 the first week, $7 the next week, $9 the next, etc., adding

$2 to each week's gift as long as she does every assignment. As soon as she misses one, he will start over at $5 per week. Becky thinks this is a wonderful plan and she starts dreaming about how much money she will have. She knows she can go a long time without missing an assignment with this as an incentive. She wants to know how much she will have if she gets through the 9th and 10th grades with a perfect homework record. That's 70 weeks all together!

Becky begins adding: $5 + 7 + 9 + 11 + \ldots$

Grandfather sees what Becky is doing and says, "Let me show you a trick I learned in high school. Sometimes it's helpful to write out all the parts of a problem before you do any calculations. The 70th payment will be $5 + 69(2) = 5 + 138 = 143$, so the sum of all 70 payments looks like this:

$$5 + 7 + 9 + 11 + \ldots + 139 + 141 + 143."$$

Then Becky's Grandfather suggested, "Now add the values for the first and last weeks. What do you get?"

Becky quickly answered, "$5 + 143 = 148$."

"Good, now add the amounts for the second week and the next-to-last week."

"$7 + 141 = 148$. Hmmmm . . . and $9 + 139 = \ldots 148$! And I see why! As the lower term goes up by 2, the upper one goes down by 2, and the <u>total</u> stays the same!"

"Excellent! So what is the total?"

**>>Problem continues on the next page.>>**

"Well, now I see everything in terms of pairs that make 148," said Becky, and she made the diagram at right. "Since there are 70 numbers being added, there are 35 pairs, so the total must be 35 times 148!"

$$5 + 7 + 9 + 11 + \ldots + 139 + 141 + 143$$

148

148

148

"That's easy enough to do:
35(148) = $5180. Wow! I can buy a cool old car for that much. Thanks, Grandfather."

a)   Use Grandfather's method to find the sum:

   $12 + 19 + 26 + \ldots + 257$   (There are 36 terms in the sum.)

b)   Use Grandfathers method to find the sum of the sequence $t(n) = -11 + 4n$ from $n = 1$ through $n = 100$.

c)   Add the following information to your Tool Kit:

---

### SUM OF AN ARITHMETIC SEQUENCE

If $t(n)$ is any arithmetic sequence, then the sum of the first $k$ terms of the sequence is given by the formula:

$$t(1) + t(2) + \ldots + t(k) = \frac{k}{2}[t(1) + t(k)]$$

Note that $t(1)$ is counted as the first term here. If we think of the sequence as starting with $t(0)$, then the sum of the first $k$ terms is

$$t(0) + t(2) + \ldots + t(k - 1) = \frac{k}{2}[t(0) + t(k - 1)]$$

In general the formula can be stated as, "First term plus last term, times half the number of terms."

The sum of terms of a sequence is called a **SERIES**.

---

RE-2.   Find the sum of the integers from 100 through 1000.

RE-3.   Let $p = 2 + 5i$ and $q = 3 - 4i$. Calculate the following values and simplify to $a + bi$ form:

a)   $p + q$ 

b)   $p - q$

c)   $p \cdot q$ 

d)   $\dfrac{p}{q}$

RE-4.   Twelve horses raced in the Petaluma Derby. In how many different orders could they finish?

RE-5.    Suppose someone multiplied out the polynomial $(x + 2)^{30}$. What would be the coefficient of $x^{11}$?


RE-6.    Solve for x in **degrees**.

   a)   $2 \sin x = -1$                          b)   $\cos^2 x + 5 \cos x + 4 = 0$


RE-7.    A line segment is drawn from point A(3, 2) to point B(-21, 0).  Find the coordinates of the midpoint.


RE-8.    In Unit 3 you compared the depreciation of a Mazda Miata and a Honda Civic EX.  The depreciation functions were:
$$M(x) = 19800(0.78)^x$$
$$H(x) = 16500(0.82)^x$$

In Unit 3 you used graphing and estimation to figure out when the value of the two cars would be the same.  This time solve the system of equations to find out when they will have the same value (to the nearest month).


# GEOMETRIC SERIES

RE-9.    In her math class Becky learned about the speed of exponential growth, so she decided to see if Grandfather would agree to a different plan.

"What if instead of increasing my incentive by $2 per week, you increased it by 10% each week?"

Grandfather wasn't born yesterday, however.  "First you have to figure out the most this change could cost me."

So Becky began to add again, but this time she took Grandfather's advice and wrote out everything before doing anything:

$$5 + 5(1.1) + 5(1.1)^2 + 5(1.1)^3 + \ldots + 5(1.1)^{68} + 5(1.1)^{69}$$

"I don't suppose you remember a trick for this one, Grandfather."

**>>Problem continues on the next page.>>**

"As a matter of fact, I might. Take your total and call it S. Now multiply that by 1.1 and tell me what you see."

"OK, $S = 5 + 5(1.1) + 5(1.1)^2 + 5(1.1)^3 + \ldots + 5(1.1)^{68} + 5(1.1)^{69}$,

so $(1.1)S = 5(1.1) + 5(1.1)^2 + 5(1.1)^3 + 5(1.1)^4 + \ldots + 5(1.1)^{69} + 5(1.1)^{70}$.

That looks almost like S again, but with the first term missing and an extra one on the end. So I can substitute $S - 5$ for all of the terms except the last one:

$$(1.1)S = (S - 5) + 5(1.1)^{70}$$

And now I can solve for S!" And she did.

$$(1.1)S - S = -5 + 5(1.1)^{70}$$

$$(0.1)S = -5 + 5(1.1)^{70}$$

$$S = \frac{-5 + 5(1.1)^{70}}{0.1} = \$7887.47$$

a) Use Grandfather's method to find the sum: $1 + 3 + 9 + 27 + \ldots + 3^{19}$.

b) Grandfather said he would agree to this plan only if Becky could write a formula for the sum of any geometric sequence. Fill in the missing steps to help her:

$$S = a + ar + ar^2 + ar^3 + \ldots + ar^{(n-1)}$$

(The series stops at $n - 1$ power because there are n terms, but the first one is not multiplied by r.)

$rS =$ _____

$rS =$ _____ (Substitute $S - a$.)

$rS - S =$ _____

but $rS - S$ can be factored:

$rS - S = S(\ _____\ )$, so

$S =$ _____

RE-10. Find the sum of the first 20 terms (t(0) through t(19)) of the sequence $t(n) = 16(1.5^n)$.

RE-11. **RETURN OF THE BOUNCING BALL**
A ball with a rebound ratio of 0.6 (each bounce is 0.6 times as high as the previous one) is dropped from a height of 10 meters and allowed to bounce repeatedly. When the ball hits the ground for the 10th bounce, what vertical distance has it traveled?

RE-12. Add the following information to your Tool Kit. Then solve the problem below.

---

### SUM OF A GEOMETRIC SEQUENCE

The sum of the first n terms of a geometric sequence,

$$a + ar + ar^2 + ar^3 + \ldots + ar^{n-1}$$

is called a **GEOMETRIC SERIES** and is given by the formula

$$S = \frac{a(r^n - 1)}{r - 1}$$

---

Find the sum of the sequence $t(n) = 1.4(0.8^n)$ for $n = 0$ through $n = 49$.

RE-13. Look at the differences between successive terms in the quadratic sequence 1, 3, 7, 13, 21, . . . What kind of sequence do the differences form? Use the formula for an arithmetic series to find the 75th term in the original quadratic sequence.

RE-14. Use another method to find $t(75)$ in the quadratic sequence in problem RE-13.

RE-15. 12 students will be chosen at random from the 900 students at Rolling Meadows High School to serve as the Judicial Board for minor student infractions.

a)    How many different Judicial Boards are possible?

b)    Mariko hopes to be on the Board. How many of the possible boards include her?

c)    What is the probability that Mariko is chosen for the board?

RE-16. One angle of a triangle has measure 70° and the side opposite it has length 37.2 ft. Another angle of this triangle is 30°. Find measures of the rest of its parts.

RE-17. For the following system:         $x^2 + y^2 = 25$
                                                        $y = x^2 - 36$

a)    Find the intersection of the graphs.

b)    Find the algebraic solution of the system.

RE-18. Find the equation of the line tangent to the circle $(x - 1)^2 + (y + 2)^2 = 25$ at the point $(4, 2)$.

RE-19. Of course we know that the ball in problem RE-11 would not bounce forever, but imagine that it could. Or instead of pretending that a ball could bounce forever, imagine starting at 0 on a number line and following this rule: move 20 units to the right, and then continue making moves to the right, with each move being 0.6 times the previous move.

Problems like this intrigued the mathematicians of ancient Greece. Would you eventually wind up traveling to the far reaches of the number line, or is there some point you would not get past? In short, is the sum of infinitely many terms necessarily infinite? Explore this idea in the following questions. You may be surprised!

a) You can use the formula for the sum of a geometric sequence to investigate this issue. The formula can also be written $S = \dfrac{a(1 - r^n)}{1 - r}$. Explain or show why this form is equivalent to the version in your Tool Kit.

b) The formula for the distance traveled after 10 moves (or the distance traveled by the ball after 10 bounces) could be written in this form:

$$S = \frac{20(1 - 0.6^{10})}{1 - 0.6} = \frac{20(1 - 0.00605)}{0.4}$$

Write the formula for the distance traveled after 20 moves in the same form.

c) Calculate the quantity $0.6^n$ for $n = 10, 20, 30, 40,$ and 50. What number is being approached? It may help to write out the values in decimal, rather than scientific, notation in order to answer. What number is the quantity $\dfrac{20(1 - 0.6^n)}{0.4}$ getting very close to as $n$ gets very large? If the ball could bounce forever with a rebound ratio of 0.6, essentially how far would it travel?

d) When we have a geometric series with a multiplier, or common ratio, which is between 1 and -1, adding infinitely many terms does not result in an infinite sum. Instead there is a specific number that the sums approach as the number of terms being added gets larger and larger. This number is called the **sum of the infinite geometric series**. The sum is finite because the term $r^n$ in the formula $S = \dfrac{a(1 - r^n)}{1 - r}$ approaches 0, resulting in the following formula. Add it to your Tool Kit.

---

### INFINITE GEOMETRIC SERIES

For an **INFINITE GEOMETRIC SERIES** with an initial value $a$ and common ratio $r$, with $-1 < r < 1$, the sum is given by the formula

$$S = \frac{a}{1 - r}.$$

---

e) A contest offers to pay the winner's family a monthly stipend forever, that is, as long as the winner has a living descendent, the stipend will be paid from an annuity account. The stipend is $10,000 the first month and it decreases by 1% each month. How much money must be set aside to pay the winning family?

RE-20.    A retired hiker decides to spend his days walking around the country. On the first day he walks 25 miles. On the following days he finds that he cannot keep up that pace, and that on average he travels 5% less each day than on the previous day. If he walked in a straight line, how far from his starting point would he travel?

RE-21.    Candice has two parents, four grandparents, eight great-grandparents, etc. If Candice traces her family tree back for 15 generations (with Candice as the 16th generation), how many direct ancestors will she have identified?

RE-22.    A deck of 40 playing cards has cards numbered one through ten, with each number appearing in red, blue, green, and yellow. How many different ways are there to have three of one number and two of another?

RE-23.    Find the sum of terms $a_0$ through $a_{80}$ for the sequence $a_0 = 10$, $a_n = -0.95a_{n-1}$.

RE-24.    When a closed container is heated the pressure inside will build. A closed cylinder is heated in such a way that the pressure doubles every hour. If the pressure builds to 100 times its starting pressure, the container will explode. When will it explode?

RE-25.    A 125-foot redwood tree is leaning 20° off vertical toward the north. How long will its shadow be when the noon sun is 68° above the horizon?

RE-26. In studying geometry you learned about deductive proof. After assuming a few very basic facts, called postulates, all the other true statements, called theorems, can be proved by logical argument, based on the postulates and the theorems that have already been proven. Mathematicians have also proved theorems for algebra. Many can be proven by deductive methods similar to those you used in Geometry, but some require different methods. One of these methods is called **PROOF BY MATHEMATICAL INDUCTION**. Here's an example.

If you use the formula for the sum of an arithmetic series to find the sum of n counting numbers, you get the following result:

$$1 + 2 + 3 + \ldots + n = \frac{n(n + 1)}{2}$$

The validity of this formula for every n = 1, 2, 3, . . . can be proven by mathematical induction. The proof by induction consists of two steps. Think of the formula as representing a sequence of statements:

$$1 = \frac{1(1 + 1)}{2}$$
$$1 + 2 = \frac{2(2 + 1)}{2}$$
$$1 + 2 + 3 = \frac{3(3 + 1)}{2}$$
$$\vdots$$

We can easily prove that any of these specific statements is true. Then we prove deductively that *if* any of these statements is true, *then* the next one must also be true. Since the 1st is true, so is the 2nd, hence the 3rd, the 4th, and all the rest.

We can see that the first statement is true. We call this the anchor. Next, suppose that one of the statements, say, the kth one, is true. In other words, suppose there is some value of k for which it is true that

$$1 + 2 + 3 + \ldots + k = \frac{k(k + 1)}{2}$$

(Note: this statement makes it appear that k is greater than 3, because we wrote out the first three terms to show the pattern, but the process will apply to any k = 1, 2, 3, 4, . . .)

Our goal is to transform this equation algebraically into the next one (n = k + 1). Then we can conclude that if the kth statement is true, so is the (k + 1)st. Before we start transforming, it helps to see what the (k + 1)st equation looks like. To do that we substitute (k + 1) for n in the formula, and we get

$$1 + 2 + 3 + \ldots + (k + 1) = \frac{(k + 1)[(k + 1) + 1]}{2}, \text{ which simplifies to}$$
$$1 + 2 + 3 + \ldots + (k + 1) = \frac{(k + 1)(k + 2)}{2}.$$

**>>Problem continues on the next page.>>**

This equation is the target. We need to know that if the *k*th equation is true, so is this one. Note that the target statement can also be written

$$1 + 2 + 3 + \ldots + k + (k + 1) = \frac{(k + 1)(k + 2)}{2}$$

since the term before $(k + 1)$ is $k$. Compare this statement to the sum of the first $k$ positive integers.

$$1 + 2 + 3 + \ldots + k = \frac{k(k + 1)}{2}$$

If we assume the above statement is true, then, we can add the quantity $(k + 1)$ to both sides. We get the following equation:

$$1 + 2 + 3 + \ldots + k + (k + 1) = \frac{k(k + 1)}{2} + (k + 1)$$

And this must also be true because we just added the same thing to both sides of a true equation. Now we can apply the properties of algebra to the right hand side of this equation, which does not have that annoying ellipsis (. . .).

$$\frac{k(k + 1)}{2} + (k + 1) = \frac{k(k + 1)}{2} + \frac{2(k + 1)}{2}$$
$$= \frac{k^2 + k + 2k + 2}{2}$$
$$= \frac{k^2 + 3k + 2}{2}$$
$$= \frac{(k + 1)(k + 2)}{2}$$

So now we have:

$$1 + 2 + 3 + \ldots + k + (k + 1) = \frac{(k + 1)(k + 2)}{2}$$

And this is the target statement that says that the formula is true for $n = k + 1$.

To summarize: we got to the $(k + 1)$st equation by adding the same thing to both sides of the *k*th statement, so if the *k*th equation is true, then so is the $(k + 1)$st.
In the case of $k = 1$, we *know* the statement is true, and now we know automatically it is also true for $(k + 1)$, which equals 2. But that makes it true for $k = 2 + 1 = 3$, $k = 3 + 1 = 4$, and all the rest. Here is a summary of the method.

**>>Problem continues on the next page.>>**

## PROOF BY INDUCTION

Mathematical induction is used to prove that a given formula is true for any natural number ($n = 1, 2, 3, \ldots$). It consists of the following steps:

1. Verify by substitution that the formula is true for $n = 1$.

2. Write the general statement of the formula for $n = k$.

3. Algebraically transform the statement for $n = k$ into the statement for $n = k + 1$.

   (Before doing Step 3, it is helpful to see what the statement for $n = k + 1$ should look like by substituting $(k + 1)$ in place of $n$ in the original formula.)

These steps complete the proof.

Prove the following formulas by induction:

a)   $2 + 4 + 6 + \ldots + 2n = n(n + 1)$

b)   $5 + 8 + 11 + \ldots + (3n+2) = \dfrac{n(3n + 7)}{2}$

c)   $1^2 + 2^2 + 3^2 + \ldots + n^2 = \dfrac{n(n + 1)(2n + 1)}{6}$

RE-27.   Prove by induction:  $1 + 3 + 5 + \ldots + (2n - 1) = n^2$

RE-28.   What is the fourth term in the expansion of $(x - 3)^{12}$?

RE-29.   A bag contains 4 red pens, 6 green pens, and 2 blue pens. If three pens are chosen at random, what is the probability that one of each color is picked?

**RE-30.** The graph of $g(x)$ is shown at right. Sketch the graph of:

a) $g(x) - 3$

b) $g(x + 4)$

c) $2 \cdot g(x)$

d) $\frac{1}{2} g(x - 2)$

e) $g(\frac{1}{2} x)$

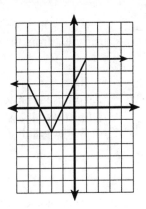

**RE-31.** A quadratic function has roots of $3 - 2i$ and $3 + 2i$. What is its equation?

**RE-32.** Factor completely: $5x^7y - 320xy$.

**RE-33.** Remember the "sleeping parabolas" of Unit 4? Write the equation for the following sideways parabola in graphing form and sketch its graph.

$$x = 2y^2 - 12y + 13$$

# ELLIPSES

**RE-34.** When you first graphed the circle $x^2 + y^2 = 25$ you may have used x- and y-intercepts or the graphing calculator.

a) What are the four intercepts?

b) What equations would you type into the graphing calculator to see the graph?

c) What are the center and radius of the graph?

**RE-35.** Now consider the equation $4x^2 + y^2 = 25$.

a) What are the four intercepts?

b) Use the graphing calculator to graph this equation. Verify that your intercepts are correct.

c) This shape is called an **ellipse**. How many points are needed to make a good sketch of this shape?

RE-36.    For the ellipse $x^2 + 4y^2 = 25$ find four points and sketch the graph. How is this ellipse different from the previous one?

RE-37.    An ellipse is basically a circle that has been stretched vertically or horizontally. Would the ellipse $4x^2 + 25y^2 = 25$ be stretched vertically or horizontally? Find the intercepts and draw the graph.

RE-38.    Here is another equation of an ellipse:     $\frac{x^2}{4} + \frac{y^2}{9} = 1$

   a)    Is it easier or harder to find the intercepts in this case?

   b)    You neither need to use the graphing calculator nor to rearrange the equation to find the intercepts. To find the x-intercepts, substitute $y = 0$ and you can determine the x-intercepts by inspection. Find the x-intercepts and then use the same idea to find the y-intercepts.

   c)    How do the x- and y-intercepts relate to the equation in this form?

RE-39.    In the previous problem you found that the x-intercepts were (±2, 0) and that the y-intercepts were (0, ±3). Find the intercepts and sketch these graphs.

   a)    $\frac{x^2}{16} + \frac{y^2}{5} = 1$          b)    $5x^2 + 4y^2 = 100$

   c)    Which form of the ellipse equation made it easiest to predict the intercepts?

RE-40.    Write an equation to represent each ellipse.

   a)    x-intercepts ±3; y-intercepts ±6          b)    x-intercepts $\pm\sqrt{10}$ ; y-intercepts ±1

RE-41.    Use what you know about locator points and what you have learned about graphing ellipses to graph:

   a)    $\frac{(x-2)^2}{16} + \frac{(y-3)^2}{25} = 1$

   b)    What are the coordinates of the four relocated intercepts? These points, at the top, bottom, left, and right extremes of the ellipse, are called its **vertices.**

   c)    Substitute two of the four points into the equation to show that they check.

RE-42. Graph the following equations. Some of them will need to be rearranged into a more useful form.

a) $\frac{(x+2)^2}{9} + \frac{(y-3)^2}{4} = 1$

b) $\frac{x^2+2x+1}{16} + \frac{y^2+6y+9}{25} = 1$

c) $4(x^2-10x+25) + 9(y^2-8y+16) = 36$

RE-43. Find the equation for each ellipse:

a)

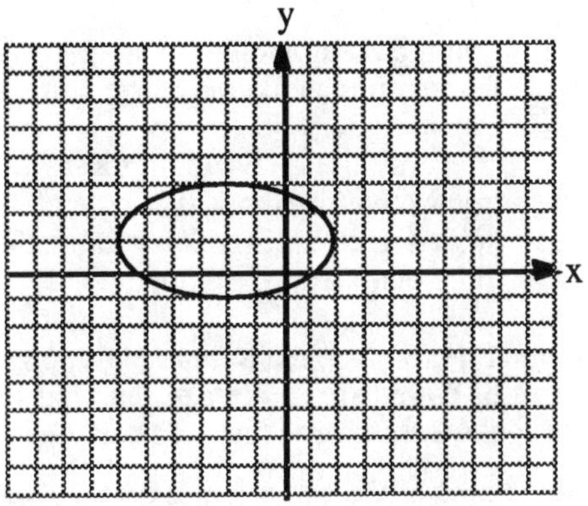

b)

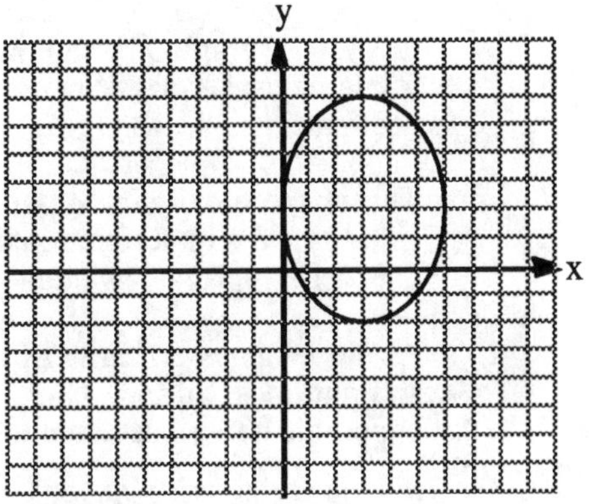

RE-44. Prove by induction that for $n = 1, 2, 3, \ldots$,

$$\frac{x^n-1}{x-1} = x^{(n-1)} + x^{(n-2)} + \ldots + x + 1$$

RE-45. Ernie and Lisa were trying to find the zeros of a quadratic function g(x) by solving the equation $g(x) = 0$. Ernie's answer was $-3\pm\sqrt{\frac{17}{2}}$; Lisa's answer was $\frac{-6\pm\sqrt{34}}{2}$. Without using your calculator, show that both could be correct and figure out what quadratic function g(x) they could have started with.

RE-46. In $\triangle ABC$, if $AB = AC$ and $m\angle ABC = 70°$ then what is $m\angle BAC = ?$

RE-47.     At the start of the previous section the problems were quadratic equations that contained sums of squares and their graphs were either circles or ellipses. We now want to look at quadratic equations involving differences of squares such as $4x^2 - 9y^2 = 36$ or $\frac{x^2}{9} - \frac{y^2}{4} = 1$.

Although the equation looks very similar to the ellipse, the graph is very different.

a)     Rearrange either equation so that it can be entered into the graphing calculator. Verify your new equation with your teacher and then enter the equation into the calculator. Be careful to use parentheses as necessary.

b)     Copy your graph on graph paper. You should have two convenient x-intercepts, no y-intercepts, and you can use the table from your calculator to get more points on the "branches."

c)     This shape is called a **hyperbola.** There are two branches that resemble a sideways V with a rounded tip. Each tip is a **vertex** of the hyperbola. What are the x-intercepts? How could you determine them from the equation?

d)     As the x-values get farther from 0, the hyperbola appears more and more like two straight lines. In fact there are two lines called **slant asymptotes** that the hyperbola gets closer and closer to. Make a table of values and use your calculator to look at the ratios $\frac{y}{x}$ for large values of x. What fraction(s) do they seem to be approaching? This number and its opposite are the slopes of the asymptotes. We can use the asymptotes and the intercepts to make a reasonable sketch of the graph without using the calculator.

RE-48.     Consider the hyperbola $\frac{x^2}{4} - \frac{y^2}{25} = 1$.

a)     From your experience in the previous problem, predict what the x-intercepts and the slopes of the asymptotes will be. Graph the asymptotes and use them along with the intercepts to sketch the hyperbola by hand.

b)     Solve the equation for y and graph it with your graphing calculator.

c)     Check to see if the x-intercepts and the slopes of the asymptotes match your predictions. Describe how the x-intercepts and slopes of the asymptotes are determined by the equation.

RE-49.    To understand why the hyperbola approaches a slant asymptote, we'll begin with an experiment. Pick a number between 50 and 100 and find the square root of that number. Now subtract 25 from your original number and take the square root of that value. Compare the two square roots. Now repeat the process several times, beginning with larger numbers. Use numbers in the following ranges: 100 to 150, 150 to 200, 250 to 300, 500 to 1000, 1000 to 10,000, above 10,000 . You may divide this work among your team and share the results. Make a table showing the results. What do you observe?

Now look at the equations that were entered into the calculator:

$$y = \pm\sqrt{\frac{25x^2}{4} - 25}$$

a)    Use the pattern you described above to estimate, *without a calculator*, the values of y  for  x = 1,000,000.

b)    Find a formula that tells the approximate values of  y  for large values of  x, and simplify this expression. How is this equation related to the graph of the hyperbola?

RE-50.    Graph each hyperbola without using the graphing calculator. Begin by graphing the x-intercepts and asymptotes to guide you.

a)    $\frac{x^2}{16} - \frac{y^2}{9} = 1$

b)    $9x^2 - 4y^2 = 36$

RE-51.    If the terms are reversed so that $\frac{y^2}{16} - \frac{x^2}{9} = 1$, the graph no longer has x-intercepts.

a)    Why is this true?

b)    Solve this equation for  y.

c)    Draw the graph. Identify the intercepts and slope of the asymptotes.

RE-52.    Using the intercepts and slope of the asymptotes as a guide, graph each hyperbola without using the graphing calculator.

a)    $\frac{y^2}{4} - \frac{x^2}{25} = 1$

b)    $x^2 - y^2 = 9$

RE-53. Use what you know about locator points and what you have learned about graphing hyperbolas to graph each of following. The following suggestions may help to organize your work.

First find the locator point. Be careful that you do not get the coordinates of the locator point reversed. Next determine the orientation (up/down or left/right) to locate the vertices. Then, starting at the locator point, use the slope to sketch the asymptotes as a guide for each branch of the graph.

Some of the equations may need to be rearranged into a more useful form

a) $\dfrac{(x-2)^2}{9} - \dfrac{(y+3)^2}{4} = 1$ 

b) $\dfrac{y^2 - 2y + 1}{4} - \dfrac{x^2 + 6x + 9}{25} = 1$

c) $4(x^2 - 10x + 25) - 16(y^2 + 6y + 9) = 64$

RE-54. Find the sums of following sequences:

a) $t(n) = 3(-2)^n, \ n = 1$ through $n = 50$

b) $t(n) = -100 + 13n, \ n = 0$ through $n = 100$

RE-55. Find an equation for the ellipse with vertices at (-4, -5), (1, 7), (6, -5), and (1, -17).

# GENERAL QUADRATIC EQUATIONS

RE-56. A **GENERAL QUADRATIC EQUATION** is an equation of the form
$ax^2 + by^2 + cx + dy + e = 0$ in which a and b may not both be equal to zero. Depending on the values of the coefficients, the equation will graph as a parabola, a circle, an ellipse, or a hyperbola. In special cases it may also be two lines, a single point, or no graph at all. Examine each of the following equations and predict what shape it will be when graphed. Give reasons for your answers.

a) $3x^2 - 3y^2 = 18$

b) $4x^2 + 9y^2 - 24x + 18y + 9 = 0$

c) $16x^2 - 4y = 0$

d) $x^2 + y^2 - 2x - 6y - 9 = 0$

e) $-2x^2 + 4y^2 - 8x - 20y + 61 = 0$

f) $8y^2 + 96y - 2x + 289 = 0$

---

$ax^2 + by^2 + cxy + dx + ey + f = 0$

is a general equation that would include all possible 2-variable quadratic relations.

In RE-56 we are considering a special case of this equation where there is no $xy$ term.

---

RE-57. To graph the ellipse $4x^2 + 9y^2 + 16x - 18y - 11 = 0$ we will need to rearrange the terms and complete the square so that the features can be recognized.

In this case we have four x-squares to complete and nine y-squares to complete.

a) Show how to change to equation above into the equation below.

$$4(x^2 + 4x) + 9(y^2 - 2y) - 11 = 0$$

b) Show how to change to equation above into the equation below.

$$4\left[(x+2)^2 - 4\right] + 9\left[(y-1)^2 - 1\right] - 11 = 0$$

c) Show how to change to equation above into the equation below.

$$4(x+2)^2 + 9(y-1)^2 = 36$$

d) Show how to change to equation above into the equation below.

$$\frac{(x+2)^2}{9} + \frac{(y-1)^2}{4} = 1$$

e) Find the locator point and vertices. Draw the graph.

RE-58. Write the original equation on your paper and fill in the steps between the ones given for rearranging the following hyperbola into graphing form. For each of steps (a), (b), and (c), write a sentence describing what was done to the equation above it to get that equation

$$25x^2 - 4y^2 - 150x - 8y + 121 = 0.$$

a) $25(x^2 - 6x \quad) - 4(y^2 + 2y \quad) + 121 = 0$

b) $25[(x-3)^2 - 9] - 4[(y+1)^2 - 1] + 121 = 0$

c) $25(x-3)^2 - 4(y+1)^2 = 100$

d) Finish the rearrangement.

e) State the locator point, the coordinates of the vertices, and the slope of the asymptotes.

f) Sketch the hyperbola.

RE-59. Show and justify each step to rearrange the parabola $x^2 - 2x - 8y + 17 = 0$ into the graphing form $(y-2) = \frac{1}{8}(x+1)^2$

RE-60. For each of the following equations, identify the curve, write the equation in graphing form, and list the following information: center, vertex or vertices, and asymptotes, if any.

a) $9x^2 - 16y^2 - 32y = 160$     b) $y^2 - 2y + 3x = 5$

c) $16 + 6x - x^2 - y^2 = 0$

RE-61. Find the equation of a hyperbola with vertices at $(0, \pm5)$ and asymptotes $y = \pm2x$.

RE-62. Find the infinite sum: $0.9 + 0.09 + 0.009 + 0.0009 + \ldots$

RE-63. Why does the formula for an infinite geometric series contain the condition that $-1 < r < 1$? Look back at how the formula was derived. What is different when $|r| > 1$?

RE-64. Find the equation of an ellipse with vertices $(-2, -3)$, $(10, -3)$, $(4, -2)$, $(4, -4)$.

# GEOMETRIC PROPERTIES OF PARABOLAS AND ELLIPSES

RE-65. Many people think that "parabola" is a name for all curves that are "sort of U-shaped." In fact, parabolas have geometric properties which are unique to curves whose parent graph is $y = x^2$ (or $x = y^2$). On graph paper, make a large, careful graph of

$y = \frac{1}{4}x^2$, for $-5 \le x \le 5$ (or your teacher may provide

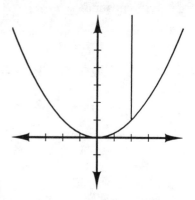

a resource page). Use a straightedge to draw several vertical lines from the top of the graph down to the parabola (see diagram). Imagine each of the lines as a beam of light striking the parabola, or as the path of an object "falling" toward the parabola from the top of the page. Suppose that the light will reflect or the object will bounce when it hits the parabola. For each vertical line segment, use your straight edge to draw a ray showing the path of the reflection from the parabola to the y-axis; the incoming ray and the outgoing ray should make equal angles with the parabola. Describe what you notice.

RE-66.

The point at which the reflected rays intersect is called the **FOCUS** of the parabola. If you drew the lines accurately in the previous problem, they will all intersect at the point (0, 1). The distance p from the vertex to the focus is called the **FOCAL LENGTH** of the parabola, and it is determined by the stretch factor. Repeat the process from the previous problem with the parabola $y = \frac{1}{2}x^2$ to estimate the focal length for that parabola.

RE-67.

What happened to the focal length when the stretch factor doubled from one-fourth to one-half? Here are some other parabolas and their foci (plural of focus): $y = x^2$, focus (0, 0.25); $y = 3x^2$, focus (0, $\frac{1}{12}$); $y = \frac{1}{8}x^2$, focus (0, 2). Find a formula relating the focal length, p, and the stretch factor, a.

RE-68. The reflective property of parabolas make them very useful. Reflecting mirrors and dishes are made in the three-dimensional shape called a paraboloid whose cross-sections are parabolas. In a high-beam light the bulb is placed at the focus, causing the out-going rays of light to be parallel. In a satellite dish, the antenna is placed at the focus where all the incoming electromagnetic waves converge. Find the equation of the parabola shown in the cross-section of the satellite dish in the drawing at right.

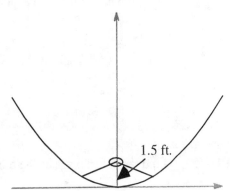

1.5 ft.

RE-69.

Ellipses also have unique geometric properties; not every oval is an ellipse. Suppose an ellipse has its center at the origin, with x-intercepts at ($\pm$a, 0) and y-intercepts at (0, $\pm$b), where a > b. Then there are two points on the x-axis at ($\pm$c, 0), with $c^2 = a^2 - b^2$, which are called the **FOCI OF THE ELLIPSE**. To understand the geometric properties of the ellipse, imagine a pool table in the shape of an ellipse, with only one pocket, located at one focus. If you place a ball on the other focus and hit it *in any direction*, it will bank off the rail and go into the pocket. In addition, no matter where the ball hits the rail, it will always travel the same distance in reaching the pocket.

a) An ellipse has equation $\dfrac{x^2}{16} + \dfrac{y^2}{9} = 1$. What are the coordinates of the foci?

b) Where should the foci be in the ellipse $\dfrac{x^2}{9} + \dfrac{y^2}{16} = 1$?

c) **Extension:** Make a careful sketch of an ellipse and draw lines to show the path of a ball hit from one focus in a variety of directions. What is the distance traveled by the ball to the pocket at the other focus?

RE-70. Find the coordinates of the focus of each parabola:

a) $y = 3x^2 - 12x$

b) $x^2 + 7x - 3y - 5 = 0$

RE-71. Find the coordinates of the foci of each ellipse:

a) $\dfrac{x^2}{16} + \dfrac{y^2}{36} = 1$

b) $9x^2 + 25y^2 - 225 = 0$

c) $4x^2 + 16y^2 - 8x - 12 = 0$

RE-72. A ship exits its home port with a heading N23°E and travels this direction for 2 miles where it stops at a neighboring island. It leaves the island with a heading of S45°E and travels for 8 miles. The ship begins to have engine problems and needs to return back to its home port. What heading does it need to take and how far will it need to travel to get to the home port?

Note: N23°E means moving 23° towards the East from a North heading. Headings are given with a starting position of North or South followed by the number of degrees heading toward the east or west.

RE-73.    Solve the system:    $\frac{x}{4} + \frac{y}{3} = 1$

$2x - \frac{y}{3} = 17$

## ECCENTRICITY

RE-74.    Did you ever know anyone who was eccentric?  In mathematics, eccentric means "out of round," and eccentricity is a measure of how far an ellipse is from being round. To define this we need some terminology.

---

### EQUATIONS FOR ELLIPSES

The line through the two ends of the ellipse in the long direction is called the **MAJOR AXIS** of the ellipse, and the distance from the center of the ellipse to one end of the major axis is called the **SEMI-MAJOR AXIS**. If  a  is the semi-major axis,  c  is the distance from the center to either focus, and (h, k) is the center, the equation of the ellipse can be written

$$\frac{(x-h)^2}{a^2} + \frac{(y-k)^2}{b^2} = 1,\ \text{if the major axis is horizontal, or}$$

$$\frac{(x-h)^2}{b^2} + \frac{(y-k)^2}{a^2} = 1,\ \text{if the major axis is vertical.}$$

The formula for **ECCENTRICITY** in either case is:  $e = \frac{c}{a}$, where $c^2 = a^2 - b^2$.

---

a)    Find the eccentricity of the ellipses in problem RE-71.

b)    Find the eccentricity of the ellipse in problem RE-41, part (a).

c)    Find the equation of an ellipse whose major axis is 10 units long with an eccentricity of 0.8.

d)    Suppose an ellipse has eccentricity = 0.  What would it look like?  Where would the foci be?  Would it still be true that a ball hit from one focus would rebound to the other focus?

RE-75.

---

## EQUATIONS FOR HYPERBOLAS

A hyperbola has relationships similar to those of an ellipse. The line connecting the vertices of the two branches is called the **TRANSVERSE AXIS**, and the letter a is used to represent the distance from the center to either vertex. In this case, if the center of the hyperbola is at the origin, the equation can be written in the form:

$$\frac{x^2}{a^2} - \frac{y^2}{b^2} = 1$$

(We use $a^2$ and $b^2$ for the numbers in the denominators because we see the square roots of those numbers on the graph.)

The vertices are ($\pm a$, 0) and the asymptotes have equations $y = \pm\frac{b}{a}x$. The foci are on the transverse axis, in this case the x-axis, at ($\pm c$, 0), with c given by the equation

$$c^2 = a^2 + b^2.$$

The eccentricity is again a measure of the shape of the curve; the larger the eccentricity the more quickly the branches spread apart. The formula is again $e = \frac{c}{a}$ (since c > a, the eccentricity of a hyperbola is always greater than 1; ellipses have eccentricity less than 1). If the vertices are on the y-axis, the equation becomes $\frac{y^2}{a^2} - \frac{x^2}{b^2} = 1$ and everything else is the same _except_ the asymptotes have slopes $\pm\frac{a}{b}$.

To shift the center (or locator point) to (h, k) replace x and y in the equations with (x – h) and (y – k), respectively, and adjust the equations of the asymptotes to go through the point (h, k) instead of (0, 0).

---

Find the eccentricity and the coordinates of the foci for each hyperbola in problem RE-52.

RE-76.    Even though they knew no algebra, the ancient Greek mathematicians knew about circles, ellipses, hyperbolas and parabolas. They called these curves the **conic sections** because they are created by the intersection of a cone with a plane. (To the Greeks a cone had two sections which extended infinitely, as shown in the drawing at right.) When placed in a 3-dimensional coordinate system as shown below, the "double cone" has an equation of the form $z^2 = ax^2 + by^2$. For this question, let a = b = 1, so $z^2 = x^2 + y^2$. Planes in 3-space have equations of the form ax + by + cz = d.

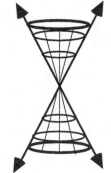

**>>Problem continues on the next page.>>**

a)  The equation $z = 4$ is a plane parallel to the x-y plane (formed by the x- and y-axes), so it only intersects the upper section. Show that the intersection of this plane with this cone is a circle by finding the equation of the intersection of the plane $z = 4$ with $z^2 = x^2 + y^2$.

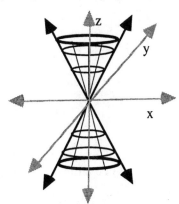

b)  The equation $x = 2$ is a plane parallel to the y-z plane  Show that the intersection of this plane with this cone is a hyperbola by finding the equation of the intersection of the plane and the cone.

c)  What will be the intersection if the plane in part (a) is tilted slightly?  Don't try to do the algebra; just see if you can visualize it.

d)  What will be the intersection if the plane in part (b) is tilted just to the point where it only intersects one branch of the cone?  Do not try to do the algebra here either.

RE-77.  Find the coordinates of the foci and the eccentricity of each ellipse in problem RE-42. Find the approximate value for the eccentricity for each ellipse and explain how the size of the eccentricity is related to the shape of the ellipse.

RE-78.  Find the coordinates of the foci and the eccentricity of each hyperbola in problem RE-53. Calculate the approximate value of the eccentricity for each hyperbola and explain how the eccentricity of the hyperbola is related to its shape.

RE-79.  For each of the following equations, identify the curve, write the equation in graphing form, and list the following information:  center, focus or foci, asymptotes, and eccentricity.

a)  $2x^2 + y^2 - 4x + 6y - 7 = 0$     b)  $3y^2 - x^2 + 12y = 0$

c)  $12x^2 + 8y^2 + 48x - 48y + 24 = 0$

RE-80.     Andy and Laurie were challenged by their teacher to factor the expression $x^3 + x^2 - 5x + 3$. For a while they were stumped, but then Andy got an idea.

"Think about the function $y = x^3 + x^2 - 5x + 3$. If we knew the roots, we could find the factors."

"I see one easy root," said Laurie. "If $x = 1$, you get 0."

"Great, now we know that one of the factors is $(x - 1)$, but what are the chances we can guess the other roots?"

"Maybe we don't have to," said Laurie. "Maybe we can use what we know about multiplying polynomials to figure out the other factor. That would be a quadratic, and we know how to factor those."

"Great idea," said Andy, "You start."

"Okay, let's try this: we know we need $x^2$ in the other factor to make $x^3$, so let's multiply by that $(x - 1)(x^2) = x^3 - x^2$ and compare it to $x^3 + x^2 - 5x + 3$."

"It's a start; we got one term right, and the next one wrong. Can we fix that without messing up the $x^3$?" Andy asked.

"Yes," Laurie responded, "If we add terms with powers less than 2 to the $x^2$ we multiplied by, the cubed term won't be affected. What we need is two more $x^2$. Whatever we put in will be multiplied by $x$, so let's put in $2x$ and see what we get.

$$(x - 1)(x^2 + 2x) = x^3 - x^2 + 2x^2 - 2x = x^3 + x^2 - 2x$$

"How does that compare to $x^3 + x^2 - 5x + 3$?" asked Laurie.

"Cool. Now we have the first two terms right, and I'll bet we can fix the $x$ term, too. We need another $-3x$, so let's put in $-3$:"

$$(x - 1)(x^2 + 2x - 3) = x^3 + x^2 - 2x - 3x + 3$$

"That's it!" they yelled in unison. "The $-3$ not only made the $x$ term right, it also gave us the constant term we needed."

Then they factored the quadratic to get:    $(x - 1)(x - 1)(x + 3) = x^3 + x^2 - 5x + 3$ and they had met the challenge.

a)     Why is it appropriate to call the process they discovered for finding the missing quadratic factor **POLYNOMIAL DIVISION**?

b)     Use their process to divide $x^3 + 4x^2 - 7x - 10$ by $(x - 2)$.

RE-81.    Andy and Laurie were talking about the polynomial division process they developed.

"There has to be a better way to organize the information," said Andy.

"It reminds me of the generic rectangles we used to multiply polynomials in Algebra 1," replied Laurie.

"Oh yeah. . .?"

"Well, look at the multiplication problem

$(x + 4)(2x^2 - 7x + 9) = 2x^3 + x^2 - 19x + 36.$

Do you see how all the terms that have the same power of x are along a diagonal?"

"Yes, and the highest and lowest powers appear only once, in the upper left and lower right corners."

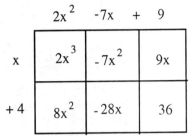

"Right, and we can use that pattern to organize the information in division. Watch. Suppose you want to divide

$(x^3 + x^2 - 14x + 6)$ by $(x - 3)$.

We know the upper left has to be $x^3$, the diagonals add up to $x^2$ and $-14x$, and the lower right is 6.

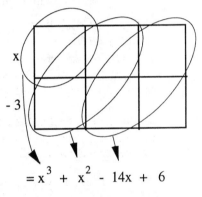

"And since we need $x^3$ in the upper left, we know that $x^2$ goes above the 1st column as the multiplier. That puts $-3x^2$ in the lower left"

"Okay, and since that diagonal has to add up to $1x^2$, we need $4x^2$ in the middle of the top row, and to get that we need $+4x$ above the second column as the multiplier."

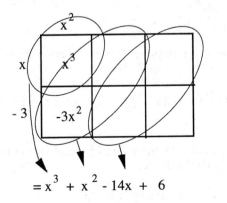

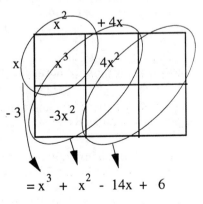

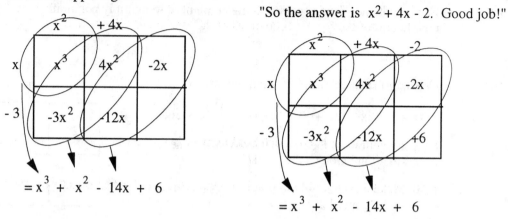

"Now we're rolling. That puts -12x in the middle of the bottom row, and since that diagonal has to equal -14x, we get -2x in the upper right..."

"And that means put -2 at the top of the last column, which gives us +6 in the lower right!"

"So the answer is $x^2 + 4x - 2$. Good job!"

$$= x^3 + x^2 - 14x + 6$$

$$= x^3 + x^2 - 14x + 6$$

Use the generic rectangle method for the following problems.

a) Divide $2x^3 + x^2 - 19x + 36$ by $(x + 4)$.

b) Divide $x^4 - x^3 - 11x^2 - 5x + 4$ by $x^2 + 2x - 1$.

RE-82. Divide $6x^3 - 5x^2 + 5x - 2$ by $(2x - 1)$.

RE-83. The next problem was to divide $x^4 - 7x^2 + 3x + 18$ by $x + 2$.

"Wait," said Andy, " there's no $x^3$ term!"

"That's easy," Luís chimed in, "Just add in $0x^3$."

Use Luís's idea to complete the division problem.

RE-84. Sarina wondered, "What will happen if the divisor does not divide evenly, that is, if it is not a factor of the other polynomial?" Each of the following division problems will have remainders, but you can use the same method to do the division.

a) Divide $2x^4 - x^2 + 3x + 5$ by $x - 1$.

b) Divide $x^5 - 2x^3 + 1$ by $x - 3$.

RE-85. Latisha had graphed the polynomial $y = x^3 - 5x^2 + 8x - 6$ during class and she remembered that it had one real root when $x = 3$. Explain how you could use division to find the other roots and find them.

RE-86.    A parabola has vertex (-3, -7) and focus (-3, -7.1).  Find its equation.


RE-87.    Find the locator point and sketch the graph of $y^2 - 2x^2 + 28x + 2 = 0$.  Find the coordinates of the foci and equations of the asymptotes, if any, and state the eccentricity.


RE-88.    Consider the functions

$$y = \sin x$$
$$y = 3 \sin 2 \left(x - \frac{\pi}{2}\right)$$

a)    Explain the effect of each **bold** number in the second function on the graph of the first function.

b)    Make a sketch of both graphs on the same set of axes.  Be sure to show your scale.


RE-89.    Suppose that $|x| < 1$.  Consider the sum  $1 + x + x^2 + x^3 + x^4 + x^5 + \ldots$

a)    Use the formula for the infinite geometric series to find the sum.

b)    Use multiplication to verify that this formula is correct.

c)    When dividing polynomials, you began by getting the highest power term right and then correcting the lower power terms in order.  It can also be done the opposite way:  starting with the constant term and going up.  Use this process to divide 1 by (1 - x), and see what happens.  The table is set up to get you started.  Since the product must equal 1, all the diagonals must add to 0.

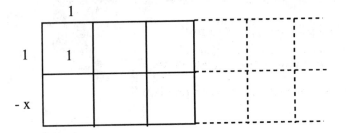

RE-90.    As they got used to using the generic rectangle to divide polynomials, Andy and Laurie started noticing some patterns.

"Look back at RE-81 part (a)," said Laurie. "The coefficients in the answer are the same as the numbers in the top row of the rectangle!"

"Hey, I'll bet we could save ourselves some writing!" said Andy, who never liked to write things down. "Look. All I have to write are the numbers."

| x | 2 | -7 | 9 | 0 |
|---|---|----|---|---|
| +4 | 8 | -28 | 36 | |

"Then you know the answer will start with $2x^2$ because you are dividing $2x^3$ by x. So you can just write the answer $2x^2 - 7x + 9$ and no remainder."

a)    "That's pretty slick," said Laurie, "will it work for RE-81(b)?" Try it yourself.

b)    Using just the numbers see what happens when you divide $\left(x^4 - x^3 - 11x^2 - 5x + 4\right)$ by $\left(x^2 + 2x - 1\right)$.

c)    Now try $\left(x^4 - x^2 + x - 5\right) \div (x - 1)$. Remember the $x^3$ term is $0x^3$.

RE-91.    **TOOL KIT CHECK-UP AND UNIT SUMMARY**

For this unit your summary could just as well be your Tool Kit . For each of the topics listed you should include the general formula or description as well as at least one example.

- Formula for an Arithmetic Series

- Formula for a Finite Geometric Series

- Formula for an Infinite Series
- Description of Proof by Induction
- General Equation for Conics

- Standard Equation for an Ellipse and the Relationship of its Coefficients to its Graph

- Standard Equation for a Hyperbola and the Relationship of its Coefficients to its Graph

- Eccentricity
- Asymptotes
- Division of Polynomials

## RE-92. END OF COURSE SUMMARY

The most useful way to summarize the course for yourself and to prepare for future mathematics courses will be to CLEAN UP YOUR TOOL KIT!  Get it ready to use in your next mathematics course.  At this point you should probably give it a complete overhaul.  Review your entries, unit by unit, and check with your team to make sure you have covered all the important concepts.  Then get rid of all the entries that you no longer need because they are tools you use so regularly that you hardly have to think about them.  Keep a succinct set of notes and examples for topics you are most likely to forget or mix up.

Many of the ideas we have studied are interconnected.  Many of your old entries may be consolidated under new headings.

In cleaning up your Tool Kit unit-by-unit you should review your strengths and weaknesses and make a note of any problems that have caused you difficulty over the year.  For these problems, choose some examples and work through them now.  If you are still having difficulty with any of them, now is the time to ask the questions that will help clear up that difficulty.

# ALGEBRA 2 MILEPOST PROBLEMS

Notes to Students
(and their Teachers)

Different students master different skills at different speeds. No two students learn exactly the same way at the same time. However, at some point you will be expected to perform certain skills with good accuracy. In Algebra 1, your teacher did not want you to grab for your calculator if you needed to calculate $-16 + 9$ or $\sqrt{81}$. The same thing is true of your Algebra 2 teacher. There are certain algebra skills that you need to be able to do on your own and with good accuracy. Most of the Milepost problems are skills that you should have been developing in Algebra 1 and Geometry. If you have not mastered these skills by now it does not necessarily mean that you will not be successful in this class. However, it does mean that to be successful you are going to need to do some extra work outside of class. You need to get caught up on the algebra skills that this year's teacher and possibly next year's pre-calculus teacher expect.

Starting in Unit 2 and finishing in Unit 9, there are twenty one problems designated as Milepost problems. Each one has an icon like the one above. After you do each of the Milepost problems, check your answers. If you have not done them correctly, this is your reminder that you need to put in some extra practice on that skill. The following practice sets are keyed to each of the Milepost problems in the textbook. Each of the Milepost practice sets has the topic clearly labeled, followed by some completed examples. Next, the solution to the Milepost problem from the book is given. Following that are more problems to practice with answers included.

Warning! Looking is not the same as doing. You will never become good at any sport just by watching it. In the same way, reading through the worked out examples and understanding the steps are not the same as being able to do the problems yourself. An athlete only gets good with practice. The same thing is true of your algebra skills. If you did not get the Milepost problem correct you need the extra practice. How many of the extra practice problems do you need to try? That is really up to you. Remember that your goal is to be able to do that skill on your own confidently and accurately. Another warning! You should not expect your teacher to spend time in class going over the solutions to the Milepost practice sets. After reading the examples and trying the problems, if you still are not successful, talk to your teacher about getting a tutor or extra help outside of class time.

Two other sources for help with the Milepost problems and the other new topics in Algebra 2 are the *Parent's Guide with Review to Math 1 (Algebra 1)* and the *Parent's Guide with Review to Math 3 (Algebra 2)*. Information about ordering these supplements can be found inside the front page of the student text. These resources are also available free from the internet at *www.cpm.org*.

## Milepost Topics

1. x- and y-intercepts of a quadratic equation
2. Graphing lines using slope and y-intercept
3. Simplifying expressions with exponents
4. Solving systems of linear equations
5. Multiplying polynomials
6. Factoring quadratic expressions
7. Solving multi-variable equations
8. Slope of the line and distance
9. Function notation; domain and range
10. Writing equations of lines given two points
11. Slopes of parallel and perpendicular lines

12. Graphing linear inequalities
13. Multiplication and division of rational expressions
14. Solving rational equations
15. Addition and subtraction of rational expressions
16. Integral and rational exponents
17. Completing the square; locator points for parabolas
18. Absolute value equations and inequalities
19. Writing and solving exponential equations
20. Finding the equation for the inverse of a function
21. Solving a system of equations in three variables

## BB-62

## Finding the X- and Y-Intercepts of a Quadratic Equation.

The y-intercept of a equation is the location where the graph crosses the y-axis. To find the y-intercept of an equation, substitute $x = 0$ into the equation and solve for y. For example:

Find the y-intercept for the equation $y = x^2 + 4x - 12$.
If $x = 0$, then $y = (0)^2 + 4(0) - 12 = -12$. The y-intercept is $(0, -12)$.

The x-intercept of a equation is the location where the graph crosses the x-axis. To find the x-intercept of an equation, substitute $y = 0$ into the equation and solve for x by factoring or using the quadratic formula. Here are two examples:

Find the x-intercept for the equation $y = x^2 + 4x - 12$.

If $y = 0$, then

$$0 = x^2 + 4x - 12$$

By factoring and using the zero product property

$$0 = (x + 6)(x - 2)$$
$$x = -6 \text{ or } x = 2$$
The x-intercepts are $(-6, 0)$ and $(2, 0)$

Find the x-intercept for the equation $y = 2x^2 - 3x - 3$.

If $y = 0$, then

$$0 = 2x^2 - 3x - 3$$

Since we cannot factor the trinomial we use the Quadratic Formula to solve for x. If $ax^2 + bx + c = 0$, then

$$x = \frac{-b \pm \sqrt{b^2 - 4ac}}{2a}.$$

substitute for a, b, and c

$$x = \frac{-(-3) \pm \sqrt{(-3)^2 - 4(2)(-3)}}{2(2)}$$

simplify and add

$$= \frac{3 \pm \sqrt{9 + 24}}{4} = \frac{3 \pm \sqrt{33}}{4}$$

find $\sqrt{\phantom{xx}}$ value

simplify the fractions

$$\approx \frac{3 \pm 5.745}{4} \text{ or } \frac{3 + 5.745}{4} \text{ and } \frac{3 - 5.745}{4}$$

and the x-intercepts are approximately $(2.19, 0)$ and $(-0.69, 0)$.

Now we can go back and try the original question. Find the x- and y-intercepts for the graph of:
$$y = x^2 + 4x - 17.$$

To find the y-intercept let $x = 0$ so $y = (0)^2 + 4(0) - 17 = -17$ .

To find the x-intercept let $y = 0$ so $0 = x^2 + 4x - 17$.

Since we cannot factor we use the Quadratic Equation with $a = 1$, $b = 4$, and $c = -17$

$$x = \frac{-(4) \pm \sqrt{(4)^2 - 4(1)(-17)}}{2(1)} = \frac{-4 \pm \sqrt{16 + 68}}{2} = \frac{-4 \pm \sqrt{84}}{2} = \frac{-4 \pm 2\sqrt{21}}{2} = -2 \pm \sqrt{21},$$

The answers are $(0, -17)$, $(-2 \pm \sqrt{21}, 0)$ or $(2.58, 0)$, $(-6.58, 0)$

Here are some more to try. Find the x- and y-intercepts for each equation,

1) $y = 2x^2 - 9x - 35 = 0$

2) $y = 2x^2 - 11x + 5$

3) $3x^2 + 2 + 7x = y$

4) $8x^2 + 10x + 3 = y$

5) $y + 2 = x^2 - 5x$

6) $(x - 3)(x + 4) - 7x = y$

7) $-4x^2 + 8x + 3 = y$

8) $0.09x^2 - 0.86x + 2 = y$

9) $y = 2x^3 - 50x$

10) $y = 3x^2 + 4x$

**Answers:**
Note that the coordinates of the intercepts are $(x, 0)$ and $(0, y)$.

1. $x = 7, -\frac{5}{2}$  $y = -35$

2. $x = 5, \frac{1}{2}$  $y = 5$

3. $x = -\frac{1}{3}, -2$  $y = 2$

4. $x = -\frac{3}{4}, -\frac{1}{2}$  $y = 3$

5. $x = \frac{(5 \pm \sqrt{33})}{2}, \approx 5.37, -0.37$  $y = -2$

6. $x = \frac{(6 \pm \sqrt{84})}{2} \approx 7.58, -1.58$  $y = -12$

7. $x = \frac{(-8 \pm \sqrt{112})}{-8} \approx -0.32, 2.32$  $y = 3$

8. $x = 5.56, 4$  $y = 2$

9. $x = 0, 5, -5$  $y = 0$

10. $x = 0, -\frac{4}{3}$  $y = 0$

# BB-66

## Graphing a Line using Slope and Y-Intercept

If an equation of a line is written in the form $y = mx + b$, then the y-intercept is the point $(0, b)$. The slope of the line is the coefficient of x, represented in the general form of the equation as m. So in the equation $y = \frac{2}{3}x + 7$, the slope is $\frac{2}{3}$ and the y-intercept is $(0, 7)$.

Let's first see how to use the information in slope-intercept equations to graph a line.

<u>Without making a table,</u> graph each line. Start with the y-intercept, then use the slope.

a)  $y = \frac{2}{3}x - 2$            b)  $y = 4 - 2x$

In part (a), we start by identifying the slope and y-intercept. The slope is $\frac{2}{3}$ and the y-intercept is $(0, -2)$. To graph the line we plot the y-intercept. (Before continuing, imagine what the line will look like.) .The fact that the slope is positive tells us the direction of the line is upward left to right. Then, knowing that the slope is $\frac{2}{3}$, we can find another point on the line by <u>starting</u> at the y-intercept, moving our pencil up vertically two units and then horizontally (to the right) two units. Just remember that the slope is positive! After moving vertically 2 units and horizontally 3 units, we arrive at another point on the line.

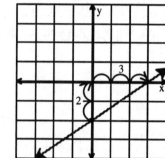

In part (b), $y = 4 - 2x$, don't let the form of the equation fool you. The slope is -2 or $-\frac{2}{1}$ and the y-intercept is $(0, 4)$. The slope is always the coefficient of x and the y-intercept is always the constant. Rearranging their order doesn't change their meaning.

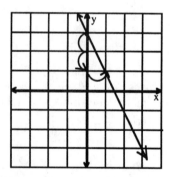

If the equation is not already in slope/intercept (y-form) then the equation must first be solved for y. If the equation to graph is $2x + 5y = 10$, then after solving we get $y = \frac{10-2x}{5}$ or $y = \frac{-2}{5}x + 2$ so the y-intercept is $(0, 2)$ and the slope is $\frac{-2}{5}$ .

Two other special cases to remember are vertical and horizontal lines.

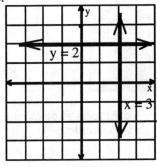

$y = 2$ is a horizontal line (slope equal to zero) passing through the y-axis at (0, 2).

$x = 3$ is a vertical line (undefined slope) passing through the x-axis at (3, 0).

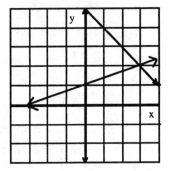

Now we can go back to the original question.
Graph each line and find the intersection.

$$x + y = 5$$
$$y = \frac{1}{3}x + 1$$

The first equation needs to be solved for y: $y = -x + 5$ so the y-intercept is (0, 5) and the slope is -1 or $\frac{-1}{1}$. The second equation has a y-intercept of (0, 1) and a slope of $\frac{1}{3}$. After graphing the two lines you see that they intersect at the point (3, 2).

Here are some more to try. Use the slope and y-intercept to graph each line and tell the point of intersection.

1)  $y = -x + 8$
    $y = x - 2$

2)  $y = -x + 3$
    $y = x + 3$

3)  $y = -3x$
    $y = -4x + 2$

4)  $y = -x + 5$
    $y = \frac{1}{2}x + 2$

5)  $y = -2x - 1$
    $y = -4x + 3$

6)  $3x + 3y = 4 + x$
    $4 - 2x = 3y$

7)  $y = 2$
    $2x + y = 4$

8)  $x = 3$
    $2x + 3y = 0$

9)  $2x + 3y = 0$
    $2x - 3y = 0$

10) $3x - 2y = 4$
    $2y = 3x - 6$

**Answers:**
  1. (5, 3)    2. (0, 3)    3. (2, -6)    4. (2, 3)    5. (2, -5)

  6. same line   7. (1, 2)    8. (3, -2)    9. (0, 0)    10. no solution-parallel lines

BB-107

## Simplifying Expressions with Positive Exponents

There are three basic patterns for expressions with positive exponents. They are summarized below with some examples.

1) $x^a \cdot x^b = x^{a+b}$     examples: $x^3 \cdot x^4 = x^{3+4} = x^7$;     $2^7 \cdot 2^4 = 2^{11}$

2) $\dfrac{x^a}{x^b} = x^{a-b}$     examples: $x^{10} \div x^4 = x^{10-4} = x^6$;     $\dfrac{2^4}{2^7} = 2^{-3}$

3) $(x^a)^b = x^{ab}$     examples: $(x^4)^3 = x^{4 \cdot 3} = x^{12}$;     $(2x^3)^4 = 2^4 \cdot x^{12} = 16x^{12}$

Now we can go back and try the original problem. Simplify each expression.

a)   $(2x^2y)^4 = 2^4 x^8 y^4 = 16 x^8 y^4$

b)   $\dfrac{-3x^2y^3}{(-6x)^2} = \dfrac{-3x^2y^3}{36x^2} = -\dfrac{y^3}{12}$

c)   $\dfrac{(2x^2y)^4}{3xy^5} = \dfrac{16x^8y^4}{3xy^5} = \dfrac{16x^7}{3y}$

d)   $5(5xy)^2(x^3y) = 5(25x^2y^2)(x^3y) =$
                     $125x^5y^3$

Here are some more to try. Use the properties of exponents to write each of the following expressions in a simpler form.

1.   $3x^2 \cdot x$

2.   $\dfrac{n^{12}}{n^3}$

3.   $(x^3)^2$

4.   $(-2x^2)(-2x)$

5.   $\dfrac{-8x^6y^2}{-4xy}$

6.   $(2x^3)^3$

7.   $(10^3)^4$

8.   $3^2 \cdot 3^5$

9.   $10^5 \div 10^3$

10.   $x^2y^3 \cdot x^3y^4$

11.   $(x^3)^4$

12.   $\dfrac{6x^2y^3}{2xy}$

13.   $-3x^2 \cdot 4x^3$

14.   $(2x^2)^3$

15.   $(x^3y)^2(2x)^3$

16.   $\dfrac{m^{16}y^{31}}{m^{12}y^{17}}$

17.   $\left(6x^3z\right)^3$

18.   $\left(3x^2\right)^2 \div \left(6x^4\right)$

19.   $(5x)^2(3y)^3$

20.   $\left(3x^{11}z^5\right)^2$

21.   $(2b)^5\left(3k^2\right)^2$

22.   $\left(\dfrac{3x^2}{6x^5}\right)^3$

23.   $(6x)^2 \div \left(24x^3\right)$

24.   $\dfrac{6x^2y^3}{2xy}$

**Answers:**

1. $3x^3$    2. $n^9$    3. $x^6$    4. $4x^3$    5. $2x^5y$    6. $8x^9$

7. $10^{12}$    8. $3^7$    9. $10^2$    10. $x^5y^7$    11. $x^{12}$    12. $3xy^2$

13. $-12x^5$    14. $8x^6$    15. $8x^9y^2$    16. $m^4y^{14}$    17. $216x^9z^3$    18. $\frac{3}{2}$

19. $675x^2y^3$    20. $9x^{22}y^{10}$    21. $288b^5k^4$    22. $\frac{1}{8x^9}$    23. $\frac{3}{2x}$    24. $3xy^2$

Milepost Number 4

FX-36

Solving Systems of Linear Equations in Two Variables

You can solve systems of equations with a variety of methods. You can graph, use the Substitution Method, or the Elimination Method. Each method works best with certain forms of equations. Here are some examples and then we can return to the original problem.

For each system below, determine which method would be best (easiest) to use. Then solve the system to find the point of intersection.

a)　$x = 4y - 7$
　　$3x - 2y = 1$

b)　$y = \frac{3}{4}x - 1$
　　$y = -\frac{1}{3}x - 1$

c)　$x + 2y = 16$
　　$x - y = 2$

d)　$x + 3y = 4$
　　$3x - y = 2$

Although the method that is easiest for one person may not be the easiest for another, the most common methods are shown on the next two pages. You should use the method you are comfortable with and with which you are most successful.

a) $x = 4y - 7$
$3x - 2y = 1$

**Substitution:** Substitute $4y - 7$ for x in the second equation.

$3(4y - 7) - 2y = 1$
$12y - 21 - 2y = 1$
$10y - 21 = 1$
$10y = 22$
$y = \frac{22}{10} = 2.2$

Find x:
$x = 4(2.2) - 7$
$x = 8.8 - 7 = 1.8$

Solution: $(1.8, 2.2)$

b) $y = \frac{3}{4}x - 1$
$y = -\frac{1}{3}x - 1$

**Graphing:** Normally graphing is not the best way to solve a system of equations, but since both equations are in y-form and if you happened to notice that they have the same y-intercept, you can tell that they cross at $(0, -1)$ the y-intercept. We did not actually graph here, but we used the principles of the graphs to solve the system of equations. Substitution will work nicely as well.

Solution: $(0, -1)$

c) $x + 2y = 16$
$x - y = 2$

**Elimination:** Subtract the second equation from the first.

$0 + 3y = 14$
$3y = 14$
$y = \frac{14}{3}$

Find x by substituting $y = \frac{14}{3}$ into the second equation:
$x - \frac{14}{3} = 2$
$x = 2 + \frac{14}{3} = \frac{20}{3}$

Solution: $\left(\frac{20}{3}, \frac{14}{3}\right)$

d) $x + 3y = 4$
$3x - y = 2$

**Elimination with a multiplication first.** Multiply the bottom equation by 3 and add it to the top equation.

$\phantom{+}\quad x + 3y = 4$
$+\quad 9x - 3y = 6$
$\phantom{+}\quad\overline{\phantom{x}10x\phantom{xxx} = 10}$
$\phantom{+}\quad\phantom{xx}x = 1$

Find y by substituting $x = 1$ into the second equation:
$3(1) - y = 2$
$3 - y = 2$
$1 = y$

Solution: $(1, 1)$

Now we can go back and look at the original problem.
Solve this system of linear equations in two variables:  $5x - 4y = 7$
$2y + 6x = 22$

You may use substitution or elimination but both methods need a little work to get started.

## Substitution method:

Before we can substitute we need to isolate one of the variables. Solve the second equation for y and it becomes

$y = 11 - 3x.$

Now substitute 11 - 3x for y in the first equation and solve.

$5x - 4(11 - 3x) = 7$
$5x - 44 + 12x = 7$
$17x - 44 = 7$
$17x = 51$
$x = 3$

Solve for y;
$y = 11 - 3(3) = 2$

Solution (3, 2)

## Elimination method:

Before we can eliminate we need to rearrange the second equation so that the variables line up.

$5x - 4y = 7$
$6x + 2y = 22$

Now multiply the second equation by 2 and add to eliminate y.

$$\begin{array}{r} 5x - 4y = 7 \\ + \ 12x + 4y = 44 \\ \hline 17x \qquad = 51 \\ x = 3 \end{array}$$

Solve for y in the first equation:
$5(3) - 4y = 7$
$-4y = -8$
$y = 2$

Solution (3, 2)

---

Here are some more to try. Find the solution to these systems of linear equations. Use the method of your choice.

1. $y = 3x - 1$
   $2x - 3y = 10$

2. $x = -\frac{1}{2}y + 4$
   $8x + 3y = 31$

3. $2y = 4x + 10$
   $6x + 2y = 10$

4. $3x - 5y = -14$
   $x + 5y = 22$

5. $4x + 5y = 11$
   $2x + 6y = 16$

6. $x + 2y = 5$
   $x + y = 5$

7. $y = 2x - 3$
   $x - y = -4$

8. $y + 2 = x$
   $3x - 3y = x + 14$

9. $2x + y = 7$
   $x + 5y = 12$

10. $y = \frac{3}{5}x - 2$
    $y = \frac{x}{10} + 1$

11. $2x + y = -2x + 5$
    $3x + 2y = 2x + 3y$

12. $4x - 3y = -10$
    $x = \frac{1}{4}y - 1$

---

Answers:

1. (-1, -4)   2. (7/2, 1)   3. (0, 5)   4. (2, 4)   5. ( -1,3)   6. (5, 0)

7. (7, 11)   8. (-8, -10)   9. ( $^{23}/_9$, $^{17}/_9$) 10. (6, 1.6)   11. (1, 1)   12. ($\frac{-1}{4}$, 3)

Milepost Number 5

FX-112

Multiplying Polynomials

The product of polynomials can be found by using the distributive property or using generic rectangles. If you are multiplying two binomials, you can also use the F.O.I.L. method.

Let us look at an example for each of the three methods before returning to the original problem.

In multiplying binomials, such as $(3x - 2)(4x + 5)$, you might use a generic rectangle.

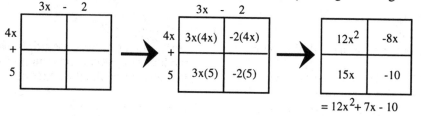

$$= 12x^2 + 7x - 10$$

You might view multiplying binomials with generic rectangles as a form of **double distribution**. The $4x$ is distributed across the first row of the generic rectangle and then the $5$ is distributed across the second row of the generic rectangle. Some people write it this way:

$$(3x - 2)(4x + 5) = (3x - 2)(4x) + (3x - 2)(5) = 12x^2 - 8x + 15x - 10$$
$$= 12x^2 + 7x - 10.$$

Another approach to multiplying binomials is to use the mnemonic 'F.O.I.L.' F.O.I.L. is an acronym for First, Outside, Inside, Last:

**F.**  multiply the FIRST terms of each binomial $\qquad (3x)(4x) = 12x^2$
**O.**  multiply the OUTSIDE terms $\qquad\qquad\qquad (3x)(5) = 15x$
**I.**  multiply the INSIDE terms $\qquad\qquad\qquad\quad (-2)(4x) = -8x$
**L.**  multiply the LAST terms of each binomial $\qquad (-2)(5) = -10$

Finally, we combine like terms: $12x^2 + 15x - 8x - 10 = 12x^2 + 7x - 10$.

Now we can go back and try the original problem again using a variety of methods.

Multiply and simplify.

a) $(x + 1)(2x^2 - 3)$
We can use F.O.I.L. here.

$$F \quad O \quad I \quad L$$

$(x)(2x^2) \quad (x)(-3) \quad (1)(2x^2) \quad (1)(-3)$

$2x^3 - 3x + 2x^2 - 3 = 2x^3 + 2x^2 - 3x - 3$

b) $(x + 1)(x - 2x^2 + 3)$

Using generic rectangles

$$x^2 - 2x + 3$$

| | $x^2$ | $-2x$ | $3$ |
|---|---|---|---|
| x | $x^3$ | $-2x^2$ | $3x$ |
| + 1 | $x^2$ | $-2x$ | $3$ |

$$x^3 - x^2 + x + 3$$

c) $2(x + 3)^2$
Write our the factors and distribute.

$2(x +3)(x +3) = (2x + 6)(x + 3)$
$(2x + 6)(x) + (2x + 6)(3)$
$2x^2 + 6x + 6x + 18 = 2x^2 + 12x + 18$

d) $(x + 1)(2x - 3)^2$
Write out the factors. Multiply two of the factors together and then multiply that answer by the third factor.

$(x + 1)(2x - 3)(2x - 3)$
$(2x^2 - x - 3)(2x - 3)$
$4x^3 - 6x^2 - 2x^2 + 3x - 6x + 9$
$4x^3 - 8x^2 - 3x + 9$

Here are some more to try.  Multiply and simplify.

1.  $(2x + 3)(x - 7)$

2.  $(4x - 2)(3x + 5)$

3.  $(x - 2)(x^2 + 3x + 5)$

4.  $(x + 8)(x - 12)$

5.  $4(3x - 5)^2$

6.  $(2x + y)(2x - y)$

7.  $(2x + 3)^2$

8.  $(5x - 8)(2x + 7)$

9.  $(x + 3)(x^2 - 4x + 7)$

10.  $(x + 7)(x - 11)$

11.  $-8x^3(5x^2 + 7)$

12.  $(2x + y)(x + 1)^2$

Answers:

1. $2x^2 - 11x - 21$   2. $12x^2 + 14x - 10$   3. $x^3 + x^2 - x - 10$   4. $x^2 - 4x - 96$

5. $36x^2 - 120x + 100$   6. $4x^2 - y^2$   7. $4x^2 + 12x + 9$   8. $10x^2 + 19x - 56$

9. $x^3 - x^2 - 5x + 21$   10. $x^2 - 4x - 77$   11. $-40x^5 - 56x^3$

12. $2x^3 + 4x^2 + 2x + x^2y + 2xy + y$

Factoring quadratics means changing the expression into a product of factors or to find the dimensions of the generic rectangle. You can use diamond problems with generic rectangles or just guess and check with F.O.I.L. or the distributive property. Here are some examples using diamonds and generic rectangles:

Diamond Problems can be used to help factor easier quadratics like $x^2 + 6x + 8$.

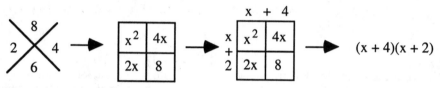

We can modify the diamond method slightly to factor problems that are a little different in that they no longer have a "1" as the coefficient of $x^2$. For example, factor:

$2x^2 + 7x + 3$

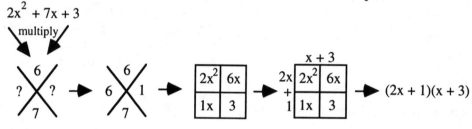

Another problem: $5x^2 - 13x + 6$. Note that the upper value in the diamond is the <u>product</u> of 5 and 6.

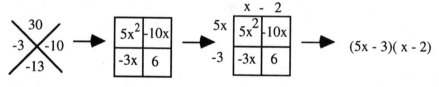

Now we can go back and try the original problem. Factor each quadratic.

a) $4x^2 - 1$

b) $4x^2 + 4x + 1$

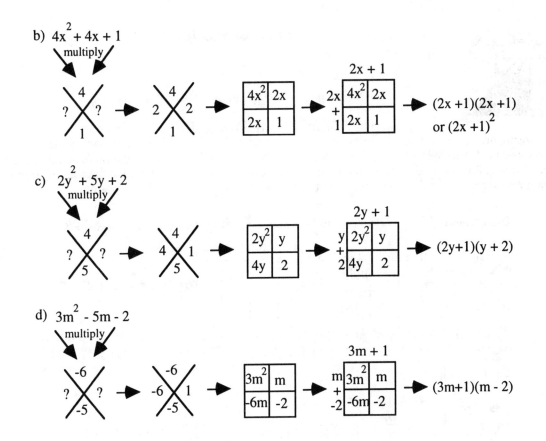

c) $2y^2 + 5y + 2$

d) $3m^2 - 5m - 2$

Here are some more to try. Factor each expression

1.  $2x^2 + 7x - 4$

2.  $7x^2 + 13x - 2$

3.  $3x^2 + 11x + 10$

4.  $x^2 + 5x - 24$

5.  $2x^2 + 5x - 7$

6.  $3x^2 - 13x + 4$

7.  $64x^2 + 16x + 1$

8.  $5x^2 + 12x - 9$

9.  $8x^2 + 24x + 10$

10. $6x^3 + 31x^2 + 5x$

**Answers:**

1. $(x + 4)(2x - 1)$          2. $(7x - 1)(x + 2)$          3. $(3x + 5)(x + 2)$

4. $(x + 8)(x - 3)$  5. $(2x + 7)(x - 1)$   6. $(3x - 1)(x - 4)$          7. $(8x + 1)^2$

8. $(5x - 3)(x + 3)$                          9. $2(4x^2 + 12x + 5) = 2(2x + 1)(2x + 5)$

10. $x(6x^2 + 31x + 5) = x(6x + 1)(x + 5)$

Milepost Number 7

PG-30

# Solving for One Variable in an Equation

# or Formula with Two or More Variables

When you solve for one variable in an equation with two or more variables it usually helps to start by simplifying, for example, removing parentheses and fractions. Then isolate the desired variable in the same way as you solve an equation with only one variable. Here are two examples.

Solve for y: $\frac{x - 3y}{4} + 2(x + 1) = 7$

First multiply all terms by 4 to remove the fractions and then simplify.

$$(4)\frac{x - 3y}{4} + (4)2(x + 1) = (4)7$$
$$x - 3y + 8x + 8 = 28$$
$$9x - 3y = 28$$

Then solve for y.

$$-3y = -9x + 28$$
$$y = \frac{-9x + 28}{-3} = 3x - \frac{28}{3}$$

Solve for y: $x + 2\sqrt{y + 1} = 3x + 4$

First isolate the radical.

$$x + 2\sqrt{y + 1} = 3x + 4$$
$$2\sqrt{y + 1} = 2x + 4$$
$$\sqrt{y + 1} = x + 2$$

Then remove the radical by squaring both sides. Remember $(x + 2)^2 = (x+2)(x+2)$.

$$(\sqrt{y + 1})^2 = (x + 2)^2$$
$$y + 1 = x^2 + 4x + 4$$
$$y = x^2 + 4x + 3$$

Now we can go back and look at the original problem.

Rewrite the following equations so that you could enter them into the graphing calculator. In other words, solve for y.

a)  $x - 3(y + 2) = 6$
    $x - 3y - 6 = 6$
    $x - 3y = 12$
    $-3y = -x + 12$
    $y = \frac{-x + 12}{-3}$ or $y = \frac{1}{3}x - 4$

b)  $\frac{6x - 1}{y} - 3 = 2$
    $\frac{6x - 1}{y} = 5$
    $(y)\frac{6x - 1}{y} = (y)5$
    $6x - 1 = 5y$
    $y = \frac{6x - 1}{5}$ or $y = \frac{6}{5}x - \frac{1}{5}$

c)  $\sqrt{y - 4} = x + 1$
    $(\sqrt{y - 4})^2 = (x + 1)^2$
    $y - 4 = (x + 1)^2$
    $y = (x + 1)^2 + 4$ or $x^2 + 2x + 5$

d)  $\sqrt{y + 4} = x + 2$
    $(\sqrt{y + 4})^2 = (x + 2)^2$
    $y + 4 = x^2 + 4x + 4$
    $y = x^2 + 4x$

Here are some more to try.  Solve for y.

1.  $2x - 5y = 7$  2.  $2(x + y) + 1 = x - 4$

3.  $4(x - y) + 12 = 2x - 4$  4.  $x = \frac{1}{5}y - 2$

5.  $x = y^2 + 1$  6.  $\frac{5x + 2}{y} - 1 = 5$

7.  $\sqrt{y + 3} = x - 2$  8.  $(y + 2)^2 = x^2 + 9$

9.  $\frac{x + 2}{4} + \frac{4 - y}{2} = 3$  10.  $\sqrt{2y + 1} = x + 3$

11  $x = \frac{2}{4 - y}$  12.  $x = \frac{y + 1}{y - 1}$

**Answers**:

1.  $y = \frac{2}{5}x - \frac{7}{5}$  2.  $y = -\frac{1}{2}x - \frac{5}{2}$  3.  $y = \frac{1}{2}x + 4$  4.  $y = 5x + 10$  5.  $y = \pm\sqrt{x - 1}$

6.  $y = \frac{5}{6}x + \frac{1}{3}$  7.  $y = x^2 - 4x + 1$  8.  $y = \pm\sqrt{x^2 + 9} - 2$  9.  $y = \frac{1}{2}x - 1$

10.  $y = \frac{1}{2}x^2 + 3x + 4$  11.  $y = \frac{4x - 2}{x}$  12.  $y = \frac{x + 1}{x - 1}$

# Milepost Number 8

## PG-53

## Find the Slope of the Line Through Two Given Points

## and the Distance Between the Two Points

To compute either the slope or the distance determined by two points, a generic right triangle provides a good diagram. The slope is the ratio of the vertical leg over the horizontal leg. (Remember to check whether it is negative or positive.) The distance is the length of the hypotenuse which is found by using the Pythagorean theorem. Here are two examples.

Use a generic triangle to find the slope and the distance between the given points.

a)    (-2, 3) and (3, 5)

b)    (-7, 20) and (3, -5)

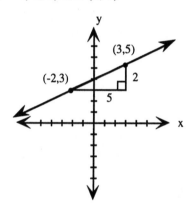

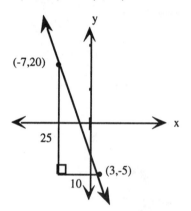

Using an accurate graph the length of the legs can be seen as 2 and 5. The line slopes in the positive direction.

slope = $\frac{\text{vertical change}}{\text{horizontal change}} = \frac{2}{5}$ . The distance is found by $d^2 = 2^2 + 5^2 = 29$. So the distance $d = \sqrt{29} \approx 5.39$.

A point moving from left to right along this line moves up, a positive direction.

Sketching a generic graph, the vertical change or difference in y-values is 25. The horizontal change or difference in x-values is 10. The line slopes in the negative direction.

slope = $\frac{\text{vertical change}}{\text{horizontal change}} = -\frac{25}{10} = -\frac{5}{2}$. The distance is found by $d^2 = 25^2 + 10^2 = 725$. So the distance $d = \sqrt{725} \approx 26.92$.

A point moving along this line from left to right moves down in a negative direction.

We can now go back and try the original problem. Use a generic triangle to find the slope of the line through the two given points and then find the distance between the two points.

a)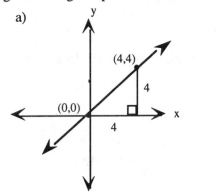

slope = $\frac{4}{4}$ = 1

d = $\sqrt{4^2 + 4^2}$ = $\sqrt{32}$ ≈ 5.66

b)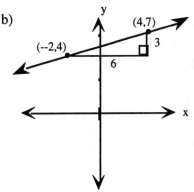

slope = $\frac{3}{6}$ = $\frac{1}{2}$

d = $\sqrt{6^2 + 3^2}$ = $\sqrt{45}$ ≈ 6.71

c) Sometimes people like to use formulas that represent the diagram. Using the points (12, 18) and (-16, -19):

slope = $\frac{y_2 - y_1}{x_2 - x_1}$ = $\frac{-16 - 12}{-19 - 18}$

$= \frac{-28}{-37} = \frac{28}{37}$.

distance = $\sqrt{(y_2 - y_1)^2 + (x_2 - x_1)^2}$

$= \sqrt{(-28)^2 + (-37)^2}$ = $\sqrt{2153}$ ≈ 46.40.

$y_2 - y_1$ and $x_2 - x_1$ represent the lengths of the vertical and horizontal legs respectively.

d) Using the formulas again, this time with the points (0, 0) and (25, 25):

slope = $\frac{25 - 0}{25 - 0}$ = 1

distance = $\sqrt{(25)^2 + (25)^2}$

$= \sqrt{1250}$ ≈ 35.35.

Here are some more to try. Find the slope of the line through the two given points and then find the distance between the two points.

1.  (1, 2) and (4, 5)      2.   (7, 3) and (5, 4)      3.   (-6, 8) and (-4, 5)

4.  (5, 0) and (0, 1)      5.   (10, 2) and (2, 24)      6.   (-6, 5) and (8, -3)

7.  (-3, 5) and (2, 12)      8.   (-6, -3) and (2, 10)      9.   (-15, 39) and (29, -2)

**Answers**:

1. m = 1   d = $\sqrt{18}$      2. m = $-\frac{1}{2}$   d = $\sqrt{5}$      3. m = $-\frac{3}{2}$   d = $\sqrt{13}$

4. m = $-\frac{1}{5}$   d = $\sqrt{26}$      5. m = $-\frac{11}{4}$   d = $\sqrt{546}$      6. m = $-\frac{4}{7}$   d = $\sqrt{260}$

7. m = $\frac{7}{5}$   d = $\sqrt{74}$      8. m = $\frac{13}{8}$   d = $\sqrt{233}$      9. m = $-\frac{41}{44}$   d = $\sqrt{3617}$

Milepost Number 9

PG-149

Using Function Notation and Calculating the Domain and Range

We should first review some vocabulary and notation.

An equation is called a FUNCTION if there exists no more than one output for each input. If an equation has two or more outputs for a single input value, it is not a function. The set of possible inputs of an equation is called the **DOMAIN**, while the set of all possible outputs of an equation is called the **RANGE**.

Functions are often given names, most commonly "f," "g" or "h." The notation **f(x)** represents the output of a function, named f, when x is the input. It is pronounced "f of x." The notation g(2), pronounced "g of 2," represents the output of function g when x = 2.

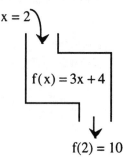

$x = 2$

$f(x) = 3x + 4$

$f(2) = 10$

Similarly, the function y = 3x + 4 and f(x) = 3x + 4 represent the same function. Notice that this notation is interchangeable, that is, y = f(x). In some textbooks, 3x + 4 is called the **RULE** of the function. The graph of f(x) = 3x + 4 is a line extending forever in both the x and y directions so the domain and range of f(x) are both all real numbers.

For each function below, tell the domain and range. Then find f(2) and solve f(x) = 3.

f(x) = | x - 1 | - 2

Since you can use any real number for x in this equation, the domain is all real numbers. The smallest possible result for y is -2, so the range is y ≥ -2. By looking at the graph or substituting x = 2 into the equation, f(2) = | 2 - 1 | - 2 = -1. To solve f(x) = 3, find the points where the horizontal line y = 3 intersects the graph or solve the equation.

$$3 = | x - 1 | - 2,$$
$$x = -4 \text{ or } 6.$$

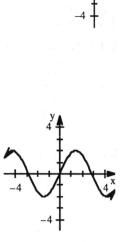

f(x) is an unknown equation.

Any real number can replace x, so the domain is all reals. The y-values are between -2 to +2 so the range is -2 ≤ y ≤ 2. By inspection f(2) ≈ 1.8. Since -2 ≤ y ≤ 2, f(x) = 3 has no solution.

$f(x) = \sqrt{x} + 3$

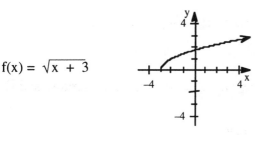

You can only use numbers -3 or larger for x-values so the domain is $x \geq 3$. The smallest possible y-value is zero. The range is $y \geq 0$. Looking at the graph gives an approximate answer when $x = 2$, $y \approx 2.25$ or substituting $x = 2$ into the equation, $f(2) = \sqrt{2+3} = \sqrt{5}$. To solve $f(x) = 3$, find the point where $y = 3$ intersects the graph or solve

$$3 = \sqrt{x} + 3$$
$$x = 6$$

Now we can go back and try the original problem.

Given $g(x) = 2(x + 3)^2$. State the domain and range. The graph is a parabola opening upward with locator point (-3, 0). The domain is all real numbers and the range is $y \geq 0$.

a)  $g(-5) = 2(-5 + 3)^2 = 2(-2)^2 = 8$

b)  $g(a + 1) = 2(a + 1 + 3)^2 = 2(a + 4)^2 = 2(a^2 + 8a + 16) = 2a^2 + 16a + 32$

c)  If $g(x) = 32$, then
$$32 = 2(x + 3)^2$$
$$16 = (x + 3)^2$$
$$\pm 4 = x + 3$$
$$x = 1 \text{ or } -7$$

d)  If $g(x) = 0$, then
$$0 = 2(x + 3)^2$$
$$0 = (x + 3)^2$$
$$0 = x + 3$$
$$x = -3$$

Here are some more to try.

For each graph, tell the domain and range

1.   2.   3.

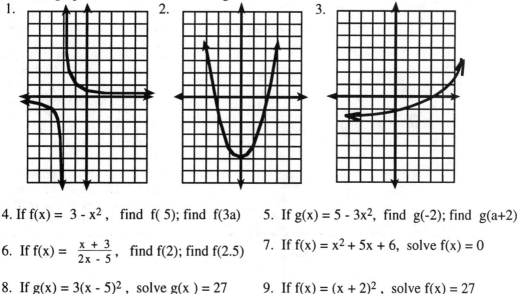

4. If $f(x) = 3 - x^2$, find f( 5); find f(3a)

5. If $g(x) = 5 - 3x^2$, find g(-2); find g(a+2)

6. If $f(x) = \dfrac{x + 3}{2x - 5}$, find f(2); find f(2.5)

7. If $f(x) = x^2 + 5x + 6$, solve f(x) = 0

8. If $g(x) = 3(x - 5)^2$, solve g(x ) = 27

9. If $f(x) = (x + 2)^2$, solve f(x) = 27

**Answers**:

1. D: all x ≠ -2, R all y ≠ 0.   2. D: all x, R: all y ≥ -5   3. D: all x, range y > -2

4. -22, 3 - 9a²        5. -7, -3a² - 12a - 7        6. -5, not possible

7. -2, -3            8. 8, 2                9. -2 ± √27

Milepost Number 10

LS-53

Writing the Equation of a Line Given Two Points

The equation of a line is y = mx + b where m represents the slope and b represents the y-intercept. One way to find the equation is to calculate the slope and then solve for the y-intercept. A second method is to use the two points to write two equations involving m and b and then solve the system. Here is an example of each method.

Find an equation of the line passing through (9, 5) and (6, 2).

Method One

Using the points we make a generic slope triangle and find the slope to be m = -$\frac{3}{3}$ = -1. The equation now looks like y = -1x + b.

We can use either one of the two original points here; I will use (9, 5). Substitute the x and y values into the equation to give:

$$5 = -1(9) + b$$

which we can solve for b.

$$5 = -9 + b$$
$$14 = b$$

Therefore the equation of the line is y = -1x + 14.

Method Two

Substitute the 2 points in for x and y in the equation y = mx + b:

$$5 = 9m + b$$
$$2 = 6m + b$$

Subtracting the second equation from the first gives:

3 = -3m so m = -1. We can now find b by substituting m = -1 into either equation. Using the first equation:
5 = 9(-1) + b
which we can solve for b.

$$5 = -9 + b$$
$$14 = b$$

Therefore the equation of the line is y = -1x + 14.

Now we can go back and try the original problem. Write an equation for each line defined below.

    a)    The line through points (-1, 4) and (2, 1).

    b)    The line through points (6, 3) and (5, 5).

Using the first method for part (a). For the points we make a generic slope triangle and find the slope to be

$m = -\dfrac{3}{3} = -1$. The equation now looks like $y = -1x + b$.

We can use either one of the two original points here; I will use (-1, 4). Substitute the x and y values into the equation to give:

$$4 = -1(-1) + b$$

which we can solve for b.

$$4 = 1 + b$$
$$3 = b$$

Therefore the equation of the line is $y = -1x + 3$.

Using the second method for part (b). Substitute the 2 points in for x and y in the equation $y = mx + b$:

$3 = 6m + b$
$5 = 5m + b$

    Subtracting the second equation from the first gives:

$-2 = 1m$ so $m = -2$.

We can now find b by substituting $m = -2$ into either equation. Using the first equation:

$3 = 6(-2) + b$

which we can solve for b.

$$3 = -12 + b$$
$$15 = b$$

Therefore the equation of the line is $y = -2x + 15$.

Here are some more to try. Find an equation of the line through the given points.

1. (2, 3) and (1, 2)        2. (-3, -5) and (-1, 0)        3. (4, 2) and (8, -1)

4. (1, 3) and (5, 7)        5. (0, 4) and (-1, -5)        6. (-3, 2) and (2, -3)

7. (4, 2) and (-1, -2)        8. (3, 1) and (-2, -4)        9. (4, 1) and (4, 10)

**Answers:**

1. $y = x + 1$    2. $y = \dfrac{5}{2}x + \dfrac{5}{2}$    3. $y = -\dfrac{3}{4}x + 5$    4. $y = x + 2$    5. $y = 9x + 4$

6. $y = -x - 1$    7. $y = \dfrac{4}{5}x - \dfrac{6}{5}$    8. $y = x - 2$    9. $x = 4$

# LS-110

## Slopes of Parallel and Perpendicular Lines

Parallel lines have the same slopes. For perpendicular lines, the product of the slopes equal negative one. Here are two examples of problems involving parallel and perpendicular lines.

Find the equation of the line that is parallel to $y = \frac{1}{2}x - 5$ and passes through the point $(4, 10)$.

Any line parallel to the line $y = \frac{1}{2}x - 5$ which has slope $\frac{1}{2}$, must also have slope $\frac{1}{2}$. The equation must look like $y = \frac{1}{2}x + b$. Substituting the given point in place of x and y we have:
$$10 = \frac{1}{2}(4) + b$$
Solving we find that $b = 8$ so that the equation is $y = \frac{1}{2}x + 8$.

Find the equation of the line that is perpendicular to $y = \frac{1}{2}x - 5$ and passes through the point $(4, 10)$.

Since the original line has slope $\frac{1}{2}$, a perpendicular line must have slope -2. The equation must look like $y = -2x + b$. Substituting the given point in place of x and y we have:
$$10 = -2(4) + b$$
Solving we find that $b = 18$ so that the equation is $y = -2x + 18$.

We will now go back and solve the original problem

Find an equation for each of the lines described below.

The line with slope $\frac{1}{3}$ through the point $(0, 5)$.

The slope and the y-intercept of the line are both given so the equation is:

$$y = \frac{1}{3}x + 5.$$

The line parallel to $y = 2x - 5$ through the point $(1, 7)$.

The slope must be 2 so the equation must look like $y = 2x + b$. Substituting the point for x and y we have:
$$7 = 2(1) + b.$$
Solving we find that $b = 5$ so that the equation is $y = 2x + 5$.

The line perpendicular to $y = 2x - 5$ through the point $(1, 7)$.

The slope must be $-\frac{1}{2}$ so the equation must look like $y = -\frac{1}{2}x + b$. Substituting the coordinates of the point for x and y we have:

$$7 = -\frac{1}{2}(1) + b.$$

Solving we find that $b = 7\frac{1}{2}$ so that

the equation is $y = -\frac{1}{2}x + 7\frac{1}{2}$.

The line through the point $(0,0)$ so that the tangent of the angle it makes with the x-axis is 2.

The tangent of the angle is the same as the slope. The y-intercept is given so the equation must be:
$$y = 2x$$

Here are some more to try. Find an equation for each of the lines described below.

1. The line with slope $\frac{1}{3}$ passing through $(-2, 5)$

2. The line through the point $(3, 0)$ so that the tangent of the angle it makes with the x-axis is -2.

3. The line parallel to $y = \frac{2}{3}x + 5$ passing through $(3, 2)$

4. The line perpendicular to $y = \frac{2}{3}x + 5$ passing through $(3, 2)$.

5. The line parallel to $3x + 4y = 4$ passing through $(-4, 2)$.

6. The line perpendicular to $3x + 4y = 4$ passing through $(-4, 2)$.

7. The line parallel to the line determined by $(-3, -2)$ and $(2, 4)$ passing through $(0, -1)$.

8. The line perpendicular to $2x - 3y = 6$ passing through $(0, 3)$.

9. The line parallel to $y = 7$ passing through $(-2, 5)$.

10. The line perpendicular to $y = 7$ passing through $(-2, 5)$.

**Answers**:

1. $y = \frac{1}{3}x + 5\frac{2}{3}$    2. $y = -2x + 6$    3. $y = \frac{2}{3}x$    4. $y = -\frac{3}{2}x + 6\frac{1}{2}$

5. $y = -\frac{3}{4}x + 1$    6. $y = \frac{4}{3}x - \frac{22}{3}$    7. $y = \frac{6}{5}x - 1$    8. $y = -\frac{3}{2}x + 3$

9. $y = 5$    10. $x = -2$

# Graphing Linear Inequalities

Graphing inequalities is very similar to graphing equations. First you graph the line. With inequalities you also need to determine if the line is solid (included) or dashed (not included) and which side of the line to shade. Here are two examples together in a system of inequalities.

On graph paper, graph and shade the solution for each of the systems of inequalities below. Describe each resulting region.

$$y \leq \frac{2}{5}x$$
$$y > 5 - x$$

First, we treat the inequality as an equation: $y = \frac{2}{5}x$. We can graph it using the slope, $\frac{2}{5}$, and the y-intercept, $(0, 0)$. This line divides the grid into two regions. Choose a point in either region and check whether or not it makes the original inequality true. If the point $(0, 1)$ is the test point.

$$1 \overset{?}{\leq} \frac{2}{5}(0) \quad \text{FALSE!}$$

Since points above the line make the inequality false, points below the line must make it true. Therefore we shade all the points below the line to represent the solution.

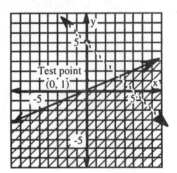

Next we do the same thing for the second inequality. First treat it as an equation and graph it on the same set of axes. The slope is -1 and the y-intercept is $(0, 5)$. This line is dashed (not solid) because the inequality is strictly greater than, not greater than or equal to. The line has divided the grid into two regions and we will chose a point on one side as a test point. You can use the same point as last time. (This is not necessary and may not always be feasible. Here it is a convenient point.)

$$1 \overset{?}{>} 5 - 0 \quad \text{FALSE!}$$

Since our test point made the inequality false, the opposite side would make the inequality true. For the second inequality we shade above the line and to the right.

Putting these two inequalities together with their overlapping shading gives us the solution to the system of inequalities. In this case the solution is the darkest region, with a solid line above the region and a dashed line bordering below (left).

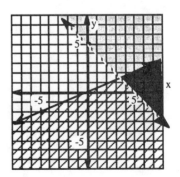

Now we can go back to the original problem. For this system of inequalities:

$$y \leq -2x + 3 \qquad y \geq x \qquad x \geq -1$$

a) Draw the graph.

b) Find the area of the shaded region.

Start by looking at the equation of the line that marks the edge of each inequality. The first has slope -2 and y-intercept (0, 3). Checking (0, 1) gives a true statement so we shade below the solid line. The second has slope 1 and y-intercept (0, 0). Again checking (0, 1) gives a true statement so we shade above the solid line. The third is a vertical line at x = -1. Checking the point tells us to shade the right side. The overlapping shading is a triangle with vertices (-1, 5), (1, 1), and (-1, -1). The shaded area $= \frac{1}{2}(6)(2)$.

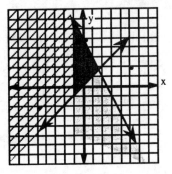

Here are a few more to try. Graph and shade the solution for the system of inequalities below.

1.  $y \leq -x + 2$
    $y \leq 3x - 6$

2.  $y > \frac{2}{3}x + 4$
    $y < \frac{7}{12}x + 5$

3.  $x < 3$
    $y \geq -2$

4.  $y \leq 4x + 16$
    $y > -\frac{4}{3}x - 4$

**Answers:**

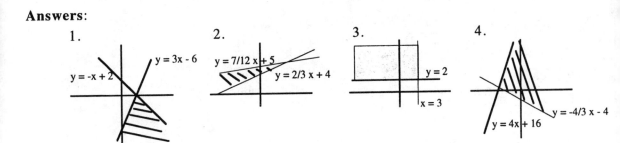

# Multiplication and Division of Rational Expressions

To multiply or divide rational expressions you follow the same procedures as you did with numerical fractions. However, you need to first factor in order to simplify. Here are two examples

**Problem A:** Multiply $\dfrac{x^2+6x}{(x+6)^2} \cdot \dfrac{x^2+7x+6}{x^2-1}$ and simplify your result.

After factoring, our expression becomes: $\dfrac{x(x+6)}{(x+6)(x+6)} \cdot \dfrac{(x+6)(x+1)}{(x+1)(x-1)}$

After multiplying, reorder the factors: $\dfrac{(x+6)}{(x+6)} \cdot \dfrac{(x+6)}{(x+6)} \cdot \dfrac{x}{(x-1)} \cdot \dfrac{(x+1)}{(x+1)}$

Since $\dfrac{(x+6)}{(x+6)}=1$ and $\dfrac{(x+1)}{(x+1)}=1$, simplify: $1 \cdot 1 \cdot \dfrac{x}{x-1} \cdot 1 \Rightarrow \dfrac{x}{x-1}$.

**Problem B:** Divide $\dfrac{x^2-4x-5}{x^2-4x+4} \div \dfrac{x^2-2x-15}{x^2+4x-12}$ and simplify your result.

First, change to a multiplication expression: $\dfrac{x^2-4x-5}{x^2-4x+4} \cdot \dfrac{x^2+4x-12}{x^2-2x-15}$

After factoring, we get: $\dfrac{(x-5)(x+1)}{(x-2)(x-2)} \cdot \dfrac{(x+6)(x-2)}{(x-5)(x+3)}$

Reorder the factors: $\dfrac{(x-5)}{(x-5)} \cdot \dfrac{(x-2)}{(x-2)} \cdot \dfrac{(x+1)}{(x-2)} \cdot \dfrac{(x+6)}{(x+3)}$

Since $\dfrac{(x-5)}{(x-5)}=1$ and $\dfrac{(x-2)}{(x-2)}=1$, simplify: $\dfrac{(x+1)(x+6)}{(x-2)(x+3)}$

Thus, $\dfrac{x^2-4x-5}{x^2-4x+4} \div \dfrac{x^2-2x-15}{x^2+4x-12} = \dfrac{(x+1)(x+6)}{(x-2)(x+3)}$ or $\dfrac{x^2+7x+6}{x^2+x-6}$

Now we can go back and try the original problem

Think about factoring first, then perform each operation. Simplify when it is helpful.

a) $\dfrac{x^2+5x+6}{x^2-4x} \cdot \dfrac{4x}{x+2} = \dfrac{(x+2)(x+3)}{x(x-4)} \cdot \dfrac{4x}{(x+2)} = \dfrac{4(x+3)}{(x-4)}$

c) $\dfrac{x^2-2x}{x^2-4x+4} \div \dfrac{4x^2}{x-2} = \dfrac{x(x-2)}{(x-2)(x-2)} \cdot \dfrac{(x-2)}{4x \cdot x} = \dfrac{1}{4x}$

Here are some more to try. Perform each operation.

1. $\dfrac{x^2-16}{(x-4)^2} \cdot \dfrac{x^2-3x-18}{x^2-2x-24}$

2. $\dfrac{x^2-x-6}{x^2+3x-10} \cdot \dfrac{x^2+2x-15}{x^2-6x+9} \cdot \dfrac{x^2+4x-21}{x^2+9x+14}$

3. $\dfrac{x^2-x-6}{x^2-x-20} \cdot \dfrac{x^2+6x+8}{x^2-x-6}$

4. $\dfrac{x^2-x-30}{x^2+13x+40} \cdot \dfrac{x^2+11x+24}{x^2-9x+18}$

5. $\dfrac{15-5x}{x^2-x-6} \div \dfrac{5x}{x^2+6x+8}$

6. $\dfrac{17x+119}{x^2+5x-14} \div \dfrac{9x-1}{x^2-3x+2}$

7. $\dfrac{2x^2-5x-3}{3x^2-10x+3} \cdot \dfrac{9x^2-1}{4x^2+4x+1}$

8. $\dfrac{x^2-1}{x^2-6x-7} \div \dfrac{x^3+x^2-2x}{x-7}$

Answers:

**1.** (x+3)/(x-4)  **2.** (x-3)/(x-2)  **3.** (x+2)/(x-5)  **4.** (x+3)/(x-3)

**5.** -(x + 4)/x  **6.** 17(x - 1)/(9x - 1)  **7.** (3x+1)/(2x+1)  **8.** 1/x(x+2)

## Solving Rational Equations

To solve rational equations (equations with fractions) usually it is best to multiply everything by the common denominator to remove the fractions. This process is called FRACTION BUSTERS. Then solve the equation in the usual ways. Here are two examples.

$$\frac{24}{x + 1} = \frac{16}{1}$$

Multiply both sides by the common denominator $(x + 1)$

$$(x + 1)\left(\frac{24}{x + 1}\right) = (x + 1)\left(\frac{16}{1}\right)$$

Then simplify.

$$
\begin{aligned}
24 &= 16(x + 1) \\
24 &= 16x + 16 \\
8 &= 16x \\
\frac{8}{16} &= \frac{16x}{16} \\
x &= \frac{1}{2}
\end{aligned}
$$

$$\frac{5}{2x} + \frac{1}{6} = 8$$

Multiply each term by the common denominator $6x$.

$$\frac{5}{2x} + \frac{1}{6} = 8$$

$$6x\left(\frac{5}{2x} + \frac{1}{6}\right) = 6x(8)$$

Then simplify.

$$6x\left(\frac{5}{2x}\right) + 6x\left(\frac{1}{6}\right) = 48x$$

$$
\begin{aligned}
15 + x &= 48x \\
15 &= 47x \\
x &= \frac{15}{47}
\end{aligned}
$$

Now we can go back any try the original problem. Solve each of the following rational equations.

a)

$$\frac{x}{3} = \frac{4}{x}$$

$$(3x)\left(\frac{x}{3}\right) = (3x)\left(\frac{4}{x}\right)$$
$$x^2 = 12$$
$$x = \pm\sqrt{12} = \pm 2\sqrt{3}$$

b)

$$\frac{x}{x - 1} = \frac{4}{x}$$

$$x(x-1))\left(\frac{x}{x - 1}\right) = x(x-1))\left(\frac{4}{x}\right)$$
$$x^2 = 4(x - 1)$$
$$x^2 - 4x + 4 = 0$$
$$(x - 2)(x - 2) = 0$$
$$x = 2$$

c)

$$\frac{1}{x} + \frac{1}{3x} = 6$$

$$3x\left(\frac{1}{x} + \frac{1}{3x}\right) = 3x(6)$$

$$3x\left(\frac{1}{x}\right) + 3x\left(\frac{1}{3x}\right) = 18x$$

$$3 + 1 = 18x$$

$$4 = 18x$$

$$x = \frac{2}{9}$$

d)

$$\frac{1}{x} + \frac{1}{x+1} = 3$$

$$x(x+1)\left(\frac{1}{x} + \frac{1}{x+1}\right) = x(x+1)3$$

$$x(x+1)\left(\frac{1}{x}\right) + x(x+1)\left(\frac{1}{x+1}\right) = x(x+1)3$$

$$x + 1 + x = 3x^2 + 3x$$

$$0 = 3x^2 + x - 1$$

using the quadratic formula
$$x \approx -0.43, -0.77$$

Here are some more to try.  Solve each of the following rational equations.

1. $\frac{3x}{5} = \frac{x-2}{4}$

2. $\frac{4x-1}{x} = 3x$

3. $\frac{2x}{5} - \frac{1}{3} = \frac{137}{3}$

4. $\frac{4x-1}{x+1} = x-1$

5. $\frac{x}{3} = x + 4$

6. $\frac{x-1}{5} = \frac{3}{x+1}$

7. $\frac{x+6}{3} = x$

8. $\frac{2x+3}{6} + \frac{1}{2} = \frac{x}{2}$

9. $\frac{3}{x} + \frac{5}{x-7} = -2$

10. $\frac{2x+3}{4} - \frac{x-7}{6} = \frac{2x-3}{12}$

Answers:
  1. $-10/7$    2. $1/3, 1$    3. 115    4. 0, 4    5. -6

  6. $\pm 4$    7. 3    8. 6    9. $\frac{3 \pm \sqrt{51}}{2}$    10. -13

# Addition and Subtraction of Rational Expressions

Addition and subtraction of rational expressions is done the same way as addition and subtraction of numerical fractions. You change to a common denominator (if necessary), combine the numerators, and then simplify. Here is an example:

The Least Common Multiple (lowest common denominator) of $(x + 3)(x + 2)$ and $(x + 2)$ is $(x + 3)(x + 2)$.

$$\frac{4}{(x + 2)(x + 3)} + \frac{2x}{x + 2}$$

The denominator of the first fraction already is the Least Common Multiple. To get a common denominator in the <u>second</u> fraction, multiply the fraction by $\frac{x + 3}{x + 3}$, a form of one (1).

$$= \frac{4}{(x + 2)(x + 3)} + \frac{2x}{x + 2} \cdot \frac{(x + 3)}{(x + 3)}$$

Multiply the numerator and denominator of the second term:

$$= \frac{4}{(x + 2)(x + 3)} + \frac{2x(x + 3)}{(x + 2)(x + 3)}$$

Distribute the numerator.

$$= \frac{4}{(x + 2)(x + 3)} + \frac{2x^2 + 6x}{(x + 2)(x + 3)}$$

Add, factor, and simplify.

$$= \frac{2x^2 + 6x + 4}{(x + 2)(x + 3)} = \frac{2(x + 1)(x + 2)}{(x + 2)(x + 3)} = \frac{2(x + 1)}{(x + 3)}$$

Now we can go back and try the original problem. Add or subtract and simplify.

a) $\dfrac{2 - x}{x + 4} + \dfrac{3x + 6}{x + 4} = \dfrac{2 - x + 3x - 6}{x + 4}$

$= \dfrac{2x - 4}{x + 4}$

$= \dfrac{2(x - 2)}{x + 4}$

b) $\dfrac{3}{(x + 2)(x + 3)} + \dfrac{x}{(x + 2)(x + 3)}$

$= \dfrac{3 + x}{(x + 2)(x + 3)}$

$= \dfrac{1(3 + x)}{(x + 2)(x + 3)}$

$= \dfrac{1}{x + 2}$

c) $\dfrac{3}{x-1} - \dfrac{2}{x-2}$

$= \dfrac{(x-2)}{(x-2)} \cdot \dfrac{3}{x-1} - \dfrac{(x-1)}{(x-1)} \cdot \dfrac{2}{x-2}$

$= \dfrac{3(x-2)}{(x-1)(x-2)} - \dfrac{2(x-1)}{(x-1)(x-2)}$

$= \dfrac{3x - 6 - 2x + 2}{(x-1)(x-2)}$

$= \dfrac{x-4}{(x-1)(x-2)}$

d) $\dfrac{8}{x} - \dfrac{4}{x+2} = \dfrac{(x+2)}{(x+2)} \cdot \dfrac{8}{x} - \dfrac{x}{x} \cdot \dfrac{4}{x+2}$

$= \dfrac{8(x+2)}{x(x+2)} - \dfrac{4x}{x(x+2)}$

$= \dfrac{8x + 16 - 4x}{x(x+2)}$

$= \dfrac{4x + 16}{x(x+2)}$

$= \dfrac{4(x+4)}{x(x+2)}$

Here are some more to try.  Add or subtract  and simplify.

1. $\dfrac{x}{(x+2)(x+3)} + \dfrac{2}{(x+2)(x+3)}$

2. $\dfrac{8x+3}{2x+3} - \dfrac{2x-6}{2x+3}$.

3. $\dfrac{6}{x(x-3)} + \dfrac{2}{x+3}$

4. $\dfrac{3x+1}{x^2-16} - \dfrac{3x+5}{x^2+8x+16}$

5. $\dfrac{7x-1}{x^2-2x-3} - \dfrac{6x}{x^2-x-2}$

6. $\dfrac{3}{x-1} + \dfrac{4}{1-x} + \dfrac{1}{x}$

7. $\dfrac{3y}{9y^2-4x^2} - \dfrac{1}{3y+2x}$

8. $\dfrac{2}{x+4} - \dfrac{x-4}{x^2-16}$

9. $\dfrac{5x+9}{x^2-2x-3} + \dfrac{6}{x^2-7x+12}$

10. $\dfrac{x+4}{x^2-3x-28} + \dfrac{x-5}{x^2+2x-35}$

**Answers:**

1. $\dfrac{1}{x+3}$

2. $\dfrac{3(2x+3)}{2x+3} = 3$

3. $\dfrac{2(x^2+9)}{x(x-3)(x+3)}$

4. $\dfrac{4(5x+6)}{(x-4)(x+4)^2}$

5. $\dfrac{x+2}{(x-3)(x-2)}$

6. $\dfrac{-1}{x(x-1)}$

7. $\dfrac{2x}{(3y+2x)(3y-2x)}$

8. $\dfrac{1}{x+4}$

9. $\dfrac{5(x+2)}{(x-4)(x+1)}$

10. $\dfrac{2x}{(x+7)(x-7)}$

CC-136

Integral and Rational Exponents

There are some basic rules for integral and rational exponents. The patterns are summarized below with some examples:

$x^0 = 1.$

Examples: $2^0 = 1,$  $(-3)^0 = 1,$  $(\frac{1}{4})^0 = 1.$

$x^{-n} = \frac{1}{x^n}.$

Examples: $x^{-3} = \frac{1}{x^3},$  $y^{-4} = \frac{1}{y^4},$  $4^{-2} = \frac{1}{4^2} = \frac{1}{16}.$

$\frac{1}{x^{-n}} = x^n.$

Examples: $\frac{1}{x^{-5}} = x^5,$  $\frac{1}{x^{-2}} = x^2,$  $\frac{1}{3^{-2}} = 3^2 = 9$

$x^{\frac{a}{b}} = (x^a)^{\frac{1}{b}} = \sqrt[b]{x^a}$

Examples:  $5^{\frac{1}{2}} = \sqrt{5},$

or

$16^{\frac{3}{4}} = (\sqrt[4]{16})^3 = 2^3 = 8$

$x^{\frac{a}{b}} = (x^{\frac{1}{b}})^a = (\sqrt[b]{x})^a$

$4^{\frac{2}{3}} = \sqrt[3]{4^2} = \sqrt[3]{16} = 2\sqrt[3]{2}$

We can now go back and try the original problem. Use integral or rational exponents to write each of the following as a power of x.

a)  $\sqrt[5]{x} = x^{1/5}$
(using the fourth property above)

b)  $\frac{1}{x^3} = x^{-3}$
(using the second property above)

c)  $\sqrt[3]{x^2} = x^{2/3}$
(using the fourth property above)

d)  $\frac{1}{\sqrt{x}} = \frac{1}{x^{1/2}} = x^{-1/2}$
(using properties four and two above)

Here are some more to try. Use integral or rational exponents to simplify each expression. You should not need a calculator for any of these.

1. $x^{-5}$

2. $m^0$

3. $4^{-1}$

4. $y^{-3}$

5. $5^{-2}$

6. $5^0$

7. $y^{-7}$

8. $(x^3 y^4)^{-2}$

9. $x^{-1} y^{-8}$

10. $x^{-4} y^{-2} (x^{-3} y^{-6})^0$

11. $25^{1/2}$

12. $25^{-1/2}$

13. $2^{1/2}$

14. $\left(\frac{1}{27}\right)^{-1/3}$

15. $x^{3/2}$

16. $9^{3/2}$

17. $\left(x^3 y^6\right)^{1/3}$

18. $16^{-3/4}$

19. $\left(m^2\right)^{-3/2}$

20. $\left(x^3 y^6\right)^{1/2}$

21. $\left(9 x^3 y^6\right)^{-2}$

**Answers:**

1. $\frac{1}{x^5}$

2. 1

3. $\frac{1}{4}$

4. $\frac{1}{y^3}$

5. $\frac{1}{5^2}$

6. 1

7. $\frac{1}{y^7}$

8. $\frac{1}{x^6 y^8}$

9. $\frac{1}{x y^8}$

10. $\frac{1}{x^4 y^2}$

11. 5

12. $\frac{1}{5}$

13. $\sqrt{2}$

14. 3

15. $\sqrt{x^3} = x\sqrt{x}$

16. 27

17. $x y^2$

18. $\frac{1}{8}$

19. $\frac{1}{m^3}$

20. $x y^3 \sqrt{x}$

21. $\frac{1}{81 x^6 y^{12}}$

## Completing the Square and Locator Point for a Parabola

If a parabola is in graphing form then the locator point or vertex is easily found and a sketch of the graph can quickly be made. If the equation of the parabola is not in graphing form the equation needs to be rearranged. One way to rearrange the equation is by completing the square. Here are three examples:

Note that first two examples are in your book problem PG-46 shown with algebra tiles. You might like that way better because you can "see it" or the way shown below which just gives a rule.

First recall that $y = x^2$ is the parent equation for parabolas and then the graphing equation for that function is given by
$$y = a(x - h)^2 + k$$
where $(h, k)$ is the locator point, and relative to the parent graph the function has been:
vertically stretched, if the absolute value of a is greater than 1
vertically compressed, if the absolute value of a is less than 1
reflected across the x-axis, if a is less than 0.

Example 1: $y = x^2 + 8x + 10$

We need to make $x^2 + 8x$ into a perfect square. Taking half of the x coefficient and squaring it will accomplish the task.

$y = x^2 + 8x + 10$
$y = (x^2 + 8x + ?) + 10$

$$? = \left(\frac{8}{2}\right)^2 = 16$$

The 16 that was put into the parenthesis must be compensated for by subtracting 16.

$y = (x^2 + 8x + 16) + 10 - 16$

Factor and simplify

$y = (x + 4)^2 - 4$.  The locator is $(4, 4)$.

Example 2: $y = x^2 + 5x + 2$

We need to make $x^2 + 5x$ into a perfect square. Again, taking half of the x coefficient and squaring it will always accomplish the task.

$y = x^2 + 5x + 2$
$y = (x^2 + 5x + ?) + 2$

$$? = \left(\frac{5}{2}\right)^2 = \frac{25}{4}$$

The $\frac{25}{4}$ that was put into the parenthesis must be compensated for by subtracting $\frac{25}{4}$.

$y = (x^2 + 5x + \frac{25}{4}) + 2 - \frac{25}{4}$

Factor and simplify.

$y = (x + \frac{5}{2})^2 - 4\frac{1}{4}$.  The locator is $(-\frac{5}{2}, -4\frac{1}{4})$.

Example 3:  $y = 2x^2 - 6x + 2$

This problem is a little different because we have $2x^2$.  First we must factor the 2 out of the x-terms.  Then we make $x^2 - 3x$ into a perfect square as before.

$y = 2x^2 - 6x + 2$
$y = 2(x^2 - 3x \quad ) + 2$
$y = 2(x^2 - 3x + ?) + 2$

The $\frac{9}{4}$ that was put into the parenthesis must be compensated for by subtracting $2(\frac{9}{4}) = \frac{9}{2}$.

$? = \left(\frac{-3}{2}\right)^2 = \frac{9}{4}$

$y = 2(x^2 - 3x + \frac{9}{4}) + 2 - \frac{9}{2}$

Factor and simplify

$y = 2(x - \frac{3}{2})^2 - \frac{5}{2}$.  The locator is  $(-\frac{3}{2}, -\frac{5}{2})$. and there is a stretch factor of 2.

We can now go back to the original problem.  Write the equation in graphing form and sketch a graph of  $y = 2x^2 - 4x + 5$.

First we must factor the 2 out of the x-terms.  Then we make $x^2 - 2x$ into a perfect square as before.

$y = 2x^2 - 4x + 5$
$y = 2(x^2 - 2x \quad ) + 5$
$y = 2(x^2 - 2x + ?) + 5$

The 1 that was put into the parenthesis must be compensated for by subtracting  $2(1) = 2$

$? = \left(\frac{-2}{2}\right)^2 = 1$

$y = 2(x^2 - 2x + 1) + 5 - 2$

Factor and simplify

$y = 2(x - 1)^2 + 3$.  The locator is  $(1, 3)$ and there is a stretch factor of 2.

You might also do this problem by completing two perfect squares using the algebra tiles.  You will have three extra ones, giving the +3 on the end of the graphing form.

The graph of the parabola passes through $(1, 3)$, $(2, 5)$, $(3, 13)$, $(0, 5)$, and $(-1, 13)$.

Here are some more to try.  Write the equation in graphing form.  Tell the locator and stretch factor.

1.   $y = x^2 - 6x + 9$        2.   $y = x^2 + 3$        3.   $y = x^2 - 4x$

4.   $y = x^2 + 2x - 3$        5.   $y = x^2 + 5x + 1$        6.   $y = x^2 - \frac{1}{3}x$

7.   $y = 3x^2 - 6x + 1$        8.   $y = 5x^2 + 20x - 16$        9.   $y = -x^2 - 6x + 10$

**Answers**:

1.  $(3, 0)$ normal size        2.  $(0, 3)$ normal        3.  $(2, -4)$ normal        4.  $(-1, -4)$ normal

5.  $(-\frac{5}{2}, -5\frac{1}{4})$ normal        6.  $(\frac{1}{6}, -\frac{1}{36})$ normal        7.  $(1, -2)$ stretch by 3

8.  $(-2, -36)$ stretch by 5        9.  $(-3, 19)$ normal size but upside down

## CT-76

## Absolute Value Equations and Inequalities

Absolute value means the distance from a reference point. There is a pattern used to solve absolute value equations and two patterns used for the different inequalities. They are shown below and then some examples are solved.

Examples

$|x| = k$ means: $x = k$ or $x = -k$

$|x| = 5$ means $x = 5$ or $x = -5$
(5 or -5 are 5 units from zero)

$|x| < k$ means: $-k \leq x \leq k$

$|x| < 5$ means $-5 < x < 5$
(the numbers between -5 and 5 are less than 5 units from zero)

$|x| > k$ means: $x > k$ or $x < -k$

$|x| > 5$ means $x > 5$ or $x < -5$
(the numbers greater than 5 or less than -5 are more than 5 units from zero)

If the expression inside the absolute value is more complicated, you still follow one of the three basic patterns above. Also $\leq$ and $\geq$ use the same patterns as the pure inequality.

If $|2x + 3| = 7$, then the quantity $(2x + 3)$ must equal 7 or -7.

$$2x + 3 = 7 \quad \text{or} \quad 2x + 3 = -7$$
$$2x = 4 \quad \text{or} \quad 2x = -10$$
$$x = 2 \quad \text{or} \quad x = -5$$

If $|2x+3| \leq 7$, then the quantity $(2x + 3)$ must be between -7 and 7.

$$-7 \leq 2x + 3 \leq 7$$
$$-10 \leq 2x \leq 4$$
$$-5 \leq x \leq 2$$

Now we can go back and try the original problem.  Solve each absolute value equation or inequality.

$2|2x + 3| = 10$

(isolate the absolute value)
    $|2x+3|=5$

(using the first pattern )
    $2x +3 = 5$ or $2x + 3 = -5$
    $2x = 2$ or $2x = -8$
    $x = 1$ or $x = -4$

$-|x + 3| < 10$

(isolate the absolute value)
    $|x+3| > -10$

(dividing by a negative changes the sign)  Since any absolute value is never negative, the solution is all numbers.


Here are some more to try.   Solve each absolute value equation or inequality.

1.   $|x - 2| + 10 = 8$

2.   $15 - |x + 1| = 3$

3.   $-3 \cdot |x + 6| + 12 = 0$

4.   $|2x + 7| = 0$

5.   $|x + 4| \geq 7$

6.   $|x| - 5 \leq 8$

7.   $|4r-2| > 8$

8.   $-2|x - 3| + 6 < -4$

9.   $|4-d| \leq 7$

**Answers**:

1. No solution

2. $x = 11, -13$

3. $x = -2, -10$

4. $x = -\frac{7}{2}$

5. $x \geq 3$ or $x \leq -11$

6. $-13 \leq x \leq 13$

7. $r < -\frac{3}{2}$ or $r > \frac{5}{2}$

8. $x > 8$ or $x < -2$

9. $-3 \leq d \leq 11$

## CT-111

## Writing and Solving Exponential Equations

Exponential functions are equations of the form $y = km^x$ where k represents the initial value, m represents the multiplier, x represents the time. Some problems just involve substituting in the information and doing the calculations. If you are trying to solve for the time (x), then you will usually need to use logarithms. If you need to find the multiplier (m), then you will need roots. Here are some examples.

Lunch at our favorite fast food stand now cost $6.50. The price has steadily increased 4% per year for many years.

What will lunch cost in 10 years?

The initial value is $6.50, the multiplier is 1.04, and the time is 10 years. Substituting into the formula:

$$y = 6.50(1.04)^{10} = \$9.62$$

What did it cost 10 years ago?

$$y = 6.50(1.04)^{-10} = \$4.39$$

How long before lunch costs $10?

The initial value is $6.50, the multiplier is 1.04, and the time is unknown but the final value is $10. Substituting into the formula:

$$10 = 6.50(1.04)^x$$

This time we must solve an equation.

$$(1.04)^x = \frac{10}{6.50} = 1.538$$

$$x = \frac{\log(1.538)}{\log(1.04)} \approx 11 \text{ years}$$

Tickets for the big concert first went on sale three weeks ago for $60. This week people are charging $100.

What was the weekly multiplier and weekly percent increase?

The initial value is $60, the time is 3 weeks, and the final value is $100. Substituting into the formula:

$$100 = 60k^3$$

$$k^3 = \frac{100}{60} \approx 1.667$$

$$k = \sqrt[3]{1.667} \approx 1.186$$

The multiplier was about 1.186 so it was a weekly increase of about 18.6%.

Write an equation that represents the cost of the tickets w weeks from the time that they went on sale. Assume that they continue to increase in the same way.

The initial value is $60 and the multiplier is 1.186 so the equation is:

$$y = 60(1.186)^w$$

We can now go back and solve the original problem parts (b), (c), and (d).

When rabbits were first brought to Australia, they had no natural enemies. There were about 80,000 rabbits in 1866. Two years later, in 1868, the population had grown to over 2,400,000!

b)  Write an exponential equation for the number of rabbits t years after 1866. For 1866, 80,000 would be the initial value, time would be 2 years, and the final amount would be 2,400,000. Here is the equation to solve:

$$2,400,000 = 80,000m^2$$
$$30 = m^2 \text{ so the multiplier } m = \sqrt{30} \approx 5.477.$$

The desired equation is:  $R = 80,000(5.477)^t$

c)  How many rabbits do you predict would have been present in 1871? The initial value is still 80,000, the multiplier $\approx 5.477$ and now the time is 5 years.

$$80,000(5.477)^5 \approx 394 \text{ million}$$

d)  According to your model, in what year was the first pair of rabbits introduced into Australia? Now 2 is the initial value, 80,000 is the final value, the multiplier is still 5.477 but the time is not known. Here is the equation to solve:

$$80,000 = 2(5.477)^x$$
$$40,000 = (5.477)^x$$
$$x = \frac{\log(40000)}{\log(5.477)} \approx 6.23 \text{ years, so some time during 1859.}$$

Here are some more to try.

1.  A video tape loses 60% of its value every year it is in the store. The video cost $80 new. Write a function that represents its value in t years. What is it worth after 4 years?

2.  Inflation is at a rate of 7% per year. Janelle's favorite bread now costs $1.79. What did it cost 10 years ago? How long before the cost of the bread doubles?

3.  Find the initial value if five years from now, a bond that appreciates 4% per year will be worth $146.

4.  Sixty years ago when Sam's grandfather was a kid he could buy his friend dinner for $1.50. If that same dinner now costs $25.25 and inflation was consistent, write an equation that will give you the costs at different times.

5.  A two-bedroom house in Omaha is now worth $110,000. If it appreciates at a rate of 2.5% per year, how long will it take to be worth $200,000?

6.  A car valued at $14,000 depreciates 18% per year. After how many years will the value have depreciated to $1000?

**Answers:**

1.  $y = 80(.4)^x$ , $2.05

2. $.91, 10.2 years

3.  $120

4.  $y = 1.50(1.048)^x$

5.  24.2 years

6.  13.3 years

# Finding the Equation for the Inverse of a Function

To find the equation for the inverse of a function just interchange the x and y variables and then solve for y. This also means that the coordinates of points that are on the graph of the function will be reversed on the inverse. Here are some examples:

If $y = 2(x + 3)$ then the inverse is:
$$x = 2(y + 3).$$

Solving for y to get the final answer:

$$(y + 3) = \frac{x}{2}$$

$$y = \frac{x}{2} - 3$$

If $y = -\frac{2}{3}x + 6$ then the inverse is:

$$x = -\frac{2}{3}y + 6.$$

Solving for y to get the final answer:

$$-\frac{2}{3}y = x - 6$$

$$y = -\frac{3}{2}(x - 6) = -\frac{3}{2}x + 9$$

If $y = \frac{1}{2}(x + 4)^2 + 1$ the inverse is:

$$x = \frac{1}{2}(y + 4)^2 + 1.$$

Solving for y to get the final answer:
$$\frac{1}{2}(y + 4)^2 = x - 1$$
$$(y + 4)^2 = 2x - 2$$
$$y + 4 = \pm\sqrt{2x - 2}$$
$$y = \pm\sqrt{2x - 2} - 4$$
Note that because of the ±, this inverse is not a function.

If $y = \sqrt{x - 2} + 5$ then the inverse is:

$$x = \sqrt{y - 2} + 5.$$

Solving for y to get the final answer:
$$\sqrt{y - 2} = x - 5$$
$$y - 2 = (x - 5)^2$$
$$y = (x - 5)^2 + 2$$

Note that since the original function is one half of a parabola, the graph of the inverse function is also only one half of a parabola.

We can now go back and try the original problem:

Find the equation for the inverse of the following function: $y = 2\sqrt{3(x-1)} + 5$. Sketch the graph of both the original and the inverse.

Interchanging x and y we get $x = 2\sqrt{3(y-1)} + 5$. Solving for y to get the final answer:

$$2\sqrt{3(y-1)} = x - 5$$

For the original function:
Domain: $x \geq 1$; Range: $y \geq 5$

$$\sqrt{3(y-1)} = \frac{x-5}{2}$$

Some points on the original graph are:

$$3(y-1) = \frac{(x-5)^2}{4}$$

$(1, 5)$, $(\frac{7}{3}, 9)$, $(4, 11)$--half a parabola.

$$y-1 = \frac{(x-5)^2}{12}$$

For the inverse function:
Domain: $x \geq 5$; Range: $y \geq 1$.

$$y = \frac{(x-5)^2}{12} + 1$$

Some points on the inverse graph are:

$(5, 1)$, $(9, \frac{7}{3})$, $(11, 4)$--half a parabola.


Here are some more to try. Find the equation for the inverse of each function.

1. $y = 3x - 2$

2. $y = \frac{x+1}{4}$

3. $y = \frac{1}{3}x + 2$

4. $y = x^3 + 1$

5. $y = 1 + \sqrt{x+5}$

6. $y = 3(x+2)^2 - 7$

7. $y = 2\sqrt{x-1} + 3$

8. $y = \frac{1}{2+x}$

9. $y = \log_3(x-2)$


**Answers:**

1. $y = \frac{x+2}{3}$

2. $y = 4x - 1$

3. $y = 3x - 6$

4. $y = \sqrt[3]{x-1}$

5. $y = (x-1)^2 - 5$

6. $y = \sqrt{\frac{x+7}{3}} - 2$

7. $y = \left(\frac{x-3}{2}\right)^2 + 1$

8. $y = \frac{1}{x} - 2$

9. $y = 3^x + 2$

## ST-12

## Solving a System of Equations in Three Variables

To solve a system of equations in three variable using elimination you use the same basic process as you do with two variables only you have to do it twice. Choose any variable to eliminate and then you are left with two equations in two variables. Continue to solve in the usual way. To solve using matrix multiplication you need to change the system into matrices and then isolate the variable matrix by using the inverse matrix on the graphing calculator. Here is an example of each method.

Solve for $(x, y, z)$

$$5x - 4y - 6z = -19$$
$$-2x + 2y + z = 5$$
$$3x - 6y - 5z = -16$$

### Method One--Elimination

Choose a variable to eliminate. Any is possible. We choose $z$. Use the first two equations. Multiply the second equation by 6 and add it to the first.

$$6(-2x + 2y + z = 5) = -12x + 12y + 6z = 30$$
$$\underline{5x - 4y - 6z = -19}$$
(**) $\qquad -7x + 8y = 11$

Then we must also eliminate $z$ using two other equations. Multiply the second by 5 and add it to the third.

$$5(-2x + 2y + z = 5) = -10x + 10y + 5z = 25$$
$$\underline{3x - 6y - 5z = -16}$$
(***) $\qquad -7x + 4y = 9$

Now we have two equations with two variables. Using lines (**) and (***) we can subtract the second line from the first to eliminate $x$ and find y.

(**) $\qquad -7x + 8y = 11$
(***) $\qquad \underline{-7x + 4y = 9}$
$$\qquad\qquad 4y = 2$$
$$\qquad\qquad y = \frac{1}{2}$$

Using our answer for $y$ in (**) we can find $x$.

$$-7x + 8\left(\frac{1}{2}\right) = 11$$
$$-7x = 7$$
$$x = -1$$

Finally go back to any of the original equations to find z. Using the first one:

$$5(-1) - 4\left(\frac{1}{2}\right) - 6z = -19$$
$$-7 - 6z = -19$$
$$-6z = -12$$
$$z = -2$$

The solution is $(-1, \frac{1}{2}, -2)$

Method Two--Matrices

Write the problem as a matrix equation.

$$\begin{bmatrix} 5 & -4 & -6 \\ -2 & 2 & 1 \\ 3 & -6 & -5 \end{bmatrix} \cdot \begin{bmatrix} x \\ y \\ z \end{bmatrix} = \begin{bmatrix} -19 \\ 5 \\ -16 \end{bmatrix}$$

Left multiplying both sides of the equation by the inverse of the coefficient matrix gives:

(You may need to refer to you calculator directions or your resource page from unit 5 for help with entering this in your graphing calculator.

$$\begin{bmatrix} x \\ y \\ z \end{bmatrix} = \begin{bmatrix} 5 & -4 & -6 \\ -2 & 2 & 1 \\ 3 & -6 & -5 \end{bmatrix}^{-1} \begin{bmatrix} -19 \\ 5 \\ -16 \end{bmatrix}$$

The solution is $(-1, \frac{1}{2}, -2)$

$$\begin{bmatrix} x \\ y \\ z \end{bmatrix} = \begin{bmatrix} -1 \\ .5 \\ 2 \end{bmatrix}$$

We can now go back and solve the original question.

Use elimination or matrix multiplication to solve this system of equations:

$$\begin{aligned} x + y - z &= 12 \\ 3x + 2y + z &= 6 \\ 2x + 5y - z &= 10 \end{aligned}$$

Method One

Adding equations one and two eliminates z.
$$\begin{aligned} x + y - z &= 12 \\ \underline{3x + 2y + z} &= \underline{6} \\ 4x + 3y &= 18 \quad (**) \end{aligned}$$

Adding equations two and three also eliminates z.

$$\begin{aligned} 3x + 2y + z &= 6 \\ \underline{2x + 5y - z} &= \underline{10} \\ 5x + 7y &= 16 \quad (***) \end{aligned}$$

Now we have two equations in two variables. Multiplying (**) by 5 and (***) by -4 eliminates x.

$$\begin{aligned} 5(4x + 3y = 18) = \quad 20x + 15y &= 90 \\ -4(5x + 7y = 16) = \underline{-20x - 28y} &= \underline{-64} \\ -13y &= -26 \\ y &= -2 \end{aligned}$$

Using y = -2 into (**) gives x = 6.
Using y = -2 and x = 6 in any of the original equations gives z = -8

The solution is (6, -2, -8).

Method Two

Write the system in matrices.

$$\begin{bmatrix} 1 & 1 & -1 \\ 3 & 2 & 1 \\ 2 & 5 & -1 \end{bmatrix} \cdot \begin{bmatrix} x \\ y \\ z \end{bmatrix} = \begin{bmatrix} 12 \\ 6 \\ 10 \end{bmatrix}$$

Isolate the variable matrix.

$$\begin{bmatrix} x \\ y \\ z \end{bmatrix} = \begin{bmatrix} 1 & 1 & -1 \\ 3 & 2 & 1 \\ 2 & 5 & -1 \end{bmatrix}^{-1} \begin{bmatrix} 12 \\ 6 \\ 10 \end{bmatrix}$$

Use the graphing calculator to multiply.

$$\begin{bmatrix} x \\ y \\ z \end{bmatrix} = \begin{bmatrix} 6 \\ -2 \\ -8 \end{bmatrix}$$

x = 6  y = -2  z = -8

Here are some more to try. Use elimination or matrix multiplication to solve
these system of equations. Most teachers expect their students to be able to use both methods
successfully.

1.  $x + y + z = 34$
    $3x + 2y + 4z = 95$
    $x + 2y + 3z = 56$

2.  $x - 2y + 3z = 8$
    $2x + y + z = 6$
    $x + y + 2z = 12$

3.  $5x + y + 2z = 6$
    $3x - 6y - 9z = -48$
    $x - 2y + z = 12$

4.  $4x - y + z = -5$
    $2x + 2y + 3z = 10$
    $5x - 2y + 6z = 1$

5.  $x + y = 2 - z$
    $-y + 1 = -z - 2x$
    $3x - 2y + 5z = 16$

6.  $a - b + 2c = 2$
    $a + 2b - c = 1$
    $2a + b + c = 4$

7.  $-4x = z - 2y + 12$
    $y + z = 12 - x$
    $8x - 3y + 4z = 1$

8.  $3x + y - 2z = 6$
    $x + 2y + z = 7$
    $6x + 2y - 4z = 12$

9.  $4x + 4y - 5z = -2$
    $2x - 4y + 10z = 6$
    $x + 2y + 5z = 0$

**Answers**:

1. $(17, 12, 5)$    2. $(-1, 3, 5)$    3. $(-1, -3, 7)$    4. $(-1, 3, 2)$

5. $(-3, 0, 5)$    6. no solution    7. $(-3, 5. 10)$    8. infinite solutions

9. $(\frac{1}{2}, -\frac{3}{4}, \frac{1}{5})$

# Glossary

**absolute value**   The absolute value of a number is the distance of the number from zero.  Since the absolute value represents a distance, without regard to direction, it is always positive. (139-40)

**additive identity**   The number 0 is called the additive identity because adding 0 to any number does not change the number. (185)

**additive inverse**   The additive inverse of a number is the number we can add to that number to get the additive identity, zero.  So, for the number 5, the additive inverse is -5; for the number -13, the additive inverse is 13.  For any x, the additive inverse is -x. (185)

**amplitude**   The amplitude of a graph is one-half the distance between the highest and lowest points on a cyclic graph. (248)

**angles of rotation**.  Angles formed by rotation from the positive x-axis are referred to as angles of rotation in standard position.  When we draw an angle in standard position, the positive x-axis is called the initial ray and the radius that determines the angle determines the terminal ray. (299)

**appreciation**   An increase in value. (100)

**Arccosine of x**   The arccosine of x is the measure of the angle with cosine x.  We can write $y = \arccos x$ or $y = \cos^{-1} x$.  Note that this last notation refers to the inverse of the cosine function, **not** $\dfrac{1}{\cos x}$.  When we want the arccosine to be a function we write $y = \text{Arccos } x$ or $y = \text{Cos}^{-1} x$, and this is the principle angle with cosine x; we restrict the domain and range of this function so that $0 \le y \le \pi$. (349-51)

**Arcsine of x**   The arcsine of x is the measure of the angle with sine x.  We can write $y = \arcsin x$ or $y = \sin^{-1} x$.  Note that this last notation refers to the inverse of the sine function, **not** $\dfrac{1}{\sin x}$.  When we want the arcsine to be a function we write $y = \text{Arcsin } x$ or $y = \text{Sin}^{-1} x$, and this is the principle angle with sine x; we restrict the domain and range of this function so $-\dfrac{\pi}{2} \le y \le \dfrac{\pi}{2}$. (349-51)

**Arctangent of x**   The arctangent of x is the measure of the angle with tangent  x.  We can write $y = \arctan x$ or $y = \tan^{-1} x$.  Note that this last notation refers to the inverse of the tangent function, **not** $\dfrac{1}{\tan x}$.  When we want the arctangent to be a function we write $y = \text{Arctan } x$ or $y = \text{Tan}^{-1} x$, and this is the principle angle with tangent x; we restrict the domain and range of this function so $-\dfrac{\pi}{2} < y < \dfrac{\pi}{2}$. (349-51)

**area model**   An area model is one way to represent the probabilities of the outcomes for a sequence of two events. (358)

**arithmetic sequence**   In an arithmetic sequence the difference between sequential terms is constant.  Each term of an arithmetic sequence can be generated by adding the common difference to the previous term. (47, 51, 466)

**asymptote**   A line that a graph of a curve approaches as closely as you wish.  We often graph functions which have vertical and/or horizontal asymptotes. (103)

**The Binomial Theorem**   The method of using combinations to write the expansion of $(x + y)^n$ is called the Binomial Theorem. (455)

$$(x+y)^n = {}_nC_n x^n + {}_nC_{n-1}x^{n-1}y + {}_nC_{n-2}x^{n-2}y^2 + \ldots + {}_nC_1 xy^{n-1} + {}_nC_0 y^n$$

For example, $(x + y)^3 = {}_3C_3 x^3 + {}_3C_2 x^2 y + {}_3C_1 xy^2 + {}_3C_0 y^3 = 1x^3 + 3x^2 y + 3xy^2 + 1y^3$

**box-and-whisker diagram**   To display statistical data a rectangular box is drawn above a number line so that the box spans the region from the first to the third quartile. The median is marked within the box. Lines (the whiskers) are drawn from each end of the box to the highest and lowest data points. (449)

**circle (equation)**   The general equation of a circle is $(x - h)^2 + (y - k)^2 = r^2$ where the point $(h, k)$ is the center of the circle of radius r. (150)

**circular functions**   The periodic functions based on the unit circle, including $y = \sin x$, $y = \cos x$, and $y = \tan x$. (286)

**coefficient**   The numbers which multiply the variables in a polynomial are called the coefficients of the polynomial. For example, 3 is the coefficient of $3x^2$. (240)

**combination**   A combination is the number of ways we can select items from a larger set without regard to order. For instance, choosing a committee of 3 students from a group of 5 volunteers is a combination since there is no order involved in the committee. The order of selection does not matter. We write ${}_nC_r$ to represent the number of combinations of n things taken r at a time. For instance, the number of ways to select a committee of 3 students from a group of 5 is ${}_5C_3$. You can use Pascal's Triangle to find ${}_5C_3$ or you can calculate $\dfrac{5!}{3!2!}$ which is $\dfrac{{}_5P_3}{{}_3P_3}$. Formulas for combinations include:.

$$_nC_r = \frac{{}_nP_r}{r!} = \frac{n!}{r!(n-r)!} . \quad (406\text{-}07)$$

**common difference**   The number added to get the next term of an arithmetic sequence is called the common difference. If a number is subtracted to get the next term, the common difference is negative. The common difference is the generator for an arithmetic sequence. (51)

**common ratio**   Common ratio is another name for the multiplier or generator of a geometric sequence.

**complete graph**   A complete graph is one that includes everything that is important about the graph, and everything off the paper is predictable based on what is there. (12)

**completing the square**   The standard procedure for rewriting a quadratic equation from standard form to graphing (or vertex) form is called completing the square. Completing the square is also used to solve quadratic equations in one variable. (121)

**complex conjugates**   The complex number $a + bi$ has a complex conjugate $a - bi$. Similarly, the conjugate of $c - di$ is $c + di$. What is noteworthy about complex numbers and their conjugates is their products. $(a + bi)(a - bi) = a^2 - abi + abi - b^2 i^2 = a^2 + b^2$ which is a real number. Also, if a complex number is a zero (or root) of a real polynomial function, then the complex conjugate is as well. (257)

**complex numbers**   The sum of a real number and an imaginary number is neither real nor imaginary. Numbers such as these that can be written in the form $a + bi$ where a and b are real numbers, are called complex numbers. Each complex number has a real part, a, and an imaginary part, bi. Note that real numbers are also complex numbers with $b = 0$. (254)

**complex plane**    A set of coordinate axes with all the real numbers on the horizontal axis (the real axis) and all the imaginary numbers on the vertical axis (the imaginary axis) defines the complex plane. Complex numbers are graphed in the complex plane using the same method we use to graph coordinate points. Thus, the complex number $1 + 3i$ is located at the point $(1, 3)$. (254).

**composition**    When we push two (or more) function machines together so that the output of the first becomes the input of the second, we create a new function which is the composition of the two functions. If the first function is $g(x)$ and the second is $f(x)$, the composition can be written as $f(g(x))$ or $f \circ g(x)$. Note that the order in which we perform the functions matters, and $g(f(x))$ will usually be a different function. (206)

**compound interest**    Interest paid on both the principle and the accrued interest. (74)

**conditional probability**    The probability of event B occurring, given that event A has already happened is called the conditional probability of B, given A. One way to calculate the conditional probability of B given A is $P(B|A) = P(A \text{ and } B)/P(A)$. In many situations it is possible to calculate the conditional probability directly from the data by counting the number of possibilities for event B once event A has occurred. (367, 371)

**conic section**    Circles, ellipses, hyperbolas and parabolas are known as conic sections. They are called conic sections because each curve can be found by taking a section or slice of a cone. (480, 485-87)

**continuous**    When the points on a graph are connected and it makes sense to connect them, we say the graph is continuous. Such a graph will have no holes or breaks in it. This term will be more completely defined in a later course. (56)

**cosine**    In a right triangle (as shown at right) the ratio $\frac{\text{adjacent side}}{\text{hypotenuse}}$ is known as the cosine of the acute angle. At right, $\cos B = \frac{a}{c}$ since the side length a is adjacent to angle B. (20)

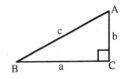

**cosine function**    The cosine of $\Theta$, denoted $\cos \Theta$, is the x-coordinate of the point on the unit circle reached by a rotation angle of $\Theta$ radians in standard position. (307, 315)

**cosine function (general equation)**    The general equation for the cosine function is $y = a \cos b(x - h) + k$. This function has amplitude a, period of $\frac{2\pi}{b}$, and locator point $(h, k)$. (315)

**cubic**    A cubic polynomial is a polynomial function with degree 3. (130)

**cycle**    The cycle of a graph is the section that is repeated. (248)

**decision chart**    A decision chart is a method for organizing a counting problem that could be represented by a symmetric tree diagram. Begin by asking how many decisions need to be made, and then mark a space for each decision. Fill in each space with the number of possibilities for that decision. For example a child has a set of 26 blocks, each with a different letter of the alphabet on it. How many three letter arrangements could he make by lining up any three of his blocks in a 3-letter "word?" There are three decisions, with 26 choices for the first letter, times 25 for the second, and then times 24.

$$\underline{26} \cdot \underline{25} \cdot \underline{24}$$

The decision chart is a short way to represent a tree with 26 branches at stage one, 25 at stage two, and 24 at stage three. (394)

**degree of a polynomial in one variable**   The exponent of the term containing the highest power of the variable is the degree of a polynomial expression in one variable. The degree of a polynomial function also tells you the number of factors and provides information for interpreting the number of "turns" the graph can take. (240)

**dependent variable**   In an ordered pair, the variable occurring second is the dependent variable. For a given value of the independent variable, or input, the value of the dependent variable is the output. (15)

**depreciation**   A decrease in value because of normal wear and tear, age, decay, decrease in price. (100)

**direct variation**   Linear functions with y-intercept (0, 0) represent direct variations. The equation of a direct variation has the form $y = mx$. (54)

**discrete**   We describe a graph that is made up of separate points as discrete. (56)

**discriminant**   For any quadratic equation $ax^2 + bx + c = 0$, $b^2 - 4ac$ is called the discriminant. If $b^2 - 4ac \geq 0$, the roots of the quadratic are real. If the discriminant is less than 0, the roots include an imaginary part. (272)

**domain**   The domain of a function is the set of possible values for the independent variable. It consists of every number that x can represent for the function. (14)

**double root**   If an expression of the form $(x - a)^2$ is a factor of a polynomial, then the polynomial has a double root at $x = a$. The graph of the polynomial does not pass through the x-axis at $x = a$ but is tangent to the axis at $x = a$. (244)

**eccentricity**   The eccentricity of an ellipse is a measurement reflecting the "roundness" of an ellipse. The eccentricity, e, is found with the formula $e = \frac{c}{a}$, where $c^2 = a^2 - b^2$, and a and b are the lengths of the semi-major and semi-minor axes. For a hyperbola, the eccentricity is a measure of the shape of the curve; the larger the eccentricity the more quickly the branches spread apart. The formula is also $e = \frac{c}{a}$. Note that since $c > a$, the eccentricity of a hyperbola is always greater than 1; ellipses have eccentricity less than 1. Parabolas have eccentricity 1, and circles have eccentricity 0. (485)

**ellipse**   You can think of an ellipse as a circle that has been stretched vertically or horizontally. The general form of the equation of an ellipse is $\frac{(x - h)^2}{a^2} + \frac{(y - k)^2}{b^2} = 1$. The line through the two ends of the ellipse in the long direction is called the major axis of the ellipse, and the distance from the center of the ellipse to one end of the major axis is called the semi-major axis. If a is the length of the semi-major axis, c is the distance from the center to either focus, and (h, k) is the center, then the equation of the ellipse can be written

$$\frac{(x - h)^2}{a^2} + \frac{(y - k)^2}{b^2} = 1, \text{ if the major axis is horizontal, or}$$

$$\frac{(x - h)^2}{b^2} + \frac{(y - k)^2}{a^2} = 1, \text{ if the major axis is vertical.}$$

In either case, the eccentricity is $e = \frac{c}{a}$, where $c^2 = a^2 - b^2$. (485)

**expected value**    The expected value of an outcome is the product of the probability of the outcome and the value of that outcome. The expected value of an event is the sum of the expected values of its outcomes. (373)

**exponential function**    An exponential function has an equation of the form $y = k(m^x)$, where k is the initial value and m is the multiplier. (87, 130)

**factorial**    Factorial is a shorthand notation for the product of a list of consecutive positive integers from the given number down to 1:  $n! = n(n - 1)(n - 2)(n - 3) \bullet \ldots \bullet 3 \bullet 2 \bullet 1$. For example, $5! = 5(4)(3)(2)(1) = 120$. (398)

**fair game**    In a fair game with several people, the expected values are equal. If you pay to play a game then the game is fair if the cost to play equals the expected value. (373)

**focal length (parabola)**    The distance c from the vertex to the focus of a parabola is called the focal length. (483)

**foci of an ellipse**    Ellipses have unique geometric properties; not every oval is an ellipse. Every ellipse has two points on the major axis called the foci of the ellipse. For any point (x,y) on the ellipse, the sum of the distances from each foci to (x,y) is a constant. Also, an ellipse with its center at the origin, x-intercepts of ($\pm$a, 0) and y-intercepts (0, $\pm$b), where a > b, has its foci at ($\pm$c, 0), with $c^2 = a^2 - b^2$. (484)

**focus of a parabola**    A point that defines a parabola in the following way: A parabola is defined to be the set of points in the plane, each of which is the same distance from a fixed point, the focus, as it is from a fixed straight line (the directrix). Also, if rays parallel to the line of symmetry enter into the interior of the parabola to intersect the parabola and reflect so that the angle of incidence equals the angle of reflection, then all such rays intersect at the focus of the parabola. (483)

**"fraction busters"**    "Fraction Busters" are methods for simplifying expressions and equations containing fractions by multiplying by the common denominator. (207)

**fractional exponents**    Raising a number to a fractional exponent indicates a power as well as a root.  $x^{a/b} = \sqrt[b]{x^a} = (\sqrt[b]{x})^a$. (101)

**function**    A relationship in which for each input there is one and only one output is called a function. (143)

**function notation**    Function notation is a convenient way to represent a function and show what a function machine does. We write the name of the function (the letter f is commonly used) next to the independent variable as f(x). This does not mean "f times x;" we read it "f of x" and it means the output of the function when f is performed on x. (21)

**general equation**    A general equation is written with additional variables which are the parameters that determine the type of equation or location and shape of its graph. If y = f(x) is a parent equation, then the general equation for that function is given by y = af(x - h) + k where (h, k) is the point corresponding to (0, 0) in the parent graph and, relative to the parent graph, the function has been: 1) vertically stretched if the absolute value of a is greater than 1; 2) vertically compressed if the absolute value of a is less than 1; and/or 3) reflected across the x-axis if a is less than 0. (112-13, 150)

**general quadratic equation for conic sections**   The equation $ax^2 + by^2 + cx + dy + e = 0$, in which a and b are not <u>both</u> equal to zero is a general equation that could represent a parabola, an ellipse, a hyperbola, a circle, or a pair of lines depending on the values of the coefficients.  In future courses, you will use the general equation $ax^2 + bxy + cy^2 + dx + ey + f = 0$  which includes conics with axes that are not parallel to the x- or y-axes.  (480)

**generator**   The generator of a sequence tells what you do to each term to get the next term.  Note that this is different from the function for the $n^{th}$ term of the sequence.  The generator only tells you how to find the following term, when you already know one term.  In an arithmetic sequence generator is the common difference; in a geometric sequence it is the multiplier or common ratio. (42)

**geometric sequence**   A geometric sequence is a sequence that is generated by a multiplier.  This means that each term of a geometric sequence can be found by multiplying the previous term by a common multiplier. (47, 51)

**geometric series (sum)**   The sum of the first n terms of a geometric sequence,  $a + ar + ar^2 + ar^3 + \ldots + ar^{n-1}$  is given by the formula at right. (469)   $$S = \frac{a(r^n - 1)}{r - 1}$$

**graph**   To graph an equation or draw a graph means we expect you to use graph paper, scale your axes appropriately, label key points, and plot points accurately.  This is different from **sketching** a graph. (21)

**graphing form for a quadratic function**   The graphing form for the equation of a quadratic function (also called vertex form) is  $y = a(x - h)^2 + k$. (116)

**histogram**   A histogram is a bar graph showing the frequency with which data values occurred. (434)

**hyperbola**   A hyperbola has relationships corresponding to those of an ellipse.  A hyperbola is made up of two branches.  The line connecting the vertices of the two branches is called the transverse axis, and the letter a is used to represent the distance from the center to either vertex. For the equation at right the center of the hyperbola is at the origin.   $$\frac{x^2}{a^2} - \frac{y^2}{b^2} = 1$$

The vertices are $(\pm a, 0)$ and the asymptotes have the equations $y = \pm\frac{b}{a}$ x.  The foci are on the transverse axis, in this case the x-axis, at $(\pm c, 0)$ with c given by the equation  $c^2 = a^2 + b^2$.  For a hyperbola, the eccentricity is a measure of the shape of the curve; the larger the eccentricity the more quickly the branches spread apart.  The formula is  $e = \frac{c}{a}$.  Note that since $c > a$, the eccentricity of a hyperbola is always greater than 1.  If the vertices are on the y-axis the foci are on the y-axis at $(0, \pm c)$, and the equation is written as shown at right.   $$\frac{y^2}{a^2} - \frac{x^2}{b^2} = 1$$

Everything else is the same <u>except</u> the asymptotes have slopes $\pm\frac{a}{b}$. (130, 486)

**identity element**   The identity element for addition is the number we can add to any number and not change that number's "identity" or value.  For addition, the identity element is 0,  $a + 0 = $ a for any number, a.  For multiplication, the identity element is 1,  because $1(x) = x$ for any number x. (185)

**identity matrix**   An identity matrix, often labeled I, is an m x m matrix with zero in every entry except those on the upper left to lower right diagonal.  On that diagonal, each entry $m_{i,j} = 1$. (187)

**imaginary numbers**   The set of numbers that are solutions of equations of the form $x^2 = $ (a negative number) are called imaginary numbers.  They are not positive, negative, or zero. The imaginary number i  is a solution of the equation $x^2 = -1$, so $i^2 = -1$  In general, imaginary numbers follow the rules of real number arithmetic (e.g. $i + i = 2i$).  Multiplying the imaginary number i by every possible real number gives us all the imaginary numbers. (253)

**independent events**   When the probability of two events happening equals the product of their probabilities, the events are said to be independent. (365)

**independent variable**   The variable occurring first in an ordered pair.  In a function, the independent variable is the input variable. (14)

**index (plural indices)**   One use of indices is with summation notation. The indices are the numbers below and above the sigma in the summation notation that indicate at what value the series is to start and where it will end. (435)

**inequalities with absolute value**   If k is any positive number, an inequality of the form: 1) $| f(x) | > k$ is equivalent to the statement $f(x) > k$ or $f(x) < -k$;  2) $| f(x) | < k$ is equivalent to the statement $-k < f(x) < k$. (158)

**infinite geometric series**   An infinite geometric series is a geometric series which never ends.  The sum of such a series with an initial value a and common ratio r, with $-1 < r < 1$, is given by the formula at right. (470)     $S = \dfrac{a}{1 - r}$

**inflection point**   An inflection point is a point where a graph changes concavity.  Concavity refers to whether or not the graph opens upward or downward.  So an inflection point is where a graph changes from opening upward to downward, or vice versa.  The graph of $y = x^3$ has an inflection point at $x = 0$. (126)

**initial ray**   When we draw an angle of rotation in standard position, the positive x-axis is called the initial ray. (299)

**initial value**   The initial value of a sequence is the first term of the sequence. (42, 74)

**intercepts**   Points where the graph crosses the axes.  x-intercepts are where the graph crosses the x axis and y-intercepts are where the graph crosses the y axis. (7, 11)

**interest**   An amount paid which is a percentage of the principle. (73-74)

**inverse circular functions**   $y = \text{Arcsin } x$, $y = \text{Arccos } x$ and $y = \text{Arctan } x$ are inverse circular functions. (351)

**inverse function**   A function that "undoes" what the original function does.  It can also be called the x-y interchange of the function.  The inverse of a function performs in reverse order the inverse operation for each operation of the function. (201)

**inverse operations**   Subtraction is the inverse operation for addition and vice versa, division for multiplication, square root for squaring, and more generally taking the nth root for raising to the nth power.

**inverse trigonometric functions**   For each trigonometric function we have studied (sin (x), cos (x), and tan (x)), there is an inverse trigonometric function written $\text{Sin}^{-1}$, $\text{Cos}^{-1}$ and $\text{Tan}^{-1}$.
Note:  this symbol does not mean $\dfrac{1}{\sin (x)}$ .  It is a new function that "undoes" the original trig function, thus giving a specific angle measure when the input is  sin x, cos x, or tan x.  For example: $\text{Sin}^{-1}\left(-\dfrac{1}{2}\right) = -\dfrac{\pi}{6}$. (115)

**investigating a function**   To investigate a function means to make a complete graph of the function and to write down everything you know about the function. Some things to consider are: intercepts, domain, range, asymptotes. (6, 20)

**Law of Cosines**   For any ΔABC,

$$a^2 = b^2 + c^2 - 2bc \cos A \quad (337)$$

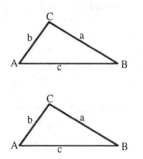

**Law of Sines**   For any ΔABC,

$$\frac{\sin A}{a} = \frac{\sin B}{b} = \frac{\sin C}{c} \quad (326)$$

**left-multiply**   Since multiplication of matrices is not commutative the product AB may not equal BA. If we want the product AB we can left-multiply matrix B by matrix A. The order of the multiplication matters; therefore, we specify whether we are left-multiplying or right-multiplying. (188)

**line of best fit**   A line of best fit is the line that best approximates several data points. For this course we place the line by visually approximating its position. (53)

**line of symmetry**   A line of symmetry divides a figure into two congruent shapes which are reflections of each other across the line. (32, 111)

**linear programming**   A method for solving a problem with several conditions or constraints that can be represented as linear equations or inequalities. (167)

**locator point**   A locator point is a point which gives the position of a graph with respect to the axes. For a parabola, the vertex is the locator point. (119)

**logarithm**   A logarithm is an exponent. In the equation $y = 2^x$ x is the logarithm, base 2, of y. (213)

**logarithmic and exponential notation**   $m = \log_b(n)$ is the logarithmic form of the exponential equation $b^m = n$ (if b > 0). (218-19)

**logarithmic functions**   The inverse of the exponential function is a logarithmic function or logarithm. The base of the logarithm is the same base as the exponential function. For instance, the inverse of $y = 2^x$ is inverse exponential function, base 2, better known as logarithm, base 2. The short version is stated "log, base 2," and written $y = \log_2 x$. (218)

**Markov Chain**   A Markov Chain is a method using matrices to model certain situations involving change over time and the probability of that change. (383)

**mathematical induction**   Mathematical Induction is a method of proof that can be used to prove that a formula is true for any natural number (n = 1, 2, 3, ....) Such a proof by mathematical induction consists of the following steps: 1) Verify that the formula is true for n = 1. 2) Write the general statement of the formula for n = k. 3) Demonstrate how to algebraically transform the statement for n = k into the statement for n = k + 1. (474)

**matrix**   A matrix is a rectangular array of numbers or algebraic expressions enclosed in square brackets.  Usually a matrix is denoted by a capital letter.  The plural is "matrices."  Each matrix has horizontal rows and vertical columns.  The number of rows and columns describe the matrix, so if a matrix has m rows and n columns we say the matrix has dimension m x n.  We often write that $m_{i,j}$ is the entry in the ith row and the jth column. (169, 171)

**mean**   The average for a set of data.  The mean is found by summing all the numbers and dividing the sum by the number of numbers. (433)

**mean deviation**   The mean deviation is used to measure the spread of the data.  It calculates the average (mean) distance from the mean and can be represented algebraically as

$$\text{mean deviation } = \frac{\sum |(x - \bar{x})|}{n} = \frac{\sum_{i=1}^{n} |x_i - \bar{x}|}{n}. \quad (440)$$

**median**   The middle score of a set of data.  The median is found by arranging the numbers from highest to lowest and finding the number in the middle.  If there is no middle number find the average (mean) of the two middle numbers. (433)

**multiplicative inverse**   The multiplicative inverse for a number is the number we can multiply by to get the multiplicative identity,  1.  So for the number 5, the multiplicative inverse is $\frac{1}{5}$;  for the number $\frac{2}{3}$  the multiplicative inverse is the number $\frac{3}{2}$. (185, 187)

**multiplier**   In a geometric sequence the number multiplied times each term to get the next term is called the multiplier or the common ratio.  The multiplier is also the number you can multiply by in order to increase or decrease an amount by a given percentage in one step.  For example, to increase 89 by 4%, the multiplier is 1.04.  We would multiply 89 x 1.04 = 92.56.  The multiplier for decreasing by 4% would be 0.96. (51, 60)

**negative exponents**   Raising a number to a negative exponent is the same as taking the reciprocal of the number.  $x^{-a} = \frac{1}{x^a}$ for $x \neq 0$. (101)

**outliers**   Data points that are quite removed or distant from the rest of the data are called outliers. (434)

**parabola**   The general equation for a parabola, also known as the graphing form, is  $y = (x - h)^2 + k$.  Standard form of a quadratic equation is  $y = ax^2 + bx + c$. (116, 134)

**parent graph**   The simplest version of a family of graphs is called the parent graph.  For instance, the graph of $y = x^2$ is the parent graph for parabolas which are functions.  See problem PG-74 for a list of the parent equations for different families. (130)

**Pascal's Triangle**   The array of numbers at right is known as Pascal's Triangle.  The triangular pattern continues downward.  This array shows all the values of $_nC_r$  where n is the row number when the vertex is $_0C_0$.  r is the number of places to the right in row n (begin counting with 0).  For instance, $_5C_2$  is equal to 10. (421)

```
        1
      1   1
    1   2   1
  1   3   3   1
 1  4   6   4  1
1  5  10  10  5  1
```

**percentile**   A percentile ranking indicates the percentage of scores which are below the score in question.  For example, if you scored at the 90th percentile on a test, your score was higher than the scores of 90% of the other test takers. (448)

**period**   The period is the length of one cycle of a graph. (248)

**periodic function**   A periodic function is a function which has a repetitive section or cycle. The pattern continues forever both to the left and to the right. (248, 281)

**periodic functions (the five point method for graphing)**   To sketch the graph of a periodic function: 1) find the locator point (the start of the first cycle);  2) find the end of the first cycle;  3) find the middle point of the first cycle;  4) the point one-fourth of the way through the first cycle (this is half way between the first point and the middle point);  and 5) find the point three-fourths of the way through the first cycle (this is the point half way between the middle point and the last point of the cycle).  (289)

**permutation**   A permutation is an arrangement in which the order of selection matters.  For example a batting line-up is a permutation because it is an ordered list of players.  Here is another example.  If each of five letters, A, B, C, D, E is printed on a card, how many 3-letter sequences can you make by selecting three of the five cards?  Permutations can be represented with tree diagrams, decision charts or the use of formulas for $_nP_r = \dfrac{n!}{(n-r)!}$ .  In the example $_5P_3 = 5(4)(3)$ or $\dfrac{5!}{2!}$  (402, 406)

**polynomial**   A polynomial in one variable is an expression that can be written as the sum of terms of the form:  (any number) $\bullet$ x $^{(\text{whole number})}$ .  Polynomials involve only the operations of addition, subtraction and multiplication and are usually arranged with the powers of x in order, starting with the highest, left to right.  The numbers that multiply the powers of x are called the coefficients of the polynomial. (240)

**population**   In statistics, the population is the entire group under consideration. (438)

**principle**   Initial investment or capital.  An initial value. (74)

**probability**   The probability that an event A will occur is the number of equally likely outcomes for event A, divided by the total number of equally likely outcomes.  This can be written as $\dfrac{\text{number of outcomes for event A}}{\text{total number of possible outcomes}}$ .  A probability p is a ratio,  $0 \le p \le 1$.

**Pythagorean Identity**   For trigonometric functions, $\cos^2 x + \sin^2 x = 1$ for any value of x. (320)

**quartile**   The first quartile ($Q_1$) is the median of the data that are below the median.  The third quartile ($Q_3$) is the median of the data that lie above the median.  The first and third quartiles with the median (which can be called $Q_2$) divide the data into four parts. (449)

**quadratic formula**   This formula gives you the solutions for x in a quadratic equation.

$$\text{If } ax^2 + bx + c = 0, \text{ then } x = \frac{-b \pm \sqrt{b^2 - 4ac}}{2a}. \quad (30)$$

**radian measure**   To locate a point on a unit circle, we can trace along the unit circle and measure the distance along the circle to the point from the positive x-axis.  The radian measure of the angle formed by the radius to the point and the positive x-axis is the distance along the unit circle. (300)

**range**   (a) In statistics, the range is (the highest data value) - (the lowest data value). (440)
(b) Of a function, the set of possible outputs for a function.  It consists of all the values of the dependent variable, that is every number that y can represent for the function, f(x) = y. (15)

**raw score**   The raw score is a score earned without any adjustments. (446)

**real numbers**   The set of all rational numbers and irrational numbers are referred to as the real numbers. (253)

**rebound height**   The height a ball reaches after a bounce is the rebound height. (53)

**rectangular numbers**   The terms of the sequence 0, 2, 6, 12, 20, ... are known as the rectangular numbers. (61)

**recursive definition**   For a sequence, a recursive definition is a rule that tells us how to get a term of the sequence from the term or terms that precede it. (426)

**reference angle**   For every angle of rotation there is an angle in the first quadrant $0 \le \theta \le \frac{\pi}{2}$ whose cosine and sine have the same absolute values as the cosine and sine of the original angle. (304)

**relative maximum (minimum)**   A function that has a "peak" (or "valley") at a point x is said to have a relative maximum (minimum) at the point x. This is the point where the function changes direction. (315)

**right-multiply**   Since multiplication of matrices is not commutative the product AB may not equal BA. If we want the product BA we can right-multiply matrix B by matrix A. The order of the multiplication matters; therefore, we specify whether we are left-multiplying or right-multiplying. (188)

**roots of a function**   The number r is a root (or zero) of the function f(x) if f(r) = 0. A root may be either a real or complex number. Real roots occur where the graph of the function f(x) crosses the x-axis. Complex roots must be found algebraically. (239)

**sample space**   The set of all possible outcomes of an event is called the sample space. (376)

**sequence**   A function in which the independent variable is a positive integer (sometimes called the "term number"). The dependent variable is the term value. A sequence is usually written as a list of numbers. (42, 47)

**series**   A series is the sum of the terms of a sequence. (435); arithmetic (466); geometric (469)

**simple interest**   Interest paid on the principle alone. (73)

**sine**   In a right triangle (as shown at right) the ratio $\frac{\text{opposite side}}{\text{hypotenuse}}$ is known as the sine of the acute angle. At right, $\sin B = \frac{b}{c}$ since the side length b is opposite angle B. (20)

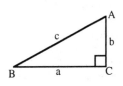

**sine function**   For any real number $\Theta$, the sine of $\Theta$, denoted $\sin \Theta$, is the y-coordinate of the point on the unit circle reached by a rotation angle of $\Theta$ radians in standard position. (285, 307, 315)

**sine function (general equation)**   The general equation for the sine function is $y = a \sin b(x - h) + k$. This function has amplitude a, period of $\frac{2\pi}{b}$, and locator point (h, k). (315)

**sketch**   To sketch the graph of an equation means you show the approximate shape of the graph in the correct location with respect to the axes and that you clearly label all key points. (6)

**"sleeping" parabola**   A "sleeping" parabola is a parabola which opens to the left or right instead of upward or downward. These parabolas <u>are</u> <u>not</u> functions. (125-26)

**slope-intercept form**   A linear equation written in the form y = mx + b is written in slope-intercept form.  In this form, m is the slope of the line and the point (0, b) is the y-intercept. (31)

**standard deviation**   The standard deviation is used to measure the spread of the data.  It can be represented algebraically as

$$\text{standard deviation} = \sigma = \sqrt{\frac{\Sigma(x - \bar{x})^2}{n}} = \sqrt{\frac{\sum\limits_{i=1}^{n}(x - \bar{x})^2}{n}}$$

In any set of data at least 75% of the points will lie within two standard deviations of the mean and if the data are normally distributed 68% will be found within one standard deviation of the mean and 95% will be within two standard deviations. (441)

**standard form for a quadratic function**   The standard form for the equation of a quadratic function is  $y = ax^2 + bx + c$ where $a \neq 0$. (46)

**standard form of an equation**   A linear equation written in the form Ax + By = C is written in standard form.  A quadratic equation in one variable is in standard form when it is written as $ax^2 + bx + c = 0$. (31)

**statistical variables**   Some standard statistical variables are listed below. (438)

| | |
|---|---|
| **n** | In statistics, n represents the total number of data values in the sample. |
| **x** | In statistics, x represents an individual value from a set of data. |
| **$\bar{x}$** | In statistics, $\bar{x}$ represents the sample mean. |
| **μ** | In statistics, μ represents the population mean. |
| **s** | In statistics, s represents the sample standard deviation. |
| **σ** | In statistics, σ represents the population standard deviation. |

**stem-leaf plot**   A useful organizational tool for representing data is the stem-leaf plot.  A common example of this is the recording information about two-digit data.  The tens digits are listed vertically in order while the ones digits are recorded to the right of their corresponding tens digits. (444)

**subproblems**   A large problem can sometimes be separated into smaller or simpler problems called "subproblems" so that the solution of these subproblems leads to the solution of the larger problem. (17)

**summation notation**   A convenient way to represent a series is to use summation notation.  The Greek letter sigma, $\Sigma$, indicates a sum.  For example, $\sum\limits_{n=1}^{4} 3n = 3(1) + 3(2) + 3(3) + 3(4) = 30$.  The number below and above the sigma are called the indices.  The index below, n = 1, tells us at what value to start with for n.  The top index tells us how high the index can go.  In the example, n started at 1 and increased to 4. (435)

**system of equations**   A system of equations is a set of equations with more than one unknown or variable.  The systems we solve most often in this course have two equations and two unknowns, x and y.  Systems of equations are often solved by using the substitution method or the elimination method. (44-45)

**tangent**   In a right triangle (at right) the ratio $\frac{\text{opposite side}}{\text{adjacent side}}$ is known as the

tangent of an acute angle. At right, $\tan B = \frac{b}{a}$ since the side of length $b$ is opposite angle B and the side length $a$ is adjacent to angle B. (20)

The function $f(\Theta) = \tan \Theta = \frac{y}{x}$ where (x,y) are the coordinates of the point on

the unit circle where the radius makes an angle of $\Theta$ with the positive horizontal axis. (320)

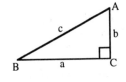

**tangent function**   For any real number $\Theta$, the tangent of $\Theta$, denoted $\tan \Theta$, is the slope of the line containing the ray which represents a rotation of $\Theta$ radians in standard position. (320)

**tangent function (general equation)**   The general equation for the tangent function is

$y = a \tan b(x - h) + k$. This function has period of $\frac{\pi}{b}$, vertical asymptotes at $\frac{\pi}{2b} + h \pm \frac{n\pi}{b}$ for

$n = 1, 2, \ldots$, and locator point (h, k). (320)

**terminal ray**   When we draw an angle of rotation in standard position, the positive x-axis is called the initial ray and the ray that determines the angle is called the terminal ray. (299)

**transverse axis**   In a hyperbola, the line connecting the vertices of the two branches is called the transverse axis. (486)

**tree model**   Tree models are useful for representing possible outcomes of probability experiments. A sequence of events, the first consisting of two outcomes and the second of three can be represented by a tree starting with two branches. Each branch would then have three branches, for a total of six endpoints. Tree models can be extended. For example a sequence of three events with two, then three, then four outcomes would start the same as the two event tree but would then have four branches stemming from each of the six endpoints to yield (2)(3)(4) = 24 possible three-part outcomes. (358)

**triangular numbers**   The terms of the sequence 0, 1, 3, 6, 10, ... are known as the triangular numbers. (70, 383)

**triple root**   If an expression of the form $(x - a)^3$ is a factor of a polynomial, then the polynomial has a triple root at x = a. The graph of the polynomial has an inflection point at x = a. (244)

**unit circle**   A circle with a radius equal to 1 is called a unit circle. (248)

**variance**   In statistics the variance is a measure of spread or dispersion of the data. It is the square of the standard deviation.

$$\text{variance} = \sigma^2 = \frac{\Sigma(x - \bar{x})^2}{n} = \frac{\sum\limits_{i=1}^{n}(x - \bar{x})^2}{n} \quad (442)$$

**vertex**   The vertex of a parabola locates its position with respect to the axes. It is the lowest or highest point of the graph of the parabola. It is also called a locator point. (119)

**vertex form**   The vertex form for the equation of a quadratic function (also called graphing form) is written $y = a(x - h)^2 + k$. (116)

**x-y interchange**   The x-y interchange of the function is the result of exchanging the x and y variables and then solving for y. It is the inverse of the function. (204)

**zero power**   The result of raising any number (except zero) to the zero power is 1. $x^0 = 1$ for any number x, x ≠ 0. (81)

**zeros of a function**   The x-intercepts of the graph of a function in the real plane are the zeros of the function. These are also called the roots of the function. A function can have complex zeros. These complex zeros cause $y = 0$, but they are not x-intercepts since they don't exist in the real plane. (239)

**z-score**   Raw scores are often converted to z-scores. Z-scores tell how far away a score is from the mean. A z-score of 1 is one standard deviation above the mean. A z-score of -2.5 is two and a half standard deviations below the mean. (446)

# Some Ways to Get Started and Some Answers

EF-7.    The negative sign is not distributed.

EF-8.    a)  $x = -\frac{1}{17} \approx -0.059$

b)  $x = \frac{66}{13} \approx 5.08$

c)  $x = -1, 3$

EF-15.    10.87

EF-17.    a)  21; 15; (0, 15)

EF-18.    e)  (-2, 9)

EF-19.    Need to multiply both sides by x

EF-27.    i)  y-axis doesn't start at 0;
extend graph in both directions

EF-28.    a)  $x = \frac{5(y-1)}{3}$

b)  $x = \frac{-2y+6}{3}$

c)  $x = \pm\sqrt{y}$

EF-29.    a)  (0, 6)
b)  (0, 2)

EF-30.    a)  (-2, 0)

EF-39.    b)  (-1, -5)

EF-52.    d)  $A = \frac{1}{2}(12)(4.8) = 28.8$
square units

EF-55.    The population is 1550.

EF-56.    b)  $\approx 42.148$

EF-57.    b)  $D : -1 < x < 1, R : -1 < y < 2$

EF-63.    $\approx 478.384384$

EF-64.    Solve the equation:  $x^2 + 2x + 1 = 1$

EF-66.    Draw a diagram.
Label the sides W and 4W.

EF-69.    $x = 2.72; y = 1.27$

EF-77.    a)    48.1131

EF-82.    $x = 1, -\frac{4}{7}$

EF-83.    First find the height.

EF-95.    a)    (3, 2)    b)  no solution

EF-96.    a)    t(4) = 1

EF-104.    a)    $x = \frac{y-b}{m}$    b)  $r = \sqrt{\frac{A}{\pi}}$

EF-106.    a)    $z = \frac{40}{3}$

EF-112.    $m = -\frac{3}{4}, (4, 0), (0, 3)$

EF-113.    a)    $y = \frac{5}{3}x + 5$
b)    $5x - 3y = 15$

EF-115.    a)    $\frac{8}{27}$

EF-118.    a)    1    b)  12

BB-4.    a)    $x^5$    b)  $y^3$

BB-8.    b)    $y = -\frac{3}{2}x + 6$

BB-11.    $\frac{3y}{2xy} + \frac{8}{2xy} = \frac{3y + 8}{2xy}$

BB-17.    a)    (-1, -2)

BB-19.    Find the slope between pairs of
points.

BB-20.    57.99

BB-22.    b)    $\frac{8+3x}{12}$

BB-28.    $y = 4x - 5$

BB-33.    (0, 0), (-6, 0)

BB-35.    b)    $2y^3$      d)  $-8x^6$

BB-46.    a)    10 cards

BB-48.    b)    $\frac{12-5y}{4y}$      c)  $\frac{m^2}{2n^2}$

BB-49.    (-2, 0), (-4, 0), (0, 8);  $x = -3$

BB-60.    a)    sequence 1:  add 4,
                $t(n) = 4n + 2$

BB-62.    (0, -17), $(-2 \pm \sqrt{21}, 0)$
          or (2.58, 0), (-6.58, 0)

BB-63.    a)    $x = 3$

BB-66.    (3, 2)

BB-68.    d)    $t(n) = 17 + 13n$

BB-70.    a)    $1.03y$

BB-72.    a)    $\frac{16\pi - 4\pi}{16\pi} = \frac{3}{4}$

BB-79.    Start with $100 and figure it each
          way.

BB-80.    c)    1.07

BB-81.    a)    1, 8, 15, 22, 29

BB-83.    a)    110

BB-89.    a)    $t(40) = 285$

BB-90.    c)    0.85

BB-93.    34.08

BB-95.    One equation is $4s + 3b = 4.36$.

BB-96.    b)    $18x^2$    c)  $\frac{6}{x}$

BB-104.   $(x + 3)^2$ is not the same as $x^2 + 9$!

BB-105.   a)    x: 0, 1, 2;  y: -2, 0, 1

BB-106.   a)    $\frac{2x-3}{15}$      d)  $\frac{1}{3m^2}$

BB-108.   $\frac{1}{8}$

## UNIT 3

FX-7.     b) $277.64

FX-9.     $\frac{3 \pm \sqrt{65}}{4}$, or 2.77 and -1.27

FX-10.    a)  $2^6$      d)  $2^{(4x+4)}$

FX-12.    a)    x: (6, 0) & (-12, 0);
                y: (0, -72)

FX-13.    a)    $2x^2 + 6x$
          c)    $2x^2 - 5x - 3$

FX-14.    a)    (x + 7)(x - 7)
          c)    (xy +9z)(xy - 9z)

FX-21.    a)    1.05
          c)    $1.03^{12} = 1.426$

FX-23.    a)    3    c)  80

FX-25.    a)    2(x + 4)
          d)    (y - 5)(y + 2)

FX-27.    $\triangle ACB$ is isosceles,
          so $m\angle ABC = m\angle BAC$

FX-35.    a)    0.96; 126,000; 5 years

FX-36.    (3, 2)

FX-38.    $x = -1.25$

FX-41.    a)    28°

FX-48.    b)    $3^{-2x}$

FX-51.    c)    $x^2 - 6x + 9$
          d)    $4y^2 - 9$

FX-52.    d)    $t(42) = -21$

FX-53.    no x-intercept; y: (0, -5)

FX-60.    a)    no   b) yes  c) yes

FX-63.    a) 3    b) 4    c)  $-\frac{3}{2}$

FX-66. Start by factoring out the common factor of 5xy

FX-69. b) $\approx 30.8$

FX-83. a) $3y(y + 2)$
c) $(x + 2)(x - 2)$

FX-85. a) 0

FX-86. a) $6y^2 - 19y - 7$
d) $x^3 - x^2 - 6x$

FX-94. a) 120

FX-95. b) $6x(x + 8)$
c) $2(x + 8)(x - 1)$

FX-98. b) $4m^2 + 4m + 1$
c) $x^3 - 2x^2 - 3x$

FX-99. b) $\frac{xy}{y+x}$

FX-110. a) 2   b) 3   c) -3

FX-112. a) $2x^3 + 2x^2 - 3x - 3$
c) $2x^2 + 12x + 18$

FX-113. $(31)^2 = 961$

FX-116. 0.16

FX-121. a) 2   b) $\frac{8}{3}$   c) $\frac{13}{3}$

FX-122. b) $(3x + 10)(3x - 10)$
c) $2(x + 2)(x - 2)$

FX-125. You know $D = 3$; substitute for D in each of the other equations.

FX-135. $x = \frac{24}{7}$ and $y = \frac{18}{7}$

FX-136. same shape but (b) is discrete and (c) is continuous

FX-140. $x = 3$, $y = 2$

FX-142. a) $5600   b) $5627.54
c) $5634.13

FX-143. $f(0) = 100$ tells you the value of k.

FX-144. $y = \frac{2}{3}x - 2$, $y = \frac{1}{2}x + 4$, (-60, -26)

<h2>UNIT 4</h2>

PG-5. parabola with vertex (2, 0)

PG-7. a) $y = -\frac{2}{3}x - 4$   b) $y = 2$

PG-8. a) cylinder

PG-11. about $182.50

PG-15. a) vertex at (-3, -8), opens up, vertically stretched

PG-16. a) $4 = 2^2$ and $8 = 2^3$
b) $z = -\frac{18}{5}$

PG-17. a) 0.625 hours or about 37.5 min

PG-18. $3p + 3d = 19.50$ and $p + 3d = 12$

PG-19. b) $30°$   d) $60°$

PG-20. c) $72 = 36$ times 2

PG-21. a) $y = (x - 8)^2 - 5$
b) $y = 10(x + 6)^2$

PG-27. a) $y = 0, 6$

PG-28. b) $y = (x - 2)^2 - 16$; (2, -16)

PG-31. a) 8.577 gigatons

PG-38. a) x: (1, 0), $(-\frac{5}{2}, 0)$, y: (0, -5)

PG-39. b) parabola, inverted, vertex (3, -7)

PG-40. b) $g(h + 1) = h^2 + 2h - 4$

PG-41. a) $x = \pm 5$

PG-42. $y = -\frac{8}{25}(x - 5)^2 + 8$ standing at (0, 0).

PG-45. b) $\sqrt{145}$

PG-49. c) $y = (x + 5)^2 - 25$ ; (-5, -25)

Selected Answers

PG-52.  a)  $2\sqrt{6}$

PG-53.  b)  $\sqrt{45} = 3\sqrt{5} \approx 6.71$; m = $\frac{1}{2}$

PG-54.  Choose variables for the weight of each type of coffee and write two equations: one for weight and one for cost.  10.5 lbs. of Colombian and 7.5 lbs. of Mocha Joe

PG-62.  a)  $y = (x - 3)^2 - 11$

PG-69.  b)  $y = (x - 2)^3 + 3$

PG-71.  b)  $(x - 2)^2 - 6$

PG-73.  (0, -4)

PG-78.  c)  $x^3 - 2x^2 - x + 2$

PG-79.  a)  $y = \frac{1}{x+2}$

d)  $y = 2^x - 3$

f)  $y = (x + 2)^3 + 3$

PG-81.  a)  $4.116 \times 10^{12}$

PG-82.  c)  5      d)  $\frac{\sqrt{3}}{2}$

PG-91.  a)  $y = 2x^2 - 4x + 6$

PG-92.  $y = (x - 2.5)^2 + 0.75$, vertex (2.5, 0.75)

PG-102.  a)  It only has two--at (-2, 0) and a double root at (3, 0).

PG-103.  b)  $x = -\frac{3}{4}$

PG-107.  a)  iii) 30
c)  Factor numerator and simplify.

PG-118.  a)  both equal 6

PG-119.  d)  no solution
h)  $|x - (-9)| = 15$;  $x = 6, -24$

PG-124.  d)  $11 + 6\sqrt{2}$

PG-131.  $4x^3 + 23x^2 - 2x = x(2x^2 + 23x - 2x)$

PG-132.  b)  x: (0, 0), (2, 0), y: (0, 0), V: (1,1); $y = (x - 1)^2 + 1$

PG-133.  21.14 and 528.39

PG-135.  a)  $x = \pm\sqrt{\frac{y}{2}} + 17$

PG-136.  b)  $x^{14}y^9$      c)  $\frac{x+3}{2}$

PG-137.  d)  -1

PG-144.  b)  $2x^3(2 + x^2)(2 - x^2)$

PG-147.  $x = \frac{-by^3 + c + 7}{a}$

PG-149.  b)  $2a^2 + 16a + 32$

PG-156.  a)  $4\pi + \frac{4}{3}\pi \approx 16.755 \text{ m}^3$

PG-157.  b)  $(x - 2)^2 + (y - 3)^2 = 25$

PG-159.  g)  no solution

PG-161.  $y = -\frac{5}{9}(x - 3)^2 + 6$

## UNIT 5

LS-7.  $y = 2$

LS-8.  a)  combining the equations leads to an impossible result, so there is no solution

LS-12.  $-20 < 5x + 8 < 20$, $-28 < 5x < 12$, $-5.6 < x < 2.4$

LS-13.  a)  $-13 < x < 5$
b)  $x > 250$ or $x \leq -70$
c)  $x \geq \frac{3}{2}$ and $x \leq \frac{7}{2}$

LS-19.  b)  (2, 6)

LS-20.  c)  20 months

LS-22.  c)  Graph (b) is like (a) rotated 90° counterclockwise.

LS-24.  b)  $9^{1/3}$

LS-30. Solve first equation, then apply answer to second equation.

LS-32. a) 9

LS-33. a) $\frac{1}{25}$  b) $\frac{x}{y^2}$

LS-34. a) -4 > x > 1
b) x ≤ -4 or x > 1

LS-39. 19.79 ft

LS-40. Shaded triangle with vertices at (5, -2), (-4, -2) and (-1, 4). area 27 square units

LS-41. b) 0

LS-42. express 16 and $\frac{1}{8}$ as powers of 2

LS-45. a) x(b + a)  c) $\frac{a}{x+1}$

LS-47. first solve first two equations for x and y

LS-48. (a - b) -2 = (a + b) - (a - b) = 35 - (a + b)

LS-50. recall that $x^2 - 8x = (x - 4)^2 - 16$

LS-53. a) y = -x + 3

LS-60. a) -4

LS-61. a) $C + F = \begin{matrix} \\ af \\ df \end{matrix} \begin{matrix} e & s & b \\ [8 & 2 & 7] \\ [4 & 3.5 & 8] \end{matrix} =$

ingredients for each cake with frosting

c)  $LC = \begin{matrix} af & df \\ [3 & 2] \end{matrix}$

$\begin{matrix} \\ af \\ df \end{matrix} \begin{matrix} e & s & b \\ [6 & 1 & 5] \\ [3 & 1.5 & 4] \end{matrix} =$

$\begin{matrix} e & s & b \\ [24 & 6 & 23] \end{matrix}$

LS-62. There is no solution, so the lines are parallel.

LS-63. c) 32 sq. units

LS-71. b) They all make 17 bouquets.

d) 5W

LS-72. a) Flowers;        Bouquet Styles
L  R  D

$\begin{matrix} \#1 \\ \#2 \\ \#3 \end{matrix} \begin{bmatrix} 5 & 4 & 3 \\ 4 & 3 & 3 \\ 4 & 6 & 6 \end{bmatrix}$

LS-73. WB makes sense. It represents the number of flowers each worker will use in a day. Notice that (workers x bouquets) x (bouquets x flowers) = (workers x flowers)

LS-83.        a)        Cost
Flowers  $\begin{matrix} L \\ R \\ D \end{matrix} \begin{bmatrix} 0.30 \\ 0.45 \\ 0.60 \end{bmatrix}$

LS-84. $\begin{bmatrix} 33 \\ 26 \end{bmatrix}$

LS-86. c) Impossible
d) Impossible

LS-88. (25, -3); new system (5,-3), (-5, -3)

LS-90. Red = 10 cm, Blue = 14 cm

LS-97. c) $x = \frac{b}{1+a}$

LS-100. c) w = 0, 6

LS-106. substitue z = 7 into any two of the original equations and solve the resulting system for x and y

LS-107. $x = \frac{b}{1-a}$

LS-110. c) y = –0.5x + 7.5

LS-118. c) $\begin{bmatrix} -23 & 8 \\ -29 & -16 \end{bmatrix}$

LS-119. a) $\begin{bmatrix} 1 & 2 \\ 3 & 4 \end{bmatrix}\begin{bmatrix} p \\ q \end{bmatrix} = \begin{bmatrix} 7 \\ 11 \end{bmatrix}$

d) A is a 4x4 matrix with several 0 entries

$

LS-120. b) $\begin{matrix} Pc \\ Pn \end{matrix}\begin{bmatrix} 0.10 \\ 0.25 \end{bmatrix}$

LS-124. b) $5x(x + 5)(x - 5)$

LS-132. multiply them together

LS-133. a) $\begin{bmatrix} -2 & 1 \\ 1.5 & -0.5 \end{bmatrix}\begin{bmatrix} 7 \\ 11 \end{bmatrix} = \begin{bmatrix} -3 \\ 5 \end{bmatrix}$,

so p = -3, q = 5

LS-134. b) 15

LS-135. b) $\begin{bmatrix} 1 & 0 \\ 0 & 1 \end{bmatrix}$

LS-137. a) $\frac{6x-21}{x^2-3x-4}$    c) $\frac{5}{x^2-9}$

LS-142. first substitute for g(-2)

LS-143. 60°

LS-146. a) circle: center (2, -3) radius 3

# UNIT 6

CC-6. ≈ 48.59°

CC-10. b) $\frac{5}{2}$    d) $\frac{80}{3}$

CC-13. a) $\begin{bmatrix} 4 & -17 & 3 \\ 11 & -19 & 5 \end{bmatrix}$

CC-15. ≈ 17.74 feet

CC-20. (-3, 0, 5)

CC-25 Tangent means that the graph just touches so you know the radius.

CC-26. a) $\frac{x-3}{x(x-4)}$
c) 2

CC-34. b) 30

CC-35. 121

CC-37. a) $f(g(x)) = f\left(\frac{1}{2}x^2\right) =$

$2\left(\frac{1}{2}x^2\right) + 1 = x^2 + 1$

CC-38. b) $\frac{1}{3}$, 1    c) 115

CC-40. a) $\frac{x^2}{x-1}$

CC-41. After completing the square, the equation becomes
$(x - 2)^2 + y^2 = 20$.

CC-42. a) $\frac{4(x+3)}{x-4}$    c) $\frac{1}{4x}$

CC-46. a) $e(x) = (x - 1)^2 - 5$

CC-49. b) 3    d) 6

CC-54. a) $-3 < x < 3$
b) $-2 < x < 1$
c) $x \le -2$ or $x \ge 1$

CC-61. $g(x) = \frac{x^2-10}{5}$; be sure the domain and range are properly restricted to x≥0 and y≥-2.

CC-67. a) $(x - 1)^2 + y^2 = 9$

CC-68. a) $x + 5$    c) $x - y$

CC-74. a) 36.78

CC-76. c) $\frac{2}{9}$    d) ≈ 0.43, -0.77

CC-77. c) 0.084x = 5000; $59,524

CC-82. $(x + 2)^2 + (y - 3)^2 = 4r^2$

CC-86. One equation is $5T + 6B = 8.58$.

CC-90. a) ≈12,353
b) He will increase the size.

CC-93. a) $\frac{6x-21}{(x-4)(x+1)}$    b) $\frac{5-6x}{2x-10}$

CC-104. a) $\frac{1}{2} \le x,\ 3 \le y$

b) $g(x) = \frac{(x-3)^2 + 1}{2}$

CC-105. a) true    b) false

CC-116. b) 2    d) $\sqrt{3}$

CC-121. a) $k = \frac{y}{m^x}$

CC-123. a) 10, -8    c) $-2 < x < 4$

CC-124. a) 2    c) $\frac{x-4}{(x-2)(x-1)}$

CC-133. e) Take the $a^{th}$ root or $x = b^{1/a}$

CC-135. b) Infinitely many solutions

CC-136. c) $x^{2/3}$

CC-140. a) 5.717

CC-142. b) $\frac{1}{3}$

CC-146. b) xy

CC-155. c) $9,625.60   d) $\approx 6.12$ years

CC-157. b) 4.230  c) 0.316  e) 3.673

CC-158. c) $f(x) = \frac{x+1}{x-1}$    d) $g(x) = \frac{3x-2}{x}$

CC-162. a) $\approx 0.0488$ grams
b) $\approx 6640$ years

# UNIT 7

CF-7. c) 0, 1, 2, 3, or 4

CF-8. (-2, -1), (3, 4)

CF-12. all except (c), (f), and (g) are polynomials

CF-14. a) $x = -26$    b) $x = \frac{15}{4}$

CF-19. use the quadratic formula

CF-20. parabolas, lines, and cubics are polynomials

CF-23. $x = -1$ or 5

CF-32. b) 5    c) 3

CF-35. 20 days; arithmetic

CF-46. area = 25 sq. units

CF-54. a) $x = 3$

CF-63. Fred is correct.

CF-64. first find AB

CF-72. a) $(1 + 2i, -3 + 4i),\ (1 - 2i, -3 - 4i)$

CF-73. c) $5 + i\sqrt{6}$

CF-75. express 16 and 8 as powers of 2

CF-78. c) -16

CF-79. a) $\frac{x+3}{2}$

CF-85. b) 34    e) 3 - 2i

CF-86. a) 4 - i

CF-87. c) -22 + i

CF-89. a) perform the inverse operations in the reverse order

CF-91. b) $\frac{3}{16}$

CF-92. a) be sure to use some negative numbers

CF-100. $(1 + 2i, 2 + 4i),\ (1 - 2i, 2 - 4i)$

CF-101. solve in terms of b using the quadratic formula

CF-103. a) Center: (3, 7), radius: 5
b) Center: (0, -5), radius: 4

CF-111. a) (3, 0), (0, 0), (-3, 0)

CF-114. a) $b^2 - 4ac = -7$; complex

CF-115. b) 1, i, -1, -i

CF-116. b) i

CF-118. x + y = 685, 5x + 8.5y = 5000, so 450 adult tickets would have allowed them to meet their goal.

CF-119. b) x: -3, $\frac{15}{2}$ (dbl root); y: 675

CF-120. b) $2x^2 + 12x + 18$

CF-127. assuming each ball takes up the space of a 3.7 cm cube, the cost is over $19,600

CF-128. c) about 0.004

CF-131. b) $(x - (-2 + \sqrt{3}))$ and $(x - (-2 - \sqrt{3}))$

c) $2 - \sqrt{3}$ and $2 + \sqrt{3}$

d) $(x - \sqrt{10})(x + \sqrt{10})$

e) $\left(x - \dfrac{3 + \sqrt{37}}{2}\right)\left(x - \dfrac{3 - \sqrt{37}}{2}\right)$

CF-139. 23.1 meters

CF-141. $\frac{8}{12}$

CF-143. b) $4 \pm 3i$

CF-152. d) average is 3; x coordinate of vertex

CF-156. $(x + 4)^2 + (y - 7)^2 = 16$

CF-157. $\frac{2(x-5)^2}{3} + 1$

# UNIT 8

CT-5. $2x^2 - 4x = 2(x^2 - 2x)$; complete the square in the parentheses, but remember what you add inside the parentheses is multiplied by 2.

CT-6. $y = 6x - x^2$

CT-8. x: none, y: (0, 88)

CT-9. a) 30-60: hypotenuse = 2, leg = $\sqrt{3}$; isosceles: hypotenuse = $\sqrt{2}$, leg = 1

CT-10. b) 176.88

CT-11. $26 + i$

CT-17. 45-45: $\frac{1}{\sqrt{2}}$, $\frac{1}{\sqrt{2}}$

CT-18. 17.46°

CT-19. 4; double root at x = -1, simple roots at -4 and 2, both ends go up.

CT-21. Write expressions for: how far the officer has traveled after x hours, and how far Sally is from where the patrol car started x hours after it started traveling.

CT-26. a) $\frac{\sqrt{2}}{2} \approx 0.707$

CT-27. a) subtract π from 4 to see how far into the third quadrant you are, then divide that by π to see what fraction of the lower semi-circle the angle with the negative x-axis is. That number times 180° is the angle you need.

CT-30. d) distance = $\frac{300}{360}(2\pi)$

CT-41. The area below the parabola and above the line y = 2x – 5.

CT-43. Transform the equation so that the fractions which have x in them are on the same side, then use a common denominator to add them together.

CT-44. $\approx 82.4$ ft.

CT-49. The graph includes points (0, -1.5), ($\frac{\pi}{2}$, -0.5), (π, 0.5), ($\frac{3\pi}{2}$, -0.5), (2π,–1.5). Now write an equation to represent this graph.

CT-50. use method from CT-40

CT-53. a) x: $\frac{-3 \pm \sqrt{6}}{3}$, y: 1

b) x: $\frac{5 \pm i\sqrt{31}}{4}$, y: -7

CT-54. average of roots $= \frac{5}{4}$.

CT-62. a) amplitude of 3, period of $4\pi$

CT-63. The period is 1.
a) locator (0, 0), period 1
b) locator (0, 0), period 2, amplitude 3
c) locator (0, 1), period 1, amplitude 3

CT-66. b) $\frac{5 \pm \sqrt{57}}{4}$    c) no solution

CT-68. a) y = sin (x + $\frac{\pi}{2}$) or y= -sin (x - $\frac{\pi}{2}$)

d) y = sin $\frac{1}{3}$(x - $\frac{\pi}{2}$)

CT-71. a) x ≈ 2.5121

CT-74. 4.73% annual interest

CT-76. a) x = 4 or -2

CT-81. a) (0.3420, 0.9397)

CT-84. a) 180°    c) $\frac{\pi}{6}$ radians

e) $\frac{5\pi}{4}$ radians

CT-85. b) $-18x^3y + 6x^5y^2z$

CT-86. y = $\sqrt[3]{2x}$ - 1

CT-87. f(x) = 2(x - 4)$^2$ + 2

CT-99. sine: 0, $\pi$, $2\pi$; 0°, 180°, 360°
cosine: $\frac{\pi}{2}$, $\frac{3\pi}{2}$ ; 90°, 270°

CT-100. b) locator ($\frac{\pi}{2}$, 1), period = $\frac{2\pi}{3}$

CT-101. a) 2i

CT-108. y = 2 + 4 sin x

CT-109. a) 210°    e) $\frac{9\pi}{2}$

CT-111. c) ≈ 394 million

CT-113. y = $-\frac{3}{3125}$(x - 125)$^2$ + 15

CT-118. a) factor out x

CT-123. a) $\frac{1}{5}$    c)    27

CT-133. Sketch graphs of the two functions.

CT-134. c) $\frac{200\pi}{3}$ ≈ 209.44 sq. units

CT-136. a) 7    b) 6

CT-142. solve one equation for x$^2$, and substitute for x$^2$ in other equation

CT-143. negative orientation, double roots at (-2, 0), (0, 0), and (2, 0)

CT-144. y = $\frac{(x-5)^2}{12}$ + 1

CT-151. locator points ($\pi$, -2) ($4\pi$, -2) asymptotes x = -$\pi$/2, 5$\pi$/2, 11$\pi$/2

CT-152. $\pm\sqrt{\frac{8}{9}} = \pm\frac{2\sqrt{2}}{3}$

CT-156. (-1 + i, 3),(-1 - i, 3)

**UNIT 9**

ST-6. a) 36.12 cm.

ST-10. a) a cone

ST-12. (6, -2, -8)

ST-20. a) 96.9 sq. units

ST-22. x ≈ 2.714, h ≈ ±4.199

ST-24. a) y = x$^{2/3}$

ST-33. a) y = 1368(0.9366)$^x$

ST-34. $\frac{ab}{a+b}$

ST-36.   a) $\frac{1}{4}$

ST-38.   b) $(\pm\sqrt{7}, 3)$, $(0, -4)$

ST-46.   a) $56.3°$

ST-48.   incorrect order of operations; $a \approx 57.23$

ST-52.   $\approx 1465.74$ sq. feet

ST-53.   a) $-2 + 2i\sqrt{3}$

ST-60.   No, the lot is $\approx 7367.19$ sq. ft.

ST-62.   a) $z \approx 20.05°$

ST-64.   b) $b^2 - 4ac > 0$

ST-65.   b) $\frac{4}{x^2 - 4}$

ST-66.   c) $(10 - 0.5n)(10 - 0.5n)(10 - n)$

ST-73.   $\approx 899.28$ feet

ST-74.   b) $\$5.46$

ST-75.   Start by factoring into $x(x^2 + 4) = 0$.

ST-77.   CD is $\$12.99$; Cassette Tape is $\$7.79$

ST-79.   a) $2^{2x}$   b) $2^{(x-1)}$

ST-91.   a) $84$ cm$^2$

ST-92.   b) $270$ gm

ST-93.   b) $\frac{x^3 - 2x - 2}{x^2 + x}$

ST-95.   b) $50°$, $3.13$, $8.59$

ST-104.  $m\angle A = 29.7°$, $m\angle B = 116.6°$, $m\angle C = 33.7°$

ST-105.  b) $y = \log_2(\frac{x}{4})$

ST-106.  (a) and (b) only

ST-107.  a) $0.2$

ST-117.  c) $k > 4$

ST-119.  a) locator $(\frac{\pi}{4}, -2)$ amp$=1$, period $2\pi$

ST-120.  $m\angle A \approx 119.6°$, $m\angle B \approx 38.4°$, $m\angle C \approx 22.0°$

ST-128.  c) $z \approx 7.75$ or $1.17$
         $m\angle Z \approx 118.4°$ or $7.6°$
         $m\angle Y \approx 34.6°$ or $145.4°$

ST-130.  $\sqrt{800} = 20\sqrt{2} \approx 28.28$

ST-131.  $1 = 3^0$

ST-132.  $\frac{1}{(\sin x)(\cos x)}$

ST-133.  b) $\frac{-1 \pm \sqrt{13}}{6}$

ST-137.  a)   $x \approx 24.49$   b) $x \approx 17.15$
         c)   $x \approx 30.90°$

ST-138.  b)   $\cos x$ is a common factor

# UNIT 10

PM-4.    a) $(4, -4)$

PM-6.    a) $(x + 3)^2 - 2$

PM-8.    $x^2 - 6x + 25 = 0$

PM-9.    b) $\frac{\pi}{3}, \frac{5\pi}{3}$   c) $\frac{\pi}{4}, \frac{5\pi}{4}$

PM-19.   a) $\frac{3 \pm \sqrt{51}}{2}$   b) $-13$

PM-20.   b) Multiply each equation by the common denominator to remove the fractions.

PM-21.   a) one answer is $(2, 8)$

PM-23.   Perpendicular slopes are opposite reciprocals; $y = -\frac{x}{3}$

PM-25.   a) $x = \frac{a+b}{c}$

PM-32.   b)  $(x + 3)^2 + (y - 4)^2 = 25$

PM-33.   one equation is
$0.15x + 0.22y = 513.01$

PM-35.   306.3 feet

PM-38.   Square both sides carefully

PM-47.   c)  15.5°

PM-48.   Use the descriminant $b^2 - 4ac = 0$.

PM-51.   b)  (3, 4) and (5, 0)

PM-52.   a)  $3a - 4b = 5$, $3b + 4a = 6$;

$a = \frac{39}{25} = 1.56$, $b = -\frac{2}{25} = -0.08$

PM-53.   a)  $3 + 4i$

PM-54.   a)  $\begin{bmatrix} 12 & -3 \\ -2 & 1 \\ -7 & -1 \end{bmatrix}$

PM-61.   1148 cu. cm.

PM-62.   Refer back to PM-23.

PM-63.   b)  $(-\frac{2}{5}, 19.2)$  $y = 5(x + 0.4)^2 + 19.2$

PM-66.   b)  120°, 240°     c)  45°, 225°

PM-72.   b)  The sides of the diagram are
labelled x; $\frac{1-x}{2}$; and $\frac{1-x}{2}$.

PM-74.   ≈1.29

PM-76.   Use slope to determine the angle.

PM-78.   a)  $\frac{x+1}{x^2}$

PM-84.   a)  start at (0,0); amp =2; period = $2\pi$
b)  start at (0,0); amp =1; period = $\pi$
c)  start at (0,0); amp =2; period = $2\pi$
d)  same graph as (c)

PM-88.   $6.36

PM-90.   a)  $7\sqrt{6}$     b)  $10\sqrt{3} + 10\sqrt{2}$

c)  $\frac{\sqrt{2}}{2}$

PM-97.   $y = -\frac{5}{12}x + 19$

PM-98.   e)  $x = 0, -2, \frac{4}{3}$

PM-105.  b)  $a + b + c = 1$, $4a + 2b + c = 3$,
$9a + 3b + c = 6$

PM-106.  b)  [ 0.1  0.2  0.6  0.1 ]; after one
day there is a 10% probability
that she will be well, a 20%
probability that she will be in
good condition, a 60%
probability that she will still be
critical, and a 10% chance that
she will have died.

PM-116.  a)   $T = \begin{array}{c} \text{rain} \\ \text{none} \end{array} \begin{array}{cc} \text{rain} & \text{none} \\ \begin{bmatrix} 0.7 & 0.3 \\ 0.2 & 0.8 \end{bmatrix} \end{array}$

d)  Find $D_4 = D_0(T^4)$ and look at
the "rain" column entry, which
≈ 37.5%.

PM-117.  d)  0.875

PM-120.  a)  0.6764          b)  82.8%

# UNIT 11

IC-9.    0.190

IC-10.   c)  8.3

IC-13.   $y = 5$, $z = 3$

IC-14.   b)  $\frac{5\pi}{12}$

IC-15.   b)  only one

IC-27.   Blue weighs 8 g and red weighs 16 g.

IC-28.   $\frac{5}{x+4}$

IC-29.   $\frac{x}{x+2}$

IC-30.  b)  $\left[\dfrac{16\pi}{9}\right]$    c)  140°

e)  1530°

IC-32.  rectangle with vertices (2, 0), (3, 1), (-1, 3), (0, 4); area = 6 square units

IC-33.  c)  It is not changing; $\approx$ 68.20°

IC-40.  $\dfrac{1}{10!}$

IC-44.  c)  56

IC-46.  $\dfrac{19}{29} - \dfrac{4}{29}i$

IC-59.  a)  1326  b)  P(2 diamonds) = 0.0588

c)  $\dfrac{_{13}C_2}{_{52}C_2}$

IC-60.  a)  21

IC-65.  $-\dfrac{9}{2}$

IC-67.  a)  i

IC-75.  a)  1000

IC-76.  a)  0.45

IC-78.  a)  Experiment with n = 3, 4, 5. What is the pattern?  Why?

IC-79.  $\dfrac{\pi}{6}$ and $\dfrac{5\pi}{6}$ or 30° and 150°

IC-88.  a)  120

IC-92.  x = 2  or  x = -1

IC-93.  9.10

IC-95.  $\approx$ 10.8 m

IC-103.  a)  875

IC-106.  a)  the answer is **not**  $\dfrac{x^1 + y^1}{x^2 - y^2}$

b)  the answer is **not**  $x^2 - 5y$

IC-110.  b)  $x^2 + 2xy + y^2$

IC-114.  0.000001539

IC-116.  $x^7 + 7x^6y + 21x^5y^2 + 35x^4y^3 + 35x^3y^4 + 21x^2y^5 + 7xy^6 + y^7$

IC-117.  b)  The coefficients of $(x + y)^n$ are the elements of the nth row of the triangle.

IC-118.  151,200

IC-120.  78 months

IC-122.  Factor out  x  to begin.

IC-124.  a)  0.0253

IC-125.  b)  $\dfrac{1}{156000}$

IC-130.  a)  4

IC-137.  Only 3, 4, 5 makes a right triangle; how many ways can that occur?

IC-144.  First factor out cos x.

## UNIT 12

DS-9.  a)  50 mph is not the answer. Continue with parts (b) through (d) to calculate the correct average speed.

f)  48 mph

DS-11.  b)  24

DS-13.  c = 3

DS-23.  They are using two different averages.  Which group is using the median?

DS-25.  50

DS-29.  sum = 70.5

DS-30.  b)  $\dfrac{2x^2 - 3x}{4}$

DS-39.  b)  22.5

DS-54.  a)  5.96 mph

DS-56.  y = a(x - 3)$^2$ + 3; substitute (7, 5) for (x, y) and solve for  a.

DS-57. b) $x \approx -1.839$  c) $x \approx -1.839$

DS-66. The answer is not 70.

DS-67. c) $y = 0.2(x - 2)^2$

DS-69. a) Find the radius first.
b) 247.403° or 112.597°; 4.318 rad or 1.966 rad
d) $\approx 0.85$

DS-81. b) 0 or $\frac{3}{5}$

DS-84. 9

DS-85. The y-intercept is 5.4.

DS-86. -1

DS-87. b) (-0.08, 7.51), (6.08, 7.51)

DS-94. b) $x^3 - 8$

DS-95. c) $(2x - y)(4x^2 + 2xy + y^2)$

DS-96. a) Notice that $x^2$ is a common factor.
b) $8y^6 = (2x^2)^3$, and $125x^3 = (5x)^3$, so this is a difference of cubes.
c) Step one is $(x^3 - y^3)(x^3 + y^3)$; both factors can be factored again.

DS-101. a) Factor the denominator; what do the factors tell you?
b) D: $[0, 25)$ and $(25, \infty)$;
R: $f(x) \leq -\frac{1}{5}$ or $f(x) > 0$

DS-113. c) There are 10 paths to 3rd and D.

DS-116. $g = 4$

DS-118. d) 64   g) 0.5   i) no answer

DS-127. d) Sometimes, when $x \leq 0$
i) S, when $y = \frac{-9}{4}x$

DS-128. The fourth term is $-32ab^3$.

DS-131. b) same as for part (a)

DS-143. $(\pm\sqrt{7}, 3)$, $(0,-4)$

DS-144   24 sq. units

DS-145. Use the points (0, 6), (2, 102), (4, 70), and the equation $y = ax^2 + bx + c$.

# UNIT 13

RE-2. 495,550

RE-3. d) $-0.56 + 0.92i$

RE-4. 479,001,600

RE-6. b) Solve $y^2 + 5y + 4 = 0$, then let $y = \cos x$.

RE-8. 3.64 yrs.

RE-12. 6.9999

RE-13. 5551

RE-14. Use the general equation $y = ax^2 + bx + c$, substitute for $x$ and $y$ and solve for a, b, and c.

RE-15. b)   $_{899}C_{11} \approx 7.3 \times 10^{24}$

RE-16. 19.8, 39.0, 80°

RE-17. b)   $\dfrac{1 \pm i\sqrt{43}}{2}$

RE-18. The tangent line is perpendicular to the radius.

RE-20. 500 miles

RE-22. 2160

RE-23. This is a geometric sequence with 80 terms and sum 5.2087.

RE-25. 90.2 ft.

RE-28. $-5940x^9$

RE-29. $0.2\overline{18}$

RE-31. $y = x^2 - 6x + 13$

RE-32. Remember to factor out the common factor 5xy first. Then factor the difference of two squares, but don't stop yet. You can factor each of those factors again.

RE-33. Remember to start by factoring out the 2 so $x = 2(y^2 - 6y + \ ) + 13$. And when you complete the square, what are you really adding to the whole expression?

RE-41. (2, -2), (2, 8), (-2, 3), (6, 3)

RE-42. b) center (-1, -3), length 8 units, height 10 units

RE-43. a) $\dfrac{(x+2)^2}{16} + \dfrac{(y-1)^2}{4} = 1$

RE-44. First show that the relationship works for n = 1, and possibly n = 2 and n = 3 to convince yourself. Then write
$$\dfrac{x^k - 1}{x - 1} = x^{k-1} + x^{k-2} + \ldots + x + 1$$
and add $x^k$ (which is the next term or k+1st term) to both sides. The rest is careful algebra.

RE-46. 40°

RE-52. a) (0, ±2); $y = \pm\tfrac{2}{5}x$; up/down
b) (±3, 0); $y = \pm x$; left/right

RE-53. a) center (2, -3); vertices (5, -3), (-1, -3); asy: $y = \pm\tfrac{2}{3}(x - 2) - 3$

RE-54. a) $\approx 2.25 \times 10^{15}$    b) 55,550

RE-60. a) hyperbola, center (0, -1)
b) sleeping parabola
c) circle, radius 5

RE-70. a) $(2, -11\tfrac{11}{12})$

RE-71. a) $(0, \pm\sqrt{20})$    c) $(1 \pm\sqrt{3}, 0)$

RE-73. (8, -3)

RE-77. b) (-1, 0) (-1, -6), e = 0.6

RE-78. a) $(2 \pm \sqrt{13}, -3)$, e = $\dfrac{\sqrt{13}}{3}$

RE-79. a) ellipse, center (1, -3), e = $\dfrac{\sqrt{2}}{2}$
b) hyperbola, center (0, -2), e = 2

RE-82. $3x^2 - x + 2$

RE-83. $x^3 - 2x^2 - 3x + 9$

RE-84. a) $2x^3 + 2x^2 + x + 4$ with remainder 9
b) $x^4 + 3x^3 + 7x^2 + 21x + 63 + \dfrac{190}{x-3}$

RE-87. asymptotes $y = \pm\sqrt{2}(x - 7)$, e = $\sqrt{3}$, foci $(7 \pm 5\sqrt{6}, 0)$

RE-89. a) $\dfrac{1}{1-x}$

RE-90. c) The remainder is -4.

RE-91. b) $x^4 - x^3 + 2x^2 - 7$

## About the Index

Each entry of the index is in alphabetical order and is referenced by the problem number in which it is discussed. In some cases, a term or idea may be discussed in several of the following problems as well. The problems are listed by two-letter code that references the unit and the problem number. Whenever possible, terms are cross-referenced to make the search process quicker and easier. For example, *cos x* could also be found under the heading *trigonometric functions*.

## Table of Unit Labels

## Index